Conflict and Identity in Romans

"Esler provides his readers with a discerning, exciting, and masterful reading of St. Paul's letter to the Romans. He hones his exegetical lenses with the full range of tools available to the modern interpreter: ancient Mediterranean history and archaeology, philology, patristics, historical and literary criticism, history of interpretation, and social science criticism. He defines terms that most interpreters leave at the intuitive level, such as ethnic and ethnicity, Greeks, Judeans, righteousness. He clearly articulates the societal processes by which groups maintain their distinctiveness and identity over against others groups (Christ-movement groups and Israel, Israelites and 'Gentiles'). He dialogues with modern commentators from Bultmann and Käsemann to Dunn and Moo. For an incisive, penetrating, and sensible grasp of Romans, there is nothing better than Esler's work. The unassuming and unostentatious style in which the book is written belies the freshness of insight and brilliance of perception that the author offers his readers."

—BRUCE J. MALINA
author of *The Social Gospel of Jesus*

"Noted for his insightful use of social-scientific methods of studying various portions of the New Testament, Esler applies his considerable skills to Paul's most famous letter. The results are both stimulating and insightful. This is perhaps the most skillful and helpful social scientific treatment of Romans thus far rendered by any one to date. Highly recommended."

—BEN WITHERINGTON III
author of *Jesus the Sage*

CONFLICT
and IDENTITY
in Romans

The Social Setting
of Paul's Letter

Philip F. Esler

Fortress Press
Minneapolis

CONFLICT AND IDENTITY IN ROMANS
The Social Setting of Paul's Letter

Copyright © 2003 Augsburg Fortress. All rights reserved. Except for brief quotations in critical articles or reviews, no part of this book may be reproduced in any manner without prior written permission from the publisher. Write: Permissions, Augsburg Fortress, Box 1209, Minneapolis, MN 55440.

Cover art © Photodisc, Inc.
Book design: Beth Wright

Scripture quotations from the Revised Standard Version of the Bible (RSV) are copyright © 1946, 1952, 1971 by the Division of Christian Education of the National Council of the Churches of Christ in the USA, and are used by permission.

ISBN 0-8006-3435-7

The paper used in this publication meets the minimum requirements of American National Standard for Information Sciences — Permanence of Paper for Printed Library Materials, ANSI Z329.48-1984.

Manufactured in the U.S.A.
07

to Robert Morgan

Contents

Preface   ix
Abbreviations   xi

1. Romans and Christian Identity   1

2. Explaining Social Identity   19

3. Ethnicity, Ethnic Conflict, and
   the Ancient Mediterranean World   40

4. The Context: Rome in the 50s CE   77

5. The Letter's Purpose in the Light of Romans 1:1-15
   and 15:14—16:27   109

6. Common Ingroup Identity and Romans 1:1—3:20   135

7. The Foundations of the New Identity
   (Romans 3:21-31)   155

8. Abraham as a Prototype of Group Identity
   (Romans 4)   171

9. The New Identity in Christ: Origin and Entry
   (Romans 5–6)   195

10. Pauline Leadership and Group Exemplification
    in Romans 7   222

11. The Exalted Character of the New Identity
    (Romans 8)   243

12. Israel and the Christ-Movement (Romans 9–11)   268

13. Descriptors of the New Identity (Romans 12–13)   308

14. The Weak and the Strong
        (Romans 14:1—15:13)   339

Epilogue: Conflict and Identity   357

Notes   366
Bibliography   416
Index   447

Preface

This book represents the present culmination of my thought on Romans, the text that has been my main research interest since 1998, when I published a book on Galatians using a similar theoretical framework. I wrote most of it in the academic year 2001–2002 during a year's research leave funded by the Leverhulme Trust in the U.K.; I am most grateful to the Leverhulme Trust for their assistance.

I have given papers on some aspects of the project at the Society of Biblical Literature meetings in Boston (1999) and Denver (2001), at a conference on early Christian spirituality in Melbourne in July 2002, at the meeting of the British New Testament Society in Cambridge in September 2002, at the Universities of Heidelberg and Bonn in October and November 2002, and in the University of Aberdeen in December 2002. On each occasion I profited greatly from discussion during and after my presentation.

I am particularly grateful to Scott Bartchy, Dennis Duling, Sean Freyne, Jack Elliott, Bruce Malina, Jerome Neyrey, Carolyn Osiek, and Ben Witherington for reading and commenting on sections of the text. John Barclay offered valuable advice at an early stage. Barry Matlock helped me clarify my thoughts on two important issues. Anselm Hagedorn has provided specific help on numerous occasions. Bill Campbell, David Horrell, Halvor Moxnes, and Gerald Downing offered very pertinent comments after the lecture in Cambridge.

Conversations I have had at various times over the last few years with my St. Andrews colleagues, especially Ron Piper and Richard Bauckham, have helped me develop my thinking on many aspects of this project. During my all too short visit to Heidelberg, I learned much from Peter Lampe, Robert Jewett, and Gerd Theissen, while Gunnar Garleff, then a doctoral student of Professor Theissen, alerted me to rich strands of German material on identity. In my visit to Bonn I was greatly helped by Ulrich Volp, Axel von Dobbeler, Michael Wolter, and Jochen Flebbe. In Aberdeen I benefited much from discussion with Francis Watson and from the assistance of Stephen Catto. Social psychologists Steve Reicher and Alex Haslam guided me in certain areas of social identity theory. None of them, it hardly needs saying, is responsible for the views expressed in this book.

At Fortress Press, biblical studies editor K. C. Hanson made some fundamentally useful suggestions about the overall shape of this book, while Beth Wright efficiently oversaw the production process.

The library staff at St. Andrews have come to my aid on more occasions than I care to think about—especially Colin Bovaird and Linda Kinloch in the St. Mary's College Library, and Katrina Acland, Sheena Fraser, and Margaret Grundy, who staff the St. Andrews end of the superbly quick and efficient Web-based U.K. interlibrary loan service.

My deep thanks go to Susan Millar, administrative officer of St. Mary's College, who helped me get through so many tasks necessary to see this book written and through the publishing process.

Finally, about the dedication of this book: When I was beginning postgraduate research in Magdalen College, Oxford, in October 1981, on my first Saturday morning in town I walked out to meet the academic who had agreed to supervise me—the Reverend Robert Morgan, of Linacre College. I arrived at his house while he was conducting a tutorial with an undergraduate student on Romans. So it was that my academic career in New Testament study began with the text that is the subject of this volume. If Bob Morgan had not in so many ways encouraged me along the path of New Testament research, this book would never have been written. While he may not agree with everything in it, I dedicate *Conflict and Identity in Romans* to him, as a small token of a debt larger than words.

Abbreviations

AB	Anchor Bible
ABD	*Anchor Bible Dictionary.* Edited by D. N. Freedman. 6 vols. New York: Doubleday, 1992
ANRW	*Aufstieg und Niedergang der römischen Welt*
ASA	Association of Social Anthropologists
Bib	*Biblica*
BibInt	*Biblical Interpretation*
BR	*Biblical Research*
BSac	*Bibliotheca sacra*
BTB	*Biblical Theology Bulletin*
BZNW	Beihefte zur Zeitschrift für die neutestamentliche Wissenschaft
CBQ	*Catholic Biblical Quarterly*
CIL	*Corpus Inscriptionum Latinarum*
CSEL	Corpus scriptorum ecclesiasticorum latinorum
EJSP	*European Journal of Social Psychology*
ERS	*Ethnic and Racial Studies*
ERSP	*European Review of Social Psychology*
ET	English translation
EvT	*Evangelische Theologie*
GNS	Good News Studies
HBT	*Horizons in Biblical Theology*
HTR	*Harvard Theological Review*
HTS	Harvard Theological Studies
HvTSt	*Hervormde teologiese studies*
ICC	International Critical Commentary
ILS	*Inscriptiones Latinae Selectae*
Int	*Interpretation*
JB	Jerusalem Bible
JBL	*Journal of Biblical Literature*
JPSP	*Journal of Personality and Social Psychology*
JSNT	*Journal for the Study of the New Testament*
JSNTSup	Journal for the Study of the New Testament Supplements
JTS	*Journal of Theological Studies*
Jub.	*Jubilees*
LCL	Loeb Classical Library

LEC	Library of Early Christianity
LXX	Septuagint
NICNT	New International Commentary on the New Testament
NovT	*Novum Testamentum*
NovTSup	Novum Testamentum Supplements
NT	New Testament
NTS	*New Testament Studies*
RSV	Revised Standard Version
SBL	Society of Biblical Literature
SBLDS	SBL Dissertation Series
SBLSymS	SBL Symposium Series
SBT	Studies in Biblical Theology
SNTSMS	Society for the Study of the New Testament Monograph Series
T. Ash.	*Testament of Asher*
TDNT	*Theological Dictionary of the New Testament.* Edited by G. Kittel and G. Friedrich. Translated by G. W. Bromiley. 10 vols. Grand Rapids: Eerdmans, 1964–76
T. Naph.	*Testament of Naphtali*
TynBul	*Tyndale Bulletin*
WBC	Word Biblical Commentary
WMANT	Wissenschaftliche Monographien zum Alten und Neuen Testament
WUNT	Wissenschaftliche Untersuchungen zum Neuen Testament
ZNW	*Zeitschrift für die neutestamentliche Wissenschaft*
ZPE	*Zeitschrift für Papyrologie und Epigraphik*
ZTK	*Zeitschrift für Theologie und Kirche*

Romans and Christian Identity

Romans as a Religious Classic

The texts we call classics have intrinsic qualities that endure and also possess a vitality that allows them to speak afresh to their readers under continuously changing circumstances for generation after generation. They mediate between the past and the present, the ancient and the modern, the permanent and the transient.[1] The canonical texts of the Old and New Testaments are classics so described,[2] yet they are also quite distinctive in referring their hearers and readers beyond their pages to acts of divine intervention in history and their ongoing significance for human beings.[3] Their canonicity embodies the culmination of a gradually unfolding ecclesial recognition that they relate the actual events of a sacred past while having the power in the present to seize the minds and hearts of those exposed to their message.[4] They remember the past for the sake of the present and the future.[5]

Paul's letter to the Romans is a classic in this sense probably without equal among New Testament texts. Its capacity to yield new insights has been repeatedly demonstrated at pivotal moments of Christian experience. Thus Augustine turned to Romans in the 390s CE to provide him with an exegetical answer to the problem, posed to all human beings by Manichean determinism, that would demonstrate the reality of human free will,[6] even if balancing free will with divine grace proved quite a struggle.[7] In the early sixteenth century, Martin Luther, agonized by the need to discover a basis for a certain belief in salvation not provided by the penitential beliefs and practices of late medieval Catholicism, found in Romans (with some help from Augustine)[8] fundamental evidence for his understanding of righteousness by faith.[9] Luther was rightly absorbed with Romans as a source of life and sustenance: "It is the soul's daily bread, and can never be read too often, or studied too much. The more you probe into it the more precious it becomes, and the better its flavour."[10] Four centuries later, Karl Barth, surveying a world brought to its knees by the Great War, published the first edition of his Romans commentary in 1919. In this work he attacked both the notion of the individual human being as the creative subject of culture and history and the religion that had provided bourgeois culture with crucial ideological support, proposing instead a God who is complete and whole in himself prior to all knowledge of him and who stands over the world in condemnation of it.[11] An even more devastating second edition was to appear in 1922. Responding to suggestions that he was opposed to historical criticism, he decried the sterile prolegomena that often passed for such interpretation of Paul and insisted on the need for "genuine understanding and interpretation," the "creative energy" that characterized the best interpretation of the apostle.[12]

The nature of a biblical text both to relate primal events of the past and to address each new generation of readers in their own situation raises questions as to the significance of those historical foundations. In particular, Paul Achtemeier argues that the fact that the traditions contained in biblical texts are "not primarily concerned with historical fact so much as they are concerned with the significance of those past events for the present, and the promise they hold for the future," entails that the past is of great but not conclusive importance.[13] Nevertheless, Achtemeier still insists on the necessity of the most detailed historical-critical understanding of the texts in their original contexts. The people responsible for shaping the traditions now represented in the biblical texts existed in a cultural context significantly different from ours. Since for a contemporary witness to be faithful to the intention of the original witness it is necessary to understand that intention, historical investigation of biblical traditions in their unique first context remains essential,[14] for such work allows us to avoid imposing modern presuppositions on the ancient word of God to his people. Achtemeier rightly asks that if we are unaware of the profound cultural differences between ourselves and those who produced the biblical texts, "how can we hear anything but familiar things, in that case familiar because they have been distorted by the modern frame of reference we bring to those ancient accounts?"[15] This view is essentially the same as that powerfully expressed by Krister Stendahl in his classic essay on contemporary biblical theology to the effect that the church at times needs to hear the biblical message in all its strangeness, "its cutting edge not blunted by the familiarity of hallowed religious expectations."[16]

Yet the cultural distance of a biblical text from each new generation of readers and listeners does not mean that they are thereby precluded from understanding what was originally conveyed in that text. Across the world today we see that communication is possible between people of different cultures, at least where those involved make an effort to understand the social script in which the discourse of the other party is necessarily embedded and do not ethnocentrically assume that the others must be just like them. There is no difference in principle when it comes to reading biblical texts, except that here we can only listen to what those who composed them sought to communicate, not reply to them concerning the subject of their messages. For this reason, reading a biblical text in a way that does justice to its historical context and yet speaks to its subsequent readers in their own very different cultural context is necessarily an exercise in intercultural communication, as I have proposed elsewhere in detail in relation to Galatians.[17]

"Theology" and "Religion" in Romans?

When a classic religious text like Romans is being considered as having a bearing on a Christian context, however, its historical dimension cannot be all that is addressed. As Robert Morgan has rightly written, "no one who is stirred by the question of God can stop there when studying a religious text."[18] Whatever message Paul intended to communicate to his immediate audience in Rome (a question examinable by historical criticism), the status of this letter as a classic testifies to the fact that for nearly two thousand years Christians have found it capable of addressing their own concerns in settings very different from the one that confronted Paul.[19] This is a text that for century after century Christians in widely diverse situations have found to say something crucial about the relationships between human beings and God. One particular reason for this may be that God and the gospel of God have a more central role in Romans than anywhere else in the Pauline correspondence.[20] In addition, there is rich teaching on subjects such as the redemptive role of Christ (Romans 5), baptism (6:2-11), the activity of the Spirit (8:1-30), the condition of the Christ-follower (8:31-39), and the characteristic love of the Christ-movement (ἀγάπη; 12:9-21) that it is easy to imagine would be valid for Christians in any time or place.

For many writers on Romans the introduction of God also signals the entry of "theology" onto the stage. Morgan states, for example, that seeking to understand the epistle with the question of God in mind "will lead us, however tentatively, in the direction of theological interpretation."[21] Many scholars, however, would replace his "however tentatively" with "inevitably." For the study of Pauline "theology" is a flourishing industry in New Testament studies, as witnessed by the succession of meetings conducted by the Pauline Theology Group at the annual meetings of the Society of Biblical Literature from 1986 to 1995 and the four volumes of essays in which many of the contributions were published.[22] A central focus of this discussion, in which many of the world's leading Pauline scholars participated, was the extent to which Paul's theology was coherent, even "systematic," when set against the contingency involved in its appearance in letters sent at various times and to groups of differing character. The fourth volume of the Pauline Theology Group's work bore the revealing subtitle "Looking Back, Pressing On,"[23] and since 1996 "Pauline theology" has continued to be a regular subject of discussion at meetings of the SBL. Romans has figured prominently in this discussion, and in James D. G. Dunn's monumental 1998 work *The*

Theology of the Paul the Apostle this letter is used "as a kind of template on which a fuller exposition of Paul's whole theology should be attempted."[24]

A most curious feature of this whole enterprise, however, is that hardly anyone ever seems to ask whether investigating Paul's writings under the rubric of "theology" is itself a good idea. Although a sense of ennui is detectable in the preface to the final (1997) volume of the SBL essays, with Dunn actually questioning the letter-by-letter approach that had been the basic premise of the group over its ten-year course, and Steven Kraftchick defending it, Dunn was taking issue only with the way the task was undertaken, not with its fundamental utility.[25] More recently, Calvin Roetzel, in an influential work on Paul, has also found the notion of "theology" unproblematic for Paul, even though he prefers the term "theologizing" to emphasize that Paul's "theology" emerged throughout the course of his ministry.[26]

So what is wrong with "theology"? I need to note at the outset that it is a word that conveys at least two meanings. It is possible, first, to speak of "theology" as "the sum of the beliefs held by an individual or group regarding matters of religious faith or of ultimate concern: the ideational element in religion." "Theology" in this sense could occur in a text that represented the views of an individual or group. A more common meaning for theology, however, is "the systematic study of the role of God in relation to human beings."[27] Whereas the first meaning refers simply to the existence and character of data in a text or other context bearing on the interactions between God, human beings, and the world or on other matters of ultimate concern, the second meaning denotes the systematic investigation of such phenomena. The first meaning relates to the *designation and description* of data, the second to their *interpretation and explanation*.

Although one could imagine "theology" in the first sense featuring in texts of many types, such as letters, political speeches, poems, and novels, in which case we would not designate the author a "theologian," "theology" in the second sense is produced by people who are "theologians" by profession and usually appears in the form of articles or monographs. The profession of "theologian" today is one that encapsulates an expository role with a certain structure and shape derived from the centuries of social and historical processes that have produced it, while Christian "theology" has a well-articulated set of doctrines. Given their focus, theologians are mainly interested in ideas, even if this means neglecting other areas of interest to Christians, such as experience.

This distinction allows us to isolate the mischief in speaking of Paul's "theology." It is beyond doubt that "theology" in the first sense is to be found in the letters of Paul. He had matters of utmost importance to convey of God's dealings with men, women, and the cosmos. But he did so in occasional letters covering a wide range of issues that were sent to this or that community of Christ-followers. Although I return to this issue below, it is worth noting that Gerd Theissen has insisted that "theology" is incapable of dealing with the whole of life that is the subject of the early Christian writings.[28] Paul did not restrict himself to the ideational dimensions of being a follower of Christ, nor did he produce systematic treatises of "theology," and it is therefore anachronistic to describe him as a "theologian." It is difficult not to gain the impression that to refer to Paul as a "theologian" serves the useful social purpose of enrolling him as an honorary member of the same club to which those who wield such designations already belong. I am sure that Paul, however, given his immense cultural and intellectual distance from anyone working today as a theologian, would have much preferred the view of Groucho Marx: "I wouldn't want to belong to any club that would have me as a member."

Why, then, are these designations used of him and his epistles? The sociology of suspicion suggests a possible answer in the professional practice of modern scholars, many of whom classify themselves as "theologians," to interpret his writings as "theology" since this is the framework they themselves are primarily interested in and employ. Trained and socialized to focus on the ideational dimension of religious life (generally to the exclusion of its many other aspects), they inevitably apply this grid when reading Paul, even though it filters out only a section of the data in the texts. Thus to interpret Paul in their own image means squeezing his message and his role into modes of conceptuality that postdate his writings by centuries and that are quite possibly alien to the purpose and meaning of those writings. The problem, then, is one of pronounced theological reductionism or, in the colorful North American expression, of theological "cookie-cutting."

Yet to restrict one's interest in the Pauline corpus to material that can be subsumed under modern "theological" agendas is not problematic merely for what it omits. In addition, there are serious question marks hanging over the quality of what is produced. To witness—in the secondary literature or at academic conferences—the seemingly endless manipulation of Pauline data within a limited and fairly constant set of theological categories ("eschatology," "apocalyptic," "soteriology," and the like) rarely disturbed by the entrance of genuinely new ideas can be disappointing. Is this all that a man of Paul's Promethean intellect, passion, and power of self-expression deserves by way of understanding? Are these the letters wherein Augustine, Luther, and Barth found such life and stimulus for genuine Christian experience and reflection? Where in research of this kind is the "creative energy" that Barth correctly saw as characterizing the best Pauline interpretation?

Even James Dunn, the author of one of the finest books ever written on religious *experience* in the early Christ-movement[29] as well as a work (on

Pauline theology) of notable erudition and insight where the liveliness and elegance of the discussion prevents it from succumbing to the problem identified in the preceding paragraph,[30] illustrates some of the problems here. Echoing Anselm's definition of theology as "faith seeking understanding," he describes Paul's purpose as having been "to articulate their faith in writing and to instruct others in their common faith," meaning that Paul was engaged in "the articulation of common faith," and suggests that from "the perspective of subsequent generations Paul is undoubtedly the *first* Christian theologian."[31] Here it is apparent that Dunn has a view of Paul that is both too narrow, since the apostle had many more purposes in writing than this, and also anachronistic in attributing to Paul the expository role of subsequent Christian theologians. Dunn himself, admittedly, is one of only a small number of scholars to recognize the problems inherent in the "theology" paradigm for Paul. At one point he commendably interprets "theology" in a broad way, so that it is not just theoretical in interest but also concerns itself with praxis.[32] Elsewhere he tantalizingly asks, was Paul "first and foremost a theologian or a missionary, church founder, and pastor? Is a focus on the *theology* of St Paul inevitably too restrictive?"[33] Yet Dunn unfortunately fails to recognize that the answer to this latter question is emphatically yes, while each of the four possible roles he lists here for Paul, although certainly positing a different framework of interpretation, is anachronistic in relation to him.

If "theology" represents a mode of understanding incapable *ab limine* of addressing the richness we find in a Pauline letter, what perspective can guide us in an investigation of Romans in a manner that does justice both to its historical dimension and also to its startling capacity to speak of matters concerning God in a way that has repeatedly transcended the circumstances of its original production? While Morgan accurately writes that reading "this weighty epistle without the customary spectacles of a Christian doctrinal framework may avoid some of the distortions arising from later tradition and experience,"[34] we are still left with identifying what positive program we may put in its place.

Morgan's own preferred framework for the study of Romans is that of religion, although he does not develop a comprehensive theory. One attraction of this model is that the language used by anthropologists in relation to religion provides an alternative vocabulary for interpreting what Paul wrote.[35] At the same time, when religion is the focus of interest, it is impossible to avoid the experiential dimensions of the early Christ-movement that are often overlooked by those concentrating on "theological" ideas. Since the early 1990s the potential for a movement from "theology" to "religion" as a dominant paradigm has been advocated by Hans Dieter Betz, amply demonstrated in a theory- and data-rich work by Gerd Theissen setting out a "theory of primitive Christian religion," and activated by John Ashton in a provocative volume devoted to Paul's religion.[36]

Yet in spite of the obvious attractions of religion over theology as a theoretical framework (and the skill with which Theissen and Ashton, for example, develop it), its introduction, although defensible, is not unproblematic for reasons initially explained by Wilfred Cantwell Smith in a work first published in 1962 that has become a modern classic in religious studies, *The Meaning and End of Religion*. At the heart of this book lies Smith's careful historical demonstration that our notion of "religion," essentially meaning a specific system of belief embodied in a circumscribed community, which seems entirely natural to us and which we automatically apply to ancient Mediterranean data, is a modern concept that dates from the Enlightenment.

The Latin word *religio* covered a variety of meanings, but seems primarily to have meant either a power outside a person obligating him or her to certain behavior under pain of retribution (a kind of taboo) or a feeling of human beings toward such powers. The *loci religiosi* were places where such powers were thought to reside, and *viri religiosi* were devout persons who fulfilled their obligations to them. In addition, the *religio* of a particular god meant the traditional cultic observances carried out at his or her shrine.[37] During the patristic period the word was used in a number of senses, including (often in the plural) specific Christian ritual practices, the attitude of a particular worshiper to God, and the name of the bond between him or her and God.[38] Augustine's *De Vera Religione* is best translated "On Genuine Worship."[39] For Aquinas the word meant the outward expression of faith, the inner motivation that prompts the worship of God, the worship itself, and the bond that unites the soul with God.[40] Calvin's influential *Christianae Religionis Institutio* (first published in 1536) is best translated "Grounding in Christian Piety," rather than "Institutes of the Christian Religion," a translation that first appeared in the nineteenth century.[41] Whereas some Protestant reformers had adopted a concept of religion to represent an inner piety, "in the seventeenth and early eighteenth centuries this was largely superseded by a concept of schematic externalization that reflected, and served, the clash of conflicting religious parties, the emergence of a triumphant intellectualism, and the emerging new information from beyond the seas about the patterns of other men's religious life."[42] Given the particular (and historically contingent) meaning the word had come to acquire, embracing both the personal faith of men and women and the cumulative traditions (the inner and outer aspects of religious life), Smith advocated discontinuing use of it altogether, although he did not consider that the same problems beset the adjective "religious."[43] On this basis the noun "religiousness" may at times be useful.

The mere fact that our modern notion of "religion" was not found in the ancient world would not necessarily preclude our using it. The whole process of translation between cultures necessitates that one culture use its concepts in relation to the other. This is why the distinction between "etic" (referring to the systematic set of concepts used by one culture to understand others) and "emic" (referring to the insider or indigenous point of view) is a useful one and, indeed, why the process of the application of social-scientific insights and models to biblical texts is valid.[44] Yet there must be a reasonable correspondence between the etic concept and the emic data upon which it will be employed, to avoid doing violence to the latter. While this is an area where agreement is not always possible, Smith is making a case for the lack of fit between religion and the premodern world being so great as to caution against its use in relation to data drawn therefrom.

Bruce J. Malina has sounded a further reason for caution. He points out that the existence of religion in modern cultures in a state of separation from other institutions, especially politics and economics, makes it notably different from the position in the ancient Mediterranean world, where what we would call "religious" phenomena tended to be embedded in politics ("political religion" or better, "political religiousness") or the family ("domestic religion" or better, "domestic religiousness").[45] One only has to consider the case of the temple in Jerusalem to see the complex interconnections that were possible. The temple was at the same time the center of the sacrificial cult to God, a repository for tithes and hence an economic power base for the high priests, a market for sacrificial animals, a place where records of debts were stored, and the site of a Roman garrison, the Antonia.

None of this entirely disqualifies religion, properly modeled and at an appropriate level of abstraction, as useful in the study of early Christian texts. Theissen and Ashton have gotten considerable mileage from this approach. But it certainly raises grave caveats over the usefulness of the notion of religion as an interpretive category and provides a good reason for trying something else. Before I set out an alternative perspective, however, it will help to situate this enterprise within recent developments in Romans research.

Romans in Its Historical Setting

In spite of the profound theological dimensions of Romans, some of which I mention below, current scholarship on the letter is thoroughly alive to the historical situatedness of the letter, in particular its connection with the experience of Christ-followers in Rome in the mid-fifties of the first century CE. Such is the approach in this volume. But it is easy to forget that this is a fairly recent development.

The German Protestant reformer Philipp Melanchthon (1497–1560) had characterized Romans as a *christianae religionis compendium,* and although this formulation was challenged by F. C. Baur in the mid-nineteenth century, its influence reached into the twentieth.[46] In a succinct survey of recent Romans research W. S. Campbell has noted that until the 1950s there was little interest in anything beyond Romans 1–8, and this section of the letter was regularly interpreted as a summary of Paul's gospel or theology, unaffected by time or history—a view fostered by the length of the letter and the shortness of university terms![47]

Yet in the 1920s and 1930s advances in historical criticism that focused on the connection between the products of the early Christ-movement and their social settings (evident, for example, in the rise of form criticism) began to make scholars aware of the importance of local context in understanding New Testament works. This perception received further stimulus with the development in Germany in the late 1940s and early 1950s of redaction criticism, which was in part alert to the particular community setting, the *Sitz im Leben,* of whole Gospels. It was inevitable that this changed outlook would sooner or later be brought to bear upon Romans.[48]

In 1954 N. A. Dahl, reviewing Rudolf Bultmann's *Theology of the New Testament,* had criticized him for virtually ignoring Romans 9–11. In the same year major stimulus to change came with Johannes Munck's *Paulus und die Heilsgeschichte* (translated into English in 1959 as *Paul and the Salvation of Mankind*) in which Munck argued against Romans being a theological presentation unaffected by time and history and argued that it was to be interpreted in the light of Paul's missionary situation.[49] For Munck, Romans 9–11 was important as Paul's reconstruction of the order of events in salvation history in the light of the Jewish failure to believe in Jesus as Messiah and in the face of Paul's own successful gentile mission.[50] In a number of essays Ernst Käsemann analyzed Romans 1–11, thus indicating his recognition of the importance of chapters 9–11.[51] But it was only with Paul S. Minear's *Obedience of Faith* (1971) that a full-blown situational reading of the letter appeared, based mainly on Romans 14–15.[52] We will return to Minear often.

The revolution in Romans research that was begun especially by Munck and Minear continues without pause. The explorations in this volume fall squarely within this effort to read the letter closely in connection with its original context, both its Roman destination and the immediate circumstances in Paul's life that he directly mentions or alludes to in the text. Yet the approach taken here differs from existing research in adopting explicitly social-scientific ideas and perspectives. While these allow a different type of historical research to be conducted into the letter, they also offer an alternative framework to that of religion.

Ethnic Conflict and Identity

So what model should we adopt? At this point I should drop the veil of
authorial anonymity in order to disclose the particular interest that has motivated my work on Romans throughout the preparation of this volume and
that has, accordingly, guided the theoretical framework I have adopted. And
in a market as crowded as the *Römerforschungsplatz* it is probably beholden on
anyone wishing to set up a new stall to explain what new product might justify such audacity.

The contemporary issue driving the current study of Romans is the nature
of Christian identity—that is, the question of what it means to be a Christian—in a world rent by violent, often murderous conflict between groups, in
particular those of an ethnic kind. Since the late 1980s we have witnessed a
horrifying upsurge in ethnic conflict. The breakup of Yugoslavia during the
years 1991–1994 led to war between Serbs, Croats, and Muslims that produced numerous episodes of mass murder, rape, and ethnic cleansing, culminating in atrocities committed on the Muslim population of Kosovo in 1999.
In 1994 approximately 800,000 Tutsis were killed by Hutus in Rwanda, many
of them hacked to death with machetes.[53] For Christians one of the most dis-
turbing features of this genocide was that some Roman Catholic religious took
an active part in it.[54] Throughout much of this period people in Northern Ireland were being killed by Unionist and Republican gangs, while Palestinians
and Israelis died at one another's hands. The lingering animosity between
India and Pakistan over Kashmir has led to many atrocities and has at times
threatened to break out into a nuclear exchange between the two nations.

It has become commonplace to speak of a "resurgence of ethnicity" in relation to these events. Yet no less an authority than Fredrik Barth has suggested
that this notion may be misplaced. According to him, this notion is based "on
impressions created by mass media reporting activism and conflict where they
were formerly silent on both issues and places." It is possible that what we "are
seeing may not be the reassertion of identities that had been attenuated, so
much as their greater visibility following on from the enhanced freedom to
express them after the fall of the former repressive regimes." The issue may be
the battleground of information control rather than one of substantive ethnicity. Repression by a regime stops people from displaying their own identity, and it also impedes them from knowing about the commitment of
others.[55] Thus Barth suggests that the salience of ethnicity and the imagined
community that it asserts intermeshes with the power and information structure of the context.[56]

However we are to understand the visibility of ethnic conflict, it clearly
constitutes one of the most pressing evils in our world and, not surprisingly,
has begun to attract significant theological analysis.[57] There are certainly

other moral disorders in the world, to do with sexuality for example, but these seem to pale into insignificance before the aggressive displays of power and the violence witnessed in the ethnic conflicts just mentioned. It is interesting to note that while Paul criticizes the Corinthian members of the Christ-movement in connection with various aspects of sexual relations, he has no such charge to bring against the Christ-followers of Rome,[58] whereas he does have a great deal to say about ethnic tension and conflict among them.

The twin and related issues that arise in connection with the warring pairs of groups just mentioned are *identity* and *ethnicity*. Each of these groups installs in the hearts and minds of its members a distinctive identity, a sense of who they are that derives from belonging to such a group, and that identity is distinctively ethnic in character. These two words, for each of which there exists a considerable social-scientific literature, have now begun to be thrown around in biblical research with considerable abandon. It has been widely and correctly realized that these concepts are as applicable to the ancient world as to the modern, as Christopher Stanley's useful article on the numerous outbreaks of ethnic violence between Greeks and "Jews" goes some way to demonstrate.[59] Regrettably, however, among English-speaking scholars attempts to indicate precisely what is meant by "identity" and "ethnicity" are notable for their rarity.[60]

The need is particularly acute in the case of "identity," which has been described as having broken out like an epidemic in daily speech and as being a "plastic word."[61] It is frequently used, rarely defined, and has an alarmingly high coefficient of elasticity. In Germany, however, many scholars, perhaps inspired by the nature of the European Union and its imminent expansion, have gone to some lengths to utilize notions of "identity" that draw upon the rich theoretical resources available.[62] Chapter two below is devoted to presenting a particular model of identity that is the dominant theoretical perspective used here in relation to Romans.

The heart of this approach is that every group generates a sense of belonging, an identity, into which its members are socialized. This means that thereafter their sense of who they are as individuals includes that aspect derived from belonging to the group. In the theory I explain in chapter two, this part of their sense of self is referred to as "social identity." This approach originated in social-psychological research, and both the social and the individual dimensions are central to its formulation. While at times external circumstances, such as the group being oppressed, may magnify the extent to which the social identity its members gain by belonging is salient in their individual experiences, their status as individuals is not forgotten. On other occasions, such as those of intragroup dissension, other aspects of the members' identities may rise to prominence.

In relation to Romans, I argue that central to Paul's communicative purpose is to strengthen the social identity that his addressees in Rome gain from belonging to the Christ-movement, particularly by emphasizing its supremacy over other identities, ethnic especially, on offer. To this extent his activity can be construed as an attempt to exercise leadership over groups of Christ-followers in Rome, torn by division related at least in part to their ethnic status as either Judeans or Greeks, in order to influence his audience in a manner that is likely to enhance their contribution to the enhancement of group goals. This is not Paul's only purpose in the letter, but it is a vital one.

As far as "ethnicity" is concerned, books have also appeared on Romans that either have "ethnic" in the title or use the notion in the text, but fail to explore the meaning of that concept.[63] Unlike the case with "identity" (which can arguably serve as a focus for integrating rival groups), social-scientific notions of ethnicity have not been much utilized so far in biblical research in Germany, perhaps because ethnicity is so invested in conflict—to which there exists a pronounced Western European aversion born of the continent's bloodstained history until the end of the Second World War. In chapter three below I model the concept of "ethnicity" and argue for its relevance to phenomena in the ancient Mediterranean world relevant to Romans.

A serious interest in the question of ethnic identity necessitates that we pay close attention to the nature and names of the ethnic groups and phenomena within our gaze. I argue later, for example, that the current habit of translating Ἰουδαῖοι as "Jews" and ἔθνη as "gentiles" is indefensible in its anachronism and that more appropriate renderings are "Judean" and "non-Judean" (or "foreigner" or even "heathen" when the word is being deployed by a Judean). Related to this argument is the proposal that the concept of "anti-Semitism" developed as recently as the second half of the nineteenth century in relation to an emerging pseudoscience of human "races." To use the word in relation to first-century social attitudes is grotesquely anachronistic. It also serves to perpetuate anti-Jewish prejudices in our society by encouraging the untenable view that the identity of twentieth- and twenty-first-century Jews is the same as that of first-century Judeans and that the former may therefore be held liable for the alleged sins of the latter.

The need to be accurate in designating identities, even if they are not ethnic, also demands that we eschew the word "Christian" in relation to first-century CE phenomena. The Greek word *Christianos* appears only three times in the New Testament (Acts 11:26; 26:28; 1 Pet. 4:16). It is the Greek version of *Christianus* that was coined by speakers of Latin, among whom the suffix *-ianus* classified "people as partisans of a political or military leader, and is mildly contemptuous."[64] An apt translation is "Christ-lackey."[65] It does not appear to have been used as a self-designation by the group until after the

New Testament period. Even in the three places just mentioned where it does appear, it reflects outsider use. In addition, the words "Christian" and "Christianity" convey more recent associations alien to the first century. In place of these inappropriate and anachronistic expressions, I prefer "Christ-follower" or "Christ-believer," "in-Christ," and "the Christ-movement" when speaking of first-century data.

The Theological Dimension

Yet reliance on social perspectives relating to identity and ethnicity is in no way prejudicial to an acknowledgment of Paul's absolute conviction in the transcendental foundations of the message he is imparting to the Romans or to the fact that it is this perceived dimension to the letter that has ensured its continued power among Christians from his day to this. It is necessary to emphasize this point, since in some quarters there still lingers the unfounded perception that approaches to a Pauline letter that utilize social theory are in some way inconsistent with an interest in what Paul has to say about the role of God.

An unfortunate stimulus to such a view has possibly been provided by the ending to Francis Watson's significant 1986 monograph *Paul, Judaism and the Gentiles: A Sociological Approach*. Having vigorously argued against the Lutheran reading of Romans and having proposed instead that Paul was seeking to persuade the "Jewish Christians" of Rome to separate themselves in sectarian fashion from the synagogue, Watson poses two questions in relation to which his readers may conclude that he considers there to be a reasonable chance that they should be answered in the negative. First, if such was Paul's aim, could he "still be seen as the bearer of a message with profound universal significance?" And, even more negatively: "Should Paul's thought still be a major source of inspiration for contemporary theological discussion? Or should it be rejected as a cul-de-sac, and should one seek inspiration elsewhere?"[66] Later in this volume I take up Watson's historical interpretation of Paul's message in Romans, but for the present I submit that what Paul says in this letter does most assuredly transcend the exigencies of its original setting, and the trenchant skepticism Watson entertained as a possibility in 1986 represents too extreme a position to be taken seriously. In addition, Watson's own more recent work on Romans shows its continuing centrality to theological discussion.[67]

In 1980, at a time when the social-scientific interpretation of the New Testament was just beginning, Halvor Moxnes had much more plausibly argued that Paul did not pursue the subject of God as an abstract theological topos, but (like Israelites contemporary with him) took the view that "the question of God and the identity of his people were inextricably bound up with one another."[68] This meant that to distinguish theological issues (in the first sense outlined above) from social ones was a difficult task. We will see in chapter two that the particular social-psychological approach to identity adopted for use in this volume encompasses the notion of bringing together groups in conflict (including ethnic groups) under a new common or superordinate identity to resolve the differences between them. As far as Romans is concerned, I submit throughout this volume that Paul is pursuing such a strategy and that the common identity he proposes is intimately associated with being in Christ in accordance with the purposes of God expressed in the gift of the Spirit. Nowhere is this clearer than in the programmatic statement at 3:29-30: "Is God the God of Judeans only? Is he not also the God of non-Judeans? Yes, also of non-Judeans, since God is one and he will righteous the circumcised by faith and the uncircumcised through faith." Here, and throughout this volume, *righteous* is used as a verb to maintain the unity of the semantic field to which it belongs, as explained in chapter seven. In 3:29-30, as Moxnes has noted, Paul begins with a primary "theological" view, that God is one, and draws from it a conclusion that God will righteous both Judeans and non-Judeans through faith.[69] The overlooking of ethnic difference is presented as a concomitant of divine monotheism. How does one separate the social from the "theological" here?

Fundamental to the question of monotheism in Romans is the role Christ plays in relation to the one God. This relationship has been the subject of an important proposal by Richard Bauckham. For some time scholars have widely accepted that there were two approaches to the nature of monotheism among Judeans in the Second Temple period. On the first view their monotheism was strictly construed so as to make it impossible to attribute any real divinity to a figure other than the one God; in this perspective, divinity could be attributed to Jesus Christ only if there was a divergence from this strict monotheistic position. On the second view, Judean monotheism was not so strict and a number of intermediary figures were afforded a semidivine status; Jesus Christ was capable of being understood in this light. In the 1996 Didsbury Lectures Bauckham argued that "Jewish" monotheism was indeed strict and that the intermediary figures were either simply attributes of God (Wisdom, for example) or were unambiguously creatures. He offered the new proposal that Jesus Christ was identified directly with the one God of Israel, that he was included in this unique identity. This reflected the Israelite understanding of God as a person rather than as a particular kind of nature. Israelites were interested in *who* God was, not *what* he was. Identifying features predicated of their personal God in "Jewish" belief were also predicated of Jesus.[70] At the annual SBL meeting in Toronto in November 2002, Bauckham applied this theory specifically to Paul's Christology and effectively answered criticism from a panel of exegetes and theologians invited to consider it. With help from the research of D. B. Capes's 1992 monograph *Old Testament Yahweh Texts in Paul's Christology*, Bauckham has persuasively argued that "Paul's christological interpretation of scriptural passages about YHWH, taking the name YHWH (κύριος in the LXX) to refer to Jesus Christ, is an important phenomenon that has often been underestimated both in extent and in significance."[71] This is all part of Bauckham's general belief in "early high Christology," which Leander Keck, one of the panelists at the Toronto meeting, engagingly referred to as "the Big Bang." According to Bauckham, the christological debates among the fathers in the third, fourth, and fifth centuries reached an understanding of Christ's divine nature using philosophical ideas that largely replicated the position Paul had reached in the first century through Israel's personalist understanding of God.[72] For his model of (individual) "identity" in this context, Bauckham utilizes ideas of Paul Ricoeur.

In this volume, I adopt the position that Bauckham is probably correct in his understanding of Pauline Christology, and I refer to his view where relevant. As a result, the extent to which Paul advocates in Romans a certain relationship to God and Christ in the interest of social reconciliation means that this dimension of his thought is drawn even more closely into what I have been describing as "theological" in the first sense. Very noticeable is the way in which the righteousness of God is imparted to those who have faith in Christ and in God himself. Paul describes a process whereby God communicates an aspect of his own identity, righteousness, to those who have faith. This represents further support for the view that this is a letter where the social and "theological" dimensions of membership of the Christ-movement are closely intertwined.

The Character of Paul's Rhetoric

That Paul is attempting in Romans to persuade his audience to embody a particular vision and praxis of identity in Christ inevitably raises the issue of rhetoric. In the ancient Greco-Roman world people who sought to persuade their listeners or readers to take some action or adopt a particular view habitually utilized the rich array of rhetorical techniques that had originated in the Greek polis.[73] Since the 1970s there has been an explosion of interest in the role of rhetoric in the persuasive strategies of various New Testament texts, which has in part been stimulated by the rehabilitation of rhetoric as an intellectual exercise.[74] As far as the Pauline epistles are concerned, Galatians has been the focus of greatest interest,[75] but Romans has also attracted attention.[76]

In writing on Galatians I have expressed caution in relation to excessively technical uses of rhetoric (especially the habit of labeling various features of a Pauline letter under rhetorical headings to the neglect of paying proper attention to their function in the text) and also in relation to assuming too great an appropriation of rhetoric in epistolary contexts.[77] Further reason to be wary about application of the full panoply of technical rhetorical language to New Testament texts now exists in the growing awareness that ancient rhetoric was much more varied than is generally appreciated. In particular, the tradition developed by Aristotle and his successors represents only one strand; approaches developed by Gorgias and others before his time may have persisted into the New Testament period, even though they are not as well represented in the sources that have survived.[78] In particular, a strand of rhetoric developed in Asia Minor during the Hellenistic period characterized by emotional effect, bombast, rhythm, and wordplay.[79] Paul was probably influenced by this style of rhetoric if he was born in Tarsus.[80]

Central to the current discussion of Pauline texts has been the need to identify the "rhetorical situation" of the communication represented in a particular text. This useful notion, which is broad enough to embrace pre- and post-Aristotelian types of rhetoric, refers to an array of social phenomena provoking the communication that comprises an "exigence" (meaning some disorder in social relationships marked by urgency), an audience (persons capable of being influenced by discourse to modify their views or actions in some way), and certain constraints (such as persons, events, beliefs, values, and interests) having the power to interfere with or block any decision or action necessary to rectify the exigence.[81]

Although knowledge of any particular rhetorical situation to which a speaker or writer is responding derives most securely from the communication itself, at times other relevant information may be provided by sources external to it. Thus, to investigate the rhetorical situation (its exigence, audience, and constraints) addressed by Paul in Romans there is nothing to exclude and everything to recommend, for example, the careful use of information we possess from elsewhere concerning the character of Rome and the condition of its diverse inhabitants in the 50s of the first century CE.[82]

This consideration also entails that we should not draw a sharp distinction between rhetorical and historical analysis of the letter, by suggesting that the former is how a particular speaker perceived the rhetorical situation and responded to it, while historical analysis is restricted to establishing "the historical circumstances lying behind a text."[83] The fundamental task of historical criticism as it applies to a New Testament text is not to investigate what lies "behind" or "beneath" it. Rather, it consists in exploring what it meant—that is, what message it conveyed—to its initial audience when it was first published to them. This task necessarily involves exploring the interrelationship between the communication, here Paul's rhetorical discourse, and the context in which it was delivered.[84] An appropriate analogy is thus sociolinguistics, not archaeology.

Two Final Points

Romans as a Text from an Oral Culture

Of fundamental importance for the interpretation of Romans is that Paul must have assumed that those who first encountered it would have done so aurally, gathered together in some place in Rome while it was read out to them. This was mandated by the low literacy rates in the ancient world, probably lower than 5 to 10 percent for both Greco-Roman and Judean populations.[85] It requires a great leap of imagination for us to comprehend what it was for a group living in an oral culture to receive a communication like Romans. Yet it is an effort we must make.

Paul certainly devoted a great deal of time and effort to writing Romans, and the cost of parchment or papyrus on which it was first written and of the services of Tertius the scribe (unless he donated them) would have been considerable. Perhaps Paul thought that his Roman audience would hear the text more than once and that the few literate members of the congregations would have had it copied so that they could pay it even closer attention (but by having slaves reread it to them). It is unlikely he assumed the letter would simply disappear after its first publication.[86] Nevertheless, he also knew that there would be a first time for all the Roman Christ-followers to encounter its message, and he must have wanted the letter to make reasonable sense on that occasion. He would be helped by the extremely retentive memories of his audience; such memories are exceedingly rare in a literate culture like ours.

I argue later that it is likely that Paul had some notion of affairs in Rome and that he tailored the letter to accord with what he knew. He and his audience were also persons socialized into the Greco-Roman and Judean worlds of the first century, so he could rely on them to understand its basic cultural discourses, in areas such as honor and shame, for example. Yet his knowledge of those who would hear his letter and of the particular circumstances that would affect their initial reception of it was still very limited. Leaving aside the small possibility that Paul had confided some collateral instructions to Phoebe (Rom. 16:1-2), the probable bearer of the letter, the letter itself obviously constituted the firmest basis of knowledge he could be sure they would receive. Such a setting meant that his safest course was for the letter to be as self-contained as possible, with its various parts making sense within the total framework it provided. One dimension to this experience of which we can be quite sure, for example, is that the best guide to the meaning of an expression in the letter is what Paul has said earlier, since this would still be fresh in their minds. The next best guide is what he says after the point in question, since he could assume that the audience would end up hearing the letter as a totality in its correct sequence.

Pauline scholarship is littered with the results of critics allowing considerations (often the product of great ingenuity) derived from outside a particular letter to displace meanings that are available from closely attending to Paul's argument in the letter. I comment later on a number of instances of this tendency, most notably the postulation of the presence of Adam in Rom. 1:18-32 and Romans 7 on the strength of alleged allusions to the Old Testament in those passages, even though the introduction of Adam into either passage is flatly antipathetic to what Paul is attempting to communicate. On the other hand, as we will see in chapter five below, when we interpret the "difficult" material in 16:17-20 on the basis that the Roman Christ-followers had just heard 14:1—15:13, many of the supposed difficulties evaporate.

These considerations provide the foundation for my broad approach to reading this letter, which I now outline.

A "Reading" of Romans

To do justice to the original oral mode of delivery and aural mode of reception of the letter, it seems advisable to examine its sections in sequential order from the beginning to the end. This is the approach taken in this volume (as in my earlier book on Galatians),[87] except for an initial chapter that deals with the "framing" passages of Romans (1:1-15 and 15:14—16:27). But this work is not a "commentary" so much as a "reading." For it will be evident from the introductory observations on identity and ethnicity set out above that the interpretation offered here is shaped by a particular theoretical framework that, although derived from the social sciences, incorporates a strong interest in the "theological" dimensions of this text. At the same time, I have not engaged exhaustively with the whole body of secondary literature on this letter in the manner typical of the many excellent commentaries that exist. Rather, I interact with a selection of social scientists or biblical scholars throughout the text in a way aimed at helping me formulate a distinctive argument rather than cover all of the issues that have been raised in relation to Romans so far.

2

Explaining Social Identity

In the previous chapter I introduced the central role that notions of identity, both ethnic and the different form of identity obtained by belonging to the Christ-movement, would play in this book. As noted there, "identity" has become something of a "plastic word," rarely defined and dangerously elastic. But as Regina Börschel has rightly noted, it makes sense to use the word as long as one explains what one means by it.[1] The time has now come to provide a detailed model of the type of identity to be used in this book. In Germany recent New Testament research employing notions of identity drawn from various reaches of the social sciences (especially the sociology of knowledge) has highlighted a number of insights likely to be applicable in any research into identity. The foundational concept is that of difference as constituting identity, since something only *is* to the extent that it is distinguished from something else.[2]

Yet this view obtains with respect to a wide variety of phenomena in the early days of the dispersion of the gospel around the Mediterranean. More focused perspectives seem necessary for Romans. In particular, the material in the letter pointing to tension and even conflict within the Christ-movement in the capital calls for a theory of identity that is embedded in the processes of intergroup differentiation and hostility. I will now set out such a theory.

Social Identity and Self-Categorization Theory

Social Identity Theory and Intergroup Phenomena

A General Outline

The central theoretical perspective employed in this volume is an area of social psychology known as social identity theory, which was developed by Henri Tajfel, together with collaborators such as John C. Turner, at the University of Bristol in England in the 1970s and 1980s and is still flourishing, in the United Kingdom and Europe especially.[3] Social identity theory was initially elaborated by Tajfel in 1972 to differentiate between intergroup and interpersonal relations and also to lay the foundation for a social psychology of intergroup relations and group processes that was nonreductionist in the sense that these phenomena were seen as having psychological properties quite distinct from those of a collectivity of individuals merely acting together.[4]

Underlying this theory was the fundamental discovery that merely categorizing people into distinct groups resulted in behavior in which members of one group favored one another over members of other groups. An early manifestation of this discovery came in research undertaken on boys in U.S. summer camps in the 1950s, where researchers led by M. Sherif found that as soon as the boys were allocated into groups, the groups began strenuously competing with one another, even though their members had friends in the other groups.[5] Elegant research, the so-called minimal-group experiments conducted by Tajfel in the 1970s, carefully stripped away all bases for differentiation other than belonging to a group and provided strong empirical support for this phenomenon by showing that group members still discriminated in favor of fellow members.[6]

"Social identity" refers to that part of a person's self-concept (admittedly from a much larger whole) that derives from his or her membership in a group. It encompasses three aspects: the cognitive recognition of belonging to the group, connotations of the value attached to such belonging, and emotional dimensions—aspects that generally tend to coalesce, as shown in self-definitions such as "us women" or "we Americans."[7] The theory is especially concerned with the ways in which the members of one group seek to differentiate it from other groups so as to achieve a positive social identity.

Connecting this form of social identity with the Christ-movement in Rome means investigating the unique kind of identity that Paul was proposing its individual members obtained by belonging to it, whatever their ethnicity. Social identity is genuinely sociopsychological since it covers the group experience but also interests itself in how this affects the hearts and minds of individual Christ-followers in the cognitive, emotional, and evaluative dimensions of group belonging.

Norms/Identity Descriptors

Social identity theory has sought to be more precise concerning how a group installs its distinctive identity on individual members. Perhaps the most prominent way is by the generation and inculcation of what it calls group "norms." Although this word is not entirely appropriate, for reasons I set out in chapter thirteen below (where I propose "identity descriptors" as an alternative), "norms" may be described provisionally as the values that define acceptable and unacceptable attitudes and behaviors by members of the group. They tell members what they should think and feel and how they should behave if they are to belong to the group and share its identity. They thus bring order and predictability to the environment, especially by narrowing down social and moral choices from the vast range of possibilities on offer to those that accord with the group's sense of who and what it is. Although in ordinary daily life members may live in accord with the group norms on a kind of autopilot and without giving them too much thought, they reveal their true worth in new and ambiguous situations, helping the members to determine appropriate outlooks and behaviors. In sum, norms maintain and enhance group identity.[8]

Norms within a social identity framework provide a useful alternative to the (almost universal) use of "ethics" in relation to parts of New Testament texts (such as Romans 12–15) that relate to how Christ-followers should behave. There are two major problems with employing the term "ethics." First, since the Enlightenment it has become a separate province of inquiry indelibly stamped by its link to that part of moral reasoning largely derived from Kant and the utilitarians that focuses on the solution of moral dilemmas. The recent renaissance of interest in Aristotelian virtue ethics, with its concern for the larger framework of the good life, has somewhat diminished but not entirely eliminated this constriction of focus. Second, contemporary "ethics" is largely preoccupied with actions of individuals; this may suit the intensely individualistic societies of North America and northern Europe (and their ex-colonial offshoots), but is far less comfortable in strongly group-oriented cultures, such as those which were the context for the New Testament texts. Social identity theory avoids both problems by treating norms as an aspect of group identity and vital to its continuation.

In spite of the importance of norms in maintaining and implementing group identity, they only form part of a much larger whole. Moreover, it is essential to reach a firm view about the nature of the identity in view before proceeding to specify values and behavior that will sustain it. As we will see, this is the route Paul charts in Romans, with chaps. 1–8 (and 9–11 to a lesser extent) being taken up with questions of identity, while chaps. 12–15 are largely taken up with "norms," or, as I prefer to call them, "identity descriptors."

Stereotyping

A phenomenon that frequently accompanies ingroup/outgroup differentiation is that of stereotyping. Within a social identity perspective stereotypes are social categorical judgments, perceptions of people in terms of their group memberships (rather than as unique individuals). "When we stereotype people we attribute to them certain characteristics that are seen to be shared by all or most of their fellow group members."[9] They are deployed in the context of intergroup relations, almost always as a way of describing outgroups. Stereotypes are not unchanging and inflexible, not fixed mental images stored in people's heads, but vary depending on the realities of any particular social context and the state of intergroup relations in which they are deployed. Like all perceptions, they vary in accordance with the circumstances of the perceiver. This has the result that there can be disputes over the validity of stereotypes within and between groups, and such disputes are a normal part of political and historical processes through which groups and society at large must move.[10] The species of stereotyping relevant to Romans is that which occurs between ethnic groups, as explained in chapter three below, and the poor relations between Judean and Greek Christ-followers in Rome seem to have weighed heavily on Paul when he was writing the letter.

Social Identity and Time

One important dimension of social life in Romans is that of time, since this letter looks to the past (especially in chaps. 5 and 6) and future (especially in chaps. 8 and 11) as well as to the present in shaping the identity of the Christ-followers in Rome. Yet time has not been the subject of much discussion by social identity theorists, as opposed to the intense interest shown by anthropologists and sociologists. In 1996, however, Susan Condor offered a useful formulation of the problem. She noted that most empirical social-psychological research had achieved an image of social life composed of discrete moments and contexts, a situation rather in tension with Tajfel's own interest in how social phenomena such as intergroup differentiation, prejudice, and conflict endured and developed over time. To generate such a perspective it is necessary to emphasize social life as a temporal trajectory rather than as a static set of positions, a reality in which social agents take up identities, ideas, and practices and hand them on to others, often transforming them in the process.[11]

Social groups should be regarded as ongoing processes, extending over macrotime, not as reified entities existing in a single moment of microtime, divorced from the historical dimension of social life. Such an emphasis would correspond more closely with the way people experience themselves—not as radically decentered subjects whose being is limited to the transitory, ephemeral moment, but "as coherent beings-over-time."[12] Similarly, people see the groups to which they belong as being generated over time. Our very possession of identities depends on our capacity to relate fragmentary experiences across temporal boundaries: "Even momentary self-images involve a simultaneous awareness of the present (self-in-context), the past and the anticipated future. . . . A sense of identity—of being oneself—hence necessitates both retroactive and proactive memory."[13]

This experienced sense of continuity is not confined to individual ("personal") identity, but also constitutes an important dimension of that part of our identity that we derive from group membership—social identity. As social actors we understand the groups to which we belong as historical phenomena, stretching backward and forward in time. As to the past, such collective identities are nourished by collective memory (encompassing events and people such as treasured ancestors), the invention of tradition and history writing, while an interest in the future of the group generates anticipatory behavior in the form of precautionary measures, plans, and strategies. In making the point that groups provide their members with a serial connectedness with other group members, Condor quotes D. Carr:

> my social existence not only puts me in contact with a co-existing multiplicity of contemporaries: it connects me with a peculiar form of temporal continuity . . . which runs from predecessors to successors. This sequence extends beyond the boundaries of my life, both into the past before my birth and into the future after my death . . . the *we* with whose experience the individual identifies can both pre-date and survive the individuals that make it up.[14]

Having cited other views as to the fact that group identities can transcend individual mortality, Condor says: "The significance of this to an understanding of social behaviour becomes apparent when we consider how the (future-oriented) actions of collectivities are often directed towards an imaginary distal future beyond the lifetimes of existing category members."[15]

The exploration of temporal aspects of social identity has been taken still further by Marco Cinnirella.[16] He builds on earlier research of H. Markus and P. Nurius (from outside the social identity tradition) that develops the notion of "possible selves," meaning the beliefs held by an individual as to his or her self in the past and what it might become in the future, together with some estimate of the probability that different possible selves will be realized. In this phrase Cinnirella applies the notion of cognitive alternatives. He is particularly concerned to develop social identity theory so it may be able to address *past* social identities and the manner in which past, present, and future may be reconstituted to create meaningful "stories" at both the individual and group levels.[17]

A helpful concept in this area proposed by Glynis Breakwell is that of "social time."[18] Social time marks the passage of items of meaningful social change. It means time that records significant social events. At a macrosocial level these include such things as the start and finish of a war, a technological revolution, a major piece of legislation. One might add that at a group level social time includes the foundation of the group, important early successes or reverses, internal or external threats posed to it at particular points in the past, and even the destiny its members envisage for themselves. Of fundamental importance is that what happens to be held significant as an event in social time "will depend upon the interests and purposes of those groups or social categories which have enough power to impose their interpretation of current and past events upon others."[19] Thus, as power relations in society at large or within a particular group change, modifications are made to the patterning of social time. Those in power rewrite the meaning of some events, erase some, and invent others. Stalin's commitment to this process was satirized in George Orwell's novel *Nineteen Eighty-Four*.

Remembering is the process by which past persons or events are brought into awareness in the present. Individuals remember people or events they have personally experienced or they have learned about from others, the latter case even covering phenomena occurring before they were born. A strong case that many of our memories are collective, that is, are derived from the groups to which we belong, was made by sociologist Maurice Halbwachs.[20] Collective memory covers a range of related phenomena, including the situations in which memory is mobilized, the process by which this happens, and the contents of what is remembered.[21] Collective remembering is certainly central to the experience of a community.[22] Efforts to control the past frequently take the form of a struggle for the possession and interpretation of collective memory.[23] At stake in such struggles is often the identity and status of groups and communities. This means we need to consider the extent to which a person's account of a past event should not be treated as a window onto the cognitive workings of his or her memory but as a description designed for a specific pragmatic and rhetorical purpose.[24]

There has been great interest lately in the functioning of collective memory, largely inspired by Halbwachs, with Jan Assmann of the University of Heidelberg being an influential voice.[25] Hitherto, however, this field has not been integrated with the rapidly evolving concern for the past being expressed by social identity theorists. Paul's discussion of Abraham in Romans 4 offers an opportunity to integrate the sociology of collective memory with social identity theory in the interests of assessing Paul's understanding of Abraham as a prototype of the identity of the Roman Christ-movement.

Self-Categorization Theory and Intragroup Phenomena

The early work on social identity focused on relations *between* groups and mechanisms of social change, as formulated in an essay written by Tajfel and Turner in 1979, rather than on phenomena *within* groups.[26] This approach was particularly useful to me in my 1998 interpretation of Paul's letter to the Galatians, given my view that Paul's dominant concern was to present the identity of an ingroup (or ingroups) of Christ-followers in Galatia in a positive light in the face of a threat originating in an outgroup of local Israelites, in which perspective the emphasis fell on intergroup rather than intragroup relationships. My reading of the Galatian situation was that Paul's addressees were, in effect, being asked to become Israelites, and from his perspective this would have meant that they had left the ingroup of Christ-followers to join the outgroup of Israelites. Although I was certainly interested in what was occurring, and what Paul exhorted should be occurring, within the Galatian congregations, especially in relation to Gal. 5:13—6:10,[27] my aim was to show how Paul advocated an identity for all his Christ-followers distinct from Israelite and non-Israelite outgroups, rather than engaging in processes of intragroup differentiation.

But in Romans Paul confronts other issues, and, while the core insights of social identity theory remain relevant, it is necessary to consider further developments of the theory that have particular application to the communicative strategy he devises in this letter. The developments in question relate especially to how to bring and hold together two subgroups of a larger group or movement that exist in a state of tension or even conflict with one another—which raises the issues of intragroup phenomena—and the role of a leader in achieving this result.

In the late 1970s some social identity theorists had indeed begun to turn their attention towards intragroup processes and the group as a psychological entity worthy of attention in its own right.[28] John Turner led the way in this development by insisting on the distinction between social identity (self-definitions based on social-category memberships) and personal identity (self-definitions based on personal or idiosyncratic attributes). He relied on experimental results indicating that a person's self-concept tended to vary in particular group situations, notably by movement along a continuum from pronounced personal identity at one end to pronounced social identity at the other. Turner described the central idea as that of "self-categorization," meaning that people define themselves in terms of membership in particular shared social categories. In his preface to the 1987 work that represents a full expression of the approach at that time, Turner relates social identity theory and self-categorization theory as follows:

> The self-categorization theory is . . . the product of a distinct European tradition of research on social categorization processes and social identity. . . . [It] is an attempt to spell out in explicit fashion the assumptions we need to make about psychological group formation. . . . In doing this it makes use of and develops . . . the concept of social identity itself and the assumption of an "interpersonal-intergroup continuum" of social behaviour.[29]

Turner notes that since both theories rely on the key notion of social identity, there is a tendency to lump them together; this is convenient but should not obscure that they are substantively different theories aimed at distinct problems.[30]

An important stimulus to self-categorization theory was the recognition that where people define themselves in terms of a shared category membership, they tend to stereotype themselves in terms of such membership, and in so doing enhance the sense of identity shared with ingroup members, while heightening the sense of contrast between themselves and members of outgroups. Most importantly: "Where social identity becomes relatively more salient than personal identity, people see themselves less as differing individual persons and more as the similar, prototypical representatives of their ingroup category. There is a depersonalisation of the self—a 'cognitive re-definition of the self'—from unique attributes and individual differences to shared category memberships and associated stereotypes."[31]

Self-categorization theory postulates a fairly mobile sense of self, with different situations leading to personal and/or group-derived characteristics becoming dominant for a time: "In many situations there will be factors making for the salience of both the personal and the social categorical levels of self-definition. It is the relative salience of different levels of self-categorization which determines the degree to which self-perception is personalized or depersonalized, the degree to which behaviour expresses individual differences or collective similarities."[32] It is worth noting here that in self-categorization theory "salience refers to the conditions under which one or the other type of identity becomes cognitively emphasized to act as the immediate influence on perception and behaviour."[33]

Whereas social identity theory has proved useful in understanding Galatians,[34] its self-categorization cousin, with its focus on intragroup processes, can lend great assistance in the interpretation of Romans. The reason for this is that Paul is not writing to Christ-followers in Rome who are at risk of having themselves circumcised and joining an Israelite outgroup, but rather he is sending a letter to the Christ-movement in the city that is experiencing internal problems, notably those involving tension between Judean and non-Judean members. Above all Paul is trying to bring them together by reminding them of the single category they have in common—faith and righteousness in Christ. From his perspective, the context in Rome is characterized by problematic beliefs and behavior located within one group, at least to the extent that there is no sign that non-Judean members are likely to become circumcised. Accordingly, a theory that focuses on the psychology of the group and the respective salience of personal vis-à-vis group-oriented self-definitions seems to have much to offer in elucidating the message Paul sent to Rome.

On the other hand, if the situation in Rome had reached such a pass (whatever Paul thought about it) that the Christ-movement had fractured into congregations whose members had little or nothing to do with one another, we would indeed be faced with a situation that was verging on intergroup rather than intragroup. Although I argue later that the Roman Christ-followers had not reached such an extreme of animosity toward one another, that there were divisions and disagreements among them, with schism always a possibility, means that it will not be possible entirely to abandon an interest in intergroup phenomena such as characterized social identity theory before the development of its self-categorization offshoot. Sometimes it is difficult to decide whether we are dealing with two subgroups of one group or whether schismatic pressures have become so pronounced that it is preferable to speak of two separate groups.

Contesting Identity within Groups

Although I take up various aspects of self-categorization (and, indeed, social identity) theory where appropriate in later chapters, one recent development relevant to the points just mentioned concerning dissent among Christ-followers in Rome has such wide-ranging significance for every part of this book that I should mention it here. It is the extent to which identity may be contested within a group.

A number of social psychologists have recently challenged a tendency among proponents of social identity theory to take for granted the existence of intragroup consensus, in other words, to assume that people converge upon a common category definition when they identify with a given group. This has the result, as Sani and Reicher note, that "the group definition—and hence group behaviour—is taken as monolithic. If intragroup consensus is presupposed, then there is no place for intragroup division."[35] Yet failure to address the question of divisions within groups is not surprising in relation to social identity theory, which focuses after all on intergroup relationships. But this issue is naturally at home within self-categorization theory, which contests the notion of group identity as an inflexible construct, and in the last few years has begun to receive close attention from researchers.

An essential step has been taken by Haslam et al.[36] They note that when people perceive that they share group membership with other people in a particular context, they expect to agree with those people on issues relevant to the shared identity and actively strive to reach such agreement. The means they adopt include argument, negotiation, and persuasion. Rather than assuming, therefore, that group membership results in automatic agreement, these authors propose that it leads to a shared quest for agreement. On this view, a group will be engaged in a process of consensualization rather than subsisting in a state of consensus.

While agreeing with Haslam and his colleagues on the importance of debate in framing group identity and group action, Sani and Reicher nevertheless question their limitation of debate to the attempt to reach consensus.[37] In raising this challenge, they appeal primarily to the work of Billig, who—in the course of an historical survey that begins with Greeks like Socrates and Protagoras—insists that all mental activity is structured in argumentative form.[38] But Sani and Reicher also cite other researchers who have shown that people deploy definitions of social identity flexibly and fluidly so as to manage social relations and social reality. This leads them to suggest that "because there are no *a priori* limits to arguments over identity, there may be times where at least some group members see certain positions as incommensurable with their own. When the opposing position is seen as fundamentally incompatible with in-group identity such that to accept it in any way would be to subvert the very nature of the group, compromise becomes impossible and negotiation is blocked."[39]

Such a condition may result in a schism occurring in the group. As an example of this process, Sani and Reicher discuss the way in which the decision of the General Synod of the Church of England on 11 September 1992 to ordain women priests led to such a pitch of debate within the church that some opponents of this decision contemplated schism. Disavowing a potential objection that all they are saying is the self-evident truth that when people disagree over what their group is about, they split, Sani and Reicher insist that their point "is not that there is a pre-given set of core issues relating to group identity and that, when differences relate to this core, schism ensues." Rather, they follow Billig by suggesting that it "is matter of argumentative accomplishment to characterize something as essential to group identity, and it is equally an accomplishment to construe a given concrete measure as embodying or subverting that essence."[40] They insist on the many and creative ways in which members of groups mount arguments in relation to issues alleged to embody or subvert group identity. The nature of identity can be contested at all levels.

It is worth recalling here the close connection between social identity and time. A group's sense of identity is tied to the social time in which it sees itself located. Accordingly, the extent to which social time can be reinterpreted by people in power within a group, or by those seeking power to persuade the members that their vision of its identity is the correct one, suggests that the past of a group is likely to be a focus of vigorous contestation, as proponents of rival views reinterpret past events and explain the significance of their reinterpretations for the group's present and future.

The pertinence of this for Romans is that the identity appropriate to membership of the Christ-movement was being contested in Rome (and elsewhere in the Mediterranean region), and Paul himself took part in this process. With some people in Rome (and elsewhere) actively seeking to subvert what he thought was essential to identity in-Christ, he needed to engage in argument, negotiation, and persuasion in order to have his vision of what it meant to be a Christ-follower prevail. His argument also needed to provide a good explanation for the past, present, and future of the group. Romans 14–15 suggests believers in Rome were already arguing about group identity.

Reducing Tension and Conflict between and within Groups

As already noted, the mere categorization of people into distinct groups is enough to arouse intergroup bias. Over the years social psychologists have become increasingly interested in how to reduce or eliminate such bias. The organizers of the U.S. summer camp experiments in the 1950s mentioned above became so concerned at the divisions that had opened up between the boys that before they returned home they exposed them to contrived social interactions aimed at bringing them together again. One device the researchers employed was to have a truck containing two groups "break down" some distance short of camp, where lunch was waiting, and to tell the boys that unless they cooperated to get the truck back to camp, they would not eat.[41] In the last two decades the reduction or elimination of intergroup hostility has attracted considerable attention from social identity theorists.

Although the research into conflict has usually been directed to the memberships of two distinct groups, it has also been applied, as we will see below, to a situation where two subgroups of one group or movement have become sufficiently estranged as to require reconciliation.

From a social identity perspective there are three major approaches to reducing conflict between groups (or subgroups). The first, known as *recategorization* or the *common ingroup identity model,* refers to redefining a situation of conflict so that the members of rival groups (or subgroups antagonistic to one another) are subsumed into a larger single, superordinate category.[42] Thus R. D. Minard showed in a classic 1952 study that black and white coal miners who were normally in conflict with one another on the surface left such hostility behind when they were working in dangerous conditions underground, where their common category membership as miners became salient.[43] Often associated with this approach is the study of the best conditions under which contact between the members might occur, since bringing them together into one category will often be accompanied by close personal contact. The second, "decategorization," consists of dissolving the problematic group (or subgroup) boundaries altogether so that the participants in the social interactions are less interested in group-based and hence stereotypic information about others and more interested in the idiosyncratic features of each individual. Discussion of this approach is also often associated with the study of the best conditions under which contact between the members might occur.[44] The third approach, "crossed categorizations," involves using one category membership that people share to cancel out another categorization where they differ.[45]

In subsequent chapters in this volume I suggest that the first of these approaches, "recategorization," the "common ingroup identity model," offers useful insights into understanding how Paul crafts his argument in Romans. Accordingly, it is useful to explore this approach in a little more detail to highlight aspects that are likely to bear upon Romans.

Reducing Group Conflict by Means of a Common Ingroup Identity

One group of researchers has noted that "recategorization from two groups to one group can be achieved by increasing the salience of existing common superordinate group membership," as is the case where the problem lies with two subgroups that have become alienated from one another, or "by introducing new factors (e.g. common tasks or fate) that are perceived to be shared by the memberships."[46] We will see that although in Romans Paul is mainly interested in the first of these methods, the various references to the destiny of his addressees and to the ultimate fate of Israel in Romans 11 show that he is also concerned with the second. Once members of two groups or subgroups are included securely in a superordinate group, the model suggests that they will treat one another favorably as ingroup members rather than engage in the patterns of devaluation and even rejection accorded to outgroups. Thus it has been suggested that a "common ingroup identity may prime the occurrence of a bi-directional sequence of perceptions, feelings, and actions" that can contribute to the development of more harmonious and constructive relations within and between groups.[47]

Additionally, over time, once people previously at odds recognize that they now share a group membership, they will engage in more open communication and self-disclosing interaction that will increase the personalized knowledge they have of one another. This will further reduce the old hostility.[48]

An important issue in relation to developing, or reinvigorating, a common ingroup identity is the ongoing status of the groups or subgroups that constitute it. One possibly surprising research result has been that the process of recategorization can be impeded, not helped, if the participants are encouraged to abandon their original (sub)group identities entirely. The reason for this seems to be that if the participants feel their original identities are under threat they will react strongly to maintain their viability and distinctiveness, a result that will exacerbate bias toward members of the other (sub)group.[49] "When the groups are not differentiated in their roles or experience, positive social identity may be threatened, . . . and bias may be exacerbated rather than reduced."[50] This means that "establishing a common superordinate identity while simultaneously maintaining the salience of subgroup identities (i.e., developing a dual identity as two subgroups within one group . . .) would be particularly effective because it permits the benefits of a common ingroup identity to operate without arousing countervailing motivations to achieve positive distinctiveness."[51] The benefits of a dual identity may be particularly relevant to interethnic group contexts. Ethnic identity is a fundamental aspect of an individual's self-concept and esteem and is thus unlikely to be abandoned.[52]

Accordingly, someone—like Paul in his letter to the Roman Christ-followers—attempting to bring two groups together under one superordinate category may need, at the very least, actively to engage with the different identities they represent and may even have to go further, for example, by demonstrating his or her respect for them. This is not to suggest that Paul was a good social identity theorist. I am rather suggesting that his familiarity with the pronounced inter- and intragroup phenomena of his culture probably taught him lessons about reconciling mutually antipathetic groups that we are now learning through empirical research. In particular, J. Louis Martyn has plausibly suggested that Paul's letter to the Galatians had been badly received in Galatia and perceived as anti-Judean, on account, for example, of his apparent suggestion that only non-Judean Christ-followers were the descendants of Abraham and of Sarah.[53] This may have led to the refusal of the Galatians to go along with his collection for Jerusalem.[54] Paul could therefore be reasonably sure when he wrote to the Roman congregations that if he did not build up the Judean side he would face the same attacks as he had in the past. Thus we have a different Abraham in Romans 4 (discussed in chapter seven below) and pro-Judean sentiments in various part of Romans 9–11 (discussed in chapter eleven below). In the end, we can see that Paul was in a position to know the difficulties of trying to accommodate two ethnic subgroups in one superordinate group and to have learned from experience how to achieve this in a manner that matches the findings of social identity theorists.

In a case, however, in which the original (sub)group identities are going to be maintained in the process of erecting a new overarching identity, the question arises as to whether it is necessary for them to be (at least roughly) equal in status. Studies conducted into reducing tension between groups by bringing representatives into contact with one another have identified certain conditions as necessary to achieve a successful result, and one of them is that the contact should take place between participants of equal status.[55] Yet it does not necessarily follow from this that the development of a common ingroup identity (as opposed to the reduction of hostility and the generation of good relationships between groups) will be assisted by the (sub)groups concerned being equal in all respects. Bringing groups together that are similar on an important dimension (for example, their ability to perform a certain task) might provoke group-based competition between them aimed at showing their superiority in relation to the task and thus demonstrating the positive distinctiveness of their original identity. As a consequence, inter- or intra-group bias might increase rather than decrease. The answer to this seems to be to ensure that the areas of experience of the two (sub)groups are distinct and equally valued (the so-called equal-status–different-dimensions condition). "Only when both groups are equal in status but share different experiences or expertise can both groups readily respect and value the other's unique contribution and believe that each group could benefit from the presence of the other."[56] On the other hand, one might expect that the problem of equal status on one dimension will arise most acutely in circumstances where, if the two (sub)groups do share a dimension, it is positive, not negative, in nature. It is possible, however, that two groups that have in common some *negative* attribute will compete by claiming that the other group is worse in this respect than they are, but this seems less likely than that they would both leave the issue well alone, or at least that claims that might be raised in such a doubtful cause would not be sufficiently strong to derail the construction of a common ingroup identity.

One final point needs to be considered here. If those who join the new and inclusive group abandon their memberships in the original group, this means that the benefits of the recategorization process, especially the reduction of bias, will not carry over to the outstanding members of the original outgroups.[57] Thus in some contexts the "dual identity" phenomenon mentioned above, in which both the subgroup and the superordinate group identities are salient simultaneously, may maximize the chance that the benefits of intergroup contact may extend to others not present during that contact.[58]

Later we will observe in detail how these ideas assist in understanding Paul's message for the Christ-movement in Rome. For the moment, however, it is helpful to explain their usefulness in general terms. The principal point of contact is that Paul's enthusiasm for reminding his audience of their status in relation to God, Christ, and his gospel can be interpreted as an attempt to revitalize their common ingroup identity in the face of the threat posed to it by their original identities of Judean or non-Judean. At the same time, this does not seem to be a case where Paul could simply ignore those earlier identities. In fact, the issues identified by social identity theorists in this area, such as the relative status of these two subgroups in respect of one another, the dimensions on which they stood to be compared, and the extent to which Paul's efforts at reconciliation were capable of extension to outgroups like Israel, all find responsive material in the letter. An awareness of some of the details of this area of social psychology thus permits a fresh agenda of issues to be posed heuristically to the text of Romans in the interests of understanding what it would have communicated to those who first heard it or read it in the imperial capital in the 50s of the first century. Although the idea that Paul was seeking in Romans to reconcile Judeans and non-Judeans is not new, social identity theory offers a new way to explore this question.

Leadership in a Social Identity and Self-Categorization Perspective

Paul's interest in Romans in persuading his audience to adopt certain views and to act in certain ways raises the question of his authority or, as I prefer to call it, his leadership. Leadership may be defined, generally at this stage, as "the process of influencing others in a manner that enhances their contribution to the realization of group goals."[59] This is also an area in which social identity theory has a decisive contribution to make. Before explaining this, however, it is helpful to set out current views on Pauline "authority" as the context within which the strengths of the social identity approach will be quite evident.

Current Approaches to Authority and Leadership in Paul's Letters

Existing scholarship on Paul's influence over congregations of Christ-followers is concerned especially with the notions of authority and power, as can be seen in the titles of two influential monographs, J. H. Schütz's *Paul and the Anatomy of Apostolic Authority* (1975) and B. Holmberg's *Paul and Power: The Structure of Authority in the Primitive Church as Reflected in the Pauline Epistles* (1978). Their notion of authority covers rather different ground than leadership as defined above, since it is concerned with the nature and foundation of Paul's rights in relation to the churches (especially as an apostle entrusted by God to preach the gospel), rather than with influencing others so as to enhance their contribution to realizing group goals. Both Schütz and Holmberg, however, utilize social-scientific ideas in their investigations, especially Max Weber's views on charismatic authority and its institutionalization.

The explorations of both scholars have a particular bearing on Paul's authority over the communities he himself had founded.[60] This emphasis is partly attributable to this being the context of most of his letters; but it is also due, especially in Holmberg's case, to the use of Weber's ideas on charismatic leadership, which presuppose a fairly full relationship between leader and followers, in analyzing the texts. Not surprisingly, therefore, they have little to say about Paul in relation to the Roman Christ-followers (except to the extent that his general understanding of the gospel and his apostleship also emerges in Romans). Romans 7, indeed (which will later be a focus for discussion of Pauline leadership), is a notable victim of this attitude; it is mentioned on only three occasions by Schütz and does not appear at all in Holmberg's list of biblical citations. This means that they regard the "I" voice in Romans 7 as almost or completely irrelevant to the issue of Paul's authority. That it is actually of fundamental importance to his attempt at leadership in Rome I argue in chapter ten below.

More recently, however, critics have begun to interest themselves in the question of leadership. In 1984 Helen Doohan published *Leadership in Paul*. Although Doohan certainly deserves great credit for discussing insights from a handful of general works on the management of organizational behavior and several on leadership in the church, she applies these perspectives only sporadically thereafter.[61] Brian Dodd begins his 1999 monograph *Paul's Paradigmatic 'I': Personal Example as Literary Strategy* with a concern for Paul as a leader: "Paul's success depended upon the applicability of his message as well as his *ability to influence others as an effective leader*."[62] He notes that none of the New Testament sources for Paul seeks to describe his practice of leadership as such, so that it must be culled from the evidence, and then reasonably suggests that a description would include: "his views and practice of succession planning, organisational administration, management of personnel and finance, vision casting and goal setting, to name a few issues."[63] "This study is intended as a contribution to the interest in Paul's leadership style."[64] In a rather odd burst of epistemological minimalism, however, he proposes that the available sources "limit my enquiry to a literary examination, though it is likely that Paul's literary practice reflects something of the leadership style of the historical Paul." Yes indeed—unless Paul was a completely incompetent communicator! Yet Dodd fails to utilize any of the recent social-scientific research on leadership or even to recognize that his work might profit from interaction with such literature, save for referring to Doohan, whom he (rather inaccurately) describes as treating Paul's leadership "through the lens of recent leadership theory."[65] Indeed, Dodd next mentions leadership at the end of his book, but only in general terms, especially to suggest in a tantalizing way that personal example, "intrinsic to Paul's leadership and literary style, may be foundational to the leadership—and certainly the missionary—enterprise where all who follow expect those who lead to embody the values they represent and proclaim."[66] Dodd's apparent disinterest in the theoretical dimensions of the notion of leadership means that his exegesis of particular passages (including Rom. 7:7-25) is never prompted or enriched by the insights or fresh questions that the theory might suggest. He has forfeited the chance to interrogate the text in the light of contemporary social-scientific ideas on what makes someone an effective leader, relying instead on broad generalizations about effective leadership that are loosely attached to the beginning and end of his book. It is now time to consider the social-scientific resources available to help us investigate Paul's attempt to exercise leadership in Romans.

Some Social-Scientific Approaches to Leadership

An Overview of Approaches to Leadership

So how did Paul seek to influence the members of the Christ-movement in Rome in a manner that would enhance their contribution to the realization of its goals? Over the last century social-scientific researchers have developed a number of ways of understanding leadership, usually in the process of discovering how it might be improved in corporate and public-sector management contexts. This is a vast field of which only a sample can be considered here.[67] Approaches to leadership tend to focus either on (a) the specific characteristics of individual leaders (the "Great Man" approach), (b) features of the context in which those characteristics (or others) come to the fore, or (c) some combination of these elements.[68]

Illustrative of type (a) are models that draw on Weber's idea of the charismatic leader.[69] Another example can be seen in the Ohio State studies of the 1950s and 1960s,[70] which canvassed views on what made an effective leader and settled on the two key issues as "consideration," meaning the leader's openness to looking after the interests of those he or she led and also to showing them respect, and "initiation of structure," meaning the leader's capacity to define and structure the roles in a group so as to achieve its objectives.[71]

Type (b), or "situationalist," approaches focus on the extent to which certain people make good leaders because of the particular context in which they operate (war, for example), that is, more by their being the right people for the task at the right time than through any personal qualities they represent.[72]

Both "Great Man" and situationalist theories of leadership suffer from the fact that they fail to help in identifying any constant factor that distinguishes leaders from nonleaders a d they lack predictive power. For example, the charisma imputed to a leader is often the effect rather than the cause of an effective leadership process.[73]

Some studies have suggested that good leadership is a combination of personal qualities and contextual features (type [c]). F. E. Fiedler, for example, has integrated these dimensions in his influential "contingency model" of leadership that predicts what type of leaders will be most effective in particular situations,[74] although the model has been criticized as failing to capture the dynamic essence of leadership.[75]

Another version of type (c) approaches to leadership, known as "transactional," is interested in the relations between leaders and other group members and the extent to which they provide intangible benefits to one another.[76] E. P. Hollander, a leading proponent of this approach, makes the simple—but often neglected—point that without dedicated followers there is little prospect of successful leadership. Thus it is just as important to study the psychology of effective *followership* as it is to study the psychology and behavior of leaders.[77] S. Alexander Haslam interprets Hollander as suggesting that "leaders cannot simply barge into a group and expect its members to embrace them and their plans immediately. Instead, they must first build up a support base and win the respect of followers."[78] This statement has obvious application to Romans from its first verse onward. Addressing congregations in Rome that he did not establish but wishing to solicit the support of the Roman Christ-followers for his plans in relation to the Jerusalem collection and the foreshadowed journey to Spain, Paul writes to them to garner their support and win their respect.

"It thus appears," Haslam notes, "that unless they have the backing of followers, leaders are unable to display genuine leadership in their management of the group's interests and that the group as a whole will suffer."[79] This brings us to social identity theory.

A Social Identity and Self-Categorization Approach to Leadership

Social identity theory and self-categorization theory, as previously described in this chapter, offer a fertile theoretical framework for examining an organizational issue such as leadership. Raising the question of social identity salience in relation to a leader and the members of his or her organization means asking the fundamental question of whether they will act as members of a team, that is, in terms of the organization as a whole (= social identity salience) or as individuals pursuing their own interests (= personal identity salience). Alexander Haslam and Michael Platow make four predictions about an organization where social identity is salient:

1. Individuals will see themselves as relatively interchangeable representatives of a particular social category, sharing self-defining norms, values, and goals with other members of that category, that is, the ingroup members. To this I add that the members will also share a common experience or even history where the group has been in existence for a considerable period.

2. The organization will provide its members with a common perspective on reality that leads them to expect to agree with one another on matters connected with their group membership and actively to seek agreement through processes of mutual influence.

3. It will provide the members with motivation (and expectations of an ability) to coordinate their behavior in relation to emerging group norms (which define the group as different from and better than outgroups).

4. It will lead group members to work collaboratively to further the interests of the group as a whole (their collective self-interest) rather than of themselves as individuals (their personal self-interest).[80]

By integrating the overall leadership aim of motivating members to achieve group aims with this social identity and self-categorization perspective, it follows that leaders and followers must define themselves in terms of a shared social identity so that the activities of each are seen as collective rather than personal in nature. More specifically: "leadership centers around the process of creating, coordinating, and controlling a social self-categorical relationship that defines what leader and follower have in common and that makes them 'special.'"[81]

Hollander's ideas, mentioned above, fit nicely into such a social identity approach to leadership. If a group is to function as a group, with a lively and committed sense of "followership," and not just an aggregate of individuals, its leaders must represent the interests of the collective as a whole rather than just their personal interests or those of a powerful elite:

> Consistent with this perspective, one important way in which self-categorization theory conceptualizes the leader (the group member who is likely to exercise most influence in any given instance) is as the *ingroup prototype*. As the (most) prototypical group member the leader best epitomizes (in the dual sense of both *defining* and *being defined by*) the social category of which he or she is a member. This means that to be seen as displaying leadership in a given context a person needs to be maximally representative of the shared social identity and consensual position of the group.[82]

We will see in chapter ten below how this particular insight helps in unraveling the meaning of Paul's "I-statements" in Romans 7, and in chapter twelve how it throws light on Paul's statements about his connection with Israel in Romans 9–11.

None of this, however, is "to suggest that the emergence of a leader is an entirely passive process, dictated purely by the whims of the group and the tides of changing circumstance. . . . The leader is an *active* constituent of the group, who is simultaneously defining of and defined by the group." Indeed, the dynamic and dialectical nature of the process, the extent to which it requires the argumentative accomplishment mentioned above, must be emphasized. Where, for example, would-be leaders espouse views that are not necessarily representative of their group:

> one strategy they might pursue is to seek to restructure the social context that defines the group, as a way of increasing

the prototypicality of their own candidature. They might do this by, for example, arguing for the appropriateness of particular categorizations—especially those that distinguish between "us" and "them" in a manner that defines the leader and the ingroup positively and as distinct from the outgroup.[83]

In addition, hopeful leaders of a group can be aided by developments among the membership as well as by their own efforts. Alexander Haslam follows Michael Hogg in observing that "as individuals identify more strongly with a group they increasingly confer leadership on those who are perceived to be prototypical of the ingroup's position."[84] Thus a dynamic develops in which as *attributions* of leadership escalate, so also does the ability of the leader to influence the group as a whole: "Having acquired power in these ways, the person occupying the leader position will be able to adopt the more active aspects of being a leader, including the power to maintain his/her leadership position by influencing the social comparative context and thus his/her prototypicality."[85] All of this means that within a social identity perspective the preference of group members for leaders is not a function of those leaders' qualities in the abstract, but of their capacity positively to differentiate between ingroup and outgroup and to make their group "special."[86] At the same time, the position any leader needs to adopt to embody the ingroup prototype is not fixed but varies with context.[87]

In short, leaders must be "entrepreneurs of identity," capable of turning "me" and "you" into "us" in relation to a particular project in a particular context that will bestow on the shared social identity meaning, purpose, and value.[88] The notion of "entrepreneurs of identity" emerged in relation to research published by Reicher and Hopkins in 1996 to describe the ways in which Margaret Thatcher (then British prime minister) and Neil Kinnock (then leader of the Opposition) sought to mobilize opinion in the United Kingdom during the protracted and bitterly contested miners' strike of 1984–1985.[89]

It now remains to consider two issues mentioned earlier in this chapter but that are of direct relevance to how a leader might successfully become an entrepreneur of identity: the extent to which group identity is likely to be actively contested by the members, and the temporal dimension to social identity.

It is unrealistic to expect too many groups to have reached agreement as to their identities. A more likely scenario is that they will be engaged in a process aimed at such a result, a shared quest for agreement undertaken by negotiation, argument, and persuasion—consensualization rather than consensus. But even this picture will too optimistic for some groups, where different members entertain competing views of the group identity that are sometimes so antipathetic as to raise the prospect of schism. A group such as the Christ-movement in Rome of the 50s CE, with two ethnic subgroups frequently at loggerheads elsewhere constituting the membership, is obviously a likely candidate for this type of problem. Groups such as this are battlegrounds of discursive argument, with the proponents of various views putting forth their vision as embodying the group identity and castigating their rivals as seeking to subvert it. We may incorporate these insights into our evolving picture of leadership by proposing that in a situation where there is or is likely to be disagreement (certainly the context in which Paul operated) a leader is someone who is highly adept through argument, negotiation, and persuasion at managing the debate, by neutralizing views antagonistic to his or her own and by stimulating a process of consensualization around a particular vision of group identity. This suggestion confirms the potential importance of Paul's rhetoric as integral to the dynamics of creating, installing, and maintaining a particular social identity in the minds and hearts of the Christ-followers of Rome.

The connection between social identity and time, especially as seen in the social time a group regards itself as having experienced—a form of time open to continuous reinterpretation by people jockeying for power and influence—implies that a potential leader of a group will need to include the group's past, present, and future within the conception of its identity that he or she propounds through the rhetorical processes of argument and persuasion.

3

Ethnicity, Ethnic Conflict, and the Ancient Mediterranean World

A central concern of this reading of Romans is the issue of ethnic conflict, both because of the signs of it in the letter, where the two subgroups that Paul is trying to bring together under an overarching common identity are ethnic in nature, and because it is a pressing problem in today's world. Since it is unhelpful and, indeed, irresponsible for interpreters to employ concepts such as ethnicity without explaining what they mean by them, especially when they are the subject of flourishing research by social scientists, I devote this chapter to this task. My aim is to model ethnicity, to explain how it differs from the pseudoscientific and discredited notion of "race," and to apply the resulting perspectives to ethnic groups in the ancient Mediterranean world, especially Greeks and Judeans and the relationships between them.

Modeling Ethnicity

An "ethnic group" may be described, provisionally at this stage in line with nonspecialist usage, as one whose members believe they share a common history or even descent, often in relation to their present or past occupation of a particular territory and their practice of similar customs. We will soon see, however, that such a description does little justice to more complex notions of "ethnic" developed in recent social-scientific research. "Ethnicity," a word that first appeared in English in 1941,[1] refers to the condition of belonging to an ethnic group. The French word for ethnic group, *ethnie*, now appears occasionally in English, mainly in social-scientific writings. Underlying these expressions is the Greek word ἔθνος, to which we will return later.

In the modern world ethnic groups include Serbians and Croatians, Flemings and Walloons, Hutus and Tutsis, Nationalists and Unionists in Northern Ireland, Palestinians and Israelis, and so on. That it is easy to produce numerous examples of pairs of ethnic groups in conflict with one another is a useful reminder of the distressing prevalence of ethnic conflict in the modern period.[2] Indeed, whereas scholars used to think that the emergence of the modern nation-state would gradually lead to the decline in importance of rival ethnic groups within national borders, the resurgence of ethnic tension in the 1960s and 1970s produced a renewal of interest in ethnicity among social scientists, both anthropologists and sociologists, that continues to this day.[3] Yet many of today's ethnic conflicts have antecedents going back centuries,[4] and, as we will see later, the ancient Mediterranean world accommodated ethnic groups often at one another's throats in ways notably similar to what we have seen in the last decade in Rwanda, Bosnia, Kosovo, Northern Ireland, Sri Lanka, and Israel/Palestine, to name only the most egregious examples.

We must now consider the nature of ethnicity more closely, drawing on the social-scientific (largely anthropological) debate that has raged around the topic during the last few decades and that shows no early signs of abating, given the continuing significance of ethnic issues in conflicts across the world.

The Interactive and Self-Ascriptive Approach to Ethnicity

Although the eminent Norwegian anthropologist Fredrik Barth has been the most influential theorist in the area of ethnicity in the last few decades, before we consider his contribution and the discussion it has fostered, it will help to consider two precursors to some of his main ideas—Max Weber and Everett Hughes.[5] Weber, writing in 1922, noted that "the *belief* [emphasis added] in group affinity, regardless of whether it has any objective foundation," can have important consequences. He insisted that ethnic groups were characterized by their belief that they shared common descent ("because of similarities of physical type or of customs or both, or because of memories of colonization and migration"); it did not matter whether an objective blood relationship existed. Ethnic membership differed from membership in a kinship group precisely by being a presumed identity, rather than the concrete social action of the latter. Weber argued that ethnic membership was likely to be a consequence of political action rather than its cause—"it is primarily the political community . . . that inspires the belief in common ethnicity." On the other hand, such a belief tends to persist even after the disintegration of the political community.[6] Weber thought that belief in common ethnicity often delimits "social circles," or, as Richard Jenkins interprets him, produces a form of monopolistic social closure—social circles (and closure) ultimately resting on "the belief in a specific 'honor' of their members, not shared by outsiders, that is, the sense of 'ethnic honor,'" which finds expression in a variety of cultural forms, such as common language and religiously inspired ritual regulation of life.[7]

In 1948 the Chicago sociologist Everett Hughes, under the influence of Weber, followed a similar approach to the relation of the basic sense of ethnic solidarity and its cultural indicia:

> An ethnic group is not one because of the degree of measurable or observable difference from other groups: it is an ethnic group, on the contrary, because the people in it and the people out of it know that it is one; because both the *ins* and the *outs* talk, feel, and act as if it were a separate group. This is possible only if there are ways of telling who belongs to the group and who does not, and if a person learns early, deeply, and usually irrevocably to what group he belongs. If it is easy to resign from the group, it is not truly an ethnic group.[8]

Jenkins paraphrases this view as meaning that "ethnic cultural differences are a function of 'group-ness,' the existence of a group is not a reflection of cultural difference."[9]

The view of ethnicity Fredrik Barth espoused in his introduction to *Ethnic Groups and Boundaries* (1969) was in some respects similar to that of Hughes.[10] Barth was reacting against a view that the persistence of ethnic groups and the cultural diversity they exhibited were a result of geographic and social isolation. He proposed instead that ethnic distinctions existed in a context of lively social interaction, that they were aspects of social organization, not culture.[11] For Barth, the core of ethnicity was the sense shared by the members that they belonged to it, with cultural features constituting the means by which this collective identity was expressed.

Ethnic groups were categories of ascription and identification wielded by the actors themselves with a view to organizing interaction between themselves and others. In his 1969 essay Barth attributed to them considerable freedom of action in defining themselves as a group of a particular type: "It makes no difference how dissimilar members may be in their overt behaviour—if they say they are A, in contrast to another cognate category B, they are willing to be treated and let their own behaviour be interpreted and judged as A's and not B's; in other words, they declare their allegiance to the shared culture of A's."[12]

A critical issue was the nature of the boundary between the ethnic group and outsiders, a boundary that was more a process than a barrier, allowing some interactions across it and prohibiting others. One aspect of Barth's position was that cultural features did not constitute but did *signal* ethnic identity and boundaries, although always subject to the qualification that the features taken into account were those that the actors themselves regarded as significant: "some cultural features are used by the actors as signals and emblems of differences, others are ignored."[13] So understood, cultural features of the ethnic group are the visible and variable manifestation, but not the cause, of an ethnic boundary and identity. They signal to the members their distinctiveness, meaning their similarity to one another and their differences from out-siders. Important confirmation of this view came in the fact that cultural indicia might change over time and yet the ethnic group could still retain a sense of its own distinctiveness: "The cultural features that signal the bound-ary may change, and the cultural characteristics of the members may likewise be transformed, indeed, even the organizational form of the group may change—yet the fact of the continuing dichotomization between members and outsiders allows us to specify the nature of continuity, and investigate the changing cultural form and content."[14] I am reminded of my paternal grand-father's axe, which over its working life had five new handles and two new heads.

None of this meant that Barth was not interested in the common culture of an ethnic group; on the contrary, he described it as a "very important fea-ture." His point was rather that culture was an "implication or result, rather than a primary and definitional characteristic," of ethnic group organiza-tion.[15] It does seem, however, that Barth's disentangling of the notions of eth-nicity and culture resulted for a time in a certain neglect of the study of culture, a neglect now being redressed.[16] One aspect of this problem was that Barth's analysis of ethnic groups as dependent on their members' sense of belonging to the group applied to all groups. Boundaries may create identi-ties, but which identities are *ethnic*? Barth did not offer much assistance on this question, although he did not entirely ignore it. As just noted, he was open to the possibility of investigating the changing cultural form and con-tent of an ethnic group. More specifically, at one point he stated that an ascription of someone to a particular social category was an ethnic ascription "when it classifies a person in terms of his basic, most general identity, *pre-sumptively determined by his origin and background.*"[17] Thus it is appropriate even on Barth's approach to look at cultural content, and we will now do so.

Cultural Features Commonly Associated with Ethnic Groups

Since an ethnic group is distinctive from other groups, such as families or football teams or school classes, there must be some limited repertoire of cul-tural features that capture this distinctiveness, even though from a Barthian perspective they will be "diagnostic" for, not constitutive of, the identity and boundary in question.[18]

Hutchinson and Smith usefully list six common features, some of which occur in other sorts of groups: (1) a common proper name to identify the group; (2) a myth of common ancestry (note "myth," since the genealogical accuracy of the claimed descent is irrelevant); (3) a shared history or shared memories of a common past, including heroes, events, and their commemo-ration; (4) a common culture, embracing such things as customs, language, and religion; (5) a link with a homeland, either through actual occupation or by symbolic attachment to the ancestral land, as with diaspora peoples; and (6) a sense of communal solidarity.[19]

Perhaps the most widespread of these features is the myth of common ancestry.[20] As already noted, Weber suggested that ethnic groups were characterized by their belief that they shared common descent, whether or not an objective blood relationship actually existed. Barth himself, as noted above, favored origin and background as presumptive indicators of ethnic identity. Such descent typically relies on a common real or fictitious ancestor. A related notion—of an ethnic group as one that has a distinctive identity based on some form of distinctive sense of its history—is central to Talcott Parsons's understanding of this subject. For Parsons, "the cultural history of the community" refers to "a series of events and symbolic outputs of the past which have contemporary significance because those who experienced them were 'our' forebears," even though there will often be no biological lineage.[21]

The second most common feature is probably the connection with a homeland, either presently occupied by some or all of the group, or the subject of memories of when they once dwelt there. The latter option represents the experience of diaspora peoples, and I will return to this feature in more detail below, in connection with Judeans in the first century CE.

These indicia of ancestry and territory will recur frequently in the discussion. The two of them can fuse in a general notion of "origin" that Roosens has emphasized as powerfully manifesting ethnic identity among immigrant populations in present-day Belgium.[22]

Religion is often one element in ethnic identity, although it is unhelpful to exaggerate its importance. Thus to interpret tension in Northern Ireland between Unionists and Nationalists as simply a battle between Protestants and Roman Catholics, a claim frequently made by advocates of the "Christianity has done more harm than good" persuasion, is to oversimplify and distort an ethnic conflict that involves all six indicia listed above.

Nevertheless, the argument above demands that no one feature can be determinative of, or a sine qua non for, ethnicity. In each case one needs to observe the nature of the boundaries that the group in question relies on to distinguish itself from other groups, sometimes using some of the above features and sometimes others, thus establishing the patterns of similarity and difference that allow its identity to persist.

The Question of Primordialism

One particular debate concerning Barth's position relevant to the cultural indicia of ethnicity requires further consideration. In 1957 Edward Shils sought to distinguish the various ties to which human beings are subject as primordial, personal, sacred, and civil, where each type referred to a cognitive perception and an associated affective dimension. In 1963 Clifford Geertz developed this notion, using the expression "primordial attachments":

> By a primordial attachment is meant one that stems from the "givens"—or, more precisely, as culture is inevitably involved in such matters, the assumed "givens"—of social existence: immediate contiguity and kin connection mainly, but beyond them the givenness that stems from being born into a particular religious community, speaking a particular language, or even a dialect of a language, and following particular social practices. These congruities of blood, speech, custom, and so on, are seen to have an ineffable, and at times overpowering, coerciveness in and of themselves.[23]

Here ascription may be not so much a matter of choice, still less rational choice, but of tradition and emotions provoked by a common ancestry.[24]

Yet the context in which Geertz described these attachments should be noted. He was presenting them as the source of serious disaffection in the new states, something he deplored: "In modern societies the lifting of such ties to the level of political supremacy—though it has, of course, occurred and may again occur—has more and more come to be deplored as pathological." He was greatly concerned with the "havoc wreaked, both upon themselves and others, by those modern (or semimodern) states that did passionately seek to become primordial rather than civil political communities."[25]

Thus Geertz was by no means endorsing such attachments. But nor was he holding them up as a social-scientific concept to be deployed by anthropologists and sociologists in understanding ethnicity, as Eller and Coughlan suggest.[26] He was merely stating that ties of blood, language, and culture are regarded by the actors concerned as ineffable and coercive, as, in fact, natural.[27] He was speaking of how the ethnic groups saw reality, not how the social scientist did: "To insist that actors perceive co-ethnics as sharing biological descent is to describe the manner in which individuals cognize the ethnies they participate in."[28] Geertz was offering a descriptive account. He even noted that these allegedly "primordial attachments" were likely to be stimulated and fostered by nation-building, which brings his position closely into line with that of Weber. Nothing Geertz wrote suggested that these sentiments were impervious to social analysis, a view Eller and Coughlan attribute to researchers influenced by Geertz, if not to Geertz himself.[29] On the other hand, Geertz's well-known advocacy of the emic perspective, of getting very close to the subjects of investigation, and dislike for theorizing at too high a level of generality has left him rather exposed to claims such as those made by Eller and Coughlan. Without an etic apparatus set at a reasonably high level of abstraction it is difficult to translate between cultures and to engage in intercultural communication.[30]

The notion of primordial attachments, therefore, is one where we are able to draw the standard anthropological distinction between the emic (insider or indigenous) and etic (outsider or social-scientific) points of view. While, in so distinguishing, trained outsiders must be concerned not to patronize the insiders under discussion, the whole intent of social-scientific research to mediate the advance of knowledge about and between differing human cultures necessitates this difference of outlook on particular phenomena. And if the practices of ethnic groups pursuing primordial attachments lead to atrocities, such as those we have seen in Israel/Palestine and in the instances of "ethnic cleansing" in Rwanda, Bosnia, and Kosovo, the proponents of etic views on such manifestations of ethnicity may well develop a critical edge (clearly seen in Geertz's analysis). We need not be distracted by misplaced concerns such as those of J. M. Hall that this would represent the generation of value judgments on the basis of "western cultural arrogance."[31]

None of this means denying the potency that primordial attachments often have for the members of an ethnic group. This was precisely Geertz's point. Indeed, the members of an ethnic group, particularly one under threat, are far more likely to adhere to a primordialist view of ethnicity—closely aligned to particular cultural indicia prominent at that time—than to a Barthian approach, and still less to an "instrumentalist" one, which sees the shared, ancestral association of ethnicity as something to be exploited in the pursuit of the real purpose, the achievement of political and economic interests through rational and self-interested processes.[32] Although Jones classifies Barth as an "instrumentalist,"[33] that word is better applied to those who have adopted Barth's key insights but have added to them analysis of the ways in which ethnic identities are deliberately mobilized for specific purposes, especially to gain access to economic and political resources.[34]

There is widespread recognition among social scientists that it is necessary to propose some reconciliation between the interactive and self-ascriptive approach of Barth and the continuing importance of primordial dimensions of ethnicity.[35] Such a reconciliation should avoid stereotyped and inaccurate views of both Barth and Geertz. As just noted, Geertz's concern was with how ethnic actors viewed the situation, while Barth himself was well aware of the power of ethnic identifications—he acknowledged that "the ethnic boundary canalises social life—it entails a frequently quite complex organization of behaviour and social relations."[36] His point was that, in certain circumstances, ethnic change can occur, not that it must.[37] My position seeks to incorporate both sets of insights and is employed in the discussion that follows.

First, as Jenkins notes: "there is good cause to reject totally any strongly primordialist view. Too much ethnographic evidence exists of the fluidity and flux of ethnic identification, and of the different degrees to which ethnicity organizes social life in different settings, for any other position to be sensible, and the theoretical argument in favour of a constructivist view is too well founded."[38] Or, as J. M. Hall puts it in relation to ancient Greek ethnicity, "there is . . . no doubt that ethnic identity is a cultural construct, perpetually renewed and renegotiated through discourse and social practice."[39] It is worth noting that F. Gil-White, who asserts the validity of a certain type of primordialism, agrees with the broad Barthian standpoint: "Following publication of *Ethnic Groups and Boundaries*, the idea that ethnies are in the first instance collections of individuals sharing a common self-ascription, but with no necessary relation to any particular cultural content, became accepted by all . . . that point, a full thirty years after its initial submission, is not contested."[40]

The second aspect, however, is the manner and freedom with which individual members of a particular ethnic group operate as they manipulate cultural features in the overall task of maintaining its existence and identity. Barth is often alleged to hold that actors in ethnic groups behave on the basis of untrammeled, personal decision making, possibly even rational self-interest, and that, accordingly, he underestimated the affective power of ethnic ties, and the extent to which ethnic actors (for example, minorities) encounter external restraints on their behavior. This criticism probably derives from his statement, quoted above, concerning the freedom with which a group could constitute themselves as A's and not B's. On the other hand, in fairness to Barth, we should recall that in 1969 he acknowledged in regard to complex polyethnic societies that "ethnic identity implies a series of constraints on the kinds of roles an individual is allowed to play, and the partners he may choose for different kinds of transactions." He went so far as to add: "The constraints on a person's behaviour which spring from his ethnic identity thus tend to be absolute and, in complex poly-ethnic societies, quite comprehensive; and the component moral and social conventions are made further resistant to change by being joined in stereotyped clusters as characteristics of one single identity."[41] When Barth revisited this debate in 1993 at a conference in Amsterdam celebrating the twenty-fifth anniversary of *Ethnic Groups and Boundaries*, he rightly complained that this aspect of his thought had been "too frequently overlooked."[42]

Do the members of ethnic groups proceed as if they were rational associations of self-interested actors, although subject to some restraints, or are they driven by the emotional, even irrational, power of primordial attachments, as suggested by Gil-White?[43] The best answer is that either option is possible but that local and individual circumstances will affect which mode is in action at any particular time. Ethnic identifications are often insisted upon either by the ethnic group itself in the pursuit of its overarching interests or, perhaps more commonly, by outsiders seeking to keep such a group in a subordinate position. Primordial attachments also often carry significant emotional overtones that can give them considerable power. In any particular case, therefore, we need to be open to the possible stubbornness of ethnic affiliation, while not underestimating the power of individuals and groups to modify ethnic identity for particular social, political, or religious ends.

To bring some order to such analysis—by investigating an ethnic group from the differing perspectives of those involved with it—we may utilize a helpful elaboration of his earlier views pertinent to this point that Barth himself has proposed. He recommends that we model the processes of ethnic identity on three separate though connected levels of abstraction: micro, median, and macro. These levels correspond to the ordinary members of the group, the leaders of the group, and outsiders with power over the group.

The micro level models the processes effecting experience and the formation of identities: "It focuses on persons and interpersonal interaction: the events and arenas of human lives; the management of selves in the complex context of relationships, demands, values and ideas; the resultant experiences of self-value, and the embracements and rejections of symbols and of social fellowships that are formative of the person's consciousness of ethnic identity."[44] This formulation nicely encapsulates the focus on the individual self and his or her consciousness actively called for by Anthony Cohen in his paper at the same 1993 Amsterdam conference and elsewhere.[45] This level deserves more attention than it has been given hitherto.

The median level (which has been the focus of most work on ethnicity) depicts the processes that create collectivities and mobilize groups for various purposes and in various ways: "This is the field of entrepreneurship, leadership and rhetoric; here stereotypes are established and collectivities are set in motion. . . . Processes on this level intervene to constrain and compel people's expression and action on the micro level; package-deals and either-or choices are imposed, and many aspects of the boundaries and dichotomies of ethnicity are fashioned."[46] This is the level that corresponds to what Paul is attempting to achieve in Romans; in terms of leadership he is an entrepreneur of group identity, as explained in the previous chapter.

The macro level is that of the apparatus of the state—its ideological, legal, and administrative framework—which allocates rights and obligations according to formal criteria or the arbitrary exercise of force. Ideologies like nationalism affect the identities arising from ethnicity.

Dual and Multiple Ethnicity

Given the socially constructed and transactional nature of ethnicity, that some people manifest more than one ethnic identity should occasion no surprise.[47] The most common example is the child of parents from different ethnic groups who will face the issue of whether to keep both identities alive or to let one or indeed both languish. A second manifestation is that of immigrants in a new land, learning to subscribe to the identity of their country of adoption but still manifesting some of the indicia associated with the place from which they have come. Third, it is common for people in multiethnic nation-states to claim more than one identity—to be, for example, British and Scottish, or Italian and Sicilian, or American and Jewish.[48] This latter type is sometimes referred to as "nested" identity, since it is possible to imagine the more local or limited identity nesting within the larger and more general one. It is possible to have two, three (as with a Japanese American living in Hawaii), or even more levels of ethnicity. In 1990 the U.S. government census authorities recognized the reality of dual ethnicities by allowing those completing that part of the form headed "Ancestry or Ethnic Origin" to report two (rather than one) ancestry groups, and 28 percent of respondents did so.[49]

In all of these cases, one ethnic identity is usually prominent at any one time, either because of the choice of those concerned or, more typically, because external social pressures and circumstances produce such a result. Thus Sicilians watching a football game between Italy and Germany usually support Italy in demonstration of their Italian ethnicity, but activate Sicilian ethnicity when a team from Palermo takes on another from Milan.[50] Sometimes the bearers of multiple identities highlight one to conform to the local context and sometimes to express their distinction from it.[51] This perspective has now acquired the designation "situational ethnicity," which is "premised on the observation that particular contexts may determine which of a person's communal identities or loyalties is appropriate at a point in time."[52] At the same time, this phenomenon is really only one variety, expressed in an ethnic context, of the processes of self-categorization, the manner in which different aspects of a person's sense of self can become salient in particular situations, which we have already observed in chapter two. All of this indicates that ethnicity forms one part of the larger arena for the expression of self and identity: "According to identity theory, the self is composed of a series of identities, each of which corresponds to a role played by the individual. Identities form a salience hierarchy, with highly salient identities being those to which the individual is most committed."[53]

Ethnic Conflict

In a substantial and empirically rich investigation, D. L. Horowitz draws on the social identity theory of Henri Tajfel to explain the conditions that lead to ethnic conflict.[54] The following sets out the core of this approach, applicable to many types of human groups, including ethnic groups:

> Group allegiances and comparisons are a fundamental aspect of social life. There is now a rapidly accumulating body of evidence that it takes few differences to divide a population into groups. Groups can form quickly on the basis of simple division into alternative categories. Once groups have formed, group loyalty quickly takes hold. In interactions between groups, favoritism towards ingroups and discrimination against outgroups are demonstrated. What group members seem to desire is a positive evaluation of the group to which they belong. A favourable evaluation is attained by comparison with other groups in the environment.[55]

One useful concept to denote attitudes such as these as they apply to an ethnic group is "ethnocentrism," although this term was coined by William Grant Sumner in 1906, long before the recent upsurge of interest in ethnicity:

> Ethnocentrism is the technical name for this view of things in which one's own group is the center of everything, and all others are scaled and rated with reference to it. . . . Each group nourishes its own pride and vanity, boasts itself superior, exalts its own divinities and looks with contempt on outsiders. Each group thinks its own folkways the only right ones, and if it observes that other groups have other folkways, these excite its scorn. Opprobrious epithets are derived from these differences. . . . Ethnocentrism leads a people to exaggerate and intensify everything in their own folkways which is peculiar and which differentiates them from others.[56]

Most of the examples of ethnic conflict that Horowitz cites originate in the colonial experience of indigenous peoples, given that colonial policy helped to sharpen group juxtapositions and clarify the field in which comparisons were made, typically by bringing various ethnic groups together under a new regional government.[57] Sometimes this encouraged ethnic tensions and sometimes reduced them. Problems were frequently caused, however, when a group that was able to benefit more from the commercial and educational opportunities offered by the colonizers advanced more rapidly than other groups in the same broad area.[58] This resulted in the juxtaposition of "advanced" and "backward" groups leading to comparison, generation of stereotypes about one another, and conflict.[59] "Backward" ethnic groups suffered from a diminished sense of group honor and often felt the need to "catch up," lest they become merely "hewers of wood and drawers of water," or even see their ethnic identity disappear entirely.[60]

Finally, a notable feature of ethnic conflict mentioned by Horowitz is that despite the plurality of ethnic groups in any particular environment, most conflicts involve only two groups, and participation by other groups tends to be minor. He offers two reasons for this. First, an argument can be made for "an economy of antipathy. It is dangerous to have multiple enemies and more efficient to concentrate on the main problem." His second reason takes us back to the realities of intergroup tension explained by Tajfel: "Group juxtapositions and comparisons . . . all emphasize the dichotomous aspect of interactions, since they call attention to perceived polar types of behavior. Pairs of antagonists emerge as comparative reference points."[61]

Ethnicity and Race

The popularity of the discourse of ethnicity among social scientists in part reflects the widespread rejection of the notion of "race." It is necessary to explain what race means, especially as the widespread tendency to discern "race" and racial issues in the ancient world has been quite destructive to our understanding of how ancient Judeans, Greeks, and Romans interacted among themselves, most notably in the bizarre view that "anti-Semitism" was in existence at that time.

The theory of permanent racial types that appeared in the 1840s and 1850s presented racial differences as stemming from objective zoological characteristics, which on the social level gave rise to particular subjective perceptions and reactions.[62] This idea of race was given its clearest expression by Robert Knox in his 1850 work *The Races of Men*.[63] "Race" combined several features: (a) humankind is divisible into a certain number of "races" with fixed characteristics that defy the modifying influences of external circumstances; (b) the intellectual and moral capacities are unevenly spread within the races; and (c) certain physiognomic features characteristic of different races reveal the inward nature of the individual or population in question.[64]

The concept of race grew up hand in hand with the scientific explorations of human origins.[65] It frequently developed into racist theory that legitimated (explained and justified) the exploitation and subordination of indigenous peoples by Europeans on the basis that the former were biologically and socially inferior. Matthew Kneale's novel *The English Passengers* features as one of its characters a racist (rather like Knox) who sees a voyage to Tasmania in the mid-nineteenth century as an opportunity to gather specimens of human bones that will sustain his views.

The problem with racial theories is that they pretend that divisions between people that are socially constructed, nearly always to allow one group to subjugate another, have some biological basis. They are a form of pseudoscience. David Mason explains that modern biologists and sociologists do not deny that phenotypical variation is genetically founded. Rather they argue that the combination of intragroup variation with the polygenetic basis of phenotypical difference means that it is not possible to develop a scientifically founded racial classification, so that "'race' can never signify anything more than socially constructed ideal types in terms of which people are categorised."[66] The use of "race" to justify oppression of one group by another is the reason that it has now been questioned as an analytic category in sociology just as it was in biology.[67] The concept of ethnicity has become popular as a way of talking about differences among peoples that does not depend on the discredited notion of race.

The notion of "anti-Semitism" is a modern one that sprang from the ideas of racism as they were developing in the nineteenth century. The expression itself was coined by the German Wilhelm Marr in 1878 in *Sieg des Judenthums über Germanenthum* (Victory of Judaism over Germanism), which was aimed at eliminating Jewish influences in German culture. Marr tried to achieve this by showing that Jews were racially inferior. It was a matter of their "blood."[68] His ideas were influential in the formation of Nazi attitude to Jews.

Given the inherent connection between racism, a concept that arose in the nineteenth century, and anti-Semitism, which is really just an example of racism, it is grossly anachronistic to use the expression "anti-Semitic" or "anti-Semitism" in relation to any phenomena whatever in the ancient Mediterranean world, even though it is common to do so.[69] The Greeks and the Romans were certainly ethnocentric; they did dislike other peoples, including Judeans and one another, but they did not do so on "racial" grounds.[70] The basis of these entirely predictable stereotypifications was what I am here calling ethnicity, usually that part of an ethnic boundary constituted by a distinctive culture. Thus the Romans thought the Greeks were characterized by *levitas*, that is, flightiness, lack of determination and grit.[71] They found the

Judeans antisocial, and hence misanthropic, especially because of their refusal to participate in imperial feast days.[72] The Greeks found the Romans vulgar and lacking in taste.[73] Philo probably mouths views typical of Judeans generally when he says, "It has been said then that the disposition of the Egyptians is inhospitable and intemperate; and the humanity of him who has been exposed to their conduct deserves admiration."[74] Similarly, although in medieval and early modern times the Jews were subjected to oppression and persecution (some of the most egregious examples of which are described in the collection of essays edited by S. Almog),[75] this was not on racial grounds, since, to repeat, that notion was invented only in the nineteenth century.

To project the comparatively recent ideas of race and anti-Semitism back onto the ancient Mediterranean world invests them with an aura of antiquity that they do not deserve and allows them to interfere with our comprehending the real nature of intergroup relations in that time and place. At the same time, however, such blatant anachronism also gets in the way of our understanding the different forms of hatred of this people that have manifested themselves in the centuries since. In spite of the Holocaust, anti-Semitism still exists in our world. The first step in meeting an evil like this is to understand it. Such understanding is only possible via a clearheaded investigation of phenomena in their own historical context, not by the sloppy application of concepts appropriate to another time and place, however well intentioned.[76]

Having now distinguished ethnicity and racism, I turn to the ancient world.

Ethnicity in the Ancient Mediterranean World

To what extent was ethnicity characteristic of the ancient Mediterranean world? The reason for devoting some attention to this question is to consider important aspects of the broader Mediterranean setting in which Judeans found themselves, in particular with reference to the Greeks and Romans, who had a direct impact on Judean experience.

Barth's ideas on ethnicity, which form the core of the approach adopted here, are not restricted to modern societies or specific historical periods.[77] This is surely a strength, even though his approach has been criticized as "formalist" and as employing a universal and ahistorical idea of ethnicity.[78] There seems no reason in principle, accordingly, not to apply the formulation of ethnicity based on Barth to groups in the ancient Mediterranean. I may provisionally note that phenomena that announce themselves most volubly as "ethnic" in the present age, such as the atrocities associated with the breakup of Yugoslavia in the period 1991–1994 or the mass murder of Tutsis by Hutus in Rwanda in 1994 or mutual killings in Israel/Palestine, find reasonably close parallels in the Mediterranean world of the first and second centuries CE. In addition, a number of writers have profitably applied interactive understandings of ethnicity to various sets of primary data from the Greco-Roman world.[79] Irad Malkin, the editor of a collection of essays on ancient Greek ethnicity, has noted that "ethnicity, we all conclude, is a viable and significant concept in its more precise signification."[80] That these ancient peoples did not have a concept of ethnicity such as this is no barrier; this is simply one more area where we observe the difference between etic (social-scientific and often cross-cultural) and emic (indigenous and intracultural) modes of understanding.[81]

The various cultures of the ancient Mediterranean region were strongly group oriented.[82] The family was the most important group, and ties of kinship were the strongest social ties of all. Yet other groups also carried weight. A person's army unit, the voluntary association representing his trade or profession, the village where he or she was born, the city in which he or she lived, and the wider group inhabiting the larger region in which one's village or city was located all constituted groups heavy with social consequence. Groups representing the citizens and inhabitants of a city or a larger territory, whether actually in occupation or living somewhere else but still in some way marked by their connection, are candidates for discussion as "ethnic groups." Although to suggest that the population of a city could constitute an ethnic group may initially sound surprising to modern ears, further analysis will reveal that the designation is appropriate. To keep the discussion within manageable scope and to keep attention focused on the ethnic group with whom the Judeans of the Christ-movement in Rome had to deal, I focus on ethnicity in the Greek world. After this I consider the question of ancient Judean ethnicity.

Greek Ethnic Identity

Ethnos and Ethnicity

Although the word "ethnicity" derives from the Greek word ἔθνος, the Greek usage of the word is much broader than our "ethnic group." In Homer the word ἔθνος designates a class of beings who share a common identification, such as warriors, the dead, flocks of birds, and swarms of insects, and this meaning persisted into the fifth century BCE.[83] But the word also included collectivities of people who came from the same place. Thus Herodotus employs the word of the Attic ἔθνος (1.57) and of the various groups inhabiting regions of the Peloponnese (8.73), but he also uses it in reference to the inhabitants of a city, as with the Athenian ἔθνος (7.161). Aristotle considered that ἔθνη were characterized by their large populations.[84] Furthermore, while ἔθνος need not always denote what we mean by an ethnic group, many of the populations referred to as ἔθνη are also often described as γένη. Γένος is related to γίγνεσθαι, meaning to be born. It can refer either to the mechanism by which one's identity is ascribed (that is, by birth) and also to the collective group in which membership is thought to be ascribed by birth.

The latter is especially seen in the case of the family unit, but γένος can be applied to a category of any size that recognizes that its members are enlisted automatically by birth.[85] So the Hellenes can be described by Herodotus as both an ἔθνος (1.56) and a γένος (1.143), since one of the defining criteria of being a Greek was shared blood (8.144). J. M. Hall explains the relation between the two words in this way: "Thus while ἔθνος can be substituted frequently for γένος, it is the latter term which has the more specialized meaning, with its focus on the notion (however fictive) of shared descent."[86] For reasons set out earlier in this chapter, the discredited concept "race" should not be used to translate γένος; "descent group" is an appropriate designation.

Greek Ethnic Identity in Barthian Perspective

This discussion leads us to look more closely at how the people who called themselves Hellenes (Ἕλληνες) but whom we call "Greeks" (from the Roman word for them: the *Graeci*, who originated in *Graecia*) were named. In the *Iliad* the collective names for the peoples who came to war with Troy are the "Achaeans" (occasionally "Panachaeans"), "Argives," and "Danaans." The Hellenes are still the inhabitants of the original Hellas, a particular district in Thessaly. The word "Panhellene," which occurs only once (2.530), may refer only to the population of northwest Greece as opposed to the Peloponnese. But the name Ἕλληνες, for reasons that are uncertain, came to be that by which the Greeks called themselves. This had happened as early as Hesiod (c. 700 BCE), who knew that the whole people were called Ἕλληνες.[87] This also means that the concept of an extended Hellas must have existed by the beginning of the seventh century and possibly earlier.[88]

Herodotus of Halicarnassus was the author of a long history, certainly in existence by 425 BCE,[89] whose main subject was the war between the Greeks and the Persians. In book 8 of the *Histories* Herodotus describes how the Athenians, in explaining to Spartan envoys before the battle of Plataea in 479 BCE why they have rejected an offer of peace from Xerxes king of Persia, state that they would never do anything that would result in Greece (Ἑλλάς) becoming enslaved. Among the reasons they offer for taking this course is the following: "Then there is the Greek people (τὸ Ἑλληνικόν), which has the same blood (ὅμαιμον) and the same language (ὁμόγλωσσον), together with the common cult places, the sacrifices and the similar customs (ἤθεά τε ὁμότροπα), which it would be ignoble for Athens to betray" (8.144.2).

Of the six cultural features listed by Hutchinson and Smith above as characterizing ethnic groups, the following four appear here: a common proper name to identify the group; a claim to common ancestry; a common culture, embracing customs, language, and religion; and a sense of communal solidarity. Here the notion of common blood is not some early expression of a theory of race constituted by physical characteristics and that arranges the various "races" hierarchically. Rather, as J. M. Hall notes,[90] common blood, consanguinity, functions to express kinship, just as Homer uses blood to refer to kinship relationships (*Odyssey* 8.853). The priority afforded here to (fictive) consanguinity illustrates the widespread prominence of shared descent in ethnic claims. Although Herodotus does not expressly mention in this quotation the remaining two features, namely, a shared history and a link with a homeland, the latter (Ἑλλάς) is implied in the name Ἑλληνικόν, and Ἑλλάς itself was mentioned a little earlier in this same section of the work (8.144.1).

As noted above, however, to refer to cultural features such as these, which even Barth did to an extent, is not at all inconsistent with an approach to Greek ethnicity that stresses its interactive and self-ascriptive dimensions. Indeed, in this Herodotean passage we see the Athenians acting at what Barth calls the median level of ethnic processing—using leadership expressed in rhetoric to mobilize all Greeks against the Persians by signaling the boundary they have in common in relation to the enemy host.

Here, then, we find evidence of a strong form of Greek ethnic identity in the fifth century BCE. What happened later? In particular, does it make sense to speak of an Hellenic (or Greek) ethnic identity in the first century CE? Not according to Hall. He is aware of the notion of "nested identity," where one person can claim to belong to more than one ethnic group. Thus he proposes that a member of a Greek city-state could also belong to one of the "intrahellenic" ethnic identities of Ionian, Dorian, Aiolian, and Akhaian. Hall also considers that an ethnic Hellenic identity did exist in the sixth century BCE and claimed mythic legitimation in the idea that all Ἕλληνες were the descendants of a male progenitor called Hellen. This is an important point, since it represents the tendency of people living in an ancestral culture who have developed an ethnic identity tied to place to engage in the post hoc generation of an eponymous ancestor to legitimate (that is, explain and justify) that identity.

Yet Hall then suggests: "there is some evidence that by the fourth century BCE it was conceived more in cultural terms," a proposition for which he cites a single passage in Isocrates (*Panegyricus* 50). By the Hellenistic period, moreover, "cities from Spain to Afghanistan could participate equally within a cultural-linguistic (though not ethnic) paradigm of Hellenism."[91] The latter aspect of Hall's case is entirely unpersuasive. For all his explicit acceptance of the situational and ascriptional approach stemming from Weber and Barth,[92] underlying this view is an unstated and inconsistent adherence to primordialism, in particular the exaggeration of the role of descent in the determination of ethnicity—something for which others have criticized him.[93] Hall cannot accept that people living in Spain or, say, in Alexandria, Syrian Antioch, or even in Rome, calling themselves Ἕλληνες, educated in Greek literature and rhetoric, speaking Greek, attending the gymnasium and the theater, participating in the worship of Greek gods, and, most importantly, engaged in conflict with other groups in their city, are "ethnically" Greek unless presumably they have a physical lineage from Greek colonists. The self-ascriptive and boundary-maintaining nature of ethnicity demands, on the contrary, that we regard such people as indeed possessing Greek ethnicity, whatever other ethnic identities they might claim. A transition from ancestry to culture and language does not solemnize the disintegration of Greek ethnicity, but simply represents an alteration in the cultural indicia by which the boundaries of that ethnic group are negotiated.

Hall's attempt to defend the indefensible with reference to Isocrates also fails. The passage in question is as follows: "Athens has become the teacher of other cities, and has made the name of the Hellenes (τὸ τῶν Ἑλλήνων ὄνομα) no longer a mark of descent (γένους) but of intellect (διανοίας), so that it is those who share our education (τῆς παιδεύσεως) rather than our common nature (κοινῆς φύσεως) who are called Hellenes" (*Panegyricus* 50). Taking this statement as one of general application, Hall interprets Isocrates' extension of the description "Hellenes" from those who are so by ancestry (meaning physical descent) to those Hellenic by education (that is, culture) as eradicating the ethnic nature of the designation, even though such a conclusion is viable only if Isocrates shared the same primordial perspective as Hall. Petrochilus (not cited by Hall) more reasonably sees in this passage "some uncertainty, even in Greece itself, as to who and what might properly be called Greek."[94] It is, indeed, just as likely that Isocrates, if he was entering upon this large issue, recognized that the nature of Greek ethnicity had now expanded to include Greeks by culture rather than to suggest that such people were not Greek. Yet perhaps Isocrates cannot be said to support either interpretation, but is making the narrow and rhetorically contrived point that henceforward the only people who can describe themselves as Greek are those who have gone to school in Athens![95] But even on this view, the situational and self-ascriptive nature of ethnicity reveals itself.

It is worthwhile noting that the Romans used the word *Graecus* to refer both to a person from Graecia itself and also someone from the hellenized peoples of the East. Cicero's *Pro Flacco* is a revealing source here. He uses

Graeci both of the inhabitants of old Greek collectivities, such as Athens, Sparta, Achaia, Boeotia, Thessaly, and even Massilia, and also of the inhabitants of Phrygia and Mysia. Even though he deprecates the claims of the latter peoples to "Greekness," he acknowledges that they did claim this for themselves. An interactive approach to ethnicity would not deny them the Greek identity that they ascribed to themselves. The key element relied on by the Romans in classifying people as *Graeci* was their use of Greek, if not always as their mother tongue at least as their primary language.[96] Yet it is unrealistic to limit the basis of a claim to ethnic identity to the issue of linguistic competence, for we should remember that the capacity to speak Greek must have been accompanied by some familiarity with the Greek literary tradition, especially Homer, and hence with central features of Greek culture. Any ethnic group, for example, the inhabitants of a city in Asia Minor, that spoke Greek and practiced Greek customs would almost certainly have claimed or invented an ancestral link to Greek founders of their πόλις from mainland Greece.

The Territorial Dimension to Greek Names for Ethnic Groups

One of the six diagnostic indicia of an ethnic group is the name they apply to themselves, which may differ from that used by outsiders to designate them. Since the ingroup name plays an important role in the processes of self-ascription underlying ethnic identity, we must now consider whether there were any principles or, at least, tendencies operative in the way the Greeks referred to themselves. I will also compare their usage in this area with that of the people who lived in or traced their origins to Judea.

It is worth noting at the outset that the principal name by which the Greeks have referred to themselves—῞Ελληνες—from as early as the seventh century BCE to the present day, derives from the name of their home territory ῾Ελλάς. At base, the explanation of the name is territorial. Yet at a fairly early stage, as mentioned above, the Greeks produced a myth of origin that sought to explain their name as the product of a common ancestor, namely, a king called Hellen. In the Pseudo-Hesiodic *Catalogue of Women* it is said that Hellen had three sons: Aeolus, Doros, and Xouthos.[97] These became the progenitors of the three broad descent groups making up the Greeks—the Aeolians, Dorians, and Ionians, a division established in antiquity.[98] Hall has accurately noted that the invention of such a myth (which was itself subject to continuous variation as relationships between groups referred to in it changed) indicates the value of an interactive and organizational approach to ethnicity; it shows "that ethnicity is not a primordial given but is instead repeatedly and actively structured through discursive strategies."[99] The claim of συγγένεια, meaning the existence of a kin relationship, either a close one or one, however remote, that depends on a belief in a shared ancestor, was frequently made in Greek political rhetoric as a way of winning support from potentially useful outsiders.[100] This phenomenon is a reflection of the extent to which this was a heavily group-oriented culture where the family was the most important group of all.[101]

A rich resource for early Greek practices of ethnic nomenclature is the *Catalogue of Ships* in the *Iliad* book 2, which contains parallel lists of the twenty-nine contingents of the Achaeans who sailed to Troy (2.494–759), with the number of ships for each contingent, and of the Trojans and their allies (2.816–77).[102] The way the *Catalogue of Ships* is organized, namely, by reference to the leaders, men, and number of ships from a list of places, inevitably emphasizes the territorial nature of the description. Every contingent commences with a reference to the relevant place, either in the form "the men from X," "those who inhabit Y," or suchlike, or with a collective name that itself refers to the territory inhabited by that group. Here are the main examples of the latter type: Boeotians (494), Phocians (517), Locrians (527), Athenians (551), Arcadians (603), Cephallenians (631), Aetolians (637), Cretans (645), Rhodians (654), Hellenes and Achaeans (684), and Magnesians (756). Only a few names do not have a territorial dimension; these include the Myrmidons (684), the Enienes, and Peribaioi (749).

By way of comparison, here is a list of the various peoples (approximately forty in all) mentioned in a late-first-century CE Greek work *Against Apion*, by the Judean historian Josephus:[103] Greeks (literally "Hellenes"), Egyptians, Chaldeans, Phoenicians, Sicilians, Attikoi (people of Attica), Argolikoi (people of Argolis), Athenians, Arcadians, Babylonians, Galileans, Romans, non-Greeks *(barbaroi)*, Medes, Persians, Thracians, Scythians, Galatians, Iberians, Hyksos, Assyrians, Arabians, Syrians, Tyrians, Colchians, Ethiopians, Macronians,[104] Indians, Macedonians, Alexandrians, Antiocheans, Romans, Tyrrhenians,[105] Sabines, Idumeans, Lacedaimoneans, Locrians, and Cretans. With only two exceptions—that of the Hyksos (a name Josephus translates as "king-shepherds" and whose origins no one knew)[106] and the somewhat exceptional (since generic) case of "non-Greeks" *(barbaroi)*—all these groups have acquired a name from the territory they inhabit.

One particular dimension to ancient Greek (and indeed wider Mediterranean) understandings of the link between a group and a particular territory deserves further attention: the widespread belief that environment affects the character of a people. While Herodotus attributes to the Persian king Cyrus the Great the view that "soft (μαλακός) regions breed soft (μαλακός) men" (9.122.3), this outlook finds ample expression in the fifth-century BCE text attributed to Hippocrates, *Airs, Waters, Places*. One section of this work is devoted to a comparison between Asia (that is, Asia Minor) and Europe, aimed at showing how they differ in every respect and how the peoples (ἔθνη) of each differ entirely in physique from those of the other. Thus Asia has a more temperate climate, with plentiful harvests and men who are well nourished. Under such conditions, courage, endurance, industry, and high spirit could not arise, but pleasure must be supreme (12). Shortly after we find him saying that just as variability in the seasons (especially as to the degree of violent and frequent changes they experience) affects human beings, so too it affects the topography of the land itself (13). The Phasians, whose land is marshy, hot, wet, and wooded, with heavy rains in every season, and who live in dwellings of wood and reed built in the water, are a good example (15): "For these causes, therefore, the physique of the Phasians is different from that of other folk. They are tall in stature, and of a gross habit of body, while neither joint nor vein is visible. Their complexion is yellowish, as though they suffered from jaundice. Of all men they have the deepest voice, because the air they breathe is not clear, but moist and turbid."[107] The people of Asia are less warlike and more gentle in character than Europeans because of "the uniformity of seasons, which show no violent changes either towards heat or towards cold, but are equable" (16).[108] Yet he also suggests that living under despots has produced a less warlike disposition in Asia than the courage fostered among independent Europeans. In addition, the variability of the climate produces among Europeans a great variety of statures and shapes—city by city (23).

Although ancient Greek beliefs in the influence of climate and topography on the character of human populations gave particular force to naming an ethnic group in relation to a specific territory and in raising expected ethnocentric claims to superiority in this or that respect, we should be open to the possibility that this set of ideas could have had a wider application around the Mediterranean. Although in *Airs, Waters, Places* Hippocrates articulated a rhetoric concerning the impact of environment on a group that was heavily Eurocentric, it is easy to imagine how an educated Syrian or Egyptian could adapt such a discourse for quite different purposes. This is a text committed to contested ethnic claims that, once promulgated, would have given others the means to turn the argument back on the Europeans who had first formulated them.

Multiple Identities

Irad Malkin has noted that ancient Greek ethnic identities are not exclusive, nor can one point to a priori hierarchies among them. Thus a citizen of ancient Syracuse could be articulated as "Syracusan," "Siceliot" (a Greek living in Sicily of whatever origin), "Dorian," or "Greek."[109] This equates with the phenomena referred to as "situational ethnicity" and "multiple or nested identities" earlier in this chapter.

Attitudes to Non-Greeks

As is the case with all groups, the members of one ethnic group tend to stereotype other ethnic groups, that is, treat all their respective memberships as sharing the same (usually negative) characteristics. This is a prominent dimension of ethnocentrism. Edith Hall has shown, however, that in the mythic portrayals of archaic Greek epic poetry foreigners were not treated as different from and inferior to Greek heroes on account of their ethnicity. Trojans were not cast as "barbarians." The nature of Greek lifestyle and identity was brought out by contrast with "supernatural barbarians," such as giants, centaurs, cyclopes, or amazons. The "barbarian," presented as the opposite of the Greek ideal in an exercise in Greek self-definition, entered the scene only in the fifth century BCE as a result of the (ultimately successful) combined Greek efforts against the Persians and also because of the development of Athenian democracy and imperial rule in the Aegean.[110]

Information on other ethnic groups was provided in abundance by Herodotus, a greater part of whose *Histories* consists of the so-called barbarian *logoi*, detailed descriptions of various peoples such as Egyptians or the Libyans. Edith Hall notes that "it is unlikely that before Herodotus' *Histories* the Greeks could distinguish the Taurians as an ethnic group from the Scythians or the Cimmerians."[111] The Athenian tragedians drew on this early (and emic form of) ethnography in a context where antipathy to non-Greeks had become established. A common line of attack was in regard to the values and qualities of Greeks versus outsiders. The cardinal Greek virtues as defined in fourth-century philosophy normally included wisdom or intelligence, manliness or courage, discipline or restraint, and justice.[112] In line with a common strategy in stereotyping of projecting the opposite of insiders' values onto outsiders, the tragedians defined the nature of Greek morality by attributing the vices that corresponded to these virtues, such as stupidity, cowardice, abandonment, and lawlessness,[113] to "barbarian" characters in drama.[114] All of this led to the development of ingrained stereotypes: "The 'truths' that Thracians were boors, Egyptians charlatans, and Phrygians effeminate cowards were deemed self-evident, and came to affect the tragedians' recasting of myth; tragic drama therefore provided in its turn cultural authorization for the perpetuation of the stereotype."[115] This practice, in due course adapted by certain groups for their own purposes, is predicated upon an underlying sense of ethnic superiority that must be viewed as a rhetorical and discursive strategy in the contested field of ethnic interaction and boundary maintenance. Later in this chapter I outline how such attitudes when manifested by Greeks and Judeans toward one another led to violent outbreaks of interethnic conflict between the two groups in the period 100 BCE–100 CE.

Judean Ethnic Identity

How does the Barthian perspective on ethnicity help us to understand the identity of the people for whom "Israelites" is a designation not subject to the same problems as "Jews"? The question may be posed in this way: Were they a distinct people first of all and formulated their ethnic identity—realized in boundaries between themselves and outsiders—in relation to certain cultural indicia (which changed over time), or did their sense of being an ethnic group depend on a collection of particular cultural features? Did their status as a distinct group in the Mediterranean world lead them to select cultural features that changed over time in response to challenges to their uniqueness, even their existence, or was it their possession of cultural features that determined the very fact of their being a group and the kind of group they were? This question could be answered only by examining what happened to this people and their identity across a reasonably long period of time, and that task is beyond the scope of this volume. Nevertheless, the former set of options seems to be much closer to the truth. The flexible and heroic way in which they responded to catastrophes and crises in their history, such as the destruction of Solomon's temple in 587/586 BCE[116] and the exile that followed, the return toward the end of the sixth century BCE, and rebuilding of Jerusalem and the temple, the persecution of Antiochus IV Epiphanes in 167–164 BCE, and the sacking of the Second Temple by the Romans in 70 CE, indicates that this was a people well capable of reengineering the cultural indicia that kept them distinctive. All this fits in well with Barth's approach.

Two issues, however, are of pressing relevance to the interpretation of Romans presented in this reading of the letter. The first concerns the most appropriate way to designate the people of Israel, in particular by examining the case to be made for using "Judean" instead of "Jew" (and here I draw on the results of my investigation of Greek ethnicity) as the best translation of the word Ἰουδαῖος. This is not simply a question of nomenclature, since it goes to the heart of how the identity of the people was understood by themselves and by their contemporaries. Viewing this matter from a Barthian perspective necessitates that we remain open to the possibility that although they may be a group that has maintained a sense that it is a group for millennia, the cultural indicia used in delimiting its boundaries may have changed dramatically over time. This means that to treat modern understandings of Jews as equally applicable to the Ἰουδαῖοι of the first century CE—on the basis that the people has remained essentially the same across the centuries—runs the risk of ignoring features of the identity of this ancient people that they themselves saw as foundational for their sense of self. To overlook the way the cultural features expressing their boundaries with outgroups have changed across the centuries also encourages the anti-Semitic notion of "the eternal Jew" who, it is alleged, killed Christ and is still around, to be persecuted if possible. The second issue is the history of conflict between Greeks and Judeans in the period preceding Paul's dispatch of the letter to Rome.

Translating Ἰουδαῖοι *as "Judeans" and Not "Jews"*
Let us begin by recalling that among the Greeks it was the practice to name ethnic groups in relation to the territory in which they originated. This practice goes back as far as the *Catalogue of Ships* in book 2 of the *Iliad* and is evident on most pages of the *Histories* of Herodotus. Moreover, of the forty or so individual ethnic groups mentioned by Josephus in *Against Apion,* only one of them is nonterritorial, the Hyksos, and the origins of this people were shrouded in mystery. It is worth mentioning in passing here that among the Romans as well ethnic designations nearly always derived from the territory occupied, or once occupied, by the group in question.

This phenomenon is a reflection of the fact that a link with a homeland, either through actual occupation or by symbolic attachment to the ancestral land (as with diaspora peoples), is one of the six features that commonly indicate ethnic identity. Yet a particular feature of the ancient Mediterranean world made this territorial dimension to ethnicity even more significant than it might be in other contexts. This was the widespread belief that environment affects the character of a people, which belief finds clearest expression in Hippocrates' *Airs, Waters, Places.* For the people who lived around the Mediterranean in the ancient period, a territorial designation for an ethnic group did not merely indicate place of origin, but also conveyed the possibility that this group might have a certain character by reason of the environment—the geography and weather—of the land from which they sprang.

To translate Ἰουδαῖοι with a word such as "Jews" in this context therefore represents a particularly blatant type of exceptionalist argument that is probably reason enough to reject it. But one can say more. Consider the likely Greek (and, for that matter, Roman) reactions to the name Ἰουδαῖοι. One would expect them to connect this name with the territory called Ἰουδαῖα that this people inhabited, and that is what we usually find. A sample of Greco-Roman authors illustrates the point. Hecataeus of Abdera (c. 300 BCE), in an important passage cited by Diodorus Siculus,[117] describes the Ἰουδαῖοι as a people who left Egypt during a time of pestilence and settled in Ἰουδαῖα. Clearchus of Soli (c. 300 BCE), in a passage cited by Josephus,[118] says that "among the Syrians the Ἰουδαῖοι take their name from the place, for the area which they inhabit is called Ἰουδαῖα." This is a particularly clear example of an ethnic group being named in reference to the territory they inhabit. Both Lysimachus, an author of unknown date but cited by Josephus, and Apion (first half of the first century CE) attribute the name Ἰουδαῖοι to the people while they were still living in Egypt, from where they say Moses led them to the country now called Ἰουδαῖα.[119] This relates the name of the people to the name of the territory, but in the opposite direction to that already noted in Hecataeus of Abdera and Clearchus of Soli.

On the other hand, Pompeius Trogus, who lived around the turn of the era, says that Israel named the *Iudaei* in honor of his son Judah, who died soon after he (Israel) had divided the people into ten kingdoms.[120] This seems, however, to reflect the common practice of generating an eponymous ancestor as the basis for a name that is actually territorial; there are many instances of this in Greece, most notably with the development of the mythical ancestor Hellen.

An examination of Judean sources reveals that the link between the people and the land is even closer. In the *Judean Antiquities* of Josephus, for example, the word Ἑβραῖοι is most commonly used of the people in the patriarchal and Egyptian period, while Ἰσραηλίτης comes to be used most frequently of them when Joshua has led the people across the Jordan; but from the time, in book 11, when Cyrus gives them permission to return to Ἰουδαία to rebuild the temple, they are referred to on most occasions as Ἰουδαῖοι. The link between the name of the people and its homeland containing the capital city and temple of their God is unmistakable.

Although the Ἰουδαῖοι were a people who became widely scattered around the Mediterranean, that in no way diminished the extent to which their identity was linked to their Judean homeland and its temple where they worshiped their God in aniconic magnificence. In the discussion above of the features that indicate ethnic identity, I mentioned the importance of a link with a homeland, either through actual occupation or by symbolic attachment to the ancestral land, as with diaspora peoples. Max Weber brilliantly formulated the experience of a people in diaspora:

> Wherever the memory of the origin of a community by peaceful secession or emigration ("colony," ver sacrum, and the like) from a mother community remains for some reason alive, there undoubtedly exists a very specific and often extremely powerful sense of ethnic identity, which is determined by several factors: shared political memories or, even more importantly in early times, persistent ties with the old cult, or the strengthening of kinship and other groups, both in the old and the new community, or other persistent relationships. Where these ties are lacking, or once they cease to exist, the sense of ethnic group membership is absent, regardless of how close the kinship may be.[121]

This description, which brings out the intense focus of a diaspora people on their homeland, is eminently appropriate for the millions of Judeans in the ancient Mediterranean world who lived outside Judea, as the primary evidence reveals. In the ancient Mediterranean, it should be noted, the Judeans were not the only ethnic group who preserved strong links with their homeland. Many Greek colonists did so, and Sean Freyne has usefully pointed out that the Phoenicians maintained close ties with the worship of their ancestral god, Melqart, in Tyre.[122]

There are many signs of the overwhelmingly powerful attachment of the 'Ιουδαῖοι to the temple in Jerusalem. Chief among them was that each year they sent the temple tax to Jerusalem. Cicero states in *Pro Flacco* (delivered in 59 BCE), and there is no reason to disbelieve him, that every year this gold was taken to Jerusalem from Italy and all the provinces.[123] Philo of Alexandria, in *On the Embassy to Gaius*, written in the late 40s CE,[124] at one point describes how Augustus (emperor 31 BCE–14 CE) showed his approval of the 'Ιουδαῖοι of Rome. Included in the emperor's acts of benevolence was that he "also knew that they collect sacred money from their 'first-fruits' [here a reference to the temple tax] and send it up to Jerusalem by the hand of envoys who will offer sacrifices."[125] Donald Binder, in an important monograph on Judean synagogues during this period, has gathered a large body of evidence for other links between those in the diaspora and the temple in Jerusalem. He mentions, for example, the practice of holding meetings in these synagogues on the days that feasts were occurring in the temple, that worshipers in them offered prayers facing Jerusalem, and that in some cases at least (for example, at Ostia) the synagogue was oriented toward the city. He concludes that "the diaspora synagogues provided a means for Jews to be connected to the central sanctuary while still residing in distant cities throughout the Greco-Roman world."[126] At one point, in a revealing statement, Philo notes that while diaspora 'Ιουδαῖοι counted their adopted countries as their "fatherland" (πατρίς), they held "the holy city where stands the temple of the Most High God to be their mother city (μητρόπολις)."[127]

Another sign of the orientation toward Judea and its temple was the habit of thousands of 'Ιουδαῖοι from around the Mediterranean to travel there for the great feasts, especially Passover. This confirmed the strength of their relationship to the temple in the best way possible, by going there and taking part in the cultic sacrifices. Some diaspora 'Ιουδαῖοι went even further by settling in Jerusalem. These people are mentioned in Acts 2:5 ("There were 'Ιουδαῖοι dwelling in Jerusalem, pious men from every people under heaven"), and their presence in the city at that time is confirmed by first-century tombs that have been found around Jerusalem that contain or once contained their remains.

None of this lessens the role of the Mosaic law in the life of diaspora communities. In chapter four below I quote a surviving fragment from a work by

Philo, the *Hypothetica;* that describes what happens at a Sabbath service, and we will see that the law is central to it. It is simply the case that before the destruction of the temple in 70 CE the law and the temple were twin foci of the Judeans. Indeed, the law itself contained many requirements relevant to the temple cult, so that separating the two is not easy.

All of these phenomena are readily explicable for the reason set out by Weber, in that here we have people who have emigrated (or were sometimes forcibly removed) from their mother community, but among whom the memory of their origin remains very much alive and engenders and maintains a specific and extremely powerful sense of ethnic identity. It stands to reason, one might add, that an ethnic group living away from their homeland and wishing to maintain their distinctive identity would have to work harder at it than those of their community who do live there and who are not surrounded by members of other ethnic groups holding out the prospect of assimilation. In 1987, discussing the question of Hellenists in Luke-Acts, I made this suggestion (in refutation of the common but wildly implausible view that diaspora "Jews" would be more "lax" than those born there) and used it to explain the fact that the opposition to Stephen arose in synagogues whose members came from outside Judea (Acts 6:8-15).[128]

This discussion, necessary in terms of explaining how this people saw their identity, also has consequences for how we translate Ἰουδαῖοι. At present, with a few notable exceptions, especially Bruce J. Malina, Richard L. Rohrbaugh, John J. Pilch, and Richard A. Horsley (since the early 1990s),[129] the word chosen is "Jews," with "Jewish" as its adjective. For some years I have been concerned with the problems surrounding this translation, and in my 1998 reading of Galatians I avoided using "Jews" and employed the word "Israelites" instead, which remains an acceptable designation. At that time I hesitated to take the further step and translate Ἰουδαῖοι as "Judeans" for the reason that I considered the translation "Judean" was "somewhat misleading in English, since we already use 'Judean' in a limited sense to designate the actual inhabitants of Judea."[130] I was not alone in this view.[131] Further reflection on the issue in the light of the primary sources (some of which are set out immediately above) and the discovery of a particular passage in Josephus, which I will now mention, have convinced me that failing to press on—by translating Ἰουδαῖοι as "Judeans"—would be inappropriate.

The major problem is that to translate Ἰουδαῖοι as "Jews" removes from the designation of this ethnic group the reference to Judea, to its temple and the cult practiced there, that both insiders and outsiders regarded as fundamental to its meaning and that accorded with the almost universal practice of naming ethnic groups after their territories. The second problem is the extent to which the words "Jews," "Jewish," and even "Judaism" now carry meanings indelibly fashioned by events after the first century, including the development of a different identity for the people around the Mishnah, the conversion to Judaism in the ninth century CE of the Khazars (a Turkic group from southern Russia) who became ancestors of Ashkenazi Jews,[132] the experience of Jews in medieval Europe, and the murder of millions of Jews in Germany and Eastern Europe during World War II, so that they are anachronistic in connection with the ancient period. All of this is part of the larger reality that meanings come from social systems and that any use of "Jew" today inevitably reflects what it means to belong to that social system, for insiders and outsiders.

Should the fact that using "Judean" as the translation for Ἰουδαῖος means losing a distinctive way of referring to an inhabitant of the geographic region of Judea discourage us from adopting this version generally, as I myself thought in 1998? That this question should be answered with an emphatic no emerges in a passage in the *Judean War* where Josephus himself faces exactly this issue but is not deterred from using Ἰουδαῖος more generally. He describes the crowds gathering in Jerusalem both from outside and inside Judea in 4 BCE after the people had been provoked by the actions of Sabinus, the Roman procurator of Syria: "When Pentecost arrived . . . it was not the customary ritual as much as indignation which drew the people together [sc. in Jerusalem]. A countless multitude flocked in from Galilee, from Idumea, from Jericho, and from Perea beyond the Jordan, but it was the membership of the people from Judea itself which, both in numbers and in ardor, was preeminent."[133] In the Greek original the phrase that I have translated as "the membership of the people from Judea itself" is ὁ γνήσιος ἐξ αὐτῆς Ἰουδαίας λαός. Although Thackeray offers the version "the native population of Judea itself,"[134] this does not quite convey the correct meaning. For Josephus does not have in mind simply those who happened to live within Judea, "natives" in that sense, which could include ethnic Greeks. He is referring to such of the people as belonged to the particular ethnic group in question who lived in Judea, as opposed to those who did not. Hence the translation I have offered.

The critical point in this passage is that the existence of a segment of this people who lived in Judea itself was irrelevant to the fact that all those of its members who came to Jerusalem were Ἰουδαῖοι. They all have an ethnic identity, focused on the temple in Judea, whether they happen to live there or not and whether or not they happen to have ethnic identities derived from other places of residence (nested identity). In a context where it is necessary to refer to both groups, Josephus does not designate the diaspora representatives by some other name (Galileans, etc.) but invents a periphrasis to describe those who do live in Judea. Accordingly, there is no justification for refusing to translate all representatives of this people as "Judeans" just because some live in Judea. Rather, when referring to the latter group we should follow the example of Josephus and employ a periphrasis. It is beside the point that it is convenient in English to have two words, "Judean" in connection with the people living in Judea and "Jews" for all the rest, if such a usage does violence, which it does, to the historical meaning of the word Ἰουδαῖοι in its first-century context.[135]

It is arguable that translating Ἰουδαῖοι as "Jews" is not only intellectually indefensible, for the reasons just given, but also morally questionable. To honor the memory of these first-century people it is necessary to call them by a name that accords with their own sense of identity. "Jews" does not suit this purpose, both because it fails to communicate the territorial relationship they had with the land of Judea and its temple and because it inevitably imposes on them associations derived from the troubled, indeed, often terrible history of the Jews. As long as the temple—the sacred heart of the land and its chief attraction—stood, and even between 70 CE and 135 CE when there was a hope that it might be rebuilt, "Judeans" is the only apt rendering in English of Ἰουδαῖοι.[136] Perhaps in relation to texts from subsequent centuries, when they had no real hope of a return to the homeland and the cultural indicia by which they expressed their identity changed dramatically, as (in Barthian fashion) the Mishnah was developed and they became a people characterized not by their links to a functioning temple cult but by the quiet fulfillment of ethical obligations,[137] it may be appropriate to translate Ἰουδαῖοι or *Iudaei* as "Jews," but certainly not in the first century CE.

Answering Objections to Translating Ἰουδαῖοι as "Judeans" and Not "Jews"
Prior to concluding this section, I find it useful to consider a case made by Shaye Cohen for the appropriateness of "Jews" in relation to the people in the first century CE. Although I argue that Cohen has fallen into error on this point, he has at least sought to defend an interpretation that has now been challenged yet to which most scholars continue to adhere, it seems to me, more from intellectual inertia than for any considered reason. In addition, since most of the arguments he floats have parallels in other writers on this period, although less well developed than his ideas, responding to him means covering the main dimensions of the discussion at present.

Part of Cohen's monograph, significantly entitled *The Beginnings of Jewishness*, consists of a study of how Ἰουδαῖοι should be translated in the ancient world.[138] His thesis is that all instances of Ἰουδαῖοι (or the Latin version thereof, *Iudaei*) before 100 BCE should be translated "Judean," since they have an "ethnic-geographic" sense not conveyed by "Jew," but that thereafter there are occasions when the word is best translated "Jew," where it has a "religious" or "political" sense. As recently as 1989 Cohen could speak of "Jews" from "the sixth century BCE to the twentieth century CE."[139] But he now differentiates himself from Morton Smith, who held the view that "Judean" was the appropriate translation up to the Babylonian and Persian period when it had a tribal or territorial meaning, but from that time onward it acquired the new religious meaning of "Jew." Cohen has thus performed a useful service in pushing the time at which the territorial dimension allegedly disappears from Ἰουδαῖοι from 587 BCE to 100 BCE. Moreover, the manner in which he mounts his case, by arguing in relation to examples of Ἰουδαῖοι after 100 BCE that a "religious" or "political" sense requires "Jew," also indicates that he has correctly appreciated that the onus of proof rests on those who would translate Ἰουδαῖοι as "Jews"—and thus remove the prima facie territorial meaning of the word—to show why this is so. In fact, however, Cohen has not discharged this onus, since an analysis of his argument and the data he cites indicates that Ἰουδαῖοι does not lose its territorial connotation so as to justify the translation "Jews" until well into the third century CE, if not two or three centuries later.

The root of the difficulty with Cohen's argument lies in his adoption of a confused approach to the meaning of ethnicity, a confusion that seems to have three main dimensions. I will consider these and then observe how they render his view that in the first century Ἰουδαῖοι should be translated as "Jews" unconvincing.

The first problem arises from the fact that Cohen favors a primordial approach over a Barthian one. He interprets Barth as suggesting that "the boundary makes the group" and that the culture of a group (its customs, values, habits, language, etc.) is separate from its identity, indeed "almost accidental" to that identity.[140] We have already seen that this view is not fair to Barth, whose essential point is that a sense of the separateness of the group is antecedent to the (changing) ways in which that separateness is expressed. Cultural features are needed to signal the boundary, even though those features may change over time.[141] Cohen defines ethnicity in terms of an ensemble of cultural features (notably a belief in a common and distinct origin). This represents a return to the approach to ethnicity as the product of primordial cultural features that the majority of social scientists, even (qualified) primordialists like Gil-White, agree with Barth in rejecting. Moreover, Cohen's view is especially surprising in relation to the Judeans, whose experience in the period from the 530s BCE to 100 CE, when they maintained a strong sense of identity in relation to outsiders in spite of radical changes in the cultural features by which that separation was expressed (none of them, by the way, relating to a common and distinct origin), is obviously explicable within a Barthian perspective.

Second, when Cohen comes to nominate the features that for him qualify a group for ethnic status, he relies on a 1981 collection of four such elements by A. D. Smith that did not include a common proper name or, more seriously, a territory.[142] Nor did Smith specifically mention religion, although it may have lurked behind the feature entitled "one or more dimensions of collective cultural identity."[143] Smith's omission of territory as a feature of ethnicity, given its appearance in virtually every conflict reasonably called ethnic from ancient times to the present, was preposterous. But Smith himself soon realized his mistake. As early as 1986 he was promoting another definition that now included "an association with a specific territory," with religion seen as distinct from ethnicity but sometimes fusing with it.[144] Even though Cohen is aware of Smith's inclusion of territory, as shown by his mentioning it in the introduction to the collection of essays that includes the one under discussion,[145] he has largely ignored its significance in his discussion of Ἰουδαῖοι. Moreover, since 1996 Smith, in the book he jointly edited with John Hutchinson, has also made explicit that religion is frequently a component of the common culture that characterizes an ethnic group (at any given time).[146] Again, this clarification merely recognizes the obvious fact that religion is prominent in many ethnic situations, even though other indicia of ethnicity are in play as well. While Cohen pays lip service to the inclusion of religion in ethnicity by noting that "'religion' is only one of many items that make a culture or a group distinctive,"[147] he follows quite a different path when discussing Ἰουδαῖοι, as we will soon see.

A third source of difficulty with Cohen's position is that he seems to assume that from the first century BCE onward it is possible to speak of "religion" existing as a realm of human experience distinct from other realms such as kinship, politics, and economics in a manner similar to modern understandings of religion. This is fundamental to his assertion that "Jewishness," a religious expression, began in the first century BCE and has continued to the present. The better view, however, for the reasons set out in the introduction to the present volume, is that "religion" is a post-Enlightenment concept having no application to ancient phenomena and that in the Mediterranean world of the first century CE the features that we refer to as "religious" ideas and institutions were primarily embodied in structures of the political and domestic realms.[148]

We may now consider particular features in Cohen's argument to see how these problems blow it off course. I focus first on his attitude to territoriality as it affects ethnic identity and then religion. In one place he gets off to an unimpeachable start: "First and foremost, a *Ioudaios* is a Judaean—that is, a member of the Judaean people or nation (*ethnos* in Greek, or a similar term) living in the ethnic homeland of Judaea (*Ioudaia* in Greek)."[149] But his argument soon begins to falter: "As an ethnic-geographic term, *Ioudaios* is parallel to terms like Egyptian, Cappadocian, Thracian, Phrygian, and so forth, which are both ethnic and geographic. In certain contexts, of course, the ethnic meaning may have primacy over the geographic, while in other contexts the geographic may have primacy over the ethnic, but both meanings are present."[150] Cohen's attempt to distinguish between "ethnic" and "geographic," indeed, to set them in opposition to each other, reflects his problematic reliance on Smith's 1981 formulation of ethnicity that Smith himself later dropped (as Cohen acknowledges in the same volume),[151] and flies in the face of the almost universal recognition that territory is frequently a dimension of ethnicity.

The difficulties with his position become even more apparent in his treatment of the important passage in Josephus's *Judean War* (2.43), which I have considered above. Cohen translates the relevant part of what Josephus says as follows (although I have added the critical words in the Greek): "A countless multitude ran together [to Jerusalem] from Galilee and from Idumaea, from Jericho and from Peraea beyond the Jordan, but the genuine nation from Judaea (ὁ γνήσιος ἐξ αὐτῆς Ἰουδαίας λαός) itself exceeded them in both number and eagerness." He then comments:

> The nation from Judaea itself is genuine in that the name Judaeans is entirely appropriate to them, while it is only partly appropriate for Galileans, Idumaeans, and Peraeans. The latter groups are Judaeans insofar as they inhabit the land of Judaea broadly defined and are members of the nation of the Judaeans broadly defined, but insofar as they do not live in Judaea narrowly defined and are not members of the nation of the Judaeans narrowly defined—Galileans like Idumaeans can be said to constitute an *ethnos* of their own—they are not Judaeans. Only the Judaeans narrowly defined are Judaeans in all respects.[152]

The critical issue is how to translate ὁ γνήσιος ἐξ αὐτῆς Ἰουδαίας λαός as one group among a multitude of Ἰουδαῖοι coming to Jerusalem to confront the Romans at Pentecost. The word γνήσιος is an adjective derived from γένος, which fundamentally means "physical descent."[153] Thus the original meaning of γνήσιος is "by physical descent," or "by birth," although the processes of semantic development do produce other meanings, such as "genuine" or "legitimate." Prima facie, then, Cohen's use of "genuine" in relation to the phrase ὁ γνήσιος ἐξ αὐτῆς Ἰουδαίας λαός might seem justified, but it is extremely implausible and entirely subverts the intention of Josephus.

As I have argued above, Josephus is describing an occasion when numerous Ἰουδαῖοι were coming to Jerusalem from various parts of the region beyond Judea. He then encounters a problem: some of them were from Judea itself, that is, they were Ἰουδαῖοι just like the others and devoted to Jerusalem, its temple and cult, but were apparently born within the borders of Judea. How could he distinguish this latter group from the others? He opts for a periphrastic explanation, literally "the people by physical descent from Judea itself," although the phrase is better expressed as "the membership of the people from Judea itself."

Cohen's notion (possibly driven by his unjustifiable favoring of descent as the prime test of ethnicity) that these Judeans constitute "the genuine nation" is entirely absent from this passage. Josephus does not subscribe to a hierarchical order of Judeans with privileged status to those actually born in Judea. They are all Judeans, all part of the people (δῆμος, 2.42) drawn to Jerusalem and its temple as the center of their socioreligious world wherever they live. Yet, as a matter of convenience only, when Josephus wishes to refer specifically to a particular segment of the people (merely to differentiate them from other segments), he will specify "the membership of the people from Judea itself." All of this is confirmed by the parallel passage to this one in the *Judean Antiquities* (17.254), which according to Cohen "is worded somewhat differently but probably means the same thing."[154] Here, speaking of those who came to Jerusalem at Pentecost on this occasion, meaning Judeans, Josephus says: "There were Galileans and Idumeans and a multitude from Jericho and from those who lived beyond the Jordan River, and a multitude of Judeans themselves (αὐτῶν τε Ἰουδαίων πλῆθος) who joined all these." There is nothing here about a "genuine nation." Just as in the *Judean War* passage, Josephus merely wishes to differentiate one group of Judeans among a number and uses the fact of their birth or residence in Judea (he does not even bother with γνήσιος here) as the way to do it.

One further issue arises from Cohen's comment on this Josephan passage. Apart from the error of supposing Josephus is suggesting that Judeans from outside Judea are not genuine Judeans, Cohen also fails to recognize the reality of dual or nested ethnicity. He is correct in describing Galileans and Idumeans as ethnic groups. This is because people born in or dwelling in those regions ascribed to themselves, and no doubt had ascribed to them by outsiders, a group identity properly described as ethnic in the sense set out above. On two occasions Josephus uses the word ἔθνος in relation to the Galilean.[155] Here the particular ethnic features of relevance comprise a common proper name, a connection with a particular territory having a distinctive landscape and climate, and certain cultural features, including a local dialect or at least a particular accent of Aramaic (such as Peter's in Matt. 26:73).

But this does not prevent Galileans and Idumeans also being a member of the Judean ethnic group. Sean Freyne has also pointed out that Josephus refers to the people of Galilee as Galileans and Judeans.[156] Dual ethnicity is a common phenomenon. Pace Cohen, such people were also Judeans, full members of a people worshiping God above all through a cult conducted in the temple in Jerusalem. If pressed, they would probably have proffered their membership of the Judean ethnic group as more central to their existence than Galilean or Idumean ethnicity, especially given the passion they clearly felt for the temple and its cult, but both were real aspects of their lives nevertheless. Having thus covered the issue of territoriality in Cohen's notion of Judean identity, I may finally assess his position on religion.[157]

It is notable that in dealing with the religious dimension of Ἰουδαῖοι, Cohen treats "religion" as capable of separation from ethnic and geographic realms, attributing to it a separate province of meaning. Thus he suggests that gentile converts to "Judaism," not Ἰουδαῖοι by birth and not living in Judea, are not Judeans but are "Jews," to reflect the "religious meaning."[158] His argument is unconvincing for three reasons.

First, whereas Cohen has earlier (correctly) acknowledged that religion is just one of many items that make an ethnic group distinctive,[159] when he is faced with instances where the full panoply of ethnic features is not present, rather than simply appealing to the elasticity of ethnic indicia, he dumps ethnicity altogether and invents a new type of affiliation that is solely religious. Second, Cohen has overlooked the phenomenon of dual (let alone multi-) ethnic identities. Third, the thought that a purely religious affiliation allegedly discovered in the ancient world may be an anachronistic illusion has not occurred to him. Religion as we understand it did not exist in the ancient world, and the religious dimensions of human experience had a very different status then, being embedded in other areas of human experience, especially the family and the city-state.

Take the case of Atomos, whom Josephus describes as a Ἰουδαῖος and Cyprian by birth (τὸ γένος), whom Felix sent to Drusilla. Here each of these three problems with Cohen's position is evident.[160] Cohen comments that this "is the only Josephan passage in which a person is said to be both a *Ioudaios* and a member by birth of another ethnic-geographic group (in this case, Cyprians)." I observe at the outset that there are other Judeans of this type in Josephus's *Judean Antiquities* 17.254, as mentioned above. Leaving this aside, however, according to Cohen, since the man was not born a Ἰουδαῖος but a Cyprian and presumably does not live in Judea, "surely it is much simpler to take *Ioudaios* as a religious term (Atomos is a Cyprian but a Jew)." We see immediately the unjustified and unjustifiable refusal even to countenance the possibility that Atomos could be ethnically Cyprian *and* Judean. Atomos was most probably born of

Judean parents who lived in Cyprus. Cohen imagines a person can only have one ethnic identification, and since he favors ancestry, Atomos must be ethnically Cyprian and a new, de-ethnicized meaning for Ἰουδαῖος needs to be pulled out of the hat, even though one that anachronistically introduces the modern notion of religion as a stand-alone phenomenon.

This analysis graphically reveals the fatal weaknesses in Cohen's attempt to justify translating Ἰουδαῖοι as "Jews" on occasion from 100 BCE onwards. The arguments for translating the word as "Judeans" have force until at least 135 CE. Some possibilities for various meanings of Ἰουδαῖος and *Iudaeus* in Greco-Roman inscriptions dated to the second century CE or later have been covered by Ross Kraemer and Margaret Williams, but since both of these authors conduct their investigations without the assistance of theories of ethnicity and are happy to use the words "Jews" and "Jewish" as if they were unproblematic, this material would probably repay further consideration in the light of the theoretical sophistication now available in this area.[161]

Greek and Judean Ethnic Conflict and Its Bearing on Romans

The picture of social conflict outlined in chapter two above was fundamentally one in which members of groups found identity for themselves in differentiation from outgroups, typically expressed in the stereotypification of outgroup members but occasionally in conflict with them. The particular field of social identity represented by ethnicity with which we have been concerned in the present chapter is one in which conflict is especially common. The 1990s witnessed numerous examples, in Africa, in the Middle East, and even in Europe, in spite of its horrifying history of four centuries of warfare culminating in the Second World War. We should expect, therefore, that the closely analogous ethnic phenomena of the ancient Mediterranean region would also produce its share of such conflict between groups, and that is what we find. In particular, the remarks of Horowitz, who (as set out earlier in this chapter) treats ethnic conflict within a framework of social identity theory, fit the data well.

Of particular relevance here is that Christopher Stanley has plotted the broad outlines of conflict between Judeans (he calls them "Jews") and Greeks from the mid-first century BCE to 117 CE. A striking feature of the story is how frequent and widespread such conflict was. All of these episodes can be seen as the product of two ethnic groups jockeying for power and status within the framework of new (or fairly new) government, a factor isolated by Horowitz as important in the modern period.

Stanley divides the incidents into four main periods. The first extends through the latter half of the first century BCE and is limited mainly to the cities of Asia Minor. There were outbreaks of conflict in Sardis (49 BCE, 11 BCE?), Miletus (46), Laodicea/Tralles (46/45), Parium (44?), Ephesus (43, 42, 14, 11?, 7/6), Halicarnassus (40s?), the cities of Ionia (14) and the province of Asia in general (12?), in addition to Cyrene in North Africa (13?).

Second, some fifty years later there was another, more violent wave of conflict in several cities of the Near East. Judeans and their neighbors battled it out in Syrian Antioch (39–40 CE), Seleucia-on-Tigris and Ctesiphon in Babylonia (41), Jamnia (39), Dora (41) and Philadelphia in Palestine (44), and Alexandria in Egypt (38–41). In most of these cities, notably Alexandria, substantial populations considered themselves "Greeks," that is, they had this ethnic identity, marked by the use of the Greek language and involvement in other features of Greek culture, whether or not they might also have possessed some other ethnic identity. This mutual hostility between Judeans and Greeks would have formed part of the living memories of most of the people to whom Paul wrote Romans, and some of them may have experienced it in other cities of the Mediterranean region.

There was a third outbreak of violence at the time of the Judean revolt in 66–70 CE, affecting the cities of Palestine containing Judeans and Greeks and also Damascus, Antioch, Alexandria, and Cyrene. Finally, the Judean communities of Mesopotamia and North Africa sustained heavy losses during the diaspora revolt of 115–117 CE.[162]

Stanley notes properly that it is wrong to talk about these conflicts as occurring between "Jews" and "gentiles" since this entails ignoring that "gentiles" is a "Jewish" way of categorizing these other peoples, not their own way, and that we should therefore refer to them by the name of the particular ethnic group in question.[163] The same point has been made by Bruce Malina, who has pointed out that τὰ ἔθνη is the Israelite designation for all peoples other than Israel, for all non-Judeans.[164] The intensity of the conflict between Judeans and Greeks, rarely involving other combatants, brings to mind Horowitz's view that in spite of the plurality of ethnic groups in any given setting, most conflicts involve only two groups, and participation by other groups tends to be minor. The group juxtapositions and comparisons—central to social identity theory as here applied to ethnic relations—emphasize the dichotomous aspect of interactions and call attention to perceived polar types of behavior that naturally tend to produce pairs of antagonists.

Horowitz has also suggested that one of the causes of ethnic conflict in the modern period has been the tensions produced where, in a context of a new form of regional government, one ethnic group sensed it was falling behind another in the allocation of resources, including honor. Its efforts to catch up led to the generation of stereotypes and conflict between the groups. This view bears closely upon the rivalry between Judeans and Greeks. As to the explanation for this conflict, rather than following the Judean authors Josephus and Philo, who present it almost universally as the product of Greek oppression and victimization of Judeans, Stanley realistically points to the fact that in the cities of the East these two ethnic groups were competing for scarce jobs and resources including, we might add, citizenship and civic honors, which were sources of great contention in Alexandria in the period leading up to the conflict of 38 CE. Second, the very different cultural indicia exhibited by Judeans and Greeks to define their ethnic boundaries meant trouble given their sheer proximity. The powerful forces of ethnocentrism suggest that strongly ethnocentric groups living next to one another are likely to find reason to quarrel. These problems were compounded by a third factor: whereas Greek populations had leveled off by the first century BCE, it is possible that Judean numbers continued to grow through immigration from Palestine and a higher birth (or survival) rate. None of this is to deny that other causes may have figured in the numerous ethnic clashes between Judeans and Greeks, as with unrest caused across the Mediterranean during the Roman Civil War of the mid-first century BCE.[165]

Stanley offers a few valuable remarks about the relevance of such interethnic animosity to Paul. Raised in a Greek city of Asia Minor, Paul would have been aware of the "anti-Jewish" sentiments of many Greeks in the eastern Mediterranean basin and had perhaps suffered himself. Stanley then notes: "He was also aware of the inevitable tensions that would result from his efforts to unite 'Jews' and 'Greeks' into a novel social institution, the Christian house-church. . . . Both Jewish and Greek converts brought heavy loads of ethnic prejudice with them into the new Christian house-churches."[166] While the argument developed in this book will demonstrate the general accuracy of this view and its relevance for understanding Romans, one can appreciate the precise nature of the tension and conflict between Judeans and Greeks in Rome that Paul faced only by attending closely to social features that were specific to that city. That subject, the 50s CE Roman context of the Christ-movement to which Paul wrote, is dealt with in the next chapter.

4

The Context: Rome in the 50s CE

Paul's letter was written to a set of individuals in Rome in the 50s CE to whom he refers in Romans 16, some by name and some by generic designation. Since I have already proposed in chapter one that Paul's communication did have specific relevance to Rome, and was not just some generalized tract that could have been sent to virtually any group of Christ-followers anywhere around the Mediterranean, it becomes necessary to consider more closely the nature of the context into which the letter was dispatched—Rome in the 50s CE—in relation both to the issue of ethnic relations considered in the previous chapter and also more to the specific features of life in the capital. This is the subject of the present chapter. Exegesis of the letter begins in the next chapter, focusing on the material relating to Paul's context and purpose in writing in 1:1-15 and 15:14—16:27.

The inquiry into the Roman context begins with the fundamental division in Roman society, based on differentiation of levels of wealth and honor, between the elite and the nonelite, especially as it emerged in the styles of housing utilized by each and in the nature and function of associations known as *collegia*. I next consider the ethnically diverse nature of the population of Rome (which represents a specific area for the application of the nature of ethnicity and ethnic conflict in the context of the ancient Mediterranean). This leads into the history and character of the Judean communities in Rome as comprising one such ethnic group, with special focus on their *proseuchai*, the buildings in which they met. The Judeans require special attention as the people from which the Christ-movement arose and with whom it continued to have a troubled association, as can be seen unambiguously in Romans. Lastly, I bring these threads together as they pertain to what we can learn about the character of the Christ-movement in Rome, first, by comparison with the Judean communities of the city (covering its history and other factors such as the role of contrasting architectural contexts); second, in relation to the structures and values of wider Roman society. I will be especially alert to the possibility of conflict being provoked through differentials of ethnicity and honor in the public and private settings in which the various component groups of the Christ-movement in Rome found themselves.

Elite and Nonelite

Two models are helpful in guiding us into basic dimensions of the Roman context, the first from macrosociology and the second from cultural anthropology.

This reflects the fact that a rounded analysis of ancient complexes of data will often (if not always) derive assistance from various reaches of the social sciences and that an investigation tied to just one such discipline may prove inadequate to the task.

The basic social division in the ancient Mediterranean world, according to a useful macrosociological model developed by Lenski and Lenski,[1] was between the elite and nonelite sections of society. The elite comprised a small proportion of the population, probably between 2 and 5 percent, based in cities, mostly literate, and everywhere styling themselves in ways we designate as "aristocratic," who controlled much of the economic production (especially in agriculture) and lived a luxurious lifestyle in cities, Rome preeminently, maintained and protected by the retainers who served them. The nonelite formed the rest of the population, nearly all of them illiterate,[2] and included peasants working on farms in the countryside (often owned by the elite or, where they were not, subject to heavy rents and taxes) and also urban populations of retainers, officials (like *apparatores* and *scribae*), craftsmen, traders, laborers, and slaves needed to keep the whole system turning. Some of the nonelite accumulated considerable wealth, while, at the other extreme, others were beggars. There was no "middle class" in this type of culture, and it is a serious anachronism to speak of one. This stratified population is reflected in the hierarchies found in ancient Mediterranean cities, such as Rome.[3]

Within this broad structural position it is helpful, second, to examine Mediterranean culture, as modeled by Bruce Malina on the basis of research by cultural anthropologists into the region in recent decades that characterized elite and nonelite sectors of the population. Central features of this culture include its pronounced group orientation (with family as the main group), its fixation on honor as the preeminent social good and competed for in every possible social arena, and its use of patron and client relationships. Just as individuals competed for honor, so too did groups in the same social arena, since they were the bearers of a collective honor that needed to be maintained against threats and challenges.[4]

Both of these models are heuristic tools (not social laws) located at a reasonably high level of abstraction and must be modulated to the particular facts of any given setting (although critics of the use of models in biblical interpretation often seem surprisingly immune from understanding this point).[5]

Indeed, the two models just described work well with Rome in the period of the late Republic and early Empire, for which a profusion of data can be discussed and illuminated in relation to them. Since much of the evidence we have for Rome is extant in the literary productions of Roman aristocrats, our understanding of that section of the population is necessarily richer than for the nonelite. Nevertheless, the nonelite population does sometimes appear in our sources (with Justin Meggitt having demonstrated that the available material is more informative than usually supposed),[6] and some epigraphic and archaeological evidence is available.[7] The graffiti from Pompeii, a city not far south of Rome and destroyed in 79 CE, only some twenty years after Paul wrote to the Romans, is a particularly valuable source.[8]

The relevance of the elite/nonelite distinction is that Romans was written to a nonelite audience. To gain some sense of how this affects our interpretation of the letter we need to consider their position in Rome, especially the values likely to have motivated them and their way of life.

The Roman Elite

We must now consider certain the features of these models as they relate to the elite in Rome that I argue below have a bearing on Paul's message in Romans. First, support for an elite/nonelite social differentiation similar to that of the Lenski and Lenski model comes from no less an authority than Averil Cameron, who argues that the Roman Empire was characterized by a strong demarcation between an educated elite and the rest of society during the first two centuries CE, even if things changed later under the influence of a rising Christian elite.[9] There was certainly a decline in the position of the urban aristocracy between the first and fourth centuries CE.[10] The distinctive feature of the Roman elite was that it comprised an upper nobility (the *senatores*) and a lower nobility (the *equites*), largely (but not exclusively) tied to particular levels of wealth (at least one million sesterces for *senatores* and 400,000 sesterces for the *equites*).[11] Mark Reasoner has examined the fundamental status division in Roman society and noted the use of the language of "strong" and "weak" to designate the two sections.[12] The role of the elite in ancient Mediterranean cities has been usefully explained by Richard Rohrbaugh and Bruce Malina.[13]

Second, Malina's discussion of the "agonistic," or competition-ridden, nature of Mediterranean culture[14] is amply illustrated among the Roman aristocracy in the first century CE, before its position had deteriorated as noted above. A passionate concern for one's *fama*, "reputation," was one of the most characteristic features of the Roman aristocracy and was reflected in the competitive practices that occurred among them. Keith Hopkins and Graham Burton have shown that fierce competition to be successful in election to the various administrative and judicial posts available in Rome was characteristic of the late Republic and early Empire,[15] even though under Augustus the elections were transferred from the popular assemblies to the Senate. Competition between senators and equestrians did not disappear under the emperors; it merely changed its character. Hopkins and Burton have shown that in the early Empire membership of the Roman Senate was not hereditary, as in medieval and early modern Europe. A large percentage of the children of praetors and consuls did not follow them into office, since this was earned by success in vigorously fought elections, even though a noble lineage was no doubt an advantage.[16] From the age of 25 to 40 senators competed with one another for important posts: "In the meantime, many spent a fortune on an ostentatious life-style commensurate with their social position and with their ambitions, in the pursuit of prestige, honours and royal favour. Divisive ambition thus supplemented terror as a mechanism of control."[17]

Third, an important feature of Mediterranean culture outlined by Malina is that a man whose honor has been desecrated must seek to restore it, typically by taking vengeance on the person responsible.[18] In Rome this process took a distinctive social form well explained by David Epstein: members of the elite who were shamed by others fostered *inimicitiae* ("enmity") toward them. *Inimicitiae* represented the polar opposite and dark side of the *amicitia*, the strong ties of friendship and patron-client relations, which often tied together members of the elite and their clients.[19] They represented a state of animosity, usually made public, that signaled that the person bearing *inimicitia* toward someone else would do all he could to stop that person achieving any objective or winning any honors. The Roman public expected a man to have a good reason for taking up *inimicitiae,* but, if he did, regarded him as having a duty of honor to pursue them. "A Roman risked losing a great deal of prestige if he gained a reputation for reconciling hostilities too easily."[20] The only notable exception was where reasons of state intervened, as when the two consuls in charge of a Roman army in the field harbored *inimicitiae* for one another. The first sign of entry upon *inimicitiae* between two men was usually "the complete suspension of all social contact."[21] But this was commonly only the prelude to attacks "on what a Roman guarded most, his honour, his property and civic rights."[22] A typical ploy was the institution of legal proceedings against someone for his management of a province or conduct of military authority, often with exile as the aim. Sometimes acts of physical violence were employed.

Fourth, as Richard Saller has pointed out, the house or *domus* was a fundamentally important arena for the Roman elite (whether in the capital or the provinces) to advertise their honor. A *domus* was a large house built around a courtyard (*atrium*) and often possessing a garden. Such a house "daily provided the stage for assertion of status and influence."[23] It was vital for a Roman aristocrat to have a fine house because, unlike his classical Athenian counterpart, he carried out most of his dealings with his public there.[24] The morning *salutatio*, for example, was a way of demonstrating a man's position as an honorable patron to his clients. This is why a crowded house *(domus fre-quentata)* appears as an index of power in an active social life.[25] I will return to the subject of Roman housing, currently the subject of extensive reexamination by Ray Laurence, Andrew Wallace-Hadrill, and others, later in this chapter.

Fifth, the house of the Roman aristocrat was also heavily implicated in the dark side of the habitual competition for positions and honor—the *inimicitiae* and the acts of aggression and even violence they encouraged. As David Epstein has reminded us, where *inimicitiae* supplanted a former friendly relationship, the public declaration "would be accompanied by the announcement that the new *inimicus* was no longer welcomed in one's house."[26]

The Nonelite in Rome

When we turn to the nonelite in Rome, the initial point to be made is that they shared the same social system as the elite, even if they had neither the resources nor leisure to play prevalent social games, such as *inimicitiae,* to the same extent. That the culture described by Malina—in its particular Roman configuration—also encompassed the nonelite population in Rome is strongly suggested by a number of factors. First, there is the sheer unlikelihood of a radically bifurcated set of basic social values given that the elite were in a position to socialize the rest of the population into their values, for example, through military service and religious cult. Second, the notions of honor and dishonor, often connected with kinship groups, are prevalent in the plays of Plautus, written between 205 and 184 BCE but performed for some two centuries thereafter; he reworked examples of Greek New Comedy in a manner that made them accessible to a wide audience in Rome. Third, there is the appearance of agonistic patterns of conduct, as in the graffiti of Pompeii, which must have been similar to the outlook of comparable types of population in Rome,[27] and also the prevalence of envy seen in the widespread use of curses *(defixiones)* inscribed on small tablets and often aimed at harming one's competitors, at whatever social level they might be located.[28] The fourth relevant factor is the widespread tendency for urban nonelites to mimic the attitudes and manners of the elites as a way of promoting their own status. In Rome this can clearly be seen in numerous phenomena, such as the extent to which freedmen in the capital around the turn of the era copied the funeral monuments (with their highly realistic portraiture) of the aristocracy[29] and the fact that the titles of offices in the *collegia,* the trade associations to be mentioned again below, imitated the offices of the Roman state, a phenomenon well observed by Wayne Meeks.[30]

This does not mean that the attitudes and values of the nonelite were identical to those of the elite. Clearly the active defense of one's *fama* was possible only if one enjoyed considerable leisure, which the nonelite did not. Meggitt rightly urges us not to forget the ludic and subversive character of popular culture, especially as it emerges in the graffiti from Pompeii and elsewhere.[31]

Nonelite Housing

Given the usual proclivity of lower social groups to ape the customs of the elite, we would expect wealthier members of the nonelite possessed of reasonably large houses to use them in the same way as centers for social networks and demonstrations of largesse likely to promote their honor among their peers. A famous inscription left on his tombstone by a certain Mactar in North Africa relates how he moved from being a harvester working hard under the strong sun to becoming a decurion in his local town council, a progress that made him master of his own *domus*, which lacked nothing.[32] Saller notes that the "physical house in itself marked the harvester's wealth and also provided a domain in which he could exercise social power as *dominus*. Clearly, the *domus*, apart from kinship, was central to the Roman construction of social status."[33] Moreover, "the honor of the *paterfamilias* depended on his ability to protect his household, and in turn the virtue of the household contributed to his prestige."[34] Such a reciprocal relationship existed both between the paterfamilias and his kin and other household members and also between him and his clients, who were in effect fictive kin.

Although evidence is hard to come by, we would expect that a man like Mactar would also follow the aristocracy by using his house as an arena for demonstrating the institution of *inimicitiae* with people at his social level, by shutting its doors against them. But what was nonelite housing like in Rome?

Because of Rome's huge population, settled on a comparatively small area, there was always a shortage of land for housing it. While the elite lived in their atrium-style *domus*, the rest of the population generally made do by renting apartments in the numerous tenement blocks called *insulae*, often built many stories high over narrow streets. *Insulae* varied in quality. Wealthier members of the population not able to afford spacious atrium style housing rented *insulae* of the best quality.[35] The standard of the accommodation decreased in the upper levels, where the rents were lower and the poor rented rooms. The poorest made do with miserable garrets at the tops of dirty stairs. For everyone rents were high, and falling into debt to pay them was a common problem for the urban poor, and even for wealthy tenants.[36]

The poorer tenements were often badly built, owing to their greedy builders having economized on construction costs. New stories were frequently added to existing buildings,[37] although Augustus prohibited tenements beyond a maximum of seventy feet.[38] Construction techniques were poor, with foundations too shallow and walls too thin, and, not surprisingly, the tenements often collapsed and were always exposed to great risk from fire. The inhabitants of the upper floors had less chance of escape if fire took hold.[39]

It was common for the street level of the tenements to be occupied by small shops of craftsmen, often with rooms behind where the craftsman's family lived.[40] The craftsmen were mainly foreigners from the provinces and those involved in the same craft tending to congregate in the same street or area.[41]

In the next chapter, when I begin interpreting the text of Romans, I set out a case for the early Christ-movement in Rome having met in houses or perhaps in small commercial premises.

Voluntary Associations (Collegia)

A notable feature of life in Rome (and elsewhere in the Mediterranean) was the interest of various groups in the population, especially from the nonelite, in coming together to form associations or clubs (collegia) as a more or less permanent focus for their shared interests and aspirations.[42] This phenomenon reflects the pronounced group orientation of ancient Mediterranean culture. Collegia were formed from the members of the same trade, profession, or religion; from the inhabitants of the same districts (vici) in Rome; from the poor, so as to provide burials to the members (collegia tenuiorum); and even from among the freedmen and slaves of particular households (collegia domestica). La Piana has noted that collegia domestica encompassed people of different ethnic groups who belonged to the same owner. Yet they also had a religious and funerary character.[43] Such collegia were relevant to the book of Romans, as we will see later. In addition, the common interests that bound members of foreign groups together led them also to organize into associations and clubs.[44]

They usually had written constitutions and regular meeting places. There was nearly always some religious dimension to their activities.[45] Usually they had wealthy patrons and officeholders whose names sometimes matched those of Roman magistracies. Thus, as well as fostering goodwill among their members, collegia allowed them access, admittedly on a small scale, to some of the honors achieved by the elite.[46]

Yet the collegia could easily become foci of dissent, and for this reason the state frequently acted against them. Thus Julius Caesar, after he had defeated his competitors, issued a decree dissolving all collegia, except those of ancient foundation,[47] those spared apparently including the collegia of Judeans.[48] In the period of anarchy after Caesar's assassination, however, the collegia quickly returned, prompting Augustus to promulgate a decree dissolving all collegia except those that were ancient and legitimate, provided they received the necessary permit from the Senate.[49] During the empire political associations *(factiones)* were forbidden, so that associations had to have economic, religious, or social purposes.[50]

Ethnic Groups in Rome

When Paul wrote to the Christ-followers of Rome, the largest city in the Western Mediterranean by far, with a population of approximately 800,000 to 900,000 in the mid-first century CE,[51] he used Greek, not Latin. This insufficiently appreciated fact reminds us that Paul was directing his letter to Greek-speaking immigrants in the city, or to their descendants who still spoke this language. Some of them were now perhaps citizens,[52] but many would have had the lesser status of *peregrini*, resident aliens, for which the Greek word was *paroikoi*.[53] Accordingly, we must pay some attention to the situation of Greek-speaking residents of the city,[54] especially since the transition from Greek to Latin would have marked a sign of increased wealth and status.[55]

During the last century of the Republic and the early centuries of the Empire the population of Rome increased rapidly, largely due to the influx of outsiders from Italy, Asia Minor, Syria, Egypt, Greece, Africa, Spain, and eventually Germany and the lands along the Danube. A large part of this population was made up of slaves and ex-slaves. So many Syrians came to Rome that in the early second century CE the Roman satirist Juvenal could complain that "the Syrian Orontes discharges into the Tiber."[56] Among the foreign groups in Rome the Judeans were the most noticeable, because of their social exclusiveness and distinctive religious practices and beliefs. By the mid-first century CE the foreign element formed a large part of the *plebs urbana,* most of the servile class, and a large proportion of the *peregrini,* while some of its representatives had begun to enter the equestrian and senatorial orders.[57] Except in rare cases, therefore (and there are no such *aves rarae* in sight in Romans), these were members of the nonelite.

A number of areas in Rome housed concentrations of foreigners. A popular site in the early Republic was the Aventine, close to the docks on the Tiber and outside the *pomerium,* the sacred precinct of the city from which foreign cults were excluded. Only under Claudius was the Aventine finally included in the *pomerium,* at which time the Aventine was still an unfashionable area inhabited mainly by plebeians of foreign extraction. Later Christian tradition placed one of the first groups of Christ-followers on the Aventine.[58] The area beyond the Tiber and within a bend in its course (now called the Trastevere) was a site of the earliest substantial Judean settlement (as we know in particular from *On the Embassy to Gaius* of Philo of Alexandria, to which I return below). But in the first century CE another Judean settlement was formed outside the Porta Capena. Others settled in the Subura and others still on the outskirts of the Campus Martius. During the first century CE large numbers of Alexandrians and Greeks settled in the area of Campus Martius.[59] The way in which Judean catacombs were later to be scattered around the outskirts of Rome reflects this distributed settlement pattern.[60]

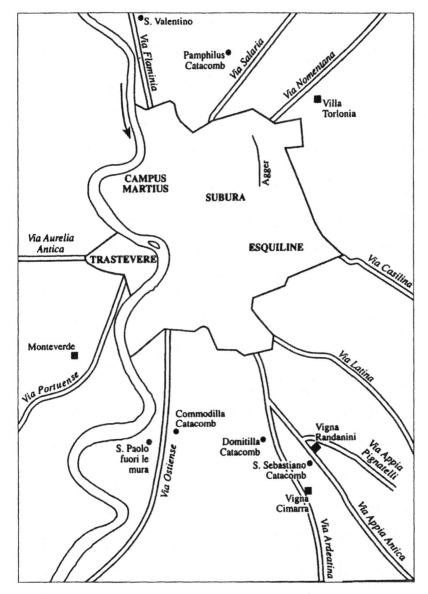

Figure 1: Judean Catacombs in Rome[61]

The action of foreigners in Rome in joining voluntary associations (collegia) was noted above. Another particular form of foreign engagement with Rome requires mention. Groups of merchants from particular places in the provinces who set up business in Rome itself and in the Italian ports for Rome, first Puteoli and then Ostia (after the improvements begun by Claudius), established bases of operations called *stationes*. The members of these *stationes* maintained loyalty to the cities from which their members came and occasionally even appealed to them for support.[62] The *stationes* were the centers of activity of the groups to which they belonged; there matters of common interest were discussed and provision was made for the erection of temples to their national gods.[63] Later in this chapter I consider the evidence for the mid-first-century Judean building at Ostia possibly built for one such *statio*.

Although Rome was utterly dependent on foreign workmen of free and servile status, and its elite citizens had been schooled in literature and philosophy by the Greeks, native-born Romans (and Italians) had a strong tradition of disdain for them. For example, the Romans stigmatized the Greeks as unreliable, irresponsible, flighty, and verbose people to whose *levitas* Roman sturdiness, *gravitas*, stood in marked contrast. The glories of Greek civilization were regarded as things of the past.[64] While to an extent this reflects the inevitable processes of stereotyping of ethnic outgroups that we discussed in chapter three, the vehemence of Roman dislike for Greeks and other ethnic groups, amply attested in their writers, is worth noting: "In their eyes Rome had become the dumping-place of the whole world, and there was no vice, no corruption, no ill practice that these foreign crowds had not imported with them."[65] The Roman dislike for foreigners may well have been one of the reasons that stimulated them to form associations.[66]

But since ethnic stereotypification is a two-way street, Roman dislike for others was matched by antipathy the Greeks and other ethnic groups felt toward them and their perceived faults, such as the way they exercised power to extract wealth from subject populations and their offensiveness and insensitivity abroad.[67] Indeed, the Greeks regarded all non-Greeks as uncivilized (barbaroi).

The Judeans in Rome

The History and Organization of Judeans in Rome

There had been Judeans in Rome since at least 139 BCE.[68] Possibly at first they comprised traders and merchants. In the next century the Judean population was enlarged with the captives whom Pompey brought back to Rome in 61 BCE from his campaign in Palestine. In 59 BCE when Cicero was defending

Lucius Valerius Flaccus, a former governor of the province of Asia, against charges of embezzlement, he referred to the crowd of Judeans in Rome, saying they were close-knit with influence in the public assemblies.[69] During the reign of Augustus (31 BCE–14 CE) the Judeans of Rome seem to have enjoyed good relations with the regime, as seen in an important passage in Philo's *Embassy* (155-57), to which I return below. Under Tiberius (emperor 14–37 CE), however, their position deteriorated. In 19 CE he deported some four thousand Judeans to Sardinia for military service, and they could only have been a fraction of the total Judean population.[70] Barclay interprets this action as the first sign on the part of the Romans that the Judeans posed a threat to their way of life.[71] Although Gaius Caligula (emperor 37–41 CE) did nothing to support the Judeans of Alexandria in relation to the actions of the Greek population against them, and at his death was even planning to install a statue of himself in the temple in Jerusalem, there is no evidence that he moved against the Judeans of Rome. The events of the reigns of Claudius (41–54 CE) and Nero (54–68 CE) I defer to later in this chapter, in view of their possible bearing on relations between the Judeans and the Christ-movement in Rome.

By the mid-first century CE the Judeans were well established in what had been their first place of settlement in Rome, in a low-lying area beyond the western bank of the Tiber—the Transtiberim, now called the Trastevere. Yet during the first and second centuries CE they had also begun to spread into other parts of the city, like the Subura and the district near the start of the Appian Way.[72] Discovered in various parts of Rome, three large Judean catacomb complexes that have produced a wealth of funerary remains reflect this distribution. These are the Monteverde (southwest part of the city), Nomentana (northeast), and Appian (south) catacombs, which are also known respectively as the catacombs of the Via Portuense, Villa Torlonia, and Vigna Randanini (see fig. 1, p. 85).[73] The Monteverde would have been convenient to the Trastevere community, the Nomentana to the Judeans of Subura, and the Appian to those dwelling in that region.

Many scholars, such as Frey in relation to the Montevede catacomb,[74] believe that bricks impressed with dated stamps, some going back to the first century BCE, found in these catacombs allow them to be dated to the first century CE or earlier, which would make them contemporaneous with the first house churches of the Christ-movement. L. V. Rutgers, however, has shown that the use of brick-stamps in this way is unreliable, principally for the reason that old bricks were regularly recycled into new locations, such as in catacombs, so that their date of production tells one little, if anything, about the date of the context in which they were ultimately found.[75] On his analysis, the most likely date for the beginnings of the Judean catacombs is the late second or early third century CE.

Nevertheless, the epigraphy found in these catacombs does bear upon the position of the Judeans during the first century CE. This material has been treated in a number of studies and need be considered only briefly here.[76] We know the names of some thirteen Judean congregations, συναγωγαί, from Rome,[77] of which eleven are represented by epigraphic remains containing the word συναγωγή.[78] This word always refers to the congregation of Judeans concerned, never to the building in which they met.[79] Support for a first-century CE date for some of these Judean congregations exists in the names they adopted for themselves. Thus the "synagogue of the Augustesians" was probably named in honor of Augustus, and the "synagogue of the Agrippesians" was possibly named after Marcus Vipsanius Agrippa (62 BCE to 12 BCE), both of whom stood up for the rights of Judeans on many occasions.[80] Naming a synagogue after an eminent Roman was a sensible way of demonstrating loyalty to the state.

These congregations seem to have been set up at various times. Earlier views that they were largely homogeneous in relation to their organization and the titulature of their array of officials are now being increasingly challenged. Newer research has pointed to the considerable variations in their structure and the titles of their officials, many of which reflected the titulature in other forms of Greco-Roman organizations.[81] Many of the titles reflect hierarchical distinctions that were a common feature of the Greco-Roman environment (*archisynagogos, gerousiarches, archigerousiarches, archon, pater/mater synagogae*), and there seems little doubt that these congregations had a strongly developed hierarchy of power and honor. There does not appear to have been a central governing body for the Judeans of Rome.[82]

Judean *Proseuchai* in Rome

In a footnote to his challenging discussion of the Claudian edict of expulsion, Mark Nanos notes, "There is no evidence of independent synagogue structures in the Diaspora during this period. Private homes were adapted for meetings, and since the Jews of Rome of this period were not often wealthy, most if not all of their homes would have accommodated only small groups."[83] He has expressed a similar view elsewhere.[84] The issue is very important, for if the Judeans of Rome did meet in privately owned houses that continued to function as such at other times, the social and architectural setting of their meetings would have been similar to that of gatherings of the Christ-movement, which certainly occurred in houses in Rome at this time. Yet Nanos is in error here, a lapse explicable in that he was following specialists on Judean and Christ-movement architecture who themselves make the same mistake[85] and was writing before this view had been subjected to a recent probing reexamination against the primary data by Donald Binder and Anders Runesson.[86]

One must grant that at the very outset of a Judean settlement in a diaspora city Judeans would have likely conducted meetings, including the most important one on the Sabbath, in the houses of individual members, probably the wealthier ones who had dwellings large enough to accommodate everyone. At this time in the history of the community there may have been no other building to use. Yet in light of the practice of benefaction so common in the Mediterranean world[87]—itself an attribute of a culture where honor was the primary value and where persons with material and social resources made gifts to others to promote their own honor and to generate reciprocal feelings of goodwill and loyalty—we would expect that at a fairly early stage wealthy Judeans or well-disposed outsiders (like the centurion in Luke 7:5) would dedicate an existing building, or part of one (probably a house but also perhaps a warehouse), or have a new edifice erected for use as a meeting place. In short, it is not impossible that in the mid-first century CE some Judean congregations were meeting in what once were or may still have been domestic dwellings; but, as we will see, this was not the dominant architectural context.

Perhaps not surprisingly in view of the antiquity of Judean settlement in Egypt, our earliest evidence for Judean meeting places comes from Egypt during the third and second centuries BCE.[88] This view assumes that the expression προσευχή, originally meaning "prayer" but used in this material with reference to a building, is actually an abbreviation for οἶκοι τῇ προσευχῇ, "house of prayer." The word προσευχή is never found in Egypt except in a Judean context.[89] *Proseucha*, as we will see, was borrowed into Latin and is used hereafter in the singular in the Latin form.

Some of the synagogues that have been excavated in the diaspora, for example, at Dura (on the Euphrates), Priene (western Asia Minor), and Stobi (in modern Yugoslavia), started life as houses.[90] In each case the synagogue was gradually remodeled into a larger and more differentiated structure. A critical point came when such a domestic building or building segment was no longer used by a family but was reserved exclusively for the community— a transformation we can witness quite starkly at Stobi, where the synagogue began as a domestic dwelling but part of it was eventually dedicated exclusively to community use.[91] But *proseuchai* could also be adapted from other types of buildings or be built specifically for that purpose. At Delos, for example, in spite of Michael White's argument to the contrary, the synagogue building was not originally a domestic dwelling. It was either a custom-made *proseucha* or a pagan cultic hall, later abandoned and then rebuilt by the Judeans.[92] We will see below that the Judean *proseucha* in Ostia functioned as such from its initial construction. Even in a densely settled part of a city characterized by tenement buildings (such as Rome), a benefactor could provide quite a large meeting space by purchasing or renting two or three adjacent houses or shops and modifying them for meetings by Judeans. Apart from the case of Stobi, plaques and other epigraphic remains recording dedications of *proseuchai* are extant from Egypt.[93]

When one recalls that there had been a sizable Judean population in Rome since the mid-first century BCE, it is inconceivable that, a hundred years later when Paul came to write Romans, the Judeans in the capital had not reached the stage where they had buildings specially dedicated to, or even constructed for, their use. Wayne Meeks accurately captures the position in this way (except in relation to Delos):

> The practice of meeting in private houses was probably an expedient used by Jews in many places as it was for the Pauline Christians, to judge from the remains of synagogue buildings at Dura-Europus, Stobi, Delos, and elsewhere that were adapted from private buildings. *In the cities where Paul founded congregations, however, the Jews had probably already advanced to the stage of possessing buildings used exclusively for the community's functions.*[94]

As far as Rome is concerned, we are able to reach this conclusion not merely on the basis of overwhelming historical probability, but by reason of unimpeachable literary and epigraphic data. Above all, there is convincing evidence in Philo of Alexandria (although it has been surprisingly neglected hitherto) that, at the time Paul wrote Romans, the Judeans of Rome, just as in Alexandria and elsewhere, were meeting in buildings specifically devoted to that purpose, not in the homes of some of their members. In addition, we will see later that the remains of a mid-first-century CE synagogue, specially built for the purpose, found at nearby Ostia afford a clear picture of what these buildings looked like.

This view, which I must now justify, means that the social and architectural context of Judean assemblies was very different from that of the communities of Christ-followers in Rome, who were (as I argue in the next chapter) gathering in the houses of some of them. This point has far-reaching implications for the respective identities of Judeans and Christ-followers, as we will see later in this chapter, and constituted a foundational dimension to the Roman embodiment of the Christ-movement to which Paul actively responded in his letter to them.

The Evidence in Philo for the *Proseuchai of Rome* and Its Implications
Among the extant works of Philo of Alexandria (c. 15 BCE–50 CE) is *On the Embassy to Gaius*, a work describing an embassy (of which he himself was a member) from the Judeans of Alexandria to the emperor Gaius Caligula in early 40 CE to complain of their persecution by the Greeks of the city.[95] At

one point in the *Embassy* Philo describes how Augustus showed his approval of the Judeans ('Ιουδαῖοι) of Rome:

> He knew that the large district of Rome beyond the river Tiber was owned and inhabited by Judeans ('Ιουδαῖοι). The majority of them were Roman freedmen. They had been brought to Italy as prisoners of war and manumitted by their owners and had not been made to alter any of their ancestral customs. Augustus therefore also knew that they have προσευχαί and meet in them, especially on the Sabbath, when they are publicly instructed (δημοσίᾳ ... παιδεύονται) in their ancestral philosophy. He also knew that they collect sacred money from their "first-fruits" (ἀπαρχαί) and send it up to Jerusalem by the hand of envoys who will offer sacrifices. But despite this he did not expel them from Rome or deprive them of their Roman citizenship because they remembered their Judean citizenship also. He introduced no changes into their προσευχαί, he did not prevent them from meeting for the exposition of the Law, and he raised no objection to their offering of the "first-fruits."[96]

Fortunately Philo elsewhere describes what happened at these Sabbath gatherings. In *Hypothetica*, no longer extant in toto but quoted by Eusebius in the *Preparation for the Gospel* 7.8, he provides the following details of the Sabbath service:

> What then did he [sc. Moses] do on these seventh days? He required them to assemble in the same place, and to sit down one with another in reverent and orderly manner, and listen to the laws, in order that none might be ignorant of them. And so in fact they do always meet together and sit down one with another, most of them in silence, except when it is customary to add a word of good omen to what is being read. But some priest who is present, or one of the old men, reads to them the holy laws, and explains each separately till nearly eventide: and after that they are allowed to depart with a knowledge of their holy laws, and with great improvement in piety.[97]

Having then described in the *Embassy* the reverence of Augustus for the temple in Jerusalem, where he ordered sacrifices to be offered daily (157), Philo goes on:

> Moreover, at the monthly distributions in Rome, when all the people in turn receive money or food, he never deprived the Judeans

(Ἰουδαῖοι) of this bounty, but if the distribution happened to be made on the Sabbath, when it is forbidden to receive or give anything or to do any of the ordinary things of life in general, especially commercial life, he instructed the distributors to reserve the Judeans' share of the universal largesse until the next day.[98]

This section of the *Embassy to Gaius* represents an invaluable historical source for the situation of Judeans in Rome up to the time of the Judean embassy's visit to the city in 40 CE.[99] While it is the only certain evidence for *proseuchai* in Rome before 70 CE, the passage is particularly valuable given its status as the product of eyewitness testimony by someone who had visited the city at the time. Nevertheless, below I deal with two other references to Roman *proseuchai* outside the works of Philo.

What did Philo have in mind when he referred to the *proseuchai* in Rome? While the text certainly indicates that they provided the architectural context for meetings of the Judeans in the Trastevere region of the city that they inhabited, this result itself leaves many questions outstanding. Chief among them, perhaps, is whether Philo was referring to private houses in which Judeans met occasionally, in particular on the Sabbath, but which otherwise continued as buildings inhabited by particular Judean families, or to buildings or parts of buildings specifically dedicated to common use by the Judeans.

Fortunately, we have an invaluable indication of what Philo had in mind by *proseuchai* from the way he uses the word with respect to the Judean community in Alexandria, both in *On the Embassy to Gaius* and also in another work that covers their persecution in the city, *Against Flaccus*. Although the relationship between the undoubtedly Philonic *Against Flaccus* and *Embassy* and even their respective order of composition have proven hard to determine,[100] they both mention *proseuchai* in Alexandria several times in relation to the events of 38 CE when the Greeks of that city perpetrated various acts of outrage upon the *proseuchai* in the context of a wider campaign against the Judeans.[101] On the assumption that what Philo tells his readers about the *proseuchai* in Alexandria provides a valuable guide to what he means by the same term used twice in connection with the Judeans inhabiting the Trastevere area of Rome, especially when the same word is used in relation to the two cities in the same work, *Embassy*, his usage repays close attention. I will not set out a full analysis here, but summarize the position as follows:

1. Judean houses (οἰκίαι) and *proseuchai* were different buildings: in the *Embassy* the οἰκίαι were attacked first, and then the *proseuchai*, although this order is reversed in *Against Flaccus*.[102]
2. *Proseuchai* existed in every quarter of the city.[103]

3. The *proseuchai* were open to the public and classed as "public" (δημό-σιοι), while the Judean houses (οἰκίαι) were private and classed as "pri-vate" (ἰδιωτικοί).[104]

4. The *proseuchai* were probably all reasonably respectable buildings or it might have been hazardous for the Greeks to seek to honor Gaius by putting his portraits in them.[105]

5. At least one of the Alexandrian *proseuchai* was large enough to contain a bronze statue of someone riding a four-horse chariot.[106]

6. Some οἰκίαι containing large numbers of Judeans were built right next to *proseuchai* (so that if the latter were burned, the former might also catch fire).[107]

7. The *proseuchai* contained objects that the Judeans had erected (or per-mitted to be erected) in honor of the emperors as benefactors, such as shields, crowns, monuments, and inscriptions (but not portraits).[108]

8. The *proseuchai* were known by particular names.[109]

9. One use of the *proseuchai* was as a place to offer prayers of thanks.[110]

This summary indicates what Philo had in mind for the *proseuchai* of Alexan-dria. It is interesting that in a rabbinic tradition one of the *proseuchai* in Alexandria had been particularly large. It was reputed to have been a basilica, a stoa within a stoa capable of holding twice the number of those who had left Egypt. A hazzan stood on a wooden platform in its center, and when someone took hold of the scroll to read he would wave a kerchief and they would answer "Amen" for each benediction.[111] Since both Rome and Alexandria contained large and long-established populations of Judeans in contact with one another, and since Philo offers no sign that the *proseuchai* of Rome he mentions in the *Embassy* were any different from those of Alexandria, it is reasonable to con-clude that this picture would also be applicable in Rome. This view is con-firmed by two further sets of data, the first consisting of two items of non-Judean epigraphy from Rome and the second the *proseucha* at Ostia.

The Two Non-Judean References to Proseuchai

First, in Juvenal's *Third Satire* (line 296) the narrator, Umbricius, explains how a poor man like him is liable to be accosted on the way home one night by an aggressive, drunken bully who, among other insults, will ask: "ede ubi consis-tas: in qua te quaero proseucha?" ("Tell me where you have your stand [i.e., as a beggar]?[112] In what *proseucha* am I to seek you?"). Since Juvenal probably wrote his *Satires* between 100 and 130 CE, but probably closer to 100 CE,[113] this evidence relates to a time some sixty to seventy years after Philo, yet it is still important. The question "In what *proseucha* am I to seek you?" is revealing and indicates (a) that at this period there were a number of them, (b) that their locations were not a secret, (c) that they were open to the public, and (d) that they formed such a distinctive type of building in Rome as to require the use of *proseucha* as a Greek loanword in Latin to refer to them.[114] All of this is in accord with what I have suggested was the case in Rome in the 40s. Since elsewhere in the *Satire* Umbricius reveals his hatred of immigrants (including Judean beggars: 3.13-16),[115] it is possible that he finds these questions particularly offensive as predicated on his being a Judean himself, even if the attitudes of both Umbricius and his assailant reflect ethnic stereotypes and not necessarily the actual behavior of the Judean population of Rome. On the other hand, perhaps because Judean *proseuchai* were open to the public even non-Judean beggars could take up position there, while the almsgiving habits of Judeans may have meant that such places offered excellent opportunities to beg.

The second reference to a *proseucha* outside Philo consists of a non-Judean epitaph, possibly to be dated to the first or second century CE:[116] "Dis M. P. Corfidio Signino Pomario De Aggere A Proseucha Q. Sallustius Hermes Amico Benemerenti Et Numerum Ollarum Decem" ("To the divine shades: Quintus Sallustius Hermes to his well-deserving friend Publius Corfidius of Segni, fruit seller at the rampart by the *proseucha,* and the number of urns is ten").[117] The *agger,* or rampart, refers to that part of the wall of Servius Tullius between the Esquiline and Colline Gates. This is the epitaph on the grave of a gentile fruit seller whose place of work is identified by reference to a *proseucha.* Once again, this means that the location of the *proseucha* was in the public domain, that it was an accepted part of the local scene, and that it was distinctive enough in Roman architectural and social terms as to require a Greek loanword to designate it.

It is, therefore, most likely sheer coincidence that the word *proseucha* has not turned up in the Judean catacomb epigraphy from Rome. The evidence just presented suggests that, at least in the first and early second centuries CE, the congregations referred to themselves as synagogues but to the buildings in which they met as *proseuchai.* There is epigraphic evidence for precisely this distinction elsewhere in the Mediterranean in the first century CE.[118]

Archaeological Evidence: The Proseucha at Ostia

Unfortunately, no archaeological evidence is extant for any *proseucha* from ancient Rome, either in the period under discussion or later. Particularly noticeable by their absence are inscriptions on structural stonework, recording benefactions, for example, which specifically mention *proseuchai* of the sort known from Alexandria and elsewhere. Given the literary evidence for their existence just discussed, however, we may be confident that this absence of archaeological evidence is simply an accident of history and cannot be tendered as an argument in favor of their nonexistence. In view of the prevalence of patterns of benefaction and patron/client in the ancient Mediterranean, it would have been remarkable if wealthy persons (either Judean or gentile) had not given the *proseuchai* to the Judeans and if such gifts had not been commemorated in stone on their walls.

All of this is strongly confirmed by the extant remains of a synagogue from Ostia, Rome's port at the mouth of the Tiber; from our previous discussion this building might be more accurately referred to as a *proseucha*. In its present state, the synagogue (discovered in 1961) dates to the fourth century CE, but this building represents the third phase of the structure, with the first stage securely dated to the mid-first century CE.[119] Although Michael White has argued that the building started life as a house, and was only converted to synagogal use in the second century CE,[120] this opinion has been conclusively refuted by Binder and Runesson. The original, first-century CE form of the Ostia synagogue bore no relation whatever to domestic architecture in the town at that time.[121] It consisted of an entry court with adjoining dining room (large enough to accommodate about thirty people), a propyleum, and a main hall (measuring approximately 12 by 15 meters) with benches on three sides. It contained handsome marble columns and a triportal gateway recalling the triple gate of the Jerusalem temple. These features can be seen in a plan and artist's reconstruction of the site (see figs. 2 and 3, pp. 96–97). An inscription found on site (the first clause in Latin and the rest in Greek) states: "For the safety of the Emperor. Mindis Faustus with his family built and made (it) from his own gifts, and set up the ark for the holy law."[122] Another inscription, in Latin and to be dated to the first or early second century CE, refers to an *archisynagōgus* named Plotius Fortunatus. A third inscription featuring a gerusiarch called Gaius Julius Justus has also been found.[123]

The synagogue building at Ostia is precious evidence of what the *proseuchai* in Rome mentioned by Philo may have been like. As Binder plausibly comments, given Ostia's relatively small size it is unlikely that the synagogue there was the prototype: "It must have been fashioned at least partly in imitation of synagogues from nearby Rome, which may have been built to an even grander scale."[124] Two more suggestions can be made. First, if a small city like Ostia had enough Judean inhabitants in the mid-first century CE to require a *proseucha* of this size, very possibly forming a *statio*, we must assume that Rome, with a population approaching a million, would have required *proseuchai* with at least fifty times this capacity—either fifty buildings the size of the Ostian example or, more likely, a somewhat smaller number, with some of them larger than this. Either way, we are surely looking at a much greater number than the eleven congregations known from Judean catacomb epigraphy. Second, if the Judeans of Ostia, or their non-Judean patron or patrons, could produce the resources necessary to build this fine structure, we must assume that the Judeans of Rome were equally capable of doing so. Suggestions that their alleged poverty would have stood in the way[125] cannot be sustained in the face of the Ostian evidence.

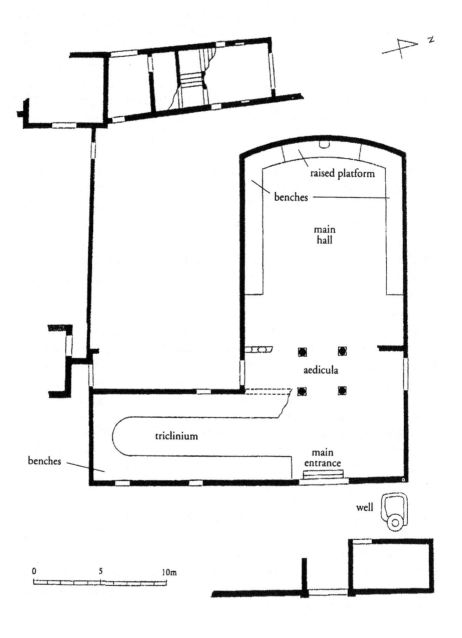

Figure 2: Plan of Ostia Synagogue in the First Century CE[126]

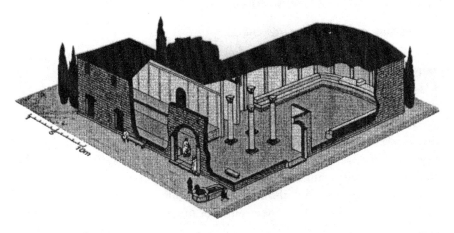

Figure 3: Artist's Reconstruction of Ostia Synagogue in the First Century CE[127]

On the other hand, this does not mean that all of the *proseuchai* of Rome were tailor-made buildings of the Ostia type. It is possible that some of them were converted domestic premises. This might have been the case where there was a congregation made up of Judeans comparatively new to Rome who had yet to acquire the resources needed for a *proseucha* of the Trastevere type mentioned by Philo, and also known from the archaeological remains in Ostia and from the two Latin references just mentioned. Yet even here the pressures to move to a more fashionable building of the type possessed by Judean congregations with a longer history in the capital, no doubt through the aid of someone wishing to promote his or her honor by making such a gift, must have been strong.

For all these reasons, accordingly, the only credible conclusion is that the majority of Judeans of Rome in the mid-first century CE met in buildings specially built or adapted for that purpose—*proseuchai*—and not in the houses of members. There is good reason to believe that some, at least, of these structures were larger and more elaborate than the imposing *proseucha* of precisely the same period known from Ostia. While such an architectural setting for Judean social and religious life is dramatically different from the domestic context of the Christ-movement in Rome, it remains to explore the ramifications and significance of this difference and assess how it might relate to the existence of conflict within the Christ-movement in Rome. But before doing so, I must comment briefly on what can be learned of the history of relations between Judeans and Christ-followers in the period leading up to Paul's dispatch of his letter to the capital.

Judeans under Claudius and the Early Stages of the Christ-Movement in Rome

The Judeans under Claudius (41–54 CE)

There are four ancient sources for the interaction between Claudius, emperor in the years 41–54 CE, and the Judean community in Rome in the 40s. As we will see, these references may have a bearing on the beginnings of the Christ-movement in the city. The first is Dio Cassius (164–after 259 CE), the author of an eighty-volume history of Rome from its foundation to 229 CE, which is reasonably extant for the period 69 BCE–46 CE.[128] Dio Cassius records in connection with the accession of Claudius (in 41 CE): "As for the Judeans, who had again increased so greatly that by reason of the multitude it would have been hard without raising a tumult to bar them from the city, he [Claudius] did not drive them out, but ordered them, while continuing their traditional mode of life, not to hold meetings."[129] Second, Suetonius, in his *Life of Claudius* (written early in the second century CE), states briefly and without offering any date: "Since the Judeans constantly made disturbances at the instigation of Chrestus (*impulsore Chresto*) he expelled them from the city."[130] Third, Acts 18:1-2 reports that Paul left Athens and went to Corinth, where he found a Judean named Aquila, a native of Pontus, who had recently come from Italy, and Priscilla his wife, "because Claudius had commanded all Judeans to leave Rome." Paul stayed with them and they worked together in their shared trade of tentmaking (18:3). Lastly, the late Christian apologist Orosius, writing a work "Against the Pagans" shortly after 417 CE, noted:

> Josephus reports, "In his ninth year [sc. of Claudius's reign] the Judeans were expelled by Claudius from the city." But Suetonius, who speaks as follows, influences me more: "Claudius expelled from Rome the Judeans who were constantly rioting at the instigation of Christ *(Christo)*." As far as whether he had commanded that the Judeans rioting against Christ *(Christum)* be restrained and checked or also had wanted the Christians, as persons of a cognate religion, to be expelled, it is not at all to be discerned.[131]

These references bristle with difficulties, the extent of which is insufficiently appreciated in work on the beginnings of the Christ-movement in Rome, especially as it relates to Paul's letter to the Romans. First, how secure is the evidence for an expulsion of Judeans under Claudius. Second, if there was such an expulsion, when did it occur? Third, who did Claudius expel on this occasion; in particular, were followers of Christ involved? The fourth issue is whether the ban on Judeans meeting that Dio Cassius records Claudius introducing in 41 CE refers to the same event as the expulsion described by Suetonius or was a separate measure. I will deal with these in turn.

First, that there was an expulsion of Judeans of some sort from Rome in the reign of Claudius seems highly likely given that Suetonius and Acts agree on this point. Although Slingerland raises the possibility that these sources (which are not exactly the same, especially because Chrestus is not mentioned in Acts) could refer to two different expulsions,[132] this seems unlikely. Acts is obviously a briefer account, referring to the bare fact of the expulsion in consequence of the Claudian edict, while Suetonius seeks to offer the reason behind this action. More importantly, however, Slingerland's two-expulsion hypothesis requires us to accept the improbable scenario that after the Judeans had been expelled by Claudius they ran the risk of returning to Rome *in that emperor's lifetime* and were then expelled by him for a second time. Slingerland tries to answer this objection by noting that Paul's letter indicates that Aquila and Priscilla had returned to Rome (Rom. 16:3-5),[133] but this event could have occurred (and almost certainly did occur) early in the reign of the next emperor, Nero (54–68 CE), whose first years as emperor were universally hailed as a period of excellent rule. Suetonius notes that in his first speech to the Senate Nero promised to rule according to Augustan precedent, and the reign of Augustus had been a good one for the Judeans of Rome, as we have seen earlier in this chapter.[134] The idea that Judeans driven out of Rome by Claudius waited until his death and the accession of an emperor likely to be much more favorable to their cause to return to the city is plausible. Accordingly, the most satisfying solution is that Suetonius and Acts 18:1-2 refer to the same expulsion.

But when the expulsion took place, the second issue, is much more difficult. Unfortunately, the date of 49 CE given by Orosius and the date commonly calculated with reference to Acts 18, also about 49 CE, become insecure on closer inspection. Slingerland has mounted an effective demolition of Orosius on this point, by showing that the date is a creation fully explicable within the tendentious historiography of this author.[135] The date of 49 CE also faces the obstacle that Tacitus, whose *Annals* cover that year, does not mention any expulsion of Judeans, Christ-followers or otherwise, which he probably would have done if this had occurred, at least if it was a large-scale affair. Certainly when he mentions the *Christiani* in connection with the events of Nero's reign he rather gives the impression of speaking of them for the first time. Slingerland has also offered reason to doubt the common view that the correlation between the Gallio, Roman proconsul of Achaia, mentioned in Acts 18:12-17, and the Lucius Iunius Gallio Annaeanus mentioned in inscriptional evidence as holding this post around 52 CE necessarily indicates an expulsion in 49

CE.[136] The result of his arguments is that a range of dates from 47 to 50 is possible for the Claudian expulsion on the basis of Acts 18:1-3.[137]

Third, who was expelled—Judeans *simpliciter*, Judeans who were Christ-followers, or both? It is common to assume that Suetonius includes the phrase "at the instigation of Chrestus" to explain the cause of the disturbances and that he was under the mistaken impression that Chrestus (= Christus) was in the city during the reign of Claudius. To this is added that in Acts 18:1-3 Paul begins to live and work at his craft with Aquila and Priscilla. As Raymond Brown perceptively noted, they are subsequently described as active in the Christ-movement, yet their conversion by Paul is never reported, which would have been strange if they had converted after he came to live with them. In addition, if they had been expelled from Rome because they were involved in disturbances among Judeans, it is most unlikely that they would have exposed themselves to the same risk by offering hospitality to a Judean who had stirred up trouble in the synagogues of Asia Minor and Greece.[138] A plausible explanation is that Paul chose to dwell with them because they were already Christ-followers and had been while still in Rome. Yet, as Slingerland has pointed out, the first assumption means that Suetonius did not know that Chrestus/Christus had been executed in Judea during the reign of Tiberius (as his contemporary Tacitus certainly did).[139] Slingerland treats Chrestus as a freedman who was advising Claudius and influenced him to expel the Judeans. It is possible to interpret Acts 18 as meaning that Aquila and Priscilla had not already joined the Christ-movement when they left Rome.[140] While Slingerland's position is perhaps a little strained, it represents a significant challenge to the *interpretatio Christiana* of the Claudian expulsion.

Fourth, was the ban on gatherings mentioned by Dio Cassius a separate and probably earlier act by Claudius, or a reference to the expulsion? This question is virtually impossible to determine. In favor of two events are Barclay (hesitantly) and Slingerland (strongly).[141] This version has the benefit of pointing to a gradual escalation of activity by Claudius. Certainly the way he dealt with the Judeans of Alexandria early in his reign, by guaranteeing them their rights but stating that he was willing to "proceed against them in every way as fomenting a common plague for the whole world,"[142] indicated that this was an ethnic group for whom he had little love. Fortunately, not as much turns on this issue as the others.

I will now correlate the results of this analysis with what else can be known or deduced about the origins of the Christ-movement in Rome.

The Origins of the Christ-Movement in Rome, Its Impact and Early Character

We have no idea when the first Christ-believer reached Rome.[143] Neither Paul in Romans nor Luke in Acts 28 names any prominent evangelist who first preached the gospel there. In his account of Pentecost in Acts, however, Luke tells us that among the devout Judeans living in Jerusalem were Romans (2:10), meaning "Rome-born Judeans," possibly possessing Roman citizenship. Many Judeans from around the Mediterranean did settle in Jerusalem, and given the size of the Judean population in Rome at that time (40,000–50,000),[144] it would be most surprising if some of them had not come from Rome. They were in the city at the dawn of the Christ-movement and could well have joined it. Similarly, non-Judean synagogue-attenders and reverers of the Judean God (called "God-fearers" in the NT) also visited Jerusalem, and it is possible that Romans were among them. They could either have returned to Rome taking the gospel with them or passed it on to Roman visitors to Jerusalem.[145] The very first Christ-followers whom we know of from Rome are Aquila and Priscilla, who were among the Judeans expelled from Rome by Claudius, probably between 47 and 50 CE, and whom Paul met in Corinth (Acts 18:2).

Yet at some point the first Christ-followers, Judean or non-Judean, and in the latter case probably God-fearing synagogue-attenders, must have reached Rome. What happened then? Across the Mediterranean the gospel of Christ had soon exhibited the capacity to arouse intense antagonism on the part of Judeans.[146] Before his conversion, presumably in the 30s of the first century, Paul himself had persecuted the "assembly of God" and tried to destroy it (Gal. 1:13; Phil. 3:6). The original source of this antagonism is one of the most difficult questions in New Testament scholarship. We are presumably looking for some breach of the Mosaic law, and my own view is that this was seen in the idolatrous or potentially idolatrous practice of table fellowship in Christ's name between Judeans and non-Judeans.

It is likely that in Rome also the arrival of the Christ-movement produced dissension and conflict among the Judean population. Even if the disturbances among the Judeans that induced Claudius to expel at least some of them did not originate in disputes about the Christ-movement, that was certainly the kind of trouble Luke describes as occurring across the Greek East in the Acts of the Apostles, and there is no reason to doubt that it happened there and that it could also have happened in Rome.

Yet Romans was written between about 55 and 58 CE, in the early years of Nero's reign, perhaps fifteen or even twenty years after the gospel had reached Rome. There are clear signs in the text (to which I return in later chapters) both that Paul is writing to a movement with strongly articulated beliefs and practices and that animosity (manifested in behavior) is being expressed between its Judean and non-Judean members. A group and a group identity have clearly developed distinctive from that of the Judean communities (although merely to state this is not to foreclose on the degree of separation between Judean synagogues and Christ-following congregations),[147] but they are being disturbed by the presence of subgroups and subgroup identities.

The challenge is to offer a satisfactory explanation for this state of affairs, since it almost certainly represents an important dimension of the context and exigence influencing Paul's communicative strategy in the letter.

The Thesis of Wolfgang Wiefel

A particular thesis, especially as propounded by Wolfgang Wiefel,[148] has become popular in explaining what happened in Rome. It draws heavily on the data discussed above relating to the reign of Claudius. In brief, the presence of Christ-followers in the *proseuchai* of Rome produced such disturbances that Claudius expelled Judeans (including Christ-followers) from the city in 49 CE. This left only non-Judean Christ-followers there, and they began to develop their own version of the movement independent of the synagogal form and adverse to the Mosaic law. Upon the accession of Nero in 54 CE, however, the Judeans returned in great numbers, and the Christ-followers among them now found a non-Judean Christ-movement in the ascendant, meeting in house congregations and ill disposed to Judean members. To such a context Paul writes Romans.

This is a reasonable and creative hypothesis and the fact that when Paul writes Prisca and Aquila are back in Rome (Rom. 16:3) fits in well with the idea of a return of Christ-following Judeans to Rome early in Nero's reign. Nevertheless, the counterarguments posed by Slingerland to many of the historical judgments upon which this hypothesis is based, especially the issue of whether the Claudian expulsion had anything to do with Christ-followers and that it may have been very small in scope if it did occur, suggest caution in its wholesale adoption.

Another major problem with Wiefel's theory is that it is unnecessary. For it is possible to explain both the features of Romans just noted, an identity for the Christ-movement distinctive from the Judean synagogues and the existence of dissent and conflict among its members, without reference to speculative reconstruction of this kind but rather by assessing how the various dimensions of the Roman context outlined earlier in this chapter would have affected the formation and character of Christ-following congregations. I will deal first with the specifically Judean context and then with the issues of nonelite lifestyle and ethnicity that took characteristic shape in Rome.

The Identity of the Christ-Movement in Relation to the Judeans of Rome: The Role of Architecture

For reasons set out in chapter five below (based largely on Romans 16), it is highly likely that the congregations of Christ-followers in Rome in the mid-first century CE met in houses owned or rented by members, or in private space in small domestic premises. While it is clear that this must have differentiated the Christ-movement from assemblies of Judeans who gathered in their custom-made *proseuchai*, not in houses, what was the precise nature of such differentiation and how did it affect the respective identities of the two groups?

As a prelude to this discussion, it is worth recalling the account of Paul's early missionary efforts in Corinth (Acts 18:1-17). Luke describes how Paul, after unsuccessfully attempting to win over the Judeans in the synagogue, "went away from there and moved into the house that belonged to a God-worshiper called Titius Justus, whose house was next to the synagogue" (Acts 18:7). When, in the next verse, Luke relates that Crispus, the leader of the synagogue, came to believe in the Lord with all his household, and that many of the Corinthians who heard this believed and were baptized, it is surely significant that he has Paul securing these conversions (including the synagogue leader himself) from a base in a non-Judean household after failing to do so in the synagogue. Is this incident, with its stark juxtaposition of two entirely different architectural contexts and different results for Paul's evangelism, emblematic of issues of fundamental importance in the early development of the Christ-movement in the diaspora, in Rome as much as Corinth?

Yet other questions cascade from this one as soon as one introduces insights derived from the sociology and anthropology of space. Architecture shapes and constrains human experience.[149] There is a dialectical relationship between the nature of space contained and expressed in particular architectural forms and the modes of sociality conducted within such space. Space that has been embodied in particular architectural forms is not simply a passive background for human action, but rather actively contributes to the maintenance of social order and social meaning, such as by legitimating (that is, explaining and justifying) particular values, roles, institutions, power relations, and hierarchies.[150] Architectural space used for a religious group in private houses that continued to function as such is likely to have a radically different impact on the group than space in buildings entirely dedicated to, or even built specifically for, their meetings. Such considerations emphasize the need closely to attend to what Philo meant by the *proseuchai* he saw in the Trastevere in 40 CE and how they differed from the congregations of the Christ-movement in the 50s.

This area has received extensive theoretical elaboration from social scientists in the last two decades. Yet in spite of the widespread recognition of the role of house churches in Rome, New Testament scholars have largely ignored the challenge such research poses to the interpretation of Romans.[151] By way of contrast, archaeologists, including those dealing with ancient Roman housing, have been alive to the need for adequate theoretical resources to enrich their empirical research. As Andrew Wallace-Hadrill has noted, we have recently witnessed "the generation of new approaches and theoretical frameworks which see in the shaping of social space not merely an incidental reflection of social practices and traditions, but a primary means of structuring social encounters and so of producing and reproducing social relationships."[152] Such research has led to a radical reappraisal of many key issues in the study of Roman houses.[153] Given the use of members' houses by the Christ-movement in Rome, this new fusion of spatial theory and empirical data cannot be ignored in tracking the links between the Roman context and what Paul was communicating in the letter.

At a most general level we are dealing with what Robert Sack has called "territoriality."[154] Sack is interested in examining how space is used and who controls whom thereby and how. "Territoriality" refers to the ways in which people use the power they possess to delimit and control an area of space for security, defense, and the display of social hierarchy. It is a strategy to establish different degrees of access to people, things, and relationships. Sack mainly has in mind territoriality over considerable stretches of space, but his insights can apply to architectural space as well, as Young-Sung Jung has pointed out.[155] For example, architectural space may be divided at a general level into monumental space, as in large buildings that arouse a sense of awe and that produce a sense of the power and status of those who erect and control them, and human space, which promotes a sense of unity and interrelationship.

Moving into theory more specifically devoted to architecture I begin with Edward Hall's distinction between sociofugal and sociopetal space. Sociopetal space creates a sense of intimacy by closely binding people together; typically, this is private space. Sociofugal space, on the other hand, tends to keep people apart; typically this is public space, which even inside buildings may be powerfully articulated into different zones.[156]

Hillier and Hanson, second, ask the critical question of how and why different forms of social reproduction become embodied in different types of spatial order. They distinguish, for example, a distributive arrangement of space, which facilitates movement from any one area to another, from a nondistributive arrangement, which generates hierarchies and restricts movements.[157]

A particular example from Hillier and Hanson, relevant to the present discussion, will help. At one point they discuss buildings used for institutionalized religious observation.[158] They describe how these buildings establish a spatial system that moves from a courtyard space open to visitors, as well as members of the socioreligious group ("bipermeable space"), through a series of rooms until one reaches a deepest space, which is the shrine room, the domain controlled exclusively by the members themselves ("unipermeable space"). Such a building assembles the members and the visitors into a direct interface. They suggest that this pattern (a single, deep unipermeable space coupled to a large bipermeable space) is "the underlying genotype for a vast family of buildings for religious observance across many cultures and times."[159] Although they do not mention it, the Second Temple in Jerusalem was built on these lines, with its nested sequence of courts beginning with one open to non-Judeans and culminating in the Holy of Holies open only to the high priest on the Day of Atonement. The various degrees of spatial proximity to the heart of the building permitted to various persons replicated their positions on the social hierarchy. Showing the same pattern, although with nothing like the same degree of differentiation, is the first-century *proseucha* from Ostia, especially if the *bema* (the raised point from which the Law was read) was at the point represented in figure 2. Here the area around the well and basin no doubt functioned as a courtyard for visitors, including beggars,[160] an aspect more fully articulated in subsequent phases of construction,[161] while the inner recesses would have been open to Judeans themselves, with only those at the top of the synagogue hierarchy being permitted to mount the *bema*. These features almost certainly characterized the *proseuchai* of Rome as well, which were open to the public.

Let us now relate these architectural considerations to the arrival of the Christ-movement in Rome. The gospel was almost certainly first proclaimed in the capital in one or more of the numerous Judean communities by Judean or non-Judean God-fearers arriving from Jerusalem. This happened in large and tailor-made *proseuchai* that were in part open to the public and that were run by a hierarchically organized group of officials. Such an architectural context must have had a direct impact on the Christ-followers and their movement as long as they were permitted to remain there. In line with Sack's notion of territoriality, the *proseuchai* represented "monumental space," which conveys a sense of the power and status of its controlling officials. The different zones in which the *proseuchai* were at least roughly divided created what Hall has called sociofugal space, which tends to keep people apart rather than to bring them together. The same divisions also represented an impetus toward nondistributive space, of a sort that hinders movement and generates hierarchies.

At some stage, however, as we will see in chapter five, the followers of Christ began to hold their meetings in the houses (or possibly small commercial premises) of some of their members. Nanos has made the interesting suggestion that Christ-followers in Rome could not have met outside synagogues because a decree of Julius Caesar (mentioned above) had proscribed the assembly of religious societies except for the Judeans in the city of Rome.[162] The initial problem with this idea is that, whether the law permitted it or not, Romans 16 provides irrefutable evidence of Christ-followers meeting in domestic contexts having nothing to do with the Judean *proseuchai*. Indeed, Caesar's decree seems not to have been enforced in relation to the category of *collegia* most relevant to Romans, for reasons explained by La Piana: "The *collegia domestica* were very numerous in the time of Augustus, and it is very probable that the law governing associations was not applied to them, and that they were not dissolved. But whether they were assimilated to the *collegia tenuiorum* and required authorization we do not know. The master's house was the official location of a *collegium domesticum*."[163]

Although not all the private spaces used by the Christ-movement may have constituted a house church in the full sense of the word as represented by Prisca and Aquila (Rom. 16:5), it is important that we recognize how different was such an architectural context and the distinctive forms of social and religious life associated with it from that offered by the Judean synagogues, with their monumental architecture and hierarchical organization. Some of these places were perhaps only a single room, like that under the high altar of San Clemente in Rome that may well have accommodated a house church in the late first century CE.[164] In relation to Sack's notion of territoriality, these private settings represented human space, rather than monumental space, and would have promoted a sense of unity and interrelationship. Employing Hall's distinction, we can say that they were examples of sociopetal space, closely binding the members together with feelings of intimacy. Finally, we can say with Hillier and Hanson that they were examples of distributed space, facilitating movement among and interrelationships between all the members. In the case of a house congregation in the full sense, an ἐκκλησία . . . κατ' οἶκον, the members would also have been brought into the familial and patron-client relationships of the house, even if these were at times unusual in giving leadership to the senior woman of the house, as in the case of Prisca and Aquila.

Such a pronounced differentiation in the architectural and social setting of the Christ-movement vis-à-vis the Judean congregations was no doubt a powerful stimulus for the development of a distinctive identity for Christ-followers in toto. The stimulus would have been even stronger if, as is possible, they held their meetings on a day other than the Sabbath observed by the Judeans.

But at the same time, it is easy to see how the existence of impressive *proseuchai* in Rome would also have exacerbated ethnic tensions between Judean and Greek Christ-followers that were likely to have preexisted their conversion to Christ. The critical issue is the probability that some Christ-followers, Judeans or even Greek God-fearers, also continued to attend the *proseuchai*, while others, Greeks (whether former God-fearers or one-time idol worshipers) more likely than Judeans (whose original socialization in the Judean ethnic group gave them greater reason to do so), did not. A continued attachment to the Judean ethnic group by some members would no doubt have encouraged the ethnocentric attitudes the Greek members felt and expressed toward non-Greeks *(barbaroi)*. Traditional forms of denigration were possibly enriched by theological arguments similar to that raised by Paul in Gal. 2:21: If the Mosaic law was still necessary, what role did that leave for Christ? In the usual course, we would expect such antipathy to be reversed, with the Judean members falling back on time-honored and stereotypical criticism of the Greeks. In subsequent chapters we will see the extent to which the text of Romans yields data that seems to reflect this scenario.

Yet further reasons for tension and conflict within the Judean and Greek subgroups are also to be found in the unique social setting that was Rome.

Dissension within the Christ-Movement in Its Roman Context

We will see in the next chapter that the early Christ-movement in Rome was situated among the nonelite. Prisca and Aquila no doubt had some resources, but they were not members of the Roman elite. Aquila was certainly neither a Roman *senator* nor an *eques*. We must therefore picture the membership as living in the dangerously high and overcrowded *insulae*, tenement blocks, of Rome described earlier in this chapter. Possibly the wealthier Christ-followers, like Prisca and Aquila, were able to rent larger apartments on the more salubrious ground floors of these buildings. Some of the members possibly had ground-floor rooms where they conducted their crafts, with living quarters for them and their families at the back. The poorest Christ-followers must have rented rooms in higher levels of the *insulae*, possibly even in the worst space of all, the tiny garrets at the very top. Failure to pay rent meant eviction and, in the worst case, a life of beggary, sleeping under whatever cover was to be found. Some of Paul' s intended addressees, however, were slaves or freedmen of named persons who were apparently not Christ-followers. These are described Rom. 16:10-11 as the people from the households of Narcissus and Aristobulus, who may well have been wealthy freedmen. The slaves of these men would have been housed and fed by them, but we should not forget that the living quarters of slaves were austere at best.

The congregations of Christ-followers meeting in these various domestic contexts could have constituted *collegia domestica,* as mentioned above, or were possibly regarded as veering so close to that type of association as to avoid trouble with the authorities. Only a slight modification would have been needed for this type of association to embrace the Christ-movement. All of these household congregations would have been shaped by the distinctive patterns of architecture and sociality that they represented in sharp juxtaposition to the character of the Judean *proseuchai.*

That groups of Christ-believers were scattered around in nonelite households in the unique social setting that was Rome brought with it consequences that could only have been inimical to the unity of the movement. Rome was a city where the competitive interactions between persons and groups in the pursuit of honor characteristic (then and now) of Mediterranean culture had assumed a particularly florid shape in the *inimicitiae,* the publicly announced hostilities between members of the elite, the inception of which was signaled by the men concerned barring one another from their homes. Just as the house of a member of the elite was the venue in which he maintained his relationships of *amicitia* with friends and clients, paraded his wealth and honor, and made displays of benevolence, so too it could become his headquarters and supply base in the ongoing battle for honor and position, a place from which his enemies were banned as long as hostilities should last.

For the nonelite, admittedly within their much more straitened social and economic circumstances, on the basis of the arguments set out above for their sharing in or emulating the values of the elite, it is likely that their houses, too, were contexts within which they made good their own social status and also engaged in competition with rivals. This is the setting within which the Christ-movement was located, and while it is possible that some of the different households engaged in *amicitia* toward one another, it is also possible that they were affected by forms of *inimicitiae* practiced by nonelite persons and groups. The existence of such hostilities is suggested by Paul in Romans 15, and I leave my explanation until I deal with that chapter of the letter.[165] For the moment it is enough to present this dimension of the Roman setting as providing a realistic social context for households of the Christ-movement in Rome having been riven by enmity rather than quietly unified around their common identity in Christ.

Yet along with the competition and dissension between individuals and groups that was a prominent feature of Roman social life even among Romans themselves, I must add a further factor to the households of the Christ movement, namely, the existence of ethnic differentiation. It is highly probable that the bad relationships between Judeans and Greeks across the Mediterranean region were replicated in the capital. These antipathies were the result of the ethnocentrism habitual to the ethnic groups being played out in particular contexts under the Roman imperial government. One needs to suppose only that some households of Christ-followers comprised (solely or mainly) Judeans and (solely or mainly) Greeks to understand how this extra ingredient would have made relationships between the households even more strained or actually hostile.

5

The Letter's Purpose in the Light of Romans 1:1-15 and 15:14—16:27

The Significance of the Letter Frame (Rom. 1:1-15 and 15:14—16:27)

In chapter one I introduced the questions that have motivated this new reading of Romans and the broad approach I adopted in seeking to answer them. The distinctive methodological resources necessary for this task were set out and applied to the Mediterranean and Roman contexts of the letter in chapters two, three, and four. Above all, I am concerned with the way in which Paul sought to exercise leadership in relation to the Roman congregations by reinforcing the fundamental common identity his addressees shared in relation to God and Christ, especially to the extent that his success in such a strategy would mean creating a particular form of unity between Judean and Greek ethnic subgroups previously accustomed to mutual hostility and conflict. I am proposing that Paul was acting as an entrepreneur of identity. The time has now come to begin examining the text of the letter.

As previously noted,[1] a feature of this reading of Romans is a determination to interpret the letter in the same order that Paul intended to unfold its message to its first recipients and in which they would have heard it, namely, passage by passage from what we call Romans 1 right through to Romans 16. Attempts to understand Paul's meaning that jump backward and forward, now lighting on one issue and now on another, and that have no relationship to the circumstances of the letter's actual promulgation seem less likely to discover the apostle's communicative strategy. In the current chapter, I diverge from this policy in one respect, by considering both 1:1-15 and 15:14—16:27.

This divergence, however, is justifiable. In both of these passages, often referred to as the "frame" of the letter, Paul is speaking expressly of the personal circumstances of himself and his addressees, while he also details his plans for the future. They contain statements in which he offers explicit reasons for writing the letter and which reveal a great deal of information about the identities, ethnicity, and social status of a number of Christ-followers in Rome—assuming that Romans 16 was originally part of this letter (an assumption I defend below). The richness of detail provided by Romans 15–16 is the foundation for Paul Minear's sensible advice that Romans is a text where it is best to read the last two chapters first.[2] There was presumably a reasonable match between the actual situation of the Christ-movement in Rome and what Paul has to say in Romans 1, 15, and 16—a correlation made possible by information he either received in Corinth, from where he wrote the letter, or already possessed—since otherwise his letter would have been dismissed as an ignorant irrelevance. A sure sign that Paul was in receipt of information from Rome emerges when he describes Mary in 16:6 as someone "who has worked hard among you." In saying this, however, we must still be open to the probability that there was more to the movement in Rome than Paul knew of or reveals in Romans 16.[3]

Romans 1:1-15 and 15:14—16:27 provide our most direct access to the nature of the Christ-movement in Rome at this time. For this reason these passages have figured most prominently in the debate about the purpose of the letter, even though one can use the rest of the text (the "body" of the letter), with caution, to furnish further information of this type, while one can rely somewhat—admittedly with even greater caution—on what can be garnered from explorations into the Roman context of the sort conducted in chapter four above. Although a full account of the purpose of Romans must successfully integrate all three sources of information, a consideration of the material in 1:1-15 and 15:14—16:27 is the best place to start. Such a discussion also serves as a good opportunity to consider the general debate surrounding the purpose of the letter, admittedly in a less than exhaustive manner (for which the numerous commentaries can be consulted). Many of the key questions are set out in *The Romans Debate*, of which a revised edition appeared in 1991.[4]

In starting with 1:1-15 and 15:14—16:27, I assume that the material contained in these passages bears on the rhetorical situation that Paul faced in Rome and his response to it, a notion I introduced in chapter one. Paul wrote the letter to actual persons to address a particular exigence (some existing factual state of affairs requiring attention), knowing that certain constraints would affect whether they accepted what he said. This approach entails that as someone seeking to persuade his audience to a particular viewpoint Paul needed to be sensitive to their peculiar circumstances and to tailor his discourse accordingly. For Paul to have written a letter that did not address his intended audience would have represented a catastrophic failure of communication on his part. For this reason the proposal of Stanley Stowers, based on modern literary theory, that we must distinguish between "encoded" readers of the letter (readers the text itself explicitly addresses or inscribes) and "empirical" readers (persons who actually read it), who might be quite different, is singularly unhelpful. These considerations suggest at the level of principle that ancient rhetorical practice is a better guide to Paul's strategy in his predominantly oral culture than the modern literary theory favored by Stowers. In addition, however, analysis of the text indicates that Paul was not guilty of the communicative incompetence implied as a possibility on Stowers's view, since the people to whom the argument of the letter is addressed (including, as we will see, Judeans and non-Judeans, not just the latter) are the same as those whom Paul intended would, and most probably did, read it. The evidence for this, moreover, comes from the letter itself, especially from the rather special material in the greetings section in chap. 16, not from hypothetical reconstructions generated from data beyond its pages whose usefulness in this regard Stowers is right to question.[5]

The Central Issues in Romans 1:1-15 and 15:14—16:27

Connecting with the Judeans and Non-Judeans of Rome (Rom. 1:1-15)

Reaching a view on whom Paul was addressing in Romans is essential to understanding the rhetorical situation (as explained in chapter one above) he faced and the persuasive strategy he crafted in response to it. The debate in this area, which has proved to be hotly contested, has identified three broad options for Paul's audience: non-Judean Christ-followers, Judean Christ-followers, or a mixture of these two groups (with non-Judeans usually regarded as being in the majority). It is not uncommon for advocates of either of the first two options to qualify their view by suggesting that there may have been Christ-followers in Rome from among the other category who are nevertheless not addressed in this letter. This position, for example, is represented by those who argue that Paul was writing to non-Judean Christ-followers even though there were also Judeans among the Christ-movement in Rome.[6] Since proponents of each option tender a variety of textual (and extratextual) evidence in support, usually privileging particular verses (such as 1:5-6, 13 to argue for an audience of non-Judean Christ-followers, or "gentile Christians," as they label them) as being of decisive importance, it is not easy to select the best starting point for this discussion. Nevertheless, I will adhere to the general policy in this volume of following Paul's argument in the order in which it would have impressed itself on its first audience and thus start with Romans 1.

Paul begins the letter (1:1-4) by announcing his commission as an apostle to preach the gospel of God that was promised beforehand in the scriptures concerning his son Jesus Christ, descended from David and designated Son of God in power through the Spirit of holiness by his resurrection.[7] Paul continues by saying that through him, "we have received grace and apostleship to bring about the obedience of faith for the sake of his name among all the foreigners (ἐν πᾶσιν τοῖς ἔθνεσιν), among whom are you also (ἐν οἷς ἐστε καὶ ὑμεῖς) called to belong to Jesus Christ" (1:5-6). It is noteworthy that here Paul employs the word ἔθνη, which is the Judean expression for all non-Judeans and is not a self-designation among such people. He is looking at the world from a Judean perspective. He then greets them, inclusively, as *all* those in Rome who are loved by God and called holy, wishing them grace and peace from, significantly, "God our Father and the Lord Jesus Christ" (1:7).

After saying that he thanks God for their faith that is proclaimed throughout the whole world (κόσμος), meaning that distinctive area comprising the Mediterranean Sea and the regions around it,[8] he states that he mentions them continually in his prayers (1:8-9), praying that by God's will he may somehow succeed in coming to them (1:10). He desires to see them in order to impart some spiritual gift to strengthen them but then, perhaps sensing that this may appear presumptuous (by implying that they need strengthening), he tones his message down a little by suggesting that he means they may be mutually encouraged by one another's faith (1:11-12). These two verses can also be explained as Paul's use of diplomatic language in a way that will avoid affronting the independence of the congregations in Rome, as Robert Jewett has suggested.[9]

Next he conveys the more specific information that he has often intended to come to them (but has so far been prevented) "in order that I might reap some fruit also among you (καὶ ἐν ὑμῖν) just as also among the rest of the foreigners (καθὼς καὶ ἐν τοῖς λοιποῖς ἔθνεσιν)" (1:13). He then says: "Both to Greeks and barbarians, to the wise and the foolish, I am indebted, so I am eager to preach the gospel also to you who are in Rome" (1:14-15).

It is widely believed that 1:1-15 provides strong evidence for the view that Paul's audience was composed of non-Judeans, even if there were Judean Christ-followers in Rome.[10] Many commentators think that 1:5-6 and 1:13d-15 indicate that Paul was writing to non-Judean Christ-followers. Douglas Moo, for example, notes that while ἔθνη in 1:5 could mean "nations" in a strictly geographic sense, that would run contrary to the semantic focus of the term in Paul, whose "call was not so much to minister in many different nations as it was to minister to Gentiles in distinction from Jews."[11] In relation to 1:6, Moo rejects the suggestion that Paul is simply identifying the Romans as living in the midst of non-Judeans. Similarly, James Dunn comments on 1:5 that ἔθνη "certainly means 'the Gentiles' (and not 'the nations' including Jews)" and "that this apostleship was absolutely fundamental in Paul's self-understanding."[12] Joseph Fitzmyer expresses much the same view.[13] Dunn considers that 1:6 indicates that Paul's addressees were mostly "Gentile."[14] These scholars reach the same conclusions in respect of 1:13d. Moo states that Paul "makes clear again that he views the Roman Christians as belonging to a 'Gentile' church."[15] Dunn asserts that here again "the strongly Gentile composition of the Roman congregation is clearly implied."[16] Not surprisingly, proponents of these views see 1:14, where Paul apparently expresses indebtedness to the non-Judean world, as supporting such views.

I submit, however, that these views are seriously flawed. They depend on both an insensitivity to the ethnic implications of Paul's language (produced by a failure to utilize theoretical insights of the sort set out in chapter three) and a faulty grasp of the meaning of his mission in its socioreligious context.[17] These issues are closely related.

First-century Judeans divided their world into two realms distinguishable on (what we would describe as) the geographic and religious dimensions of ethnic criteria. There was Judea—the sacred homeland of the people and the site of its capital city and the temple of its God—where they were in a preponderant majority and then there was the rest of the Mediterranean region, inhabited by numerous foreign peoples (ἔθνη) who idolatrously worshiped false gods. The word ἔθνη inevitably carried negative connotations for Judeans, although these varied from context to context. At its most extreme the appropriate translation for ἔθνη is "heathen," while in a less antipathetic situation "foreigners" captures the sense of the word. The peoples so categorized, moreover, did not describe themselves in this way; they called themselves "Greeks," "Romans," and so on. Complicating the picture, however, was that numerous Judeans were living among these foreigners in most of their cities, with particularly large Judean populations in Alexandria, Antioch in Syria, and Rome. Accordingly, Paul's reference at 1:5 to his work "among all the foreigners," the first ethnic expression in the letter, immediately characterizes the situation as one seen from a Judean perspective. Indeed, whenever we hear Paul describing his mission as being to proclaim the gospel among (ἐν) the ἔθνη (Gal. 1:16; Rom. 1:5) or, which is much the same thing, simply as "to" or "unto" (εἰς) the ἔθνη (Gal. 2:8; Rom. 15:16), or "to (bring about) the obedience of the ἔθνη" (Rom. 16:18), or "to preach to the ἔθνη so that they may be saved" (1 Thess. 2:16), we must keep this picture in mind.

It is impossible to exclude a geographic dimension from Paul's mission. His apostleship entailed preaching the gospel outside Judea in the lands inhabited by idolatrous non-Judean peoples (but which also contained minority populations of Judeans).[18] The use of the phrase "among (ἐν) the ἔθνη" (Gal. 1:16; Rom. 1:5) precisely expresses this aspect of his work.

It is reasonable to accept, however, that Paul was primarily interested in bringing non-Judeans to faith in Christ. They were in the majority everywhere outside Judea, and their idolatry meant that they constituted a unique challenge to someone proclaiming Christ and the gospel. Paul certainly wanted to bring about their obedience to the faith (Rom. 16:18), to preach so that they might be saved (1 Thess. 2:16). In at least one place, Thessalonika, he had previously founded a congregation that consisted solely of ex-idolaters with no Judean representation.[19]

Yet the case of Thessalonika seems unusual. It was inevitable that as Paul traveled through foreign lands he would encounter some of the numerous Judeans living in them. At times they must have provided him with useful networks in a strange city.[20] There was nothing to prevent him also preaching the gospel to them, and he certainly did so. "To the Judeans I became as a Judean," he tells us in 1 Cor. 9:20, "in order to win Judeans." So serious, indeed, was his engagement with Judean synagogues in the diaspora that he was subjected to their punishment of thirty-nine lashes on five occasions (2 Cor. 11:24).[21]

The result of this evangelism to Judeans was that Pauline congregations were routinely composed of non-Judeans and Judeans. This phenomenon emerges with notable clarity in Galatians. When Paul states in Gal. 2:2 that (in Jerusalem) he presented the gospel that he proclaimed "among the non-Judeans" ($\dot{\epsilon}\nu$ τοῖς ἔθνεσιν), he is speaking in the context of discussions (and heated debate) where the whole point at issue was the relationship between Judeans and non-Judeans in the Christ-movement, especially as to whether the latter had to be circumcised. In addition, no sooner has Paul mentioned the agreement he struck with James, Cephas, and John in Jerusalem that recognized that he had been entrusted "with the gospel of the uncircumcised just as Peter had been of the circumcised" (Gal. 2:8), than he is describing an incident in Antioch in which the congregational table fellowship between Judeans and non-Judeans is sundered by the withdrawal of Peter, Barnabas, and the other Judeans. From all this it is beyond dispute that inherent in Paul's understanding of his having been sent to the non-Judeans is that his congregations will often embrace them and Judeans and, furthermore, that his vision of the manner in which the Christ-movement will incorporate Judean and non-Judean components (without the latter being circumcised) should prevail.[22] Thus Judean membership of his congregations will be integral to their nature (except in the possibly rare case of a wholly non-Judean congregation, as in Thessalonika), even in the context of his being sent "to the non-Judeans."

With all this in mind I can offer an interpretation of the data in Romans 1 just mentioned quite different from that in most current discussion. When Paul speaks, first, in 1:5-6, of his mission being "among all the foreigners, among whom are you also," he is referring to his work among the non-Judean peoples of the region, now extending to Rome.[23] Nothing in this excludes the fact that Judeans regularly formed part of this congregation. Nor would any Judean or non-Judean Christ-followers in Rome listening to the letter as it was read deduce from this expression that the Judean members were excluded, especially since this would entail that they had somehow slipped out of the category of "all the beloved of God in Rome, who are called holy," mentioned in the very next statement (v. 17). Similarly, when in v. 13 Paul explains that he wants to come to them "in order that he might reap some fruit also among you just as also among the rest of the foreigners," this simply constitutes an acknowledgment that he wants to have a successful mission in Rome, just as he has had elsewhere, even though his congregations were often composed of Judeans as well as non-Judeans. None of this suggests he is not speaking to Judeans, nor does his statement in the next verse of the debt he owes (that is, because of his success) to "Greeks and barbarians" (meaning non-Judeans of all ethnic groups, although using language that typified the way that Greeks themselves divided their social world) and whether educated or not. He wants to have the same success in Rome, which is why he says, "So I am eager to preach the gospel also to you who are in Rome" (vv. 14-15). There is no justification for claims that these expressions in any way exclude Judeans from Paul's address or would have been so understood by the recipients of the letter. This conclusion is confirmed by his statement in the very next verse that the gospel is the power of God unto salvation for everyone who believes, "Judean first and also Greek" (1:16).

Paul's Future Plans (Rom. 15:14-33)

In 15:23 Paul repeats from 1:11-15 that he has long wished to visit believers in Rome but has not been able to. Now, however, he has the opportunity and wants to see them "in passing as I go to Spain, and to be sped on my journey there by you, once I have enjoyed your company for a little" (15:24, RSV). First he is going to Jerusalem to make a contribution to the destitute among the saints there that has been collected by the congregations of Macedonia and Achaia (15:25-29), a contribution, remarkably, he is not certain will be accepted by the Jerusalem saints (15:31), just as he is fearful of the unbelievers in Judea (15:30-32).

We should not underestimate the importance of the Roman congregations in assisting Paul to have a successful mission in Spain. First, they could shore up his financial resources (he would be "sped" on his journey). Yet there is a second factor well expressed by Minear: "we may suppose that Paul wanted to avoid the catastrophe of having his work in Spain ruined by opposition from the Roman congregations. He had learned how important for missionary activity is a loyal base, a city where various congregations share wholeheartedly in a common enterprise. Nothing more quickly jeopardized the survival of infant churches than strife among supporting churches."[24] Robert Jewett has highlighted a third area of concern. There is no evidence for Judean synagogues in Spain that could have provided Paul with a base for operations once he arrived there. Much of the population spoke native languages, and while there was a growing familiarity with

Latin, Greek would not have been widely known. Accordingly, Paul was going to require material support when he was in Spain and also translation services if he was going to make himself understood by the inhabitants. These resources would need to be provided through the agency of the Roman congregations, as Paul's logistical base, even if people like Phoebe also contributed funds.[25]

Jerusalem presents another problem. He anticipates trouble there from unbelievers and Christ-followers. It is not too much of a stretch of the imagination to assume that the source of Paul's fears that the Jerusalem church would turn up its nose at the money he was bringing them was somehow related to the slander current about him that he advocated doing evil so good might come (Rom. 3:8), slander probably originating in a distorted view of his attitude to the law. Luke reports, after all, that when Paul arrived in Jerusalem he was regarded as someone who taught diaspora Judeans to forsake the Mosaic law (Acts 21:20-21). Such rumors about Paul were probably also current in Rome.

Romans 16 as an Integral Part of the Letter

Central to the argument concerning the context and purpose of Romans is whether chapter 16 was originally part of the letter. Over the years many scholars, including T. W. Manson and Willi Marxsen, have thought that chap. 16 represents a later addition to the letter to adapt it for dispatch to another community, perhaps at Ephesus.[26] Such theories were given a fillip in the early twentieth century by the discovery of a Chester Beatty papyrus, P46, which placed the doxology now located at 16:25-27 between chaps. 15 and 16. Harry Gamble has persuasively demonstrated, however, that chap. 16 did indeed form part of the letter Paul sent to Rome and has comprehensively refuted alternative theories, such as an original Ephesian destination for this section.[27] An additional reason for doubting the notion of an Ephesian provenance for Romans 16 is that the greetings the chapter contains are highly inappropriate for Ephesus or any other congregation where Paul had been active in person. The personal details relating to those whom he greets are of a form suggesting that the movement as a whole was not aware of their achievements, while others are named without any personal details, which would have been insulting if Paul had worked among them. Nor does Paul ever refer to his past experience among them. The details in chap. 16 are therefore much more suitable to an audience Paul has not visited, and Rome is the only candidate.[28] To this one might add that the sheer number of the people Paul mentions in chap. 16 strongly points to his desire to create relationships in advance of his arrival.

Having defended the status of chap. 16 as originally part of the letter Paul sent to Rome, I may now consider the main issues that arise in this section of the letter, paying particular attention to the character of the audience Paul is addressing, including its ethnic dimensions.

Ethnic Subgroups and Romans 16

Paul begins by commending to his audience one Phoebe, a deaconess of the community in Cenchreae and a person of considerable social standing there of whom he has a very high opinion, and by exhorting them to help her in any way she may require, for she had been a προστάτις of many, including himself (16:1-2). The word προστάτις means patroness.[29] Cenchreae was a seaport on the Saronic Gulf seven kilometers from Corinth, the city in which Paul probably wrote the letter.[30] In this culture her status as patroness, and of many, meant that she must have had quite considerable resources. R. A. Kearsley has analyzed inscriptions from Corinth on women who acted as patronesses in a way that casts considerable light on the role of Phoebe. Carolyn Osiek has well explored the entire phenomenon of women's patronage.[31]

While it is almost certain, as scholars often point out,[32] that it was Phoebe who brought Paul's letter to Rome, we can proffer little more about her and her activities in Rome than this. In 1971 Minear criticized the notion current then that there was only one congregation in Rome and insisted that there were several—at least six could be seen in Romans 16.[33] Along similar lines, Peter Lampe has proposed that it is possible to identify in 16:3-15 at least seven different groups of Christ-followers, probably meeting in domestic dwellings, like that of Prisca and Aquila mentioned first in 16:3-5, or in some other private space.[34] While I will return to this issue below, the relevant point here is that since there is no sign that the individuals and groups named gathered in one place or constituted one ἐκκλησία (with the reference to the specific house congregation of Prisca and Aquila suggesting that they did not), we should envisage Phoebe carrying the letter to various groups of Christ-followers in Rome seriatim and no doubt waiting in each instance while it was read to them, a process that my own experiments reading the Greek text suggest would have taken between sixty and ninety minutes, assuming no interruptions. As she had almost certainly discussed its contents with Paul, she would have been able to answer questions relating to its contents.[35] It is not impossible that the Roman Christ-followers gathered somewhere in extraordinary session to hear her, but this seems less likely than separate meetings, given the evident signs of division among them (to which I return later in this volume) and the number of people involved. In any event, Phoebe would have needed to ensure that the letter was read in the presence of all individuals and groups in Rome that Paul mentions, otherwise his recommendation of her and his greetings to them would not have found their mark.

In addition, it is probable that Phoebe herself was the lector on these occasions. As a patroness of the congregation in Cenchreae she must have been a woman of considerable wealth and was therefore probably literate. She would have been the most suitable person on whom Paul might safely devolve the task of reading the letter around Rome. He had probably gone over it with her, and perhaps his mysterious request that they help her in any way she might require of them (16:2) related to them complying with her suggestions as to practical measures to implement Paul's message, as contained in Romans 12–15 especially. It is possible that she had come to Rome with a scribe who was to read the letter in her presence (and hence under her control), but in that case Paul would probably have commended him to the Romans as well.[36]

Of paramount importance here is that the people Paul mentions in 16:3-16—twenty-four by their own names and two more by relationships (the mother of Rufus and the sister of Nereus)—include Judeans and non-Judeans, all of whom he must have envisaged listening to the body of the letter before they encountered his particular greetings to them at the end. Prisca and Aquila, who are mentioned first, were almost certainly Judeans.[37] Second, Paul calls three of them "my kins(wo)men" (συγγενεῖς): Andronicus and Junia in v. 7 and Herodion in v. 11. Since Paul uses the word συγγενεῖς at 9:3 unequivocally of fellow Judeans, these three are best regarded as Judeans too. Junia, properly interpreted as a woman of that name (and not a man called Junias),[38] may have been the wife of Andronicus. Whether she was or not, she is also accorded the privilege of being described with him as "outstanding among the apostles." They were even Christ-followers before Paul. Rufus, described as "chosen in the Lord," and a woman Paul describes as "his mother and mine" (16:13) are probably Judeans, because Judeans often adopted the Latin name Rufus as a sound-equivalent of the Hebrew name Reuben[39] and because Paul's own closeness to this woman seems to indicate an ethnic connection.

Thus, of the twenty-six individuals named or identified, seven are probably Judeans, and Paul commends four of these more than the others (Prisca and Aquila, Andronicus and Junia). Yet there could well have been more Judeans among the other nineteen people mentioned individually. The suggestion that the specification of συγγενεῖς in relation to three of them exhausts the Judean Christ-followers in the list is unconvincing,[40] since Prisca and Aquila are not so designated even though they are Judeans. Paul may have failed to mention the Judean ethnicity of some of the others, as with Prisca and Aquila, simply because he had other interesting things to say about individuals,[41] as indeed he had with respect to nine of them. That most of them have Greek names is no bar to their having been Judeans. On the other hand, Mary (16:6) is such a common Judean name (even if it appears in Latin as the feminine form of Marius) that she could also have been a Judean.[42] Putting all these considerations together, we conclude that of the twenty-six people greeted by Paul the most prominent four were Judeans, while the over-all proportion of Judeans may have approached 50 percent.

With this analysis in mind, we may now consider the suggestion encapsulated in the remark by Moo that the "greetings in chap. 16 show that there were Jewish Christians in the Roman community, but they do not require that the letter be addressed to them."[43] Other commentators, notably Stowers, have expressed similar views.[44] Yet how feasible is this idea? Let us imagine the scene on one of the occasions when Paul's letter was first read in Rome. Phoebe (or maybe someone else), holding the letter, stands before a group of Christ-followers that possibly includes such eminent Judeans as Prisca and Aquila, or perhaps Andronicus and Junia, or other Judeans. They are all eager to hear his message. Some of them (like Prisca and Aquila) are on very close terms with Paul, and he obviously intended that they would hear the letter read.

How can one seriously maintain that the letter was not addressed to such Judeans? Are we to suppose that very early in the reading (by 1:5-6, 13 on many accounts) these Judeans must have realized, and Paul intended them to realize, that he only had non-Judean Christ-followers within the scope of his discourse and not them? This in spite of the fact that in v. 7 he greets "all those in Rome beloved of God, who are called holy"? Did they then sit or stand patiently for over an hour while the letter was read, all the while saying to themselves something like "Very interesting, but of course Paul did not intend this teaching for us," even though the status of Israelites and Israel is prominent in many parts of the text and at its very end Paul greeted them in the warmest terms? The notion becomes even stranger if we include the question of honor in the discussion.[45] If on any occasion when the letter was read to a group of Judeans and non-Judeans, it appeared that Paul had ignored the former, that is, even though knowing they would be present (with some of them very close to him) he had still chosen to omit them from the scope of his concern, this would have been a cause of deep shame to them. It would, in particular, necessitate that they were not "all the beloved of God in Rome, who are called holy," since Paul explicitly greets all of the people in this group in v. 7. Why would Paul permit such a result, when it would have been cause for further division among the Roman Christ-movement and for some of his own friends being grievously dishonored? These considerations predispose me strongly toward the prima facie view that Paul must have had both Judean and non-Judean Christ-followers in mind as his target audience.

The final point to be raised here is that although Judeans are among the people addressed in Romans 1 and 16, there is no reference to Judean synagogal congregations, or any of the rich array of officeholders that characterized them, or to the *proseuchai* ("prayer halls") where they met in Rome that were discussed in chapter four above. Paul's failure to mention any connection with the social and architectural forms typical of the Judean community in Rome in the mid-first century in Romans 16 poses a significant obstacle to the pioneering thesis of Mark Nanos that the Roman Christ-movement was still included within "Judaism" at this time.[46] Although some critics have claimed that the synagogues of the "Jews" in Rome were private houses that continued to be used outside meeting times by the families who owned them, we have seen in chapter four above that there are compelling grounds to reject that view. Judeans typically gathered in the numerous, purposely built, large and publicly accessible *proseuchai* of the capital. On the other hand, the Christ-movement appears to have held its meetings in private domestic space—a topic I must now address.

Romans 16 and the Question of House Churches in Rome

Minear's 1`971 book, *The Obedience of Faith: The Purposes of Paul in the Epistle to the Romans,* conclusively marked the transition from an interpretation of Romans as a general treatise to one that was fully absorbed with seeking to understand the letter in relation to the situation in Rome. Building his thesis mainly on Romans 14–15, Minear argued that the Christ-movement in Rome contained five different groups characterized by mutual disregard and conflict relating to lifestyle and theological differences.[47] Although not many have followed the precise details of Minear's proposal, his book is full of perceptive insights into the social and religious situation Paul addressed in Rome. One such insight, which has assumed ever greater significance since 1971, is the consideration that, unlike the position elsewhere in his letters, where it was possible to speak, in the singular, of the congregation (ἐκκλησία) of a city,[48] Paul nowhere uses such an expression in Romans, but instead addresses a diversity of house churches as the locus of the Christ-movement in Rome. "It is probable," Minear notes, "that these various cells were brought into existence at diverse times, by diverse leaders, with diverse conceptions of the Gospel." Since the disputes described in Romans 14 would have made common meetings involving these house congregations impossible, Paul could not hope to gain their support unless he first produced among them "a new sense of interdependence."[49]

This line of research was subsequently developed by Peter Lampe in an important monograph published in 1989,[50] the central results of which in relation to the question of houses have appeared separately.[51] Minear had noted that although Paul uses the expression "house church" (κατ' οἶκον . . . ἐκκλησία) in relation to that of Aquila and Prisca (16:5), by mentioning this particular church Paul implies that there were others in Rome.[52] Lampe identifies at least seven house congregations from Romans 16. These are (a) the house church around Aquila and Prisca (16:5); (b) the Christ-followers around Asyncritus, Phlegon, Hermes, Patrobas, and Hermas (16:14); (c) the Christ-followers around Philologus, Julia, Olympas, Nereus, and his sister (16:15); (d) the Christ-followers in the household of Aristobulus (16:10); (e) the Christ-followers in the household of Narcissus (16:11); and (f) and (g), the two house churches (at a minimum) that he postulates as needed for the other fourteen named individuals in Romans 16. To these he adds an eighth, the congregation that developed around Paul in his rented lodgings when he finally got to Rome as mentioned in Acts 28:30-31. One could adopt a slightly more conservative approach to the data and reduce Lampe's seven house congregations to five by interpreting the individuals mentioned in Rom. 16:5b-10a as actually members of the house church of Prisca and Aquila, and Herodion in 16:11 as belonging to the group associated with the house of Aristobulus mentioned in 16:10. Yet even on this basis we would still have five irreducible groups, and Lampe's general position would not be threatened.

In view of the subsequent lack of any central worship place in Rome for several centuries, Lampe concludes that these congregations worshiped in separate dwellings located in different quarters of the city. Most importantly, however, he adds that this result "does not exclude that some of them were also held together by kinship or household-ties."[53] Other writers on Romans have supported the importance of houses as the architectural and social setting of the Christ-movement in Rome.[54]

There have, nevertheless, been some dissenting voices. Chris Caragounis has argued that the Roman Christ-followers of Paul's time did constitute one church for the whole city, not just a collection of house churches or house groups.[55] He rejects the idea that Paul's failure to address the Romans as ἐκκλησία is significant, since he does not use this word when writing to the Philippians. Noting that in Romans 16 Paul refers only to the "house church" (κατ᾽ οἶκον . . . ἐκκλησία) of Prisca and Aquila (16:5), Caragounis proposes that this should not be taken as an invitation to assume there were others, but rather as a sign that this was the only one—otherwise Paul would have mentioned them.

The main problem with Caragounis's thesis is that there is no sign of a single church in Rome, to the extent that there was no monarchical bishop who could bring the various groups in the city together until much later, possibly as late as about 235 CE, as Brent (whom he fails to cite) has pointed out.[56] In spite of this, Caragounis usefully reminds us of the need to be more sensitive to a possible diversity of meeting places for the Christ-movement.

In what type of architectural settings did the various groups comprising the Christ-movement in Rome each meet? First, Paul's semi-technical expression κατ' οἶκον . . . ἐκκλησία presumably covers the case where the owner or tenant of domestic premises large enough for the purpose hosts the meetings there. In this situation, he or she is the host (a ξένος like Gaius in Corinth, mentioned in Rom. 16:23) or patron to the community, which would have brought the members within the patronage relationships common among the wealthier families in Roman contexts.[57] This would have been the best possible arrangement, and Paul mentions Prisca and Aquila and their house church first for this reason, as well as the importance of its members (especially if those listed in 16:5b-10a were members). Guided by the discussion in chapter four above, I can say with some confidence that their house was not of the atrium style. It almost certainly formed part of an *insula,* the accommodation in which varied greatly in size and quality. But it also possible that their house comprised living accommodations next to or over some form of commercial premises. In the *Acta Justini* 3.1 we learn that Justin had meetings of his congregation where he lived, over the bath of Martin, the son of Timothy.[58] In either case, the setting was probably not characterized by the poverty and equality of status among members that Jewett has rightly observed could have characterized "tenement churches" in some settings, as seems to have been the case, for example, in Thessalonika.[59]

Second, however, we must envisage the possibility of other groups gathering in less advantageous settings, often just a single room, either in more impoverished circumstances in an *insula* (akin to Jewett's "tenement church") or in any other space, residential or commercial in nature, that would have allowed the group to meet in some privacy. The two groups described as belonging to the households of Aristobulus and Narcissus were probably domestic slaves or perhaps freedmen. They were living in houses they neither owned nor rented. Their masters may have permitted them to hold meetings there or they may have been forced to go somewhere else; in either case theirs was not a κατ' . . . οἶκον . . . ἐκκλησία. Fitzmyer notes that Paul does not greet Aristobulus and Narcissus;[60] all we can say is that they were probably not Christ-followers.

It is quite possible that house churches that developed among the Roman Christ-followers to whom Paul writes or among others in the capital lay at the base of the *tituli* churches, like that at San Clemente. These were a feature of the capital for many centuries and were so named because the owner or tenant of the premises had his name *(titulus)* inscribed over the front door.[61] But that subject lies beyond the scope of this book.

The use by the Roman Christ-movement of domestic premises of various types, some of it probably very humble indeed—in contrast to the impressive *proseuchai* in use by the Judean congregations of Rome and the fact that there was nothing comparable to the rich elaboration of officeholders in the synagogues—necessitates that we now return to the important question of the relationships between social (and religious) life and architectural form discussed earlier in this volume. Two issues in particular demand attention.

First, how, if at all, does the domestic setting of the Roman Christ-movement differentiate it from the Judean communities of the city? The key to answering this question is found in the circumstance that not only did Judeans meet in publicly accessible buildings exclusively devoted to, and often specially constructed for, the use of the Judean communities (paralleling the custom-made mid-first-century CE synagogue at Ostia known to have existed from excavations there), but that the architectural and social differentiation of such a setting from the house churches of the Christ-movement has major implications for the distinct identities of Judeans and Christ-followers. Using Sack's notion of territoriality, we may say that these private settings represented human space, rather than monumental space, and would have promoted a sense of unity and interrelationship. In relation to Hall's distinction, they were examples of sociopetal space, closely binding the members together with feelings of intimacy. Finally, we can say with Hillier and Hanson that these places, often perhaps just a single room, would have constituted examples of distributed space, facilitating movement among and interrelationships between all the members. In the case of a house congregation in the full sense, an κατ' . . . οἶκον . . . ἐκκλησία, the members would also have been brought into the familial and patron-client relationships of the house, even if these were at times unusual in giving leadership to the senior woman of the house, as in the case of Prisca and Aquila, which were very different from the hierarchical arrangement of offices among Judean synagogues known to us from catacomb inscriptions.

All of these issues directly relate to the identity of the various groups that made up the Christ-movement and—because a group inevitably socializes its members, installing in their hearts and minds its own unique ways of seeing themselves and outsiders—also to the identities of individual Christ-followers. The answer they would have given to the question of who they were in such a context, an answer straddling the cognitive, emotional, and evaluative dimensions of group belonging, would have been very different from that which a *proseucha*-attending Judean would have provided. Yet because it is possible for one person to possess multiple identities (see chapters two and three above), we must acknowledge that a Judean Christ-follower who attended meetings of the Christ-movement but also went along to his or her *proseucha* on the Sabbath or on feast days could have experienced both identities, with one being salient on any given occasion.

Second, given that the nature and function of house and family vary from culture to culture,[62] and that Rome of the mid-first century CE represented a particularly distinctive instance of such social and architectural adaptation (see chapter four above), what relevance do such factors have for the house churches of Rome? We have already considered the architectural nature of, and living conditions in, the nonelite tenement blocks, or *insulae,* which probably accommodated one or more of the house churches, in contrast to the atrium-style houses of the elite.

The critical issue is how one household related to others, with the opposite poles being represented by interfamilial cooperation or competition. As noted in chapter four above, houses and households played a central role in the pursuit of honor that was characteristic of Mediterranean culture in general and Roman culture in particular, among both individuals and groups.[63] This led to interactions between families that were far more often competitive than cooperative. The phenomena in question are revealed most clearly in practices of competition and conflict between elite families that produced the social and political convulsions that had shaken and ultimately destroyed the Roman Republic, but that were also evident in the context of elections for high office during the Empire. Moreover, the well-documented propensity of the nonelite for copying the habits of the elite suggests that competition was also likely among families and households at much lower socioeconomic levels. This cultural context implies that the default position inter se for differing households hosting congregations of the Christ-movement was far more likely to be one of competition, even conflict, than of amity and friendship. One has only to compare the state of affairs in the Roman colony of Corinth, where various groups of Christ-followers (possibly reflecting household loyalties) were torn by strife and dissension,[64] to discover how prevalent conflict was among people socialized into this cultural world.

To this already volatile situation one more ingredient must be added. When we consider that elite families in Rome of old and unimpeachable Latin lineage were perfectly capable of finding arenas of social activity in which to compete vigorously, even ferociously, it is not difficult to imagine the incendiary effect that the addition of ethnic difference might have on relationships between households. Yet the Christ-movement in Rome was divided ethnically along Judean and non-Judean—in this case, Greek—lines. In view of the wider animosity between Judeans and Greeks that had fomented frequent outbreaks of violence between the two groups by the time Romans was written, and would continue to do so thereafter,[65] it is far more likely than not that their representatives in Rome cultivated toward one other attitudes that were similarly stereotyped and negative. While there may not be much data in Rom. 1:1-15 and 15:14—16:27 suggesting such conflict, for anyone attuned to the realities of ethnicity in the Mediterranean world of the first century CE, merely to mention that this was a movement made up of

Judeans and Greeks would have been enough to suggest to Paul's contemporaries the likelihood of trouble between them. As we will see, there is much evidence in the body of the letter that this was indeed the case. While the wider issue of relationships between Judeans and Greeks has been the subject of consideration in Romans research, the issue needs to be pursued in a more methodologically focused way, with the aid of theory relating to ethnic conflict as applied to the particular empirical setting of first-century Roman households.

In addition, however, the frame of the letter itself does also contain some data suggesting ethnic conflict, in the widely misunderstood passage 16:17-20, that we must now consider.

Ethnic Conflict in Romans 16:17-20

Romans 16:17-20 has long been regarded as an extremely puzzling passage. While the primary reason for this is its apparently awkward position toward the end of the long list of greetings running from v. 3 to v. 23, many critics have also found the subject and tone of these four verses difficult to relate to Paul's message in the rest of the letter. A common view is that here Paul has suddenly launched upon a new topic—his apprehension that opponents would arrive in Rome from elsewhere and begin speaking against him and his gospel. While reasons of space prevent a full treatment of this passage here, I will outline my position.

Three broad difficulties have been discerned in these verses. First, they seem to be awkwardly intruded between greetings that run from 16:3-16 and are then resumed at 16:21. Lagrange represents the view of many on this point: "On est étonné de trouver après les salutations aux Romains, et avant les salutations des compagnons de Paul, un avis dirigé contre des semeurs de discorde. . . . Le contexte n'est assurément pas naturel."[66] The answer to this point is that the greetings in 16:21-23 are quite different in character from those up to 16:16, because they are the very personal and individual greetings from named persons, so that the inclusion of the material in 16:17-20 is not as awkward as Lagrange believed. The second and third difficulties probably carry more weight.

Second, to many writers on Paul, this passage represents a sudden change in "tone" and/or "style" from the previous part of the letter. Ziesler well expresses this point of view: "In vv. 17-20 we have a denunciatory passage unlike anything else in the letter. Elsewhere, differences of opinion are tackled discursively, by reasoned argument and persuasion. Here there is simply a brief and unexplained tirade."[67] Many other scholars have expressed similar views.[68]

The third area of difficulty concerns the contents of these verses, with scholars considering that here Paul is moving away from the previous message of Romans, notably 14:1—15:13, to an entirely new topic. Dunn is typical: "the dangers addressed here are not those of 14.1—15.6, despite the use of σκάνδαλον."[69] Fitzmyer puts the point even more strongly: "The paragraph has . . . nothing to do with the problem addressed in 14:1—15:13."[70] Moo, similarly, considers that "Paul's strong denunciation in this text is completely different from anything" to be found in 14:1—15:3.[71] Frequently associated with the idea that these verses are unrelated to the rest of Romans in tone and content is the notion that they are similar to passages elsewhere in Paul's correspondence where he warns of people who might disturb the communities, such as Phil. 3:2-21 (especially 3:17-19), 2 Cor. 11:12-15, and Gal. 6:12-17.

Yet if one holds as the fundamental canon of interpretation that the main resource we have for judging the plausibility of the interpretation of any aspect of a Pauline letter, including the context into which it was sent, is the letter itself, it is relatively easy to construe these verses as largely summarizing points that Paul has made earlier in the letter. The only other contemporary scholar I have found subscribing to a view similar to mine is Karl Donfried, who offers a few short observations directed to showing that Rom. 16:17-20 is not a new topic but rather a summary of what Paul has said in Romans 14, especially because a key theme of Romans 14 is that concern for food, for the stomach, can be a stumbling block to the weak brother (14:2-23).[72]

I now provide some evidence in support of this position, merely a sample of the data available and focusing on 16:16-17, which commentators have found most problematic: "I urge you, brothers (Παρακαλῶ δὲ ὑμᾶς, ἀδελφοί), to keep an eye on (σκοπεῖν) those who are producing dissensions (διχοστασίας) and stumbling blocks (σκάνδαλα) contrary to the teaching (διδαχή) you learned, and turn aside (ἐκκλίνετε) from them." To begin, the statement at the start of 16:17 (Παρακαλῶ δὲ ὑμᾶς, ἀδελφοί) is very similar to the expressions Paul used at 12:1 and 15:30. The original audience of Romans, therefore, would not have found the start of (what we call) v. 17 in any way innovative or surprising. Here again they would have heard Paul exhorting them to particular types of behavior and, for the third time, introducing his advice with the words Παρακαλῶ . . . ὑμᾶς, ἀδελφοί.

Second, it is commonplace for σκοπεῖν in 16:17 to be translated as "look out for"[73] or "watch out for."[74] This translation, with its connotation of looking or watching out for someone not currently in view but who may be soon, is necessary for those who regard Paul's advice as directed to people not currently present in Rome. Unfortunately for these interpreters, this is not the meaning of σκοπεῖν in the Pauline letters. In three of its four other occurrences it refers unequivocally to looking at someone or something already in view, not who or which might come into view. In these cases the correct translation is "keep an eye on," whereas "look" or "watch out for" would be incorrect (Gal. 6:1; Phil. 2:4; 3:17). While the fourth occasion is more complicated (2 Cor. 4:18), the same point can be made in relation to it. Providing strong corroboration is that Paul employs another word entirely to express the precise meaning "to look out for" (someone currently absent): βλέπειν. He uses this word three times in Phil. 3:2 to warn the Christ-followers of Philippi to be on the lookout for people who might turn up in that city advocating that they be circumcised. This is precisely the scenario that many advocate Paul has in mind in Rom. 16:17-20. Without reiterating the case against this view set out above, it is surely of great moment that where he is clearly talking of such a possibility Paul uses βλέπειν and not σκοπεῖν. At the same time, the use of the present (ποιοῦντας), rather than a future participle, confirms that the problem is already present, not about to arrive.

Third, Paul had referred to behavior that could be regarded as constituting "dissension" (διχοστασίας) earlier in the letter (11:17, 20; 14:1-5, 10, 13) or had advocated its peaceful counterpart (12:16; 14:19), even if the word itself had not been used previously. The same considerations apply a fortiori to "stumbling blocks" (σκάνδαλα), since the singular form of that word appears at 14:13.

Fourth, 16:17 concludes with a direction from Paul: "and turn aside (ἐκκλίνετε) from them," that is, from those producing dissension and scandals. Although this introduces a new issue, it is explicable on the basis of earlier statements relating to pursuing peace and harmony (as just noted) and can hardly be said to generate a change of tone. It is a gentle imperative, especially since the sentence in which it appears begins with Παρακαλῶ δὲ ὑμᾶς, ἀδελφοί, which adds the flavor of exhortation to this verb, even if a still more low-key injunction could have been produced by use of the infinitive. Nor is Paul's direction here inconsistent with his earlier advice to welcome (προσλαμβάνεσθαι) one another (14:1; 15:7). Paul has previously said that if people come to you, you must make them welcome; but this does not mean that you must seek out troublemakers, that is, go to them, and that is the burden of his instruction here.

Fifth, and most importantly, is the matter raised in v. 18a: "For such people are not serving Christ our Lord but their own stomach (κοιλία)." Paul has previously suggested that some in the Roman house churches were causing others distress by what they ate (14:15); that there was a chance that they would do something they thought was good that would be reviled as evil (14:16); and, most pertinently, that that they needed to avoid demolishing the work of God for the sake of food (14:20). Romans 16:18a is naturally explicable as a pithy summary of these statements, especially that concerning the conflicting demands of God's work and food in 14:20. Attempts to link v. 18a to Phil. 3:19 (in spite of the coincidentally similar remark in that verse that "their God is their stomach [κοιλία]") are unnecessary distractions.

This brings us to Rom. 16:18b: "and through smooth talk (χρηστολογία) and flattery (εὐλογία) they are deceiving the hearts of the guileless (ἀκάκων)." Explicit reference to persuasive talk and to the guileless being deceived is new to the letter at this point. Nevertheless, Paul has earlier mentioned arguments about disputable matters (14:1) and expressed concern that certain of the weak are at risk of adopting views expressed by the strong, even against their conscience (14:22-23). Such passages suggest that the strong are exercising their powers of persuasion against the weaker members and are deceiving them. This is almost certainly how the original audience of the letter would have understood v. 18b, and there is no need to go beyond its borders for a different interpretation.

From this analysis I conclude that 16:17-20 relates directly to affairs in Rome and that the problems it warns against relate directly to issues Paul has ventilated earlier in the letter, notably in 14:1—15:13. Since that section of the letter concerns ethnic and domestic conflict in a manner that I explain in chapter fourteen below, I further conclude that this issue is also present in 16:17-20. Although these four verses occur, admittedly, just near the end of the letter, their presence testifies to the deep-seated nature of Paul's concern with the relationship between Judean and Greek that appears first in Romans 1, recurs (as we will see) throughout the body of the letter, and, at last, stages a final rally here.

The Purpose of Romans: Some Preliminary Observations

Having analyzed data in 1:1-15 and 15:14—16:27, especially as it relates to the ethnic composition of the Christ-movement in Rome, its probable organization into house churches, and the signs of conflict among its members, I am now in a position to make some preliminary observations about the purpose of the letter to bear in mind as we follow the course of Paul's argument in the body of the letter (1:16—15:13).

Those who believe that the letter was not meant as a timeless theological treatise on the nature of the gospel have proposed three broad solutions to the problem of why Paul wrote it: (a) because of his concerns for his own future ministry in Jerusalem and then Spain; (b) to resolve problems he knew existed among the Christ-followers of Rome (in the mid- to late 50s of the first century CE); and (c) some combination of (a) and (b).[75] The "frame" sections of Romans (1:1-15 and 15:14—16:27) clearly contain abundant data relevant to (a), but also contain material that bears upon (b), especially in 16:17-20, while the close juxtaposition of Judeans and Greeks in a single group in the first century made difficulties between them likely, even without signs of this in these four verses. My own (strong) preference is for solution (c), which attributes a number of purposes to Paul in writing. Indeed, it is difficult to disentangle solution (a) from solution (b). As Minear has noted, if there was strife among the Christ-followers in Rome, Paul's desire to use the city as a base for his mission to Spain would be badly compromised.[76] I can add that this was a culture where one's reputation was vital, but where the forces of slander that imperiled it were, as Richard Rohrbaugh has shown,[77] powerful and ubiquitous, so that rumors about Paul (such as the one evident in 3:8) could easily pass between Jerusalem and Rome and other places around the Mediterranean. This meant that Paul could expect that if he offered guidance to the Christ-followers of Rome and in so doing allayed suspicions that might be in circulation there about his teaching and activity, the word of this would spread, with beneficial consequences when he visited other cities.

An examination of what he says about his planned visit to Jerusalem highlights some of Paul's difficulties. Consider the first part of his statement:

> At present I am on my way to Jerusalem undertaking a ministry for the holy ones (τοῖς ἁγίοις).[78] For Macedonia and Achaia were pleased to make a contribution (κοινωνία) among the destitute (τοὺς πτωχούς) among the holy ones in Jerusalem. They were pleased, for indeed they are in debt to them, for if the foreigners have shared (ἐκοινώνησαν) their spiritual gifts, they ought also to be of service to them in material matters. (15:25-27)

Beneath the surface of these superficially sunny remarks there lurk unmentioned depths of bitterness and conflict. Paul was originally to assist the destitute (πτωχοί) in Jerusalem as part of the agreement he and Barnabas reached in Jerusalem with James, Cephas, and John. As I have argued elsewhere, this agreement allowed Paul to continue evangelizing outside Israel on the basis that Judean and non-Judean members of his congregations would be able to participate in joint eucharistic table fellowship (Gal. 2:1-10). Yet Peter, at the behest of James, himself prompted by the extreme Judean Christ-followers of Jerusalem, broke the agreement in Antioch, and took Barnabas and the other Judean members of the movement with him (Gal. 2:11-14).[79] In spite of this, Paul continued to take up the collection. In 1 Cor. 16:1 Paul says, "Now concerning the contribution (λογεία) for the holy ones (τοὺς ἁγίους), just as I directed the congregations of Galatia, so you do also." Extensive details of the arrangements for the collection in Macedonia and Achaia appear in 2 Corinthians 8–9.[80] Yet from Rom. 15:26 we gain the remarkable piece of information that the Galatians had not contributed after all, only Macedonia and Achaia. J. Louis Martyn has reasonably surmised that the Galatian churches refused, under the influence of Paul's opponents (whom he calls "the Teachers"), to participate in the collection Paul proposed to assemble from his churches for delivery to the church in Jerusalem, presumably because they did not want to be perceived in Jerusalem as belonging to the orbit of Paul's circumcision-free mission.[81]

But a consideration of the nature of gifts in Mediterranean culture allows us to say more than this. In the pervasive social dynamic regulating the acquisition of honor that we call "challenge-and-riposte," the delivery of a gift represented a challenge to the recipient requiring an appropriate response if shame was to be avoided and honor maintained.[82] To make a gift was not an innocuous and friendly social gesture (as in most northern European and North Atlantic cultures today), but the opening gambit in an exchange that could soon take a nasty turn. Even if Paul intended bringing his collection to Jerusalem in the absence of the history of his relationship with the Jerusalem pillars just mentioned, it would have been a risky business. But with that history, it became perilous indeed. For every coin that dropped into Paul's collection bags was a physical reminder that the Jerusalem leaders had breached the Jerusalem agreement. Paul's delivery of the money had the deliberate intention, or the anticipated effect, of pushing them back toward honoring that agreement. That Paul well understood the agonistic dimension to gift giving even appears in the text of Romans, when he says at 12:20 (quoting the LXX of Prov. 25:21-22a closely): "No, if your enemy is hungry, feed him; if he is thirsty, give him drink; for by so doing you will heap burning coals upon his head." This was another reason, therefore, why opponents of Paul in the Galatian congregations would have brought pressure to bear on their members to prevent a collection being taken up for Jerusalem. For later evidence that the collection was an embarrassment and probably a cause of conflict when Paul finally reached Jerusalem, I may cite Acts 21, where it is not even mentioned as the reason for Paul's visit to the city (although Luke later forgets himself and makes passing reference to it in Acts 24:17).

Paul's own appreciation of the challenge the collection would pose to the Jerusalem church surfaces in Romans itself. After the passage just cited (Rom. 15:25-27), he mentions his plans to deliver the collection and then to visit them on his way to Spain (15:28-29) and continues: "I appeal to you, brothers, through our Lord Jesus Christ and through the love of the Spirit to strive together with me in your prayers to God on my behalf, so that I may be delivered from the unbelievers in Judea and so that my ministry (διακονία) for Jerusalem might be acceptable to the holy ones, so that by God's will I might come to you in joy and be refreshed in your company" (16:30-32). Paul's apprehension that his offering would be refused and the reasons for entertaining such a fear deserve more attention than they currently receive.[83] The most likely context is the one just described, that the collection constituted a slap in the face to the leaders of the Jerusalem congregation, James especially, and that Paul well knew that it was likely to be rejected. Accordingly, Moo's comment that "Paul's relationships with the Jerusalem apostles were apparently cordial enough at this point" (for which view he cites Acts 21:18-25 and Gal. 2:1-10), so that the problem really lay with "various conservative Jewish-Christian groups" who continued to be hostile toward him, is wide of the mark.[84] The leaders of the Christ-movement in Judea would have been Paul's main opponents, though some of the rank and file were no doubt also antipathetic toward him.

The chief motivation for opposition to Paul on the part of the Christ-followers in Jerusalem was probably the same problem that had exploded in Antioch (Gal. 2:11-14)—their unhappiness with the practice of mixed eucharistic table fellowship between Judean and non-Judean members where those present passed around one loaf and one cup (see 1 Cor. 10:16-17). As a result of the Jerusalem agreement (Gal. 2:1-10), the Jerusalem authorities had decided to permit this, but they soon reneged on their promise, in Antioch. Thereafter mixed table fellowship was an anomaly for which there was only one solution: the non-Judeans must get circumcised and take on the Mosaic law, that is, become Judeans. This was precisely the battle that Paul was fighting in Galatia. Having himself established congregations of Judeans and non-Judeans, he had now learned that people were trying to impose circumcision and the Mosaic law on his non-Judean converts. This was the context in which he wrote Galatians.[85]

I have previously used that part of social identity theory which describes how groups maintain a sense of identity for their members by strengthening the boundaries separating them from outgroups to explain the situation in Galatia and Paul's response to it.[86] While this is an approach to the letter derived from one area of social psychology, it would also make sense to analyze the situation using the sociology of sectarianism. This theory can be usefully focused on the manner in which a group that starts as a reform movement within a dominant religious group can foster such antagonism that it eventually secedes or is expelled, thereafter having a sectarian status in relation to the mother group, meaning that membership of both organizations is no longer possible. This process can be observed with some clarity in both Luke-Acts and John's Gospel.[87]

Yet Rome is different. There is no sign in the framing passages of the letter (Rom. 1–15 and 15:14—16:27) that the Judean Christ-followers are being pressured into accepting circumcision and the law. Nor, as we will see, is there any such indication in the body of the letter. Thus the particular resolution of the ethnic problem in the Christ-movement favored by the Jerusalem church ("Let these foreigners become Judeans") is not being proposed.

This is the main reason why Francis Watson's significant attempt at a social explanation of Romans may be ultimately unsuccessful, even though, in the clarity of its argument, it represents a helpful point of entry into the position taken in the letter on the question of the relation of Judeans and Greeks in the Christ-movement. He utilizes the model of transition from reform movement to sect (which would work well on Galatians) with respect to Romans, a text to which it is not well suited.[88] Watson argues that in Romans Paul is seeking to "legitimate the social reality of sectarian Gentile Christian communities in which the law was not observed." The particular means Paul chose to achieve this result, according to Watson, was by persuading "the Jewish Christians to recognize the legitimacy of the Gentile congregation and to join with it in worship, even though this would inevitably mean a final separation from the synagogue."[89] The major problem with Watson's view is whether his insistence that Paul is seeking to persuade his Judean readers to drop their Judean identity can be correlated with the data in the text where Paul seeks to establish an overarching common identity that embraces Judean and Greek subgroup identities without extinguishing either.

At the other end of the spectrum from Watson is the thesis of Nanos that Paul is seeking to remind the "gentile Christians" of Rome of their position as "righteous gentiles" within Roman "Judaism" and its synagogues, that is, to have them become more securely within the Judean fold.[90]

A long way from Watson and somewhat closer to Nanos is the well-developed opinion of W. S. Campbell (unfortunately expressed in nomenclature that now seems increasingly indefensible), to the effect that Paul did not seek to discourage "Jewish Christians" from following a "Jewish" lifestyle after they became "Christians." For Campbell the notion that there is no distinction between "Jew" and "Greek" (cf. Gal. 3:28; 1 Cor. 12:13), or rather that both groups are the recipients of divine impartiality, constitutes an assertion concerning God; it is "theology" rather than "anthropology."[91] His steadfast insistence on the need continually to relate Paul's position on this subject to his understanding of the nature of God, something I have flagged in chapter one, is an attractive feature of his approach. Campbell poses the strongest opposition to the possibility that Paul eradicates the difference between Judeans and non-Judeans by attacking Judean ethnic identity: "Then, as now, it is precisely in the reconciliation of differing peoples, of Jews and Gentiles—that the grace of God is made visible. Reconciliation consists not in the elimination but rather in the overcoming of differences in Christ. Its goal is the eradication of the hostility that springs from differences."[92] Campbell has not managed to convince Daniel Boyarin, who believes that Paul, while not "anti-Semitic,"[93] wants "Jews" to abandon their separate cultural identity.[94] As we will see, data in Romans suggests that Paul does not envisage the disappearance of a distinctive Judean subgroup identity among the Judeans who have turned to Christ.

Somewhere between Watson on the one hand and Campbell and Nanos on the other lies Paul's attitude to the Judean ethnic group,[95] and having considered the data in the body and frame of the letter I express a view on this subject in the final chapter below. The varieties of opinion represented by these critics have in common, however, that Paul is trying in some way to bring together Judeans and non-Judeans in the Christ-movement: on one view by eliminating the former as a distinct identity (Watson), on another by maintaining ethnic differences in full while insisting on a unity between the two subgroups existing at the theological level (Campbell). The view that Paul is, in some way, seeking to effect the reconciliation of the two groups is frequently heard in Romans research.[96] The approach I take in this volume is to explore the precise mode in which Paul seeks to reconcile Judeans and Greeks by reminding them of the new common ingroup identity that they share. This is the principal issue explored below, although this investigation inevitably also leads us to a conclusion on the particular question of the attitude Paul had to Israel and the position of Israelites in the Christ-movement.

I suggest, moreover, that Paul had a particular purpose in writing to the Judean and non-Judean Christ-followers in Rome, in that he was attempting to exercise leadership over them. As noted in chapters one and two above, leadership is a notion that encompasses the various levels at which Paul is operating in a way that interpretations fixing upon his "theology" singularly fail to do. I define leadership, in a general fashion, as "the process of influencing others in a manner that enhances their contribution to the realization of group goals."[97] Such a focus plainly bears upon many of the issues hitherto raised in the secondary literature concerning the purpose of Romans but approaches them in a fresh way. I will deploy a particular model of leadership—one which, among a number of possibilities, derives from the social identity theory inaugurated by Henri Tajfel and John Turner at Bristol University in the United Kingdom in the 1970s and 1980s. A model of leadership based on this theory fixes upon the ways in which leaders present themselves as prototypical of the values and experience of the groups they seek to lead.

Whatever the precise situation of the believers in Rome, Paul clearly believes that he has a right to speak to them. Ann Jervis notes correctly that Romans is the only letter that Paul sends in a solo capacity, even though Timothy was with him when he dictated it (Rom. 16:21); he wants his authority to be plain from the start.[98] As early as 1:5-7 he announces that his apostleship involves bringing about "the obedience of faith" among all the "foreigners," including the Christ-followers of Rome. This role that he assumes he has in relation to them comes out clearly much later in the letter:

> I myself am satisfied about you, my brothers, that you yourselves are full of goodness, filled with all knowledge, and able to instruct one another. But on some points I have written to you very boldly by way of reminder, because of the grace given me by God to be a minister of Jesus Christ to the foreigners in the priestly service of the gospel of God, so that the offering of the foreigners may be acceptable, sanctified by the Holy Spirit. (15:14-16, RSV, modified)

Let us now see what he said to them.

6

Common Ingroup Identity
and Romans 1:1—3:20

Establishing His Leadership Credentials:
Paul's Purpose in Romans 1:1-15

Let us picture the scene when Paul, in Corinth some time in the mid-50s CE, starts to dictate to Tertius the scribe his letter to the Christ-followers of Rome. He knows that Phoebe, or someone else, will soon be standing up to read it in some private space in the capital before a group of them, some known to him but some not, some Judean and some non-Judean. This will happen in a city he has never visited, whose congregations he has not founded, where some word about him has reached his target audience, just as he knows certain things about them, especially the tensions present among them. It is a moment when he is preparing to undertake a journey to Jerusalem critical to his mission and its reputation but whose outcome is not necessarily going to be happy. Afterward he hopes to visit Rome itself on his way to evangelize in Spain. The epistolary conventions of his time require that he name himself as sender and the letter's intended recipients, as well as sending them greetings.

In these complex circumstances he nevertheless wants to persuade the Christ-movement in Rome to adopt certain views that, we will see, overwhelmingly involve the nature and demands of their identity in Christ. He wishes, in short, to assume a leadership role in relation to them, that is, to enter upon the process of influencing them in a manner that will enhance their contribution to the realization of group goals.[1] He probably realizes from his own experience that leaders "cannot simply barge into a group and expect its members to embrace them and their plans immediately," that instead "they must first build up a support base and win the respect of followers."[2] How will he begin? We find the answer in 1:1-7.

His Initial Greetings (Rom. 1:1-7)

He does so by crafting a single sentence (comprising vv. 1-7) that is of a structure, content, and length without parallel in the openings of his letters.[3] His self-designation (v. 1) is unique among his correspondence in naming him alone as sender and in mentioning his status as an apostle devoted to God's gospel, a feature that implies at the outset that the letter will involve an eluci-dation of that gospel.[4] That he describes himself as a slave of Christ Jesus underlines that he defines his identity primarily as being totally at the disposal of Christ.

More importantly, however, Paul diverges from his typical pattern of spec-ifying himself and a fellow worker or workers as senders and then immedi-ately naming the recipients and greeting them. For here he inserts between the first two elements of the standard form of greeting a lengthy statement—first about his gospel and Christ (vv. 2-4), second, concerning his apostleship (vv. 5-6), before proceeding to the third element, the actual greeting in v. 7.

The features mentioned in vv. 2-4 are that God promised the gospel through his prophets in the Holy Scriptures and that it concerned his son, "Jesus Christ our Lord," who was a descendant of David and who was appointed Son of God with power according to the Spirit of holiness by res-urrection from the dead. Here Paul is doubtless summarizing fundamental aspects of the beliefs of the Christ-movement (some of them predicted in Israelite scripture) that he knew would also be accepted by his Roman audi-ence. Commentators have correctly noted that he cited such traditional mate-rial as a means to establish some element of common ground with the Christ-movement in Rome, with which he had hitherto had no direct con-tact.[5] We can add to this from a social identity perspective. Someone wishing to exercise leadership needs to "be maximally representative of the shared social identity and consensual position"[6] of the group in question. Paul has realized that he will be unable to push them in a particular direction unless they are confident that he subscribes to the foundational beliefs for their iden-tity. He needs to assure them that he and they worship the same Jesus Christ—hence his statement that Christ is *our* Lord (1:4).

The subject of v. 2, that God promised the gospel through his prophets in the Holy Scriptures, requires attention. Of the forty-eight instances of "gospel" (εὐαγγέλιον) in the seven Pauline letters universally accepted as genuine, this is the only occasion on which it is explicitly said to be foretold in Israelite scripture. Moreover, this unique connection is enhanced by his use of the word "foretold,"[7] προεπηγγείλατο, which partially rhymes with εὐαγγέλιον in the previous verse, since it is built on –αγγέλλομαι, a paronym of εὐαγγέλιον. The idea of God's fulfilling promises in relation to Christ and his gospel made long ago in Israelite scriptures is an important theme in Romans. This is not because of some interest on Paul's part in promise and fulfillment as a theological topos, or in scripture as authoritative text, or because Paul was someone who enjoyed the literary delights of inter-textuality (see chapter eight below). Rather, Israelite scriptures matter to Paul and his largely illiterate audience because they contain collective memories of

God's dealings with his people, in this case words he spoke through his prophets.

This record of the past was inevitably going to be a lively field of contestation between proponents of the gospel of Christ and Israelites who rejected it, and between Christ-followers of various beliefs themselves. As I noted in chapter two, efforts to control a group's past and hence its present identity frequently involve a struggle for the possession and interpretation of its collective memory, and here we see Paul's appetite for this battle, very near the start of the letter. Central to his campaign is the argument that these written records of God's promises themselves predict and promise Christ and, as he will develop later, the inclusion of non-Judeans within the ambit of divine mercy. Paul needs to be able to show that the gospel he preaches exists in continuity with the memories of God's dealings with his people commemorated in Israelite scripture. The fact that Judean Christ-followers form part of the audience he is addressing in Rome must figure among the reasons for his emphasis on such continuity.

In vv. 5-6 he develops this line by the assertion that it is from Christ that he has received grace and apostleship to bring about obedience to the faith in the non-Judean world, where his Roman addressees are located. We have seen in chapter five above that Paul's mission entails the conversion of both non-Judeans and Judeans; in diaspora situations both groups were often associated, leading to the creation of mixed Christ-following congregations. By insisting on Christ as the source of his apostleship Paul stakes his claim to be a leader in relation to the new identity Christ has made possible by his life, death, and resurrection.

In v. 7 Paul finally names the recipients of the letter as "to all those in Rome beloved of God, who are called holy," and wishes them grace and peace "from God our Father and the Lord Jesus Christ." He does not address them as an ἐκκλησία as he does to the congregation of Corinth (1 Cor. 1:1; 2 Cor. 1:1), Thessalonika (1 Thess. 1:1), and the house church of Philemon (v. 2), possibly because they did not comprise one congregation.[8] In saying they are "called holy" and "beloved of God" Paul not only emphasizes the exalted nature of their status but also underlines the demands that it imposes on them.

Building an Emotional Bond (Rom. 1:8-15)

If in vv. 1-7 Paul is seeking to persuade his Roman audience in a rather formal tone that he has an unimpeachable divine warrant for his activities in spreading the gospel, the next section of the letter (1:8-15) continues his effort as a potential leader to build a support base and win their respect by touching their emotions through reference to the warm feelings he has for them. In v. 8 he turns a thanksgiving formula customary in letters of his day into flattery by first expressing his thanks to God through Jesus Christ *for all of them* because their faith (πίστις) is proclaimed in all the world. Then he adds that, as God is his witness whom he serves in his spirit through the gospel of his Son—thus reiterating his role as slave of Christ to proclaim his gospel—he prays for them unceasingly, asking that he may eventually, by God's will, succeed in coming to them (vv. 8-10).

He next says he desires to see them so that he may share with them some spiritual gift, which sounds perfectly appropriate from someone who prided himself on the gifts of the Spirit he had received and which characterized his congregations,[9] except now he slips a little by adding "so that you may be strengthened" (v. 11), thus suggesting that they are suffering from some weakness that needs his help and representing the kind of direction more suitable to a congregation he had founded.[10] Immediately aware that this is not quite the right tone in the circumstances, Paul changes tack a little. "That is," he begins, before continuing in a rather clumsy fashion that reveals his discomfiture, "to be mutually encouraged among you through the faith of one another, yours and mine" (v. 12). But in so saying he is not undermining his apostolic status, as Käsemann has suggested,[11] but rather he strengthens his bid for leadership by defining himself and his audience in terms of a shared social identity, here centering on the mutuality of their faith (πίστις).

In v. 13 he continues his quest for their goodwill by addressing them, for the first time in the letter, as "brothers" (ἀδελφοί), which here must cover men and women given the prominence of women in his greetings in chap. 16, and by stating that he has often wanted to come to them but was prevented. His purpose was to harvest some fruit among them as also among the other non-Judeans. I have explained in chapter five that this statement is to be understood as indicating his interest in making converts in the world of non-Judeans beyond the borders of Judea, even though some of those converts were routinely Judean, with Paul insisting that they form congregations in Christ without circumcision or the Mosaic law being imposed on non-Judean members.

In v. 14 he acknowledges that he is under obligation to "Greeks and barbarians, to the wise and foolish." By this Paul means that he has been successful in securing converts from among these two groups, the first focusing on ethnicity and the second on level of education. To speak of "Greeks (Ἕλληνες) and barbarians (βάρβαροι)" is to adopt, for a moment, the stereotypical way in which people claiming for themselves Greek ethnicity, whether originating in Greece itself or from other parts of the Mediterranean claiming "Greekness" in the manner I have described in chapter three, see all other outgroups as uncivilized people speaking outlandish languages (= βάρβαροι). Paul is claiming he has been successful with people of all sorts. This does not weigh against his having made Judean converts; indeed, from the Greek point of view evident here, they would be numbered among the βάρβαροι. But even if Paul is mentally excluding Judeans from the ranks of the βάρβαροι,[12] this statement would still not weigh against my view that Judean Christ-fearers formed part of his Roman audience. Paul is simply making a factual statement that his preaching has led to people from many ethnic groups turning to Christ. In the second half of v. 14 he offers a further measure of his success: he has converted people who were highly educated and people who were not. There is no need to assume that he is here speaking of the same groups.[13] He is merely offering another criterion against which to measure his success.

The contents of both vv. 13 and 14 seem to be in Paul's mind when he concludes this section with the assertion: "hence (οὕτως) my eagerness also to preach the gospel to you who are in Rome" (v. 15). He has previously wanted to come to them; he has been successful in other parts of the non-Judean world, whatever their ethnicity or level of education; now he wants to preach the gospel to them in Rome, where the population exhibited marked differentiation in ethnicity and degrees of education. Again, none of this necessitates altering my view that there were Judean Christ-followers among his addressees. Rather unusually for Paul, here "to preach the gospel" (εὐαγγελίσασθαι) does not mean to undertake initial evangelization but to expound its meaning to people who already have faith in Christ. Yet this will presumably involve little more than developing the process he has begun by sending them this letter, for the letter itself probably represents a proclamation of his gospel, as we will now see.

The Gospel and Social Identity (Rom. 1:16-17 and 18)

Paul concludes the opening section of the letter with a statement (vv. 16-17) that has generally been held to contain a summary of its main themes. He thus rounds off the initial attempt to establish his leadership credentials that he began in v. 1.

His first claim, "For I am not put to shame by the gospel," must be understood within its ancient Mediterranean context, where to be dishonored publicly by some event, person, or (as here) a group affiliation with unique beliefs and practices was a grievous social ill. The Vulgate has the vivid translation: "Non enim erubesco evangelium" ("For I do not blush because of the gospel"). Carlin Barton has aptly written of the ancient Roman world that in the "delicate physics of honor, the pivotal mechanism was the blush."[14] But what could there be about the gospel that would shame Paul, cause him to blush? He probably means that it has never let him down, that it has always stood firm against challenges.[15] He then offers

a theological reason to explain this: "for it is the power (δύναμις) of God."
That it has this fundamental character goes far to explaining the reliability
and resilience of the gospel.

Yet that is not the end of the story. This is a divine power of a very special
sort: "for salvation for everyone who has faith, to the Judean first and also the
Greek." Here Paul identifies the gospel with God's power to save a certain
category of people, all those who have faith, but it is a category comprising
two subcategories, Judeans and Greeks. His ancient readers, well used to
belonging to groups, would have appreciated the sense of group belonging
Paul was conveying. From our modern perspective, we may analyze this
statement in terms of the group differentiation described by social identity
theorists: there are those who do have faith (with salvation in store) and, by
necessary implication, those who do not, ingroup and outgroup, "us" and
"them." The group to which Paul refers, however, exists because representatives of two other groups, Judeans and Greeks, have been recategorized to
belong to it. The bare facts known of it so far, that it is characterized by faith
and destined for salvation, require that it has a distinct identity, one that will
be lodged as social identity in the minds and hearts of its members—meaning that part of their sense of who they are as individuals that derives from
belonging to this group. Yet such identity will need to coexist with whatever
remains of the members' original Judean and Greek identities. This
inevitably raises the question of how the life experiences and loyalties represented in this conjunction of identity and subidentities might be balanced, a
point I return to below.

The issue becomes even more complex with Paul's next assertion: "For in
it [sc. the gospel] the righteousness (δικαιοσύνη) of God is being revealed by
faith for faith, just as it stands written, 'The righteous person (δίκαιος) by
faith will live'" (v. 17). Paul's original audience would have heard in these
words the beginning of his talk of righteousness in the letter, of divine righteousness being somehow revealed to human beings through faith so that they
might become righteous. From the viewpoint of the social theory being
employed in this volume, the issue is how Paul's vision of righteousness relates
to his understanding of the identity of the Roman Christ-followers. To what
extent does it contribute to the cognitive, emotional, and evaluative dimensions of group belonging? In writing to the Galatians some time previously,
Paul had described righteousness as a form of privileged identity, essentially
equivalent to life and blessing.[16] Romans 1:17, especially with its claim that
"the righteous person by faith will live," seems to raise the prospect of similar
issues. That the righteousness on offer to Christ-followers stems from "the
righteousness of God," that God imparts a vital dimension of his own character to those who believe, raises an important theme of the letter mentioned
in chapter one above. Paul takes such great lengths to show how closely

related are God and those who accept the gospel of Christ, even rival groups of Judeans and Greeks, that it is difficult to disentangle what we would call the "theological" and "social" dimensions of his understanding.

Yet we must wait until Rom. 3:21-31 before Paul begins to elaborate more fully on what this kind of righteousness is and how it is related to faith. I defer a discussion of that righteousness until chapter seven below.

In the meantime Paul is about to explain the terrible plight for which the righteousness available to the Christ-follower is the solution. He begins this large theme in the very next verse of the letter (1:18): "For the anger of God is being revealed from heaven on all godlessness (ἀσέβεια) and injustice (ἀδικία) of human beings who by their unrighteousness (or 'injustice,' ἀδικία) suppress the truth."

Thus in consecutive verses Paul enunciates the revelation of God's righteousness (δικαιοσύνη) on those who have faith and the revelation of God's anger on those who practice godlessness and unrighteousness. Paul will work out the implications of these statements, with their dramatic juxtaposition of divine righteousness on the one hand and divine anger at godlessness and unrighteousness on the other, in 1:19—3:20. The discussion of that section, which I must now undertake, provides the context for an explanation of 3:21-31.

The Common Plight Needing a New Solution: Recategorization in Romans 1:18—3:20

The Dilemma of Romans 1:18—3:20

Although there is a closely argued development from 1:16-17 to 1:18, 1:18—3:20 constitutes a recognizably distinct section in the letter, as most commentators agree. Here, despite the complexity of the argument, Paul is preoccupied with one broad subject—the sinful condition in which all human beings find themselves prior to the revelation of God's righteousness.[17] That revelation, indeed, sharply defines this section in the form of an *inclusio*, since it is announced in 1:17 and repeated in 3:21. Most commentators also point out that Paul differentiates the experience of Judeans and non-Judeans (whom most call "Jews" and "gentiles") within the large canvas on which he is portraying human sinfulness.

Yet Douglas Moo rightly asks what is the purpose of this protracted indictment of humanity.[18] Why has Paul thought it necessary to interpolate such a discussion into the midst of a treatment of righteousness begun at 1:17 and not returned to until 3:21, a full sixty-four verses later? After all, A. J. M. Wedderburn has pointed out that "Galatians lacks any equivalent to the sustained argument of Romans 1.18—3.20 to show that 'all sinned and lack God's glory'" (3:23).[19]

It is probably best not to see 1:18—3:20 as part of Paul's gospel but as a preparation for it, given his generally positive use of gospel language. While this is an explanation at a general level, Moo amplifies it by arguing that only if sin is seen to be the dominating force as Paul presents it will it become clear why God's righteousness can be experienced only as a gift, that is, by faith. Moreover, he suggests, this will occur only if "Jews" as much as "Gentiles" understand that they are both equally under the power of sin (as stated in 3:9).[20]

Yet this explanation might apply to any congregations comprising both Judeans and non-Judeans. Is there anything relating to the situation of the Roman Christ-movement, or to Paul's status among Christ-followers and his plans for the future, especially his forthcoming visit to Jerusalem and, after that, to Spain via Rome, that might help explain the insertion of this passage and the particular arguments in it? Thomas Tobin has suggested that underlying 1:18—3:20 was the fact of Paul's being a controversial figure in the early Christ-movement and his attempt to defuse some of this controversy especially as to the relation between the Mosaic law and faith in Christ.[21] Tobin argues that Paul sought to ensure his friendly reception by the Romans when he eventually got to their city and even to win their intercession with the Jerusalem community so that the latter would accept the collection he was bringing to them. One might ask, however, if this view focuses too much on Paul's concern for his own position and status (which is certainly part of the picture) and underestimates the extent to which he was genuinely concerned to make a positive intervention in the affairs of the Christ-movement in Rome (the need for which is evident in Romans 14–15).

I am now ready to suggest a new way of addressing the dilemma posed to interpreters by the presence of 1:18—3:20 in the letter.

Eliminating Obstacles to Recategorization

In chapter two I set out (in the context of explaining social identity theory) the method of reducing intergroup conflict known as recategorization or the common ingroup identity model. In essence, the idea is that when members of two groups or subgroups are incorporated within a superordinate group, they will treat one another favorably as ingroup members rather than engage in the practices of stereotyping and antipathy accorded to outgroups, in time getting to know one another as individuals rather than just as representatives of a social category in ways that will further help break down old attitudes. Paul's intention to persuade his Judean and Greek addressees of the significance of what (I later argue) is a new identity derived from the righteousness of God through faith in Christ is evident in the verses that frame the passage under consideration, 1:17 and 3:21.

Yet although the goal might be to include all within a new ingroup identity, modern research has shown how the original group memberships of those whom it is hoped can be brought together can seriously interfere with the process of recategorization. In particular, it has emerged that the process can be impeded if the participants are encouraged to abandon their original (sub)group identities entirely. It appears that if the participants feel their original identities are under threat they may react strongly to maintain their viability and distinctiveness, a result that will exacerbate any bias they feel and exhibit toward members of the other (sub)group.[22]

I submit that in seeking to recategorize Judeans and Greeks into a new group in Christ, or to bring home to them forcefully the meaning of their having been so recategorized, Paul faced precisely this problem of persisting subgroup loyalties. We have seen in chapter two above that Paul's previous experience in Galatia had probably taught him to be more sensitive to subgroup identities.

Although more details are provided below, the Judeans had clearly been socialized to accept that their worship of the one true God and obedience to him through the commandments of the Mosaic law made them superior to other peoples, who were by and large mired in the snares of idolatry. Within the Christ-movement such an attitude toward non-Judeans would constitute a force against acceptance of non-Judean Christ-followers, including the Greeks of Rome.

At the same time, the Greek members of the Roman congregations must have taken pride in their Greek ethnicity, just like other Greeks around the Mediterranean. This pride was associated with stereotypical attitudes to non-Greeks, the βάρβαροι whom Paul mentions in 1:14, including Judeans. These attitudes were likely to be vented upon Judeans with whom they came into contact, for example in meetings of Christ-followers. It is even possible that such contact enhanced negative stereotypes on both sides, giving both subgroups further areas of activity in which to devalue and discriminate against the other.

The force of these subsisting ethnic allegiances would have made it unrealistic for Paul to suggest that his addressees abandon them; nor does he do so, but rather he self-consciously preserves the two social categories, as in the programmatic affirmation of 1:16, where he describes his gospel as "the power of God for salvation for everyone who has faith, to the Judean first and also the Greek." William B. Campbell has reached a similar conclusion in his insistence that Paul is not seeking to remove diversity between Judeans and Greeks among the Christ-movement in Rome, but rather his intention is "to promote harmony *within* diversity."[23]

applic.

The Equality of Greeks and Judeans in Relation to Sin

What answer is there, then, to the problem of building or maintaining a common ingroup identity if the members are not going to abandon their subgroup identities? As noted in chapter two, the solution, especially in the challenging context of interethnic conflict, seems to be to make a virtue out of necessity, by establishing "a common superordinate identity while simultaneously maintaining the salience of subgroup identities." This permits "the benefits of a common ingroup identity to operate without arousing countervailing motivations to achieve positive distinctiveness."[24] Paul, brought up in a group-oriented culture, educated by his previous experience, and hence no doubt far more alert to group dynamics than his modern readers, seems to have instinctively grasped the necessity of adopting this approach to the mixed Judean/Greek Christ-movement in Rome.

Yet now we encounter a further complication, namely, the relative status of each of two subgroups vis-à-vis the other if the process of bringing them together in a new group is to succeed. To summarize the position expressed in chapter two above, this result is only likely if the two groups have an equal status but on different dimensions, since if they were equal in precisely the same quality or activity, they might tend to compete in a fashion destructive of the single ingroup identity sought to be achieved. As one group of researchers has expressed it: "Only when both groups are equal in status but share different experiences or expertise" can they readily respect and value the other's unique contribution and believe that they will benefit from the presence of the other.[25]

Paul's strategy in dealing with his two subgroups of Judeans and Greeks seems, again, instinctively to accord with this position. To anticipate the results of my analysis of 1:18—3:20 for the moment, his aim is to show that they are both equal in respect of their subjection to the power of sin but they are different in the way they have reached that result—Judeans under the law of Moses and Greeks in the absence of that law (a situation precisely expressed in 2:12-13). The difference between Paul's approach and that suggested by the model is that whereas the latter looks to an equivalence on different dimensions in respect of some positive attribute, Paul is equating them in respect of a negative condition—domination by sin. Accordingly, rather than each subgroup thinking it will benefit from the presence of the other, in Paul's scheme they realize that they are each precluded from suggesting they will be harmed by the presence of the other, since they are both equally under the dominion of sin. The result, however, is exactly the same. Paul knocks away the respective foundations each group has for harboring feelings of ethnic superiority over the other that would get in the way of their accepting the value of the new common ingroup identity on offer.

With the aid of this social-scientific framework I will now explore 1:18—3:20. Although many ways have been put forward for subdividing this passage, I adopt the following, explaining why in the course of the discussion: (a) 1:18—2:5; (b) 2:6-16; (c) 2:17-29; (d) 3:1-8; and (e) 3:9-20.

Sodom and Social Identity: Romans 1:18-32

Central to the meaning of 1:18-32 and then 2:1-5 is the question of whom Paul is targeting in these sections. The debate is most intense in relation to 1:18-32. The three possibilities are non-Judeans alone, Judeans and non-Judeans, or all human beings irrespective of their ethnic origins and Paul's own temporal context. Critics who favor either of the second and third options frequently find in the passage references to Adam and the fall. I have argued elsewhere at some length that in 1:18-32 Paul is referring only to Judeans contemporary with him, that the master metaphor for their portrayal is the Israelite tradition of Sodom, and that his presentation is deliberately exaggerated as part of his overall strategy of recategorizing Judean and non-Judean Christ-followers into their new identity in Christ.[26] I now briefly discuss the passage in this light, summarizing features of the fuller argument where necessary.

We have just seen that Paul does not seek to achieve the difficult task of erasing the two broad ethnic identities present in the Roman Christ-movement, Judean and Greek. Instead, he crafts an argument that will establish that they are both equally subject to sin but in entirely different ways. Romans 1:18 represents the beginnings of this process. The divine wrath is being revealed over all godlessness and unrighteousness. We shall observe in chapter seven below that Proverbs 10–15 and Psalm 36 (LXX) provide the richest sources in Israelite scripture for the antithetical relationship of righteousness, on the one hand, and godlessness and unrighteousness on the other. While that antithesis provided Israelites with a powerful means to stereotype foreigners, Paul will insist that unrighteousness (if not godlessness) is also a feature of Israelite experience (explicitly at Rom. 3:5). Thus the blanket combination of 1:18 covers Judeans as well as non-Judeans.

Nevertheless, Paul does begin his onslaught with a stinging attack on non-Judeans. This is the point of 1:19-32. That he should do so probably reflects his own Judean outlook on the world (which had been evident in Gal. 2:15 when he referred to himself [and possibly also Peter] as "Judeans by birth and not sinners from among the non-Judeans" and which will burst into prominence later, in Rom. 9:1-5), the fact that the gospel was initially for Judeans (1:16), and the presence, and perhaps prominence, of Judeans in the Christ-movement in Rome.

Like other ethnic groups then and since, Paul and the other Judeans of his time were ethnocentric, that is, they were strongly socialized to consider that they were superior to the other ethnic groups who surrounded them. Giving Judean ethnocentrism its distinctive cast was the fact that they worshiped the one true God in his temple in Jerusalem and obeyed his commandments, while all other peoples were immersed in sinful and foolish idolatry. They knew from Deuteronomy 28 that God provided blessings and life for adhering to the law and curses and death for not keeping it and for worshiping idols. This gave them powerful warrant for holding negative views on peoples who were idolatrous. Such an outlook is reflected in the *Letter of Aristeas*, a Judean text written sometime in the fourth to second centuries BCE, which highlights righteousness as a salient and treasured feature of identity and which serves to differentiate the Judean ingroup from the evil, unjust, idolatrous, and polluted outgroups among whom they lived. In time there even developed a "two ways" tradition to epitomize this differentiation, of which there is a formative statement in Ps. 1:6: "For the Lord knows the way of the righteous (ὁδὸν δικαίων), but the way of the wicked (ὁδὸς ἀσεβῶν) will perish." Similar sentiments can be found in other texts, such as Sir. 15:11-21, *T. Ash.* 1:3-5, Philo's *Hypothetica*, Josephus's *Against Apion*, and the *Sentences of Pseudo-Phocylides*.[27]

Some Judean texts focused specifically on the ignorance and folly involved in worshiping idols when those who did so should have been able to discover God in his creation. A good example can be found in the Wisdom of Solomon, probably written in the mid-to-late first century BCE:[28]

> For all those are foolish (μάταιοι) by nature who have suffered ignorance (ἀγνωσία) of God and who, from the good things that are seen (ἐκ τῶν ὁρομένων ἀγαθῶν), have not been able to discover Him-who-is, nor, by studying the works, have recognized the Craftsman. . . . Even so, they are not to be pardoned; if they were able to acquire enough knowledge to investigate the world, why have they not more quickly discovered its Master? But wretched are they—in dead things putting their hopes—who have given to things made by human hands the title of gods, gold and silver, finely worked, likenesses of animals or some useless stone, carved by some hand long ago. (Wis. 13:1, 8-10; JB modified)

In another place the author notes: "As their foolish and wicked notions led them astray into worshipping mindless reptiles (ἑρπετά) and contemptible beasts, you sent hordes of mindless creatures to punish them" (Wis. 11:15-16, JB). Occasionally Israelites laughed at the fact that those who made the idols had to clamp them upright with iron bands lest they fall over and be damaged, so useless were the "gods" they had carved in protecting themselves.[29] This type of mordant humor probably characterized first-century Judean attitudes to the idolatry that surrounded them.

Ingroup/outgroup differentiation of this sort represents a form of stereotyping, which essentially means treating everyone in the outgroup solely in terms of their group membership rather than as distinctive individuals.

Stereotypes are fluid, variable, and context dependent.[30] They are not rigid or fixed, but vary with the current state of intergroup relations, the context in question, and the perspective of the perceiver. In any given case, the nature and force of the stereotype represents a balance between the individuals involved and the social context in which they are operating.[31]

Paul draws on this bountiful stock of Judean stereotypes and engages in a fairly extreme type of stereotyping that he no doubt judged necessary to his context in Rom. 1:19-23:

> For what can be known (τὸ γνωστόν) about God is mani-
> fest (φανερόν) among them, because God has manifested
> (ἐφανέρωσεν) it to them. For his invisible attributes (τὰ
> ἀόρατα), that is, his eternal power and deity, have been visible
> since the creation of the world, being intelligible in the things he
> has made, so that they are without excuse. For although having
> known (γνόντες) God, they did not honor him as God or give
> thanks, but they became foolish (ἐματαιώθησαν) in their
> thinking and their senseless heart was darkened. Claiming to be
> wise, they became fools (ἐμωράνθησαν), and exchanged
> (ἤλλαξαν) the glory of the immortal God (ἀφθάρτου Θεοῦ)
> for the likeness of an image (ἐν ὁμοιώματι εἰκόνος) of mor-
> tal man (φθαρτοῦ ἀνθρώπου) or of birds or animals or reptiles
> (πετεινῶν καὶ τετραπόδων καὶ ἑρπετῶν).

Here we have a similar idea to that in Wis. 13:1 that the good things of God's creation are visible (ἐκ τῶν ὁρομένων ἀγαθῶν). In addition, the notion that non-Israelites have been stupid and reduced to foolishness (ἐματαιώθησαν in Rom. 1:21 and ἐμωράνθησαν in 1:22) parallels the foolishness of Wis. 13:1 (μάταιοι). In both cases they are without excuse (Wis. 13:10; Rom. 1:20). The paraphernalia of idol worship mentioned in Rom. 1:23 probably derives from a source like Deut. 4:16-18, where Moses records God's commandment to the Israelites not to make a graven image (ὁμοίωμα), any kind of figure (εἰκών) for themselves, either of male or female, or of any creature, bird, rep-tile, or fish. It is noteworthy that the words ὁμοίωμα and εἰκών appear in Rom. 1:23 in the same order.

This material has suggested to many critics that Paul has non-Judeans in sight here.[32] The people in view apparently do not possess the Mosaic law as a means to know God (1:19-20) and they practice idolatry (1:22-23). There is no sign in Romans that Paul attributes idolatry to the Israel that is con-temporary with him; such a view would stand in blank contradiction to the way he describes the Judean in 2:17-29 (especially in 2:22, where Paul states the obvious by acknowledging that Judeans abhor idols) and to his passionate statement about Israel in 9:1-5. The non-Israelite humanity in view in 1:18-32 includes but is probably a more comprehensive group than the Greeks whom Paul has just announced as the recipients, second after Judeans, of God's saving power (1:16).

In spite of the power of these arguments, others are of the view that Paul is referring to Judeans as well as non-Judeans. One influential reason adduced for this position is the alleged reference to the story of Adam's fall in 1:23. If Adam is referred to here, it is hard to resist the conclusion that Paul is referring to all who stem from him, Judeans and non-Judeans. Morna Hooker proposed a reference to Adam in 1960.[33] Her view has been accepted by Barrett, Wedderburn, and Dunn, to cite a few.[34] Hooker contended that in 1:18-32, especially at v. 23, Paul had Adam in mind and that in these verses he deliberately described humankind's predicament in terms of the biblical story of Adam's fall. She suggested that the language of the passage echoed Genesis 1–3 and that its sequence of events is reminiscent of the narrative of Adam in Genesis 1–3. As supporting evidence she cited the fact that the order of the living things mentioned as the object of idolatry in Rom. 1:23 was the same as in Genesis, rabbinic traditions associated the fall with sexual desire and idolatry, and the two passages had similar vocabulary (including the use of εἰκών in Rom. 1:23). Although she acknowledged that nothing in Genesis suggested that Adam ever worshiped idols, Hooker proposed that he could "be justly accused of serving the creature rather than the creator, and that it is from this confusion between God and the things which he has made that idolatry springs."[35] Another ground for regarding Israelites as included in 1:18-32, proposed by Wedderburn, is the possibility of allusions to Israelite scripture that include Israelites in idolatry (Jer. 2:5, 11; Ps. 105:19-20 LXX).[36]

But Hooker's case is weak. Fitzmyer has explained the linguistic similarities she cites on other grounds and rejects her rabbinic materials as too late to assist. Käsemann finds her reference to Adam "arbitrary" and reasonably states "that there can be no reference to making an image of this man."[37] Dale Martin suggests that Romans 1 has to do with "the invention of idolatry and its consequences, not the Fall of Adam," and that Paul refers to a plurality of persons in the passage, not to one.[38] Stowers attacks the attempts to tie 1:18-32 to the fall story in Genesis as "profoundly unconvincing" for the reason that they assume the existence and obviousness of cultural codes, especially those which propose Adam's fall as the explanation for the human predicament, even though those codes developed only centuries after Paul wrote the letter.[39] Lastly, in answer to Wedderburn, the possibility that there are echoes of Jeremiah and Psalm 105 (LXX) in Rom. 1:18-32 proves little, since there was nothing to stop Paul applying to non-Israelites derogatory descriptions previously used of Israelites, especially when the language in question concerned idolatrous activity by Israelites. In short, given the obvious connections of 1:18-32 to non-Israelites and non-Israelite idolatry, a point I substantiate further below, it is far-fetched to introduce Adam into the picture.

As well as rejecting any allusion to Adam and the fall in 1:18-32, Martin also suggests that "Paul apparently presupposes a Jewish mythological narrative about the origins of idolatry." He refers to rabbinic sources that ascribe the invention of idolatry to Kenan, Enosh (son of Seth), or the people of Enosh's generation, and follows Stowers in proposing that a narrative about the decline of human civilization provides the context for 1:18-32.[40] While it is useful to look to some body of Israelite tradition other than the fall as underlying this passage, this is probably the wrong one. Paul is not concerned with the invention of idolatry for its own sake, although he does explain how it came about (1:21-23), nor does he put forward some diachronic narrative of decline. Rather, using the aorist tense he describes in vv. 21-27 events in the past, the origin of idolatry and same-sex relations between women and men, which, in themselves (apparently) and in their effects (clearly), continue into the present and are falling under the sway of divine wrath, as unequivocally revealed in the present tenses in the framing verses, 18 and 32. A plausible prima facie candidate as a tradition that Paul might have relied on that can be reconciled with these features is the biblical and extrabiblical material bearing on Sodom and its destruction.

Since I have developed the details of this argument elsewhere,[41] I will only summarize them here. The main Old Testament source is the account of events in Sodom in Genesis 19, when the men of the town wanted to engage in a sexual assault on Lot's guests, unfortunately for them, two angels. This account clearly had a major impact on the Israelite imagination.[42] Other scriptural references to it can be found in Deut. 29:23-28; 32:32; Isa. 1:2-11; 13:19-20; Lam. 4:6; Jer. 23:13-14; 27:33-40 (LXX); 29:17-18 (LXX); Ezek. 16:44-58; and Amos 4:11. There are extrascriptural references in 3 Macc. 2:4-5; *T. Naph.* 3:4; *Jub.* 16:5-8; Wis. 19:13-15; Josephus, *Judean War* 4.484; while the fullest Israelite account of Sodom outside scripture occurs in Philo, *On Abraham* 135-36 (c. 20 BCE–50 CE). Sodom and Gomorrah are also mentioned several times in the New Testament (Matt. 10:15; cf. Luke 10:12; Matt. 11:23-24; Luke 17:29; 2 Pet. 2:6; Jude 7; Rev. 11:8). Lastly, one should not forget that Paul himself refers to Sodom and Gomorrah in Rom. 9:29.

The chief features of the picture of non-Judeans presented by Paul in the passage are, first, the general assertion of God's anger being revealed on their godlessness and unrighteousness in 1:18 following right on the heels of the revelation of divine and human righteousness of 1:16-17; second, their failure to thank and honor God and their adoption of idolatry instead (1:19-23);

third, their being handed over by God to ἀκαθαρσία ("impurity") and dishonoring of their bodies manifested principally in women and men engaging in same-sex relations (1:24-27); and, fourth, their being handed over by God to the practice of a long list of vices (1:28-32). Given the representation of Sodom in Israelite tradition, beginning with its godlessness that constituted the antithesis of righteousness and its combination of idolatry, same-sex relations, and a variety of other forms of wickedness, it seems highly likely that Paul intended Sodom to form the master metaphor in this section of the letter and that his readers, some of whom must have been reasonably familiar with Israelite tradition (Judeans and any non-Judeans who had ever attended synagogue services), would have realized this.

Of particular interest is that the Sodom metaphor offers a good explanation for the fact that Paul mentions same-sex relations between women (1:26) before those between men (1:27). Ancient Mediterranean male authors were remarkably reticent about same-sex relations between women.[43] The probable reason for this was that they posed a severe threat to the hierarchical way that men of honor constructed their world.[44] Honorable men took the active role, with women (and pathic men) always being in a position of subordination, to be penetrated, not to penetrate.[45] So it is a real puzzle (although this point is insufficiently made by commentators) why Paul mentions women at all, let alone before men.

The probable solution lies in the novel way in which Ezekiel refers to the daughters of Sodom (Ezek. 16:48-50). The rest of the tradition focuses firmly on the men of the city and does not mention women. Ezekiel 16 is unique in this respect. This particular feature of Paul's account, therefore, points strongly to his use of Sodom as the master metaphor for Rom. 1:18-32. This conclusion can be strengthened by a detailed comparison of the vices in 1:24-32 with the various aspects of the Israelite understanding of Sodom just mentioned. Although the discussion is beyond the scope of this chapter,[46] most of the vices mentioned find direct or close parallels in the Sodom tradition. Paul ends on the serious note that those who do the things previously listed are worthy to die, but so also are they who approve of those who practice them (1:32).

Greeks, Judeans, and the Coming Judgment (Rom. 2:1-16)
At 2:1 Paul continues ominously and in the form of an imaginary dialogue characteristic of diatribe style: "Therefore, you have no defense, O human being (ἄνθρωπος), every one of you who judges, for in what you are judging the other person, you condemn yourself, for you do the same things you are judging." Paul goes on to warn that the judgment of God falls on those who do such things, that the man (ἄνθρωπος) who does the same as those he judges will not escape that judgment and should not presume on God's pity,

which is meant to lead to repentance, and that by his impenitent heart he is storing up wrath for himself on the day of wrath when there will be revealed the righteous judgment of God, who will repay each according to his deeds (2:2-6).[47]

For some reason that escapes me there is a fierce debate as to whom Paul is addressing here. A large number of scholars consider that the ἄνθρωπος is a typical Judean.[48] Others see a non-Judean interlocutor.[49] The latter position is correct, and the widespread support for the former is a cause for wonder. As we have already seen, 1:19-32 concerns the godless and vicious character of the idolatry typical of non-Judeans. In that passage Paul is solely concerned with the ἔθνη, "heathen" from a Judean point of view. The person referred to in 2:1-6 engages in the same practices, which can only mean idolatry (1:19-23) and the vices listed (1:26-31), while hypocritically passing judgment on others who do the same. It is implausible to imagine that a first-century CE Judean like Paul (and cf. 9:1-5 and 11:1), someone who prided himself on belonging to a people separate from sinful non-Judeans (Gal 2:15), would ever blur the fundamental distinction that separated his ethnic group from the disliked outgroups by attributing idolatry to Judeans. Not only is this view inevitable within the framework of the ethnic realities of the time, but in 2:17 Paul confirms its accuracy by indicating how he would go about accusing a Judean of hypocrisy; I come back to this below, but Paul states the obvious by making explicit that a Judean is not such as to commit idolatry, just the contrary in fact, as shown in the criticism (2:22): "You who abhor idols (ὁ βδελυσσόμενος τὰ εἴδωλα), do you rob temples?"

In 2:1-6 Paul is widening his critique of non-Judeans in 1:18-32, who could discern God in the cosmos (even if they did not possess the Mosaic law), to embrace those non-Judeans who wrongly imagined that they were not guilty of the horrors mentioned. He does not have Judeans in his sights at this stage, but soon will have.

First he must elaborate on the nature of the coming end-time events (2:7-16), which he has hitherto introduced only in general terms in 2:2-6, initially by offering generalized promises of eternal life for some and wrath and fury for the wicked (2:7-8). An important feature of his elaboration is his insistence that the divine decision (my reasons for not using "judgment" here appear in chapter seven) falls on the two broad groups of people within his purview: "There will be tribulation and distress upon every human being who does evil, the Judean first and also the Greek; but glory and honor and peace on everyone who does good, the Judean first, but also the Greek. For there is no partiality (προσωπολημψία) with God" (2:9-11).

The impartiality of God is prominent here, as Jouette Bassler has argued, but not just as a "theological axiom," as she would have it.[50] For God's impartiality is an integral component of Paul's presentation of the conditions under which two ethnic subgroups well used to conflict with one another could be made to realize that their common plight had only one solution—a new ingroup identity based on faith and righteousness. For a Judean to say that there was no προσωπολημψία with God, when Israel was built on precisely the opposite belief—that through divine election Israel had become God's own people—was a truly momentous step that had been taken as soon as the Christ-movement admitted the first non-Judeans and shared eucharistic table fellowship with them. The significance of this step can be seen by comparison with the story of Peter's conversion of Cornelius, the first non-Judean convert according to Acts, where the lesson that Peter draws from what he has experienced is this: "In truth I understand that God is not partial (προσωπολήμπτης), but that in every people (ἔθνος) he who fears him and practices righteousness is acceptable to him" (Acts 10:34-35). Here again we see that divine impartiality is not just a "theological axiom," but has profound social implications for Israel's boundaries with other peoples and for the new group of Christ-followers that straddles those boundaries.

Having laid down the basic differentiation of ethnicity ("Judean" and "Greek"), Paul now proceeds to that dimension of the differences between the two in relation to the Mosaic law: "Those who have sinned in the absence of the law (ἀνόμως) will also perish in the absence of the law (ἀνόμως); and those who have sinned under the law (ἐν νόμῳ) will be judged by the law" (2:12). Here Paul expresses their equal liability to be punished for their sins, whether they have law (Judeans) or not (Greeks). Those who have sinned in the absence of law (ἀνόμως) are the people castigated in 1:19-32; those who have sinned under the law (ἐν νόμῳ) will be described in 2:17-24. Yet Paul ends this section on an encouraging note that does something to counterbalance his intensely negative presentation in 1:19-32. For those who will be righteous before God, he insists, are those who do the law, not just hear it, and "the heathen" (τὰ ἔθνη) not possessing the law can yet do what the law requires if it is written on their hearts, and avoid judgment (2:13-16).

The Plight of the Judeans (Rom. 2:17—3:8)
Paul next takes up the question of Judean sin. Romans 2:17 addresses the Judean, just as 2:1 addresses the non-Judean. This brief treatment, occupying vv. 17-24, parallels the much fuller account of non-Judean sin in 1:19-32. He needs to have a rough equivalence between Judeans and non-Judeans in relation to sin, yet his heart is not really in the argument. The almost comic nature of the disparity, indeed, is reinforced by the particular details Paul offers. In 1:19-32 he mentions idolatry, same-sex relations between women and between men, extreme greed, wickedness, envy, murder, rivalry and

strife, treachery, malicious slander, hatred of God, violent assault, boasting, inventiveness in evil, senselessness, and lack of mercy. These are the sins of the "heathen." In 2:17-24 he mentions theft, adultery, and (wait for it) robbing from temples (really just a variation on the first charge, which is included within the general classification of "dishonoring God by breaking the law"). These paltry few are the sins of the Judeans. It is difficult to avoid the impression that Paul's heart was not in the production of such a list, even if their commission involved breaching the law and dishonoring God. The signs of his straining to produce a Judean analogy to non-Judean sinfulness for the purpose of his argument are quite visible.

In vv. 25-29 Paul explains that honorable Judean status (which he refers to here as "circumcision") is only of use if one performs the law. If one does not, "circumcision" can become "uncircumcision." Similarly, an uncircumcised man who keeps the law will be regarded as "circumcision." Genuine "circumcision," genuine Judean status, is an inward matter, of the heart, not a matter of external appearance. This is another act of ethnic redefinition by Paul. He is working on well-established themes in Israelite tradition, such as that God looks to the inward reality, not the appearance of a person (as with David at 1 Sam. 16:7), but reusing them in the particular interests of bringing Judeans and Greeks together in the overarching identity of the Christ-movement.

Realizing that these statements may appear to have erased the reality of the divine election of Israel, Paul draws back a little to reassert the existence of Judean privileges (Rom. 3:1-8). He mentions that they have been entrusted with the oracles of God (τὰ λόγια τοῦ θεοῦ), and the fact that some of them have been faithless has not annulled the faithfulness of God. God will be true though every human being is false (vv. 1-4). This leads Paul into the difficult waters of seeking to balance human responsibility for sin with divine justice (vv. 5-8), during which he lets slip the important detail that some people are slandering him by saying he teaches that we may do evil so that good may come of it (v. 8).

Conclusion: Judeans and Greeks Are Equally under Sin (Rom. 3:9-20)

Romans 3:9-20 represents the conclusion of the section of the letter that began at 1:18. Paul summarizes the position in a manner that unambiguously points to the presence of Judeans among his intended audience:[51] "What therefore? Are we [sc. Judeans] better off? Not at all! For we have already said that Judeans and Greeks are all under sin" (3:9). This view is then supported by a catena of scriptural quotations from Ecclesiastes, Psalms, and Isaiah (vv. 10-18), beginning with the statement, "There is no one righteous, no not one" (perhaps taken from Eccl. 7:20). The concluding verses (Rom. 3:19-20) seem more attuned to Judean than non-Judean experience, since they assert that "no human being will be righteoused before God, since through the law comes knowledge of sin." What Paul means by this emerges in Romans 6–7.

Recategorization and Paul's Argument in Rom. 1:18—3:20

In 1:18—3:20 Paul presents a humanity in which everyone is in thrall to sin. This is the condition from which the righteousness that comes from God through faith provides liberation. For Paul, as a first-century Judean, "everyone" so affected means both Judeans and outgroups, whom Paul calls "foreigners" (ἔθνη) once (2:14) and "Greeks" three times (2:9, 10; 3:9). The first designation divides the world from a Judean ethnic perspective into a valued ingroup and negatively stereotyped outgroups. The second uses a word, "Greeks," which that people employed of themselves.

Those who have the requisite faith constitute a distinctive group with a distinctive identity, a unique and exalted sense of who they are, but they also carry the residue of their original identities. The way he mounts his argument indicates that Paul has realized that to inculcate his Roman addressees in the reality and status of their glorious new shared identity, he must persuade them of the inevitable sinfulness to which they are subject without it, yet do so in a way that is adapted to their entirely different social origins, non-Judean/Greek sinners not subject to the law of Moses and Judean sinners subject to that law. That is why he first deals specifically with non-Judeans and their characteristic sinfulness in 1:18—2:5, covering its nature in 1:18-32, and then with the Judeans and their sinfulness in 2:17—3:20, after offering a transitional passage (2:7-16) that stresses the impartiality of God in punishing and rewarding members of each group.

Paul's approach is in accord with the results of recent research on how best to recategorize members of two (generally antipathetic) groups into a new common ingroup identity that posits the need for each group to be roughly equal in status (here with respect to their subjection to sin) yet representing different experiences, here freedom from, or adherence to, the Mosaic law.

7

The Foundations of the New Identity
(Romans 3:21-31)

Righteousness through Faith in Jesus Christ (Rom. 3:21-26)

In 3:9-19 Paul had concluded his demonstration that all Judeans and Greeks were under sin with a catena of scriptural quotations beginning with the assertion: "No one is righteous (δίκαιος), no, not one" (3:9). It is fundamental to Paul's understanding of the solution that this position has changed with the manifestation of the "righteousness of God" and that there are people who already are, or are capable of becoming, δίκαιοι at the present time. This was suggested by the present-tense verb "is being revealed" (ἀποκαλύπτεται) predicated of God's righteousness in 1:17 but is strongly confirmed in 3:21-31.

With 3:21 we suddenly leave behind Paul's diagnosis of the sinful and unrighteous plight in which all Judeans and Greeks find themselves (3:9-10) and return to the solution he had briefly announced in 1:17, the righteousness of God, but now with several additional elements:

> But now, apart from the law, the righteousness (δικαιοσύνη) of God has been revealed as attested by the law and the prophets, the righteousness (δικαιοσύνη) of God through faith (διὰ πίστεως) in Jesus Christ (Ἰησοῦ Χριστοῦ) for all who have faith (πιστεύοντας). For there is no distinction (διαστολή), for all have sinned and fallen short of the glory of God. They are righteoused (δικαιούμενοι) by his grace as a gift through the redemption that is in Christ Jesus, whom God put forward as an expiation (ἱλαστήριον), through faith, in his blood as a demonstration of his righteousness (δικαιοσύνη) in overlooking sins previously committed, in the forbearance of God, as a demonstration of his righteousness (δικαιοσύνη) in the present time, that he is righteous (δίκαιον) and righteouses (δικαιοῦντα) a person through faith in Jesus. (3:21-26)

While this is an extremely rich and concentrated statement with numerous theological, moral, and social implications, it has three clusters of interest: a righteous God, the expiatory role of Jesus Christ, and sinful human beings who are now able to be righteoused through faith in Jesus Christ.

In his very first words (v. 21) Paul states that "But now" (Νυνὶ δέ) God's righteousness "has been revealed" (where the perfect tense πεφανέρωται represents a condition recently begun and continuing) and a little later adds that it has been demonstrated "in the present time" (ἐν τῷ νῦν καιρῷ, 3:26). Fitzmyer speaks of these two expressions as signifying the eschatological "now,"[1] but this notion (like most discussions of any word with as high a coefficient of elasticity as "eschatology," as I explain in chapter eleven) is not particularly helpful. More fundamentally Paul is speaking about the *actual* present. The human condition has changed *now;* people can and do become righteous (δίκαιος) *now.* The righteousness language in this passage covers three words beginning with δικ-: the noun δικαιοσύνη, the adjective/noun δίκαιος, and the verb δικαιόω. I have employed above a useful neologism of E. P. Sanders,[2] "to righteous," to translate the present participle δικαιοῦντα in a way that brings out the paronymic connection between the three words involved (δίκαιος, δικαιοσύνη, and δικαιόω) and will continue to use it throughout this volume in relation to the verb δικαιόω.

We must not forget that God is the agent of this transformation. This is clear in Paul's use of the verb δικαιόω, although we must exercise care in its interpretation. In 3:26 Paul makes clear that the demonstration of the righteousness of God involves both God's being righteous (δίκαιος) and also "righteousing" the one who has faith in Jesus, where "righteousing" translates the present participle of the verb δικαιόω. The point of this is that God's action in "righteousing" a person and that person's achieving righteousness, or becoming righteous, occur in the present. The use of the verb δικαίοω to express this phenomenon appears again later in the letter when Paul asserts that "since we are righteoused (δικαιωθέντες) by faith, we have peace with God through our Lord Jesus Christ" (5:1), and also refers to our "being righteoused (δικαιωθέντες) now by his blood" (5: 9). The aorist passive participles in both statements refer to a present state of being righteous brought about by having been righteoused (by God) at a point in the past.

I have also translated the two words referring to faith in the passage in a way that brings out their connection in the Greek by using "faith" for the noun πίστις and "to have faith" for the verb πιστεύω. In an important, although perhaps neglected, work titled *Glaube als Teilhabe* ("Faith as Participation"), Axel von Dobbeler has made a valuable contribution to the meaning of πίστις in the Pauline corpus.[3] In opposition to an intellectualizing understanding of faith that sees it as a holding fast to the truth or as a new self-understanding, von Dobbeler seeks to characterize faith as a comprehensive interpersonal occurrence encompassing two broad and inseparable dimensions: access to God and entry to the community. For von Dobbeler, faith has a powerfully social character. It permits access to God only via entry into the communal relationship of the congregation, not on an individual basis.

Faith in Jesus Christ

One further aspect of the translation requires some comment, which picks up the connection of this kind of faith with Christ. In this passage "faith" is linked first to Jesus Christ (v. 22), then to Jesus (v. 26), both in the genitive case. The traditional interpretation of these expressions, which is still dominant in Great Britain and Europe, ably championed by J. D. G. Dunn,[4] is that they are objective genitives and carry the meaning, as in the translation above, of "faith in Jesus Christ" and "faith in Jesus." On this view Jesus/Jesus Christ is the object of faith. Since the 1980s, however, a different interpretation, that the genitives are subjective, meaning "the faith of Jesus Christ" and "the faith of Jesus," has become popular in North America, where it may now well be the majority view; on this interpretation Jesus/Jesus Christ becomes the model of faith.[5] An important stimulus for this approach has been Richard B. Hays's 1983 book, *The Faith of Jesus Christ*. A central feature of this work is the argument that underlying this formula is a Pauline "narrative," never fully presented by Paul, but which Hays has been able to reconstruct and use as the basis for the subjective interpretation. Other North American scholars who have favored the subjective view include Luke Timothy Johnson and Sam K. Williams.[6]

While a full review of this much-discussed topic is beyond the scope of this volume, my view in short is that the argument for the subjective reading is so weak as to qualify as one of the "emperor has no clothes" variety. I mention here what I regard as the insuperable exegetical obstacle to its acceptance, although I also consider that this interpretation simply does not work in the context of the seven places in Paul's letters where the phrase appears.[7] If the notion of the "faith of Jesus Christ" did figure in Paul's thinking, if it was an element in some basic narrative (which, unfortunately, he has nowhere fully disclosed in his correspondence), we would expect that Christ would also appear as the subject of the verb πιστεύω or as designated by the epithet πιστός. Yet even though the verb appears forty-one times in the Pauline letters and the epithet nine times, Jesus is never the subject of the verb and is never described as πιστός, as Thomas Tobin has pointed out.[8] On the other hand, the expression "we put faith in Christ Jesus" (εἰς Χριστὸν Ἰησοῦν ἐπιστεύσαμεν) occurs in Gal. 2:16, which also contains the phrases πίστεως Ἰησοῦ Χριστοῦ and πίστεως Χριστοῦ.[9] Galatians 3:26 has the phrase "faith in Christ Jesus" (πίστις ἐν Χριστῷ Ἰησοῦ). The use of the verb πιστεύω with a pronoun clearly referring to Christ as its object occurs in Rom. 9:33 and 10:11.

As for Hays's use of a putative Pauline narrative to support his position, it is regrettable that the worrying precedent of Rudolf Bultmann's (ultimately unsuccessful) postulation of a gnostic redeemer myth to explain the central ideas of the Fourth Gospel did not alert Hays to the danger of letting one's exegesis be guided by a hypothetical source or narrative of one's own devising, especially when data of the sort just cited pointed unerringly in the opposite direction.

Yet this is an issue that also has serious theological implications. Hays has recently canvassed a selection of these and suggests that "some opposition" to the subjective interpretation "may be rooted in an implicitly docetic Christology."[10] In other words, he surmises that some of those who regard the phrase πίστις Χριστοῦ as meaning "faith in Christ" and not "the faith of Christ" may not believe in the humanity of Christ. But it is difficult to read Paul and not be convinced of his belief in the real humanity of Christ, not only because of statements like those at Gal. 4:4-5, Rom. 1:3-4, and Phil. 2:6-8 or because of his death on the cross (as mentioned by Hays), but also because Paul's theology of Christ as a second Adam (Rom. 5:12-19) depends totally on his humanity. Hays does not cite any scholarship that entertains a docetic reading of Paul's understanding of Christ, and it is hard to see how this would be possible; Hays has invented a straw opposition. Those who prefer the phrase to refer to Christ as the object of faith know that this cannot be at the expense of his humanity.

Indeed, it is the subjective interpretation that is theologically problematic. I illustrate with a quotation from Sam K. Williams, a proponent of the subjective view who takes it to its logical conclusion: "Christian-faith is Christ-faith, that relationship to God which Christ exemplified, that life-stance which he actualized and which, because he lived and died, now characterizes the personal experience of everyone who lives in him. Christ is not the 'object' of such faith, however, but rather its supreme exemplar—indeed its creator."[11] This view is maintained in spite of the data mentioned above, including the phrase "faith in Christ Jesus" (πίστις ἐν Χριστῷ Ἰησοῦ) of Gal. 3:26. In relation to Williams's views (and having quoted this very passage), Hays states that he considers that they have "considerable heuristic power," and that although he differs in some respects from Williams, "this is a matter of emphasis rather than substantial disagreement."[12] The question here is how to assess the opinion of Williams (with which Hays thus does not substantially disagree) that Christ is not the object of Christian faith. My concern is that such a reduction in the status of Christ is arguably a movement in a proto-Arian direction, in that this position is far more comfortable with Christ as a creature rather than as the creator.[13]

This is not to suggest for one moment that Williams or Hays (or any other supporter of the subjective view) is proto-Arian, or that it would matter if he or she were, given the number of committed Christians who today subscribe to that position or for other reasons reject the notion of the divinity of Christ. My point is simply that we should be alert to the theological implications of the subjective view stated in this form. After all, part of the challenge posed to Chalcedonian orthodoxy by those who question its teaching on the incarnation of Christ[14] is a similar stress on the role of Christ as a model or exemplar of Christian faith, even if God is also seen to be acting in him.[15] While we are free to regard Jesus Christ as divine in accordance with the early councils (my position) or not, we should recognize that opposing Christ as the object of faith pushes one's view in the latter direction. At the same time, however, the persuasive research by Richard Bauckham into Paul's "early high Christology" (mentioned in chapter one above) reveals the extent to which Jesus Christ is included in the identity of God, typically in that what is said of God is also said of him. This conclusion obviously accords with, indeed necessitates, Christ as the object of faith. Bauckham sees Paul as presenting a view of the divine status of Jesus Christ based on the Israelite personalist understanding of God that was later largely replicated by the councils of the church, especially Chalcedon (451 CE), using the resources of Greek philosophy.

Lastly, the curious popularity of the subjective interpretation of πίστις Χριστοῦ in North America may lie in the residual legacy of liberal Christianity, stronger than Karl Barth's influence could budge, which stressed Jesus as the model of Christian life. Perhaps in North America there is a tendency to see Jesus as our "buddy" rather than as the triumphant Lord. Empirical evidence for the prevalence of such a low Christology (Jesusology?) exists in the immense popularity of the Christian pastoral text *In His Steps: "What Would Jesus Do?"*[16] The readers of this book (still achieving healthy sales) are urged to put themselves in Jesus' place when faced with a moral or practical dilemma. This would be an area for interesting research into the North American sociology of religion.

The Meaning of Righteousness in Current Discussion

The righteousness now available to sinners whatever their ethnic background has become so through the shedding of Christ's blood acting as an "expiation." This is the commonly accepted translation for ἱλαστήριον, which is directed to sinners and refers to the removing of sin and guilt. The notion of "expiation" is preferable to "propitiation," which denotes the placating of an angry God, even if some element of propitiation cannot be ruled out entirely here. Elsewhere Paul says that Christ "died for us" (1 Thess. 5:10), "died for our sins" (1 Cor. 15:3), and died to reconcile us to God (Rom. 5:6-10). It is difficult to determine precisely how Paul understood the redemptive function of Christ's death on a cross. John Ziesler has made the following suggestion on this point: "Paul may have seen the death of Christ as the divinely provided way, in the new Christian scheme of salvation, to deal with sin and its effects, *without trying to rationalize how it worked beyond seeing God himself as its effective agent.*"[17] This is a good route to take. While Paul regarded the redeeming death of Christ as the foundation for the new dispensation, he was far less interested in probing its ontological nature than in exploring its consequences for those who came to faith in him (in the broad sense just described). In terms of group identity, I conclude that the death of Christ within God's overall plan for human beings was the occurrence that enabled the existence of the group, but that Paul focuses on its ongoing life. Righteousness was central to this, and we thus enter the territory of his understanding of this subject.

This has been a region so fought over in exegetical and theological discussion these last five centuries that no interpreter can cross the border without feelings of considerable trepidation. However, that two denominations long at odds on the character of righteousness in Paul, Lutheranism and Roman Catholicism, have reached considerable agreement on the matter has fortunately produced a much more peaceful discussion.[18] As I have set out my views on the subject in relation to Galatians,[19] I will make some general introductory remarks and develop my perspective in exposition of the text.

Luther argued that when we have faith in Christ, God accounts us righteous, so that we thereby obtain remission of our sins. Sin is still present in us, but God disregards it, or prevents it being imputed to us for Christ's sake. The core of his approach to righteousness is thus encapsulated in the phrase *simul justus et peccator:* the Christian is at the same time justified and a sinner. The Lutheran view thus generated a two-pronged approach to righteousness that still carries enormous influence.

First, God declares a sinner righteous, or "acquits" him or her, in what is generally seen as a judicial context (usually the Last Judgment). The verb used by Paul is δικαιόω, and Käsemann explained this interpretation as follows (echoing rather similar views of Bultmann earlier): "What is meant is pronouncing righteous. This is an eschatological act of the Judge at the last day which takes place proleptically in the present."[20] He considered that this aspect was strengthened by the "reckoning formula"—a reference to the phrase used of Abraham in Gen. 15:6 and prominent in Romans 4: "and it was reckoned (ἐλογίσθη) to him as righteousness."

Second, there is the separate issue of how the person thus pronounced righteous in anticipation of the Last Judgment should behave. Luther thought there need be no change of behavior, but this view has subsequently been modified in Lutheran circles. Thus Käsemann acknowledged that history-of-religions research "has shown irrefutably that δικαιοῦσθαι has also the sense of effectively making righteous as in 3:24 and as Roman Catholicism has constantly maintained."[21] But this principled concession by Käsemann necessitates the difficult task of reconciling what he calls the "declaratory" (or "forensic"—"judicial"?)[22] element with the fact that God really makes the person righteous.[23] This was the issue with which Ziesler valiantly grappled in 1972. He proposed that the verb δικαιόω had for Paul a "declaratory," "forensic," or "relational" meaning, while the noun δικαιοσύνη and the adjective δίκαιοι had "behavioral" or "ethical" meanings and embodied that truth that righteousness involved a real change of behavior. Christians were both justified by faith (acquitted, restored to fellowship)—the "forensic" or "relational" sense—and righteous by faith (leading a new life in Christ)—the "ethical" sense.[24]

One element of this explanation can be immediately excluded: that the action of God in righteousing a sinner is "an eschatological act of the Judge at the last day which takes place proleptically in the present." As we have just seen in relation to Romans 2, Paul certainly believed there would be a *future* day of anger and of revelation of the right judgment (δικαιοκρισία) of God (2:5), a day when God would judge (at least some) human beings "by Jesus Christ" (2:16). But the idea that this judgment occurs proleptically when a person is righteoused is entirely alien to his thought.[25] Not only does it have no positive textual support, but it is contradicted by what Paul says in 5:9-11. For while these verses affirm that a person who is now righteoused and reconciled to God by Christ's blood and death will stand a better chance at the end—of being saved from "the wrath" (sc. of God at the End)—they also make clear that righteousness and final judgment are distinct. Those who believe in Christ still have to face the events of the day of wrath; they have not done so already in anticipation through attaining righteousness. For Paul righteousness and reconciliation (5:11) begin in the present period. Further support for Paul's not linking the final events with righteousness comes from 1 Thessalonians, a letter with a strong assertion of the coming expression of God's anger (1 Thess. 1:10; 5:9) but no mention of righteousness. It is true that Paul does not specify exactly how God achieves this change of status gratuitously given. But that is no reason to introduce notions drawn from the Last Judgment that would distract us from righteousness being a present reality. Paul is not troubled by this question because what matters for him is not the precise divine mechanism involved but the changed condition of human beings before God that results.

Yet a far more fundamental objection emerges to the notion that in Romans Paul is proposing that God righteouses a sinner now in anticipation of an act of judgment on the last day if we seek to reconcile what he says here with a difficult passage in 8:33-34 that may refer to the day of wrath. This is the possibility that *Paul envisages no judgment for the righteous on the last day, only judgment for the wicked.* There is no doubt that Paul considered that on this occasion God would allocate to each according to his or her works (2:6), with glory and eternal life for some and wrath for the wicked (2:8). This will occur before the dais (βῆμα) of God (14:10), or the dais of Christ (2 Cor. 5:10). Everyone will have to give an account of him- or herself before God (Rom. 14:12) and receive good or evil depending on what he or she has done in life (2 Cor. 5:10). Yet a judgment requires that someone lay a charge, and I argue in chapter eleven below that Rom. 8:33 implies there is no such person as far as the righteous Christ-follower is concerned. Similarly, Paul implies in 8:34 that the elect will not be condemned, because Christ will intercede to prevent that happening. Thus the "righteous judgment" (δικαιοκρισία) of 2:5 apparently refers only to the wicked; there is no judgment for those who have attained the status of righteous in this life, because God has righteoused them. They will appear "righteous before God" (δίκαιοι παρὰ [τῷ] θεῷ), "they will be righteous" (δικαιωθήσονται), as he says in 2:13, they will give an account of themselves and will receive their reward. They are not judged, but rather are simply waved through. This view is compatible with the vision of the end in Malachi (3:16—4:3), where God distinguishes between the righteous and spares them (meaning no judgment?) but destroys the wicked (meaning they are judged, condemned, and punished).

I must now set out a defense of the translation "they will be righteous" for δικαιωθήσονται and generally consider the role that the verb δικαιόω has had in the discussion. It is worth noting initially that in the Septuagint δικαιόω is not applied to the action of God in his anger and judgment at the end.[26] But more than this, the extent to which it conveys a "forensic" sense in connection with the activity of God has been seriously exaggerated. Frank Matera expresses a widely held view (in relation to Galatians), "In the LXX *dikaioun* is primarily a forensic term, and it is the legal and forensic sense which Paul adopts: God acquits the sinner, God declares a person to be just."[27] As just noted, there is much doubt whether in Romans Paul does consider that the righteous will experience judgment, as opposed to their preexisting status simply achieving the rewards it deserves.

In addition, however, an analysis of the usage of δικαιόω in the Septuagint and in Paul (in Galatians and Romans) falsifies the view represented by Matera, as Lagrange argued in relation to the Pauline letters long ago and as I have proposed in relation to Galatians.[28] The Septuagint uses δικαιόω literally only eight times in relation to a judicial setting, seven of them involving human judges and one of "gods" who judge.[29] In many of these the word does not mean "acquit" but "find in favor of," sometimes in relation to corrupt judges who enter a verdict on the basis of bribes from the rich who are mistreating the poor where entitlement to property (not criminal culpability) is at issue.[30] At the same time, in many other instances δικαιόω refers to the announcement or demonstration of a person's status as righteous or otherwise where there is no judicial setting.[31] In particular, Sirach has a series of occurrences where the verb appears (often in the passive voice) simply with the meaning of "be righteous" or "become righteous,"[32] as Lagrange pointed out.[33] This view finds confirmation in Rom. 2:13, where Paul equates being δίκαιοι before God and the future passive of the verb δικαιόω. On occasion, the verb is used with respect to how God will be regarded by human beings; there is clearly no judicial aspect here, for God is not judged.[34] The point is that God is righteous and is the source of righteousness. Accordingly, when we turn to the (comparatively small number of) instances that do speak of God as the subject of the verb, it is a mistake automatically to introduce the judicial sense of "acquittal."[35] While these cases nearly always involve God's righteous acknowledgment of a person's status as righteous or otherwise, such declarations do not necessarily carry any judicial connotation.[36]

One further problem with the distinction between a "declaratory," "judicial," or "relational" meaning and a "behavioral" or "ethical" meaning is that it is probably anachronistic for the first century CE, since it rests on the assumption that "ethical" behavior occurs independently of its recognition or acknowledgment by others. But this is arguably a modern view, based on the generation in the last two centuries of universalist ethics, typically built on Kantian or utilitarian foundations, which transcend the values of any particular group. But in group-oriented cultures such as those of the ancient Mediterranean the position was very different, since qualities were possessed by persons to the extent that they were attributed to them by a particular group. In that context to declare righteous and to make righteous were essentially one and the same.[37]

The Meaning of "Righteousness" for Paul

What, then, does Paul mean by "righteousness" in this passage and elsewhere in Romans? While the topic is important, we should not overstate its significance. In 1 Thessalonians, a letter rich in Pauline conceptions, the language of righteousness is not only entirely absent, but at 5:8 Paul redacts out of his scriptural source a reference to righteousness. This phenomenon is explicable on the basis that 1 Thessalonians was written to a congregation consisting entirely of non-Judeans, ex-idolaters in fact (1:9). Paul employs "righteousness" when he is writing to a mixed group of Judeans (for whom, as we will see, it was central to their identity) and non-Judeans where the question of the Mosaic law is inevitably a pressing one and where there is tension between the two subgroups.[38] In Romans, indeed, as Robert Morgan has noted, righteousness almost disappears in chaps. 6–8. Morgan attributes this to Paul's not citing much scripture in this section,[39] but a better explanation is that in these chapters Paul is setting forth details of his letter relevant more to the common ingroup identity of the Christ-movement than to the precise issue of the relations of Judean and non-Judean members to one another. But as Morgan rightly notes, "That conclusion need not devalue this particular part of Paul's language which has been found to have a wider applicability than he probably intended."[40]

It is worth considering the meaning of "righteousness" in Galatians for the light it may shed here and on other "righteousness" discourse in this letter. Elsewhere I have argued against currently popular covenantal or judicial interpretations of righteousness in Galatians and suggested instead that for first-century Israelites it essentially encapsulated the privileged and blessed identity that came from being an Israelite, an identity that Paul seeks to reapply to the members of Christ-following groups in Galatia.[41] In considering the Israelite context for righteousness relevant to Galatians, I first examined the manner in which the *Letter of Aristeas* used righteousness to differentiate Israelite identity from that of idolatrous ethnic outgroups. Later I assessed the evidence from Israelite scripture bearing on the meaning of righteousness.[42] A central plank of my argument was to offer a unified understanding of the main "righteousness" expressions, with the adjective/substantive δίκαιος (Gal. 3:11) providing the fundamental clue and meaning "the privileged and blessed Christ-follower," the verb δικαιοῦν (Gal. 2:16 [thrice], 17; 3:8, 11, 24; 5:4) meaning "to be or become righteous," and the noun δικαιοσύνη (Gal. 2:21; 3:6, 21; 5:5) meaning "the state of being δίκαιος."

Without foreclosing the results of discussion of later sections of Romans where righteousness is covered in detail, nothing precludes such an understanding as appropriate for Rom. 1:16-17, and I proceed on this basis. That Paul includes in one verse (1:17) both the δικαιοσύνη of God and a reference to a man who is δίκαιος (quoting Hab. 2:4) provides some comfort in taking this route, in view of the likelihood that the notion of "being (or becoming) δίκαιος," rather than being subject to some kind of end-time judicial proceeding allegedly evoked by the verbal form δικαιοῦν, constitutes the core of Paul's thought in this area.[43]

Apart from the meaning of "righteousness," the other issue requiring immediate attention is how we should interpret the close connection between righteousness in Rom. 1:17 and godlessness and unrighteousness in v. 18. Both subjects may be examined in relation to the context of Israelite scripture.

My understanding of righteousness language in Galatians derives largely from two parts of the Septuagint revealing the greatest concentration of instances of δίκαιοι and both representing the wisdom tradition—Proverbs 10–15 and Psalm 36 (LXX), and further consideration of this material may help explain the relationship between Rom. 1:16-17 and 1:18.

Both Proverbs 10–15 and Psalm 36 (LXX) concretely illustrate the meaning of "righteousness" (δικαιοσύνη)[44] by offering numerous antitheses that contrast the happy and blissful identity of the δίκαιοι with the wretched and doomed identity of the ἀσεβής, the godless and impious person (Proverbs 10–15), or the sinner (ἁμαρτωλός, Psalm 36). For example, "The memory of the righteous (δίκαιοι) is praised, but the name of the godless (ἀσεβής) person is extinguished" (Prov. 10:7); or, again, "For the arms of sinners (ἁμαρτωλόι) shall be broken, but the Lord supports the righteous (δίκαιοι)" (Ps. 36:17 LXX).

On eight occasions in Proverbs 10–15 the words ἀδικία or ἄδικος appear as antonyms to the identity represented by δικαιοσύνη and δίκαιοι, either in close conjunction with ἀσεβής or ἀσέβεια or in substitution for them. Examples of close conjunction are: "Righteousness (δικαιοσύνη) traces out blameless paths, but godlessness (ἀσέβεια) encounters ἀδικία" (Prov. 1:5 LXX), and "God is far from the godless (ἀσεβεῖς), but he listens to the prayers of the righteous (δίκαιοι); better is a small return with righteousness (δικαιοσύνη) than abundant fruits with ἀδικία" (Prov. 15:29 LXX). Examples of ἄδικος occurring with ἀσεβής appear at Prov. 11:18; 12:21; and 13:5. Examples of ἄδικος providing the antithesis to δίκαιος instead of ἀσεβής are found at Prov. 10:31; 12:17; and 13:23.

It is important to note that Proverbs 10–15 contains the greatest concentration of δίκαιος and ἀσεβής in the Greek Old Testament. Thus, of some 375 examples of δίκαιος, 100 are found in Proverbs, with a full 50 of these in Proverbs 10–15, while 50 of the 240 examples of ἀσεβής also occur in Proverbs 10–15.[45] No other sections of the Septuagint approach such an intensity of use, apart from Psalm 36 (LXX). The other words related to ἀσεβής occur far less frequently, with ἀσέβεια ("godlessness") appearing some 75 times and ἀσεβεῖν ("to be godless") some 40 times. Both of these latter words are scattered fairly evenly across the Septuagint, except that Ezekiel has some 18 occurrences of ἀσέβεια.

In some other places in the Septuagint δικαιοσύνη, ἀσέβεια, and ἀδικία (or their paronyms) occur in close proximity. Particularly noticeable is the emblematic statement in Ps. 1:6: "For the Lord knows the way of the righteous (ὁδὸν δικαιῶν), but the way of the wicked (ὁδὸς ἀσεβῶν) will perish." Similar sentiments appear in Hos. 10:12-13; Job 36:18-19; Ps. 11:6 (LXX); and Wis. 4:16. Elsewhere ἀσέβεια and ἀδικία (or their paronyms) occur near one another, as in Deut. 19:16; Job 10:3; Ps. 73:6 (LXX); Ezek. 18:30; 21:24; and Bar. 2:12. But all of these are very short, unique statements, and nothing in any of these cases matches the sustained contrasting of righteousness and godlessness that occupies Proverbs 10–15.

This means that if one were looking to Israelite scripture for detailed information as to the meaning of δικαιοσύνη in relation to antonyms specified as ἀσέβεια and ἀδικία, that is, if one were seeking to identify a rich biblical context for such a pattern of meaning, Proverbs 10–15 is the obvious location, even though the Sodom material in Genesis provides a particular instance of the pattern, as we have seen in chapter six above.

In Rom. 1:16-17 we have an assertion of δικαιοσύνη (albeit this time of the sort characterizing the Christ-movement) in relation to ἀσέβεια and ἀδικία very similar to that found in Proverbs 10–15 and nowhere else in such detail in scripture. This both corroborates my earlier use of this material to interpret the nature of righteousness in Galatians and also further strengthens the notion that the same understanding of righteousness prevails in Romans.

Most commentators entirely miss the reference to Proverbs 10–15 in Rom. 1:18. Fitzmyer at least cites the linking of ἀσέβεια and ἀδικία in Prov. 11:5 (LXX) to support his view that in Rom. 1:18 this pair of words forms a hendiadys that sums up "the total sinfulness and rampant unrighteousness of pagan humanity,"[46] but this does not go nearly far enough. Proverbs 10–15 bears upon Rom. 1:17-18 and then 1:19-32 in a manner that is both consistent with Paul's previous use of righteousness language in Galatians and also fundamentally important to what he is seeking to convey in this section of the letter. Above all, the expression "all impiety (ἀσέβεια) and unrighteousness (ἀδικία) of human beings," used in v. 18 to introduce the cognitive, moral, and social pathologies in vv. 19-32, evokes the whole nasty world of the impious and unrighteous person so thoroughly denigrated in Proverbs 10–15.

As already noted, in discussing Paul's understanding of righteousness in Galatians, I proposed the significance of the antithetical sayings in Proverbs 10–15 and also suggested that it would have been natural for first-century Israelites to interpret the impious and unrighteous persons mentioned there as non-Israelites, given that Israelites regarded righteousness as the brightest badge of their identity as worshipers of the one true God. This means that scriptural texts that could have been applied to faithless Israelites were brought into service in negatively stereotyping non-Israelite outsiders. Paul provides an example of such interpretation since he proceeds from the general description in Rom. 1:18 to describe persons who do not have the Mosaic law and who are idolatrous (1:19-23), bringing into play, as we have seen, a further area of imagery for that purpose—the Israelite traditions concerning Sodom.

In terms of Mediterranean culture, "righteousness" as Paul describes it is a form of ascribed honor, that is, an honor gifted (cf. δωρεάν in 3:24) to someone by a notable person of authority, in this case God, as an exercise of will and choice by that person, not because the recipient of the honor has done anything to deserve it.[47] Thus the passive form of the verb, "to be (or 'to have been') righteoused," implies God as the agent, but since it designates an ascribed status, one can generally translate it "to be righteous." This phenomenon is evident in 3:24, where Paul says of those who sinned that "they are righteous as a gift (δωρεάν) by his grace through the redemption that is in Christ Jesus." Here "are righteous" (literally "are righteoused") translates δικαιούμενοι, the present passive participle of δικαιόω.

Yet righteousness already had a particular meaning within Israelite tradition. It was regarded as one of the most positive features of Israelite identity, especially in relation to outgroups perceived to be unrighteous, as I have argued elsewhere.[48] In the fullest exposition in their scriptures of what it meant to be δίκαιος, in Proverbs 10–15, the characteristics attributed to such people do not define them or specify what they are like in any functional sense, but rather commend them as possessing a desirable set of qualities and a bright destiny. Their existence is connected especially with life and blessing.[49] In short, Israelites saw righteousness as a central ingredient of their identity. In terms of Tajfel's understanding of the three dimensions of group identity, righteousness: (1) said something to Israelites about the substance of that identity (the cognitive dimension); (2) made them feel good about belonging to it (the emotional dimension); and (3) gave them a criterion against which to make negative judgments concerning outgroups (the evaluative dimension).

When writing previously to his congregations in Galatians, Paul had accepted the value of righteousness but had sought to redefine it and transfer it from Israel to his version of the Christ-movement that embraced Judeans and non-Judeans. Righteousness would still describe a privileged identity, equivalent to life and blessing, but now faith in Christ crucified would be the source of that life and the experience of the Spirit the primary content of the blessing.[50] It was by no means inevitable that Paul would despoil Israelite identity in this way. After all, when he was writing to a solely non-Judean audience of one-time idol worshipers in Thessalonika (1 Thess. 1:9), he did not employ righteousness language—at one point even redacting a passage from Isaiah to remove the word "righteousness"—and instead used the language of sanctification to express the heart of their identity. But righteousness language was necessary for Paul whenever he was writing to a mixed audience of Judeans and non-Judeans. This had been the case in Galatia and it was also true of Rome.

Righteousness language was a way Judeans had of understanding themselves that Paul reappropriated to cover Judeans and non-Judeans in a congregation of Christ-followers. It was a means of recategorizing both subgroups within the new group in relation to a prize of belonging. But for Paul to portray righteousness as produced within the congregations of Christ-followers for whoever had faith in Christ, Judean or non-Judean, represented a radical reinterpretation of the traditions of Israel in a way that would inevitably be contested by those who did not join the movement. The signs of that contestation are clear in relation to the figure of Abraham in Galatians and Romans 4, as considered in chapter eight below.

Implications for Judeans of Non-Judean Righteousness (Rom. 3:27-31)

At 3:27 Paul begins to explore the implications of what he has just said for Judeans. "Where, therefore, is the claim to honor? It is excluded." Paul is referring to Judean honor-claims, mentioned earlier in 2:17 and 23. "Boasting," typically used of these expressions, is a bad translation for the words in question, the noun καύχησις (3:27), the verb καυχάομαι (2:17, 23), and the word for a single honor-claim used later, καύχημα (4:2). In North American and northern European societies "boasting" always has a negative connotation, but in the honor cultures of the ancient Mediterranean the practice covered by these words meant the acceptable practice of publicly making claims in relation to one's honor, a phenomenon that could be seen in numerous inscriptions in any city or large town. This was not unacceptable per se, only if there was no genuine foundation for the claims, in which case the person making them would appear foolish. The Judeans had been claiming honor for themselves on the strength of their relationship to God (2:17) and their possession of the Mosaic law (2:23). This was a natural expression of Judean ethnic pride. The making of this claim to honor has nothing to do with the self-confidence of "the religious person" overly proud of his achievements, as Käsemann (and others) has suggested.[51]

The reason that the claim can now no longer be made rests in the "law of faith." This is a bold expression, and one should not make too much of the word "law" here, since Paul is just setting up a sharp juxtaposition with the phrase "the law of works." His point is that the arrival of faith on the scene has pulled the rug from under Judean claims to be privileged on account of their possession of the law, for that is no longer (as Judeans had long thought it to be) the source of righteousness.

This is shown by the way Paul continues: "For we consider that a human being is righteous[52] by faith apart from the law." As a defense of this statement, which Judeans would inevitably have interpreted as an attack on the very foundations of their ethnic identity, Paul turns to "theology," in the first sense of that term outlined in chapter one above: "the sum of the beliefs held by an individual or group regarding matters of religious faith or of ultimate concern: the ideational element in religion." He propounds one of the most important theological statements in the letter: "Or is he God of Judeans only? Is he not also (God) of foreigners? Yes, also of foreigners, since God is one who will righteous the circumcision through faith and the uncircumcision through faith" (3:29-30).

Here Paul appeals to the fundamental Judean belief in monotheism, paradigmatically expressed in Deut. 6:4, to legitimate (that is, to justify and explain) his claim that righteousness through faith comes to Judeans and non-Judeans. Paul proposes that God's equal treatment of both groups depends on his nature as one. It is a daring claim; the long history of Israelite monotheism had always coexisted with a belief in the election of Israel and their superiority over the idolatrous peoples in their environment. Among Israelites the question about God had not been theoretical but practical in nature.[53] In particular, it had been grounded in the reality of groups in conflict where the issue at stake was which group had the strongest claim to be God's people, and therefore to be the most honorable people and entitled to make the appropriate honor claims (as in Rom. 2:17 and 23). Now Paul challenges the collective memory of his own people in an area long central to their identity. Any proposal that lessened the honor of Israel by denying that they alone basked in the glow of God's election, such as Paul is clearly making in 3:29-30, inevitably tended to provoke arguments about the trustworthiness of God.[54]

As Moxnes has pointed out, here Paul begins with the foundational theological view, that God is one, and draws from it a conclusion with which most Judeans contemporary with him would have disagreed—that God will righteous both Judeans and non-Judeans through faith.[55] The unitary nature of God is demonstrated in his righteousing by the same means those who were historically the chosen people and also all other ethnic groups. How do we separate the social from the theological here? Or how deny that in such a context social-scientific ideas able to cast new light on the issue of group relations are also likely to assist in understanding its more specifically theological dimensions?

Yet this leaves an obvious and difficult question for Paul. If Judeans and non-Judeans are righteoused by faith and this reflects the unitary nature of God, where does that leave the Mosaic law, which had been the means whereby Israel demonstrated its unique status among all peoples and also maintained boundaries to keep them at a safe distance? Paul rushes in to allay Judean fears on this score (and here we see the extent to which he envisages that Judeans will be among the people who hear the letter): "Do we therefore destroy the law through faith? Emphatically not! On the contrary, we establish the law" (3:31). Yet mere assertion is not proof, and it will be difficult for Paul to demonstrate the truth of what he says. Indeed, we will see a far more negative view of the law as the letter proceeds (especially in Romans 7). For the moment, however, he has at least offered some response to this problem, and he is able to move on to a demonstration of the accuracy of his view that faith brings righteousness for Judean and non-Judean by reinterpreting one of the most important areas of the collective memory of his people—that concerning Abraham. His means of achieving this result is the subject of chapter eight below, where the issue of the impossibility of making honor claims based on the law with which this section began (3:27) appears near the beginning of Paul's exposition (4:2).

8

Abraham as a Prototype of Group Identity
(Romans 4)

Abraham and Romans 4

The focus of Romans 4 is Abraham.[1] Chapter 4 treats a number of critical themes in the letter, such as the righteousness of God and the status of non-Judean Christ-followers, and (in so doing) looks back to 3:21-31 and forward to later sections of the letter.[2] It also contains Pauline data bearing (or at least susceptible of being brought to bear) on topics such as salvation history and the nature of Christian faith. For these reasons it has attracted much attention both from interpreters and also those interested in systematic theology.[3] Romans 4 is far from being merely, as Dodd opined, "a long digression or excursus, in which Paul illustrates and confirms his doctrine of justification 'apart from Law' by a reference to Abraham."[4] Since my main interest in this volume lies in the way Paul has recategorized conflicting groups of Judean and non-Judean Christ-followers in the distinctive context of 50s CE Rome into a new identity in Christ, that perspective determines the way I approach Romans 4. This will not, however, be to the detriment of the theological dimensions of the text.

Although Romans 4 is replete with material concerning the nature of the relationship between Judeans and non-Judeans in the Christ-movement, and thus constitutes "a far-reaching reinterpretation of the figure of Abraham with important social implications,"[5] it also contains an unusually large number of statements about God. It thus provides fertile ground for developing the insight of Halvor Moxnes, worked out in relation to Romans generally but Romans 4 in particular, that the identity of the Christ-movement and how its members understood God were inextricably linked.[6] This is part of Moxnes's larger thesis, for which we have already seen considerable evidence in Romans, in 3:29-30 especially, that for the Israelites and Christ-followers of Paul's time the question about God did not involve an "idea" or "a concept" of God, but centered on the experience of interaction between God and human beings.

I begin, then, with aspects of social identity theory particularly apposite for the unique phenomenon of Romans 4. That Paul introduces Abraham in 4:1 at all is remarkable. So far his efforts to describe the new identity in Christ have occupied only two verses in Romans 1 (vv. 16-17) and ten in Romans 3 (vv. 21-30). Rather than undertake a discursive account of this novel socioreligious category, Paul proceeds to speak of Abraham in terms of what I describe as a "prototype." Many other critics before me have applied the word "prototype" to Abraham.[7] In particular, notions of prototypicality figure prominently in Axel von Dobbeler's fine analysis of the Abraham tradition in Romans 4.[8] My approach is distinctive in offering a detailed model of what I mean by this concept, in this case derived from the social identity theory developed by Henri Tajfel and others as set out in chapter two above.

Prototypes, the Past, and Common Ingroup Identity

Running through much psychological research has been the idea that information about social categories is stored in the form of prototypes that are thought to express each category. A "prototype" is a summary representation that is considered to capture the central tendency of the category and derives from multiple experiences with category members.[9] A prototype of a group of people will be a representation of a person thought to typify the group. Such a prototype will not be a current or actual member of the group, but rather the image of an ideal person who embodies its character. On the other hand, social psychologists refer to an actual person who may embody the identity of a group as an "exemplar."[10] Debate rages as to whether observers assess group members in terms of their closeness to a prototype or to individual exemplars, but that issue need not detain us here.[11]

A prototype usually refers to how an ingroup sees itself. It is generally positive in nature and its existence does not induce ingroup members to abandon their awareness and belief that they are all distinctive individuals— the so-called ingroup heterogeneity effect. In these respects, a prototype is to be distinguished from a stereotype. Stereotypes are also social categorical judgments. But they are usually negative in character. They are directed at outgroups and serve to epitomize the convictions of the ingroup as to the identity of outgroup members. They are often accompanied by the view that the members of the outgroup are all similar to one another along the lines of the stereotype—the so-called outgroup homogeneity effect.[12]

In chapter two I discussed the suggestion of Marco Cinnirella that an important feature of the way a group understands itself is by reference to "possible social identities," meaning those identities that it believes it has had in the past or may have in the future.[13] This proposal highlights the intersection between a group's sense of itself and how it is oriented to time. Since the representation of social categories is frequently effected by the use of prototypes and exemplars, one would expect that the postulation of possible past or future social identities would also draw upon such means, and empirical evidence abundantly confirms this expectation.

Groups do frequently attach their identities to outstanding members from the past, now dead, but whose remembrance lives on among the membership. We have seen in chapter two that (within a social identity framework) a person aiming at leadership in a given context needs to be maximally representative of the shared social identity and consensual position of the group, that is, to come as close as possible to a prototype or exemplar of the group. Similarly, a figure from the past will be received as a group prototype or exemplar if he or she is regarded as having represented the group identity to the maximum extent. Thus, among the people of Great Britain, Winston Churchill fulfills such a role, his courageous yet imperturbable determination to resist Nazism during World War II constituting characteristics regarded as typically British. Within the distinction just set out, Churchill is an exemplar of Britishness, a real person (although now dead) who typifies his group. Similarly, to many people in France, Charles de Gaulle represents an exemplar of the French.

On the other hand, where a person belongs to the probably legendary past of a people, say Abraham or Roland,[14] although the group members who accept his or her real existence will regard the person as (what I am calling) an exemplar, an outside observer would employ the concept of prototype. In the figure of Arthur as "the once and future king" we have a prototype straddling the past and the future.[15] To Christians, Jesus is an exemplar who covers past, present (cf. Matt. 28:20), and future.

Cinnirella has noted that the choice of prototypes and exemplars will be affected by the temporal orientation of the ingroup.[16] It is reasonable to expect that groups originating in cultures that treasure the past—shown, for example, in the veneration of ancestors—and that are not oriented to the future in the manner typical of modern North Atlantic society will be most likely to choose as prototypes people from the past, especially actual or alleged former members. That Mediterranean culture in the first century CE was traditional in this sense is hardly to be doubted. Devotion to ancestors was widespread in all regions.[17] In addition, a good case can be made for its prevailing concepts of time being far more focused on the present and the past than on the future.[18]

To raise the question of prototypes or exemplars being selected from among outstanding former members of a group constitutes one facet of adopting an emphasis on social life as a temporal trajectory rather than as a static set of positions that (as pointed out in chapter two) represents a recent development of social identity theory. In this new perspective, as advocated by Susan Condor and Cinnirella, social life is a reality in which people take up identities, ideas, and practices and hand them on to others, often transforming them in the process.[19] People generally appreciate that the groups to which they belong are phenomena in history, stretching backward in time and reaching forward into the future. As David Carr has expressed it: "my social existence not only puts me in contact with a co-existing multiplicity of contemporaries: it connects me with a peculiar form of temporal continuity . . . which runs from predecessors to successors. This sequence extends beyond the boundaries of my life, both into the past before my birth and into the future after my death."[20]

Remembering is the process by which group members bring past persons, their predecessors or ancestors, and events into recollection in the present. They remember people or events they have personally experienced or they have learned about from others, the latter case covering phenomena occurring before they were born. Many of our memories are collective, as the increasingly influential Maurice Halbwachs argued in the period leading up to World War II; that is, they derive from the groups to which we belong.[21] Collective memory covers a range of related phenomena, including the situations in which memory is mobilized, the process by which this happens, and the contents of what is remembered.[22] Collective remembering is central to the experience of a community.[23] Even though there is no assumption that members of a group or community themselves directly participated in the past events, in cases of a group's collective memory they are likely to identify with long-dead group members, typically as when "we" recall what "our forefathers" did in distant former times.[24]

In the last decade Jan Assmann, professor of Egyptology at Heidelberg, has introduced into his discipline (under the stimulus in part of Halbwachs's ideas) the related notion of "cultural memory." This embraces two areas, that of "memory culture" *(Erinnerungskultur)* and "reference to the past" *(Vergangenheitsbezug)*. Memory culture refers to the means by which a society preserves cultural continuity by protecting its collective knowledge from one generation to the next by the use of cultural mnemonics (which includes material culture); this allows later generations to reconstruct their cultural identity. Reference to the past, on the other hand, reassures members of a society of their group identity and supplies them with an historical consciousness (that is, their sense of a unity with the past and of their own particular situation in the present) by re-creating the past.[25] Assmann's approach represents a highly creative application of the notion of collective memory, with special pertinence to cases where material culture figures in the process.[26]

Yet the past is also a lively field of social contest. In any given social context individuals and groups disagree over what people and events in the past are significant in the present and on the nature of any claimed significance. In the last week of August 2002 there was controversy at the attempt by figures in the administration of President Bush, such as Defense Secretary Donald Rumsfeld, to enlist the memory of Churchill's tough line on the Nazis to legitimate their opposition to Saddam Hussein, the Iraqi leader, with British commentators being critical of the comparison.[27] Recent collaborative work between anthropologists and historians has shown the prevalence and power of "the processing of the past" and has highlighted the worldwide struggle to control voices and texts from the past in numerous settings in order to press claims about group status and identity.[28]

As already pointed out in chapter two, these contested efforts to control the past are frequently embodied in a struggle for the possession and interpretation of collective memory.[29] The identity and status of groups and communities are often at issue in such struggles. Accordingly, we need always to consider the extent to which a person's narrative of events or significant persons in the past is not so much a window onto the cognitive workings of his or her memory but rather a description or performance designed for specific pragmatic and rhetorical purposes.[30] Since prototypes frequently feature as the means by which a group reminds itself of its identity, it is inevitable that particular efforts to maintain or reinterpret an identity with reference to the past involve the manipulation of prototypes.

I have noted above that prototypes resemble stereotypes in being judgments concerning social categories. For this reason prototypes, like stereotypes, are not rigid and immutable but can be altered to suit the realities of particular social contexts and the condition of intergroup relations in which they are used. Like all perceptions, they vary in accord with the situation of the perceiver. This means that there can be disputes over the nature and validity of prototypes within and between groups.[31]

This brings us back to what Paul is up to in Romans 4, where he canvasses the position of Abraham at some length, presenting him as what we would call a prototype (although, since he accepted Abraham's real existence, he would regard him as an exemplar). That Paul should explain the meaning of the identity that comes from God's righteousness and human faith in terms of a prototype shows how embedded he was in the group-orientation characteristic of his culture.[32] To make a point about an important phenomenon to his ingroup, he recounts at length details of the life and experience of a particular person whom he treats as prototypical of that group.

But Abraham was a figure from Israel's past, and the past is not a neutral zone but an arena for vigorous contest over the status and identity of groups. In raising Abraham, Paul immediately and consciously strides onto a battleground.

Yet this is hardly the impression one gets from a consideration of current scholarship that addresses Paul's attitude to the past. Here the focus is on his attitude to Israelite "tradition" as it became embodied in Israelite scripture. There can be no doubt that "tradition" is a useful concept in social-scientific research, as the major work on the subject by Edward Shils reveals.[33] At its heart, tradition contains a *traditum*, "anything which is transmitted or handed down from the past to present."[34] In addition, however, as Sylvia Keesmaat notes, tradition also encompasses the way in which what is handed down helps to delineate the collective identity of a group, both for insiders and outsiders. In addition, tradition is not simply "handed down" but must be continuously actualized in the life of the group.[35] The word *traditio* has come to be used of this processual dimension of tradition, the diverse ways in which the *traditum* is handed down over succeeding generations.[36] Michael Fishbane has argued that a vibrant tradition is one that not only conserves aspects of the past but is a force for innovation, being reinterpreted and revivified in new social and historical contexts.[37] Applying these ideas to Paul's letters, therefore, means investigating how Paul has reinterpreted Israelite scripture to serve the particular local needs of the groups of Christ-fearers to whom he is writing. Keesmaat has pursued this approach in her proposal for Paul's use of the Exodus tradition in Romans 8.[38]

But where in all of this is the element of contestation? Where is the recognition that, although Paul was engaged in a creative process of reinterpreting scripture, he was doing so in a context where his views were likely to be powerfully contested by other groups who realized that their connection with their past through the collective memory lodged in the texts was at stake? Fishbane offers a tantalizing glimpse of this dimension: "whatever can be known of the procedures of unstable life-circumstances—like rivalries between priestly or lay groups—also greatly contributes to a historical understanding of the living pressures within which competing groups may cite (interpreted) Scripture against each other."[39] Yet this critical insight is not much developed in the text in which it appears, nor in Keesmaat's work on Romans 8. Admittedly, Fishbane finds the information for this type of investigation largely lacking in the Old Testament,[40] but that is hardly the case with Paul. When the apostle reminded the Thessalonians that he had preached the gospel to them "amid great opposition" (ἐν πολλῷ ἀγῶνι, 1 Thess. 2:2), he could just as well have been describing his experience from the beginning of his career to its end.

This and other problems surface in Richard B. Hays's elegantly written *Echoes of Scripture in the Letters of Paul*.[41] Here too the extent to which Paul was occupied in reconstruing sacred Israelite texts in an environment of fierce competition between various groups set upon retaining the collective memories of Israel inscribed there and denying them to outgroups is largely absent. Hays adopts a literary approach to the problem. Paul now becomes a "reader" (and "misreader") of scripture who, as a writer of texts that allude to or sometimes just "echo" scriptural passages, invites consideration under the rubric of "intertextuality," meaning the analysis of the way in which fragments of an earlier text are imbedded within a later one.[42] He is especially interested in the extent to which one may discern "a field of whispered or unstated correspondences" between Paul's writing and certain scriptural passages. Hays's inspiration for this approach lies largely in studies by twentieth-century American and British literary critics into the way one literary text is related to its predecessors. Yet he denies that this discipline is anachronistic, for "within Israel as a reading community, 'all significant speech is Scriptural or Scripturally-oriented speech.'"[43]

But the notion of Israel as "a reading community" is anachronistic. Since, as Catherine Hezser has exhaustively and brilliantly demonstrated,[44] the literacy rate among Judeans in Roman Palestine was very low, perhaps as low as 3 percent, Israel was certainly not a "reading community." It was, overwhelmingly, a speaking and listening community. The sophisticated literary analysis that Hays practices on Pauline epistles and that demands intensive poring over written texts was unavailable to some 95 percent of the Judean population. It is possible, nevertheless, that the Judean elite, a small number of scribes especially, could have engaged in textual analysis, but these were not the target audiences for Paul's letters. And Hays's subtle and creative interpretations are so charged with a modern sensibility as to make it extremely unlikely that anyone in the ancient world read texts as he does.

What we need, instead of "intertextuality," are ways of understanding the social (more than literary) processes involved in Paul's reinterpretation of scripture—whereby he reconstructed Israelite collective memory in a context where he knew his results would be fiercely contested—that make sense in a context of oral and aural communication. The rest of the present chapter is aimed at making a contribution to this problem in relation to Romans 4. I first briefly explain how Abraham was prototypical for Judeans contemporary with Paul, and then discuss the controversy Paul must have stirred up by how he spoke of Abraham in his earlier letter to the Galatians. After this I investigate Abraham in Romans 4.

It is worth noting at this point, however, that there is no word in Paul's vocabulary that corresponds to "prototype" as just defined. While in 5:14 he describes Adam as the τύπος of the one who was to come, this word carries the meaning of "type" in the sense of an event or person from the *Urzeit* that provides a pattern for a phenomenon in the New Testament period,[45] an example or rule, an "advance presentation" intimating "eschatological" events.[46] In 6:17 τύπος has another meaning, closer to its etymological origin, as "the mould and norm which shapes the whole personal conduct of the one who is delivered up to it and has become obedient thereto."[47] The word can also carry the meaning of a determinative example, as at Phil. 3:17; 1 Thess. 1:7; and 1 Pet. 5:3. Thus "prototype" is a useful etic expression for which there is no emic equivalent in Paul's language.

A crucial issue in considering Abraham as a prototype in Romans 4 is the extent to which Paul uses this figure from Israel's past to recategorize the Judean and non-Judean subgroups of the Christ-movement in Rome into a new common ingroup identity. I have already noted in chapter two above that a recategorization exercise such as this is likely to succeed only where the subgroup identities are not erased in the process. The participants must not be encouraged to abandon their original (sub)group identities entirely, since if they consider that their original identities are threatened they might react strongly to preserve them, a result that can intensify animosity or bias toward members of the other (sub)group.[48] This is particularly prone to occur in a context in which the subgroup identities under threat are ethnic in nature, given that ethnic identity is often fundamental to an individual's self-concept and esteem, and are not easily abandoned.[49] A common superordinate identity is likely to be established only where subgroup identities are simultaneously permitted to retain their salience.

This question is brought into sharp focus by the approach Francis Watson takes to Abraham in Romans 4. In line with his overall view on Romans, that Paul was aiming to persuade "the Jewish Christians to recognize the legitimacy of the Gentile congregation and to join with it in worship, even though this would inevitably mean a final separation from the synagogue,"[50] Watson argues that in Romans 4 Paul reinterprets the figure of Abraham so as to deny the view that he legitimates the way of life and hope of the "Jewish community." Instead, Abraham teaches that "Jewish Christians" must recognize and unite with the "Gentile Christian congregation" and separate themselves from the "Jewish community." If Watson is correct here, it would mean that Paul was attempting the form of recategorization that social theorists suggest is doomed to failure, namely, one that advocates the abandonment of an existing ethnic identity. It would also mean that Paul's presentation of Abraham constituted evidence for the position of Daniel Boyarin that Paul sought to bring about the erasure of human difference, primarily the difference between Judean and non-Judean.[51] In the remainder of this chapter, I pay attention to how Paul's argument in relation to Abraham aligns to these views. As we will see, the evidence of Romans 4 cannot easily be reconciled with Watson's view and, at the very least, fails to offer positive support for Boyarin's.

Abraham as Prototypical for First-Century Judeans

To see what a risky gambit raising Abraham must have been for Paul, I begin by noting how other Judeans of his time, including those who had not found faith in Christ, regarded Abraham. Above all, they saw him as their forefather by natural descent (Isa. 51:2).[52] They were his physical progeny, his "seed" (Ps. 105:6; Isa. 41:8). Because of Abraham they had received their distinctive identity, which came from having a covenantal relationship with God as his chosen people. This privilege gave them good reason to make the honor claims for themselves that Paul mentions in Rom. 2:17. In the words of *Psalms of Solomon* 9, an Israelite text written in Jerusalem in the first century BCE:

> For you chose the descendants of Abraham above all the nations,
> and you put your name upon us, Lord,
> and it will not cease forever.
> You made a covenant with our ancestors concerning us,
> And we hope in you when we turn our souls toward you.[53]

In addition, Abraham's life and character were regarded as models of true piety: "Abraham was perfect in all his deeds with the Lord, and well-pleasing in righteousness all the days of his life" (*Jub.* 23:10).[54] Sirach has the following to say about him:

> Abraham, the great forefather of a host of nations,
> no one was ever his equal in glory.
> He observed the Law of the Most High,
> and entered into a covenant with him.
> He confirmed the covenant in his own flesh,
> and proved himself faithful under ordeal. (44:19-20)

The confirmation of the covenant in his own flesh is a reference to Abraham's circumcision in Genesis 17. He was, in short, an exemplar who, although more glorious than they, nevertheless represented for Israelites central components of their identity. In our terms, he was a prototype of Israel.

Israelite remembrance of Abraham constituted a collective memory of critical importance, living continually in their consciousness.[55] It constituted a foundational "reference to the past" *(Vergangenheitsbezug)*, as Assmann has described such a phenomenon. By holding on to such a memory they were enabled to remain conscious of their identity over time and, importantly, to consider that it had remained the same over that period.[56] Yet this latter belief was probably an illusion, which underestimated the extent to which each generation reworks its understanding of exemplary or prototypical figures from the past in the service of existing needs.

We saw in chapter two that two contrasting analytic approaches have been identified as to the nature of collective memory as a category of knowledge. The first assumes that the past is a social construction shaped by the present, so that the primary function of memory is not to preserve the past but to adapt it in order to be able to enrich and manipulate the present.[57] The second suggests that memories serve not to transform the past by bending it to the service of the present but to make it live as it once was. Thus the image of a hero of the past is not so much conceived and elaborated anew in each generation but assumes a guiding pattern that endows different generations with a common heritage.[58] Judeans of the first century CE probably regarded Abraham as a figure serving the second type of function, yet it is doubtful if this option or their acceptance of it fits the case of Abraham.

To note how the figure of Abraham was adapted in each generation we need only consider how the rite of circumcision that he had received (Genesis 17) came into greatly increased prominence as a consequence of the Maccabean rebellion against Antiochus IV Epiphanes.[59] That is, while circumcision was always part of the picture of Abraham, it became salient only from 167 BCE onward. In the first century CE Philo of Alexandria concluded an essay on Abraham that brings out the numerous ways in which he was prototypical of Israelites with the following exalted formulation: "Such is the life of the first author and founder of our nation; a man according to the law, as some persons think, but, as my argument has shown, one who is himself the unwritten law and justice of God."[60]

Abraham in Galatia: A Contested Prototype of Identity

Before looking at Romans 4 in detail, we must consider that in Galatia Paul had previously experienced how Judeans could invoke Abraham in ways inimical to his gospel and that he had delivered a robust response. The situation in Galatia was, therefore, one in which the fluid and flexible nature of prototypes was evident. The prototype of Abraham was capable of interpretation and reinterpretation in a contest to process the past in a manner that would have it bear in particular ways upon group identity in the present. Abraham represented possible social identities in the past from which contending groups could select a particular version to suit their own immediate needs.

It is common for interpreters to suggest that the people causing trouble for Paul in Galatia by preaching "another gospel" (Gal. 1:6) were appealing to "scripture" in support of their arguments.[61] This is accurate in a sense. Prior to Paul's time Israelites had begun according a special status to the texts that would eventually form the canon of Hebrew scripture (and possibly some that did not quite make it, like Sirach and the Wisdom of Solomon). They were "holy scriptures" (Rom. 1:2) and "the oracles of God" (3:2).[62] As Ernst Käsemann has noted, "Pauline method is bound to the Scriptures and therefore does not apply to non-biblical events and figures."[63] Yet the perspective I am applying here suggests that such an appeal carried force not only because of some power thought to reside in Israelite scripture as sacred text. In addition, that scripture contained the collective memories of Israel that were essential to its identity, especially the way in which God had chosen the Israelites, and them alone, as a people for himself, and entered into a covenantal relationship with them, initially through Abraham. On at least one occasion Philo of Alexandria expressed a view similar to this: "So that a man may very properly say, that the written laws are nothing more than a memorial of the life of the ancients, tracing back in antiquarian spirit, the actions and reasonings they have adopted."[64]

Thus the use of Israelite scripture relating to Abraham by Paul's competitors in Galatia and his response thereto should not be seen so much as a dispute as to who was the best interpreter of a written text, but rather as a struggle, carried on within an oral culture, to control the past and the collective memories that embodied it so that they might be brought to bear in various and conflicting ways on matters of group identity in the present.[65] Scripture mattered as a record of the history and identity of the people in relation to their God, in addition to its status as sacred text. The current fashion for studying the use of Israelite scripture in the New Testament writings under the banner of "intertextuality" runs the risk of overlooking the actual context of social struggle within which Israelite traditions were invoked. With this caveat in mind, we may now consider some details of the role of Abraham in Galatia.

John Barclay, in his levelheaded, if overly conservative, appraisal of what can be learned from "mirror-reading" Galatians, regards it as "highly probable" that the opponents in Galatia were appealing to the Abraham narratives in scripture and "probable" that the scriptural passages they deployed were Genesis 17 and the Sarah-Hagar narratives.[66] Jeffrey Siker adopts and amplifies this view, and suggests that Paul's opponents argued that the "Gentile Galatian" converts, to be fully counted as heirs to God's promises to Abraham, had to become fully incorporated as his descendants (his seed; Gen. 13:15; 17:18) by being circumcised and observing the law. Abraham himself had been circumcised and law observant.[67] Walter Hansen notes that the opponents' resort to the Abraham tradition was likely to have been prompted by their fundamental interest in having Paul's converts circumcised. Since the connection between circumcision and the Abrahamic covenant is made so frequently in "Jewish" literature, Hansen argues, it is difficult to see how they could have promoted circumcision without referring to Abraham.[68]

While these views are helpful, they require amplification and reworking. The fundamental problem with Paul's version of the Christ-movement, according to his Galatian opponents, was the blurring of Israelite ethnic identity represented by the mixed Judean and non-Judean table fellowship he encouraged at their meetings. Their solution to this anomaly was that the non-Judean Christ-followers become circumcised. They saw circumcision as the solution, not the problem.[69] In my view, however, Abraham was not raised merely because one could not mention circumcision without mentioning him, given the connections frequently made between the two in Israelite literature, as Hansen has suggested. Rather, Abraham was offered in a positive way—as a particular reason for becoming an Israelite. "Get circumcised and become Israelites like us," Paul's opponents were saying, "and you will gain Abraham, who by the way was circumcised, as your glorious ancestor. This is the way you can become one of his descendants, share in the blessings promised to his seed and in the honor we enjoy as a people in consequence." Thus Paul's converts are being offered a form of kinship connection with an outstanding prototype of Israel. The stress on the sonship of Abraham is so strong in Galatians that it seems more probable that Paul was responding to a case put like this, with Abrahamic descent being offered as a glittering prize by the opposition, than as an issue that arose incidentally. In addition, it is likely that parallel to this argument was its converse, namely, that whereas Israelites claimed honorable lineage from Abraham and his wife, freeborn Sarah, non-Israelites were the descendants of his slave girl Hagar through her son Ishmael, an altogether dishonorable ancestry.[70]

In response, Paul mounts an argument that is more notable for its daring than its persuasiveness and that well illustrates the extent to which collective memories of the past enshrined in prototypical figures are malleable in the hands of those caught up in a conflict occurring in the present. First, he insists that those who rely on faith are the "sons of Abraham" (Gal. 3:7). That is, they "share an identity of kinship with this illustrious hero from the past."[71] Second, whereas all who rely on the law are under a curse, Jesus Christ has redeemed "us" from the curse of the law, so that in him the blessing of Abraham has come upon non-Israelites (Gal. 3:10-14). Third, Paul deals with the Genesis references to the promises made to Abraham and his seed, which were probably being proffered to non-Israelite Christ-followers in Galatia as an inducement to be circumcised.[72] His riposte is to fix, quite artificially, upon the fact that seed ($\sigma\pi\acute{\epsilon}\rho\mu\alpha$) in these passages is a singular, not plural, noun; it therefore refers to one, Christ, and not to many (Gal. 3:15-18). Lastly, Paul argues (remarkably) that he and his non-Israelite converts are the real descendants of Sarah, while he links his opponents with Hagar, implying that they are Ishmaelites (Gal. 4:24-31).[73]

Thomas Tobin has helpfully emphasized the profound (but insufficiently noticed) implications of Paul's strategy in respect of Abraham in Galatians. When Paul says non-Israelites are the "sons of Abraham," does he not necessarily imply that Israelites are not, especially by his assertion that they are under a curse and not a blessing? If the word "seed" refers only to one person,

Christ, and not to the many, how can it refer to Judeans? If his converts are the descendants of Sarah, are Judeans really Ishmaelites, descended from Hagar?

Siker warns against taking Paul's argument as intended to say anything about Judeans other than the Judean Christ-followers who were causing trouble in Galatia; he opposes the view of G. Klein that Paul's purpose in Galatians 3 was to rule out any Judean appeals to Abraham as father and to reappropriate him as the father of Christ-followers exclusively.[74] Yet Siker thus glosses over a serious issue far too easily. He underestimates the rhetorical force of the black-and-white contrasts Paul draws in Galatians. As Tobin has argued: "Paul's use of Abraham in Galatians . . . certainly left him open to the accusation or at least the suspicion that he enfranchised Gentile believers at the expense of disinheriting the Jews. Such a reputation hardly would have endeared Paul to his fellow Jews or to many of his fellow Christians, especially those who saw their own beliefs in close continuity with both the Jewish scriptures and the Jewish people."[75] Tobin plausibly suggests that the animosity Paul generated by his polarizing argument in Galatians forced him to treat Abraham differently in Romans.

It is worth considering briefly how, from a social-psychological perspective, Judeans might have regarded Paul's representation of Abraham. In essence, Paul's argument constituted a threat to Judean identity. As Glynis Breakwell has explained, a threat to identity consists of a demand of some kind that changes occur to the content or sensed value of an identity that would be inconsistent with its continued integrity. Such a threat can originate internally, when a person takes the initiative to alter his or her position in the local environment and runs into obstacles, or externally, where there is a change of some sort in the social context. Threats can challenge people as individuals or they can be attacks on a group to which various individuals belong. A threat that concerns a group attacks its value and, by denigrating the group, levels a refracted slur on the self-esteem of individual members.[76] Paul's construal of Abraham as the father of non-Judean Christ-followers, apparently even to the exclusion of Judeans (whether members of the Christ-movement or not), constituted for Judeans a threat having an external origin that impinged on their group identity. Paul's reinterpretation of Abraham, denying Judeans a relationship to him as their father, had the potential greatly to diminish the value of their belonging to Israel. Such an attack, if allowed to pass unanswered, would inevitably diminish their self-esteem.

Yet, as Breakwell has shown, a threat to identity elicits various types of activity, which she calls "coping strategies," aimed at its removal or modification.[77] The generation of negative views about Paul and his teaching, aimed at discrediting him and it and spread about by word of mouth, seems to have been the coping strategy they employed (as suggested most obviously in Rom. 3:8 and 15:31). In a face-to-face oral and honor-focused culture such as this, where one acquired or lost honor in the diverse modes of social competition known as challenge-and-riposte, the gossip network was an important means whereby individuals could be pilloried and their honor rating diminished before the relevant audience, as Richard Rohrbaugh has argued in a brilliant contribution to this neglected subject. Gossip could do tremendous damage by diminishing or destroying one's honor.[78] Paul's awareness of the danger of verbal modes of attack emerges in his inclusion of ψιθυρισταί ("whisperers") and καταλάλοι ("slanderers") in the vice list in 1:28-31.

Abraham in Romans 4: A Prototype of a Common Identity

Romans 4:1-8: Abraham's Righteousness, Its Cause and Character

Romans 4:1-8 constitutes a distinct section in Paul's discussion of Abraham.[79] It is devoted to explaining the cause and character of his righteousness. Paul does not begin to take up the representative or, as I will suggest, prototypical role of the patriarch in relation to the two subgroups of Judean and non-Judean, until v. 9. By this point, however, he will have established foundational propositions concerning the origin and nature of Abraham's righteousness, and done so in a way that demonstrates its connection with the righteousness through Jesus Christ that he has previously introduced (1:17) and then described in some detail (3:21-31).

In Romans 4 Paul begins by asking "What, therefore, shall we say Abraham our forefather in the flesh to have found [sc. to be the case]?"[80] Here "in the flesh" (κατὰ σάρκα) covers an Israelite connected to Abraham both "by natural descent" and "through circumcision," that is, a native-born Israelite and a proselyte.[81] Since Paul is addressing a mixed audience of Judean and non-Judean Christ-followers in Rome, when he refers to Abraham as "our forefather in the flesh" (προπάτορα ἡμῶν κατὰ σάρκα) he is invoking a physical connection, a kinship, with Abraham (either from birth or by proselyte circumcision) that embraces him and his Judean addressees, but also Judeans outside the Christ-movement.

It is essential not to underestimate the significance of this designation. We saw in chapter two above that the core of self-categorization theory is the fact that a person's self-concept tends to vary in particular group situations, along a continuum from pronounced personal identity at one end to pronounced social identity at the other. Self-categorization theory assumes a fairly mobile sense of self, in that different situations can lead to personal and/or group-derived characteristics becoming dominant for a time, either by a simple stress on personal over group-derived characteristics or by selection among a range of possible groups. When Paul mentions "Abraham our forefather in the flesh," he thereby brings Israelite group identity into salience. Illustrating the mobility characteristic of one's sense of self in this theoretical perspective, he categorizes himself all of a sudden in relation to ethnic Israel. He does not do so here to the same extent or with the same passion with which he will make the same gambit at the start of Romans 9, but nevertheless that he activates his Israelite identity is striking. This move on Paul's part, attesting as it does to his belief in the continuing existence and relevance of ethnic Israel, is an early sign in Romans 4 running contrary to the positions of Watson and Boyarin mentioned above.

This opening question in v. 1 immediately distances Paul's rhetoric from any suggestion in the air as a result of what he had written to the Galatians that Judeans were not the sons of Abraham. But it also signals that the problem he had faced in Galatia, of having competitors who were seeking to impose circumcision on the non-Judean Christ-followers, was not an issue in Rome. For Paul could not be so relaxed about kinship with Abraham if there were people in Rome dangling it before non-Judean Christ-followers to entice them to get circumcised.

The first point Paul makes is directly parallel to his statement at 3:21-22 that the righteousness of God is being manifested "apart from the law" (χωρὶς νόμου) through faith and also develops the claim made in 3:27 that Judean honor claims based on the law have been excluded. Using an argument based on Israelite scripture, Paul declares that Abraham would have an honor claim if he had relied on the law, but not before God. In fact, he did not attain righteousness through law but through faith in God (4:2-3). For this view Paul was extremely fortunate to have had a most apt text in Gen. 15:6 that connected faith and righteousness: "Abraham put his faith in God and it was credited to him as righteousness (δικαιοσύνη)."[82] That Paul begins his exposition with Gen. 15:6 and proffers several more explicitly scriptural references is partially explained by the last verse in Romans 3: "Do we therefore destroy the law through faith? Emphatically not! On the contrary, we establish the law" (3:31). This continues a theme he had initiated at 3:21, when he described the righteousness of God as "attested to by the law and the prophets." The position he sets out in Romans 4 serves, at least in part, to show that he upholds the law, here to the extent that Israelite scripture ("the law and the prophets" of 3:21) supports his explanation of righteousness by faith to Judean and non-Judean.

Later on in the text (15:4) he will reiterate the importance of Israelite scripture. The extent to which his method of interpretation involves reading Israelite scripture against Israel will come up at various points below. Israelite scripture becomes a battleground on which rival parties campaign to have their version of the past prevail for group needs in the present. It is evident from this insistence on the law, and elsewhere in the letter, that Paul is talking about the requirements of the Mosaic law, not about human actions generally. Interpretations that suggest that Paul is making some point about the inefficacy of human actions generally are simply untenable, whatever the theological traditions that motivate them. This is part of the perspective on the Mosaic law introduced into New Testament studies by E. P. Sanders in 1977.[83]

Paul does not mention in 4:2 a point that is implied in this assertion that Abraham was not righteoused by works, namely, that the events of Genesis 15 preceded those of Genesis 17, where indeed Abraham was circumcised. Perhaps he could rely on his audience to be aware of this hidden premise in his argument, which he does not raise explicitly until 4:11. In any event, this argument allowed Paul to align the experience of Abraham, who found righteousness through faith, with that of Paul's Christ-following addressees, which was essential to his claim for Abraham's prototypicality.

Many Judeans contemporary with Paul, however, would probably have rejected Paul's argument. As James Dunn notes, "Abraham was at this time regularly presented as a type or model for the devout Jew."[84] Certainly in some circles the Judean picture of Abraham included his devotion to God's law. This attitude is represented in Sir. 44:20, which says Abraham "observed the Law of the Most High, and entered into a covenant with him," and also in the *Damascus Document*, which states at one point that Abraham was "counted a friend of God for keeping God's precepts and not following the desire of his spirit."[85] Nevertheless, the various portrayals of Abraham in Israelite tradition were capable of generating diverse interpretations. Moxnes has shown how Philo's exposition of the Abraham story focuses less on Abraham as the first to receive circumcision and a covenant and more on his faith, even if πίστις does not have the same meaning for Philo as for Paul.[86] Paul's distinctive position reminds us of the extent to which the past is a field of lively social contest, where collective memory is mobilized in diverse ways to serve needs in the present felt by a variety of groups, some of them in conflict with one another.

In Rom. 4:4 Paul uses an analogy drawn from the economic relations of his day: "To one who works, his wages are not credited as a gift (κατὰ χάριν) but as an entitlement (κατὰ ὀφείλημα)." This implies a further aspect of the righteousness that came from God to Abraham—that it was gratuitous. Paul had previously made this point in relation to the righteousness dependent on faith in Christ by the use of the phrase "being righteoused freely (δωρεάν)" at 3:24. This dimension is assumed, not stated, in the next proposition in Paul's argument: "But to the one who does not work, but has faith in the one who righteouses (δικαιοῦντα) the godless, his faith is credited to him as righteousness." Here God is the implied subject of the transitive and present tense participle δικαιοῦντα. As we have seen in chapter seven above, this verb does not import any sense of "an eschatological act of the Judge at the Last Day which takes place proleptically in the present," as suggested by Käsemann. Rather, it refers to the ascription of honor by God to the sinner, and, this being a culture in which the announcement of a status or other good on someone by a person in authority is regarded as effectively conferring that status or good, it has the effect of making the person so honored actually righteous. In this setting, to declare righteous and to make righteous are one and the same thing. This result is confirmed by further examination of these verses.

Although what is said in vv. 4-5 on its face speaks of Abraham, it is expressed in a general way that goes beyond his experience to all those who, like him, have righteousness credited to them on account of their faith. This indicates the extent to which Paul is presenting Abraham as prototypical of all people of this kind.

It is evident here that the fact that Abraham attained righteousness, expressed by the abstract noun δικαιοσύνη, is equivalent to the aorist verb that I translate "he was righteoused" (ἐδικαιώθη) to bring out the semantic connection between the two words. Paul contends that Abraham was not righteoused by works (4:1), and, soon after, he insists that righteousness was credited to him through faith (4:3). Paul is saying that a result that did not come about from works came about by faith. This result can either be expressed by the passive verb "he was righteoused" (ἐδικαιώθη) or by the phrase "righteousness (δικαιοσύνη) was credited to him."

Here righteousness, just as in 3:21-31, is a present condition that comes into existence as soon as Abraham has faith. There is no judicial proceeding or decision in view in Gen. 15:6. Abraham has been "righteoused" in the course of his everyday human experience. On the other hand, God is most certainly the agent of this "righteousing." Divine agency is implied in Rom. 4:3 and again in 4:5, where God is obviously the "the one righteousing the godless (τὸν δικαιοῦντα τὸν ἀσεβῆ)." As in 3:21-31, righteousness is an ascribed honor from God that ennobles a particular identity. It produces a person who is thus righteous (δίκαιος) and thereby has an identity of a particularly privileged type, characterized by life and blessing. This lines up with what Paul has already said earlier via a quotation from Hab. 2:4 at Rom. 1:17: "The righteous person by faith will live." Life and blessing are described as characterizing δίκαιοι in the richest Old Testament source we have concerning them—the antithetical proverbs in Proverbs 10–15, where the extent to which δικαιοσύνη is a way of specifying a privileged identity comes through loud and clear.[87]

Not surprisingly, therefore, Paul next mentions this dimension of blessing with reference to Ps. 31:1-2 (LXX):

> So also David pronounces a blessing on the person to whom God credits righteousness apart from works:
> Blessed are those whose lawless deeds are forgiven,
>   and whose sins are covered.
> Blessed is the man against whom the Lord does not credit his sin. (4:6-8)

This statement continues the generalizing thrust of thought that began with Rom. 4:4. It seems to be said not just of Abraham but of anyone in his position. The forgiveness of sins mentioned here picks up the idea of the remission of former sins referred to earlier in connection with the expiation effected by the blood of Christ (3:24-25).

While the emphasis in this passage falls mainly on the blessing that accompanies the new identity of the righteous, Paul also makes clear that the lawless acts previously committed by the righteous person are forgiven, the sins covered, and the sinfulness not credited to him or her. Thus God's activity in righteousing effects a major change for the individual concerned—from sinner to righteous. In an honor culture, where a person's sense of worth rises or falls on manifestations of external approval, from either the local group or a person in authority, a sinner whom God righteouses will necessarily internalize that act of acceptance and forgiveness. Accordingly, I reject the argument of Douglas Moo that the process described in Ps. 31:1-2 (LXX) is "forensic" only, bringing about a change in the sinner's relationship to God (acquittal rather than condemnation) and "has nothing to do with moral transformation."[88] This view represents an ethnocentric and anachronistic imposition of a modern distinction between one's status and relations with others, on the one hand, and one's inner reality, on the other, onto the ancient Mediterranean world.

Romans 4:9-12: The Blessing Is for Judeans and Non-Judeans

With v. 9 Paul moves on to another respect in which Abraham is the prototype of the new identity, by asking whether the blessing that characterizes it fell upon the circumcised or also the uncircumcised.[89] If Paul's audience was aware of the line he had taken in Galatia, they could reasonably have supposed that at this point he was about to restrict the blessing to the uncircumcised, to non-Judeans, such as Greeks. Indeed, for the first part of this section this seems to be precisely the course he has chosen: "How was it [sc. righteousness] credited to him? When he was circumcised or uncircumcised? It was not when he was circumcised but when he was uncircumcised" (4:10). Paul's point depends on the fact the Abraham was righteoused in Genesis 15 but not circumcised until Genesis 17. Will Abraham only be prototypical for non-Judeans, as was arguably his point to the Galatians?

Far from it! For Paul's problem in Rome is very different from that in Galatia. He is not faced with a group of Judean Christ-followers applying pressure to the non-Judean members of the movement to be circumcised and become proselytes, but with the need to recategorize two subgroups in a state of tension, and even conflict, into a common ingroup identity. Once again, therefore, he chooses a prototype who will serve to typify the ingroup—Abraham. But now, in a dramatic demonstration of the flexibility of prototypes and the capacity of those seeking to influence groups to modulate their processing of the past to accord with the exigencies of the current situation, he presents Abraham not as a figure who gathers in non-Judeans and excludes Judeans, but as one who incorporates both social categories.

He takes this dramatic step by embarking on a topic not taken up in Galatians, namely, the event and effect of Abraham's circumcision (Genesis 17), an aspect of the Genesis narrative that he may have been pressed to explain, even though Abraham had attained righteousness before it happened (Gen. 15:6): "He took the sign that is circumcision,[90] a seal of the righteousness he had by faith while he was still uncircumcised, in order that he might become the father of those who have faith without being circumcised and that righteousness might be credited to them" (Rom. 4:11).

We must pause to reflect on the extraordinary nature of this claim, something insufficiently adverted to by commentators. Whereas in Gen. 17:11 circumcision is described as "a sign of the covenant" (σημεῖον διαθήκης) that God enters into with Abraham on that occasion, Paul radically reinterprets its denotative force so that it signifies the *righteousness* he had *previously* received through faith. Those who see Paul's thought in terms of the fulfillment or climax of the covenant must explain its outright replacement by righteousness here.[91] Since Abraham attained righteousness when he was uncircumcised, Paul can thus describe Abraham as the father of those who come to faith while uncircumcised and thus attain righteousness. This was an ingenious, if strained, argument that seems aimed at those (Judeans surely) who might raise the fact of Abraham's circumcision in answer to Paul's argument based on Gen. 15:6. In any event, by it Paul mounts a case for the prototypicality of Abraham for non-Judean Christ-followers and also the honor that attached in this culture to descent from someone as illustrious as him.

Yet Paul is not finished with this point. He immediately continues: "and father of those of the circumcised who rely not merely on circumcision but also walk in the footsteps of our father Abraham who had faith while he was uncircumcised" (4:12). Once again the argument is radical. Paul is saying that Judeans trace descent from Abraham not in virtue of his circumcision but from the righteousness by faith he had prior to it and of which circumcision was merely a sign. Paul has thus achieved a result fundamental to his communicative strategy in the letter. He has recategorized the two subgroups of the Christ-movement in Rome into an ingroup identity that is unified by virtue of their sharing exactly the same relationship with Abraham. He is the father of all of them in relation to righteousness that comes from faith. Axel von Dobbeler has well noted the integrative function served by calling Abraham "our father" at this point.[92] Abraham is thus the prototype of this critical dimension of their identity. In this respect, Abraham is to be distinguished from the forefather κατὰ σάρκα of 4:1.

Paul had given discursive expression to the notion that there was no distinction between the two subgroups in 3:21-31. First he had contended that in relation to sinfulness there was no distinction (διαστολή, v. 22) and that they were righteoused in Christ Jesus as a demonstration of God's righteousness (vv. 23-26), through faith and not law (vv. 27-28). Second, he had introduced the two subgroups by asking: "Or is he God of Judeans only? Is he not also (God) of foreigners? Yes, also of foreigners, since God is one who will righteous circumcision through faith and the uncircumcision through faith" (3:29-30). This last statement, from which Romans 4 follows on immediately (except for the assertion in v. 31 about Paul upholding the law), means that Paul is playing for high stakes, since he is connecting the righteousing of Judean and non-Judean by faith directly to the theological reality of monotheism.

We should not underestimate the importance of Paul's assertion of the unitary nature of God as motivation for his use of Abraham as a prototype. Granted that God is one, Paul could hardly do adequate justice to this oneness merely by asserting, as he had in 3:30, that God righteouses Judeans and non-Judeans by faith, since this articulation did not itself demonstrate a resulting unity between the two groups homologous with, and demanded by, the divine unity. The beauty of choosing a prototype to illustrate the common ingroup identity that resulted from God's righteousing of two social categories in the same way was its necessarily unitary character. In a prototype, Paul had a single, idealized individual who summarized and embodied the central tendencies and characteristics of the new group. In other words, he had a picture of one person representing the socioreligious identity of the new group that powerfully replicated the theological reality of the oneness of God. That Paul should have chosen Abraham as his prototype was the result of the centrality of kinship in Mediterranean culture and the dominant role that Abraham already played in the construction and maintenance of Judean identity. Abraham was, moreover, someone who had been on the best of terms with God. Paul's use of Abraham to represent the identity of the Christ-movement, which was itself a consequence of the unitary character and activity of the one God, indicates how closely integrated are matters of theology and social identity.

Lastly, in relation to 4:9-12, it is apparent that this passage leaves a question hanging: What is the status of Judeans who have *not* come to righteousness by faith in respect of Abraham? Is Paul insinuating that they are not really his sons, meaning he is not distinguishing between real and fictive kinship, or is it the case that nothing he has said affects their status as sons of Abraham by physical descent, as Ambrosiaster at least thought, when he said Abraham was "the father of the Judeans according to the flesh, but according to faith truly the father of all who believe"?[93] Such a view receives some support from his invocation of Abraham as "our father in the flesh" in 4:1 and even more from his acceptance of the continuing existence of Israel in 9:1-5 and in chap. 11.

Romans 4:13-22: The Fulfillment of the Promise

Verses 13-22 contain a number of arguments that largely amplify and support points Paul has already made. He begins by denying a promised blessing to those who rely on the law (vv. 13-15), then attaches the blessing to those who have faith (v. 16), and finally expatiates upon the characteristics of Abraham (vv. 17-22).[94]

In 4:13 Paul avows that "it was not through the law that the promise (ἡ ἐπαγγελία) (was made) to Abraham and his seed, that they would inherit the world, but through righteousness by faith." This statement continues Paul's effort to eliminate the law as relevant in the new dispensation. This perspective was already apparent in his insistence that righteousness is by faith, not by, but "apart from," law (3:20, 21, 28). Now it surfaces for the first time in connection with Abraham. This is another issue, therefore, in relation to which Paul imparts the prototypicality of the patriarch for Judean and non-Judean Christ-followers. In this instance, however, Paul is putting the case negatively—by telling them in relation to Abraham what is not the case rather than what is.

Yet v. 13 also contains the first of eight instances of "promise" (ἡ ἐπαγγελία) in the letter.[95] Nowhere in the Old Testament, however, does God precisely promise Abraham and his seed that they will "inherit the world"; rather, this seems to summarize the effect of three types of promises made in various places from Genesis 12 to 22: to have numerous descendants, to possess the land, and to bring blessings to all the peoples of the earth.[96] It is not impossible that having the world as one's inheritance could be another way of saying that Abraham's seed would be as numerous as the stars in heaven (Gen. 15:5), but this may be pushing the latter promise too far. In any event, an extensive inheritance of whatever type plainly represents an aspect of the blessings that are associated with the identity represented by the righteous in Israelite tradition, especially in Proverbs 10–15.

It is worth considering how such a promised inheritance relates to social identity. This dimension of group identity plainly scores highly on what Tajfel described as its emotional and evaluative aspects, that is, it makes the members feel good to belong to such a group and it enables them to rate themselves highly (in this case, very highly) in relation to outgroups. In v. 13 Paul is concerned to deny that such blessings will fall on those who rely on the law. On the other hand, he has already proclaimed the connection between righteousness and blessing a little earlier in chap. 4 (vv. 6-9) and will develop this idea further below.

Verse 14 contains a reason offered in support of the claim in v. 13: "If the adherents of the law are the heirs, faith is rendered invalid and the promise is nullified." The reasoning here is not easy to follow. It would be straightforward if the promise referred to were simply that in Gen. 15:5 (to have descendants as numerous as the stars of heaven), which could then be related directly to Abraham's faith in Gen. 15:6. This answer, however, is probably excluded given that a promise "to inherit the world" goes way beyond Gen. 15:5. In Rom. 4:15 Paul introduces another line of attack on the law that he will develop in chaps. 5–7: "For the law produces wrath, but where there is no law there is no transgression."

Having canvassed problems besetting any idea that the promise is linked to law in vv. 14-15, in v. 16 Paul offers a positive argument for the role of faith: "On account of this, it is of faith, in order that it might be in accordance with grace, so that the promise might be secure for all the seed, not only to those who are of the law,[97] but also to those who are of the faith of Abraham who is the father of us all." To what does the word "it" in the first line refer? The most likely candidates are "promise" (ἐπαγγελία), which Paul leaves out to avoid unnecessary repetition, since the word will soon reappear,[98] or "the promised inheritance."[99] The former is more likely, since it produces a nice parallel between vv. 13-15, with their assertion that the promise is not "through law" (διὰ νόμου), and v. 16, with its assertion that it (the promise) is "by faith" (ἐκ πίστεως). The promise, therefore, that Abraham and his seed would inherit the world falls on those who have faith like their father. In other words, to be a Christ-follower is to enjoy the blessings associated with that particular identity.

Since we know that Abraham's seed are those who are righteous by faith and no one, except Abraham himself, appears to fit this category until the possibility arose of faith in Christ, it follows (even though Paul does not expressly mention it) that we have a period between Abraham and Paul's time when the promise was not fulfilled by anyone; it was *de futuro* only. This would seem to produce barren ground for notions of "salvation history" or "the climax of the covenant." Thus Ulrich Luz suggested that the covenantal promise God made to Abraham remained in a sort of docetic state until the arrival of the single seed, Christ.[100] J. Louis Martyn nicely expressed this insight: "By implication the corporate people of Israel was a dance sat out by the covenantal promise as it waited for its true referent, the Singular Seed."[101]

With v. 17 Paul reverts to Abraham, with the aim of showing what sort of faith he had that resulted in its being credited to him as righteousness (v. 22). Paul begins with a quotation from Gen. 17:5, "I have made you the father of many nations," made "in the presence of God in whom he had faith, who brings the dead to life and calls the things that do not exist into existence" (Rom. 4:17). Paul is envisaging God as the one who creates and brings the dead to life. The latter element may well refer to God's actions in bringing life from Abraham's virtually dead body ($\sigma\hat{\omega}\mu\alpha$ [$\check{\eta}\delta\eta$] $\nu\epsilon\nu\epsilon\kappa\rho\omega\mu\acute{\epsilon}\nu\sigma\nu$) and from the "deadness" ($\nu\acute{\epsilon}\kappa\rho\omega\sigma\iota\varsigma$) of Sarah's womb (4:19) and in raising Christ from the dead, soon to be mentioned at 4:24.

As to God as creator, Edward Adams has suggested that underlying Paul's thought here and elsewhere in Romans 4 is a tradition depicting Abraham as a former idolater who reasoned from the creation to the creator, thus representing an antitype to the disobedience of non-Judeans in 1:18-32, especially their failure to glorify God whom they recognized in created things (1:20-21).[102] This is possible. One must grant that there is no suggestion in Genesis that Abraham was ever involved in idolatry, nor any explicit statement to that effect in Romans (thus giving support to Käsemann's view, mentioned above, that Paul restricts himself to biblical figures and events). Nevertheless, Paul seems to imply an idolatrous past for Abraham in Rom. 4:5: "But to the one who does not work, but has faith in the one who righteouses the godless ($\dot{\alpha}\sigma\epsilon\beta\hat{\eta}$), his faith is credited to him as righteousness." This is a generalizing statement, yet it must include Abraham, and $\dot{\alpha}\sigma\epsilon\beta\acute{\eta}\varsigma$ is a strong word, the nominal form of which appeared at 1:18 prior to Paul's treatment of the idolatry and other sinfulness typical of non-Israelites in 1:19-32.

Romans 4:17-21 diverges from the rather schematic treatment of the Abraham narrative upon which Paul has ventured hitherto to describe particular facets of Abraham's faith. In hope he had faith against hope that he would become the father of many nations (v. 18). He did not weaken in faith when he considered his age and necrotic physical state and the barrenness of his wife (v. 19). Nor did he distrust God's promise but grew strong in faith, glorifying God (v. 20). He was fully convinced that God was able to do what he had promised (v. 21). Therefore it was credited to him as righteousness (v. 22).

Romans 4:23-25: Abraham as Our Prototype

In 4:23-25 Paul emphasizes what has been fairly obvious throughout most of this chapter—that the righteousness which was credited to Abraham and the scriptural reference reporting this event also apply to those contemporary with Paul.[103] Their identity is his identity. But we can go a little further than this. Paul is presenting the graphic picture of Abraham's faith in vv. 18-21, tied to the exigencies of human hope and capable of growing weak yet waxing strong, as also prototypical of Christ-followers, since he writes immediately afterward in vv. 23-25: "But the words, 'it was reckoned to him,' were not written only for his sake, but for ours also. It will be reckoned to us who believe in him who raised from the dead Jesus our Lord, who was put to death for our trespasses and raised for our righteousness." In our faith we can expect to be subject to the ups and downs of human life, needing to be sustained by hope, just like Abraham, just as Paul makes clear in 5:1-5. It is an interesting question, therefore, whether it is possible to reconcile the rich picture of Abraham's faith, the prototype of ours, with Käsemann's assertion that faith "is neither a virtue, a religious attitude, nor an experience," but only a receiving and keeping of the word.[104]

A final point worth noting here and to be developed later (see chapters ten and twelve below) is that it is clear from 4:23-25 that Paul envisages that, given the failure of the Mosaic law, the only people who have achieved righteousness by faith are Abraham and the Christ-followers contemporary with him. Paul knows of no one between Abraham and Christ who pursued this type of righteousness. This has serious implications for any attempt to attribute to Paul notions of "salvation history."

Conclusion

The account of Abraham in Romans 4 thus serves many purposes. Above all, it carries forward Paul's aim of recategorizing Judean and non-Judean Christ-followers in Rome into the new ingroup identity and does so by mobilizing collective memories to explain how both subgroups claim ancestry from Abraham in the same way—righteousness credited to them through faith. Abraham thus becomes the prototype of the new identity, portrayed by Paul in a manner peculiar to the needs of this communication and in the face of many rival construals of this patriarch that were possible in the ongoing processing of the past to serve the needs of the present. Second, Abraham as a prototype is socially homologous to, and expressive of, the oneness of God, who righteouses people whatever their ethnicity without distinction. Third, the image of Abraham, who did not make any honor claim based on law, continues the explicit relegation of the Mosaic law that Paul had commenced at 3:20-21.

9

The New Identity in Christ:
Origin and Entry (Romans 5–6)

Romans 5–8 can be distinguished as a reasonably discrete unit in the letter. In theological language one might rightly say that here "Paul portrays the soteriological change that transposes man from a state of non-salvation to a state of salvation."[1] Within the framework of social identity, however, these chapters of the letter set out in some detail the origins and nature of the new common ingroup identity in Christ and emphasize its superiority over rival means to solve the dilemma of human sinfulness adumbrated in 1:18—3:20, especially the Mosaic law.

In chap. 5 Paul offers a positive and detailed exposition of the role of Christ in enabling righteousness in faith and the gift of divine grace, which clearly encompasses all who believe in him, including, as we will see, Paul himself. Thus he differentiates the ingroup of Christ-followers from outgroups, positively reinforcing their special nature and status. The role of Christ in relation to the origin of the new identity in vv. 1-11 is followed by a discussion of Adam in vv. 12-14 and a comparison of the effects of Adam's sin and Christ's redemption in vv. 15-19. Chapter 5 concludes with a statement that the (Mosaic) law arrived with the result that the (preexisting) wrongdoing (stemming from Adam) increased,[2] but that where sin increased, grace through Christ abounded all the more (5:20-21).

Chapter 6 answers two troublesome corollaries that might be thought to flow from 5:20-21 (first, that people should *continue in sin* so that grace might increase; second, that they can *commit sin* because they are no longer under law but under grace), and Romans 7 answers a third (that the law is sin). In responding to these objections, however, Paul is able to make positive statements about important areas of the experience of Christ-followers. Thus he disposes of the first corollary by reference to baptism, which applies to all Christ-followers, Judean or non-Judean (6:1-14). Yet in dealing with the second and third corollaries he returns to his practice earlier in the letter in focusing first on one subgroup (non-Judeans in 6:15-23) and Judeans (in chap. 7). Chapter 8, on the other hand, celebrates the new identity, in its present and future dimensions, in a way that is applicable to all Christ-followers, irrespective of their ethnicity.

In the current chapter our interest lies in Romans 5–6. Romans 7 and 8 are covered in the next two chapters.

The New Common Identity and Its Origin (Rom. 5:1-11)

Paul's Bid for Leadership

Romans 5:1-11 marks a major development in Paul's attempt to establish a leadership role for himself in relation to the Christ-followers of Rome. We have seen in chapter two above that a social identity approach to leadership stresses the need for leaders and followers to define themselves in terms of a shared social identity so that the activities of each are seen as collective rather than personal in nature. Leaders must create, coordinate, and control a categorical relationship that defines what they and the followers have in common and makes them special.

In this regard, Patricia McDonald has valuably observed that 5:1-11 forms a "rhetorical bridge" between Paul and the recipients of the letter in the sense that here he strengthens the links between him and them that he has begun to develop earlier. In particular, throughout 5:1-11 he does so by use of first person plural expressions, "we" and "us." These eleven verses contain eighteen first person plurals, and only vv. 4 and 7 lack a reference to "us." This usage was not common prior to this point in the letter, with 4:23-25, a link passage to chap. 5, constituting a notable exception. McDonald explains the position as follows: "In this pericope, then, the Roman Christians are viewed no longer as typical of groups (Jews and Gentiles), as was the case in 1.18—4.22. Nor are they being considered as components of an all-inclusive but still impersonal *pantes*, as they were at 3.21-26. Instead, in 5.1-11 Paul speaks for the first time in Romans of the life that he and the Roman believers share as Christians."[3]

Despite the nomenclature used of the groups in question, this statement contains significant insights into the letter. We have already seen how Paul strove earlier in the letter to acknowledge the two subgroup identities, Judeans and non-Judeans, in a way that social psychologists today consider would be necessary to avoid the perils posed to the maintenance of a common ingroup identity if either subgroup felt its own existence was threatened. In 3:21-31 he had begun to set out the basis for the new ingroup identity and in chap. 4 presented Abraham as a prototype of that identity, initially underlining his own link to one of the two groups in 4:1 with his description of Abraham as "our forefather according to the flesh." Only at the end of chap. 4, in vv. 23-25, does Paul begin to insinuate himself into that identity, that is, to define himself and them in terms of a shared identity. This process suddenly accelerates in 5:1-11 with the proliferation of first person plural expressions, as Patricia McDonald has pointed out. Paul is not only interested in saying something about the new identity, but also bolstering his claims to leadership of the group by making clear that he and his audience have it in common.

The New Identity (Rom. 5:1-5)

After a section of the letter in which God was far more visible than Christ,[4] chap. 5 begins with Jesus Christ: "Therefore, having been justified by faith we have peace with God through our Lord Jesus Christ, through him we have access to this grace in which we stand, and let us rejoice in the hope of the glory of God" (5:1-2). This statement briefly mentions the role of Jesus Christ, which will occupy the bulk of chaps. 5–6, after a number of such references to him hitherto. It also raises the issue of the future of the movement—in the form of an exhortation to rejoice in the glory of God that they hope to enjoy. As we have seen in chapter two above, the identity of a group straddles past, present, and future, although the balance struck between these three temporal dimensions will reflect the nature of the group and the attitudes to time in its cultural setting. I will consider Paul's perspective on time and the future in particular later in relation to 8:18-30.[5]

Yet in vv. 1-2 Paul also mentions aspects of the *present existence* of Christ-followers—their having been righteoused, their peace with God, and the grace in which they stand—and thus begins to reflect upon, for the first time in the letter, what it is like to belong to the group brought into existence by Christ.[6] Yet he is not chary of reminding them of the downside of belonging, in particular by mentioning that the hope they hold is the product of rather trying current circumstances: "Let us rejoice not only in that, however, but also in our afflictions, knowing that affliction produces endurance, endurance produces character, and character produces hope. Hope does not cause us shame, because the love of God is poured out into hearts through the Holy Spirit that has been given to us" (5:3-5). Here Paul emphatically draws the attention of his audience away from the joy they have when they consider their glorious future destiny by insisting, possibly to their surprise, that they should also rejoice at their present afflictions and the way these generate the very hope that sustains them. It is important to note the potency of present experience in Paul's presentation. They are righteous, they have peace with God, and they stand in grace, but at the same time they suffer afflictions, which bring about endurance as well as the character that produces hope. Joy is the appropriate response to the present as well as to what the future holds.

In addition, God's love (meaning God's love for us, not ours for him)[7] and the Holy Spirit have been given to them. This is the second reference to the Spirit in the letter, the first appearing at 1:4. The occasion for their initial reception of the Spirit, in an explosion of charismatic phenomena, was baptism, a subject discussed below in connection with 6:1-14. The nature of a life lived in the power of the Spirit is dealt with in 8:1-17.[8]

All these characteristics represent a group experience of a particular type, with an undoubtedly exalted identity. The emotional dimension of identity, the way one feels about belonging to a group such as this, is very positive; indeed, it is difficult to envisage how it could be more positive.

Paul's insistence in v. 5 that "hope does not cause us shame" reflects a sentiment expressed in Israelite scripture, particularly the Psalms,[9] that those who hope in the Lord will not be put to shame. Yet Paul's reiteration of this biblical theme here depends on its relevance to the current situation of his addressees and the extent to which their membership of the Christ-movement involved them in a loss of honor among outgroups. In an honor-shame culture such as this, the afflictions that Paul has just mentioned would inevitably have been accompanied, perhaps occasionally constituted, by attempts by outsiders to blacken their name. Psalm 21:4-8 (LXX) brings out the social dynamics and the theological response involved:

> Our fathers hoped in you, they hoped and you delivered them.
> They cried to you and they were saved. They hoped in you and
> they were not put to shame. But I am a worm and not a human
> being, an object of contempt among human beings and a matter
> of disgrace among the people. All who saw me mocked me; they
> spoke with their lips; they shook the head (saying), "He hoped in
> the Lord. Let him deliver him, let him save him, because he takes
> pleasure in him."

Paul's point is that although in relation to outsiders they are dishonored and dishonorable, they belong to a group that derives its identity (characterized by righteousness, peace, and grace) and its hope for vindication from God, and that in the meantime they will be sustained by God's love and the presence of the Holy Spirit. It is not easy to imagine how one could do more to laud the exalted character of a group, and the desirability of belonging to it, than by insisting on its direct relatedness to God, as Paul does here.

Christ and the New Identity (Rom. 5:6-11)

With v. 6, Paul at last begins to expand on the precise role of Christ in the establishment of this identity. Verses 6-8 illustrate God's love that has just been mentioned: "For at the appointed time, while we were still weak, Christ died for the godless. For one would hardly die for a righteous person—although perhaps for a good person one would dare to die. But God shows his love for us in that while we were still sinners Christ died for us."

In the next section Paul moves from Christ's death in the past to the salvation this will enable in the future: "Therefore, by how much more, being righteoused now in his blood, will we be saved through him from the anger (of God). For if while we were enemies we were reconciled to God through the death of his son, by how much more being reconciled will we be saved by his life. Not only that, but we also rejoice in God through our Lord Jesus Christ through whom we have now received reconciliation" (5:9-11).

This is how God has solved the problem of the godlessness (ἀσέβεια) that Paul began to discuss at 1:18. He has demonstrated his love for us in that his own son died on our behalf, even though we were weak and sinful, his enemies in fact, and thus righteoused us and reconciled us to himself. He has also given us a strong hope that we will be saved (σωθησόμεθα, vv. 9, 10), another cause of rejoicing. Paul's message is that Jesus Christ is the founder of a new identity built on a transformed relationship with God that has past, present, and future dimensions.

Adam, Sin, and Christ (Rom. 5:12-21)

Romans 5:12-14 explains how sin came into the world through one man, even though in the absence of law sin was not counted. The focus is on the period between Adam and Moses. It is necessary to note the details of 5:12-14 to prepare for later discussion, especially of chap. 7.

Paul states initially that sin came into the world through one human being (ἄνθρωπος) and death through sin. Paul is presumably speaking only of Adam. There is no sign that he attributes any responsibility to Eve. In Genesis God commanded (ἐνετείλατο) Adam that he could eat of every tree in the garden except that of the knowledge of good and evil, and that if he did eat from that tree he would die (2:16-17). Then God created Eve, and, when the serpent came to tempt her, Adam had apparently passed on to her God's direction about the tree of good and evil (3:1-4). The woman was persuaded by the serpent, ate of the tree, and gave some of its fruit to Adam, who, without further ado, ate it (3:5-8). Later, when God asked Adam why he had eaten of the tree, he replied that the woman gave him some of its fruit and he ate it (3:13). God then asked the woman why she had done this and she replied, "The serpent deceived (ἠπάτησε) me and I ate" (3:14). Thus Genesis does not suggest that Adam was deceived, merely that he did what the woman suggested, in breach of God's direction. Reconciling these details with Paul's concern to fix all responsibility on one person, Adam, renders Eve's being deceived by the serpent less central to the outcome.

The result for Adam and Eve was that they were driven out of the garden that contained the tree of life from which they needed to eat to live forever

(3:23-25). Thus "death," which primarily means actual, literal death, although it probably also covers spiritual death,[10] came into the world. In the ancient Mediterranean world, as Clifton Black has argued,[11] there was a wide diversity of perspectives on death clustering around two broad options. Death was seen, first, as depletion (which encompassed treating it as a terrible thing to be feared, the loss of the richness of life, an intrusion into the order of creation, a tyrannous cosmological power, and a result of sin), and, second, as completion (which encompassed treating it as part of the natural order, a payment of an account owed to God or an atoning sacrifice offered to him, a release from suffering, an occasion for hope, witness, heroism, or glory, and the incentive for ethical behavior, and the fulfillment of the righteous life).

It is interesting to note, however, that Paul does not suggest that all human beings became liable to death solely on account of the sin of Adam, but also because they all sinned (Rom. 5:12).[12] Paul's idea seems to be that while Adam's sin unleashed death, so that he was the ultimate cause ("many died through one's person's wrongdoing," 5:15), nevertheless all other human beings still needed to subject themselves to it, and did so.

In v. 13 Paul insists that sin was in the world before the law, but sin is not taken into account (οὐκ ἐλλογεῖται) in the absence of the law. Criticism frequently leveled against Paul for the alleged unintelligibility of this statement—such as Bultmann's rebuke, "Verse 13 is completely unintelligible. . . . What sort of sin was it if it did not originate as a contradiction of the Law?"[13]— is based on an ignorance of the nature of law from which Paul himself did not suffer. As I have argued elsewhere in relation to Paul's understanding of the law in Galatians, Gal. 2:18 shows that Paul has an unimpeachably correct grasp of the effect of law. He knows that the "introduction of law into a particular context establishes a set of norms with respect to which human behavior acquires a different character."[14] Most criminal legislation is passed to restrain the commission of something already recognized as evil but which, because of the legislative act in question, will thereafter have a different character and render those who engage in it liable to punishment to which they were not subject prior to its promulgation. This is Paul's point in v. 13. In addition, the consequence of sin (in the absence of law), namely death, reigned from Adam to Moses, even over those who did not sin in the same way as Adam. Here Paul is setting the scene for the alteration of circumstances that occurred with the giving of the law to Moses on Sinai, even though it would actually make matters worse.

At the end of v. 14 Paul describes Adam as "the type (τύπος) of the one to come," meaning Christ. Here τύπος carries the meaning of "type" in the sense of a person from the primordial time who provides a pattern for a phenomenon in the New Testament period,[15] an example or rule, an "advance presentation" intimating end-time events.[16] Paul does not present Adam as a (negative) "prototype" of his audience before they turned to Christ in the sense discussed in chapter eight above, namely, as the image of an ideal person who embodies this negative character. Adam is rather the ultimate cause of the problem of sinfulness, to which all humanity contributed, even though in ways different from Adam.

This observation suggests the most fundamental level at which Adam is the "type" of Jesus Christ. In Pauline thought the life of the earthly Christ is not the prototype of the Christ-believer in relation to faith, in spite of the unconvincing attempts by several scholars, most prominently Richard Hays, to argue for the existence of the notion of "Christ's faithfulness" as the correct translation of πίστις Χριστοῦ and for its alleged exemplary character.[17] Christ is the agent who, by his sacrificial death, has broken the power of sin and enabled the creation of a new group that has him as the object of its faith and, as we will see in relation to 6:3-11, encounters him in baptism and remains in him thereafter. The role of Christ in relation to the new movement is as its enabler and Lord, not as its ideal embodiment. While baptism, as we will see below, brings a person into the closest relation with the death and resurrection of Christ, Paul does not propose Christ as the model or exemplar of faith or of daily Christian experience. There is one exception to this, and that is in relation to the only part of the life of Jesus that Paul is interested in—his death on a cross. In 15:3 Paul proposes the shame that Christ endured (on the cross) on behalf of God as exemplary for the self-sacrifice required of those who believe in him.

None of this, however, in any way diminishes the humanity of Christ; indeed, it is his humanity that permits him to act as a second Adam (5:18-19). The typological relationship between Adam and Christ, which Paul proceeds to explore in 5:15-19, subsists primarily in the fact, as James D. G. Dunn has said, "that each begins an epoch and the character of each epoch is established by their action."[18] We must add to this formulation, however, that Paul also makes much of the fact that it was a *single person* who brought about these results, with the word "one" used in relation to Adam or Christ eleven times in these five verses. The fourth-century commentator Ambrosiaster fixed upon this aspect to explain the point of the typology: "Adam autem ideo forma futuri est, quia iam tum in mysterio decrevit deus per unum Christum emendare, quod per unum Adam peccatum erat."[19]

In 5:15-19 Paul elaborates on the typology by setting out several ways in which the respective acts of the individuals Adam and Christ had spectacular consequences for the many—spectacularly bad in Adam's case and spectacularly good in Christ's. The following chart plots the structure and content of the comparison.

ONE ADAM (Wrongdoing; παράπτωμα)		ONE CHRIST (Gift; χάρισμα)	
Act of One	*Result for Many*	*Act of One*	*Result for Many*
(15) Wrongdoing	Death	Grace/gift	Abounding grace/gift
(16) Judgment	Condemnation	Gift	Righteousing
(17) Wrongdoing	Reign of death	Abounding grace/righteousness	Reign in life
(18) Wrongdoing	Condemnation	Righteous act	Righteousing of life
(19) Disobedience	Became sinners	Obedience	Will become righteous

Identity

The basic effect of the comparison is to delineate two contrasted identities and to show how one individual was responsible for the establishment of each, even though, as just noted, neither Adam nor Christ is presented as a prototype (in the social identity sense used in this volume) of that identity. The polarity Paul sets up between sin, death, and condemnation on the one hand, and grace, gift, righteousness, and life on the other nicely illustrates the power of social stereotypes as an engine of group differentiation. Paul is concerned here not so much with the substance of elements of identity he attributes to each group (although they are not ignored), but rather to press the case for belonging to one rather than the other. He is underlining the emotional and evaluative dimensions of group belonging or, more specifically, commending the remarkable benefits of belonging to one particular group, those who believe in Christ.

Romans 5:20-21 briefly looks beyond the period identified as "from Adam to Moses" in 5:14 that was the subject of 5:15-19 to see what happened in consequence of the arrival of the law (through Moses). Paul's initial point is that the law slipped in *with the result that* (ἵνα) wrongdoing increased, as John Chrysostom noticed long ago,[20] and not, as many commentators surprisingly propose, "in order that wrongdoing might increase."[21] Paul leaves his explanation of how and why wrongdoing increased with the arrival of the law until later (Romans 7). For the moment he is content to assert that grace has (that is, now through Christ) abounded even more, so that just as once sin reigned through death, grace now reigns through righteousness unto eternal life through Jesus Christ.

Romans 6: Baptism and Sin

Paul's compressed statement in 5:20-21 of how the baleful realities of sin, death, and the law had now been overwhelmed by grace, righteousness, and life, although recapitulating the effect of 5:12-19, is also the overture to the arguments of Romans 6 and 7.

In chap. 6 Paul repudiates two false notions that might be thought to flow from how he has just explained the origin of the new identity in Christ (5:1-11) and how Christ has reversed the baleful effect of Adam (5:12-19) and the law (5:20-21). These repudiations occupy vv. 1-14 and 15-23, and each of them is clearly introduced by the same device—a question that begins Τί οὖν ("What therefore . . . ?") followed by the emphatic negative μὴ γένοιτο ("Emphatically not!"). The precise issue in the second is stimulated by a statement he makes at the very end of the first, in v. 14.

In the first repudiation he disclaims any notion that his addressees should *continue in sin* so that grace might increase, and in the second he denies that they might *commit sin* because they were no longer under law but under grace. It is likely that this material represents a response by Paul to slander about him abroad in Rome and elsewhere (in Jerusalem especially) to the effect that he recommended doing evil so that good might come from it (3:8).[22] The extent to which Paul feels compelled to argue a case on these issues, and at considerable length, provides an example of the accuracy of the insight of Reicher and Sani, mentioned in chapter two above, that intragroup consensus should not be taken for granted and that it is necessary to be sensitive to possible division and dissent within groups and argue actively to achieve a consensus position.[23]

These two passages in Romans 6 also enable him to develop important aspects of his argument in a manner that is closely integrated with earlier parts of the letter and with what will come later. In chap. 7 Paul will return to the whole question of the law, how it had been used by sin to increase its power and how its inadequacies have now been solved in Christ. I deal with Romans 7 in chapter ten below.

Sin and Baptism (Rom. 6:1-14)

Paul's first disclaimer relates to his having earlier said that where sin increased (πλεονάσῃ), grace abounded (5:20). If so, should we continue in sin so that grace might increase (πλεονάσῃ)? Paul rejects this, initially by asking: "How shall we, who died to sin, still live in it?" (v. 2), and eventually by giving directions (in the imperative mood) to them not to sin (vv. 12-13). These directions are immediately followed by a statement in the indicative mood that prompts the second passage: "For sin will not reign over you, since you are not under law but under grace" (v. 14). This material relating to the destruction of sin's dominion constitutes a framework within which Paul outlines the effect of baptism (vv. 3-11).[24]

The Origin and Practice of Baptism in the Early Christ-Movement

Paul's explanation of baptism in Romans 6 needs to be set within the origin and practice of the phenomenon in the early days of the Christ-movement as they can be discerned outside this section of the letter, although here the scarcity of evidence makes detailed reconstruction difficult.[25] It is likely that the early church inherited the practice from the baptisms carried out by John on numerous people in the Jordan. These included Jesus himself, whose baptism described in the Gospels (Matt. 3:13-17; Mark 1:9-11; Luke 3:21-22; John 1:32-34) was almost certainly historical (given the embarrassment it occasioned) and not an etiological legend to explain the adoption of the rite.[26] In addition to Jesus himself having been so baptized, John's baptism, unlike Judean proselyte baptism of the first century CE, was related to the remission of sins in view of a radical and imminent transformation of the world and was carried out by a baptizer who dipped the person seeking baptism under water. The similarity of baptism of the Christ-movement to John's in each of these respects suggests its adaptation of his practice.[27]

In the early period at least, the person being baptized was probably pushed right under the water, head and all. This is strongly suggested by the Gospel accounts of Jesus seeing the heavens rent asunder when he came up out of the water, as if the fact that his face was under water would have prevented his seeing this earlier.[28] To similar effect is Philip's baptism of the Ethiopian eunuch (Acts 8:38-39): "and they both went down into the water, Philip and the eunuch, and he baptized him. But when they came up out of the water (ἐκ τοῦ ὕδατος), the Spirit of the Lord snatched Philip away." As the two were already in the water, the only further action open to Philip to complete the baptism was by pushing the eunuch right under the water.

Somewhat puzzling is the source of water used for this baptism in an urban setting. In describing what was done and said during a Pauline baptism, Wayne Meeks suggests that the "river seems our best guess, or else a tub and a bowl."[29] There was, however, a definite preference for the use of "living," that is, running, water. The *Didache*, a first- or second-century Syrian text, directs the baptizer, after having reviewed the status of the candidates for baptism, to "baptize in the name of the Father and of the Son and of the Holy Spirit in living water."[30] It is possible that those involved simply resorted to the nearest river. In Acts Paul meets Lydia on a riverbank outside Philippi, and that may be where the reader is meant to understand that her baptism occurs (Acts 16:11-15). The Christ-followers of Rome could have been baptized in the Tiber, a river in which people were accustomed to bathe during this period.[31] Indeed, there is an early tradition that Peter did precisely this, since Tertullian states at one point in *On Baptism* (the earliest Christian exposition of baptism and written in Carthage c. 200 CE) that it does not matter what sort of water is used, in that "there is no difference between those whom John 'dipped in the Jordan' and Peter in the Tiber."[32] This remark, made incidentally by Tertullian in the course of proving another point and therefore strong evidence that he thought the idea that Peter had baptized in the Tiber a reasonable one and also good evidence that Peter had done so—perhaps on the further bank in the Trastevere region that was the site of a large Judean settlement—is immensely revealing. On the assumption that the reference is to Peter's activity in Rome in the 60s before his martyrdom there during the reign of Nero,[33] we are provided with a picture of baptism in the Tiber, which the Christ-followers addressed by Paul may themselves have experienced (probably at the hands of some other baptizer) some five to ten years earlier.

On the other hand, Hippolytus presents a different mode of obtaining "living water" in his *Apostolic Tradition,* a text written in Rome in about 217 CE but that reflects practices and beliefs in the city some thirty years earlier and possibly even further back:[34] "At cockcrow prayer shall be made over the water. The stream shall flow through the baptismal tank or pour into it from above when there is no scarcity of water."[35] Immersion in the open flow of the Tiber is not in view, as a baptismal tank is mentioned, apparently in close proximity to "the church," since the newly baptized are clothed and brought into it.[36] We have moved beyond the situation of the first generation, when the building normally used by the congregation for its meetings would usually have been the house of a wealthy member. The tank may have been fed with water diverted from one of the city's aqueducts, for the tank is being fed with running water. Baptisms in the Tiber may have become too risky after Christ-followers had begun to be persecuted, in Nero's reign especially.

Another possibility is baptism in one of Rome's numerous baths. Meeks's initial reaction to this idea is that it is rather fantastic to picture Christ-followers taking over a room in a public bath. Nevertheless, he notes that the priests of Isis at Cenchreae made use of "the nearest bath" for the customary ablution of the initiate, so perhaps the idea is not so far-fetched after all, especially if the baptism occurred at times when the baths were least frequented.[37]

Hippolytus depicts a baptism where the candidates first take off their clothing, while women also loosen their hair and put aside any gold or silver ornaments, lest they take any "alien thing" down to the water with them. The nakedness of people of either sex in one another's presence for this purpose seems not to have been a matter of concern. This no doubt reflects the common practice in Rome of naked men and women bathing together in the public baths.[38] After disrobing, each candidate enters the tank with the person who will effect the baptism, the baptizer apparently pushing the candidate's head under the water. This happened three times according to Hippolytus, with the three immersions being the occasion for the candidates to declare their faith, in turn, in the Father, the Son, and the Holy Spirit.[39] Here again we have evidence for total immersion. The precedent for all these aspects of the ritual was the practice of John the Baptist immersing people in the living water of the Jordan. The early church, however, was practical. The passage from Hippolytus just cited continues, "but if there is a scarcity [of water], whether constant or sudden, use whatever water you can find." Tertullian, in addition, states: "Therefore there is no difference whether one is washed in the sea or in a pool, in a river or in a spring, in a lake or in a river bed."[40] Even more radically, the author of the *Didache* continues the passage quoted above: "But if you have no living [that is, running] water, then baptize in some other water . . . and if you have neither, then pour water on the head three times 'in the name of the Father and Son and Holy Spirit.'"[41] This appears to be the earliest reference to baptism by any means other than immersion.[42]

In the first generation or so of the Christ-movement baptism was also the occasion on which the believer received the Holy Spirit. Dunn has persuasively argued for a "conversion-initiation" complex in the early stages of the Christ-movement, in which water baptism—the expression of faith to which God gives the Spirit—and the reception of (or "baptism" by) the Spirit are closely connected but distinct events, with the former paving the way for the latter.[43] Typically, reception of the Spirit followed immediately after the believer came up out of the water.[44] That this was Paul's view emerges in 1 Cor. 12:13: "For by one Spirit we were all baptized into one body—Judeans or Greeks, slaves or free—and all were made to drink of one Spirit." The presence of the Spirit that Christ-followers experienced so powerfully at baptism may have led to the reworking of Jesus' baptism by water in the Jordan so as to include the feature of the Spirit descending like a dove upon him.

It is all too easy for modern readers familiar with the rather tame rituals of the sacrament of Christian confirmation to overlook the dramatic experiential aspects of receiving the Holy Spirit in the earliest period. Dunn accurately diagnoses the problem:

> It is a sad commentary on the poverty of our own immediate experience of the Spirit that when we come across language in which the NT writers refer directly to the gift of the Spirit and to their experience of it, either we automatically refer it to the sacraments and can only give it meaning when we do so, . . . or else we discount the experience described as too subjective and mystical in favour of a faith which is essentially an affirmation of biblical propositions, or else we in effect psychologize the Spirit out of existence.[45]

Those who received the Holy Spirit thought that God had entered them. The result was a variety of ecstatic states ("altered states of consciousness")[46] and phenomena, including trances, visions, auditions, prophecy, and glossolalia, that often produced feelings of peace and even euphoria. Analysis of charismatic phenomena in contemporary settings, especially where the most powerful dissociative states are manifested, has been of assistance in understanding similar features in the New Testament, such as in 1 Corinthians 12–14.[47] Glossolalia is a particularly useful indicator of charismatic states. It is not speech in a foreign language (= xenoglossy), but lexically noncommunicative utterances, where speech becomes musical sound.[48] Felicitas Goodman, speaking of glossolalia in Mexico, describes its power: "I can easily see now why glossolalia is so universally considered a divine inspiration, a possession by a supernatural being. There is something incredibly, brutally elemental about such an outbreak of vocalization, and at the same time something eerily, frighteningly unreal."[49] Paul himself produced potent glossolalia; at one point he says, "I thank God that I speak in tongues (γλώσσαις λαλῶ) more than all of you" (1 Cor. 14:18). There is some evidence from modern contexts that those who achieve an ecstatic state for the first time have an experience of being surrounded by light or of seeing a descending light.[50] This experience of actual illumination may lie behind the revealing statement about baptism in Heb. 6:4-5, even though there are biblical and extrabiblical sources for imagery of light and darkness:[51] "For it is impossible to restore again to repentance those who have once been illuminated (φωτισθέντας), who have tasted the heavenly gift and become partakers of the Holy Spirit and have tasted the goodness of the word of God and the powers of the age to come, but then fall away."

Meeks is skeptical about the incidence of possession by the Spirit at baptism: "We can scarcely believe that every convert on emerging from the water of baptism fell into a trance and spoke in tongues, however, if for no other reason than that it would then be hard to understand either the divisions over the practice at Corinth or Paul's arguments in trying to bring it under control." Perhaps, he suggests, the initiate shouted out "Abba" as a sign of the Spirit impelling the person to acknowledge his or her adoption by God.[52] Yet Meeks's negative assessment flies in the face of texts like 1 Cor. 12:11 and Heb. 6:4-5. Moreover, the emotionally charged atmosphere of baptism, with fellow Christ-followers present to assist the newly baptized members achieve spiritual possession, in the manner known from Goodman's investigation in modern charismatic congregations,[53] would have meant that most did receive the Spirit. Nor is there anything in 1 Corinthians 12–14 that stands in the way of baptism as the usual occasion for reception of the Spirit. In these chapters Paul is dealing with the way that spiritual gifts should be treated at regular meetings of the congregation. While it is clear that not everyone possesses every gift, this does not exclude a much more florid display of ecstatic phenomena during the ritual of baptism.

Although there is no reference to the Spirit in Romans 6, this does not count against the assumption that Paul's understanding of the connection between baptism and Spirit evident in 1 Cor. 12:13 had altered. For in Romans 8 he offers a rich presentation of the role of the Spirit in the Christ-movement. Although I deal with this material in chapter eleven below, it is worth mentioning here that Rom. 8:1-17 concerns life in the Spirit. Although Paul does not say so, it is reasonable to impute to him and his audience the belief that such life began with baptism. When he refers (8:23) to their "having the first fruits of the Spirit," we must assume a shared understanding that baptism was the occasion for first receiving that fruit. Similarly, when he mentions (vv. 9-10) that being in the Spirit means having the Spirit of God dwelling within (πνεῦμα θεοῦ οἰκεῖ ἐν ὑμῖν), of having the Spirit of Christ (these two Spirits apparently being equivalent or closely related) and belonging to Christ, the point at which this indwelling of God's Spirit, possession of Christ's Spirit, and relationship with Christ began, with all the associated charismatic excitement mentioned above, was baptism.

Oscar Cullmann has noted that whereas the eucharistic meal was a repeated event involving the whole community as a community, baptism was an event that could not be repeated and that had an impact on an individual within the community.[54] Perhaps so, yet while it is not entirely clear who attended on such occasions, that baptism occurred in the presence of the community seems highly likely, given the importance of the occasion. Hippolytus, describing the practice in Rome as it must have been in the second half of the second century CE and possibly much earlier (if one assumes a continuation of traditions in the same city), provides important information. He notes that during the protracted, three-year period of catechumenate, when they are "hearers of the word," the catechumens are not allowed to give the kiss of peace, "for their kiss is not yet pure."[55] Yet Hippolytus concludes his description of the baptism of the candidates and their anointing with oil by saying: "And immediately thereafter they shall join in prayer with all the people, but they shall not pray with the faithful until all these things are completed. And at the close of the prayer they shall give the kiss of peace."[56]

This passage is evidence for the presence of the rest of the community, with whom the intimacy and sign of full belonging to the group represented by the kiss of peace can only be shared once the candidates have been through the entire ritual. The prescription of such a gesture of inclusion was probably regarded as fundamental to the process. This practice underlines the importance of the approach taken by Axel von Dobbeler to faith mentioned in chapter seven above. In this perspective faith is a comprehensive social occurrence encompassing both access to God and entry to the community.[57] Von Dobbeler's view that it permits access to God only via entry into the communal relationship of the congregation, not on an individual basis, is confirmed in the gathering of the community for the baptism of each new member.

If the baptism was carried out in a house (or, in later centuries, a church) attended by members of the congregation, this would have been more a private than a public gathering. If it occurred in or next to a river, it seems more likely that a time or place would have been chosen so as to avoid notice by people unconnected with the Christ-movement, thus producing a comparatively private occasion. When John H. Elliott, therefore, writes that as "a ritual of conversion, baptism was the public celebration of both a personal transformation and a social transition,"[58] I must agree, save with the qualification that here "public" means "open to and witnessed by the congregation," but probably not outsiders. Concerns about the presence of nonmembers, admittedly, were probably greater after the persecution of Nero, when belonging to the movement had become much more dangerous.

Baptism and Social Identity

From the viewpoint of social identity theory, the subject of baptism falls under the rubric of joining, or becoming a member of, the group. Unfortunately, because of the neglect of the temporal and developmental dimensions to group phenomena by social identity theorists until comparatively recently, this is not an issue that has been subjected to a great deal of scrutiny. There are, however, some useful studies. Levine and Moreland, for example, have proposed a temporal model of group socialization that covers a person's initial investigation, recruitment, and (at times) eventual exit and emphasize that it is a two-way process, with new members being changed by the group but also changing it.[59] Rupert Brown has focused on three of the phenomena described by Levine and Moreland: reconnoitering the group, changes in self-concept, and initiation into the group.[60] I will briefly relate these three issues to Romans.

Reconnaissance is undertaken by people who are considering joining a group voluntarily. It essentially involves weighing benefits against costs— assessing what the group can do for them and what they will be expected to offer in return. The benefits offered by membership of the Christ-movement were many. Most dramatic was the euphoria produced by having the Spirit of God enter a person, with the usual panoply of charismatic gifts such as visions, auditions, glossolalia, prophecy, and so on. Paul speaks about life in the Spirit later in the letter (Rom. 8:1-17).[61] Another benefit was that members were expected to treat one another in a manner characterized by the type of love that typified the movement—ἀγάπη. Paul explores the dimensions of ἀγάπη in 12:9-21 and 13:8-10.[62] In a society marked by pronounced social stratification, that all members were expected to treat one another in accordance with the (often countercultural) demands of ἀγάπη must have made the movement considerably attractive, especially when the poor and destitute could also expect support and sustenance from members with more resources (see 12:3-8). The main downside to membership was that it involved severing ties with practices such as idolatry that were embedded in local patterns of familial and civic life. Christ-followers ran the risk of being treated as atheists in relation to the traditional gods and goddesses upon whose support the state relied. All this meant that they could expect to experience afflictions, the θλίψεις Paul mentions in 5:3.

I mentioned above that the *Apostolic Tradition* of Hippolytus, representing the situation in Rome in the second century CE, speaks of a three-year catechumenate before baptism. While we cannot be sure that such a period was the rule in Rome in the mid-50s, it is almost certain that potential members would have been required to spend some time in preparation for baptism. From the point of view of the movement (normally the only one considered in this discussion) this would have ensured their suitability, while from their perspective this was the time when they would have reconnoitered the movement, weighing the advantages and disadvantages in the manner just described.

Since our sense of who we are is intimately tied up with our group memberships, one of the major consequences of becoming a member is a change in the way we see ourselves—a redefinition of who we are—which has definite implications for our self-esteem. This is the second aspect of joining a group highlighted by Brown and obviously applies to a group like the Christ-followers in Rome in the 50s of the first century. Given the seriousness of the potential pros and cons of membership, there can be no doubt of the magnitude of the change in self-concept involved. New members of the movement asked to answer the question "Who am I?" would have given replies very different from those they proffered before baptism. Since they would have gradually internalized their membership of the Christ-movement as part of their self-concept, the prestige and high value that they attached to it (which encouraged them to join) would have increased their own sense of self-worth.

Brown's third issue is initiation into the group. Following Levine and Moreland, he notes that existing members of a group often signal the importance of entry by the requirement of some "ceremony" or "ritual." The preferable word for an initiation is a "ritual." Mark McVann has usefully distinguished between rituals and ceremonies.[63] Rituals are actions occurring at irregular intervals that break usual routines, are presided over by professionals, and produce transformations of status. They focus on the movement of time from the present to the future. Ceremonies occur on regular intervals and at predictable times, are presided over by people with no professional standing, and serve to confirm social values and structures. They focus on the movement of time from the past to the present. Within this distinction, examples of rituals are baptisms, weddings, and funerals, while ceremonies include birthdays, anniversaries, and annual feast days.

Rituals of initiation have been frequently analyzed as rites of passage, a perspective first developed by Arnold van Gennep and further explicated by Victor Turner.[64] The three stages of a rite of passage are *separation* (when the initiand leaves behind his or her old status or group), *the liminal stage* (when the initiand occupies an ambiguous zone between the old world and the new), and *aggregation* or *incorporation* (when, with the ritual actions completed, the initiand is accepted into the new status or group, with new rights and obligations). The liminal stage is the heart of a rite of passage, the time and mechanism of transformation, when the initiands shed an old identity and obtain a new one. Turner offers a fine description of this phase:

> They may be disguised as monsters, wear only a strip of clothing, or even go naked, to demonstrate that as liminal beings they have no status, property, insignia, secular clothing indicating rank or role, position in a kinship system. . . . Their behavior is normally passive or humble. . . . It is as though they are being reduced or ground down to a uniform condition to be fashioned anew and endowed with additional powers to enable them to cope with their new status in life.[65]

The relevance of this to baptism in the early stages of the Christ-movement, including, we may presume, the Christ-followers of Rome addressed by Paul, is clear. The period of instruction, the catechumenate, constituted the first stage, of separation from the old identities of the initiands, although here extending over a considerable time. This stage served, as Brown puts it, "as an apprenticeship for the individual, introducing him or her to the normative standards of the group and relevant skills needed for effective functioning in it."[66]

The total immersion in water that formed the heart of the ritual was the liminal stage. In line with Turner's description, the candidates stripped naked and the women had to remove any jewelry they were wearing. This symbolized the abandonment of their old existence, especially the sinfulness that had accompanied it. Then they handed themselves over to the baptizer to be subject to his will in pushing them under the water, thus humbly and passively letting themselves be fashioned anew. This event, in its sheer physicality, must have constituted a powerful cognitive and emotional experience for those undergoing it. The cleansing immersion in living water starkly underlined the distinctiveness of the Christ-movement from the world that had been, in a sense, left behind and the pervasive nature of the identity transition that had occurred. After the baptism, aggregation or incorporation occurred, since the candidates dried and clothed themselves and were brought into the church, where the faithful were gathered. This brings us to Paul.

Paul's Teaching on Baptism (Rom. 6:1-10)

The first point to notice in relation to Paul's treatment of baptism here is the proliferation of verbs with a first person plural subject, just as in 5:1-11. There are thirteen such verbs and three equivalent expressions in 6:1-8. This means, as Patricia McDonald has suggested, that there is a strongly personal dimension to what Paul writes in this first part of chap. 6. Paul and the Christ-followers of Rome have in common not only righteousness by faith (5:1) but also the "ritual by which each person entered into the mystery of Christ's death and resurrection."[67] From a social identity perspective, the repeated first person plurals are a means whereby he solidifies his claim to exercise leadership over them by making clear that he and they share the same identity and the same means whereby he acquired it.

In 6:3-10 Paul presents an explanation of baptism that focuses on how sin no longer has power over Christ-followers. Paul explains how the actions of Christ and the experience of those who believe in him are synthesized in baptism. Yet the mythos concerning Christ is fairly sparse in its details: he was crucified, he died (a death in which he died to sin), he was buried, he was raised from the dead by the glory of the Father, and he will never die again. Paul does not here say precisely how Christ's fate so described ended the dominion of sin, although that is clearly his position (see 6:14). Earlier in the letter he is similarly reticent as to how Christ's death brought about this result, saying little more than that Christ was put forward by the Father as an expiation (ἱλαστήριον) so that his blood might earn his followers their righteousness (3:24-26; 5:8-11). Paul can hardly be said to express in Romans a well-articulated soteriology.

His real interest in 6:3-10 lies not in the theological reason by which Christ's death and resurrection break the power of sin and enable human righteousness, but in describing how human beings obtain the benefits of his self-sacrifice by replicating his experience in baptism and thus being incorporated into him. Although it is not mentioned here, we may take for granted that those who were baptized had already in some way expressed their attachment to Christ, faith of some kind,[68] during the course of their preparation, otherwise they would not have been permitted to undertake the rite. As we have seen, affirmation of faith in trinitarian form was central to the baptismal liturgy described by Hippolytus in the *Apostolic Tradition,* and some affirmation of faith was probably always associated with baptism. Nevertheless, none of this runs counter to Cullmann's argument that faith in Christ in its fullness only began with baptism or to Axel von Dobbeler's insistence on faith as social rather than individual in its basic orientation.[69]

Paul begins with a general question (v. 3), which benefits from a fairly literal translation to bring out the point. His initial statement in v. 3 ("Are you unaware that all of us who have been baptized into Christ Jesus . . . ?") seems to assume that Paul is reminding his audience of at least some things they already know, the starting point of his argument.[70] At the least, he probably assumed that they would be familiar with the fact that the baptism by which they joined the group had a fundamental reference to Christ, even if in the first generation the precise nature of the connection may have been understood differently among communities of Christ-followers.[71] This view is rendered likely by the fact that here baptism "into Christ" (εἰς Χριστόν) seems to be roughly equivalent to an older and more common expression: baptism "in/into the name of Jesus Christ."[72] Paul could probably also assume, as Wedderburn notes, that his audience thought that the ritual of baptism *"somehow united one with Christ,"* possibly in the sense of entering the community formed under his lordship and protection.[73] With the next part of his question, however, "(Are you unaware that) we have been baptized into his death?" Paul appears to enter an area of interpretation with which they may not be familiar. Their current understanding requires some enhancement in how the process of baptism relates to Christ's death. Later in the letter he will have more to say about the nature of the incorporation into Christ experienced by baptized members of the movement (12:4-5).

Paul's first task is to homologate the experience of the believer in baptism with the death and resurrection of Christ by offering two parallel descriptions (vv. 4-5). The imagery involved seems to have efficacy only if Paul has in mind the baptism by total immersion described above. First, he says, "Therefore we have been buried together with (συνετάφημεν) him through baptism into death," thus indicating the immersion stage of the ritual, burial in water, "in order that just as Christ was raised from the dead through the glory of the Father, so might we also walk in the newness of life" (v. 4), thus intimating, in turn, the emergence of the believer out of the water and his or her donning clothes to commence the new life, or, in our terminology, the new identity in Christ.[74] The next verse restates this with a different emphasis: "For if we have been united with him in the likeness of his death we will also be united with him in the likeness of his resurrection." This clarifies that resurrection is involved in the new life.

In v. 6 Paul states that "we know that our old self was crucified with him, so that the sinful body might be destroyed and we might no longer be slaves to sin." Paul is still referring to baptism and its effects.[75] It is in baptism that the old self of the believer is crucified with Christ, the word συνεσταυρώθη matching "we were buried with" (συνετάφημεν) in v. 4. Paul does not specify in this verse that this old identity is replaced by a new one, but he does so in the next: "For he who has died is righteoused (δεδικαίωται) from sin." Pace Douglas Moo,[76] there is no judicial setting in view here, since Paul is simply making clear (as he does elsewhere in the letter) that the result of Christ's act (and of God standing behind it) is that a person who believes in him (expressed unequivocally in baptism) becomes a δίκαιος, a righteous person, in the present, with God being the agent of that transformation. Paul thus identifies baptism as the locus for the destruction of the old identity and the acquisition of the new, the exalted status of which is expressed by its necessary association with righteousness.[77]

Immediately after this Paul reminds his Roman audience that this identity has a future dimension: "But if we died with Christ," that is, in baptism, "we believe that we will live with him" (v. 8). It is difficult to know if the life envisaged here is the new life Christ-followers experience in the present, as Lagrange thought,[78] or to the life after their resurrection. Given the references elsewhere in the letter to life in the present (5:18; 8:6, 10), Lagrange is probably right. The reference to resurrection in v. 5, however, surely indicates that Paul has in mind an identity that extends into the future forever, that this is life without end (cf. 5:10; 6:22, 23). In vv. 9-10 Paul returns to Christ, who being raised from the dead is no longer subject to death's lordship, for he has died once and for all (ἐφάπαξ) to sin and lives for God.

Some commentators, such as Moo, consider that Paul drops the subject of baptism in 6:4, "never to resume it in this chapter."[79] On this view, in vv. 5-10 Paul is not speaking about baptism but generally about the experience of a Christ-follower, the new life made possible in baptism. Wedderburn is another representative of this opinion and supports his case by citing a number of references, several of them from Pauline texts outside Romans, where Paul mentions dying with Christ as far as sin is concerned without mentioning baptism.[80] There are two fatal objections to this position in relation to Romans 6. First, the explicit mentions of baptism in vv. 3-4 necessarily evoked images of the baptism that Paul's addressees had themselves undertaken, and in which the element of removal of sin through cleansing with living water had been central to the ritual. It is unlikely that Paul intended that his addressees, when hearing, soon after explicit mention of baptism, references to walking in new life (6:4), the crucifixion of the old man (6:6), the destruction of the body of sin (6:6), their no longer being enslaved to sin (6:6), and their being righteoused from sin (6:7), would understand that he was no longer speaking of baptism, when that was the occasion when all this became a reality for them, and regard Paul as now addressing their new life generally. The second objection is that Paul's proposal that at baptism the Christ-follower is baptized into Christ's death and burial and thus experiences new life just as he rose from the dead, involving the powerful imagery of immersion in water and elevation from it, is followed by a number of other statements with such cognate ideas and expressions that it is implausible to imagine that Paul wanted his audience to forget about baptism at v. 4 or that they did so. How could the Christ-followers in Rome, upon hearing v. 8 when the letter was read to them: "But if we died with Christ, we believe that we will live with him," which is virtually a summary of how Paul explains baptism in vv. 3-4, possibly assume that baptism was not still in view?

Indeed, the dichotomy between vv. 5-10 concerning baptism or life in Christ is a false one. For even though baptism is not forgotten in vv. 5-10, Paul also addressed here the identity that begins with that event. The aorist tenses that plainly refer back to the event of baptism (ἐβαπτίσθημεν, v. 3; συνετάφημεν, v. 4; συνεσταυρώθη, v. 6; ἀπεθάνομεν, v. 8) are matched by perfect tenses that refer to a state of affairs that began then but continues in the lives of the members of groups with faith in Christ (γεγόναμεν, v. 5; δεδικαίωται, v. 7) and by future tenses pointing to their destiny (ἐσόμεθα, v. 5; συζήσομεν, v. 8).

Yet how are we to understand the relationship between Christ and the person whose belief in him has been manifested in baptism? Commentators who believe baptism is left behind at v. 4 tend to minimize the role of the ritual in bringing the believer into contact with Christ, generally preferring faith to have that function, as if baptism and faith were somehow independent options. For example, Moo is so determined to champion what he describes as "the subsidiary role of baptism in our union with Christ" that he fixes upon the preposition διά used in v. 4 ("Therefore we were buried with him 'through' [διά] baptism into death") as showing that baptism "is not the place, or time, at which we are buried with Christ, but the instrument (*dia*) through which we are buried with him."[81] The force of the imagery, however, necessitates that baptism (understood to include baptism by water and Spirit) is indeed the place and time, as well as the mechanism, of the believer's burial with Christ. The preposition διά covers all these possibilities.[82] Wedderburn suggests that Paul believes the Christ-follower "has died with Christ and the 'dying' that takes place in baptism is but an 'echo,' a realization, of a past death with Christ, a death that took place once and for all, unrepeatable and final."[83] In other words:

> That one person died and with him all for whom he died; that past death is declared afresh in baptism, as the baptized says her or his "Amen" to the past representative act, pledging herself or

himself to live henceforth in solidarity both with the representative and all those represented by him; at the same time she or he receives the promise of new life uttered in the vindication of that same representative person by his resurrection from the dead.[84]

While this view at least sees baptism as the occasion of the believer's "death," the question remains as to whether it is just too christologically meager to do justice to Paul's vision of baptism. In particular, it ignores the presence of Christ, and the Spirit, during baptism.

Moo disavows the presence of Christ, and of his death, burial, and resurrection, in baptism on the basis of two "fatal" objections. First, the once-for-all nature of Christ's death and resurrection (ἐφάπαξ, v. 10) prevents them from being present in the act of baptism. Second, to locate these events in baptism would give it a significance that does not fit the line of thought in chap. 6.[85] Since I have already suggested above that Moo's attempt to minimize the significance of baptism in chap. 6 is untenable, I will pass over this latter argument. The former argument depends on an unacceptably literalistic understanding of ritual and a disregard for what actually happened when someone was baptized.

It goes without saying that Christ did not literally die and rise at every baptism. Yet a central part of ritual is to bring past events into the present *in a socially and religiously significant sense*. At this point it will be helpful to offer a brief prelude to the fuller discussion on time in chapter eleven below. Perhaps the most extreme version of presence of the past in ritual is represented in Lévi-Strauss's claim that "historical rites bring the past into the present."[86] In a manner reminiscent of Mircea Eliade's "myth of the eternal return,"[87] Lévi-Strauss proposed that in "historical rites" the sacred and beneficial atmosphere of the mythical period is re-created and becomes a present reality. Alfred Gell is critical of such assertions for the reason that he presents, as real, rituals that are, in terms of metaphysics, "illusions."[88] But for Gell to characterize the beliefs of peoples who seek to re-create the experience of the mythic past in the present as "illusions" is simply too extreme. For they are "illusions" only in relation to some metaphysical framework and are real enough for those who ascribe to them and for whom they serve vital social functions. That is, ritual regularly serves to make the past "present" in a manner that has real social and religious impacts. The commemoration of Passover (admittedly, as defined above, a ceremony rather than a ritual) in the Second Temple period illustrates the point. Accordingly, Gregory Baum is correct in claiming that baptism is an act of initiation "whereby the redemptive death of Christ which happened but once in history is cultically made present in the shape of a visible rite."[89] Yet it is doubtful if even this formulation goes far enough, for it does not assert the presence of Christ in the experience of the ritual. This also brings us to the second objection to Moo's position, that it overlooks what happens in baptism.

Those who were baptized received the Spirit of God within and henceforth the Spirit lived there. For Paul this was virtually the equivalent of saying that they had the Spirit of Christ (Rom. 8:10). Thus baptism was an overwhelming encounter with God and Christ, an encounter charged with visionary experiences of light and manifested in an eruption of glossolalia and other ecstatic phenomena. For his early followers, Christ was actually present in baptism and this presence was central to the ritual. Immersion in the depth and silence of the water ritually corresponded to sharing Christ's death, while elevation into the air and possession by the Spirit of God/Christ, with associated receipt of charismatic gifts, brought them into closest conjunction with the risen Lord.

Brendan Byrne has reasonably suggested that central to Paul's argument here is a concept of Christ-followers as "incorporated through faith and baptism into the person of Christ as all-embracing sphere of salvation." The reality that results can be described as "union with Christ" and is communicated by the distinctive expressions beginning or associated with συν- ("with") that run throughout the passage and serve to align the experience of the Christ-follower with that of Christ (συνετάφημεν, v. 4; σύμφυτοι, v. 5; συνεσταυρώθη, v. 6; ἀπεθάνομεν σὺν Χριστῷ and συζήσομεν, v. 8).[90]

Keeping Away from Sin (Rom. 6:11-14)

The explanation in vv. 3-10 sparks an exhortation from Paul in v. 11 that follows closely on from v. 10: "So also you consider yourselves dead to sin, but living for God in Christ Jesus." It may seem odd that Paul would even entertain the possibility that they could be anything else than dead to sin. But, as Hartman has noted, for Paul baptism "meant a liberation not from sinning, but from sin's reign, from living according to the conditions of its power. Liberation is real but not automatic; it must be realized in a life lived to God."[91] To achieve this, Paul wants his audience to treat the death and resurrection of Christ as made available to them in baptism and thus providing a new foundation for their experience and identity, which now have attached to them for the first time in the letter the expression "in Christ Jesus." Although the meaning of this phrase is much discussed, Albert Schweitzer offers a useful explanation: "Though the expression has almost the character of a formula, it is no mere formula for Paul. For him every manifestation of the life of the baptized man is conditioned by his being in Christ. Grafted into the corporeity of Christ, he loses his creatively individual existence and his natural personality. Henceforth he is only a form of manifestation of the personality of Jesus Christ, which dominates that corporeity."[92]

Schweitzer's formulation fits comfortably with efforts made since the early 1980s to emphasize the group-oriented nature of ancient Mediterranean culture, with individuals finding social meaning within the collectivities to which they belong, especially the family, to a greater extent than in modern North American and northern European cultures, where individualism is a dominant expression of human aspiration.[93] Paul takes this aspect of his social world one step further, by assimilating the group of Christ-followers to the body of Christ. Yet, as we will see in chapter thirteen below in relation to 12:4-5, the body he has in mind is one that is differentiated as to its parts, with another form of differentiation later evident in the metaphor of the olive tree in Romans 11.

In 6:12-13 Paul exhorts them not to let sin reign in their mortal flesh so that they obey its passions, nor to yield their members as weapons of unrighteousness (ἀδικία) for sin, but to present themselves to God as people who have come to life from death and as weapons of righteousness (δικαιοσύνη) to God. Paul began to establish the contrast between ἀδικία and δικαιοσύνη, respective marks of their old and new identities, as far back as 1:17-18. Here we see him still absorbed with the same pair of opposites and plainly alive to the possibility that sin and unrighteousness are still options for those who believe in Christ. In spite of Christ's death and resurrection, a certain fragility is attached to the identity he has made possible. In v. 14, however, Paul moves to a more confident statement: "For death will not lord it over you, since you are not under law but under grace."

That Paul should relate baptism in this letter to the question of liberation from the power of sin is a radically different explanation from the one he offers in Gal. 3:26-28, where he celebrates the abolition of boundaries: "For you are all sons of God through faith in Christ Jesus. For as many of you as were baptized into Christ have put on Christ. There is neither Judean nor Greek, there is neither slave nor free, there is neither male nor female, for you are all one in Christ Jesus." Daniel Boyarin uses these verses as an essential foundation for his view that Paul is concerned with the erasure of human difference, primarily between "Jew" and "gentile," but also between man and woman, freedman and slave.[94] We have already observed, however, that in other passages in Romans Paul appears to be maintaining difference, especially in relation to the significance of Judean identity, that he had arguably disregarded in Galatians. The last thing he wants to do in Romans is to say "there is neither Judean nor Greek." His treatment of baptism in Rom. 6:3-10 and the lesson he draws from it in 6:11-14 provide further evidence of this altered perspective. As already proposed in chapter six above, although Paul argues that all people are subject to sin, he takes great pains to demonstrate that non-Judeans and Judeans succumb to the power of sin via entirely different routes, non-Judeans in the absence of the law and Judeans while under it. Paul's strategy in reconciling Judeans and non-Judeans thus accords with the discovery of modern social psychologists that the establishment of a common ingroup identity will only succeed if the two subgroups concerned do not feel that their distinctive identities are threatened in the process—this is the "equal status–different dimensions condition" that is a prerequisite to their successful recategorization. Accordingly, when Paul spells out the meaning of baptism in 6:3-10 in relation to breaking the power of sin, he is not erasing the difference between Judeans and non-Judeans, because the fact that they fall victim to sin in different ways is well and truly part of the picture.

Indeed, this view finds immediate confirmation in the way Paul crafts his argument following 6:1-15, by addressing himself (primarily if not exclusively) first to the needs and situations of non-Judean Christ-followers and then to his Judean addressees—in 6:15-23 and chap. 7, respectively. That is, having spent much of chaps. 5–6 speaking of his addressees and himself as sharing the same common ingroup identity, for example by the frequent use of first person plural verbs and pronouns, he now indicates that he has not forgotten the two subgroup identities that comprise his audience in the manner that modern social psychologists have suggested is essential if a process of recategorization is to be successful.

Romans 6:15-23

In 6:15-23 Paul repudiates the second false notion that might be deduced from how he has just explained the origin of the new identity in Christ (5:1-11) and how Christ has reversed the consequences of Adam and the law (5:12-21)—that Christ-followers should sin because they are not under law but grace. His use of pronouns requires comment. After the first person plurals of 6:15, a sign that he is including himself with his audience, he suddenly moves into the second person plurals that characterize vv. 16-22 and only returns to first person plurals in v. 23, in the phrase "our Lord Jesus Christ." This probably suggested to his first audience, listening to the letter rather than reading it, that he was not necessarily including himself in the subject he describes in this passage of the letter. As we will see in a moment, when they heard the sentence we know as v. 19 they would have realized that the reason for Paul so distancing himself was that here he mainly has non-Judean Christ-followers in view. Let us take up his argument.

To rebut the notion that "we" should sin because "we" are not under law but under grace, Paul describes it as inconsistent with the identity they have now acquired, and he does so mainly through the use of images from slavery. At first glance, it may seem odd that Paul should choose servile imagery, given that slaves occupied the bottom level of the socioeconomic hierarchy in the ancient Mediterranean.[95] The reason for its selection seems to lie ultimately in that Paul saw the relationship of a believer to Christ as one of slave to Lord. He began the letter, after all, by describing himself as "Paul, a slave of Jesus Christ," and he uses this self-appellation elsewhere in his letters.[96] In addition, Paul usually operated on the basis of stark either/or dichotomies, with no room for neutral zones in the middle, and this form of conceptuality probably reflects the pronounced ingroup/outgroup categorization characteristic of Judeans and borrowed from them by the early Christ-movement. One such dichotomy is between enslavement to sin or to God/Christ. He mentions the first alternative a little earlier (6:6) when he says that "we are no longer enslaved to sin" (μηκέτι δουλεύειν ἡμᾶς τῇ ἁμαρτίᾳ). As noted above, such enslavement ended with baptism, and those so initiated into the new group, including Paul himself, are now slaves to Jesus Christ.

This is an important theme in 6:15-23. He notes that they were formerly slaves to sin (6:17) but they have now been freed from it. To designate this reality Paul uses the aorist passive participle ἐλευθερωθέντες meaning "having been emancipated," "set free," on two occasions (6:18, 22), with reference to a single event in the past, namely, baptism, although most commentators do not note this point.[97] The freedom that began at baptism continues in the present, as shown by the phrase "but now" (νυνὶ δέ) at the start of v. 22. In this regard the parallel with the emancipation of a slave is close, since the act of emancipation was a momentous event in itself that also produced a new status and hence identity for the person that persisted thereafter.

As noted already, however, the manner in which Paul depicts this transformation of masters shows that he has not forgotten that he needs to keep distinct the respective histories and situations of Judean and non-Judean believers. That he has the latter subgroup in mind becomes apparent at v. 19, when he says that "you once yielded your members as slaves to impurity (ἀκαθαρσία) and lawlessness (ἀνομία) unto lawlessness (ἀνομία)." Paul used the word ἀκαθαρσία earlier in the letter in reference to those engaged in idolatry (1:24). Similarly, the notion of lawlessness first appears in the letter in the adverbial form ἀνόμως at 2:12 (a pivotal verse) in unambiguous reference to non-Israelites: "For all those who have sinned lawlessly (ἀνόμως) will also perish lawlessly" (ἀνόμως; 2:12a). This clause probably refers back to 1:18-32, just as 2:12b ("and all who have sinned under the law will be judged by the law") looks forward to Israelite sin in 2:17-24. While the plural form of the word ἀνομία appears in 4:7 (a quotation from Ps. 32:1) in a way capable of extending to all Paul's addressees, when it is used in Rom. 6:19b the earlier appearance of lawlessness in 2:12a and its close conjunction here with ἀκαθαρσία suggest that it is more apt for the non-Israelite component of Paul's Roman audience.[98] Paul is concerned that the non-Israelite Christ-followers of Rome might lapse back into ἀκαθαρσία, just as he had been with this sort of convert in Thessalonika (1 Thess. 4:7-8).[99]

A further indication of the non-Judean referents of these verses is the word "sanctification" (ἁγιασμός) at the end of Rom. 6:19 and in v. 22. In 1 Thessalonians the language of "sanctification" (which covers ἁγιασμός, ἅγιος, ἁγιωσύνη, and ἁγιάζω) provides a semantic framework for expressing the ideal identity of non-Judean converts parallel to the language of righteousness, which does not appear in 1 Thessalonians and which, indeed, Paul consciously redacts out of a source at 1 Thess. 5:8.[100] Standing in stark contrast to sanctification is "impurity" (ἀκαθαρσία), as at 1 Thess. 4:7. Paul inherited this term from Judean tradition as "a general description of the absolute alienation from God" in which the non-Judeans of his time found themselves.[101] The reference to ἁγιασμός in Rom. 6:19, therefore, closely following and juxtaposed with ἀκαθαρσία, evokes an essentially non-Judean polarity of experience, inside and outside the Christ-movement, respectively. The references to the law in vv. 14 and 15 do not militate against Paul focusing here on non-Judeans, since in these verses the law functions to specify an alternative to grace available in the present, not an aspect of their experience in the past.

That Paul does not associate himself with those whom he addresses in 6:16-22 by use of first person plural pronominal forms makes good sense in a part of the letter where he is especially interested in the position of non-Judean Christ-followers. After all, he did not share their ethnic status or the history (probably of idol worship in some cases) that they brought with them on joining the congregations in Rome. On the other hand, he did have in common with them a shared experience of Christ in the present that he referred to with the use of first person plural verbs and pronouns (6:15, 23). I noted above the proposal that successful attempts at recategorization involve attending to both subgroups in question, and here Paul reflects on the position of non-Judeans even though he was a Judean.

10

Pauline Leadership and
Group Exemplification in Romans 7

In Romans 6 Paul dealt with two possible corollaries that those hostile to him and his gospel might deduce from what he had said in 5:20-21. He used the first ("Shall we continue in sin so that grace might increase?") as a springboard to talk about the initiation into the Christ-movement in baptism that encompasses all members, including himself (6:1-14). He related the second ("Shall we commit sin as we are no longer under law but under grace?") primarily to non-Judean Christ-followers (6:15-23). This left him with the other matter raised in 5:20-21, the relationship between sin and the Mosaic law. This issue he takes up in chap. 7.

That he should next cover this issue (which was primarily relevant to those raised as Israelites in the Roman congregations because of their actual experience of the law) was not unexpected, especially given his practice earlier in the letter of bringing forward material primarily relevant to either the non-Israelite or Israelite component in successive (or almost successive) passages.[1] Such a progression would mean that he was paying attention to the interests of the Israelite as well as non-Israelite component of his target audience in the area of sin and the contrast between past and present experience. In this regard, I argue below that his opening statement in 7:1, "Do you not know, brothers, for I speak to those who know the law," is an aural cue that he has now turned his attention away from the non-Judean Christ-followers he mainly had in mind in 6:15-23 and is focusing more on the Judean members. We should recall once again that successful recategorization is likely to require careful attention to all subgroups. Yet the nature and status of the Mosaic law would also be of at least some interest to non-Judean Christ-followers in Rome in the event that people there were to begin advocating a gospel different from his to the extent that they urged acceptance of the law in addition to faith in Christ. Although there is no sign that this had already happened in Rome, Paul must have been worried from previous experience in Antioch (Gal. 2:11-14), Corinth (2 Cor. 11:4), Galatia, and Philippi that it was likely to occur.[2] His recognition that acceptance of the law was an option for Roman Christ-followers is evident in his statements (reminders?) at Rom. 6:14-15 that they are not under law, but under grace.

Romans 7 is especially renowned for the prominence of the "I" voice in vv. 7-25. As well as considering the status of the Mosaic law in relation to Judean

Christ-followers (and possibly non-Judean believers as well), we need to interpret what Paul says here in a way that incorporates this issue into the discussion. This brings us back to the social identity and self-categorization approach to leadership set out in chapter three above.

A Social Identity Approach to Leadership in Romans

I have already proposed that Paul writes Romans to secure a base for himself in Rome for his Spanish mission, to win over hearts and minds before his visit to Jerusalem, and to address problems he has heard are affecting the congregations in Rome, especially tension between Judean and non-Judean Christ-followers. To achieve these results by his letter he needs to assume a leadership role over his Roman addressees, to succeed at "the process of influencing others in a manner that enhances their contribution to the realization of group goals."[3] To do this he must become an "entrepreneur of identity," turning himself and them into an "us" in relation to their identity as Christ-followers, thus gaining their commitment to a sense of self from which they would derive meaning, purpose, and value. This meant ensuring that the two basic subgroups among them, Judean and non-Judean, were both acknowledged and respected in relation to their own history and experience and yet recategorized more effectively into the superordinate identity they shared—of being righteous as in Christ. To achieve this Paul needed to demonstrate that he was representative of the shared social identity and consensual position of the group; in short, that he was an ingroup exemplar. As explained in chapter eight above, social psychologists define an ingroup exemplar as an actual person who embodies the identity of a group.[4] His success would depend on his powers of argument, deployed through rhetorical techniques (including diatribe style)[5] in the frail medium of a single letter.

From a social identity perspective, the function of a leader and the emergence of leadership are analyzed within a group-based social context that gives these roles and qualities expression. "Leaders and followers are transformed and energized as partners in an emerging social self-categorical relationship . . . leadership is all about the way in which this shared sense of 'us' is created, co-ordinated and controlled."[6] In particular, we have seen that for a person to exert most influence over other group members, to be an effective leader, he or she needs to be an ingroup exemplar or prototype, that is, the person who is most representative of the shared social identity and consensual position of the group as a whole.[7]

In congregations that he founded, Paul based his claim to exemplify the group on his behavior when among them. In particular, he went so far as to portray himself as the model of life in Christ that other Christ-believers should imitate. A social identity leadership model thus allows an entirely fresh approach to the mimetic strand in Paul's letters, which scholars commonly discuss.[8] Paul's position is that he epitomizes the social category of Christ-follower (that is, he both defines and is defined by it) and that other believers with personal knowledge of him should copy him; thus he exercises leadership. This means that he is an exemplar, a living example, of the identity of Christ-followers. Yet since Paul has not even visited Rome, this particular policy is not possible. This factor explains the lack of any call to imitate him in Romans.[9] All that Paul can do in connection with the Roman Christ-followers is to exercise his powers of argument, flexibly deploying notions susceptible to analysis within the framework of social identity to push their social relations toward greater harmony and to convince them of the truth of his understanding of the gospel. To do this he will need to persuade his audience that he is an exemplary Christ-follower, encapsulating all that such identity entails, even though they have not had any experience of him in person.[10] In a situation where there is or is likely to be disagreement (certainly the context in which Paul operated), a leader is someone who is adept at managing the process of consensualization in the direction of a particular vision of group identity through argument, negotiation, and persuasion. This suggestion means interpreting the rhetoric of Paul's discourse as integral to the dynamics of creating, installing, and maintaining a particular social identity in the minds and hearts of fellow Christ-followers.

The circumstance that at 7:1 Paul turns to consider the position of Judeans in relation to sin and the law, thus attesting to his capacity to move from one subgroup to the other among his addressees, tailoring his discourse and identity formulation to the needs of each, well illustrates the insight of social identity theorists that a leader needs to be flexible and accommodate him- or herself to changes in context.

Romans 7 demands consideration in the light of this model, given the prominence of the "I" voice that appears in vv. 7-25. Before considering these crucial verses, however, it is necessary to consider the way in which chap. 7 relates to the chapters in Romans preceding it and also, more importantly, the role of 7:1-6 in paving the way for the first person narration in 7:7-25. Let us now see, then, how far this model carries us in understanding chap. 7.

Social Identity and Leadership in Romans 7

Interpreting Romans 7:1-6: A Cue for Judean Christ-Followers

When Paul says in v. 1 that he is speaking to those who know the law (νόμος), it is certain that he has the Mosaic law in mind, since the example he immediately proceeds to lay out—of the woman bound to her husband while alive but free of responsibilities to him after his death—represents

Israelite law,[11] but not Roman law,[12] let alone the legal order generally.[13] This view is confirmed by the unambiguous reference to the Mosaic law in v. 6 and later in the chapter.

Yet the question arises whether in addressing "brothers" who know the (Mosaic) law in 7:1 he has in view both non-Judean believers (possibly familiar with Judean communities,[14] especially if former God-fearers) and Judean believers (who knew the law from performing it) or only the latter. It is possible that Paul includes both groups by addressing "brothers" (ἀδελφοί) in 7:1. If so, however, he soon narrows his focus to Judean Christ-followers alone—a situation probably reached in v. 4 when he addresses "my brothers" who "died to the law through the body of Christ,"[15] but certainly achieved by v. 6 where he speaks of release from the law by which they were constrained,[16] a statement applicable only to Christ-followers who had been Judeans prior to baptism. This impression is confirmed by the discussion of what it was like to be under the law that follows. All this suggests that it is more likely that Paul has the same group in mind in v. 1 as well, for nothing in the text suggests a change of the people in view from v. 1 to vv. 4-6. In this case, his qualification of brothers in v. 1 as "those who know the law" provides an aural cue to the original recipients of the letter that at this point he was about to pay particular attention to the position of Judeans among their number.[17]

When Paul begins chap. 7 with the words: "Or are you unaware, brothers, for I speak to those who know the law," he is addressing his audience as "brothers" for only the second time in the letter, the first occasion being 1:13. As we have just seen, he proffers an even more intimate address with the phrase "my brothers" in v. 4. Just as eye-catching is the transition from second person plural in vv. 1-3 to first person plural at the end of v. 4, where he concludes a statement that his brothers had died to the law so as to belong to the one who rose from the dead by saying "so that [or, 'with the result that'][18] we bear fruit (ἵνα καρποφορήσωμεν) for God." This verb is repeated in v. 5 but appears nowhere else in the Pauline corpus, although κάρπος ("fruit") occurs at 1:13; 6:21, 22; and 15:28.[19] The purpose (or result) clause ἵνα καρποφορήσωμεν does not express Paul's interest in being successful in missionary work (cf. 1:13), but signals that he is now aligning his own experience with that of the Judean Christ-followers in Rome, the "fruit" in question being that kind mentioned a little previously, in 6:22, as holiness and eternal life. This conclusion is mandated by the sentiments of 7:5-6 that are closely connected with v. 4 by the γάρ in v. 5 and by their contents and that can, indeed, be seen as an expansion of v. 4, but this time including Paul in the negatively assessed past *and* the positively valued present. For in vv. 5-6 Paul not only mentions the time when "*we* were in the flesh," with desires for sins[20] active in *our* limbs so as to bear fruit for death, but also proclaims that now (νυνὶ δὲ) *we* have been released from the law, dying to that by which *we* were constrained (presumably a reference to baptism, described in 6:3-11), so that *we* might serve in newness of spirit and not in oldness of letter. Paul's inclusion of himself via the first person plural here stands in contrast to the way he distances himself from the past experience of non-Judeans through the second person plurals of 6:16-22.

For scholars like Dunn and Fitzmyer the use of "brothers" in v. 1 is a sign that the topic is a "sensitive" one that calls for mutual trust and understanding.[21] Dunn also comments on the movement to first person plural in v. 4 as reflecting the mutual interdependence of Paul and his audience in ministry and daily life.[22] While such observations are not inaccurate, they do not go far enough. Since Dunn and Fitzmyer privilege the search for the way Paul develops cognitive patterns in chap. 7, they regard such signs of intimacy as a means to sweeten the draught.

A social identity perspective, however, produces a different view: In order to advance his bid for leadership in Rome, namely, to influence the Christ-members there to put into effect group goals, Paul needs to persuade his audience that he is in the same social category as they are—that the "me" and "you" has become "us." Social identity theorists have shown that a person's persuasive impact is often predicated on his or her status as an exemplary ingroup member. In particular, where disagreement might exist between a speaker and those he or she is seeking to persuade (surely a real possibility in the case of someone as controversial as Paul), such disagreement is more likely to generate a desirable subjective uncertainty (that is, feelings of doubt and a need for clarification) among the target recipients of the viewpoint if they perceive that the would-be persuader is a member of their own ingroup.[23]

Socialized into a heavily group-oriented culture and with long experience of seeking to persuade congregations of Christ-followers—sometimes, it appears, unsuccessfully[24]—Paul seems to have instinctively grasped such insights. This is why he introduces the word "brothers" unexpectedly in v. 1, and repeats it in v. 4, to remind his audience both that they share a group identity and that such identity has brotherhood as a fundamental dimension. He is reminding them that he and they are partners of a particularly close kind in "an emerging self-categorical relationship."[25] But he also makes clear, probably as early as v. 1 but certainly soon thereafter, that he is here interested in those brothers who constitute the Judean members of the Christ-movement in Rome. In vv. 1-6 he establishes that he has (what I am calling) a social identity in common with them, which is closely associated with particular experiences in the past and the present. Both he and they are people who have moved from the realm of the Mosaic law and passions conducive of sin, "flesh," and death to the realm of Christ and spirit—indeed, he is saying little more in vv. 1-6 than this. Yet in social identity terms this is a great deal, for he has established his identification with one of the subgroups at which he is aiming and he has set the scene for a detailed treatment (in vv. 7-25) of what it means to be under law and in the realm of sin. This represents the past for him and them, but as Cinnirella has persuasively argued, reflection on a past social identity can serve a critical role in the constitution, or reconstitution, of a present and future social identity.[26] Here the reflection takes the form of stigmatizing the past identity as something now utterly rejected, rather than (as in the case of Abraham in Romans 4) of proffering a prototype from the past who represents a source of group prototypicality in the present.[27]

The "I" Voice in Romans 7:7-25: Opening the Discussion

In 7:7 Paul adopts the stylistic feature previously seen in 6:1 and 6:15 of introducing a mistaken conclusion from his argument in question form: "What then shall we say? Is the law sin? Emphatically not!" This, accordingly, is the third issue to be explored as Paul investigates the relationship of 5:20-21 to the past and present experience of Christ-followers.

Yet his next assertion in 7:7 is surprising: "But I would not have known sin except through the law; for I would not have known covetousness unless the law had said 'You shall not covet.'" Thus Paul begins a passage in concentrated first person narration continuing until v. 25 that is unique in the letter. The data are striking. He introduces the pronoun ἐγώ, for the first time in the letter, at v. 9, and repeats it at vv. 10, 14, 17, 20, and 24, while employing the first person pronoun in oblique forms on no less than seventeen occasions in vv. 7-25.[28] How are we to explain this phenomenon?

By way of a preliminary observation, it is useful to delineate three broad possible meanings for "I" statements in Paul's letters: (a) the personal (or autobiographical) "I" where Paul is speaking of his own personal experience in distinction from others (as in 1 Cor. 15:8-9; Gal. 1:24; Phil. 3:4-6); (b) the typical "I," where Paul speaks in a way that includes himself but also others (with Gal. 2:20 as an example); and (c) the fictive or rhetorical "I," where Paul presents an idea in a lively manner but without including himself, as seen in diatribe style when Paul assumes the view of another for the purpose of argument even though he does not agree with it (as in 1 Cor. 10:29b: "For why should my freedom be determined by the conscience of someone else").[29] Clearly, the second category, the "typical" "I" statement, is imbued with a complexity absent from the other two, and it embraces a range of possible cases—including, as we shall see, assertions of exemplifying social identity aimed at claiming group leadership.

The Status Quaestionis and Social Identity Theory

Modern discussion of the "I" voice in Romans 7 dates largely from an essay by W. G. Kümmel published in 1929.[30] Prior to Kümmel, Romans 7 had been widely interpreted as a personal "I" statement, relating Paul's own experience, either his inner struggles and his despair of adhering to the Mosaic law prior to his conversion, or his life as a "Christian." Luther had given important stimulus to such views. Kümmel's influential contribution was to interpret the "I" voice as having nothing whatever to do with Paul's personal experience, either before or after his conversion. The "I" was a fictive "I," a rhetorical device for depicting the lot of humanity under the law, except Paul himself.

Not everyone has been happy with this conclusion. Many have difficulty with the idea that Paul is entirely divorced from the first person speaker in the chapter. Other approaches to the problem (canvassed below where relevant) also continue to attract support, for example, that the speaker represents Adam, Christ-followers, or humanity in general.

It is generally true that the various scholars who have contributed to the nature and function of the "I" speaking in chap. 7 have been concerned with the cognitive aspects of Paul's message. They have sought to understand chap. 7 within the larger ideational structure of Paul's argument in the letter. Viewing the passage in the light of a model of leadership derived from social identity theory, however, leads to a different emphasis. Now Paul is not merely seeking to persuade the Roman Christ-followers of the nature or truth of certain ideas—even though the ideas are necessary (since they contribute to the cognitive dimension of social identity)—but doing so within a context where he aims to establish a leadership role for himself among them (which also entails the emotional and evaluative dimensions of social identity). That is, he wants to put himself in a position where he can influence them in a manner that enhances their contribution to the realization of the goals of the Christ-movement. Such an approach demands that we pay attention to the social dimensions of Paul's discourse. Not only must we try to understand what he is saying, but how (in relation to the particular social identity and self-categorization perspectives in play) his words contribute to the establishment of his place as leader. Following this route also provides a fresh means of assessing the value of particular arguments put forward in existing scholarship.

Interpretation of Romans 7:7-13

Overview

Earlier in the letter, Paul had made clear that sin and death had come into the world with Adam (5:12), but "although sin was in the world before the law was given, sin is not taken into account (ἐλλογεῖται) where there is no law" (5:13). I have noted that prompting this statement was Paul's correct understanding of the effect of introducing a law into a particular context, namely, to establish a set of norms with respect to which existing problematic human behavior thereafter acquires a different character and its practitioners become subject to penalties not in existence before.[31] Yet Paul argues that the effects of the Mosaic law went beyond this, in that the promulgation of prohibited activity alerted people of its existence and triggered their interest in engaging in it. Thus the consequences of the Mosaic law were catastrophic, even though he insists (against a possible objector?) that the law itself is not sin (v. 7). In chap. 5 he had asserted that the arrival of the law resulted in an increase in wrongdoing but without explaining how (5:20). In 7:7-13 he returns to this idea and offers an explanation for how the introduction of the law made things worse. Paul presents the Mosaic law as resulting in the commission of the very practices it banned.

It is worth noting here, however, a point to which I return in chapter eleven below in relation to 8:12-17: Paul is notably more favorable to the Mosaic law in Romans than he is in Galatians. Central to Paul's argument in Galatians is to present the law as part of the forces (which also include the weak and beggarly elemental spirits of the cosmos: Gal. 4:4, 9) that restrict and enslave people. The high point of Paul's depiction of the Mosaic law and its proponents as representing slavery comes in the allegory of Hagar and Sarah in Gal. 4:21-31. But fortunately the law and related powers only had a limited power of operation and that time has now passed (a point made clearly in Gal. 3:23—4:7).

The picture in Romans differs radically in two respects. First, Paul never suggests in Romans that the law is a force of enslavement. In this letter that function is filled by sin (6:16-17, 20). As we will see in a moment, Paul develops the idea that although the law was holy, righteous, and good (7:11), it was not up to the task and sin got the better of it with the result that the power of sin over human beings increased. A significant corollary of this point is that whereas in Galatians the law is included among the forces from which one is liberated (Gal. 5:1), in Romans liberation is from sin (Rom. 6:18, 22; 8:2).[32] Second, Paul never suggests that the Mosaic law has now passed its expiration date. Perhaps he was forced to acknowledge that the ongoing devotion of Israel to the covenants, which he will soon mention (9:4), made indefensible the claim that the time of operation of the Mosaic law had expired.

In any event, just as Paul has been far more accepting of, and conciliatory toward, Israelites in relation to the figure of Abraham in chap. 4, so too in relation to the law his views in Romans are far more positive in the respects just described. This change of position needs to be borne in mind in the interpretation of 7:7-25.

Verses 7-13 are characterized by the use of the past tense (with the exception of the future tense of the first verb in v. 7). The (first person) speaker, the identity of whom I pass over for a moment, looks back to a time before the arrival of law (v. 9a): "I once lived in the absence of the law (χωρὶς νόμου)."

But then the law (νόμος: vv. 7, 8, 9, 12), the commandment (ἐντολή: vv. 8, 9, 10, 11, 12, 13), arrived. The result was that the speaker now "knew" sin (v. 7): "I would not have known sin except through the law; for I would not have known covetousness (ἐπιθυμία) unless the law had said 'You shall not covet (ἐπιθυμεῖν),'" which is a summary reference to the law against coveting from the tenth commandment (Exod. 20:17; Deut. 5:21). Since Paul later cites this commandment in Rom. 13:9 along with other prohibitions in the Decalogue, and since "Do not covet . . ." was regarded in wider Israelite circles as summarizing the Decalogue (4 Macc. 2:6),[33] it is clear beyond contradiction that the Mosaic law is in view.[34]

This then was the first dimension—that the law informed those subject to it of various types of evil. But there was a second, even more pernicious, dimension: "Seizing its opportunity, sin produced every sort of covetousness 'in me' through the commandment (ἐντολή)" (v. 8). His point is that sin utilizes the knowledge of evil that is produced by its legislative definition and encourages people to engage in it. The passive position of law in relation to sin presented here stands in sharp contrast to the situation in Galatians, where Paul presents the law as the active party, which locks up everything under the power of sin (Gal. 3:22).

"I" once lived in the absence of the law, but when the commandment came, sin gained a new lease of life (ἀνέζησεν). In the absence of law, on the other hand, sin is νεκρά, by which Paul means lifeless and ineffectual, not nonexistent (7:9). "I" died and a commandment meant for life produced death (v. 10).[35] By means of the commandment, sin tricked and killed "me" (v. 11). Here "death" must mean something like a moral or metaphorical death, not a physical one (which had entered human experience with the sin of Adam), just as the life offered by the Mosaic law meant not immortality but rich and righteous existence before God. Nevertheless, the law is holy, and the commandment holy and righteous and good (v. 12). It did not cause death; rather sin, so that it might manifest itself as sin, produced death through that which is good for me, in order that through the commandment, sin might be exceedingly sinful (v. 13).

This picture of the effects of the law helps to explain why Paul is so remarkably reticent about the manner or occasion of the law's arrival, which must be understood from a single clause in v. 9: "but when the commandment came." These words are all that Paul allows himself in relation to the dramatic details of the Sinai incident and God's delivery of the Decalogue to Moses. The reason for such reticence is no doubt to avoid making too much of the embarrassing fact that it was God, after all, who devised and transmitted this notably useless, indeed dangerous, law to Israel. An Israelite unhappy with Paul's account of the law's effects would no doubt object that his position, even though it granted that the increased power of sin was the result and not the purpose of God's provision of the law (5:20-21),[36] presupposed an impossibly high degree of incompetence on God's part. When Paul had previously dealt with the effects of the law in his letter to the Galatians (Gal. 3:19-20), he had sought to distance God from Sinai by attributing the giving of the law to an angel through the hand of a mediator.[37] In Rom. 7:7-13 he goes even further than this by altogether avoiding reference to the way the law was given.

The "I" Voice as Paul's before His Conversion

Who is the "I" speaking in Rom. 7:7-13? Is it, first of all, that of Paul, speaking autobiographically of his preconversion existence, as suggested by C. H. Dodd and numerous other scholars?[38] The details of the text exclude this interpretation. In particular, as insisted by Kümmel and many others since, there never was a time when Paul lived in the absence of the law (7:9a), at least not after he had been circumcised.[39] Attempts to argue for some ancient equivalent of the (comparatively modern) practice of bar mitzvah as substantiating an early period of his life when he did live in the absence of the law are unpersuasive.[40] Second, the autobiographical view necessitates a sharp break in the text at 7:7, in that Paul's determined efforts to identify with his Israelite audience in vv. 1-6 would simply be discarded in favor of an account personal to him and having no obvious bearing on what is being discussed. Lastly, scholars from Kümmel onward have proffered Paul's statement in Phil. 3:6 that he was "blameless as to righteousness under the law" as counting against any form of autobiographical reading of Rom. 7:7-13 (and, indeed, of 7:7-25). I will return to this argument in a moment, to indicate that it is unpersuasive. Nevertheless, the arguments from Romans 7 itself are quite sufficient to exclude interpretations of vv. 7-13 that treat these verses as solely autobiographical in relation to Paul's life prior to his conversion.

The "I" Voice as Paul's after His Conversion

The passage is equally difficult to reconcile with the idea that its subject is Paul's own life *after* his conversion, as suggested, for example, by Alan Segal.[41] There is the same problem with the idea of any sharp break at 7:7. In addition, as Kümmel pointed out,[42] the details of Paul's experience as a Christ-follower do not square with the picture in 7:7-13. That is, Paul did not first encounter the commandment against covetousness as a Christ-follower and it was certainly not part of his experience in Christ that sin first became active through the commandment and he died.

Does Philippians 3:6 Exclude Paul's Having Any Connection with the "I" Voice?

Although the arguments for the first person speaker in Rom. 7:7-25 not being simply that of Paul speaking autobiographically, either before or after he turned to Christ, are persuasive, Kümmel went further than this and argued that Paul was *entirely absent*, especially because of the inconsistency between a Paul who could assert that he was "blameless (ἄμεμπτος) as to righteousness under the law" (Phil. 3:6) and the speaker of Rom. 7:15 and 19 who could commit evil acts. "Paul's absolute statement in Phil. 3.6," Brian Dodd explains, "does not seem to allow for the tension and feeling of moral impotence found especially in Rom. 7.14-25."[43] Does the statement in Phil. 3:6 rule out any Pauline involvement whatever in the "I" voice in Romans 7?

Paul's autobiographical statement in Phil. 3:5-6 should be noted in full. He says that he was: "circumcised on the eighth day, of the people of Israel, of the tribe of Benjamin, a Hebrew born of Hebrews; as to the law a Pharisee, as to zeal a persecutor of the church, as to righteousness under the law blameless (ἄμεμπτος)" (RSV).

This account must be compared with what he says in two other places: "For you have heard of my former life in Judeanism, how I persecuted the church of God and tried to destroy it; and I advanced in the practices of the Judeans (Ἰουδαισμός) beyond many of my own age among my people, so extremely zealous was I for the traditions of my fathers" (Gal. 1:13-15, RSV modified); "For I am the least of the apostles, unfit to be called an apostle, because I persecuted the church of God" (1 Cor. 15:9, RSV).

These three passages all agree that Paul persecuted the Christ-movement before his conversion, two of them specifying zeal (either for the law or the traditions of his fathers) as his motivation, while one of them expressly claims he was a Pharisee, which is corroborated by his devotion to the traditions of the fathers. The Philippians statement alone mentions his having been blameless as to righteousness under the law. The dominant question is what is meant by "blameless" here. Kümmel's thesis demands that it means "never breached the Mosaic laws," or "perpetually sinless." Is this what "blameless" means?

In the Septuagint ἄμεμπτος is mainly used of Job (1:1, 8; 2:3; 4:17; 9:20; 11:4; 12:4; 15:14; 22:3, 19; 33:9), occurring elsewhere only at Gen. 17:1; Esth. 8:13; Wis. 10:5, 15; 18:21. Job is described in terms that seem to fit the sort of meaning required by Kümmel: he was "true, blameless, righteous, God-fearing, abstaining from all evil" (Job 1:1, 8; 2:3), although his inter-locutors found the idea of a blameless man hard to swallow (4:17; 11:4). It does appear elsewhere, however, that ἄμεμπτος did not necessarily mean "perpetually sinless." For example, Wis. 10:15 refers to Israel and its "blame-less seed," which Wisdom delivered from their oppressors, in spite of Israel's checkered history in relation to God's covenant. In Wis. 18:21 Aaron is described as blameless in relation to his protection of the people from divine wrath (Num. 16:41-50), even though it is said elsewhere that he had acted wrongly in relation to the incident of the golden calf (Exod. 32:25, 35). These two instances suggest that "blameless" was a relative (or comparative) rather than absolute means of expressing moral excellence, inasmuch as it differentiated someone in a particular context from others, as Israel's seed from external persecutors (Wis. 10:15) and Aaron from the Israelites whom God was about to destroy (Wis. 18:21). Similarly, in 2 Chron. 15:17 Asa is described as having a πλήρης (full, complete) heart, a meaning close to "blameless," in connection with his taking action against idolatry, yet Chronicles 16 goes on to catalogue his sins.

This analysis suggests that by "as to righteousness under the law blameless" (Phil. 3:6) Paul means to express his high socioreligious status in the period immediately prior to his conversion *in relation to other Judeans*, which would mean he is saying little more than "I advanced in the practices of the Judeans beyond many of my own age among my people" (Gal. 1:14). The other instance of ἄμεμπτος in Philippians itself corroborates this comparative sense of the word: "Do all things . . . that you may be blameless (ἄμεμπτοι) and innocent, children of God without blemish in the midst of a crooked and perverse generation, among whom you shine as lights in the world" (2:14-15, RSV). Exactly the same point can be made of Paul's other examples of ἄμεμπτος (or the adverbial form), in 1 Thess. 2:10; 3:13; and 5:23, in view of the role such language serves to differentiate the privileged ingroup of Christ-followers from sinful and doomed outgroups.[44]

I conclude, therefore, that Paul's description of himself as a devout Israelite, as ἄμεμπτος, in Phil. 3:6 does not preclude the possibility that even at that time in his life he occasionally breached the Mosaic law. If he did, the law itself provided methods of atonement by ritual bathing or sacrifice.[45] It follows a fortiori that were Paul, as a Christ-follower of many years' standing, to have looked back on his preconversion life as an Israelite, he could without prevarication have associated himself with the thrust of the experience we will soon consider in Rom. 7:7-25, even if certain details, such as 7:9a, were not relevant to him personally. There is no obstacle to Paul's being involved in some way with the "I" voice of chap. 7.

The "I" Voice as Adam or Alluding to Adam?

What about Adam, a character whom many scholars have make an entrance in Romans at virtually every difficult moment, as if he were the villain in a Victorian melodrama? Those who regard Adam as the speaker in Romans 7 include Lyonnet, Wedderburn, Watson, Dunn, and Hill.[46] Käsemann goes so far as to claim: "There is nothing in the passage which does not fit Adam, and everything fits Adam alone."[47] A significant variation on this theme, proposed, for example, by Gerd Theissen and N. T. Wright, is that although Paul does not speak directly of Adam in Romans 7, the figure of Adam stands clearly in the background and there are reminiscences of the fall in this chapter.[48] Theissen says that Adam is not the *subject* but the *model* of 7:7ff.[49] Support for a reference to Adam in Romans 7 has been found in the argument that the sin of Adam was conceived as covetousness and in linguistic and other similarities between Genesis 2–3 and Romans 7 (such as the notion of deceit in Gen. 3:14 and Rom. 7:11, and the use of ἐνετείλατο at Gen. 2:16 and ἐντολή in Rom. 7:7-13).

But the Adamic solution, in either of these two forms, is unpersuasive. Moo makes the obvious point: "How could Paul feature Adam's experience in a discussion about a law which he presents as entering the historical arena only with *Moses*?"[50] This point can be expanded with reference to an earlier section of the letter. Paul has already dealt with Adam and the fall in Romans 5. Sin did indeed come into the world with Adam, and through sin, death, including literal death, as noted above (5:12). Sin was in the world before the law but was not taken into account (5:13); indeed "death reigned from Adam to Moses, even over those whose transgressions were not like the transgression of Adam" (5:14). All this leaves hanging the question of the effect of the coming of the Mosaic law, and this is precisely the subject of 7:7-13. In these verses Paul unambiguously moves the scene on to the time when the law did come, the time of Moses and Sinai, and expresses a view on the damaging effects of its introduction, principally a form of moral death (since physical death was introduced by Adam, not by the Mosaic law).

To regard Adam as the "I" voice in Romans 7, or merely to find there allusions to Adam and the fall, would unnecessarily complicate, if not destroy entirely, Paul's vision of the stages of human history under God. For Paul carefully distinguishes between a time beginning with the transgression of Adam when sin was in the world but not active, not taken into account (5:13), a time before the (Mosaic) law (5:12-14), and a later time, of the giving of the Mosaic law, when sin came to life (ἀνέζησεν, 7:9) and would be taken into account, while those who took on the law "died." The latter set of circumstances produced a particular *and novel* dilemma. Given this careful distinction and the unique plight of those affected by the interaction of sin and the Mosaic law (soon to be described in vv. 7-25), what communicative purpose could Paul serve by speaking (in vv. 1-6) of the second event in terms that alluded to the first?

It is certainly true that from Paul's perspective all human beings became sinners and subject to death ultimately as a result of Adam's trespass (5:12, 17, 19), thus laying the foundation for a problem that could only be solved by Christ. Nevertheless, 7:1-6 (and then 7:7-25) are not concerned with this particular death, or with sinfulness generally, but with a new development in human experience, the increased ferocity that sin gained through its manipulation of the law of Moses—a development to which the fall of Adam was simply irrelevant. It was not the status of God's commandment in Eden that was the focus of concern for Paul or his audience in Rome, but the law of Moses. Indeed, when Paul *is* explicitly dealing with Adam, in Romans 5, he does not even mention the commandment of Gen. 2:16-17, being content merely to refer to Adam's "transgression" (Rom. 5:15, 17, 18).

The precise details of the alleged link between Genesis 2–3 and Romans 7 are also open to question. First, there are difficulties with the view that Paul was employing a tradition that the sin of Adam was covetousness; above all, there is no sign of such an understanding in Romans 5, which is where he would have inserted it if he did subscribe to this interpretation and wanted his readers to relate this section with the "I" voice in (what is now known as) chap. 7. Second, there are the similarities of language. That ἐνετείλατο appears in Gen. 2:16 and ἐντολή in Rom. 7:7-13 is probably coincidence or arises from the bare similarity of the two situations, with a command in each. The deceit motif is more interesting, but still unpersuasive. At Gen. 3:14 the woman says, "The serpent deceived (ἠπάτησε) me and I ate," while the "I" voice in Rom. 7:11 states, "Sin, taking its opportunity through the commandment (ἐντολή), deceived (ἐξηπάτησεν) me." The first problem for the suggested reminiscence is that, as already noted,[51] in Genesis Adam was not deceived, yet it is on Adam, and Adam alone, that Paul fixes responsibility for sin coming into the world. That Paul knew quite well that Eve, and not Adam, was the one deceived appears from 2 Cor. 11:3 ("the serpent deceived [ἐξηπάτησε] Eve by his cunning"). The better explanation is that Paul, when he wanted to describe the effect of sin on the speaker of Rom. 7:7-13, simply reached for a convenient and natural word to do so, "deceived" (ἐξαπατάω), a word he uses elsewhere in his letters—in a sense unrelated to the story of the fall—in Romans itself (16:18) and in 1 Cor. 3:18. That sin (and not a person) should be the deceiver is not a problem. Although ἐξαπατάω appears only twice in the Septuagint (Exod. 8:29 and Add. Dan. Sus. 56 [Theodotion]), the related word ἀπατάω occurs frequently, usually with a person as its subject, but deceit can also be wrought by beauty (Jdt. 13:16), a full stomach (Prov. 24:5), or, the closest parallel, trickery (δόλος, Wis. 4:11).

The most that can be said about the relationship of the Genesis account of the fall and Paul's description of the arrival and effect of the Mosaic law in Rom. 7:7-13 is that there were certain intrinsic resemblances between the two situations (a commandment by God, a breach, its consequences) and that in setting out his position in Romans 7 Paul (almost inevitably) employed similar language and concepts. He did not intend any allusion to, or echo of, the fall, nor was his audience likely to have perceived one, since the intrusion of those ideas in Romans 7 would be an unwelcome and troublesome distraction from the overall message being communicated in chaps. 5–8.[52]

Excluding Adam also means excluding the significance frequently attached to his alleged presence—that he is representative of humanity generally, a position expressed by Dunn as "I = Adam = humankind = everyman passed under the sway of death."[53] This quotation discloses the appeal of Adam in some quarters—it permits Paul's language to be universalized on the basis that Adam was the ancestor of us all, and hence a representative of all humanity, then and now. It is an appeal that we should consciously resist. If we are to interpret Romans in its historical context, we should be wary of interpretations that seem driven by a desire to make it speak to contemporary issues. The tendency to universalize statements made in another part of Romans, 1:18-32, by the introduction of Adam (again entirely without foundation, but that is another story) has been rightly criticized by Dale Martin to the extent that it provides a rationale for giving the remarks about same-sex relations in 1:26-27 a wider application than they probably had for Paul.[54]

The "I" Voice as Humanity in General

Some scholars attach a wider significance to the "I" voice in 7:7-13 while rejecting any allusion to Adam, as if Paul was speaking of humanity in general. Kümmel comes close to this position, since although he recognizes that Paul refers to the Mosaic law and makes no allusion to Adam in the passage, he nevertheless insists that Paul uses the first person pronouns to depict the lot of humanity under the law.[55] To similar effect is Fitzmyer's admittedly subtle insistence that Paul's perspective here is "that of unregenerate humanity faced with the Mosaic law—but as seen by a Christian."[56] Such views stumble over the fact that the law of Moses was given not to humanity in general, but to Israel. Paul divides humanity into those who have the law, meaning Israel, and those who do not. This viewpoint surfaces earlier in the letter: "For all those who have sinned lawlessly (ἀνόμως) will perish lawlessly (ἀνόμως), and all those who have sinned in the law will perish on account of the law" (2:12). This is a fundamental dimension to his identity, as it must have been for every Israelite of his era. In 7:7-13 Paul has in mind the Mosaic law, which was given to Israel and to Israel alone, and to suggest that he or his readers would have understood the passage to have any application to non-Israelite humanity is entirely inconsistent with this outlook. While Paul is certainly looking at things from the vantage point of his faith in Christ, he is only concerned with the consequences of Israel's receipt at Sinai of the Mosaic law (7:7-13) and, as we will soon see, with where that leaves anyone in the present who still relies on that same Mosaic law (7:14-25). In both situations, the past and the present, his focus is not on humanity, unregenerate or otherwise, but only on people who have taken on this law; and they, by definition, are Israelites.

The Identity of the "I" Voice

What then is the solution? Who is the first person speaker of the passage? When Paul states in 7:7 that "I would not have known sin except through the law; for I would not have known covetousness (ἐπιθυμία) unless the law had said 'You shall not covet (ἐπιθυμεῖν),'" it is difficult not to see this transition to the first person singular, soon to climax in a proliferation of first person singular pronouns, as the latest step in his identification with the Israelite Christ-followers of Rome that is progressively elaborated in vv. 1-6. Paul initially links his Israelite addressees and himself together by use of first person plural pronouns and then intensifies the joint identity by severing interpersonal boundaries altogether. "We" becomes "I." This is an example of a "typical" "I" statement, as discussed above, but of a particular kind. Within a social identity and self-categorization framework, someone bent on becoming a leader, which means assuming the mantle of ingroup exemplar (the person most representative of the shared social identity and consensual position of the group as a whole), could hardly take a more radical step than to assert for himself and one of the subgroups in view a single, common identity properly characterized by first person singular speech. This does not mean that the separate identities of Paul and his Israelite addressees disappear, merely that for present purposes Paul is claiming to be at one with them in relation to a particular social identity.

But what group? What identity? Kümmel argued that 7:7-25 had no relevance to Paul's experience after his conversion (or to that of any other Christ-followers in the present) because prominent features of the text simply could not be reconciled with such a hypothesis. These include the fact that they had died to the law (7:1-6) when 7:7-25 spoke of those still subject to it, and because according to 7:25a and 8:1-4 they had been set free from the various horns of the dilemma described in 7:14-24, 25b. These arguments are compelling.

The best guide to the correct interpretation, although one scholars rarely rely on, is provided by following the course of Paul's thought from vv. 1-6 into vv. 7-25. We have already seen how Paul has aligned himself with Israelite Christ-followers in vv. 1-6. Moreover, their past bitter experience of the law outlined in v. 5 bears striking similarities to the fate of the first person speaker about to be described in vv. 7-11. These considerations make it highly likely that the group in question is Israel, even though this view has received surprisingly little scholarly support.[57] It is Israel in the period up to God's provision of the law to Moses on Sinai and then afterward—an "afterward" that, we will soon see, extends right to the moment in which Paul speaks. In vv. 1-6 Paul qua Israelite speaks on behalf of himself and the Israelites among his addressees in the first person singular as Israel. One incident of such a close identification, as suggested by the insistence of Susan Condor and Marco Cinnirella that a temporal dimension is intrinsic to group identity,[58] must be the capacity to speak of everything that has contributed to that identity—its history, its present experience, and its hopes for the future.

This last consideration indicates why the statement in 7:9a, "I once lived in the absence of the law," does not constitute an obstacle to Paul being included in the speaker of Romans 7. In making the point that groups provide their members with a serial connectedness with other group members, Condor quotes David Carr:

> my social existence not only puts me in contact with a co-existing multiplicity of contemporaries: it connects me with a peculiar form of temporal continuity . . . which runs from predecessors to successors. This sequence extends beyond the boundaries of my life, both into the past before my birth and into the future after my death . . . the *we* with whose experience the individual identifies can both pre-date and survive the individuals that make it up.[59]

This means that a person like Paul can speak as one with, and as representative of, a group, even though he is aware that the group had an existence prior to him and will have a future after him. We saw in chapter eight above how important were collective memories in the maintenance of group identity, even though the "events" remembered could have happened long before the lifetimes of a current generation of members. That Paul has donned the persona of Israel to speak of its experience since Sinai now needs to be weighed against the details of vv. 14-25.

Interpretation of Romans 7:14-25

After a first person plural statement in v. 14a, "We know that the law is spiritual" (which serves to remind the Israelite component of his audience that he has not forgotten them), the "I" voice continues in vv. 14b-25, and there is no sign of any alteration in its referent. For this reason, it is safe to assume that Paul is still speaking in the persona of Israel and, indeed, that the arguments mounted above for this identification in vv. 7-13 apply with equal force in relation to vv. 14-25 and need not be repeated here. The broad subject of the passage is the plight of the speaker after the introduction of the law as described in vv. 7-13, desperately trying to live in accord with its demands but unable to do so.

In 7:14, however, the tense changes from past to present. What is the significance of this? Although some scholars argue that Paul speaks from 7:14 onward (and not just from 8:1) of the new life of the Christ-follower,[60] I have already noted the compelling arguments of Kümmel that vv. 14-23 cannot carry this meaning. Theissen further, and correctly, notes that the "scissure" (division) in vv. 13-14 "is marked too weakly to be considered the transition between pre-Christian and Christian periods of life; above all it lacks a reference to Christ, without whom this transition is inconceivable."[61] The most likely explanation is that Paul is now fixing his sights on the nature of the Mosaic law and what it is like for a person to live under it in view of the reality of sin. The present tense is appropriate for a number of reasons: because Israel continues to exist (cf. 9:3-5; 11); because he is addressing Israelite Christ-followers in Rome, some of whom were still adhering to the Mosaic law; and because a decision to take on the law of Moses remains a continuing possibility for non-Israelites, even in the new epoch inaugurated by Christ and even though there is no sign in Rome (as there was in Galatia) of a push to have them circumcised and obey the law. Paul wants to show just how terrible that option is. He wants to expatiate upon the dramatic distinction between life under the law and life under grace. Accordingly, in 7:14 Paul effects a transition from the brief narration of a past event (the giving of the Mosaic law) and its consequences related in augmented tenses (vv. 1-6) to an elaborate description of a condition, namely, being under that law, which is depicted in vv. 14-25 in the present tense.[62]

A detailed consideration of the text of vv. 14-25 allows a more thorough probing of the function of the "I" voice. Dunn comments that in this part of the letter Paul intends to provide "a defence of the law" in response to the question in v. 7 that it is equivalent to sin.[63] While other scholars also take this significant view, I cannot accept it. In Romans Paul is defending his version of the gospel, not law. He is also defending himself as part of a larger process of seeking a leadership role among the Christ-followers of Rome, including the Judean component, and to allay rumors that may be current about him elsewhere, including in Jerusalem. The notion at 7:7 that the law is sin requires his attention because it is precisely the sort of allegation that could be cast in his face as a natural corollary of his gospel. For people who were alleging that he taught "Let us do evil so that good might come" (3:8), a teaching only possible if the law was ignored, it would not have been a big step for them also to smear Paul as claiming that the law was sin. We have seen that his argument in chap. 6 was framed around two similar slurs that could possibly be leveled at his message.

In chap. 7 Paul's means of fending off such potentially troublesome slander is to appear to defend the law, to acknowledge its God-given goodness, yet all the while sticking to his case that it is no longer relevant for those in

Christ. Paul himself was almost certainly troubled, even racked, by the difficulty of reconciling his belief that the law had a divine origin with the new means of achieving righteousness and salvation offered by God through Christ. The necessarily troubled nature of his positive regard for the law, which had already appeared with the awkwardly intruded but clearly sincere result clause in v. 12, becomes even more obvious from v. 14 onward. Here remarks about the law, purportedly offered in the course of defending it against the claim that it is sin, have the effect of bringing out all the more forcefully the utter uselessness of the law in the face of human sinfulness. In this regard it appears that his interest in maintaining the salience of the identity of the Judean subgroup in Rome that is evident elsewhere in the letter and that will find powerful expression a little later (in chaps. 9–11) came into collision with deep-seated views he held about the importance and exclusivity of Christ's death and resurrection for the righteousness and salvation of human beings. It is perhaps in Galatians that he expresses his bedrock sentiment in this area: "I do not nullify the grace of God, for if righteousness came through the law, surely Christ died in vain" (Gal. 2:21). Paul's powerfully negative assessment of the law in Romans is therefore not one produced by deliberate and cynical design, but rather by irreconcilable tensions between his recognition that God had been with Israel in giving the law and his overwhelming sense that God had sent his own son to break the power of sin for the benefit of all people, Israelite and non-Israelite. This conclusion is substantiated by a consideration of the text of Rom. 7:14-25.

The passage falls naturally into three sections: vv. 14-17, 18-20, and 21-25. The most notable structural feature of vv. 7-25 (and one insufficiently adverted to in the commentaries) is the degree of repetition between the first and second sections, a phenomenon highlighted in the following synoptic chart (using the RSV, slightly modified):

14. For we know that the law is spiritual; but I am fleshly, sold under sin.	18. For I know that nothing good dwells within me, that is, in my flesh.
15. I do not understand my own actions.	I can will what is right, but I cannot do it.
For I do not do what I want, but I do the very thing I hate.	19. For I do not do the good I want, but the evil I do not want is what I do.
16. Now if I do what I do not want, I agree that the law is good.	20. Now if I do what I do not want,
17. So then it is no longer I that do it, but sin that dwells within me.	it is no longer I that do it, but sin that dwells within me.

The remarkable similarities are worth noting: (a) each section begins with a statement concerning knowledge: "For we know (οἴδαμεν γάρ)" in v. 14

and "For I know (οἶδα γάρ)" in v. 18, where the similarity in content of what follows after each verb constitutes a powerful confirmation that the "I" voice of v. 18 represents a collectivity consisting of the speaker and his addressees (in this case, Israelites); (b) both these opening "knowledge" statements refer to the fleshly condition of the speaker (σάρκινος in v. 14 and ἐν σαρκί in v. 18); (c) in each case a statement follows as to an impediment to acting (properly)—lack of understanding in v. 15a and weakness of will in v. 18c; (d) in each case there is next a statement by the speaker that he does not do what he wants but does what he does not want (vv. 15b-c and 19), in very similar language; (e) a conditional clause in virtually identical wording ("Now if I do what I do not want") begins the final sentence in each case; (f) both sections conclude with a statement to the effect that sin has taken control of the speaker's actions, in identical wording (apart from the first two words in v. 17).

The question irresistibly arises as to why Paul has included this doublet of passages very similar in content and with one immediately following the other. Yet the second passage does differ in certain respects from the first, and it is presumably the existence of these differences that explains why Paul has included the material in vv. 18-20. It is almost as if he has retransmitted a message but with a few significant alterations. This is a rare case where we are able to apply a redaction-critical analysis to one Pauline passage (vv. 18-20) in relation to another that is its source (vv. 14-17).

Apart from the transition from lack of knowledge in v. 15a to failure of will in v. 18c, the major change is the elimination of the law from the second passage. In vv. 14-17 Paul maintains an interest in defending the Mosaic law in spite of the speaker's experience under it, first by distinguishing (v. 14) its spiritual (πνευματικός) character from the speaker's fleshly (σάρκινος) nature (thus suggesting that the law is too noble for the dirty job given it), and second by agreeing (v. 16) that it is good (καλός) because the speaker recognizes he is doing what he does not want to do (with the law presumably articulating the correct course of action that he forsakes).

In spite of this praise for the law, the speaker concludes with a confession that it is sin, not the speaker, that is responsible for his actions. This is the climax of vv. 14-17, not the positive features of the law. Since Paul re-presents the same lamentable picture and arrives at the same conclusion in vv. 18-20, but without reference to the law, the conclusion is inescapable that his interest lies in the gloomy condition of human existence under the thrall of sin (which the law is powerless to affect), not in offering a defense of the law. The joint effect of the two passages can be encapsulated in an imaginary explanation of Paul: "Yes, of course the law is wonderful, but this is what our life is like, given that sin takes over in spite of the law. I repeat, this is what our life is like, given that sin takes over in spite of the law."

The third section of this part of the letter, vv. 21-25, represents a restatement of the predicament of the speaker faced with the law and sin—wanting to do good but doing evil—in terms of a distinction between the speaker's inner person (ὁ ἔσω ἄνθρωπος) and mind (νοῦς), which delight in and are in service to God's law, on the one hand, and his limbs and flesh (σάρξ), on the other, which are the site of and are subject to the law of sin that fights against the other law.

Some scholars have considered that v. 25b was originally located at the end of v. 23.[64] But although this might be thought to produce a smoother ending, there is no textual support for such an alteration and there seems no reason not to view v. 25a as a (slightly) proleptic outburst of joy in the midst of this situation through looking forward to 8:1-4. Verse 25a reads as if the speaker will not be able to keep the lid on the kettle for much longer, even though not having quite finished the tale of woe, which concludes with v. 25b. Accordingly, just like vv. 14-17 and 18-20, vv. 21-25 also terminate with sin's control over the speaker's body, the speaker being Israel.

Conclusion: Paul's Leadership Aims in Romans 7 from a Social Identity Perspective

The interpretation of chap. 7 set out above indicates the usefulness of a social identity and self-categorization approach to leadership. Paul emerges as a skilled entrepreneur of identity. Within a broad framework of seeking to make more secure the superordinate category of Christ-follower in relation to sub-categories of Judean and non-Judean in the Roman congregations, he pushes the Israelite subgroup in his target audience in a certain direction by reminding them who they are now and the historical path that got them there. He does this above all by creating an "I" voice that exemplifies Israel in its experience of the law and that incorporates himself and his fellow Judeans. That is, he makes salient this particular subgroup identity that he shares with them and demonstrates the problems that necessarily beset it through its relationship with the Mosaic law. Above all, it is in thrall to sin, from which faith in Christ offers a complete escape. He is able to speak to them, to lead them, because he shares this identity with them. While purporting to deny any charge that the law is sin (7:7), he delineates a particular problematic identity for which there now exists a new, alternate, and exciting Spirit-charged identity in Christ that liberates humanity, Judean and non-Judean, from sin and provides the route to righteousness and salvation and that he will now proceed to celebrate (8:1-11).

11

The Exalted Character of the New Identity (Romans 8)

Romans 8 constitutes a *crescendo al finale* to Paul's exploration of the foundations of the new identity shared by his Judean and non-Judean audience in Rome that occupies the first half of the letter (chaps. 1–8). For in this section he explains in some detail an indispensable issue that he has hitherto only hinted at—the glorious character of this identity, in both its present and, although to a surprisingly limited extent, its future dimensions, in contrast to life outside it. Paul has dealt with the sinfulness to which the two subgroups were, in their different ways, equally subject (1:18—3:20). He has explored the righteousness that represents the solution to this plight and the essential attribute of their common ingroup identity, both discursively (3:21-31) and in relation to that prototype in faith, Abraham (chap. 4). He has explained Christ's role in enabling the establishment of the new identity (3:21-26 and chap. 5) and how they gained access to it through baptism (6:1-10). He has expatiated upon the way in which the new dispensation has achieved what the Mosaic law could not and in the process demonstrated his leadership role as exemplar of group values (6:15—7:25). Now, at last, in a passage that falls fairly naturally into three sections (1-17, 18-30, and 31-39),[1] even though the last two are very closely connected, is the time to celebrate the nature of this new identity. In so doing, however, he touches on many of the earlier themes of the letter. In Tajfel's terminology, this involves singing a paean to the emotional and evaluative dimensions of identity-in-Christ, that is, how his addressees should feel about belonging to a group such as this and how they should rate themselves in relation to outsiders. Romans 8 is marked by language that is always passionate and, at times, exalted.

Present Identity in the Spirit (Rom. 8:1-17)

Existence and Identity according to the Spirit (Rom. 8:1-11)
Paul begins by summarizing the effect of 7:7-25 (describing the plight and solution of the ἐγώ) in a manner that picks up the theme of 5:12-21:

> There is therefore now no condemnation for those who are in Christ Jesus. For the law of the Spirit of life in Christ Jesus has

freed me[2] from the law of sin and death. For what the law was unable to do, in that it was weakened by the flesh, God did by sending his son in the likeness of sinful flesh, and concerning sin he condemned sin in the flesh, in order that the righteous requirement of the law might be fulfilled in us who walk not according to the flesh but according to the Spirit. (8:1-4)

This reiterates his understanding of Christ's role in establishing the new identity that represents liberation (ἠλευθέρωσεν, v. 2) from the realm of death-dealing sin that the law could not achieve. Yet Paul here again compliments the law (cf. 7:12) by suggesting that its "righteous requirement" (δικαίωμα) is now fulfilled; although the law was aimed at making people δίκαιος, it was simply not powerful enough for the job.

The contrast drawn at the end of this passage between those who "walk (περιπατοῦσιν) not according to the flesh (κατὰ σάρκα) but according to the Spirit (κατὰ πνεῦμα)"—Spirit having been introduced in v. 2 with the reference to "the law of the Spirit of life"—becomes the central theme in the discourse as far as v. 17. The frequency with which πνεῦμα and σάρξ are mentioned in this part of the letter is remarkable. In chaps. 1–7 there are only three references to πνεῦμα in connection with God;[3] in 8:1-17 there are six-teen. There are only seven references to σάρξ in the sense of "the flesh" hith-erto,[4] but thirteen in 8:1-17. How is this polarity of Spirit and flesh to be interpreted? What, moreover, is the significance of the similarities between 8:1-17 and Galatians 5 that have prompted some critics to the view that a common tradition must lie behind both passages?[5]

Paul's main point in Rom. 8:5-13 is to make a series of antithetical state-ments that differentiate living according to the flesh from living according to the Spirit. Those who live according to the flesh think (φρονοῦσιν) the things of the flesh. The mind (φρόνημα) that is set on the flesh is death; it is hostile to God, it is unable to obey God's law, and it does not obey it. Such people cannot please God. If the Spirit of Christ is not within you, you do not belong to Christ. If, finally, you live according to the flesh, you will die. On the other hand, those who live according to the Spirit think the things of the Spirit. The mind that is set on Spirit is life and peace. If you are in the Spirit, the Spirit of God dwells within you. If Christ is in you, although your body is dead through sin, your spirit is alive through righteousness. If the Spirit of him who raised Jesus from the dead dwells in you, he will give you life through his Spirit that dwells within you, and if by the Spirit you put to death the deeds of the body, you will live.

Why does Paul propound these antitheses? One idea worth consideration and raised by Dunn is that Paul was concerned to remind his audience that, even though they were in the Spirit following baptism, they needed to stay there.[6] Yet such a thought is not expressed here, as it was at 6:11-14 or as it will be, briefly, in 8:12-13. Paul states they have received the Spirit (v. 15) and does not raise here the (admittedly real) possibility that they would return to the flesh. When he does move into the area of moral persuasion, moreover, as in chap. 12, he leaves his audience in no doubt as to his intentions. Rather, his interest here, as Douglas Moo suggests, is "descriptive" rather than "hortatory."

But what is he describing? Moo discounts the idea that Paul is contrasting two groups of people, the converted and the unconverted, since his main purpose "is to highlight the radical differences between the flesh and the Spirit as a means of showing why only those who 'walk/think/are' after the Spirit can have eschatological life."[7] Yet as well as relying on the impossibly elastic word "eschatological," Moo's explanation (itself hardly "descriptive") assumes that to walk according to the Spirit is different from, and is the cause of, "eschatological life." In fact, they are two ways of saying the same thing. Paul is not establishing a relationship of cause but of predication between "walking according to the Spirit" and the various features described in vv. 5-13. He does the same in relation to "walking according to flesh." What he is up to?

At base, we encounter here (and in Galatians 5) an eruption of ingroup/outgroup differentiation. For the members of a group with a pronounced boundary between it and outgroups, the use of binary oppositions to praise themselves and denigrate the outside world becomes second nature. This view is a reflection of the central insight of social identity theory—that group members tell themselves who they are, that is, formulate their identity, in relation to other groups who they are not. The qualities of belonging to the ingroup are defined, interpreted, and positively evaluated by attributing the opposite of such qualities to outgroups. In Galatians, where Paul had sought to sustain the identity of his mixed congregations of Judeans and non-Judeans against pressure on the latter to be circumcised and become Judeans themselves, he had developed three binary oppositions: faith versus law, freedom versus slavery, and flesh versus Spirit.[8] Paul's determination to present his argument to the Galatians in these terms had led to the extreme of artificiality (mentioned in chapter eight above) entailed in associating Israel with Hagar and Ishmael in Gal. 4:24-31. Each of these three oppositions recurs in Romans, although Paul's aim of including Judean Christ-followers results in different emphases.

Paul's selection of the Spirit to designate the desirable pole of the contrast with the flesh is neither arbitrary nor idiosyncratic, but rooted in bedrock experience of being a Christ-follower. As noted in relation to Paul's treatment of baptism in Rom. 6:3-11 (chapter nine above), baptism was the occasion on which the person who professed his or her faith in the presence of the group and was incorporated into it received the Holy Spirit. Paul testifies to the relationship between baptism and the outpouring of the Holy Spirit in 1 Cor. 12:13: "For by one Spirit we were all baptized into one body—Judeans or Greeks, slaves or free—and all were made to drink of one Spirit."

Reception of the Holy Spirit was, however, not the rather tame affair of modern Christian confirmations. To receive the Spirit meant to have God within you. This overwhelming experience was frequently accompanied by charismatic gifts, such as prophecy, speaking in tongues, miracle working, visions, and auditions, and could result in feelings of euphoria among those involved. Such phenomena, probably unique in the ancient Mediterranean world, seem to have characterized the initial Judean followers of Christ in Jerusalem (Acts 2:14-21) and soon spread to non-Judean followers in the context of baptism (Acts 10:44-48).[9]

Charismatic phenomena were fundamental to Paul's congregations. This is most evident in 1 Corinthians 12–14, where his statement "I thank God that I speak in tongues more than all of you" (14:18) indicates both the extent of his own involvement in charismatic gifts and the value he attached to them. In addition, when Paul affirms to his entirely non-Judean congregation in Thessalonika that "our gospel came to you not only in word, but also in power and in the Holy Spirit and with full conviction" (1 Thess. 1:5), he is including reference to the manifestation of charismatic gifts and miracles. In short, whenever Paul mentions the Holy Spirit and the gifts of the Spirit in his letters, we must try to put out of our minds a purely theological understanding of the Holy Spirit that has been dominant in the modern period (at least in those reaches of Christianity to which Pentecostalism has not penetrated) and incorporate into the picture the dramatic, audible, and visible manifestations of God's presence that Paul and other Christ-followers of the first generation had in mind.

So when Paul describes members of the Christ-movement as those "who walk . . . according to the Spirit" (8:4) he is designating them with respect to the unique and exciting realm of the Spirit-charged to which they were admitted on baptism. It is a complimentary, almost eulogistic way to describe the life and identity of the ingroup. On the other hand, to "walk according to the flesh" refers to the world of sinfulness, either with or without the Mosaic law, characteristic of all outgroups. To develop the power of the opposition between the two identities Paul sets out a series of directly or indirectly antithetical statements, which differentiate between what it is like to live according to or in the flesh and the Spirit, respectively (vv. 5-13).

Sons of God in the Spirit (Rom. 8:12-17)

Verses 12-13 are an introductory statement in which Paul, addressing the recipients of the letter as "brothers" (ἀδελφοί) and moving from indicative to the imperative mood, insists that they are under an obligation not to live according to the flesh, which leads to death, but for the Spirit, which produces life.[10] He then proceeds to predicate of Christ-followers, for the first time in the letter, a further aspect of their identity—that they are sons, children, and heirs of God (8:14-17). If they are led by the Spirit, Paul asserts, they are "sons of God" (υἱοὶ θεοῦ). For the Spirit they received was not one of slavery that would make them fall back into fear but the Spirit of adoption (υἱοθεσία) that allows them to cry "Abba! Father!" Paul has drawn this convenient image of adoption from Greco-Roman legal systems, since first-century CE Judeans did not use adoption. The Spirit bears witness to their spirit that they are children (τέκνα θεοῦ) of God. If they are children (τέκνα) they are also heirs (κληρονόμοι)—heirs of God but fellow heirs (συγκληρονόμοι) of Christ, if they suffer with him in order that they might be honored with him.

The reference to fellow heirs reminds us that primogeniture (the inheritance of all the father's property by the eldest son) was not practiced among Judeans.[11] They believed in dividing property among the children. Luke's parable of the prodigal son (Luke 15:11-32) illustrates this approach to succession.[12]

In this passage Paul draws on the most powerful language of relationship in the ancient Mediterranean world to bind together the members of a group—that of kinship. In ancient Mediterranean society, kinship was the most basic social institution. Malina describes it as "the symboling of biological processes of human reproduction and growth in terms of abiding relations, roles, statuses, and the like."[13] So fundamental was connection with kin that members of groups seeking to express the close relationships they shared regularly used the language of kinship fictively in relation to one another. Israelites, for example, addressed one another as "brothers," and the same designation was used even among nonethnic groups that were not able to refer to a common ancestor as the putative basis of the relationship. The inevitable connection between the basic kinship group and a particular house and household meant that household imagery was also drawn upon to speak of the character of group belonging. The 1990s witnessed an upsurge in interest in kinship, families, and households in the first-century CE Greco-Roman and Judean world and how the relationships, roles, and statuses they represented affected the nascent Christ-movement.[14]

Why does Paul introduce the language of sonship and heirship at this point in the letter? Many commentators point to the similarity of the thought here with that in Gal. 3:23—4:7, and there is no doubt that the passages have elements in common that could derive from a Pauline teaching pattern.[15] It is certainly striking that in both places Paul refers to addressing God with the Aramaic word "Abba," the origin of which lies in intimate familial relations in Palestine.[16] Yet the real interest in the comparison between Gal. 3:23—4:7 and Rom. 8:14-17 resides not in the similarities but in the differences, although this has been insufficiently appreciated hitherto.

We have already seen how a consideration of the different way in which Abraham is portrayed in Romans 4 compared with Galatians aids in the interpretation of that part of the letter. Similarly, to be able to compare and contrast Rom. 8:14-17 with the Galatians passage offers the prospect of bringing Paul's communicative strategy here into sharper focus. That is, the Galatians passage offers a "control" for interpreting what he is seeking to achieve in Rom. 8:14-17.

I noted in chapter ten above that in Galatians Paul presented the law as being among the forces that enslaved human beings but whose time of operation has now passed. In Galatians liberation was from these forces, but in Romans liberation is from sin, a very different perspective and one far more positive toward the Mosaic law. It is within this expression of a negative attitude to the law in Galatians that Paul introduces the divine sonship of the Christ-followers. He argues that the time of the tutelary function of the Mosaic law has come to an end. Rather than being under the παιδαγωγός of the law, they are now sons of God through faith in Christ Jesus (Gal. 3:23-26). Divine sonship is thus presented, rather polemically, as the opposite of immaturity and restraint under the law. Since through baptism they are one in Christ Jesus (3:27-28), they are in Christ, and therefore the offspring of Abraham, "heirs according to promise" (3:29). Paul then expands on this to argue that an heir in his minority is little better than a slave, since he is under trustees and guardians until he reaches the age at which he will inherit (4:1-2). Until the arrival of Christ, they were infants (νήπιοι), enslaved to the elemental spirits of the cosmos, but now God's Son has redeemed those who were under the law in order that they might become adopted sons (4:3-5). Hence, because they are sons God has sent the Spirit of his Son into their hearts crying "Abba! Father!" Through God, they are no longer slaves, but sons and therefore heirs.

In Romans, on the other hand, Paul does not introduce divine sonship as the condition achieved by liberation from the law, but as a buttress for his demand that they live in the Spirit and not in the flesh. To be a son and heir of God is now interpreted as intrinsically connected with existence in the Spirit. The function of divine sonship to demonstrate the inferiority of the Mosaic law (and, by implication, any person or group advocating its adoption) is entirely absent.

Accordingly, Paul invokes sonship and heirship of God as a further means of designating the new identity they have achieved in Christ, now using imagery from the realm of kinship and household, the arena of social relations most characterized by its intimacy and fidelity. To be a member of an honorable family in the an ient Mediterranean world was itself a source of honor: "Being born into an honorable family," writes Malina (and we could add, being adopted into one), "makes one honorable since the family is the repository of the honor of past illustrious ancestors and their accumulated acquired honor."[17] It is not possible to conceive of a family as honorable as the one to which Paul is reminding the Christ-followers of Rome they belong.

Paul rounds off Rom. 8:12-17 by sounding a note that paves the way for the next section of the letter. For his addressees to be children, heirs, and coheirs of Christ, they must satisfy a condition: "if indeed we suffer with him so that we might also be glorified with him" (v. 17). This balancing of present suffering and future vindication is developed in 8:18-30.

Present Experience and Future Hope (Rom. 8:18-39)

Paul's Attitude to the Future in Current Discussion

Up to this point in the letter there have been a number of indications that the future matters for Paul. Most notably he has mentioned the day of wrath, when God's righteous judgment will be revealed and when God will render to everyone according to his or her works, with eternal life for some and wrath and fury for the others (2:6-11; 3:5). Many commentators discern in 8:18-30 the most important statement in the letter relating to the future. Thus Moo describes these verses as Paul's "moving portrait of the culmination and full benefits of that adoption that await the believer in the future" and "the exposition of the future glory to be enjoyed by the believer."[18] Meeks sees it as Paul's "picture of the future transformation of the whole creation."[19] Yet this passage also provides data, in existing scholarship, for assessing whether Paul's understanding of the radically transformed possibilities for human existence opened up by Christ's death and resurrection (usually called his "eschatology") is best described as present-oriented (or "realized"), future-oriented but imminent, or future-oriented but not necessarily imminent.

In particular, in this passage and elsewhere in Paul, Rudolf Bultmann and Ernst Käsemann had a major debate concerning the extent to which Paul's thought was oriented toward the future. Bultmann argued that the circumstance that the expected end of the world did not arrive and the "Son of Man" failed to appear in the clouds of heaven brought the early Christ-movement face to face with the fact that it had become an historical phenomenon.[20] As for Paul, although he did not abandon the "apocalyptic" picture of the future, the coming (parousia) of Christ, with the resurrection of the dead, the Last Judgment, and the glory of the righteous associated with it, he insisted that "the real bliss is righteousness, and with it freedom." Paul presented this state of bliss, according to Bultmann, as already present and as affecting believers as individuals. Believers who had been baptized were "in Christ," they were new creatures, and the Holy Spirit was upon them.[21]

Bultmann's emphasis on the centrality of the individual derived ultimately from his appropriation of the existentialist philosophy of Martin Heidegger. Before God, each individual confronts his or her life, which acquires its character by the decisions he or she makes. Such a person is continually called to be him- or herself in free decision. The life of such a person is a continuous being on the way, between the "no longer" and the "not yet." Thus the "eschatological event" is something not for the future but for the present, for in each moment in one's life a person is called to choose for life or for death.[22] The "eschatological event," at least according to Paul (and to the Fourth Evangelist), is not to be understood as a "dramatic cosmic catastrophe" but as happening within history, starting with the appearance of Jesus Christ: "It becomes an event repeatedly in preaching and faith. Jesus Christ is the eschatological event not as an established fact of past time but as repeatedly present, as addressing you and me here and now in preaching."[23]

Ernst Käsemann, a former pupil of Bultmann, was unable to accept this approach. He recognized that Bultmann's interpretation of Paul was "determined by his resolute placing of the apostle's present eschatology at the controlling centre of his thought" and that this also meant that Paul's particular contribution was to be regarded as his systematic development of the position of humanity in the new dispensation.[24] Yet Käsemann insisted on the importance of the signs of futurist "eschatology" or "apocalyptic," which were "everywhere to be found in the Pauline epistles." Käsemann regarded Paul as "anti-enthusiastic" (a topic I return to later in this chapter) and thought that his continued hold on a strong sense of the future was motivated by his desire to keep enthusiasm at bay. "Participation in the Resurrection is spoken of not in the perfect tense, but in the future. Baptism equips for it, calls to it, but does not itself convey this gift." The Spirit is "the reversionary expectation of the Resurrection." The resurrection, moreover, is primarily christological, not "anthropological." It is also a mistake to follow Bultmann in putting such emphasis on the individual, since Paul is interested in the whole "company of the obedient" who stand in succession to Christ's obedience and who comprise the body.[25]

Problems with the Current Discussion

The debate between Bultmann and Käsemann isolated a number of questions regarding Paul's understanding of the relationship between present and future for the Christ-believer that retain their importance, especially in relation to a text such as 8:18-30, written by Paul toward the end of his ministry. But there are two problems with this form of analysis.

The first such problem is that Bultmann and Käsemann were taking part in a debate using almost overwhelmingly theological concepts, long before the development of social-scientific interpretation of biblical texts. As we have already seen, not only is it difficult indeed in Romans to distinguish issues that we can label for convenience "theological" and "social," but also the 1980s and 1990s have seen a vigorous application of social-scientific ideas and perspectives to a huge range of biblical data. Few texts in either Testament remain untouched by such interpretation. Issues such as group formation and the relationships between individuals and groups to which they belong, the characteristic identity of the early Christ-movement, the role of charismatic phenomena in religious experience, and the nature of time (including the problems stemming from a strong dichotomy in modern Western cultures between present and future) have all been the subject of such considerable social-scientific scrutiny that it would now be methodologically suspect to attempt to address them without assistance from the social sciences.

The second problem is the possibility that the concepts most commonly employed in relation to phenomena of the kind found in 8:18-39, namely, "eschatology" and, perhaps to a lesser extent, "apocalyptic," have now passed their effective expiration date in this discussion, a question closely implicated in one of the social-scientific areas now important in biblical research, the nature of time. Given the fundamental importance of this in the interpretation of 8:18-39 to be set out below, it is necessary to say something about these terms.

"Eschatology" was coined in 1804 by K. G. Bretschneider and taken up by F. Oberthür in 1807–1808, and then by other German theologians, before passing to France in 1828 and England in 1844 or even sooner.[26] This was probably adapted from the traditional theological topic of *novissima*, the last things. In addition, it was not until 1852 that the word "apocalyptic" was used (by the German scholar F. Lücke) as a label for the genre of ancient texts represented by Daniel, Enoch, Ezra, and Baruch.[27] These notions burst into prominence in biblical research with the publication of works by Weiss in 1892 and Schweitzer in 1906 and have remained enormously influential ever since.[28]

But both words are now used with a great variety of meanings such that it is often difficult to know precisely what interpreters mean when they use them; they are words that often substitute for thought rather than expressing it. Indeed, in 1970 Jean Carmignac energetically argued that the word "eschatology" was employed with so many different meanings and produced such problematic distortions in the study of the first generation of the Christ-movement (such as obscuring the real nature of the kingdom of God) that it should be dropped from historical and theological discourse: "Puisque ce terme est une source de confusion, pourquoi ne pas l'abandonner? Puisque cette notion pervertit la notion biblique de la *basileia tou Theou*, pourquoi la garderait-on plus longtemps?"[29] Carmignac's strong view stands in stark contrast to the rather feeble assertion of E. P. Sanders that the "term 'eschatology' is so common and has such a long history in biblical scholarship that we cannot discard it."[30] Malina represents a more robust view when he suggests that "'apocalypse' and 'eschatology' are simply part and parcel of the theological jargon of the last century that fossilize perception and misdirect interpretation."[31]

The two expressions are also closely tied up with notions of time and history, and with the end of both, that are part of our modern understanding of reality but not necessarily apt when applied to the Mediterranean world in the first century CE. The vast majority of interpreters seem unaware of the extent to which conceptions of time vary from culture to culture.

In short, the problem with the word "eschatological" is twofold: it is arguably so capacious of meaning as to be almost vacuous, and, to the extent that it does still signify, it is riddled with implicit assumptions concerning time and the cosmos of uncertain relevance to the first century CE.

All this indicates that an alternative approach to 8:18-39 is needed, one that is open to the social dimensions of the text in a way that Bultmann and Käsemann were not and, at that time, were not able to be. This entails being open to the issues of identity that I have demonstrated are relevant to a wide range of phenomena in Romans, but here especially the particular question of the nature of time.

A Social Identity Perspective on Time

Social identity theory, as described in chapter two above, displays increasing interest in the diachronic dimensions of group identity. Susan Condor has proposed the necessity of viewing social life as a trajectory through time rather than as a static set of positions, as a continuum in which social agents take up identities, ideas, and practices and hand them on to others, often transforming them in the process.[32] This perspective matches Paul's interest in tracing a narrative from Adam to Moses, then on to Christ, and beyond to the coming judgment and, for some, future glory. The identity of Christ-followers incorporates this progress in its entirety. The "we" with whose experience members of the group identify both predates them and will survive after them.

The future dimension of group identity provides a fertile ground for what Marco Cinnirella calls "possible selves," meaning the beliefs held by members concerning themselves in the past and what they might become in the future. Moreover, the outlooks and activities of the group are commonly directed to a future beyond the lifetimes of existing category members. One might add that just as leaders of groups process the past, reworking or even inventing collective memories to serve the purposes of the group in the present, they are also able to "process the future," meaning to visualize its outcomes, often through various forms of mythopoiesis, in ways adapted to the particular needs of the group.

A typical product of such processing is the creation of myths of future world transformation and deliverance. In 1 Thessalonians Paul himself provides a detailed example of such a myth, one that speaks of the future coming of the Lord, who will descend from heaven, and of how the dead in Christ and the living will meet him in the clouds and be always with him (1 Thess. 4:15-17). He raids Israelite tradition to formulate this myth, even though he is writing to ex-idolaters in Thessalonika and avoids employing other Israelite traditions such as those relating to righteousness and the Mosaic law.[33] Yet before I ask a question that Pauline commentators rarely do ask—Why is this myth singularly absent from Romans?—a more fundamental question calls for consideration. It is the nature of time, specifically, the extent to which the sense of time is culturally conditioned.

Social identity theory provides useful insights into the relationship between groups and time, but at a fairly high level of abstraction. By moving a little closer to the subject of time (that is, by lowering the level of abstraction) we encounter the findings of anthropologists and sociologists as to the extent to which conceptions of time differ between cultures separated geographically and historically.

The issue rarely raised is whether Paul's understanding of time, which is, after all, the framework within which his views on the future must be construed, corresponded to that of his modern northern European and North American commentators. Since this is a question they rarely even ask, one presumes that they would answer it yes. Sadly, there is no basis for such complacency.

The Anthropology and Sociology of Time

A flourishing social-scientific literature demonstrates beyond the risk of contradiction that notions of time, both its nature and function, differ widely across human cultures. Munn surveys recent contributions to this area from cultural anthropologists, and Adam indicates the richness of the discussion among sociologists.[34] Although those of us socialized into northern European or North American culture tend to assume that our conceptions of time are shared across cultures and historical periods, the social-scientific material shows that this is simply ethnocentrism (and anachronism) on our part. "Combinations of past, present and future occur in culturally determined ways, rather than deriving from pan-human characteristics."[35] Only at the turn of the twentieth century was there set up a system of measured, external time on a global scale, a development stimulated especially by the invention of the telegraph and the ever-widening reach of railways.[36] We have generally failed to appreciate that "contemporary Western time needs to be understood in its historically developed uniqueness."[37]

Accordingly, it is not surprising that virtually all the North Atlantic scholars who use the word "eschatology" in relation to Romans (and other NT texts) proceed as if the understanding of time is invariable and that *their* notion of time, its future dimension especially, was shared by Paul and the initial recipients of this letter. In his usual refreshingly provocative manner, Malina has tried to shake the guild from such anachronistic and ethnocentric lethargy by calling for a movement from "Swiss" time to "Mediterranean" time;[38] perhaps nowhere is this change of perspective more urgently needed than in relation to the biblical literature usually referred to as "eschatological."

I now set out a brief introduction to some of the social-scientific research into how notions of time vary across cultures to lay the foundation for the fresh examination of 8:18-30 outlined below. It may be worthwhile to distinguish, at least loosely, between ideas as to the nature of the time—of past, present, and future—and the social function of such ideas. Consideration of the latter issue, the function of modes of temporality, will also require reflection on certain types of group behavior and the ways in which they relate to the identity of the members, such as will occupy the next broad section of this chapter.

Social-Scientific Views on the Nature of Time

The notion of time has attracted considerable attention from sociologists (such as Durkheim, Mead, Gurvitch, Sorokin, and Schutz),[39] and also from anthropologists (such as Evans-Pritchard, Lévi-Strauss, Leach, and Gell).[40] A common theme in all this literature is the extent to which the experience and understanding of time has a social dimension and varies from one culture to another. This view stems mainly from Durkheim, who expressed it, admittedly, in an extreme form. He regarded the various ways by which people divide time into various segments, such as years, seasons, months, weeks, days, hours, and so on, as a product of the social life: "what the category of time expresses is the time common to the group, a social time, so to speak."[41] This approach meant that the representations of time collectively entertained by a particular group did not reflect time but actually created it, which had the consequence (visible in the work of many social scientists influenced by Durkheim) that different societies were thought to generate diverse temporal worlds capable of being explored and even experienced.[42]

Yet Durkheim's argument was beset by a serious flaw that sprang from his epistemology, in that he sought to give social expressions of temporality a metaphysical status, thus confusing sociological and philosophical inquiry, as Gell has explained.[43] Moreover, the actual practices of human beings do not support Durkheim. Most of the temporal periodicities that affect people (such as days, seasons, and years) derive from the movements of the sun and the moon, while others, such as market days, are affected by ecological constraints, being adaptations to the physical environment. Nevertheless, while Durkheim was wrong to assert that all the periodicities that affect human life are socially derived, it is true that some of them are (such as the hourly division of a day) and that social life determines which others are to become salient. As Gosden puts it, the "divisions between day and night or the passage of the seasons represent a biological background to be played with culturally, in the same way that gender is the cultural use made of sexual differences."[44]

Subsequent research since Durkheim (even if it is sometimes accompanied by Durkheimian quasi-metaphysical claims) has revealed the diversity of social expressions of time and the extent to which social factors affect the perceptions of time operative among particular groups. Among anthropologists, for example, Evans-Pritchard was able to discern that the Nuer distinguish between "ecological time" and "structural time," the former referring to concepts derived from the adaptation of the Nuer to their environment, and the latter connected with the ways in which the Nuer organized their social and political structure, especially in relation to lineage across several generations.[45] Since the Nuer never permitted recognition of more than the six most recent generations, with all older generations being pushed back into the past, it followed that the distance between the beginning of the world and the present day remained inalterable.[46]

Lévi-Strauss differentiated between "hot" societies, such as ours, which have a conception of historical time as an enormous file into which historical events are entered and then never expunged, and "cold" societies, where the fundamental cognitive schemes are static and adverse to change, which seek to remain closed to external influence.[47] He distinguished between "synchronic" and "diachronic" time in his writings, even if the distinction is not convincing.[48] He even spoke of reversible time. "Lévi-Strauss is essentially an anti-time man. His interest in the sociology of time is focused primarily, and perhaps with a degree of envious nostalgia, on the ways in which societies can annul time and its effects."[49] His ideal is for order achieved without authoritarianism.

There is certainly much ethnographic testimony for cultures that consider that the temporal relationship of the present to the mythical/ancestral past is not affected by the passage of time. Perhaps the best-known example of this is the beliefs of Australian Aboriginal people about dream-time versus the present. Gell, relying on Strehlow, notes that all their daily activities

> are both re-enactments of the long-past prototypical activities of the ancestors in the dream-time (the noumenal, mythic period) and at the same time are contemporaneous with these same ancestral doings, in that the ancestors are considered *still* to be engaging, invisibly, in these activities at all the relevant sacred sites specified in the myths. The totemic past and the real world coalesce, but are also distinct from one another, in that the phenomenal order of things, the non-dream-time life, is only a pale shadow of the "real" world of the dream-time ancestral beings.[50]

Lévi-Strauss argued that in what he called "historical rites" the past was re-created so that it becomes the present.[51] This idea is similar to Eliade's notion of "the myth of the eternal return."[52]

Gell is critical of such claims. He considers that Lévi-Strauss has fallen prey to Durkheimian pseudo-metaphysical claims in that he presents as real, rituals that are, in terms of metaphysics, "illusions."[53] To refer to the beliefs of Australian Aboriginal people and of other groups who in some way re-create the experience of the mythic past in the present as "illusions" does, however, seem rather harsh, unless one is careful to insist that they are illusions only in relation to a metaphysical framework and that they are real enough for the peoples who ascribe to them and for whom they no doubt serve meaningful social functions.

Another provocative contribution was made by Edmund Leach. In two essays republished in 1961 he sought to debunk the idea that preindustrial hunter-gatherer and horticultural (whom he unfortunately called "primitive") peoples experience time as cyclical by proposing instead that they see it as an alternation between "opposites." According to Leach, such people experienced time as "a repetition of repeated reversals, a sequence of oscillations between polar opposites: night and day, winter and summer, drought and flood, age and youth, life and death. In such a scheme the past has no 'depth' to it, all past is equally past, it is simply the opposite of now."[54] He also sought to distinguish between "profane" time in which time goes forward and "sacred" time, when, in a ritual context, time goes backward and earlier states or conditions are restored. While these proposals, especially the idea that ritual acts produce notions of time running backward, have attracted criticism,[55] they serve as a good introduction to the whole question of how different cultures envisage past, present, and future and the relationships between them. This question has a direct bearing on the analysis of texts, such as Rom. 8:18-30, that deal with the future dimensions of the Christ-movement.

Conceiving the Future and Myth

Writers such as Durkheim, Lévi-Strauss, Eliade, and Leach have highlighted a variety of approaches to time and serve to remind us of the historically contingent nature of the sense of temporality present in North Atlantic cultures. Nevertheless, much ethnographic research, in seeking to do justice to other frameworks of thought and experience, tends to draw so sharp a distinction between the "cyclical," "mythical," or "reversible" time of preindustrial peoples on the one hand and linear or Newtonian time on the other as to produce a distorted view of the temporality characteristic of other cultures. It is, in particular, unhelpful if claims as to the cyclical, synchronic, or reversible time of preindustrial peoples lead to the conclusion that they do (or, for past peoples, did) not have a sense of the future. Many traditional societies envisage the future as well as the past, and their belief systems can span vast periods of time.[56] While we must be alert to different ways in which the future is conceived and functions, we must not deny other peoples futurity per se.

If it is reasonable to establish a spectrum of concern with the future among various cultures, we may begin with the suggestion that modern northern European and North American cultures are future oriented to an extraordinary degree. We continually reach out into the future in order to eliminate or control its uncertainties. Thus nation-states negotiate international environmental treaties to produce impacts by 2010, 2020, or even 2050. Our major organizations routinely engage in the processes of strategic planning and risk management. We build institutions in the areas of law, banking, and insurance, all based on the reality of promises made to be fulfilled in the (possibly distant) future. We contribute to pension schemes for our retirement, and we insure our lives, our health, our houses, and our cars. Everywhere we consciously seek to protect ourselves against the future and the risks it may bring. T. Hägerstrand has coined the phrase the "colonisation of the future" to characterize these pervasive efforts at control.[57]

Inevitably, other cultures see the future differently. Cultures at an agrarian stage of evolution, where the peasantry live from one harvest to the next and are largely at the mercy of the natural forces (rain or drought, pests, crop disease, etc.), have a very different attitude to the future.[58] While such people do have a sense of future, it is much more attenuated. People must accept what the future, something almost entirely beyond their control and, accordingly, in God's hands, will bring. There is little sense that one can reach into the future to control or eliminate its uncertainty and dangers.[59] To a much greater extent, people live in the present. This resistance to peering too far into the future is the context for sayings from the agrarian culture of the first-century eastern Mediterranean such as "Tomorrow will be anxious for itself" (Matt. 6:34), "Let the day's own trouble be sufficient for the day" (6:34), or "Give us this day our daily bread" (6:12). For the preindustrial, agrarian societies of the ancient Mediterranean, the connection of the future to the present was widely understood as the culmination of presently occurring natural processes. We will see the relevance of this to Romans 8 in a moment.

H.-W. Hohn has argued that the transition from human beings who are part of nature or God's creatures, living in his time and to his design, to makers of history and shapers of their own future occurred as late as the height of the Middle Ages.[60] He suggests that this entailed a movement from a unity of present and eternity (the realm of God's future) to a goal-oriented, teleological awareness. Hohn connects this development with the rise of market economies that turned the uncertainties of the future into a risk factor to be calculated and monetarized, in short, controlled, by the best means available, which has led to our contemporary view of the future.

Yet even in cultures at a horticultural or agrarian stage of development, where the future is less controllable and far less mapped and scrutinized, it is still the subject of interest. For such societies the future matters, although it is less prominent and less the basis for decision making in the present than in modern North Atlantic cultures. Thus practices connected with taking oracles of various kinds, or observing the flight of birds or the entrails of animals, in relation to the likely outcome of an imminent event, a battle especially, do reveal that a desire to reduce future risks within certain limited spheres characterizes many preindustrial societies today and was also common in the ancient Mediterranean world. Similarly, a peasant with a surplus of a particular crop one year might lend some to his neighbor, knowing that next year he might be in need of such a loan himself, thus engaging in a form of modest insurance. The major buildings of Greco-Roman cities were also built to last for a long time.

Yet perhaps the most arresting form of future speculation among preindustrial peoples consists of expectations that the existing order of things will be destroyed and replaced with a new order that will solve the problems that are thought to exist in the present. Such expectations are usually couched as myths, that is, as narratives involving the intersection of divine and human realms.[61] They are commonly (although not exclusively) found among indigenous peoples whose traditional way of life has been disturbed or even suppressed by colonial intruders. The "millennial" or "millenarian" myths, to use the designations favored by social scientists, generated in this context frequently look forward to the imminent transformation of the present situation, the destruction of the invader, the return of the ancestors, and the restoration of lands, culture, and power to the original population. Striking examples are the Ghost Dance of the Native North American[62] and the cargo cults of the South Pacific.[63] Clearly the book of Daniel is capable of being analyzed within such a perspective, as I have argued elsewhere.[64]

It is necessary, however, to emphasize how much myths such as these relating to the future transformation of a group differ from other kinds of myth.[65] Much research on myth carried out in the early and mid-twentieth century argued for its fulfilling a range of social functions. In particular, functionalists such as Malinowski argued that myth played an important role in maintaining social stability. According to him, "Myth, as it exists in a savage community . . . is not merely a story told, but a reality lived."[66] It is "a pragmatic charter of primitive faith and moral wisdom."[67] While we may wish to demur at the use of the words "savage" and "primitive" here, there are no doubt situations where myth does fulfill such a function. Similarly, Eliade's notion of "the myth of the eternal return," which proposes that myth provides access to a formative, primordial past, is closely compatible with Malinowski's functionalism.

It is worth noting that functionalist approaches to myth do have the capacity to adapt to an interest in the future. In her introduction to a collection of essays that discuss how certain contemporary cultures, some of them nonindustrial, visualize the future, Sandra Wallman lists a number of statements that encapsulate worthy lines of inquiry in relation to the understanding of the future held by any particular group. The first two are easily accommodated to the ideas of Malinowski and Eliade:

1. The future can be used to justify present action—a forward-looking version of the mythical charter.
2. Scenarios of the future function to illuminate the present and/or to offer at-a-distance and so politically and (emotionally?) safe ways of criticizing it.

In spite of all this, however, the bias of functionalists in favor of social stasis has now lost ground to models of social interaction that highlight change and conflict. The second pair of statements posed by Wallman to encapsulate contemporary ideas on the future reflect the reality of social change:

3. Belief in the future underpins the sense of self and its survival.
4. Changes in those beliefs, however generated, can work radically to alter the way individuals and groups relate to each other, to the natural environment, and to culture itself.[68]

The understanding of myth has inevitably been affected by this changing emphasis. These newer perspectives have brought out the extent to which myth can stress the goal rather than the foundation of a social order, to have a *prescriptive* rather than a *proscriptive* role.[69] In such a context, it is natural that myth addresses future events. That is, even in contexts such as the agrarian cultures of the ancient Greco-Roman East, with a strong orientation to the present rather than the future, it would not be surprising if personal or social disruption or disturbance, fostered by conquest, political oppression, famine, dissatisfaction with the prevailing moral order of society, or a number of other factors, encouraged an interest in future speculations. Thus the myth of the future in texts like Daniel reflects the fact that the transformation which the Seleucid king Antiochus IV Epiphanes sought to impose on Israel was so extreme that established mythic traditions could no longer be synchronized with the current situation. Jesus' proclamation of the kingdom of God is also susceptible to such analysis, as is Paul's teaching of the "coming'" of the Lord (1 Cor. 15:23; 1 Thess. 2:19, 3:13, 4:15, 5:23). While Paul uses the word *parousia* of the Lord's coming, and the word was employed in relation to the arrival of high officials in the cities of the East (equivalent to *adventus*), his frequent use of the word in relation to the arrival or presence of himself or fellow Christ-followers (1 Cor. 16:17; 2 Cor. 7:6, 7; 10:10; Phil. 1:26; 2:12) cautions us against attributing to it too technical a sense.

Social Identity and Time in Romans 8:18-39

Interpretation of Romans 8:18-30

When Paul begins the next section of the letter with the statement: "For I consider that the sufferings of the present time are not worth comparing with the glory about to be revealed to us" (8:18), his readers may have expected that they were about to treated to a description of this glory. Moo appears to consider that Paul does this, because he says that the focus of vv. 18-30 is "eschatological glory" and that Paul here elaborates that glory.[70] But Paul does no such thing. The most striking thing about these verses, and the closely related section that follows (8:31-39), is the extent to which Paul refuses to provide a picture of the glory that is to come. He holds out the prospect of describing the glory in v. 18 and then singularly fails to do so.

Earlier in his career Paul had been quite willing to depict in some detail events that would occur when Jesus Christ returned. He does this in 1 Thess. 4:15-17, even though writing to an audience composed of non-Judeans. It would also have been possible for him to expatiate upon the blessed state of those who, after the return of Jesus, will be "with the Lord always" (πάντοτε σὺν κυρίῳ, 1 Thess. 4:17), perhaps along lines similar to what we find in Revelation (e.g., Rev. 5:11-14). But in Romans Paul provides no such description. This is a remarkable phenomenon the significance of which is largely overlooked by commentators, even if a few, like Hans-Werner Bartsch, have noticed that "there is no consideration of the nature of the coming kingdom" in Romans.[71] Indeed, the sense of the future in 8:18-30 (and in 8:31-39) is notably attenuated. So what is Paul up to? We must pursue the course of his argument to find out.

Verses 19-22 constitute the first of a number of recognizably distinct units. Here Paul suggests that the whole cosmos has been eagerly waiting for the revelation of the sons of God (8:20), which in Paul's context meant a mere few hundred Christ-followers scattered around the Mediterranean. We should note that his interest is on the group, not on any individual. Certainly the individual members benefit from belonging, but if they did not belong they would not enjoy this sonship. To this extent Käsemann was correct in criticizing Bultmann for placing such a strong emphasis on the individual, since Paul is interested in the whole group.

Brendan Byrne rightly comments on vv. 19-22: "This is one of the most curious and fascinating passages in Romans. Its distinctiveness lies in the fact that here for the first and perhaps only time in his extant letters Paul considers human beings in relation to the non-human created world."[72] While it is not uncommon for a religious group to imagine that its membership exists at the center of the world, rarely do we find anything quite as daring as this. Creation had been subjected to futility, not voluntarily, but by the one who subjected it in hope (8:20). The one who subjected is most likely God,[73] and the futility referred to (ματαιότης), although alluding to the futility lamented in Ecclesiastes,[74] probably reflects the position that creation found itself in as a result of Adam's sin (already mentioned in 5:12-14). Now the reason for the eager expectation of creation becomes clear: it is not just an interested group of bystanders (the most extraordinary in history), but it will also be set free from its bondage to decay to partake in the freedom of the glory of the children of God. "Creation, fallen with the human race, shows a hope nonetheless that it will share also in its restoration."[75]

Then, and most significantly, Paul says: "For we know that all creation groans (συστενάζει) and suffers the pangs of childbirth together until now" (8:22). This is a revealing metaphor. Paul is linking the current suffering of creation with the expected outcome—a successful birth. Here we see graphically a conception of time quite different from that current among the societies of northern Europe and North America. We are accustomed to envisaging precise moments or events in the future, possibly a long way off, that may have no real connection with present experience, for example, the first manned space flight to Mars. The commonplace expression in New Testament studies "now and not yet" is indelibly stamped with this mind-set. It represents the "overlapping" of two time zones that in our modern perspective are distinct.

As Malina has observed, however, for the people of the ancient Mediterranean cultures (like Paul), the connection between the present and the future was regularly understood in terms of a natural process occurring in the present that would produce a particular result in the future, unless a disaster occurred. Paradigmatic examples included growing crops and a woman pregnant or in labor. In this perspective, the forthcoming was the unfolding or developing horizon of the experienced present.[76] Malina assists in grasping the effect of this. He says that what distinguishes "the forthcoming," by which he means the Mediterranean sense of the future (as in the word μέλλουσα in 8:18), from "the future," meaning the future in modern, technological societies, is "the degree of immediate and direct organic connection with some presently experienced person, event or process. When exactly that potentiality might be realized is not at issue as it would be for us. Rather the item at issue is the inevitability of the outcomes rather than how many and when."[77] In this context, to speak of "now and not yet," with its implication of two separate periods of time brought into surprising collocation or "overlap" anachronistically and ethnocentrically imposes a view alien to the Mediterranean one, where the forthcoming is a natural and organic outgrowth of the present.

In addition to this distinctive temporal dimension to 8:19-22, social identity theory helps us to appreciate the momentous nature of its relevance to the status of Paul's addressees in Rome. He is boldly personifying the whole of creation and then aligning its unhappy experience and expectation with the existence and destiny of a small band of Christ-followers. The effect of this is to magnify the various elements of their group identity. The cognitive dimension, the sheer fact of belonging to a group like this, is enhanced by the incorporation, as it were, of creation itself as an associate member. Of all the millions of people alive in the known world, creation was aligned with, and supportive of, the tiny minority constituting the Christ-movement. From this it necessarily followed that the emotional and evaluative dimensions (how they felt about belonging to a group like this and how they rated themselves in comparison with other groups) were also greatly augmented.

Verses 23-25 constitute the second unit. Paul now establishes a direct parallel between creation and the members: "And not only the creation, but we ourselves, who have the first fruits (ἀπαρχή) of the Spirit, groan (στενάζει) within ourselves as we eagerly await adoption (υἱοθεσία), the redemption of our body" (8:23). Just as creation was groaning (συστενάζει, v. 22), so too are Paul and his audience in Rome. They too have a difficult present experience (sweetened, however, with a foretaste of the Spirit) with a forthcoming transformation (sonship/redemption) that yet "stands at the concrete horizon of the present."[78] Here Paul deftly extends the imagery of birth pangs and childbirth to embrace the situation, respectively, of adversity and adoption. It would have been impossible for Paul to stretch the metaphor so far as to refer to childbirth here (as he does at v. 22), so he makes do with the analogous notion of adoption instead, a feature already mentioned at 8:15. The reference to "the first fruits (ἀπαρχή) of the Spirit" is undoubtedly to the exciting array of charismatic phenomena, such as miracle working, prophecy, and glossolalia, that characterized the early communities of Christ-followers, including Paul's, in Palestine and the diaspora (cf. 15:27) and were received initially in baptism, which I have discussed earlier in this chapter. Käsemann's argument that Paul is attacking charismatic phenomena, which he labels "enthusiasm,"[79] in this section of the letter produces a lamentable misreading of Paul.

In this context, then, 8:24a comes as no surprise: "For in terms of hope we have been saved."[80] Rather than seeing this as illustrating a tension between "the now and the not yet," we should adopt an ancient Mediterranean perspective on time. Malina brings out the dimensions of that perspective in a manner closely relevant to 8:24a: "The immediate future bound up with the present as well as previous activity still resonating in the present are all part of that present, still experienced and all actually present."[81] Paul speaks of a reality in the present, a reality marked by the experience of the Spirit mentioned in the previous verse, as shown by the causal connective $\gamma\acute{\alpha}\rho$ that links v. 24 to v. 23.[82] This reality is so powerful that Paul can speak of it in the language of salvation in the aorist tense ($\grave{\epsilon}\sigma\acute{\omega}\theta\eta\mu\epsilon\nu$), even though righteousness language is more commonly employed in this letter for present experience. This fact of salvation represents "previous activity resonating in the present," as Malina puts it. And yet the future ("hope") is closely integrated into the picture as well.

An attitude resistant to speculation about the future also emerges in what Paul says next: "For hope that is seen is not hope. For who hopes for what he sees? But if we hope for what we do not see, we wait for it with endurance" (8:24b-25). Paul is noting the contradiction involved in seeing what we hope for. Within a Mediterranean perspective on time, this means that although we know the woman is pregnant, we cannot yet see the baby; although the seed is sown we cannot yet see the grain. What is that we cannot see but hope for? He is presumably referring to phenomena such as the glorification and revelation of the sons of God (8:17, 19), adoption, and redemption of the body (8:23). These exist on the horizon of the present, organically evolving out of present experience but not yet visible. Paul is also saying that this encourages us to be patient. In addition, however, he makes no effort to describe such events, of the kind he himself had previously attempted in 1 Thess. 4:15-17 and that other New Testament writers would later also explore, notably the author of Revelation, and that we also find in florid forms in Judean writings such as *4 Ezra*. There is much to be said, accordingly, for Baumgarten's proposal that Paul is here critical of "apocalyptic" traditions and can be accurately described as "anti-apocalyptic," even if Dunn resists this view and proposes instead that Paul is "non-apocalyptic."[83] Paul is positively discouraging any effort to visualize end-time events, rather than simply failing to report them. Paul is demanding a concentration on present experience, with hope and endurance typifying the right attitude to what will be forthcoming, and discouraging attempts to reach into the future and to envisage the glories to come. The future serves to provide a particular character to existence in the present rather than to be the subject of separate speculation.

With vv. 26-27 we encounter the third unit in this section. Perhaps not surprisingly for people who have received the first fruits of the Spirit (v. 23), Paul now proceeds to specify ways in which the Spirit helps the faithful: "Likewise also the Spirit supports us in our weakness. For we do not know what to pray for as we ought, but the Spirit itself intercedes on our behalf with inarticulate groans (στεναγμοί). And he who searches the hearts knows what is the mind of the Spirit, because he intercedes in accordance with God on behalf of the holy ones" (8:26-27). The reference to "weakness" in v. 26 reminds us of the "the sufferings of the present time" in v. 18, the groaning of v. 23 (matching the groaning of creation in v. 22), and the endurance that is necessary in v. 25. Paul is now focusing entirely on the present experience of his addressees but is bringing them the good news that the Spirit, no less, is supporting them, in the sense of sharing their adversity and articulating it in prayer. As Dunn aptly notes, "The image of the Spirit shouldering the burden which our weakness imposes on us is quite a vivid one."[84] That the Spirit also utters groans (albeit "inarticulate" ones, that is, not in any human language) just like the Christ-followers (v. 23) underlines the extent to which the Spirit understands their difficulties. But God, the one who searches their hearts (cf. 1 Sam. 16:7; 1 Kgs. 8:39; Ps. 139:1-2, 23), is also involved in complex interaction with the Spirit to ensure that the necessary prayers of the holy ones reach their destination. In social identity terms, all this greatly amplifies the cognitive, emotional, and evaluative dimensions of belonging to this group. Indeed, Rom. 8:26-27 constitutes a magnificent statement of one particular way in which God expresses solidarity with his people that brings out the exalted nature of this identity.

The last unit in this section of the letter (8:18-30) consists of vv. 28-30: "We know that for those who love God, everything[85] works together for the good for those who are called according to his purpose. For those whom he foreknew, he predetermined to be conformed to the image of his son, so that he should be the firstborn among many brothers. And those he predetermined, he also called; those he called, he also righteoused; and those he righteoused he also glorified." From the viewpoint of the Christ-followers in Rome, these verses would serve to emphasize that they had always been within the loving intentions of God: known in advance, selected in advance, called, righteoused, and glorified. The last point is nearest to our purpose here. How is it that Paul can speak of the glorification as something already completed? After all, he began his section of the letter (8:18) by speaking of "the glory about to be revealed to us." Moo offers one answer: "Most interpreters conclude, probably rightly, that Paul is looking at the believer's glorification from the standpoint of God, who has already decreed that it should take place."[86] For Moo, these three verses represent the clearest example in the New Testament of the tension between the "already" and the "not yet."

Yet we have already had reason to cast doubt on this notion of the "already" and the "not yet" by reason of the modern notion of time in which it is embedded. If one adopts a more Mediterranean view of time that locks present and future far more closely together, a different solution suggests itself. Now the glory is forthcoming, rather than future, and has a direct, organic connection with present experience. It exists on the horizon of the present, even if it is not already here. While not coming at the problem from this direction, Byrne has observed that "we can admit that there is a sense in which glory, in a hidden way, is already a part of Christian life."[87] Precisely! That is why Paul can say in v. 24a: "For in terms of hope we have been saved." What we have, therefore, is the forthcoming closely integrated with the present and the recent past. The notion of a future separate from this complex, a "not yet" distinguished from an "already," is an unnecessary modern intrusion on Paul's thought. Nevertheless, this conclusion is far closer to Bultmann's emphasis on the present experience of the Christ-follower than to Käsemann's advocacy of a strongly futurist dimension of Paul's thought.

Interpretation of Romans 8:31-39
Written in an exalted (even purple) style, possibly reflecting Asiatic rhetoric, 8:31-39 has been described as "une sorte de chant de triomphe anticipé."[88] Its basic theme is the inseparable bond between God and Christ on the one hand and the followers of Christ on the other. This picks up a subject covered in the previous section (especially vv. 26-27) and binds the two of them quite closely together, in spite of the more elevated style here. When Paul asks, "If God is for us, who is against us?" (8:31), he alludes to the impotency of the unnamed agents responsible for their sufferings in the present (8:18). Whatever the character of the outgroups, in other words, the people stereotyped in 8:5 as living in accordance with the flesh, they will not ultimately prevail over the Christ-movement. If God did not even spare his own son, but gave him up for all of us, will he not also give us everything with him (8:32)? In other words, will God not do everything else that we require?

Paul now moves away from generalization to specifics in vv. 33-34. Here, as the commentators all point out, it is extremely difficult to punctuate the Greek, especially as to whether clauses are statements or questions. Nevertheless, I am guided by the fact that there are three definite questions beginning with "Who?" (τίς) at the start of vv. 33, 34, and 35. Since the answer to the third, by implication, is definitely "no one," I interpret vv. 33 and 34 accordingly as assuming the same answer: "Who will bring any charge against God's elect, when it is God who righteouses? Who condemns (κατακρινῶν), when it is Christ (Jesus) who died, rather was raised, who is also at the right hand of God, who intercedes on our behalf?" On this view, no one will bring a charge against God's elect, since God is righteousing them. Here we see Paul radically reinterpreting the collective memory of Israel to seize and reapply to the members of the Christ-movement an Israelite term of group definition that reflected their view that they were God's chosen people—"the elect of God."[89] Similarly, no one will condemn them, since Christ is sitting at the right hand of God and will intercede on their behalf (to prevent any condemnation). This brings to mind 8:1: "There is therefore now no condemnation (κατάκριμα) for those who are in Christ Jesus."

Is this a reference to some future event, especially judgment? This is possible. In chap. 2, after all, Paul had spoken of the day of wrath when God's righteous judgment will be revealed, when he will render to every human being according to his works (2:5-10). That will be a day when God judges (κρίνει) the secrets of human beings by Christ Jesus (2:16). These events will take place before the dais (βῆμα) of God (14:10). These events are possibly in mind here. If so, they are understated in a way consistent with Paul's statement that we do not hope for what we see (8:24). But if the day of wrath is in view here, it is worth repeating the unexpected and rarely commented-on issue noted in chapter seven above: Paul does not appear to envisage a judgment for the righteous, even though they will appear before God. For a judgment requires someone to lay a charge, and 8:33 implies there is no such person. Nor will the elect be condemned, because 8:34 implies that the intercession of Christ will prevent that happening. Thus the "righteous judgment" (δικαιοκρισία) of 2:5 apparently refers only to the wicked; there is no judgment for those who have attained the status of righteous. They will arrive "righteous before God" (δίκαιοι παρὰ [τῷ] θεῷ), they "will be righteous" (δικαιωθήσονται), as he says in 2:13, and will receive their reward. In effect, Christ-believers do not participate in any judicial proceeding, let alone condemnation. No one brings a charge against them and no one condemns them. It is as if they are simply passed by without further ado.

On the other hand, there is another way to interpret vv. 31-34. Given that in vv. 35-36 Paul is certainly talking about their experience in this world and assuring his audience that nothing will separate them from the love of Christ, is it not possible that he is doing the same in vv. 31-34? Is Paul saying here that in their present existence no one will be able to charge them with unrighteousness because God is righteousing them and no one will be able to condemn them since Christ will intercede on their behalf? In this case, the element of the forthcoming, which I have already suggested is not prominent in this passage, would be reduced even further.

Conclusion: Identity and Time in Romans 8:18-39

From this analysis I conclude that in these verses Paul is not offering a "moving portrait of the culmination and full benefits of that adoption that await the believer in the future" (so Moo) or an "exposition of the future glory to be enjoyed by the believer" (Meeks).[90] Nor does characterizing this passage as "eschatological" in any way further our understanding of it. Rather, if one attends to what Paul is saying in relation to the dynamics of social identity and within a context with a different attitude to time from the one with which we are familiar, we see that he is focused on the present existence of Christ-followers and, I should add, as a group, as shown by the relentless use of first person plurals throughout this section of the letter. What Paul has to say relates to the experience and destiny of the group; true, this becomes part of their identity that is then installed in the minds and hearts of the individual members as a central feature of the social identity they derive from belonging to it, but the primary reality is a social one.

There is certainly a future dimension to what Paul says. There is a glory that is going to be revealed (8:18). Hope is vital (8:24). Yet the forthcoming is organically linked to the present, as in the imagery of childbirth (8:22-23). And Paul urges them not to visualize what is to come, since this is inconsistent with hope (8:24). It is possible that vv. 33-34 refer to the final acknowledgment of the status of the righteous (and judgment and condemnation of the wicked), with Christ at the right hand of God, yet Paul is singularly sparing in his portrayal. There is nothing here to compare with 1 Thess. 4:15-17 or even with the details in Rom. 2:5-10 and 14:10. There is also the possibility that 8:33-34 refers to the present of the Christ-followers, to the way that God and Christ look after them now, a view strengthened by the reference to the vicissitudes of this life in the verses that follow (vv. 35-39).

Accordingly, the real subject of this passage is not the glory that is about to be revealed, but the character of life in the present, with the forthcoming held onto in hope, a life supported by the active presence of the Spirit (8:26-27) and the love of God in Christ Jesus (8:37-39). It is an exalted vision of life in Christ delivered with overwhelming power and eloquence.

12

Israel and the Christ-Movement (Romans 9–11)

The Problem of Romans 9–11

Romans 9–11 comprises a well-defined section of Romans. Until the mid-nineteenth century, an interpretation of this section inspired by Augustine was dominant and had found a particularly warm reception in Calvinist readings. On this view, the primary argument of the letter on righteousness concludes with chap. 8 and chaps. 9–11 were a rather unrelated treatise dealing with predestination—of some human beings to salvation and others to damnation. In 1868, however, W. Beyschlag posed a strong challenge to the Augustinian position, by arguing that these chapters did not address the fate of individuals, but instead dealt with the relative positions of "Jews" and "gentiles" in the divine plan, and focused especially on the issue of the election of Israel.[1]

But this still left the question of how chaps. 9–11, dealing with "the Israel issue," related to chaps. 1–8 and (although less interest was shown here) to chaps. 12–16. Thus C. H. Dodd found this section was originally a separate treatise by Paul having little direct relation to the rest of the letter.[2] Bultmann considered there was a sharp inconsistency between chaps. 1–8 and 9–11 and virtually ignored the latter passage in his *Theology of the New Testament*.[3] On the other hand, other scholars regarded chaps. 9–11 as far more important and well integrated in the argument of the letter. F. C. Baur, for example, found here Paul's subordination of the claims of Israel and "Jewish-Christian" particularism to the universalism of the gospel represented by "Gentile Christians," which formed an important step in the movement toward the ultimate synthesis of early theology.[4] While this particular view has fallen out of favor, the notion that chaps. 9–11 are of central importance to the argument of the letter is today widely defended.[5]

My purpose in the present chapter is to explore Romans 9–11 using the theoretical perspectives focusing on conflict and identity that have been applied to earlier sections of the letter. As we will see, this exploration produces strong support for the idea that these chapters are closely linked to chaps. 1–8 and have a bearing on chaps. 12–16; indeed, that here Paul is largely addressing the concerns of Judean/Israelite members of the Christ-movement in Rome. This analysis meshes closely with some statistics that are worth mentioning at the outset. A striking feature of chaps. 9–11, as Guerra has noted,[6] is that 39 percent of the text consists of scripture quotations, with such frequency being approached nowhere else in the Pauline corpus. In addition, 51 of the 89 scripture quotations in Paul's letters occur in Romans.[7]

Social Identity, Theology, and Romans 9–11

The best way to reach a view as to what Paul seeks to communicate in chaps. 9–11 is to offer an exegesis of the text in relationship to its most immediate context, the rest of Romans, especially chaps. 1–8, since this material (and no other) was certainly in the mind of those who first heard or (far fewer in number) first read the letter. The exegesis I offer here, however, also draws on social identity and self-categorization theory already used in this volume to interpret chaps. 1–8. To prepare for the exegetical exploration it is useful to rehearse general dimensions of this approach and the conclusions that it has produced concerning chaps. 1–8, and also to develop further certain aspects of the theory that are especially apt for chaps. 9–11.

I have already shown that Paul's strategy in the earlier parts of the letter repays examination from the part of social identity theory that deals with the reduction and elimination of conflict between groups through recategorizing two (or more) groups in conflict under a new common subgroup identity. The new ingroup identity embracing Judean and non-Judean Christ-followers had been announced in 1:16-17, further elaborated in 3:21-31, explored in relation to the exemplary figure of Abraham in chap. 4, and analyzed with great richness in chaps. 5–8. I have noted that a precondition to a successful process of recategorization is that no attempt be made to extinguish the two subgroups, since this might lead to countervailing efforts by their members to maintain their distinctive identities in a way that would render the establishment of a new common identity difficult, if not impossible.

As already seen, however, none of this is to downplay the importance of the theological dimensions of the text, for Paul intimately connects the incorporation of the two subgroups into the new entity with the very nature of God. Thus he asks at 3:28-29: "Or is God the God of Judeans only? Is he not also the God of non-Judeans? Yes, also of non-Judeans, since God is one and he will righteous the circumcised by faith and the uncircumcised through faith." Paul relates the unitary nature of God to his righteousing by the same means those who were historically the chosen people and also all other ethnic groups. This example, which goes to the heart of Romans, shows how difficult it is to distinguish the "theological" from the "social" in the letter. In interpreting chaps. 9–11 I weigh this balance between social and theological dimensions of Paul's meaning against other views, for example, the privileging of the theological evident in the writings of Elizabeth Johnson on these chapters in the letter.[8]

Other aspects of social identity theory are relevant to chaps. 9–11. One is the temporal dimension to a group's existence—its straddling past, present, and future—that I considered in detail in relation to 8:18-30. Another is the basic insight of the aspect of the theory that focuses on "self-categorization," that is (as John Turner has described it), that a person's self-concept tends to vary in particular group situations, notably by movement along a continuum from pronounced personal identity at one end to pronounced social identity at the other.[9] In varying situations a person is able to activate any one or more of the ensemble of social categorizations that form part of his or her self-concept. I return to this area later in this chapter, given its importance for understanding some unique features of Romans 9–11. Another issue is the extent to which identity within groups is contested, so that, as Sani and Reicher have proposed, for a person wanting to take a group in a particular direction "it is matter of argumentative accomplishment to characterize something as essential to group identity, and it is equally an accomplishment to construe a given concrete measure as embodying or subverting that essence."[10] Lastly, within a social identity and self-categorization approach, leadership (meaning "the process of influencing others in a manner that enhances their contribution to the realization of group goals")[11] refers to the process of establishing, coordinating, and controlling a relationship based on a particular social category that defines what the would-be leader and followers have in common and of presenting the leader as exemplifying that category.[12] A good leader must be an "entrepreneur of identity."[13] This perspective on leadership, in relation to the social category "Judean," was used in chapter ten above to explain Paul's argument in relation to the Judean subgroup in Romans 7.

Interpretation of Romans 9

Romans 9:1-5 and the Presence of Paul in Romans 9–11

Many commentators note the strong personal presence of Paul in chaps. 9–11.[14] Indeed, it is fair to say that the most striking stylistic feature of chaps. 9–11 is that each of these three chapters begins with a statement by Paul expressing his concern for Israel. Most remarkable is the start of chap. 9:

> I speak the truth in Christ; I am not lying; my conscience bears me witness in the Holy Spirit, that my grief is great and unceasing the anguish in my heart. For I could pray (ηὐχόμην)[15] that I might be accursed from Christ on account of my brothers, my

kinsmen according to the flesh, they who are Israelites, to whom belong adoption, glory, the covenants, the law, the worship, and the promises, to whom belong the patriarchs and out of whom came the Messiah according to the flesh. (9:1-5)

Paul begins chap. 10 with the statement, "Brothers, the desire of my heart and prayer to God for them is that they might be saved." Lastly, we have the opening of chap. 11: "I ask, therefore, has God rejected his people? Emphatically not! For I myself am an Israelite, from the seed of Abraham, of the tribe of Benjamin. God has not rejected his people whom he foreknew" (vv. 1-2). There is also another personal statement by Paul at 11:13-14: "I speak to you foreigners.[16] Inasmuch as I am the apostle of the foreigners, I claim honor for my ministry in the hope that I might provoke my kinspeople to jealousy and save some of them." How are we to explain this concentration of personal statements in this section of the letter, the first and third of them directly asserting Paul's status as an ethnic Judean, the second and fourth demonstrating his deep concern for them? A satisfying answer is to be found in self-categorization theory; this was just mentioned but now requires further elaboration.

Within the broad field of social psychology, the "self-concept," or "social self-concept," is the cognitive component of the psychological system or process referred to as the "self." In particular, a person's self-concept is defined as "the set of cognitive representations of self available to a person."[17] Take the example of a white, middle-aged, married, Roman Catholic, Scottish, female airline pilot: these seven characteristics (and in any such case there could well be others) constitute cognitive representations of self available to the woman in question that together contribute to her self-concept. We may add to this that associated with every such cognitive component of self are certain emotional and evaluative dimensions, meaning how the person feels about each particular component and how he or she evaluates him- or herself in relation to other people on the basis of these components.

Although there will be some unity among these representations, they can be highly differentiated and function relatively independently. This social self-concept functions in a situation-specific way. A person activates, or brings to the fore, a certain component or components of his or her self-concept in a particular context. This will affect the perceptions of the person concerned in the form of his or her producing a particular image of self, meaning a particular experience of self. A representation becomes salient as a function of the interaction between the characteristics of the person and a specific situation. In the example of the woman above, the "pilot" part of her self-image becomes salient in an airplane cockpit, her motherhood in ferrying her children around on Saturday, her Roman Catholicism in church on Sunday or evening work with a charity, and so on.[18] Sometimes various components of self may come alive, as with her being middle-aged and Scottish when she is lunching with some young English women.

All of this is directly relevant to Paul. Like every other person then and since, Paul was a "self" with a "self-concept" that included a number of cognitive representations available to him. There is no doubt that the most important such representation was his faith in Christ, but at times when he speaks about himself he mentions others, such as his status as an Israelite and his role as an apostle. While all of these components of self coexisted in the person that was Paul, they were differentiated from one another and capable of being activated in specific situations.

During the course of Romans 1–8 his faith in Christ has been the salient component of Paul's self-concept. In chaps. 9–11, however, the mobile sense of self central to self-categorization theory becomes evident in Paul's explicitly activating that part of his self derived from the group category of Israelite. This aspect of his self had also been present in the "I" voice of chap. 7, but with nothing like the force or passion present in 9:1-5 and 11:1-2. A plausible explanation for this phenomenon readily presents itself. Paul had conducted much of his career under the banner of "apostle to the non-Judeans," even though, as we have already seen, this never meant the exclusion of Judeans from his congregations. For some two decades, as he wrote his letter to the Romans, Paul had lived among and attended to a group that had a large presence of non-Judeans. He had modified his manner of life to accord with this mission, dropping, for example, the characteristic Judean ban on intimate table fellowship with non-Judeans and generally becoming "to those outside the law (ἀνόμοις)" himself "as one outside the law (ἄνομος)—not being without law toward God but under the law of Christ" that he "might win those outside the law" (1 Cor. 9:21). This meant that for much of his adult life he had, of necessity, laid aside Judean aspects of his self-concept in which he had been socialized since infancy and which he still shared with his own immediate kin and with all those who were Judean by birth who claimed kinship with and through Abraham. He must have felt that he had moved away from a part of his deepest self.

In 9:1-5 he returns to this dimension of his self, that is, makes salient his connection with ethnic Israel, with a powerful emotional intensity that will burst to the surface again at 10:1-2 and 11:1-2, and, to a lesser extent, 11:13-14. These passionate outbursts are the product of his reconnecting with the often dormant but nevertheless deeply rooted Israelite dimension to his self-concept. Enabling this reconnection is the circumstance that in this section of the letter Paul is going to say that, contrary to all appearances, the story of

Israel's relationship with God will have a happy ending: first, because a remnant of Israel has already turned to Christ; second, because in the end all Israel will be saved. Paul is like anyone who, having lived many years among a social or religious group not his or her own by upbringing, suddenly discovers a good reason to celebrate the original allegiance and his or her affiliation with it.

Such a dramatic reconnection with Israel would have struck a deep chord with the Judean members of the Christ-movement in Rome who were the first recipients of this letter. What Paul had said about his relationship with Israel also applied to them. By exemplifying an ethnic category he shared with them, Paul put himself in a good position to push their views and behavior in certain directions, that is, to exercise leadership over them. Yet at the same time, his appeal to non-Judeans in his capacity as the apostle of non-Judeans in 11:13 indicates that he was also concerned not to lose contact with, or leadership influence over, this segment of his audience.

In spite of declaring his kinship with ethnic Israel in 9:1-5, Paul also maintains his distance from it. He does this by referring to Israelites in the third person plural in v. 4: "they who are Israelites," not, for example, "we who are Israelites." Accordingly, when he lists what characterizes them, namely, adoption, glory, the covenants, the law, the worship (meaning the sacrificial cult, which probably also implies the promise of the land, since it required the temple in Jerusalem),[19] and the promises, he is also maintaining a space between himself and these features. In effect, he is saying: "This is what they have, those Israelites." The notion that Paul is looking at Israel as someone apart from it is strengthened by the fact that no parallels have been found in Israelite literature for a list of Israel's privileges that approximate to those selected here.[20] John Piper has even suggested that Paul may have composed this list himself when he first faced the reality that Israel had rejected the gospel.[21] In v. 5, however, he acknowledges that they have the patriarchs, presumably including Abraham, whom, as I argued in chapter eight above, he did not sever from the ancestry of ethnic Israel in Romans 4. He also mentions that the Messiah was an ethnic Israelite.

Romans 9:6-33

In 9:6 Paul asserts, "But it is not as though the word of God has failed (ἐκπέπτωκεν), for not all of those who are from Israel are Israel." The connection of this verse to the preceding passage is hardly self-evident. Presumably, however, two issues are implied in the space between vv. 5 and 6: first, the obvious fact that these Israelites had, in spite of all their advantages, neither responded positively to the gospel nor chosen en masse to follow Christ (hence Paul's extreme distress), and, second, the question of how it is possible to explain or make sense of this fact. The compressed and difficult nature of the argument in Romans is well illustrated by Paul's failure to formulate such issues explicitly.

The word ἐκπέπτωκεν means literally "fell off, fell from," but it has a (rarer) metaphorical meaning. At Sir. 34:7 it is said that those who put their hopes in dreams ἐξέπεσον, "went forth empty," "were deceived."[22] Other possible meanings for ἐκπέπτωκεν are "failed" or "lost force and validity."[23] There is an important use of the cognate word διαπίπτω at Josh. 21:45: "Nothing failed (διέπεσεν) from all of the good words that the Lord spoke to the children of Israel; everything came to pass."[24] The word suggests something failing to achieve or obtain the desired result. Paul is seeking to deny that the "word of God," which probably includes the promises made to Israel, has failed to produce an effect; he is not focusing on God himself, since the way the human recipients of the promises respond to them will also figure in how successfully they are fulfilled. We have already seen in Romans 7 that although God gave Israel the law to restrain sin, sin got the better of it and wrongdoing increased. There is no sign in chap. 7 that the faithfulness of God is imperiled by the failure of the law to do the job he had assigned it. This interpretation of ἐκπέπτωκεν, which inevitably brings Israel into the picture along with God, features in the discussion below.

For many commentators 9:6a, "But it is not as though the word of God has failed," exposes the main theme of chaps. 9–11.[25] Those of this persuasion often insist that Paul's concern is "theological." Thus Käsemann denies that these chapters represent "a dialogue with the Jews," "an attempt to ward off incipient anti-semitism in Gentile Christianity," the product of Paul's missionary experiences, "apologetics," or "controversy with specific opponents." In his opinion, "What we have is theological reflection, which, in the style of the diatribe, is broken up by fictitious objections and answers to them."[26] Thus, for Käsemann, no interpretation that savors of an actual connection with the social realities of Paul's situation is possible. Although this position must be tested by exegetical investigation, the extremity of Käsemann's view raises the suspicion that it represents a transparent expression of theological hegemonism, which Bengt Holmberg has labeled—accurately, although less bluntly than here—the "idealistic fallacy."[27]

Elizabeth Johnson has also argued that the real import of chaps. 9–11 is theological, in that this passage concerns the trustworthiness of God. For her these chapters represent Paul's effort to balance his belief in the impartiality of God (to Israelites and non-Israelites) with his belief in God's abiding faithfulness to Israel.[28] She overlooks that Paul is not speaking in 9:6a explicitly or necessarily of the trustworthiness of God, but rather of whether his word produced the result he intended and was not, for example, overwhelmed by the recalcitrance of Israel. An additional problem for Johnson's view and other "theological" explanations for chaps. 9–11 emerges if one reasonably asks why Paul would bother to make such an argument. Johnson, at least, recognizes this problem and answers: "In the transforming present of the Christ-event as Paul preaches it, there lurks the danger that God's past was fruitless and the consequent risk that God's future will similarly disappoint."[29]

In response to this, I can assert with some confidence that the idea that the future dimensions of the Christ-event could, or ever would, come to nothing or be undone by God is utterly alien to Paul, and there is no sign that his addressees ever entertained it either. That such a desperate notion is proffered by Johnson to support a theological explanation for chaps. 9–11 constitutes a solid basis for seeking to explain this material in some other way. In particular, we must be alert to the possibility that the close, at times almost seamless, connection between social and theological factors already observed in earlier parts of the letter will also be found here. Exegesis must provide the answer.

Situating the Question in the Relevant Socioreligious Groups

Romans 9:6-7 and the argument that follows are stimulated by Paul's anguish (expressed in vv. 1-3) at the failure of Israel, his own people, to turn to Christ. He would separate himself from Christ if only they would come to faith. Israel's failure is what he is trying to make sense of. The place to begin is by asking to whom this issue would have been a concern and for what reasons. In line with my interest in group differentiation and identity and to tie the analysis to a first-century CE setting, I isolate the four groups that would have had an interest, bearing in mind that Paul is not only speaking to the Roman Christ-movement but has in mind the views (as seen, for example, at 3:8) that are in circulation about him both in Rome and elsewhere, including Jerusalem, whither he is soon about to travel. These groups are:

1. Israelites who had not accepted Christ
2. Israelite Christ-followers (such as the church in Jerusalem) not having a close association with non-Israelite Christ-followers
3. Non-Israelite Christ-followers
4. Israelite Christ-followers who associated (even if in a troubled way) with non-Israelite Christ-followers (as in Rome) on the basis that it was not necessary for them to be circumcised and take on the Mosaic law

It may be useful to bear in mind the possibility of some difference in outlook existing, dependent on whether the groups were in Rome or elsewhere in the Mediterranean region. While one could postulate a fifth group—non-Israelites unconnected with the Christ-movement—as a theoretical possibility, it is difficult to imagine a context in which they would have been interested.

For the first relevant group, Israelites who had not been persuaded by Paul and the other apostles to become Christ-followers, the failure of the majority of Israel to turn to Christ on the basis that such an allegiance was necessary for righteousness and salvation would have been a cause for self-congratulation. They were the chosen people, they had the advantages Paul mentions in 9:4-5, plus one he does not mention, election, and Christ was irrelevant to their status and destiny. Probably they criticized Paul for precisely this reason, urging against him and his gospel that if Christ was necessary for righteousness and salvation but the Mosaic law was not, this would mean that God had not achieved what he had set out to do for Israel.[30] For them this was simply an impossible prospect. They had political power in Judea under the Romans, a magnificent temple and cult, and they were spread everywhere around the Mediterranean in thriving communities focusing on weekly synagogue attendance. What basis was there for saying God's word had not been successful among them? Here the theological argument about the nature of God (to the limited extent to which it arises) is not separable from pride in their own ethnic identity. In Rome the synagogues of the Trastevere and elsewhere in the city had thousands of Israelite members who could have expressed these views if and when they came to hear of Paul and his gospel. The gossip networks of the ancient Mediterranean world probably meant they did learn of Paul long before he first arrived in Rome.[31]

Representatives of the second group, Israelite Christ-followers, especially those comprising the church in Jerusalem (but also the people who had caused Paul trouble in Galatia), would largely have shared the views of Israelites just mentioned. This group still believed in the ongoing validity and relevance of the law of Moses, and any suggestion that it was no longer necessary would have met the same objection—that Israel under God's word expressed in the Mosaic law had been and still was flourishing. For them belief in Christ was additional to, not in substitution for, Israelite law and identity. Although they do not seem to be in Paul's purview in Rome, their opinions may well have been conveyed to Israelite Christ-believers in the city from other parts of the Mediterranean.

Non-Israelite Christ-followers, the third group, probably used the failure of the majority of Israelites to believe in Christ as a reason to condemn Israel en masse. Given the competitive nature of Mediterranean culture and its tendency to attribute the shame suffered by some members of a group to all the rest, this probably extended to criticizing Israelite Christ-followers for the failure of the other Israelites (their kinsmen) to convert. In the arena of ethnic differentiation and conflict the fact that Israel, by and large, had rejected Christ may well have been a powerful argumentative resource for Greek and Roman Christ-followers in the cultural contests of Mediterranean life.

Strong support for the existence of such attitudes among non-Israelite Christ-followers is provided by the advice Paul will offer them in 11:18-20. People in this group would have been quite happy with the notion that "the word of God has not been successful in relation to Israel." But they would not have blamed God for this, as if he had revoked his promises, but rather have blamed Israel for frustrating God's good intentions toward them. Even if they did look at the problem in relation to God rather than Israel, they could have taken the view that the promises God made to Israel in the past were no longer in force and effect, having been replaced with the new promise that comes from faith in Christ. This, after all, was essentially the argument Paul himself had run with respect to the law in Galatians—especially in the metaphor of the παιδαγωγός (Gal. 3:24-25). Non-Israelite Christ-followers represent the only group whom we can envisage as having proposed that God's promises to Israel were no longer operative, in an agonistic fashion typical of this culture.

These considerations suggest why James Dunn's view that Rom. 9:6a "responds to a question which arises naturally from a Jewish perspective on Paul's gospel" is too narrow.[32] Dunn overlooks the fact that the notion of God's promise to Israel failing could also stem from non-Israelites using this as an argument to substantiate long-standing attitudes of ethnic differentiation. It is a matter of great moment in the interpretation of Romans, however, that Paul does not adopt, or even mention, the possibility that God's promises to Israel were limited by time and the time has elapsed, even though that was what he had argued in writing to the Galatians. His approach in Romans is to argue that the word of God has achieved the result it desired, although in an unexpected way. This contention would therefore constitute a correction by Paul of non-Israelite Christ-followers who were arguing that the term of the promises made to Israel was now passed.

Israelite Christ-followers (some of whom were present in Rome) who were in contact with non-Israelite believers whom they agreed found righteousness and salvation in Christ without needing to take on the Mosaic law would have been torn in two directions on this issue. First, non-Israelite believers might have stigmatized them for their connection with an Israel that had resisted conversion. Such non-Israelites might have been saying words to the effect, "The promises that God made to Israel were thwarted by the stubbornness of the Israelites. You should have nothing to do with these people." Second, they would no doubt have been worried, even destabilized, by the failure of the majority of Israelites by natural descent to accept Christ. They were the representatives of a fragile new order that the majority of Israelites had rejected. Being in a minority must have produced some anxiety as to whether they had made the right decision. Whereas they needed to be convinced that God's word had not been fulfilled in Israel, they found themselves exposed to the argument that could have been put to them by Israelites outside the movement, or by Israelite Christ-followers who insisted on retaining the Mosaic law (such as those in Jerusalem and Galatia), that if someone could turn to Christ to be righteoused and saved without needing to follow the law, then how did one explain the flourishing state of Israel in Judea and across the Mediterranean? The Israelites of Rome could point to their synagogues as representing the fruits of the promises God had made to Abraham, Moses, and the other patriarchs. On the other hand, they had to be certain that God's word was being fulfilled among them.

All this meant that they needed to have their own choice of Christ legitimated, that is, explained and justified, in line with the theory of Berger and Luckmann.[33] They could have hedged their bets by retaining some association with non-Israelite Christ-followers, while trying to maintain Torah adherence as well, possibly associated with continued synagogue attendance. This would probably have been the situation in other parts of the Mediterranean, not just in Rome, although the presence of a significant non-Israelite presence in the Christ-movement in that city may have added new dimensions—including, perhaps, pressures to abandon any remaining features of Israelite lifestyle.

In summary, the group that was most likely to have been troubled by the failure of Israel generally to come to faith in Christ were Israelite Christ-believers who associated with non-Israelite believers on the basis that it was not necessary for them to be circumcised and take on the Mosaic law. They were caught on the horns of a dilemma. On one side, other Israelites could insist that Moses was needed for righteousness and salvation, that the flourishing status of Israel was the result of God's word (which could hardly be said not to have achieved its effect), and that Christ was not needed. On the other, the non-Israelite members of the Christ-movement could mock them for attachment to a people who had blocked God's saving will for them and (possibly) whose period of enjoyment of divine privilege had now come to an end. There was ample opportunity for all of these issues to have arisen in Rome by the time Paul wrote the letter. They cohere closely with the other group phenomena, including the clear lines of differentiation between subgroups and their respective identities, evident earlier in the letter.

We must now investigate the remainder of Romans 9 (chaps. 10 and 11 as well) against this setting. We will see that Paul essentially aims to explain how the fact that most Israelites have not converted to Christ is within the divine plan; the core of this argument is that they are not Israel or God's people but that, without any injustice on God's part, that status has passed to the (small number of) Israelites and non-Israelites, the sons of God, who have achieved righteousness by faith, though he never calls this new group Israel.

Romans 9:6-13

Paul argues in this way. He denies that the failure of most Israelites to believe in Christ means God's word has not been effective by proposing that the (presumably small number of) Israelites who have turned to Christ themselves represent the successful fulfillment of that word. Not all out of Israel are Israel (9:6b), he contends, not all physically descended from Abraham (his "seed") are "children" (τέκνα), a proposition that he then proves from scripture. For the line of Abraham passed through Isaac (Gen. 21:12) and not through Hagar's son (Ishmael) (Rom. 9:7)—a point similar to one he made in Gal. 4:21-31.

Paul explains this point by asserting that it is not descendants by flesh (τέκνα τῆς σαρκός) who are the "children of God" (τέκνα τοῦ θεοῦ), but the children of the promise (τέκνα τῆς ἐπαγγελίας; Rom. 9:8). The expression "children of God" appearing here is immensely significant. For only a little earlier, in chap. 8, Paul had used it (as well as the closely related expressions "sons of God" [υἱοὶ θεοῦ] and "children" [τέκνα]) in the climax of the passage describing their exalted status in the Spirit, now and in the future, as a self-appellation that certainly embraced Israelite and non-Israelite Christ-followers in the new common ingroup identity (8:14-17). This immediately raises the possibility that Paul is here including non-Israelite Christ-followers among those who are the "children of the promise" and he is not just speaking of Israelite Christ-followers. The previous discussion of Abraham and his descendants in chap. 4 (although infrequently mentioned by commentators in this connection) strongly confirms this suggestion. There Paul had made crystal clear that the descendants who would fulfill the promise God made to Abraham would do so through faith and would include Israelites and non-Israelites (4:11-17). Accordingly, Richard Bell is in error when he suggests that it is at 9:24 that Paul asserts for the first time in chaps. 9–11 that God has chosen "not only from the Jews but also from the Gentiles."[34] That choice appears much earlier, here in 9:8.

"In some sense then," writes Elizabeth Johnson in relation to chap. 9, "'Israel' can include Gentiles as well as Jews, because God's continuing election of Israel has always taken the same approach as it has now with Gentiles." While this is certainly correct, she then goes too far: "Israel is God's elect, and God elects because of who God is, not because of who people are."[35] For in spite of the inclusive message of 9:6-13, Paul does not identify the Christ-movement with Israel. He comes perilously close, but avoids taking that final step.

Paul then illustrates and supports the importance of being "children of the promise" by two scriptural examples. First, he refers to Gen. 18:10 and 14, which state that when the Lord returns, Sarah will have a son (Rom. 9:9). Second, he cites the example of Rebecca being pregnant by Isaac (with Esau and Jacob), inasmuch as before they were born (or had done good or evil) God chose one and rejected the other, as illustrated by quotations from Gen. 25:23 and Mal. 1:2-3 (Rom. 9:10-13). Thus Paul shows how a wide class of natural progeny can be steadily reduced by God intervening in favor of particular offspring in successive generations.

Romans 9:14-18

Paul next asks whether God is unjust, and right away denies that he is (9:14). This question most immediately arises in connection with the way that Ishmael and Esau were treated, but it also relates, by implication at least, to Paul's view on the sorry status of Israelites who have not turned to Christ that these scriptural examples serve to illustrate. While this is certainly a theological question, since it goes to the nature of God, it also has social implications. For it could be charged against Paul (by an Israelite objector, either Christ-believing or not) that his opinion about Israel, if correct (which of course it is not), would mean that God is unjust. Paul bluntly asserts in reply that God shows mercy and compassion to whomever he likes; it is not a question of human will or human activity (9:15-16). He also provides an example from scripture to illustrate this point—that of Pharaoh (from Exod. 9:16),[36] whom God raised up to show his power, so that his name might be proclaimed over all the earth (Rom. 9:17). Finally Paul notes, using an image of hardening that we will return to below, that God "shows mercy to whomever he wants and hardens (σκληρύνει) whomever he wants" (9:18).

Romans 9:19-29

This leads to a further objection with a theological aspect that soon becomes highly social. How can God blame human beings, therefore, if everything depends on his irresistible will (9:19)? Paul's initial answer (9:20) is that a human being (ἄνθρωπος) has no right to answer back to God, just as something molded cannot ask its molder, "Why have you made me like this?"

This is an answer (however unconvincing) offered at the level of theological principle. But it becomes merely a staging area for Paul to set off once more into the realm of ingroup/outgroup differentiation. A potter can use the same clay to make one vase for decorative display and another for menial use (9:21). In the same way, because he was wishing to demonstrate his anger and make known his power, God has long put up with vessels of wrath made for destruction so as to make known the riches of his glory for the vessels of mercy (9:22-23), "who are us whom he has called not only out of the Judeans but also out of the foreigners" (9:24).[37] I should note here that the language used of the vessels of wrath in 9:22 not only echoes the language Paul used of Pharaoh in 9:16 but actually imports from Exod. 9:16 an idea that Paul omitted when he used that verse in Rom. 9:22, namely, the notion of divine forbearance for a period, which emerges in Exod. 9:16 in the statement that Pharaoh had been preserved (διετηρήθης) so God could demonstrate his power. This establishes a further link between the portrayal of Pharaoh and his fate and that of the "vessels of wrath." At the same time, Paul now expressly states that the vessels of mercy include Israelites and non-Israelites, thus confirming the view reached above from the meaning of "children of God" and "children of the promise" (the latter in comparison with the promise made to Abraham in Romans 4). Yet still he refrains from calling this group "Israel."

The imagery employed here, of destruction for the vessels of wrath and glory for the vessels of mercy, graphically reveals that Paul is establishing a pair of sharply contrasted alternatives. That the vessels of mercy are the same as "the children of God" and the vessels of wrath are to be identified with those Israelites who have not accepted Christ becomes manifest from the three sets of scriptural quotations Paul summons to bolster the argument (9:25-29). First, we have Hos. 2:23 ("I will call not-my-people my-people and not-loved loved") and Hos. 1:10 ("Where they were called not-my-people they will be called sons of the living God"). Second, there is Isa. 10:22-23 ("If the number of the sons of Israel is as the sand on the seas, a remnant will be saved," for the Lord will fulfill his word over the earth).[38] Is this a recognition of just how few Judeans have turned to Christ? Third comes Isa. 1:9 ("If the Lord of hosts had not left us seed, we would have become like Sodom and been made similar to Gomorrah").

Romans 9:30-33

He concludes from the preceding passage that non-Judeans not pursuing righteousness have achieved it through faith (9:30), while Israel pursuing a righteousness based on law did not fulfill that law (9:31) because they pursued it not through faith but through works, and they have stumbled over a stumbling stone (9:31-32), as scripture has stated (9:33).

Paul explains this position using a radically reworked conflation, rearrangement, and abbreviation of Isa. 28:16 and 8:14: "Behold, I am laying on Zion a stone of stumbling and a rock of scandal, and he who believes in him will not be put to shame."[39] The major change Paul introduces here is that his "quotation" makes it necessary to believe in a stumbling stone (not an honored cornerstone as in Isa. 28:16) to avoid being put to shame. He also adds to the description of the stone in Isa. 8:14 that it is a stone of scandal. This links the view expressed in Rom. 9:33 to his description of the crucified Christ in 1 Cor. 1:23 as a scandal to Judeans and to the phrase "the scandal of the cross" in Gal. 5:11, even though the word σκάνδαλον as used here may derive from a variant reading of the Septuagint.[40] In Rom. 10:11, moreover, Paul employs unambiguously of Christ the clause from Isa. 28:16, "he who believes in me has not been put to shame" (ὁ πιστεύων οὐ μὴ καταισχυνθῇ), which in Rom. 9:33b he had used in relation to the stumbling stone. Romans 9 had begun with Paul's anguish over the Israelites, implicitly because they had not accepted Christ, and in 9:32b-33 he openly specifies this as the reason. Accordingly, the stumbling stone in 9:33 is certainly Christ, not the law, and not the law and Christ together.[41] This result is relevant to the view stated in chapter seven above, that Christ is an object of faith in Pauline thought, in spite of views to the contrary that depend, at least in part, on the untenable subjective reading of πίστις Χριστοῦ.

This conclusion also bears upon a debate over the nature of Israel's failure in 9:31-32a. We are all in debt to E. P. Sanders for demolishing the idea that the religious practice of Judeans in the first century CE was one of works-righteousness.[42] But in relation to 9:30—10:13 Sanders has unnecessarily and erroneously conceded that "at first blush" this passage offers "the best proof that Paul's argument against the law is really against a legalistic way of observing it."[43] C. B. Cranfield, Robert Gundry, and Richard Bell have all proposed (the last two well after Sanders's 1977 work had appeared) that Paul is indeed accusing Israel in 9:30-32a of seeking righteousness by observing the law in a legalistic way, not merely by observing it.[44]

It is worth noting in advance that this view, if correct, would suggest that in a letter where Paul, bent on differentiating between ingroup and outgroups, continually maintains a sharp antithesis between justification by works of the Mosaic law on the one hand and justification by faith (through grace) on the other—an antithesis that has appeared before and will appear afterward (11:5-6)—he decides at this point to introduce out of the blue (but not to mention hereafter) a complication to the picture that inevitably compromises the distinction he has been drawing, in that it suggests that there are good and bad modes of righteousness by works of the law. To this I must add that he would have done this in a communication undoubtedly meant for oral delivery in the first instance where the audience would have needed almost miraculous powers of percipience to take the (alleged) point. Raising these questions induces a sense of disbelief that scholars could have ever entertained this idea in the first place; but as they have, and in the interests of demonstrating Paul is not the incompetent communicator their view implies, a closer inspection of the evidence is required.

Romans 9:31-32a, and especially the expression in 9:32a: "not out of faith but out of law,"[45] are admittedly difficult to interpret.[46] The best approach is to read these verses in the light of what Paul says elsewhere in the letter, especially prior to this passage. Beginning with 3:21-31 and continuing in the exposition of Abraham in chap. 4, the righteousness pursued by Israelites under the law stands in contrast with the righteousness of God for those who have faith in Christ. The two forms of righteousness are ways of differentiating two groups and two identities. "Righteousness by works of the law" (3:20), and also the equivalent expressions "righteousness by works" (4:2, 6), "work(s) of law" (3:27, 28), "law" (3:21), or just "works" (11:6), are primarily labels, stereotypes attached to Israelite identity. They have as their basis the fact that Paul presents Israelites as seeking righteousness by performing the requirements of the Mosaic law. In chap. 7 Paul explains that with the arrival of the law (that is, with Moses) sin gained a new lease on life and brought death. Paul makes absolutely no suggestion that during this period Israelites could fulfill the law by one of two routes—either by faith or works, a good way or a "legalistic" way. This notion, which is required on the view of Cranfield, Gundry, and Bell, is unknown to Paul. The Israelites either obeyed the law or they did not; and, as a matter of fact and because sin turned the law to its own ends, they did not obey its demands. Then Christ's redemptive acts broke the power of sin (8:2). At this point Israel had the chance to turn to faith but did not. This is why Paul is in anguish at the start of chap. 9 and why he presents Christ as the stumbling block in 9:32-33. The purpose of 9:30-33 is to examine the situation from the time of Christ's redemptive acts onward. Non-Israelites not pursuing righteousness attained righteousness, but righteousness "from faith" (ἐκ πίστεως; 9:30).

So what happened to Israel? Paul's final point is that most of Israel has rejected Christ because they found him a stumbling block (9:32b-33), and 9:31-32a must be consonant with this result. These verses are problematic only because 9:32a is so compressed: "Israel pursuing the law of righteousness did not achieve that law. Why? Because not from faith but as it were from law (ὅτι οὐκ ἐκ πίστεως ἀλλ' ὡς ἐξ ἔργων)." Given that Paul has just mentioned "righteousness from faith" (ἐκ πίστεως) in 9:30 (and will return to this usage in 10:5-6), we may reasonably also insert "righteousness" before ἐκ πίστεως in 9:32a, thus producing the idea that Israel was unsuccessful because it pursued righteousness "not from faith as it were but from law." Paul's point is not, as Cranfield, Gundry, and Bell suggest, that Israel failed to attain righteousness because of the legalistic way they sought to fulfill the law. Rather, it is that they failed to obtain righteousness because, after the coming of Christ, they persisted with the law route rather than moving to the faith route.

Theoretically, law observance could produce righteousness (2:13a: "Those who do the law will be righteoused"). But the history of Israel after Moses as set out by Paul in chap. 7 had shown that, as a practical matter, Israel could not observe the law because of the way sin used the law to its own ends.

Therefore, righteousness was unobtainable from the law. Christ was the solution to this dilemma, but Israel had set its face against him. The idea that, in seeking to obey the law so as to achieve righteousness, the Israelites opted for a "legalistic" method based on works rather than on faith is foreign to Paul and impossibly inconsistent with what he says in chap. 7 and elsewhere in the letter, where "works" is the same as "works of the law" and simply refers to the Mosaic law, not a legalistic way of performing it, in contrast with faith or grace (as at 11:6). For Israelites in the time between Moses and Christ all that was available to attain righteousness was the law, and it had failed. This solution is in accord with what Paul has said elsewhere in the letter and avoids concluding that he has in mind some different phenomenon generalized out of the Israelite ethnic matrix such as "works-righteousness" or even less (to cite a grotesque anachronism that still occasionally rears its head) "self-righteousness." On this view, the reference to "works" in connection with Jacob and Esau in 9:11-12 is not a reason to import a notion of works-righteousness into the letter,[47] but merely an illustration of the fact that the means preferred by the Israelites for obtaining righteousness did involve performing "works," admittedly those required by the Mosaic law.

Interpretation of Romans 10

Romans 10:1-4

Romans 10 begins with another statement of Paul's deep concern for "them," meaning the Israelites outside the Christ-movement—he desires in his heart and prays to God for their salvation (10:1). While this is not as strong a statement as at 9:1-5, it is clearly of a piece with it. That Paul believes they still have salvation in prospect signals an unexpected new development in his message, since his audience may well have concluded from his earlier reference to them as "vessels of anger made for destruction" (9:22) that they had denied themselves the hope of salvation. Paul will have more to say on this in the latter half of chap. 11.

He acknowledges that they have zeal for God yet not in accordance with knowledge (10:2), for they are ignorant of God's righteousness and have not subjected themselves to it but seek to set up their own instead (10:3). Christ is the end (τέλος) of the law (almost certainly meaning the Mosaic law)[48] unto righteousness for everyone who has faith (10:4). The meaning of "righteousness" here is the same as in 9:31-33: it is simply the righteousness they pursue through the law as opposed to God's righteousness, which comes via faith in Christ. Beneath these two different banners of identity one is aware, yet again in this letter, that there subsist two clearly differentiated collectivities—the Christ-movement and Israel, ingroup and outgroup.

Debate rages as to the precise meaning of τέλος here.[49] The four main possibilities are "end/termination," "result," "goal" (the so-called teleological sense), or a polysemic combination of two or more of these meanings. Badenas has suggested that in nonbiblical Greek τέλος is a dynamic, polysemic word but that the basic connotation is "goal" rather than termination.[50] Although he also argues that this is essentially the meaning of the word in the Septuagint and the New Testament, Moo has shown that in these corpora the temporal meaning of "end/termination" predominates.[51] In spite of assertions by Badenas to the contrary, there is no instance of τέλος clearly meaning "goal" in the Pauline letters. For Paul the two most common senses are "end/termination" (1 Cor. 1:8; 10:11; 15:24; 1 Thess. 2:16) and "result" (Rom. 6:21, 22; 2 Cor. 11:15). On two occasions the word seems to convey both meanings (2 Cor. 3:13; Phil. 3:19). Although there is one possible teleological sense, at Rom. 6:22, the appearance of τέλος with an unambiguously consequential meaning in the previous verse tends to pull this example in the same direction.[52]

Badenas considers that at Rom. 10:4 the word bears the teleological meaning.[53] Moo suggests that the notion of end or termination dominates, but that the word here also has a sense of reaching a goal, so that translations such as "culmination," "consummation," or "climax" are appropriate.[54] The most probable meaning, however, is that of termination and definitive replacement. Contra Moo, there is absolutely no sense in Romans that Christ is the "natural or inevitable result" of anything to do with the Mosaic law.[55] Such a suggestion is comprehensively falsified by the picture of the law in chap. 7. Because of the overwhelming power of sin, the law proved a catastrophe, leaving Israel in a worse state than it found her. Christ did not come at the tail end of a process of which the law represented the earlier stages; he was the person who liberated Israel from the mess the law had produced (7:24-25). Paul fixes upon the radical discontinuity between the Mosaic law and Christ, not on any alleged progression from the one to the other. I have elsewhere reached a similar view in relation to Paul's statement in Gal. 5:14 that the law is fulfilled in the commandment "You shall love your neighbor as yourself." Given that love is the first fruit of the Spirit (Gal. 5:22), Paul is saying that members of the Christ-movement have the best that the law can provide but by an entirely different route.[56]

Badenas resists the notion of τέλος meaning "end/termination" and the discontinuity this implies for the reason that it "seems to contradict a main theme of Romans, namely, that salvation has always been by grace through faith (see especially ch. 4)—so that Christ could hardly put to an end what did not exist."[57] This view, apparently based on some sort of "salvation history," seriously misinterprets Romans. In chap. 4 Paul attempts rhetorically to persuade his audience that Abraham was the prototypical father of all of those who seek righteousness by faith and that promises were made to him that he would have descendants (pursuing righteousness by the same route) who would inherit the earth. Yet for Paul there was no one between Abraham and Christ who pursued righteousness by faith. That is why in 4:23-25 Paul limits the people for whom this was a possibility to Abraham and his Christ-believing addressees: "But the words, 'it was reckoned to him,' were not written only for his sake, but for ours also. It will be reckoned to us who believe in him who raised from the dead Jesus our Lord, who was put to death for our trespasses and raised for our righteousness." Sin was in the world from Adam to Moses, and with the giving of the Mosaic law sin increased its power (5:13-14). Only Abraham achieved righteousness by faith. After Abraham, the possibility of such righteousness lay dormant until the arrival of Christ, while from Moses onward Israelites en masse succumbed to the horrors of the power of sin set out in chap. 7.

This is the major reason why the notion of salvation history is inapt for Paul, in both Romans and Galatians. Paul does agree that in Christ God fulfills the promises made to Abraham, although in Rom. 4:11 he deletes the word "covenant" from his source in Gen. 17:11 in speaking of this process.[58] Yet for Paul the centuries between Moses and Christ comprised a period of unrelieved gloom. Christ is not the climax of the Mosaic law or the Mosaic covenant;[59] as far as the achievement of righteousness is concerned (and that is what Paul is speaking of in Rom. 10:4), he constitutes the replacement of the Mosaic law/covenant with an entirely new mechanism—faith. Paul could not go farther than this, however, and allege that the Mosaic law was finished for all purposes and in all contexts, since he had already acknowledged at the start of chap. 9 that Israel still existed and still held on to the covenants and the law (9:5).

Romans 10:5-13

In this passage Paul expands on 10:4 by offering some details as to what it is like to seek righteousness through faith in Christ. He begins by mentioning righteousness from the law, quoting Lev. 18:5 to the effect that one who does the law's requirements will live by them, but almost certainly implying, given his bleak view of the law in Romans 7, that no Israelite actually does obey the law and, accordingly, does not obtain life from this source (10:5). This is the gloomy reality against which he contrasts the other righteousness, by faith.

Yet his method of substantiating the contrast involves audaciously contesting a collective memory of Israel and reapplying it to serve his present purposes, a mode of processing the past we considered earlier in relation to chap. 4.[60] The collective memory in question is found in a magnificent passage in Deuteronomy 30. There Moses states that the commandment he is enjoining on Israel is not too hard for them, or too far away: "It is not in heaven, that you should say, 'Who will go up for us to heaven, and bring it to us, that we may hear it and do it?' Neither is it beyond the sea, that you should say, 'Who will go over the sea for us, and bring it to us, that we may hear it and do it?' But the word is very near you; it is in your mouth and in your heart, so that you can do it" (Deut. 30:12-14, RSV). Paul thoroughly reinterprets this passage. Now it is Christ, not the commandment, whom one might mistakenly think is in heaven needing to be brought down (Rom. 10:6).[61] Now it is Christ, not the commandment, whom one might mistakenly think is in the abyss (not beyond the sea as in Deut. 30:13) and needing to be raised from the dead (Rom. 10:7). Lastly, Paul insists that the "word" that is very near in Deut. 30:14, in one's mouth and heart, is actually "the word of faith that we preach" (Rom. 10:8).

Richard Hays rightly calls 10:6-8 "a startling reading of Deut. 30:11-14," but then goes astray when he follows Dan O. Via in advocating "a deep structural affinity between the theology of the word in Deuteronomy and in Paul" in the sense that "the presence of God's word in the community of God's people empowers the obedience of faith."[62] As we observed in chapter eight above, studies of the way Paul has utilized Israelite tradition, such as those of Hays and Keesmaat, tend to treat his readaptation of biblical texts in a manner unjustifiably divorced from its inevitable setting of contest between bitterly competitive groups.[63] In Rom. 10:6-8 we see Paul blatantly seeking to tear the Mosaic law from its place at the heart of one of the most moving passages in the Old Testament and replace it with the message of Christ. This attempt to suppress Israelite identity and promote the identity of the Christ-movement would have been bitterly resented and resisted, indeed laughed to scorn, by Israelites who came to hear of it. Between Deut. 30:11-14 and Rom. 10:6-8 there exists not so much a "deep structural affinity," but rather the highly tendentious relationship that Paul, in the course of a daring feat of argumentation, creates between this site of collective Israelite memory and the needs of his audience.

In Rom. 10:9-13 Paul initially elaborates on the idea that the word is in the mouth and heart of the Christ-follower for righteousness and salvation (10:9-11), before stressing that this applies to both Judean and Greek, for they have the same Lord (a notion that evokes the sentiment of 3:30), who enriches those who call on him (10:12). Everyone who calls on the Lord will be saved (10:13). The reference to Judean and Greek again repeats a point that has been expressed (9:24) or implied (9:8, 30) earlier in this section of the letter.

Israel's Rejection of the Gospel (Rom. 10:14-21)

The subject of the final verses in Romans 10 is the refusal of Israel to believe in Christ and to call upon him even though they have had ample opportunity to do so. Paul begins by picking up the precise notion of invocation introduced in 10:13. How will people call on Christ if they have not come to faith in him? Yet faith results from hearing, hearing occurs with proclamation, proclamation comes from those sent to proclaim, and how beautiful are the feet of those who preach good news (10:14-15). But now Paul reminds his audience of the bitter truth: not all have obeyed the gospel (10:16). He probably has Israelites in mind here, the people whose resistance to Christ has been in view since 9:1.[64] He repeats the point. Yes, faith comes from hearing, and hearing is through the word of Christ (10:17), and they have certainly heard. This is proven by the statement that their (that is, the apostles') voice has gone out everywhere on earth, citing Ps. 19:4 (Rom. 10:18). And they have certainly known. In support of this Paul first draws on Deut. 32:21, for reasons I return to below: "I will provoke you to jealousy (παραζηλώσω) at what is not a nation, I will provoke you to anger (παροργιῶ) with a nation devoid of understanding" (Rom. 10:19). He then reaches for a passage from Isa. 65:1 about God being found by those not seeking him and being made manifest to those not asking for him. This material is reminiscent of Rom. 9:24-26. Finally, having made the point that Isaiah is referring to Israel, he continues with the first part of the next verse in Isaiah 65, "All the day I stretched out my hands to a disobedient and obstinate people."

Provoking Israel to Jealousy (Rom. 10:19)

Yet in spite of this gloomy conclusion, the word παραζηλώσω in 10:19 indicates a way forward for Israel. This word reappears twice in chap. 11 and requires close attention if we are fully to comprehend the extraordinary message that Paul is about to communicate in chap. 11.

In the Septuagint the verb παραζηλοῦν occurs eight times. Two of them represent the *piel* of קנה (Deut. 32:21; 3 Kgs. 14:22), two the *hiphil* of קנה (Deut. 32:21; Ps. 77:58), and three the *hithpael* of חרה (Ps. 36:1, 7, 8), while the eighth is found at Sir. 30:3 (for which no Hebrew original is extant). It will help if, prior to examining these instances, we briefly consider the meaning of jealousy and the related concept of envy within their ancient Mediterranean social context so as to minimize the risk of semantic contamination from modern understandings of the referents of these words. Richard Bell's monograph on the jealousy motif in Romans 9–11 would have been improved if he had raised this fundamentally important sociolinguistic question of the meanings of these notions within their widely varying cultural contexts instead of contenting himself with definitions drawn largely from English and German dictionaries.[65]

If we begin at a fairly high level of abstraction, we may say that the Greco-Roman and Judean cultures of the first century CE treasured honor as a primary value and construed the world as one in which all goods, honor included, did not increase but were merely redistributed (which is the idea of "limited good"). This meant that people had to be careful about preserving what was theirs—all goods, material (such as money and land) and immaterial (such as relationships, roles, and statuses). Those who unexpectedly had a surfeit of good luck, or who deliberately embarked on a process of accumulating more and more goods, inevitably created strains in the system and aroused various forms of animosity, at least among those with whom they had been approximately equal beforehand. In this context we can distinguish two fundamental attitudes/emotions.

The first is an attitude of ill will (with associated emotional dimensions) toward those who have more goods (either material or immaterial) than oneself. The English word that comes closest to expressing this social reality (and we must avoid any notion of essentialist meaning here) is "envy." The usual Greek word was φθόνος. As Malina notes, "Envy is a feeling of begrudging that emerges in face of the good fortune of others relative to some restricted good that is equally of interest to us."[66] In the ancient Mediterranean it was widely believed that those who felt envy toward others were capable of afflicting them with the evil eye, a subject that has been brilliantly exposed by J. H. Elliott in a series of essays.[67] The evil eye was a malign force, a kind of witchcraft, that could injure or even kill people and damage their property. People who were envious of others also practiced sorcery with the aim of harming them or their property, and the widespread nature of such an attitude is seen in the huge number of small tablets inscribed with curses (*defixiones*) that have turned up across the Mediterranean region and even further afield, as in the Roman cult site at Bath in England. Those who have trouble accepting the existence of major cultural differences (at appropriate levels of generality) existing between modern northern European and North American cultures and ancient Mediterranean ones will find it rather difficult to explain the widespread use of *defixiones* (and the remarkably malign attitudes and social complexes from which they sprang) in the latter. Paul's recognition of the horror of φθόνος emerges in his mentioning it in Rom. 1:29 at the start of a list where it is immediately followed by murder and dissension.

The second attitude/emotion we can distinguish is the desire to preserve what is one's own in the face of possible threats to it. The English word closest to expressing this emotion is "jealousy." Bruce Malina and John Pilch describe it in this way: "Jealousy, in contrast to envy, refers to attachment to and concern for what is exclusively one's own: one's child, spouse, house, fields, town. . . . Jealousy is a form of protectiveness that would ward off the envious and their machinations."[68] While this is accurate, it is worth noting that the feelings associated with such concern are often passionate ones. This is why the usual Greek word for this disposition, ζῆλος, can be translated in English sometimes as "jealousy" and sometimes as "zeal." Jealousy is a social situation with three elements:

1. The person who experiences the emotion
2. The subject of his/her concern (a person or a thing, such as one's honor)
3. The person threatening that subject (either by taking it, harming it or demonstrating superiority over it)

It is important to bear in mind the distinction between envy and jealousy: "envy refers to the sentiment of begrudging the success of another. Jealousy, on the other hand, is the sentiment of concern for the well-being of whom or what one holds dear."[69] In the Septuagint φθόνος appears on several occasions but is not predicated of God,[70] presumably because there is nothing he lacks, whereas ζῆλος regularly is.[71] He is a God jealously and zealously protective of his powers, prerogatives, and people. But envy is predicated of the devil.[72]

Jealousy has two aspects. It can either be defensive, emerging in the face of a threat, or aggressive, as an expression of the value of what one has that surfaces in rivalry or competition with others, often members of outgroups,[73] although in a dysfunctional family (where the group honor was being besmirched) siblings could also jealously compete with one another. In the second sense, jealousy comes close to meaning "emulation," which derives from the Latin *aemulatio*, which means an assiduous striving to equal or excel another in some status or field of activity.

Let us examine Deut. 32:21 (LXX) within this perspective. Deuteronomy 32 consists of a song that Moses sang to the whole assembly. In vv. 19-20 Moses says that the Lord saw (sc. the idolatry of the Israelites and that they had forgotten him), was jealous (ἐζήλωσε) and provoked to anger (παρωξύνθη), and declared he would turn away from them. Here we see God passionate about protecting what was his own, in this case presumably his honor and the exclusive relationship he should have with Israel. Then the Lord says (and I separate the four stichs):

> They have provoked me to jealousy (παρεζήλωσαν) with that which is not god,
> they have provoked me to anger (παρώξυναν) with their idols,
> and I will provoke them to jealousy (παραζηλώσω) at what is not a nation,
> I will provoke them to anger (παροργιῶ) with a nation devoid of understanding.

Here we have God, in effect, angrily protective and concerned for his honor when he sees the Israelites dishonoring him by running after a nongod, announcing that he will do to them what they have done to him and pro-voke them to become angrily protective and concerned for their honor when, presumably, he attaches himself to another people who are not really a people and are devoid of understanding. In short, just as they provoked him to jealousy and anger by choosing nonexistent gods over him, he will provoke them in the same way by choosing a people not really a people and who lack understanding. This is an example of defensive jealousy; God feels a good he has is threatened and he wants to impose that same experience on Israel. The means chosen by God in Deuteronomy 32 to provoke Israel to jealousy is to inflict suffering on her and to allow her enemies, for a time, to get the better of her. But only for a time. God does not want Israel's enemies to assume that it was they and not he who did these things to Israel (32:27). The future destiny of the enemies of Israel had been decided long ago, and they will soon be devastated by the vengeance of God (32:34-35). He will eventually show compassion on Israel, who had wilted before the foreign invasion (32:36).

The same picture emerges in relation to the other instances of παραζηλοῦν. In Ps. 77:58 the situation is virtually identical to the first element in Deut. 32:21: "And they provoked him to anger (παρώργισαν) with their high places, and with their graven images they provoked him to jealousy (παρεζήλωσαν)," although here Yahweh does not repay Israel in kind. In 3 Kgs. 14:22 it is said that "Rehoboam did evil in the sight of the Lord, and the Lord παρεζήλωσεν him in all the things that their fathers did in their sins that they sinned." Here the verb means that the Lord provoked Rehoboam to passionate concern for what was his by competing with his ancestors in sin-fulness. This is an example of aggressive jealousy, in the sense of emulation, made all the more heinous by the fact that former family members are those with whom Rehoboam was provoked to compete. All three instances of the word in Ps. 36 (vv. 1, 7, and 8) consist of exhortations not to be jealous of evildoers, meaning "do not work yourself up into a state in relation to your affairs that you will seek to outdo them" (that is, by doing evil). This is another example of aggressive jealousy, emulation of a particularly bad kind, although here the psalmist is advising against it. Lastly, Sir. 30:3 states: "The person who teaches his son παραζηλώσει his enemy, and before his friends he will be happy with him [sc. his son]." Here παραζηλώσει means "he will provoke (his enemy) to passionate concern for his own affairs," presumably meaning that he would want to be able to compete on the basis that his own son is as learned as the first man, which he most probably is not. It is inter-esting to note here how utterly inapt would be the translation "will make envious" for παραζηλώσει, since the father would not wish to make his enemy look with envy on his son, with all the danger that might produce, from the evil eye especially.

We may now reexamine Rom. 10:19 in the light of this analysis. Paul employs the third and fourth stichs of Deut. 32:21, altering them only so as to remove the "and" from the beginning of the quotation and to change "them" on the two occasions the word appears to "you":

> I will provoke you to jealousy (παραζηλώσω) at what is not a nation,
> I will provoke you to anger (παροργιῶ) with a nation devoid of understanding.

The first question is why Paul offers this material as proof of the fact that Israel knew of the proclamation of the gospel. Richard Bell has suggested that Israel knew because it was aware of this particular prophecy and was aware that God would provoke Israel to jealous anger.[74] Yet this solution, focusing on mere knowledge of the prophecy (and reflecting the fact that Bell has given insufficient attention to the meaning of jealousy in this particular cultural matrix), does not address adequately the full range of material in Deuteronomy that Bell himself has rightly insisted has a wider relevance to Romans 9–11.[75] The most likely answer is that just as God's threat to Israel in Deut. 32:21 was followed by a period when he devastated Israel with military and cosmological disasters (Deut. 32:23-26) and transferred his favor to foreigners, thus, by implication, provoking Israel's passionate concern for what she had lost, *which was rightly hers,* and desire to regain it, so too Israel now sees that others are enjoying the benefits of God's favor, *which are actually or arguably rightly hers,* and thus must know that the gospel is being preached and others are accepting it.

This view is confirmed by the quotation from Isa. 65:1 in Rom. 10:20: "I have been found by those who were not seeking me; I have shown myself to those who were not asking for me." Thus Moo misunderstands the effect of the Deuteronomic quotation when he suggests in relation to Rom. 10:19 that "the inclusion of Gentiles in the new people of God stimulates the Jews to jealousy and causes Israel to respond in wrath against this movement in salvation history."[76] The point of the expressions "provoke to jealousy" and "provoke to anger" in Deuteronomy 32 is not that Israel responded in wrath against her enemies, for Israel took not a step against them, but rather her anger is closely aligned with her jealousy as a way of describing the passion with which Israel should regard the successes being achieved by her enemies as a stimulus impelling her to return to God. Similarly, Paul is not making the point here that Israel has reacted in wrath against the Christ-movement, but rather he is speaking of the emotional intensity and chagrin with which she should view the blessings bestowed on Christ-followers and desire to regain her rightful position in God's favor.

Yet the clauses emphasized above demonstrate that an unexpected light has suddenly illuminated the apparently gloomy condition of Israel. For inherent in the idea of Israel's being provoked to jealousy is the fact of her expressing concern for what is actually or arguably rightly hers. It is not simply a case that in ignoring or rejecting the gospel Israel has lost something; for what she has lost is hers! She has allowed herself to be supplanted from a privileged position and relationship that belongs to her. The picture of those who have succeeded to it is most unflattering—they are not a nation, and even though Paul could have omitted this clause, he chose not to: they are a senseless nation. Thus he describes non-Israelite Christ-followers. Moreover, if Paul's addressees had in mind the course of Deuteronomy 32 after Rom. 10:21 they would have known that the final result of Israel's being provoked to jealousy was that her enemies, who for a time were aided by God, were eventually subjected to his vengeance, whereas Israel was restored to God's favor. Thus, in a verse where Paul is in one respect castigating Israel for her obstinacy, he is, by one of the passages from scripture he selects to make this point, also indicating that Israel will finally be vindicated and her enemies defeated. This theme will be powerfully developed in Romans 11.

Israel's Present Plight and Future Hope (Romans 11)

Romans 11:1-10

The broad theme of 11:1-10 is that God has certainly not rejected his people, because he has preserved a remnant, while hardening the rest. Paul begins by emphatically rejecting the notion that God has rejected his people: "I ask, therefore, has God rejected his people? Emphatically not! For I myself am an Israelite, from the seed of Abraham, of the tribe of Benjamin. God has not rejected his people whom he foreknew" (11:1-2). As noted earlier, here we see Paul, in a particularly emotion-charged situation, activating that aspect of his self (comprising cognitive, emotional, and evaluative dimensions) that was embedded in his identity as an Israelite. Paul was a "self" with a "self-concept" that included a number of cognitive representations available to him, and here he was making the Israelite one salient. Paul may have been doing so as an expression of ethnic pride—how could I, an Israelite, from the seed of Abraham, of the tribe of Benjamin, think anything so improbable as that God would abandon his people. Alternatively, he may be suggesting that the notion of God abandoning his people is falsified by the counterexample he himself represents.

Although some commentators prefer the latter option,[77] the former is correct, and for four reasons. First, if he were not expressing his ethnic pride there would have been no need for Paul to mention, in addition to his being an Israelite, that he was descended from Abraham and of the tribe of Benjamin.

Second, his case that God has not abandoned his people is based on his having spared a limited number of Israelites, which Paul has already proposed (9:27) and which he will soon seek to demonstrate further; it is not based on the much more limited and arguably trivial circumstance of his having spared Paul. Third, this is the third statement in chaps. 9–11 where Paul has closely identified with his people. The other two embodied Paul's impassioned activation of the Israelite aspect of his personality, and there is no reason to think 11:1-2 is any different. Fourth, it would be extremely odd if Paul were putting himself forward as a single representative Israelite proving God has not abandoned Israel when he is about to relate an incident from scripture in which God will correct much the same claim from Elijah that he alone is left by insisting that there are seven thousand people who have not bent the knee to Baal (in 11:2-5).[78] This is what will prove to be Paul's first answer to the charge that God has abandoned his people—a remnant of them have survived.

As scriptural proof that God has not rejected his people, Paul refers to an exchange recounted in 1 Kgs. 19:10, 14, 18, in which Elijah pleaded with God against Israel, because Israel had slain his prophets and demolished his altars, so that he alone was left and they were seeking to take his life, but where God had replied: "I have seven thousand men left who have not bent the knee to Baal" (Rom. 11:3-4). Therefore in the present time (ἐν τῷ νῦν καιρῷ), Paul concludes (11:5), there is a remnant—chosen by grace, he adds immediately, as he continues to drive in the message of the two sharply contrasting approaches to righteousness he has been pushing throughout the letter (including at 9:30-33). Indeed, he now makes this point once more, for what, indeed, will be the last time in the letter: "If by grace, then no longer by works, since otherwise grace is no longer grace" (11:6). The alternatives are stark and there is no mediating position between them. Paul now reiterates that Israel did not obtain what it sought, but the chosen obtained it and the rest were hardened (11:7). The word "hardened" (ἐπωρώθησαν) takes us back to the theological moral he drew from the example of Pharaoh at 9:18: that God "shows mercy to whomever he wants and hardens (σκληρύνει) whomever he wants."

This point is reinforced by the first of two sets of scriptural material he supplies at this stage, a loose composite of Deut. 29:3 (LXX) and Isa. 29:10:[79] "He gave them a spirit of stupor, eyes that should not see and ears that should not hear, until this day today (ἕως τῆς σήμερον ἡμέρας)" (Rom. 11:8). The phrase "a spirit of stupor" comes from Isa. 29:10; the rest is based on Deut. 29:3, which states (just after a reference to things the Lord had done to Pharaoh and his land) that "the Lord has not given to you a heart to know and eyes to see until this day." Paul changes this to have God positively giv-

ing them eyes not to see and ears not to hear, no doubt to accord with the way
he hardened Pharaoh.

It is important to note that some may perceive some ambiguity concerning the phrase ἕως τῆς σήμερον ἡμέρας in v. 8 and, perhaps, its source in Deut. 29:3—ἕως τῆς ἡμέρας ταύτης. Does the idea expressed here suggest that the stupor, blindness, and deafness lasted up to today but has now disappeared or very soon will?[80] Whatever the Deuteronomic expression means, this does not seem to be what Paul has in mind, to judge by the similar expressions in 2 Cor. 3:14-15. Here he says that the minds of the Israelites are hardened "until this day today" (ἄχρι γὰρ τῆς σήμερον ἡμέρας) in that a veil remains on their reading of the old covenant, because only through Christ is it taken away. Until today (ἕως σήμερον) when Moses is read, the veil remains on their heart. There is no sign here that he envisages that this situation has reached its term. The same meaning is patent in Matt. 28:15, which has a similar expression (in some textual witnesses): "This rumor has been spread abroad among Judeans until this day today (μέχρι τῆς σήμερον [ἡμέρας])," where there is no sign the rumor is about to die. From this I conclude that the spiritual stupor and disabilities that Paul attributes to Israel in Rom. 11:8 are not about to vanish.

The second collection of scriptural material Paul summons in defense of God's tough stance with Israel comes from Ps. 68:22-23 and 34:8 (LXX):

> May their table become a snare for them and a trap,
> and a stumbling block and a retribution;
> let their eyes be darkened so they cannot see
> and bend their backs continually. (Rom. 11:9-10)

There is some controversy as to whether the particular details of this passage (especially the references to the table and bent backs) have any specific application to Israelites with whom his addressees in Rome might be familiar, or whether Paul is just continuing to speak in a fairly general way about them and their stubborn resistance to the gospel. In spite of skepticism in some quarters,[81] given that the reference to "table" is so prominent and unexpected, so unlike statements concerning spiritual or physical disabilities mentioned in 11:10 and previously, while also raising the topic of eating practices that will be prominent in chap. 14, it seems more likely that it is touching some raw nerve in the Roman context. Minear has a precise explanation, suggesting that Paul selected this example:

> Surely because members of Group One in Rome [sc. Christ-
> followers, mainly Israelite but some non-Israelite who accepted

the Mosaic law] were inclined to set the barriers of table-fellowship in such a way as to exclude Gentile Christians. These members were under constant pressure from the synagogue to enforce
the Torah provisions on foods and they themselves exerted constant pressure on members of Group Three [sc. those uncertain
whether to observe the law] to do so. The issues of ch. 14 are
clearly visible here in Paul's choice of citations from Scripture.[82]

This view is, admittedly, tied to Minear's problematic differentiation of groups.
Nevertheless, it seems more likely than not that underlying Paul's mention of
an Israelite table was some issue of significant socioreligious import for the
Roman Christ-movement, and we will return to this passage later in connection with Romans 14.[83]

Israel's Second Chance (Rom. 11:11-15)

Romans 11:11-15 contains the greatest surprise in the letter. Whereas he has
hitherto proposed God's preservation of a remnant of Israelites as the means
by which God's word for Israel would have an effect and as proof that God
has not rejected his people, Paul now introduces a second and entirely new
scenario. He opens up the prospect that the hardened and unbelieving "part
of Israel" (cf. 11:25) might be saved after all. Israel has a second chance!

First he backtracks a little (11:11a), by emphatically denying that they
(meaning the stubborn majority of Israelites) have stumbled (ἔπταισαν) so
that they might fall, or with the result that they fall (ἵνα πέσωσιν).[84] Yet
even this question is surprising. The notion of "stumbling" seems a rather
gentle concept with which to label the condition of Israel he has previously
been strongly lambasting. Although he had earlier used the verb "stumble
against" (προσκόπτω) at 9:32 to describe Israel's response to Christ, there is
"a certain crescendo from stumbling to falling, for the one who stumbles may
get up again, pull himself together and stand on his feet, or he may fall and
lie on the ground."[85] Paul is making clear that for Israel the former, not the
latter, possibility is in store.

In the second part of 11:11 Paul intimates how this result will be achieved:
"Through their wrongdoing salvation has come to non-Israelites so as to provoke them [sc. Israel] to jealousy." Here Paul uses the verb "provoke to jealousy" (παραζηλῶσαι) for the second time in the letter, and the discussion
above in relation to its appearance at 10:19 becomes relevant here. Although
God is not expressed as the subject of the infinitive, the issue is the same. The
situation is such that it will provoke Israel's passionate concern for what she
has lost—salvation, to which she has a prior claim—and a desire to regain it,
now that she sees others (inferior to her) attaining it. Having stated the prin-

ciple, Paul proceeds to hint at the magnitude of what is involved: "If their wrongdoing means riches for the world and their failure riches for foreigners (ἐθνῶν), how much more will their fullness mean?" (11:12). Although he denied in the previous verse that Israel had fallen, this represents the first positive indication that a glorious destiny exists for Israel, that the story of that part of Israel which has not accepted Christ will have a happy ending. At this point he is speaking as an Israelite in a manner familiar to Israelites, since the word ἐθνῶν in v. 12 carries an ethnic ingroup connotation (which is why I have translated it "foreigners").[86]

At 11:13, however, he does directly address non-Israelites, but notably using their designation among Israelites (ἔθνη), rather than their self-designation of "Greeks" that he deploys earlier in the letter (1:14, 16; 2:9, 10; 3:9; 10:12). This address to the non-Israelites is not to be taken as a sign that Paul believes that the recipients of the letter are solely or even largely non-Israelites, as it is often interpreted.[87] Rather, in speaking to a mixed audience of Israelite and non-Israelite Christ-followers in a section of the letter where he has been engaging more with the former, he now, as it were, prods the latter into wakefulness. He reminds them that now he has something to say specifically for them.

At this point, however, he says something even more strange: "Inasmuch as I am an apostle of the foreigners, I glorify my ministry, if in some way I will provoke my kinspeople to jealousy and save some of them" (11:13b-14). Paul's description of Israelites as his kinspeople is of a piece with his earlier assertions of Israelite identity at 9:1-5, 10:1-2, and 11:1-2. He is continuing to maintain the salience of this aspect of his self-concept even though he is now addressing non-Israelites directly. Here we have the third and last instance of παραζηλοῦν in the letter, and the remarks made about its meaning earlier apply equally here. Paul says he is glorifying his ministry, meaning making much of it and showing how good it is, to stir up the passions of the Israelites to reacquire what is really theirs when confronted with others who have laid hold on it instead. The signs I have noted earlier in the text that the newcomers are in certain ways inferior to the original heirs of God's promises are also implied here. Paul may not be declaring in these verses that the whole thrust of his ministry to the non-Israelites is to save Israel, but he is not far off it. How would his non-Israelite audience listening to these words in Rome have felt about these words, given their implication that Paul's work to non-Israelites is an instrument for the salvation of Israelites, who will in due course obtain what rightfully belongs to them? His heart really lies with Israel and not with foreigners.

With v. 15 Paul's enthusiasm for the ultimate vindication of Israel moves above the foothills of 11:12 to scale new heights: "For if their being discarded (ἀποβολή)[88] means the reconciliation (καταλλαγή) of the world, what will their acceptance mean but life from the dead?" The exalted nature of this destiny can be gauged initially by the correspondences between the language here and that used in connection with Christ's redemptive activity in 5:10. Most commentators, moreover, consider that the "life from the dead" in v. 15 refers to the general resurrection that will take place at the end of time. This interpretation coheres well with the prediction in 11:25-26 that Israel will attain salvation when the full number of non-Israelites has come in. Paul is therefore making the general resurrection successive, and possibly even conditional, upon the acceptance (by God) of Israel after the reconciliation of the rest of the world. This brief intimation of the future of Israel and the world is now richly developed via imagery.

The Metaphor of the Olive Tree (Rom. 11:16-24)

The section beginning with 11:16 is indelibly stamped as distinctive by Paul's use of imagery. One picture is worth a thousand words, and there are critical times in Paul's correspondence where he relies on visual images to convey a message rather than dianoetic argument. Herbert Gale has argued that a Pauline "analogy" (his word for "image") is always subordinate to Paul's thought and can only be meant to apply to it in a limited way.[89] But this is too constricted a view of the role of Pauline images. We must give them proper weight in ascertaining what Paul is seeking to communicate. Usually this means that, rather than the image being subordinate to his thought, it offers a clearer sense of his meaning and helps us to resolve difficulties and ambiguities in the thought. A good example is the metaphor of the slave who accompanied young boys to school, the παιδαγωγός, in Gal. 3:24-25. One consequence of this image is to strengthen the case that Paul did not hold the view that the function of the law was to produce or provoke breaches of it, since that was inconsistent with the role of the παιδαγωγός on any view.[90] This is far preferable to the approach adopted by Heikki Räisänen, who argues that Gal. 3:19 means that the law was added to produce transgressions, though he adds in a footnote, but does not treat with sufficient seriousness, that the image of the παιδαγωγός "suggests rather the notion of preventing transgressions."[91]

In Rom. 11:16 Paul introduces two images that share the notion of holiness spreading from a small beginning to the final totality: "If the first fruit (ἀπαρχή) is holy, so is the lump of dough (φύραμα). If the root is holy, so are the branches."[92] Somewhat surprisingly, however, these images do not primarily look backward to illustrate what has just been affirmed, that the eventual acceptance of the rest of Israel will mean life from the dead, but rather to inaugurate a sequence of imagery and argument by which Paul will demonstrate his considered view on the relationship between Israel and the Christ-movement, now and in the future, that will *ultimately* produce the result celebrated in v. 15. We must be careful not to misunderstand the images in 11:16, as Moo does, for example, when he interprets them to mean that "the holiness that characterized the beginnings of Israel is an indelible mark on that people, fraught with significance for her present and her future."[93] The referent of the holy first fruit and holy root is not "the beginnings of Israel," but that segment of Israel that forms the initial component of the Christ-movement. At this point, that is to say, Paul shifts focus away from Israel as a whole (in view up to v. 15) and back to his arguments concerning the select few whom God has chosen (9:6-13), the remnant (9:27-29) who have turned to Christ, who are descendants of Abraham. Paul may well have Abraham in mind as the "root" here.

He had previously made clear that this initial group included non-Israelites (9:8, 24-26, 30-33). One would expect, then, that the holy first fruit and holy root of the images should extend to Israelites and non-Israelites. Now, however, Paul introduces a singular modification of his position. Although in the course of a passage to the mixed audience in Rome in which he has just reminded the non-Israelites to pay attention to what he is saying (11:13), he proceeds to elaborate on the second image of v. 16, using a metaphor of an olive tree, in a manner that restricts the sacred primal group of the Christ-movement to Israelites. All aspects of the image are significant:

> Now if some of the branches were broken off and you, being wild olive (ἀγριέλαιος), have been grafted in among them and become a sharer of the rich root of the olive tree (ἐλαία), do not boast over the branches. If you boast, it is not you who supports the root but the root supports you. You will say, therefore, "Branches have been broken off so that I might be grafted in." Certainly. They were broken off because of lack of faith, while you stand through faith. Do not think arrogant thoughts but fear. For if God has not spared the natural branches, nor will he spare you. See, therefore, the goodness and severity of God. For those who have fallen there is severity, but for you the goodness of God, if indeed you remain in that goodness; otherwise you too will be cut off, while those, if they do not remain in lack of faith, will be grafted in. For God is able to graft them in again. For if you were cut off from a wild olive tree in accord with nature and contrary to nature grafted in to the cultivated olive tree (καλλιέλαιος), by how much more will these be engrafted in accordance with nature into their own olive tree. (11:17-24)

The basic image is that of the Christ-movement. The primary component is a cultivated olive tree from which branches have been broken. This represents the remnant of Israel who have turned to Christ. It must include a root (which relates it to the image in v. 16) and a trunk, possibly with some branches left, possibly not. Onto this tree are grafted wild olive branches. The result is a unity of structure—there is one tree—but a noticeable differentiation of features—the tree is part Israelite and part non-Israelite and this differentiation does not disappear. The resulting image conforms closely to the way in which I have understood Paul's attempt at recategorizing the Christ-followers of Rome throughout the present volume. Yes, Paul is advocating a common ingroup identity (here equivalent to the tree itself). At the same time, however, he does not erase the distinctiveness of the two subgroups. In short, he is establishing a common superordinate identity while simultaneously maintaining the salience of subgroup identities. I have already noted that efforts at social recategorization may fail if this strategy is not adopted by those leading the process. This dimension of the metaphor of the olive tree constitutes further evidence against Daniel Boyarin's view that Paul eliminates the difference between "Jew" and "gentile."[94]

This image of the engrafted olive tree is introduced as a device for countering the arrogance of non-Israelites toward Israel (11:17). It seems that Paul was aware of a disturbance in relations among the Christ-followers of Rome caused by non-Israelites boasting over and nursing arrogant thoughts toward Israelites who had not joined the movement, presumably in the course of conversations with Israelites who had. Paul admonishes them not to indulge themselves in such attitudes. To gauge the tone of his message in this passage, however, and to see what light it sheds on Paul's view of the respective positions of Israelites and non-Israelites in the Christ-movement, it is necessary to know more about the context of the metaphor within the varied practices of Greco-Roman oleiculture. There is plainly an issue here, since in characterizing the grafting of branches from a wild olive tree onto a cultivated olive as "contrary to nature" ($\pi\alpha\rho\grave{\alpha}$ $\phi\acute{\upsilon}\sigma\iota\nu$) in 11:24, Paul is expressing a negative view toward the inclusion of non-Israelites This is not simply a matter of ancient Mediterranean agriculture, therefore, but an issue bearing directly on themes of fundamental importance in the letter as whole. Only a brief exposition of this subject, which I have covered at length elsewhere, is possible here.[95]

This initial question is whether Paul was referring to an actual feature of ancient oleiculture. In line with his belief that Paul was "not really interested in the objects which he used as figures; they are only a transparent disguise for realities," C. H. Dodd went so far as to assert that Paul "had not the curiosity to inquire what went on in the olive-yards which fringed every road he walked."[96] Let us see.

In 1985 A. G. Baxter and J. A. Ziesler published a significant article on the olive tree metaphor in 11:17-24 that sought to situate the Pauline image in relation to the actual practices of ancient agriculture. They largely agreed with views expressed by Sir William Ramsay in 1905, especially his suggestion that Paul's metaphor reflected an aspect of ancient Mediterranean oleiculture known to us from Columella (*De re rustica* 5.9.16) whereby "well-established trees that are failing to produce proper crops can be rejuvenated and made more productive if they are ingrafted with shoots from the wild olive."[97] Baxter and Ziesler referred to modern writers who had encountered this practice around the Mediterranean and noted that "such grafting with scions from a wild olive would be done only to a tree that was exhausted, unproductive or diseased, in order to reinvigorate it."[98] Apart from a brief reference to the late Latin author Palladius, they did not cite any ancient writer on olive grafting except Columella (in the form of his *De re rustica* and *De arboribus*), whom they described as "the only writer to leave copious material about the culture of trees, including olive trees."[99] They were in error here: the extant botanical works of Theophrastus, much of them on arboriculture, cover five volumes in the Loeb series, those of Columella three. Furthermore, Baxter and Ziesler employ the word "rejuvenate" as if such a notion, namely, that it was good to become young again, would have been favorably entertained in the Greco-Roman world, just as it is in contemporary northern European and North American cultures.

For Baxter and Ziesler the cultivated olive tree and Israel whom it represents appear in a bad light, with the vigorous wild olive shoots, the non-Israelites, being introduced to bring it back to health and productivity, to "rejuvenate it." Several critics have adopted this interpretation.[100] But we must now consider an entirely different explanation for the aspect of oleiculture underlying the metaphor of the olive tree.

The olive tree (the ἐλαία of 11:17) belongs to the species *Olea europaea L.* and is usually divided into two subspecies: *Olea europaea sativa* (which includes the cultivated olive, the καλλιέλαιος of 11:24) and *Olea europaea oleaster* (the wild olive, the ἀγριέλαιος of 11:17).[101] It differs from other trees by reason of its longevity, which may extend for centuries. After planting, a young olive takes a reasonably long time to begin bearing fruit, ranging from about six years in very good conditions to fifteen to twenty years in dry areas or where the tree is neglected.[102]

In modern times in some parts of Greece (such as Methana) grafting domesticated cultivars onto wild stock is the normal method of propagation for olives.[103] Young wild olive trees are dug up in the mountains and transplanted to their permanent site and are then watered for at least two summers.[104] Later, branches from cultivated olives are grafted onto them. This method is also still practiced in Israel. Wild olive saplings taken from the forest as root stock are grafted with scions from a particular tree in the olive groves of a village known to be fruitful.[105] The rationale for this practice is that branches from cultivated olive trees produce the best fruit, whereas wild olive trees have extensive root systems (needed for taking in as much water as possible) and often also have greater disease resistance. Grafting a cultivated olive branch onto a wild olive stock gives the farmer the best of both worlds.

We know that the same practice was a feature of ancient Greek oleiculture. Theophrastus discusses the use of grafting in propagating trees, including the olive, at some length in *De causis plantarum* (1.6.1-10, and more briefly in 2.1.1-4). The passage most relevant to the present discussion is the following:

> It is also reasonable that grafted trees are richer in fine fruit, especially when a scion from a cultivated tree is grafted onto a stock of a wild tree of the same bark, since the scion receives more nourishment from the strength of the stock. This is why people recommend that one should first plant wild olive trees and graft in buds or branches later, for the grafts hold better to the stronger stock, and by attracting more nourishment the tree bears rich fruit. If, on the other hand, someone were to graft a wild scion into a cultivated stock, there will be some difference, but there will be no fine fruit. (*De causis plantarum* 1.6.10, my translation)

Three features are of critical importance. First, Theophrastus recommends that scions from cultivated trees (τὰ ἥμερα) should be grafted onto wild trees (τὰ ἄγρια) of the same species (literally "of the same bark," τῶν ὁμοφλοίων). In the case of olive trees, this means planting wild olives first and later grafting them with cultivated buds or shoots. This is still the practice in Greece and Israel. Second, Theophrastus offers a reason for this practice: wild trees (such as the olive) possess strength (ἰσχύς), which results in more food for the scion. This means both that the graft holds better to the stock and also that the tree produces rich fruit. Third, Theophrastus explicitly raises the prospect of grafting wild branches into a cultivated tree (the subject of Paul's metaphor) and rejects it since it will not produce fine fruit.

Later in this same text Theophrastus says a little more about wild trees relevant to this subject (*De causis plantarum* 1.15.3-4). In seeking to explain (the apparently undisputed) fact that wild trees, though stronger than cultivated ones (τὰ ἄγρια, τῶν ἡμέρων ἰσχυρότερα ὄντα), fail to ripen their fruit (τοὺς καρποὺς οὐ πεπαίνει), he offers two reasons. First, there is the abundance of the fruit produced by the wild tree, coupled with the fact that the fruit fails to ripen (ἅμα δὲ πλῆθος πολὺ καὶ οὐκέτι γίνεται πέψις), leading growers to prune off some fruiting parts when there are too many of them. The second reason is that wild trees are denser and drier, and so more apt to draw moisture into the tree.

These explanations accord reasonably closely with modern oleiculture in Greece and Israel. It also is worth noting that there is important archaeological evidence for the views expressed by Theophrastus in the inscriptions from Delos that refer to leases over farms owned by the temple of Apollo on that island but leased out to tenants during the period 454–140 BCE.[106] One such farm was the Thaleon farm on Mykonos. These inscriptions are fairly rare in constituting secure evidence of relatively large-scale arboriculture on ancient Greek farms, including (but only in the case of the "Thaleon" farm) olive tree cultivation.[107] The "Thaleon" farm clearly used olive trees grafted onto wild stock since included among its inventory of buildings and trees in 207 BCE were 147 cultivated olive trees (ἐλαίαι), 87 wild olive trees that had been grafted (ἐλαίοι ἐνωφθαλμισμένοι), and 200 wild olive trees (ἐλαίοι).[108]

Which of these explanations is most appropriate for Romans 11, that of Columella or Theophrastus? The principal objection to the former is simply the massive discrepancy between salient features of Paul's metaphor and the practice described by Columella. To begin with, Columella speaks of a cultivated olive that is unproductive prior to the insertion of a branch of wild olive, and that depends on that new branch. But nothing in Rom. 11:16b-24 suggests any problem with the tree or postulates its dependence on the wild olive grafted into it. In fact, the movement is all in the other direction: just as if the first fruits are holy, so too is the batch of dough, then if the root is holy, so too are the branches. Holiness passes from flour to dough and from root to branches (11:16). The same point is reinforced and developed in the next verse: the wild ingrafted olive shares in the richness of the root (11:17). Unlike in Columella's example, here the wild olive branch depends on the tree for fruitfulness, not vice versa. And again in v. 18: the ingrafted branch does not support the root but the root supports the branch. Lastly, v. 24 suggests that the olive tree would be much better off with its original cultivated branches than with the wild branches, and this factor is also inconsistent with the latter adding anything to the tree, as required in the Columella passage.

A second area of discrepancy is that whereas Columella is speaking of a recuperative measure for an unproductive tree, not "grafting" of the standard type with the aim of obtaining fruit from the grafted branch, Paul does seem to have grafting in the proper sense in mind. This is suggested by his sixfold use of ἐγκεντρίζειν, a word employed by Theophrastus to designate grafting, to express what he has in mind. On the other hand, Columella does not use the standard Latin word for graft, *inserere*, for the procedure he describes in *Res rustica* 5.9.16. Although Paul does not expressly mention the notion of fruitfulness, which was what grafting was meant to encourage, that feature is implied by the richness of v. 17 and may also be intimated in v. 24.

A third problem is that Paul regards the original insertion of the wild olive as "contrary to nature" (παρὰ φύσιν, 11:24). This may not necessarily imply that the process of grafting itself was unnatural, but it certainly indicates that Paul thought there was something peculiar about inserting a wild olive branch into a cultivated olive. But Columella has no such qualms. If Paul did have in mind the recuperative oleiculture described by the Roman author, it is difficult to see why he would categorize it as παρὰ φύσιν.

The final major objection is the uncertainty that Paul had ever even come across it. Whereas Paul was certain to have been more familiar with the agricultural practices of the eastern Mediterranean, there is no mention of this technique in the writings of Columella, and it is quite inconsistent with his views on the inability of wild olive branches to contribute to a tree's fruitfulness. Even in the west it passes unnoticed by the two other main agricultural writers, Cato and Varro. Accordingly, there is little reason to believe that Paul was even aware of it. Having excluded the phenomenon described by Columella, I now proceed to the likely explanation.

By far the most plausible view is that Paul and his Greek-speaking audience were well aware both of the widespread practice in the eastern Mediterranean of grafting wild olive branches into cultivated olive trees and of the reason for that practice—to produce more fruit. What Paul describes seems to be closely related to the practice discussed by Theophrastus. We have cuttings from one subspecies of olive being engrafted into the other for the purpose of producing fruit. It is manifest, however, that his description does not precisely correspond to such a practice; in fact, he presents its complete inversion. The explanation for this is that the very differences between the details of the metaphor and a well-known feature of oleiculture clearly bring out what Paul is intending to convey, as can be shown by examining the passage in its context. Paul may well have been led to select a metaphor of the olive tree by reason of the occasional references to Israel as such a tree in Israelite scripture (Jer. 11:16; Hos. 14:6). Perhaps, too, the long history of Israel prompted him to construe it as a cultivated olive rather than a wild one. In general, the wild olive trees used as stock will be younger than cultivated ones from fruitful specimens of which scions are taken for grafting.

But having chosen to refer to Israel as a cultivated olive tree, in circumstances where he was seeking to promote the status of Israel and take his non-Israelite addressees down a peg or two, Paul was now in the fortunate position of being able deliberately to diverge from accepted horticultural practice by describing the branches inserted into the tree as coming from the wild olive. After all, he could just as easily have described them as originating from a *young* cultivated olive, but chose not to do so. In opting for the wild olive when he and his readers well knew that its branches did not bear edible fruit, Paul was consciously building an image most unflattering to the non-Israelites. This accords closely with his admonitions to them not to make honor claims for themselves at the expense of the branches (that had been cut off) in v. 18 and not to entertain haughty thoughts in v. 20.

It is interesting to note that W. D. Davies published an important essay that referred to a number of modern writers, but not to any of the ancient Greek and Roman authorities just mentioned, in which he arrived at a conclusion similar to that reached here. Davies proposed that the wild olive was notoriously unproductive and the fact that "Paul represents the Gentiles as a wild olive is a most forceful indictment of their lives."[109] Whereas they were inclined to look down their noses at their Israelite associates, Davies asked whether Paul was not deliberately turning the tables on them: "The Gentile Christians came from a wild olive; they had nothing to contribute. To be fruitful they had to be grafted on to the cultivated olive which had Abraham, the father of Israel, as its root."[110]

There can be no doubt that the olive tree metaphor offers a textualized image of the recategorization of two subgroups in which Paul is engaged throughout Romans. But this is a form of unity that necessitates internal differentiation, just like the simile of the body he will present in 12:4-8. Moreover, by giving proper weight to this image formed of articulated parts, as understood in its ancient context, we are left with a rather negative picture of the non-Israelite members of the Christ-movement. They are attached to the olive tree in a way that is παρὰ φύσιν, and they do not contribute to it. Restoring the original (cultivated) branches to their rightful place will produce much more.

This dimension of the metaphor is closely connected to Paul's use of the verb παραζηλόω. The olive tree gives the notion of Israel's being provoked to regain what is properly hers great visual solidity and power. The nature of this image demonstrates that Paul's assertions of his Israelite ethnic identity, most recently in 11:1, have not been mere rhetorical flourishes. Paul has spent his career seeking to attract non-Israelites to the movement and has argued consistently that the Mosaic law was not necessary for them, but this has not been at the expense of his pride in his Israelite ethnicity, his belief that Israel had prior place in God's affections and one day will be restored to its privileges. That Israelites and non-Israelites form one social category in Christ in no way means that the differences between these subgroups have been erased, or that one is not superior to the other.

The Mystery of the Coming Redemption of Israel (Rom. 11:25-32)

With v. 25 Paul leaves figurative language behind to return to discursive argument. Yet he still seems to have in mind mainly the non-Israelites in his mixed audience. For his opening remark, "I do not want you to be ignorant of this mystery, brothers," is followed by a negative purpose clause, "in order that you do not become wise (φρόνιμοι) according to your own estimation," which reminds the audience of the injunction "Do not think arrogant thoughts (μὴ ὑψηλὰ φρόνει)" of v. 20, which was directed at non-Israelites. He wants them to understand a mystery: a hardening has come upon part of Israel (ἀπὸ μέρους τῷ Ἰσραήλ); they are already well aware of this but that it is clearly the massively preponderant part he does not mention. But now Paul offers some information of astonishing import: this hardening has a point of termination, in that it will last only until the full component of the foreigners has come in and "so all Israel will be saved" (11:25-26). This point is substantiated by a quotation from Isa. 59:20-21 concerning the deliverer who will come from Zion (11:26-27). This deliverer is probably Christ at his parousia. More specifically, Paul also probably has in mind that Israel will be saved by conversion to Christ.[111] The idea of Mussner and others that Paul has in mind for Israel a separate mode of salvation not consisting of such conversion seems less likely, but it is difficult to exclude entirely.[112]

Paul ends this section by noting that although as regards the gospel Israelites are enemies on account of Christ-followers, as regards election they are beloved for the sake of their forefathers (11:28). The conflict-ridden nature of Paul's world comes out clearly in the first clause in this verse. Paul justifies the second clause by a statement of fundamental theological principle: "For the gifts and the call of God are irrevocable" (11:29). God is merciful to human disobedience, whether of Judeans or non-Judeans (11:30-32).

Concluding Doxology (Rom. 11:33-36)

Paul concludes this chapter, and indeed the whole of chaps. 9–11, with a doxology. This is a natural conclusion, given the extraordinary nature of God in the face of his dealings with a difficult people that has been set out in these chapters. Dunn comments aptly on these verses that "the hope of a truly universal salvation leads into a hymn in praise of the Creator, the unknowability of his ways, and the certainty that he cannot be deterred from the accomplishment of his purpose."[113] Here Paul steps back from engagement with the socioreligious subgroups in the Roman Christ-movement to give vent to a doxology of God that rests both on age-old Israelite theology and, in v. 36, on Hellenistic, especially Stoic, philosophizing about the deity.[114]

Conclusion: The Point of Romans 9–11

I may now briefly sum up the point of chaps. 9–11. These chapters address a question left hanging from the preceding discussion that, after all, had produced a negative assessment of the Mosaic law (chap. 7). Where did this leave Israel? This mattered greatly to Paul because (1) he himself was an Israelite and immensely proud of his heritage; (2) Israel continued to exist, with its sonship, honor, covenants, law, cultic liturgy (in the temple), promises, and patriarchs (9:5); (3) some of the non-Israelite members of the Christ-movement were antipathetic to Israel on account of its failure to convert to Christ; and (4) some of his Roman addressees (including prominent ones like Prisca and Aquila) were themselves Israelites and probably on the receiving end of criticism from, on the one hand, any Israelites they encountered who had not turned to Christ and, on the other, from non-Israelite Christ-followers.

We have seen that throughout chaps. 9–11 Paul argues in a complex way that responds to the various parameters of the situation as just set out and that is closely connected with statements made earlier in the letter. For some commentators these chapters address what is essentially a theological problem: Has God's word failed?[115] This issue is indeed expressly raised at 9:6a. I submit, however, that the main point of these three chapters is more social than theological and appears at 11:18-21 and 11:25-32.

In spite of the failure of the Mosaic law, Israel is not to be scorned. In the end all Israel will be saved. Issues of divine justice do appear in these chapters, but in the course of an argument moving resolutely toward a conclusion that has direct relevance to solving ethnic tensions and conflict between Greeks and Judeans in the Roman Christ-movement. But Paul's resolution does not entail eliminating the distinction between the two subgroups. As in the metaphor of the olive tree, they are incorporated within one new identity but not at the price of losing their subgroup identities. The tree and cut-off branches are distinct from the wild olive shoots that are grafted on—one tree, but recognizably separate parts. Yet neither here nor elsewhere in Romans does Paul call the new entity Israel. He is noticeably reticent about this, unlike in Galatians, where he comes close by referring to the Christ-movement as the Israel of God (6:16).[116] This is in keeping with a more benign attitude to Israel that is also evident in the very different understanding of Abraham he propounds in Romans 4 compared with his position in Galatians.

13

Descriptors of the New Identity
(Romans 12–13)

Romans 12:1—15:13 is widely recognized to form a distinctive component in the letter. At 12:1 there is a sharp transition from the status of Israel with which Paul has been engaged in chaps. 9–11 to advice relating to the ongoing life of the congregations in Rome. Critics frequently describe the movement in terms such as from the "indicative" to the "imperative," from "theology" to "ethics," or from "doctrine" to "paraenesis."[1] A further transition is often detected between fairly general exhortation in chaps. 12–13 and the material in 14:1—15:13 that is more specifically adapted to the situation in Rome.[2]

It is not possible within the scope of this volume to consider all the rich array of issues that arise in 12:1—15:13. I have elsewhere argued for a new broad approach to this material that eschews the difficulties associated with the use of terms such as "ethics" and "paraenesis" in relation to this section of the letter and proposes instead a new approach fixing on issues of identity and the extent to which Paul's ideas on life in Christ can be related to Aristotelian notions of virtues and the good life, which have recently seen a resurgence in ethical thinking.[3] Solid support for relating Pauline moral thought to these ancient Greek traditions can be found in Ambrosiaster, the astute Pauline commentator in late fourth-century Rome, who began his treatment of chap. 12 commenting that Paul "after the treatment of law and faith and a people by nature Judean and non-Judean, offers exhortation *on how to live a good life*" (emphasis added).[4]

In another essay, however, I have argued against the thesis of Troels Engberg-Pedersen (in his important monograph *Paul and the Stoics)* that there is an underlying similarity between Stoic ethics and Pauline moral teaching. Moreover, a comparison between Paul and the Stoics is better undertaken in a form that focuses on differences as well as similarities. When such a comparison is undertaken of Romans 12 as a test case, it reveals that although Paul has interacted with Stoic ethics, he has done so in the interests of presenting a radically different moral vision.[5]

Accordingly, in this chapter, while I occasionally refer to these other issues, my aim is to offer an exegesis of Romans 12–13 that is restricted to the extent to which this section of the letter outlines identity descriptors ("norms" in the social identity sense discussed in chapter two of this volume) for the good life that is based on faith in Christ and the active influence of the Holy Spirit.[6]

Interpreting Rom. 12:1-8

Rom. 12:1-2

Paul begins this section with the clause "I exhort (παρακαλῶ) you, therefore (οὖν), brothers, through the mercies (οἰκτιρμοί) of God." This is the first of three appearances of παρακαλῶ in Romans 12–16 with the meaning "I exhort" (the others being 15:30 and 16:17). In each case Paul goes on to request his audience to engage in particular behavior or take on certain attitudes, or to avoid others.[7] The only other instances of οἰκτιρμός in Paul are at 2 Cor. 1:3 (where the word is linked with παράκλησις, and God is described as "the father of mercies and God of all comfort") and Phil. 2:1.[8] The οὖν indicates here that Paul sees this section as closely linked to what he has been discussing previously; it is not simply a transitional particle.[9] But what is the substance of Paul's exhortation prompted by divine mercy and how is it connected with chaps. 1–11?

In previous chapters I have sought to demonstrate that Paul's strategy in Romans is usefully understood as an exercise in what social identity theorists call recategorization or the development of a common ingroup identity. One factor affecting the likely success of such an enterprise is the degree to which those involved manage to pay attention to the separate needs of the two or more subgroups that are the targets of the recategorization process. We have seen how consistently Paul attends to both the Judean and non-Judean components of his audience in previous chapters of the letter. The same plan now appears in the contents of Paul's request. It has two parts. First, he exhorts them (v. 1):

> by the mercies of God,
> to present your bodies
> as a living sacrifice (θυσία ζῶσα), holy and acceptable to God,
> which is your rational worship (λογικὴ λατρεία).

Second, he continues (v. 2):

> and do not be conformed to this age (αἰών)
> but be transformed by the renewal of your mind (νοῦς),
> that you may prove what is the will of God,
> what is good, acceptable, and perfect.[10]

In these two statements Paul manages both to address the entirety of his Roman audience yet also to pitch his request in a way that is peculiarly relevant to its two subgroups, first Judeans and then non-Judeans.

In v. 1 the notion of living sacrifice and rational worship represents an unambiguous alternative to the Judean cult, with which Paul had been concerned in his discussion of the status of Israel immediately preceding this (chaps. 9–11). Thus, although pagan idolatry was designated by the verb λατρεύω much earlier in the letter (at 1:25), the precise word λατρεία appears at 9:4 ("They are Israelites, and to them belong the adoption, the glory, the covenants, the giving of the law, the worship [λατρεία], and the promises" rsv). This is the only other instance of λατρεία in Paul, and the word is uncommon elsewhere in the New Testament,[11] so its repetition at 12:1 packs quite a punch.[12] While the Judeans are undoubtedly continuing with their λατρεία (9:4), Paul's addressees themselves constitute a λατρεία of an entirely different type. This λατρεία is λογική in character. While λογική is notoriously difficult to interpret, it seems to mean "rational," as denoting worship that involves the mind (and heart) and not just external actions (a contrast made in relation to Judeans in 2:28-29), as seen in many passages in the Old Testament,[13] and is appropriate for human beings in relation to God. Sometimes λογική is translated as "spiritual,"[14] but this misses the strongly cognitive dimension to the start of chap. 12, which will be continued with "the renewal of mind" in v. 2 and further references in v. 3.

At the same time, they will be a living sacrifice, a θυσία ζῶσα, presumably as opposed to the dead animals offered on the altar of the temple in Jerusalem.[15] This is the only instance of θυσία in Romans. Elsewhere, however, Paul does use it, literally, of the sacrifices in Jerusalem: "Consider the people of Israel; are not those who eat the sacrifices partners in the altar?" (1 Cor. 10:18, rsv), and, as here, metaphorically (Phil. 2:17; 4:18).

The admonition at the start of Rom. 12:2, however—not to be conformed to this world—would have spoken especially to Paul's non-Judean listeners or readers. The expression "this age" (ὁ αἰὼν οὗτος) refers to the present period and realm inhabited by persons and powers to which the redemption offered in Christ stands in contradiction (1 Cor. 1:20; 2:6 [twice], 8; 3:18; 2 Cor. 4:4). Here "this age" must include, inter alia, the realm of violent ethnic hostility and conflict. Suggestions that Paul understood "this age" in terms of a contrast with "the age to come" (derived from Israelite "eschatology") are unnecessary and probably eisegetical;[16] Paul never uses the expression "the age to come" and no such contrast is implied here. Paul is interested in the current character of the Christ-believing congregations in relation to the world outside them. Ambrosiaster takes the (non-"eschatological" and far more plausible) view that here Paul is speaking about what we must do "if we are to keep our bodies undefiled, unlike the worldly people who devote themselves to pleasures."[17] Since the Judeans contemporary to Paul prided themselves on the extent to which the Mosaic law allowed them to keep this world at bay, Paul's warning not to be conformed to it would be more pertinent to the non-Judean component among his audience. These ex-idolaters (perhaps) were the people for whom the sinfulness described in Rom. 1:18-32 typified the age from which they had come and to which they must ensure they do not return. Instead of falling backward, they are to move forward—being transformed by the renewal of their mind.

Yet in spite of the fact that Judeans and non-Judeans would have found different parts of these two verses peculiarly relevant to their own experience, every statement had some application to each subgroup. That is, the single sentence comprising 12:1-2 spoke in its entirety to all Christ-followers in Rome, even if the Judean and non-Judean segments would each have recognized a feature distinctly apt for them. Thus the exhortation to "present" (παραστῆσαι) their bodies in v. 1 refers back to (and summarizes much of) 6:12-19, a section of the letter certainly directed to all of Paul's addressees in Rome, where this verb is used five times. Moreover, in the statement in 12:2 that they might "prove what is the will of God," Paul also has both components of his audience firmly in mind. The verb (δοκιμάζω) means "to test," "to prove" or "approve" (that is, "discover in order to carry out"),[18] though when followed by an infinitive it means "to see fit." It occurs twice earlier in the letter, first at 1:28, of non-Judeans who did not "see fit" to keep God in recognition; and second, at 2:18, of a Judean, who (allegedly) knows the will of God and "approves" what is best, but goes on to break the law. Thus at 1:28 we learn that the non-Judeans "discounted God as a factor in shaping their lives,"[19] so that God gave them over to a "worthless mind" (ἀδόκιμος νοῦς), while at 2:18 the problem was with Judeans who did test God's will but then acted contrary to it. In 12:2 Paul offers an alternative approach to both pathologies. He carves out a new modus vivendi for Christ-followers that consists of being transformed with a renewed mind (νοῦς), so that they might discover and implement God's will. Walter Grundmann comments in relation to this verse that the Christ-followers "are to test or prove what is the will of God. But to do it, they must know it by testing. In the new positing of human existence in faith, Christians are enabled to know the will of God."[20] This is accurate as far as it goes, but what function does 12:1-2 serve in terms of identity?

Paul tells the Roman Christ-followers who they are in both positive and negative terms, that is, in relation to who they are and who they are not. As explained in chapter two above, it is common for an ingroup to define itself in relation to outgroups. The outgroups here are Israelites who have not turned to Christ and who continue with the sacrificial cult in Jerusalem, with its sacrifice of dead animal carcasses, and the sinful world ("age"), especially of pagan idolatry, in which all concerned are located. The first positive dimension to their identity is that they are people who offer themselves to God as a living, holy, and pleasing sacrifice and a rational worship. The second is that they are being transfigured by a renewed mind so that they might "prove" the will of God, which is good, acceptable, and perfect. This, therefore, is an extremely broad and exalted identity. These are people who will live in tune with the will of God, embodying in their existence its goodness, acceptability, and perfection. Paul's concern is clearly with something much closer to the classical Greek interest in a cohesive account of the good life than merely with the criteria for right and wrong action. To describe these verses as "ethical" in that sense would be reductionist. Nor are any specific moral rules as yet delineated in these verses. Rather, Paul is advising on fundamental attitudes and processes of identity in Christ that will connect the lives of the Roman believers with God and will lead to their demonstrating the divine will in their daily existence.

At the same time, however, the reference to a renewed mind should not be overlooked. Julia Annas has pointed out that ancient Greco-Roman theories of ethics are conspicuous for their appeal to human rationality and that this was particularly true of the Stoics.[21] Paul engages with this dimension of Stoic thought, while presenting a vision of moral life very different from Stoicism, especially in its concern for others (inside and outside the Christ-movement).[22]

Arrogance and the Identity Descriptors of the Christ-Movement (Rom. 12:3-8)

This section begins with an admonition having a negative and a positive dimension that notably plays with four expressions containing the verb φρονεῖν ("to think") or its cognates (v. 3):[23]

> For by the grace given to me, I say to every one among you
> not to think arrogantly (μὴ ὑπερφρονεῖν)
> contrary to how you should think (παρ' ὃ δεῖ φρονεῖν),
> but think (φρονεῖν) with self-restrained thinking (σωφρονεῖν),
> just as God has assigned a measure of a faith to each.

We need to attend closely to the problem Paul addresses here, especially since most translations fail to appreciate the mischief he is confronting in the phrase μὴ ὑπερφρονεῖν. Paul is not worried about people who exaggerate their real importance, or think too highly of themselves, as if the problem was what we would call "vanity," an idiosyncrasy peculiar to an individual.[24] Moo's suggestion, similarly, that Paul is here concerned not with his addressees judging one another or the possibility of their "bickering," but with "spiritual pride," represents an individualistic and hence anachronistic reading of this passage.[25] For Paul's concern lies with the attitudes and behavior of those who promote their own importance *at the expense of others*. Although this is the only appearance of ὑπερφρονεῖν in the New Testament, it does occur three times in the Septuagint, on each occasion with the meaning "to despise," "proudly to reject,"[26] admittedly with an impersonal object. It is similar in meaning to two expressions used in Romans 11—κατακαυχάομαι ("make honor claims over") in 11:18 and, even closer, ὑψηλὰ φρόνει ("think high thoughts") in 11:20, both used of the wrong attitude of one subgroup to another. At 12:16 it will appear again, unambiguously meaning to nourish arrogant thoughts toward others (specifically, one's social inferiors) as opposed to associating with the lowly.

The cultural context in which ὑπερφρονεῖν (and the other two expressions just mentioned) must be understood is the agonistic Mediterranean world where individuals and groups endlessly compete with anyone of roughly equal status coming within their purview, with the aim of increasing their honor and shaming the other parties. These activities lead to envy,[27] a desire for revenge, and strife within groups in which they occur (the precise situation deplored in Gal. 5:26). They figure prominently in the life of "this age" to which Paul has just urged them not to be conformed. It was commonplace for people in the Greco-Roman world, Rome especially, to scorn anyone perceived to be lower in wealth and honor; this was one consequence of the pronounced social stratification of this culture. Paul wants to snuff out such behavior before it can get started, by telling his addressees not to harbor the thought that stimulates the attitude just mentioned, namely, that they are superior to others (whom, accordingly, they imagine they can despise and reject). Instead, they are to think in a moderate way, which here entails controlled and sober thoughts of others. Within the social identity framework, this admonition encapsulates a "norm" in the sense discussed in chapter two above.

It is also worth noting that here we have Paul installing very near the start of his treatment of how to live as a Christ-follower a deliberate and explicit focus on rational and self-restrained judgment analogous to that being advocated in his time by the Stoics. It is hard to resist the conclusion that he is here offering a rival vision of human behavior that picks up their best insights but integrates them into a new and distinctive product.[28]

The basis for the distinctiveness maintained by Paul appears in the last clause of v. 3, where he relates this norm to the fact that God has assigned a measure of faith (μέτρον πίστεως) to each. The precise nature of the relationship between the norm and the divine gift is, however, not easy to determine. The fundamental point seems to be that members of the house congregations in Rome who do act in an arrogant fashion to others will be challenging a divine decision, by scorning someone who has received faith from God. Yet the clause also raises the reality of the differentiation within Paul's addressees, on the broad basis of how much faith each had received. For Paul suggests that different measures of faith have been allocated to each,[29] thus paving the way for the analogy of the body he is about to provide (given that in the ancient world some parts of the body were more honorable than others, as evidenced in 1 Cor. 12:12-26) and, perhaps more significantly, the differentiation between weak and strong in faith in Romans 14–15. Sound, self-restrained thinking about other members of the congregations involves reconciling one's view to the fact that God has allocated different measures of faith to each.

At this point, however, Paul's audience would not have known what type of differentiation Paul had in mind. This is because of the lack of specificity in the notion of the "measure of faith" that God had distributed to each. The μέ-τρα πίστεως differed, but in what respect? One possibility was the differentiation between Judean and non-Judean, especially as shortly before this Paul had exhorted the non-Judeans not to "boast over" (11:18) the Judean branches cut from the tree, or "think high thoughts" (11:20)—expressions that betoken similar types of outlook and behavior to those signified by ὑπερφρονεῖν.

But Paul does not take this course and return to the dysfunctional disdain felt by non-Judeans for Judeans, at least not yet. Even in his next step he does not clarify what type of difference he has in mind. For now he proceeds to an analogy from the human body. Just as in the one body we have many members, with all of them not having the same function, so too we, though many, are one body in Christ, and individually members of one another (12:4-5). As we cannot assume that the Roman Christ-followers knew Paul's earlier letter to their coreligionists in Corinth that we now call 1 Corinthians, where Paul employs this analogy at great length to make a particular point (1 Cor. 12:4-31), they would still have been in dark as to where this was leading. Only with the next set of phrases (they lack a finite verb) does Paul's point emerge:

> Having gifts (χαρίσματα) that differ according to the grace
>   given to us,
> if prophecy in proportion to faith,
> if serving, in service,
> the one who teaches, in teaching,
> the one who consoles, in consoling,
> the one who distributes, with generosity,
> the one who leads,[30] with zeal,
> the one who does acts of mercy, with cheerfulness. (Rom. 12:6-8)

Thus Paul's readers learn that the arena in which they are not to despise other Christ-followers with which he is concerned in this passage is the way "gifts" (what we might call "ministries") are distributed among the faithful. Someone engaged in prophecy should not despise a teacher, nor someone who distributes despise a consoler, and so on. Underlying this is the fact that all of them form one body of Christ, although Paul does not offer here a lengthy explanation why this reality rules out despising one another as he does in 1 Corinthians (12:15-26).

In Rom. 12:3-8, therefore, Paul provides his first illustration of the general message of vv. 1-2: how they might offer their bodies as a living sacrifice and rational worship, prevent themselves being conformed to this age so as to demonstrate the will of God, and think in a sound and restrained fashion. He is concerned with specific ministries within the congregation, whose diversity is manifested only in relation to the fundamental unity that comes from the members forming the body of Christ. Paul is delineating and recommending a "norm" of identity (as explained earlier in this volume) for this group that consists, in part, of those of its members holding a particular ministry eschewing honor-based attitudes and practices from the surrounding culture and adopting a sober attitude toward those who hold different ministries. The activities mentioned in 12:6-8 are vital to the maintenance of community life. By way of contrast, the social dimension to Stoic thought was extremely weak.[31]

Yet making this contrast even more pronounced is the highly unusual nature of this group, as the listing of the ministries (apart from providing examples of where the correct attitude and behavior [the norm] should be demonstrated) graphically brings out. This group, uniquely in its environment, encompassed people who spoke as a mouthpiece for God under the impetus of the Holy Spirit,[32] taught, and were active in consolation and in works of mercy. These characteristics, to refer to Henri Tajfel's understanding of a group, contributed to the cognitive sense of group belonging (how they understood the utterly distinctive nature of the group), the evaluative sense (how they rated themselves in comparison to other groups), and the emotional sense (how they felt about such belonging).

But in these verses Paul does not just describe these features of the Christ-movement's identity. By virtue of the phrases he appends to the gifts, the last three in particular ("with generosity," "with zeal," "with cheerfulness"), Paul is adding a hortatory sense,[33] urging the person bearing such a gift to use it in the positive fashion mentioned. This is a good example of the difficulty in making the distinction, still common in Pauline studies, between the "indicative" and the "imperative" senses. Yet what is an embarrassment for existing scholarship is readily explicable within a social identity framework since here, as noted above, the identity of the group and its norms tend to be closely integrated. Indeed, 12:3-8 illustrates the extent to which such a perspective offers a more fertile means of commenting on the data in this text. On the other hand, to categorize 12:3-12 as "ethical" or, still less, as "paraenetic," would be reductionist, given the limited amount of material in the text that would be separated out by such conceptual "filters."

Is Paul here addressing a particular problem that he knew was current in Rome? The issue seems to concern people who are excessively proud of a particular charisma they possess (and presumably despise others who do not—although translators and commentators usually miss this negative edge to the verb ὑπερφρονεῖν). As Moo notes, there is little sign that the kind of problem Paul had encountered in Corinth in relation to spiritual gifts (1 Corinthians 12–14) was present in Rome.[34] This view is strengthened by the circumstance that the only charismatic gift per se mentioned here is prophecy, as opposed to miracle working, gifts of healing, distinguishing between spirits, speaking in tongues, and interpreting (1 Cor. 12:10, 29-30), which pass unnoticed. Similarly, the image of the body with many members is only a pale reflection of the extended treatment in 1 Cor. 12:12-26. Here the point of the body metaphor is to give substance to the injunction against pride and despising in Rom. 12:3. We seem to have here general guidance in an area Paul knew could be a problem rather than any evidence for Roman bickering or divisiveness in the area of particular ministries. Nevertheless, that Paul warns against ὑπερφρονεῖν is significant. There is no such blunt warning at the beginning of the problems he discusses at length in 1 Corinthians 12–14, which he begins at 1 Cor. 12:1 by offering teaching on the subject of spiritual gifts. In Romans, on the other hand, we have similar expressions at 11:20 and 12:16, followed by similar behavior in chaps. 14–15. This broad outlook, to despise others, is a problem, even though not in the area of the attitudes associated with the distribution of various ministries. Paul's metaphor of the body with many members for the Romans is offered as a way of exemplifying his message about not exaggerating one's own honor and despising others. In 1 Corinthians the body metaphor covers this purpose (1 Cor. 12:14-26) but in the course of a lengthy disquisition on the spiritual gifts that is also much interested in the maintenance of good order in the congregations (a topic entirely alien to Romans). Paul's point is that such a pathological attitude would be inimical to the unity in Christ founded on the fact that those who believe in him form one body. In Rom. 12:3-8 Paul strips everything down to this one issue. In short, Paul wants them not to engage in agonistic behavior by virtue of the ascribed honor attached to the possession of any one of the charismata mentioned.

Interpreting Rom. 12:9-21

The Contents and Structure of Rom. 12:9-21

At v. 9 Paul launches on a new topic, delivered in a truly remarkable style. Without any words connecting the passage with what precedes, he bluntly announces "Love (ἀγάπη) is without pretense"; then, again without any explicit link to this, he proceeds to set out thirty statements that apparently illustrate this assertion, delivered in staccato style without any connecting words among them (except for two instances of "for" [γάρ] in vv. 19-20). The following chart sets out the Greek and English in a way that reveals the individual stichs:

Romans 12:1-30

1.	Ἡ ἀγάπη ἀνυπόκριτος.	Love is without pretence:
2.	ἀποστυγοῦντες τὸ πονηρόν,	hating evil,
3.	κολλώμενοι τῷ ἀγαθῷ,	holding fast to good;
4.	τῇ φιλαδελφίᾳ εἰς ἀλλήλους φιλόσ-τοργοι,	being devoted to one another with brotherly love,
5.	τῇ τιμῇ ἀλλήλους προηγούμενοι,	giving precedence to one another in honor,
6.	τῇ σπουδῇ μὴ ὀκνηροί,	not lazy in zeal,
7.	τῷ πνεύματι ζέοντες,	being on fire with the Spirit,
8.	τῷ κυρίῳ δουλεύοντες,	serving the Lord,
9.	τῇ ἐλπίδι χαίροντες,	rejoicing in hope,
10.	τῇ θλίψει ὑπομένοντες,	being steadfast in affliction,
11.	τῇ προσευχῇ προσκαρτεροῦντες,	persisting in prayer,
12.	ταῖς χρείαις τῶν ἁγίων κοινωνοῦντες,	contributing to the needs of the holy ones,
13.	τὴν φιλοξενίαν διώκοντες.	practicing hospitality.
14.	εὐλογεῖτε τοὺς διώκοντας [ὑμᾶς],	Bless those who persecute [you],
15.	εὐλογεῖτε καὶ μὴ καταρᾶσθε.	bless and do not curse.
16.	χαίρειν μετὰ χαιρόντων,	To rejoice with those who rejoice,
17.	κλαίειν μετὰ κλαιόντων.	to weep with those who weep.
18.	τὸ αὐτὸ εἰς ἀλλήλους φρονοῦντες,	Thinking in harmony toward one another,
19.	μὴ τὰ ὑψηλὰ φρονοῦντες	not having arrogant thoughts,
20.	ἀλλὰ τοῖς ταπεινοῖς συναπαγόμενοι.	but associating with the lowly.
21.	μὴ γίνεσθε φρόνιμοι παρ' ἑαυτοῖς.	Do not be clever according to your own estimation.
22.	μηδενὶ κακὸν ἀντὶ κακοῦ ἀποδι-δόντες,	Not repaying evil for evil to anyone,
23.	προνοούμενοι καλὰ ἐνώπιον πάντων ἀνθρώπων:	taking into consideration what is noble in the sight of all.
24.	εἰ δυνατόν τὸ ἐξ ὑμῶν, μετὰ πάντων ἀνθρώπων εἰρηνεύοντες	If you are able, being at peace with all people,
25.	μὴ ἑαυτοὺς ἐκδικοῦντες, ἀγαπητοί,	not taking your own revenge, beloved,
26.	ἀλλὰ δότε τόπον τῇ ὀργῇ, γέγραπται γάρ, Ἐμοὶ ἐκδίκησις, ἐγὼ ἀνταποδώσω, λέγει κύριος.	but give opportunity for God's wrath, for it stands written: "Vengeance is mine; I shall repay," says the Lord.
27.	ἀλλὰ ἐὰν πεινᾷ ὁ ἐχθρός σου, ψώμιζε αὐτόν:	But if your enemy is hungry, feed him.
28.	ἐὰν διψᾷ, πότιζε αὐτόν: τοῦτο γὰρ ποιῶν ἄνθρακας πυρὸς σωρεύσεις ἐπὶ τὴν κεφαλὴν αὐτοῦ.	If he is thirsty, give him to drink; For by doing this you will heap coals on his head.
29.	μὴ νικῶ ὑπὸ τοῦ κακοῦ	Do not be conquered by evil
30.	ἀλλὰ νίκα ἐν τῷ ἀγαθῷ τὸ κακόν.	but conquer evil by good.

The first twelve of these are all either participial or adjectival phrases (vv. 9-13), with the adjective or participle placed at the end of the phrase in every case after the first two phrases in v. 9. No connecting words are provided. The (rather literal) translation and layout in this chart illustrate this unusual effect. These are all grammatically indicative in mood, but many commentators and translators sense imperatival force, and translate accordingly: "Let love be genuine, hate what is evil. . . ."[35] In one respect this is reasonable, given that Paul then moves on to the next eighteen such statements, again without connectives, in a mixture of explicit imperatives (vv. 14, 16, 19, 20, 21), infinitives (v. 15), and participial phrases. On the other hand, this amalgam seems to require a framework for understanding the passage that does justice to Paul's freedom in combining indicative and imperatival expressions.

For the introduction of imperatives in v. 14 does not mark any significant break in the material. All eighteen statements continue to illustrate the meaning of "love is without pretence." On the other hand, there does seems to be a division between vv. 9-16 and vv. 17-21 (which consist of the last nine injunctions), the latter section dealing solely with the question of vengeance, in the sense of responding to an evil act with an evil act.[36]

The many attempts to see a transition in the text at v. 14, on the basis that there Paul moves from purely intracommunity concerns to oppression by outsiders (and in the imperative mood), have little to recommend them. Even if outside oppressors are in view in v. 14, Paul is still concerned with how his audience, in their capacity as Christ-followers, should respond. In addition, although it is not a common interpretation, we cannot rule out the possibility that it was other Christ-followers who were doing the oppressing. Paul may even have Christ-followers in mind in vv. 17-21 as those from whom vengeance should not be sought, but to whom mercy should be extended. Lending strong support for this view is that the kind of mercy recommended—offering food and drink—connects closely with Paul's invocations at two critical points in chaps. 14 and 15 to welcome one another, in the sense of show hospitality to them (as expressed in the word προσλαμβά-νεσθαι; 14:1 and 15:7), as I discuss later in this volume.

Verses 9-16 (statements 1 to 21 in the chart) are characterized by a remarkable incidence of stylistic patterns that depend on pronounced aural repetition. The aural dimension to the structuring of vv. 9-16 has been largely overlooked by scholars, who divide the text inappropriately after v. 13 and prefer to hunt for a chiastic structure instead.[37] These patterns emerge in the presentation of the Greek text, where I have inserted a number at the start of each stich for the purposes of identification.

This passage deserves attention in relation to both its structural and aural features. The dominant structural feature is its paratactic nature. Items are added to one another with little subordination of one thought to another.

The most prominent aural feature is rhyme. This occurs in the repeated -οι sound at the ends of 4, 5, and 6, the -ουτες sound at the end of stichs 7, 8, 9, and 10, the -ουντες sound at the end of 11 and 12 and 18 and 19, and the -αιοντων sound at the end of 16 and 17. There is also patterned repetition of the article at the beginning of words; thus τῇ commences three successive stichs (4, 5, and 6), then τῷ commences two (8 and 9), and we then revert to three instances of τῇ (9, 10, and 11). There is frequent repetition of the same word or words of similar sound, as with ἀλλήλους in 4 and 5, διώκοντες / διώκοντας in 13 and 14, εὐλογεῖτε in 14 and 15, the remarkable similarities in 16 and 17, φρονοῦντες in 18 and 19, and the use of φρόνιμοι shortly after these participles in 21. There is also alliteration, as with the ἀ- sounds in 1, 2, and 3, φ- in 4 and προς- in 11.

How are we to explain this patterning? The best answer, although one rarely if ever offered as scholars strive to detect literary patterns, is that it is a product of Paul's oral proclamation. The tendency that it exhibits to add elements one after the other, rather than to subordinate some to others, represents what Walter Ong has described as the first characteristic of orality.[38] The aural features, second, almost certainly constitute an elaborate mnemonic pattern, allowing someone to hold the entirety of this material in memory. By contrast, Paul's discussion of love in 1 Corinthians 13 is a far more eloquently worked-up piece of prose that does not exhibit such mnemonic features. Whatever the source of the individual statements in Rom. 12:9-16, we seem to have in this section of the letter a chunk of teaching about ἀγάπη either exactly in the form in which Paul had memorized it and used in teaching elsewhere, or which he had composed for the Roman congregations in such a way as he hoped they would be able to remember it. The former of these alternatives is probably the more plausible. Admittedly, some of the statements, for example in v. 16, seem peculiarly apt for the situation in Rome and similar views appear earlier in the letter. On the other hand, these sentiments could have long constituted bedrock teaching for Paul, and when he came to write to Rome he developed them in ways suited to the state of affairs in that city. It is more likely that the richness of the mnemonic array in this passage depends on a period of development than that Paul composed it de novo when dictating his letter to the Romans. What we have in 12:9-21 is a precious fragment of Paul's oral proclamation on the subject of the love that must characterize the life and identity of Christ-followers.

The Meaning of Ἀγάπη Elsewhere in Romans

To appreciate why Paul is able to introduce ἀγάπη in v. 9 without explanation we need to consider his use of this and cognate words earlier in the letter. We are also able to consider his usage in other letters, but since there is no reason to believe that Paul's Roman audience had encountered them, we should assume that this letter itself conveyed enough meaning in relation to ἀγάπη for the notion to be explicable to its original addressees.

Paul had directed the letter "to all the beloved of God (ἀγαπητοὶ θεοῦ) who are in Rome" (1:7), and this is the only example of ἀγαπητοὶ θεοῦ in his correspondence.[39] On the next occasion in the letter where this or cognate expressions occur, he offers an exalted explanation of precisely what he means by it: "God's love (ἡ ἀγάπη τοῦ θεοῦ) is poured out into our hearts through the Holy Spirit who has been given to us" (5:5). It is widely agreed that "God's love" does not mean "our love of God" but "God's love for us." While the former view was favored by Augustine and others after him (and it does seem to square with "poured out *into our hearts*"), most modern commentators prefer the latter view because it is more easily reconciled with vv. 6-8, especially v. 8a: "But God shows his love (ἀγάπη) for us. . . ." On the other hand, that Paul specifies "our hearts" as the repository of God's outpoured love for us certainly seems to intimate, even at this early point, that such love will have profound consequences in the lives of those who so receive it. At the same time, this is another sign of the divine activity in the hearts of Christ-believers that has already appeared in 8:27.

This supposition that God's love will produce results is confirmed the next time this word group appears in the letter, immediately after the verse just mentioned: "We know that God works everything for the good for those who love (ἀγαπῶσιν) him, who are called according to his purpose" (8:28). This means that some human beings are characterized by their loving God, no doubt in response to his love of them present in their hearts, that is, in the depths of their being. There is no basis for seeing different types of ἀγάπη among the Roman Christ-followers here—the ἀγάπη that God pours into us results in our experiencing the same ἀγάπη for him and also for other people. Their love "is nothing but the direct flowing back of the heavenly love which has been poured out" upon them.[40]

Soon after, Paul mentions another aspect to this dynamic relationship of mutual ἀγάπη, namely, that nothing can separate "God's elect" from "the love of Christ" (ἀγάπη τοῦ Χριστοῦ;[41] 8:35) or from "the love of God in Christ Jesus our Lord" (8:39). One reason for this confidence is that they will completely prevail through him (here meaning Christ) who loved them (8:37). Now ἀγάπη is revealed as the unbreakable bond that God and Christ have for those who believe. Although it is primarily the love of God and Christ *for us* that is in view, the reference to natural or human catastrophes (8:35)—to which human beings but neither God nor Christ are subject—being unable to produce a rift between Christ's love and those who believe indicates that Paul also has in mind the reciprocal human dimension to this love mentioned just previously (8:28). Apart from two examples of the verb in Septuagintal quotations in Romans 9 not relevant for present purposes (vv. 13 and 25), the stage is now set for the appearance of ἀγάπη at 12:9.

The outline of ἀγάπη in 12:9-21 indicates that the word also characterizes the relationships among Christ-followers themselves and, possibly, their dealings with outsiders. Paul will formulate this programmatically at 13:8-10 and with almost the same force at 14:15. But here he seems confident that the Roman Christ-followers would assume that love was to govern their relationships, either as a necessary corollary of the views he had expressed earlier in the letter about love between God and Christ and Christ-followers, or because he could rely on them to be already aware of its importance in relation to human interactions.

In 13:8-10 (a passage I deal with in more detail later) Paul seeks to explain the need for them to love one another. To do so, he situates ἀγάπη in relation to four of the ten commandments of the Mosaic law (against adultery, murder, theft, and covetousness) and the injunction to love one's neighbor as oneself in Lev. 19:18. Here Paul announces that the person who loves (ἀγαπῶν) has fulfilled that law. This means, as I argue below, that Christ-believers have in ἀγάπη, which is given them directly by God and the Spirit, the best that the law can offer, but not actually produce, since the Mosaic law is used as a tool by sin. Accordingly, the Mosaic commandments become irrelevant to life in Christ. In ἀγάπη Christ-believers receive the best that the law offered—but never managed to provide—by a new and completely different route.

Ἀγάπη and the Spirit

The presence of ἀγάπη is closely linked to the Holy Spirit. At 5:5 Paul attributes the outpouring of God's love into human hearts to the agency of the Spirit "that has been given to us." The word designating this outpouring is a perfect tense of ἐκχέω, expressing a process continuing into the present. The same word is used of God's pouring out the Spirit in Joel 2:26-27, a passage quoted or alluded to at Acts 2:17, 18, 33; 10:45; and Titus 3:6, so that it may have regularly been applied to Pentecost among early Christ-followers (as Dunn aptly suggests)[42] or, one might add, to the initial experience of the Holy Spirit by any Christ-follower, at his or her baptism. Although the aorist tense at Rom. 5:5 ("has been given [δοθέντος] to us") does suggest such a discrete event, this "initial impact of divine power"[43] in no way militates against the continuing activity of the Spirit in close conjunction with God's love, from which it is, indeed, not easily distinguished. In consequence, it comes as no surprise when, later in the letter (15:30), Paul appeals to his audience "through our Lord Jesus Christ and through the love of the Spirit," where the genitive in "love of the Spirit" (ἀγάπη τοῦ πνεύματος) almost certainly conveys the meaning "the love that the Spirit produces," not love for the Spirit.[44] Paul makes this point explicitly in Galatians when in the course of running through the "fruit of the Spirit" he mentions ἀγάπη first (Gal. 5:22).

Finally, it is important to note that Paul makes clear that ἀγάπη is to be distinguished from the spiritual gifts (*charismata*; χαρίσματα). This emerges from the way they are contrasted in 1 Cor. 14:1, but also from the fact that it is possible to have χαρίσματα and yet not also have love (1 Cor. 13:1-2). Similarly, Paul employs the human body analogy in 1 Corinthians 12 in reference to the χαρίσματα, to insist on the unity holding together the diverse ministries, but not in relation to love. The χαρίσματα refer to the power of the Spirit manifested in differentiated ministries or callings within the congregations, whereas ἀγάπη is "the power which transforms character and which motivates the transformed character."[45] All of this brings us back to Rom. 12:9-21.

In Rom. 12:3-8 Paul had been concerned with the χαρίσματα and with the possibility that their various holders might despise one another. To counter this, just as in 1 Corinthians 12, he resorted to the analogy of the human body, although now in a much briefer form. Then, again as in 1 Corinthians 13 and in the same order, he took up the question of ἀγάπη in Rom. 12:9-21. Yet in Romans 12 there is nothing of the impassioned and carefully wrought eloquence of 1 Corinthians 13. Paul does not even offer connected prose. Instead, he proffers a list of thirty unadorned assertions, mnemonically linked as already discussed, to portray the meaning of ἀγάπη.

Ἀγάπη and Social Identity

General Comments

The thirty statements that Paul lists to illustrate the meaning of ἀγάπη, when understood in the context of other uses of this word or its cognates in the letter (and coupled with the parallel sequence of fifteen statements in 1 Cor. 13:4-7) and in comparison and contrast with Aristotelian and Stoic approaches to the virtues,[46] justify regarding ἀγάπη as having paramount importance for him in designating the unique identity of the Christ-movement. Its significance embraces an indispensable foundation of this identity, namely, the action of God (in association with the Spirit) in pouring his ἀγάπη into the hearts of those who have faith in Christ, and also the ongoing experience of the members of the movement. Thus, in social identity terms, ἀγάπη relates both to the creation of the group, in all three dimensions (cognitive, emotional, and evaluative) and also to its "norms" or identity-descriptors, in the sense previously explained—the acceptable and unacceptable attitudes and behaviors for the members of this particular social unit. That the word straddles these two dimensions, that there is a unity of action between the act of God in pouring love into the Christ-followers and their responding with love of God and other people, underlines the problems inherent in drawing too sharp a distinction between Romans 1–11 and this section of the letter. To distinguish sharply between the "indicative" and "imperative," or "theology" and "ethics," seems to impose too violent a disjunction upon the text and also upon the economy of salvation God has inaugurated in Christ. As we will now see, moreover, such crude schemata are also inappropriate to the details of 12:9-21.

Detailed Consideration of Romans 12:9-21
To consider the nature of the statements illustrating ἀγάπη in relation to the social identity framework already set out, it is helpful if we rearrange them in an order that brings out their variation in character and content. Among the many possible forms of classification, I employ the following (maintaining the fairly literal translations adopted above to emphasize important features of Paul's understanding):

1. Relationship with God.
The relevant statements are:

> Persisting in prayer.
> Serving the Lord.
> Being on fire with the Spirit.

It is noteworthy that these are not normative ethical statements of the sort that specify criteria for distinguishing right and wrong action. They are all descriptive, the first two characterizing both a character trait and a behavioral pattern and the third being a factual statement of possession by the Spirit (a reality expressed in the spiritual gifts/ministries listed in 12:6-8).

2. Attitudes and Dispositions Not Directed toward Others.

> Hates evil and
> holds fast to good.
> Do not be conquered by evil,
> but conquer evil by good.

> Not lazy in zeal.
> Being steadfast in affliction.
> Rejoicing in hope.

Here the first four statements, drawn from the beginning and end of Paul's list in vv. 9 and 21 (where they constitute an *inclusio*), indicate in the most general terms that ἀγάπη is realized in holding fast to goodness and hating evil. There is also a link back to the mention of goodness in 12:2.

The next two statements specify unflagging zeal and steadfastness. Again, these refer either to character traits or dispositions appropriate for this identity, or to behavioral patterns by which the virtue of love is manifested. The word "zeal" (σπουδή), meaning "eagerness,"[47] appeared in 12:8 as a characteristic of one who leads. While Paul does not specify the object of the zeal he advocates here in v. 11, it is presumably meant to have a wide application, typifying the way the Christ-follower will undertake all of the behavior listed in 12:9-21.

Lastly, hope evokes the orientation to the future, to the end-time events, which formed an essential aspect of the identity of the movement, but, as we have seen in chapter eleven above, were closely linked to the present. It may have been Paul who invented the triad of virtues, namely faith, hope, and love, that became characteristic of Christ-followers.[48] In 1 Thessalonians he is worried about the weakness of hope among the addressees of the letter.[49] But in 1 Cor. 13:13 he insists that love is the greatest of the three, while in Rom. 12:12 he subordinates hope to love by making the former a manifestation of the latter.

3. Dispositions and Practices Directed toward Others.

One type of statements ("endogenous") in this category relates to attitudes and behavior necessary to preserve the unity of the congregations. Another type relates to the appropriate response to offer to those who persecute or do evil. Although scholars generally see such persecution or evil as originating from outside the Christ-movement ("exogenous"), I later advert to the possibility that sometimes other Christ-followers may have been the cause of these problems.

The first six endogenous features (two comprising v. 10 and the next four v. 16) refer to the need to eschew cultural values relating to excessive competition over honor (which were endemic in the surrounding culture) and adopt instead the love that was supposed to exist between brothers, within the family, where such competition was entirely out of place:

> Being devoted to one another with brotherly love.
> Giving precedence to one another in honor.
> Thinking in harmony toward one another.
> Not having arrogant thoughts,
> but associating with the lowly.
> Do not be intelligent according to your own estimation.

While the notion of actual "brotherly love" was recognized by Greco-Roman authors (such as Plutarch, in his treatise *On Brotherly Love*) as the model of harmonious relations among a respectable family, throughout his career Paul was an active proponent of "fictive" brotherly love, meaning love taking its character from love between siblings, to be shown by Christ-followers to one another, as can be seen from his use of the word in 1 Thess. 4:9 and the presence of the concept in Gal. 5:13—6:10, as well as here in Rom. 12:10.[50] The strength of the ties binding the communities of Christ-followers together required for their expression a powerful metaphor from kinship patterns in the ambient culture, and brotherly love provided it. It is possible that the ultimate root of such ideas in the movement were sayings of Jesus that asserted the reality of his new family under God as Father, seen in passages like Mark 3:35; Matt. 7:3; 18:15, 21.[51]

"Giving precedence to one another in honor" may also have origins in the Jesus tradition, in sayings such as Matt. 23:12 (and Luke 14:11): "Whoever exalts himself will be humbled, and whoever humbles himself will be exalted."[52] In this respect Jesus (and Paul after him) was uttering a strongly countercultural sentiment.

Paul's direction against having arrogant thoughts is rooted in the actual experience of his addressees. In Rom. 11:20 he had used the same phrase in the context of ethnic relationships, to castigate the wrong attitude of non-Israelites to Israelites. In 12:16 the rejection of arrogant thoughts is set in a context of differentiated social status—in contrast with a commendation of associating with the humble and lowly (ταπεινοί).[53] This leaves open the possibility, to which I return in the next chapter, that there was an identity between the actual and implied Israelite victims of 11:18 and 11:20 and the social inferiors of 12:16. That Paul saw human lowliness in a positive light (unlike the Stoics, who derided non-Stoics as "worthless" and "stupid")[54] is probably due in part to his being imbued with Israelite Scriptures, where this was a common theme,[55] and also probably due to his awareness of Jesus traditions like "Blessed are the destitute" (Matt. 5:3; Luke 6:20).

The remaining four endogenous features (the first two from v. 13 and the second two from v. 15) summarize particular modes of love related to generous sharing and the practice of consolation, already mentioned as ministries in 12:8:

> Contributing to the needs of the holy ones.
> Practicing hospitality.
> To rejoice with those who rejoice,
> To weep with those who weep.

Practices such as these were necessary for maintaining and strengthening the community. This is particularly the case with material help, which is recommended in the first two statements. Contributing to the needs of the holy ones needs to be understood in the first-century context where poor and destitute people lived from day to day. In Rome, unlike other Greco-Roman cities, public distributions of grain relieved some of this distress.[56] Yet the coverage of the city's population was uneven and the amount distributed was insufficient to meet all of a family's needs.[57] Even in Rome, therefore, help from other Christ-followers would have been beneficial. It is possible that Paul also had in mind the desirability of congregations in one part of the Mediterranean helping the poor in others, just as he was intending to take a collection from Macedonia and Achaia to saints among those living in Jerusalem (15:26). Similarly, in a context like Rome and elsewhere where the Christ-movement was based in houses, the expression of ἀγάπη in a material form to others, either living locally or passing through, would necessarily take the form of hospitality, that is, the provision of shelter and food and drink to visitors. This will emerge as a theme in Romans 14–15, as we will see in chapter fourteen below. At the same time the notion of practicing hospitality had a particular relevance for Paul's relationship with the Roman Christ-followers, since he intended to avail himself of their help on his foreshadowed journey to Spain (15:24). The ultimate source for these attitudes may have been the Jesus tradition, especially as seen in statements like that in Matt. 25:35: "For I was hungry and you gave me food, I was thirsty and you gave me drink, I was a stranger and you welcomed me," even though there was also a tradition of hospitality among Judeans.[58]

The exhortation to weep with others, to engage in a visible expression of that emotion with fellow Christ-followers (for which Paul may have had an Israelite source in Sir. 7:34), can be contrasted with the attitudes to the emotions entertained by the Stoics, for whom to feel grief, pity, or anguish would have seemed pointless.[59] Ambrosiaster notes a pertinent connection between shared grief and joy in Rom. 12:15 and something Paul says in 1 Cor. 12:26, when he is expatiating on the metaphor of the one body with many parts: "If one member suffers, all suffer together; if one member is honored, all rejoice together."[60] Paul is moving easily from this description to the corresponding prescription in Romans 12. To rejoice and weep with one another is to enact the unity of the congregation in Christ.

We now come to exogenous material, although (as noted above and explored below) we need to be wary of simply assuming that insiders could not have been responsible for the persecution and evil mentioned. This comprises v. 14:

> Bless those who persecute [you],
> bless and do not curse;

and the statements in vv. 17-21:

Not repaying evil for evil to anyone,
taking into consideration what is noble in the sight of all people.
If you are able, being at peace with all people,
not taking your own revenge, beloved,
but give opportunity for God's wrath,
    for it stands written:
    "Vengeance is mine; I shall repay," says the Lord.
But if your enemy is hungry, feed him.
If he is thirsty, give him to drink;
for by doing this you will heap coals on his head.
(Do not be conquered by evil,
But conquer evil by good.)[61]

Whereas the Stoics advised the wise man not to pardon those who injured him,[62] Paul urges a different approach. But Paul is not merely saying be tolerant in the face of evil; rather, he is moving to a higher moral position by saying repay evil with good.

The origin of the exhortation not to repay evil for evil, and leave vengeance to God, requires some consideration. The principal Old Testament passage bearing upon vengeance is Lev. 19:18 (which Paul cites in Rom. 13:9), the Septuagintal version of which may be translated (fairly literally) as follows: "Your hand shall not take vengeance and you shall not be angry against the sons of your people; and you shall love your neighbor as yourself; I am the Lord." The commandment here (and also in the Hebrew version) has both a negative component (not to take vengeance on or to be angry with fellow Israelites) and a positive one (to love one's neighbor as oneself). The connection of this rule against taking vengeance on Israelites with the notion that vengeance is for God alone was not made in the Old Testament, but does appear in various intertestamental Israelite texts.[63]

Yet Paul applies the direction not to repay evil for evil to everyone (a point reinforced by his urging his addressees to take into consideration what is noble in the sight of all people and, if possible, to be at peace with all people). This universality of scope indicates that he wants the Christ-followers of Rome to apply the principle among one another and also to outsiders. When writing to the Thessalonians he had made precisely this point: "See that none of you repays evil with evil, but always seek to do good to one another and to all" (1 Thess. 5:15). How did this extension of the principle to non-Israelites come about?

In relation to the clause "Repaying evil with evil to no one" in Rom. 12:17 and with Lev. 19:18 in mind, Ambrosiaster wrote: "This is what the Lord said, 'Unless your righteousness exceeds that of the scribes and the Pharisees, you will not enter into the kingdom of God.' For it was commanded in the law, 'You will love your neighbor and you will hate your enemy.'"[64] Yet the expression "You will hate your enemy" is not found in Lev. 19:18 or elsewhere in the Mosaic law. Where does the idea come from? Ambrosiaster is quoting Matt. 5:43, which also contains this statement. In all probability it derives from the legal principle now known by the Latin maxim "unius expressio alterius exclusio," meaning that where a law expressly brings one class of person (or thing) within its ambit, a converse class (or thing) is necessarily excluded. Thus to say you shall not take revenge on Israelites but love them implies that there is no prohibition on avenging yourself against non-Israelites and on not loving them. I have suggested the pertinence of this principle, as it became enshrined later in the halakic midrashim, to understanding the legal reasoning in Luke's parable of the good Samaritan.[65] It seems, therefore, that Matthew (followed by Ambrosiaster) quotes the positive injunction in Lev. 19:18 and then offers an interpretation thereof formulated on "unius expressio alterius exclusio" lines. Matthew was helped in this view by the fact that no text in the Mosaic law prohibits taking personal vengeance against non-Israelites.

As Israelite tradition developed, however, the narrow focus of Lev. 19:18 was gradually widened in some quarters, at least. In one place a variant text form of Proverbs states, "Do not say, 'I will take vengeance on the enemy,' but wait for the Lord, so that he might help you" (20:9c). The idea also developed in intertestamental Israelite literature, although the extent of this should not be overstated. *Joseph and Aseneth* (an Israelite text probably written sometime from the first century BCE to the second century CE) is witness to this development.[66] Two types of incident require consideration. First, toward the end of the text the wicked brothers of Joseph (Dan, Gad, Naphtali, and Asher) attempt to kill Aseneth and their brother Benjamin, but God reduces their swords to ashes.[67] Aseneth then intercedes on their behalf when Joseph's righteous brothers, led by Simeon, seek to kill the wicked ones. She urges them not to return evil for evil against their "neighbors" and "brothers,"[68] but here she is really just reminding them of their obligations under Lev. 19:18. Elsewhere in the text, however, there are incidents where the principle of non-retaliation is widened to embrace non-Israelites. At one point Levi restrains Simeon from slaying Pharaoh's son, saying as he does so, "Why are you furious with anger with this man? And we are men who worship God, and it does not befit us to repay evil with evil."[69] Later in the text, Levi restrains Benjamin from killing the son of Pharaoh, with advice that adds to what he had previously said to Simeon that it is not fitting for someone who worships God to trample a fallen man or to oppress his enemy unto death.[70] One other text where something akin to this sentiment emerges is in the *Sentences of Pseudo-Phocylides*, an Israelite work probably to be dated from the first century BCE to the first century CE: "Practice self-restraint, and abstain from evil deeds. Do not imitate evil, but leave vengeance to justice. For persuasiveness is a blessing, but strife only begets strife."[71]

A respectable case can be made for the view that the sayings about blessing persecutors in Rom. 12:14 derive from the teaching of the historical Jesus, especially as later represented in Matt. 5:44 and Luke 6:27-28: "But I say to you, Love your enemies and pray for those who persecute you."[72] It is possible, however, that the presence of Israelite ideas similar to those found in Rom. 12:17-21, for example, the notion of not repaying evil with evil in *Joseph and Aseneth*, makes it more difficult to see an influence from Jesus traditions here. On the other hand, it is likely that Jesus, if he did not invent such ideas, at least adopted and taught them.[73] The notion of loving one's enemies includes not repaying them evil for evil, and the wide circulation of the latter idea among the Christ-movement (it also occurs in 1 Thess. 5:15 and 1 Pet. 3:9) makes good sense if it was associated with Jesus. Paul (or tradition before him) has sharpened the point by including a connection between nonretaliation and the idea that vengeance is God's prerogative, which developed in extrabiblical literature, admittedly there only in relation to vengeance against fellow Israelites.[74]

Kent Yinger has challenged the almost unanimous view that relations with unbelieving outsiders are in sight in Rom. 12:14-21, proposing instead that here Paul continues "the ecclesial focus of 12:1-13."[75] While Yinger has been successful in demonstrating that elements of vv. 14-21 can refer to evil perpetrated by members of the congregations (and this is a significant step forward), his proposal that Paul maintains a total focus on matters internal to the congregations from v. 14 to v. 21 is unpersuasive.[76] It cannot be the case that, when Paul's Roman audience heard the statements "Bless those who persecute you (διώκοντας); bless and do not curse," they said to themselves (or that Paul intended them to say to themselves): "Of course, this statement applies only to fellow Christ-followers, and we are free to go on cursing outside persecutors." Given that outsiders persecuted Christ-followers during this period, such a limitation would have required an emphatic and unambiguous signal from Paul, and there is none. On the other hand, Yinger's arguments do suggest that they could have imagined persecution by insiders as well as outsiders. It may seem a little messy to intrude a statement relating to persecution from outside in the midst of material dealing with the congregations, yet there is a mnemonic explanation for this—the appearance of the word διώκοντες (admittedly used in the sense of "practice") immediately before (v. 13). As already argued, the basis for the organization in 12:9-16 is mnemonic, to aid in Paul's proclaiming and his audience remembering the message about ἀγάπη, not the literary structures advocated by some. Furthermore, the reference to being steadfast in affliction earlier in the passage (v. 13) was capable of referring to both endogenous and exogenous affliction.

Clearly, however, Paul had intended to end the material on ἀγάπη with an important statement on nonretaliation (vv. 17-21). This passage does not have the mnemonic characteristics of vv. 9-16, and the way in which its theme is elaborated sets it apart from the maximlike statements of those verses. Whereas in vv. 9-16 he was using well-rehearsed material, in vv. 17-21 he seems to offer something specifically composed for the occasion, a consideration that implies the importance of this teaching in Paul's communicative strategy in Romans. The two prominent references to "all people"—taking into consideration what is noble in the sight of all people (v. 17) and being at peace with all people (v. 18)—should be given their full force. There is no basis for restricting such statements to members of the Christ-movement, as Yinger suggests.[77] On the other hand, his proposal does mean that they should not be excluded. Indeed, there are links between what is said on the subject of nonretaliation in vv. 17-21 and matters raised in Romans 14–15, especially the notion of giving food and drink to your enemy, to which I return in chapter fourteen.

Interpreting Romans 13

Appropriate Attitudes to Civic and Political Authorities (Rom. 13:1-7)

Romans 13 appears to mark a striking new development in Paul's argument:[78]

> Let every person be subject (ὑποτασσέσθω) to the governing authorities (ἐξουσίαι). For there is no authority (ἐξουσία) except under God, and those that exist have been instituted by God. Thus he who resists authority resists what God has appointed, and those who resist will receive judgment on themselves. For rulers (ἄρχοντες) are a terror not to good conduct, but to bad. Do you want to have no fear of authority? Do what is good, and you will have his praise, for he is God's servant (διάκονος) for your good. But if you do wrong, be afraid. For he does not bear the sword in vain; for he is God's servant, an avenger (ἔκδικος) for wrath on the wrongdoer. Therefore it is necessary to be subject (ὑποτάσσεσθαι), not only on account of wrath but also on account of conscience. Because of this you also pay taxes (φόρους τελεῖτε), for they are ministers (λειτουργοί) of God, attending to this very thing. Pay all their dues (ὀφειλάς), revenue

(φόρον) to whom revenue is due, tax (τέλος) to whom tax is due, fear to whom fear is due, honor to whom honor is due.

Yet a consideration of this passage in its context indicates that it is more closely integrated with what comes before and after it than at first appears. First, this passage must be seen as part of Paul's treatment of ἀγάπη, with which he had been dealing in 12:9-21, since immediately after it comes a section on the relationship of ἀγάπη and the Mosaic law (13:8-10). Second, the concluding statement in 12:21, "Do not be conquered by evil but conquer evil by good," leads naturally into a treatment of cooperation with tax-gathering authorities, who were renowned in the ancient world for their avarice and injustice, in short, for their evil. Third, there are some internal connections between 12:9-21 and 13:1-7. The first sentence establishes the connection: "Let everyone be subject to the authorities," for example, by blessing, not cursing, them if they are oppressive (cf. 12:14) and by not retaliating if they perpetrate evil (cf. 12:17-21). There is also the reference to the vengeance of God (12:19 and 13:4). Dunn well explains the broad role of this passage in relation to 12:14-21: "guidance on how to cope with opposition and hostility naturally leads into consideration of political realities" within which the Christ-followers of Rome had to live.[79]

Yet who are the authorities to whom Paul refers? The generally accepted position, reflected in the view of Dunn just cited, is that they are the political rulers in Rome. It is, indeed, possible to point to a specific reason why these verses would have been appropriate in a letter Paul wrote to the Christ-movement in Rome in the early years of Nero's reign. For around 58 CE the population of Rome expressed a clearly documented antipathy toward the tax system (in particular, the corruption of the offices responsible for tax farming in Italy) that resulted in Nero's tax reform.[80] On this view, Paul is urging his addressees not to get involved in opposition to unpopular Roman taxation.

Mark Nanos, on the other hand, has recently mounted a refreshingly innovative case that the governing authorities in 13:1-7 are those of the Roman synagogues.[81] This view forms an important element of his significant new thesis that the Christ-movement in Rome to whom Paul writes was still closely related to the Judean synagogues in that city. In this volume, however, I conceive of the situation in Rome differently. I have argued in chapters four and five that there was a substantial separation between the Judeans of Rome, meeting in large and publicly accessible prayer houses *(proseuchai)*, and the Christ-movement, meeting in the houses of their members (as reflected in Romans 16). Furthermore, the movement, in addition to a substantial proportion of Judeans (who could have retained links with the Judean synagogues) also embraced a substantial number of non-Judeans who seem (to judge by Paul's message in chap. 11) to have had a low opinion of Israel incompatible with their involvement in the *proseuchai*. A similar position emerges in 14:1—15:13, the subject of chapter fourteen below. This general view pushes me away from the particular contextualization of the letter enunciated by Nanos that is necessary to displace the prima facie likelihood that 13:1-7 refers to Roman political authorities.

While this conclusion dispenses me from a detailed dialogue with Nanos on 13:1-7, I will merely mention two individual features of the text that are difficult for his interpretation. First, there is the reference to the sword (μάχαιρα) in 13:4. Nanos faces this difficulty head-on in an able argument in which he cites a number of (mainly) scriptural references to the sword as the basis for his view that here the word has a symbolical or metaphorical sense in relation to the disciplinary authority of the synagogue authorities. Although he rejects the suggestion that this explanation is forced by reason of figurative language Paul uses elsewhere, it is still the case that his readers would more naturally have understood it as a reference to Roman power. The "sword" had a literal significance, referring to the power vested in Roman provincial governors to execute Roman citizens by the sword (the *ius gladii*),[82] but it could also thus have a figurative reference to the power of Roman officials vested with *imperium* to execute those who fell foul of them, whatever the means of death chosen. It simply seems too draconian an image for the much lower levels of discipline allowed to synagogue authorities.

The second difficulty concerns the references to the payment of φόρος and τέλος. Although Nanos suggests possible alternative meanings for these words, their most likely meanings derive from Roman taxation. Bruce Winter, following Strabo, notes that φόρος was known as "the provincial tax." It was a levy placed on people and land that was imposed on everyone in the empire, except for Roman citizens living in Roman colonies who enjoyed the *ius Italicum*. Thus any noncitizens in Rome's audience would have had to pay this. The τέλος, on the other hand, was a levy on income, goods, and services. It was common for items sold in city markets to be liable to this type of tax.[83] Paul seems to appeal to the two main forms of taxation that would have troubled his addressees in their everyday experience rather than having the internal workings of the synagogue in mind.

To conclude, the signs I have noticed in 12:9-21 indicating that Paul's instructions extended beyond the boundaries of the Christ-movement are now significantly confirmed with this set of directions in 13:1-7. Here he explains how one relates to civic and political authorities within the overarching perspective of ἀγάπη. Yet it is possible that Paul was motivated by another factor. As Reasoner has suggested, Paul may also be telling the Christ-followers of Rome to submit to the authorities (especially the emperor) in

13:1-7 as a survival strategy because the perception of Christianity as a super-stition was growing.[84] This interpretation brings out the historically contin-gent nature of what Paul is saying in 13:1-7. As Neil Elliott has eloquently shown, there is no basis whatever for finding here a "theology of the state," especially one conservative in nature.[85]

A Final Instruction on Ἀγάπη (Rom. 13:8-10)

Verses 8-10 round off the treatment of ἀγάπη that began in 12:9:[86]

> Owe (ὀφείλετε) nothing to anyone, except to love (ἀγαπᾶν) another. For he who loves (ὁ ἀγαπῶν) the other has fulfilled (πεπλήρωκεν) the law. For the commandment, "You shall not commit adultery," "You shall not kill," "You shall not steal," "You shall not covet," and any other commandment is summed up in this word, "You shall love your neighbor (πλησίος) as yourself." Love does no wrong to the neighbor. Therefore love (ἀγάπη) is the fulfillment (πλήρωμα) of the law.

Having set out some of the substance of ἀγάπη in 12:9—13:7, Paul con-cludes his treatment with a consideration of its relationship to the Mosaic law, which is indisputably in view here, given the quotations from the Ten Com-mandments at the beginning of 13:9[87] and the quotation of Lev. 19:18 at the end of the verse. Why return to the law? Dunn notes that the treatment of the law in 1:18—11:36 "was bound to raise the question of its continuing role as norm for personal and social ethics in the redefined people of God," and this is reasonable enough, subject to the difficulties that beset the use of the word "ethics" for Paul's exhortation in chaps. 12–13.[88]

The real problem arises when we seek to identify how Paul saw and pre-sented the relationship between the law of Moses and the ἀγάπη that typi-fied life in Christ. For Dunn the answer is: "With the people of God redefined in nonethnic categories it was obviously important that the law, so much identified with ethnic Israel as such, be similarly redefined—not aban-doned or attacked . . . otherwise continuity between the epochal phases of the people and purpose of God would be lost." For Dunn, the law provided "the rule of love" (12:9) with "a model and resource" that "such a demanding lifestyle" needed to be sustainable.[89] For him, "fulfillment of the law" means "a meeting of the law's demands."[90]

I submit, however, that this approach misses the point of Paul's message on the relationship between law and love. The best starting point for this subject is what Paul says in his (earlier) letter to the Galatians. At one point Paul expresses a sentiment similar to that of Rom. 13:8-10: "For the whole law is fulfilled (πεπλήρωται) in the one statement, namely, 'You will love your neighbor as yourself'" (Gal. 5:14), where Lev. 19:18 is also quoted. I have elsewhere set out my position in regard to this verse, again in disagreement with Dunn, who argues that Gal. 5:14 indicates Paul was not opposed to the ethical section of the Israelite law.[91] Dunn's view rests on an unconvincing distinction he draws between "the law" and "the works of the law"[92] and is inconsistent with Paul's strenuous efforts in Galatians to demonstrate that the law has had its day (well seen in his metaphor that its former duty as a παιδαγωγός, a moral guide if ever there were one, is now ended [Gal. 3:23-25]).

Most importantly, Dunn's position falters before the vital interconnection between ἀγάπη and the Spirit, from which we discern what Paul means by saying that love is the fulfillment of the law. Paul's point in Galatians is that the very best the law could provide, ἀγάπη of neighbor (Lev. 19:18), is now available to his congregations by an entirely different route—the Spirit. For ἀγάπη is the first fruit of the Spirit (Gal. 5:22). To say that the law is fulfilled (πεπλήρωται) by love does not affect this conclusion. This word is never used in the Septuagint for the performance of the law. It requires another sense in Gal. 5:14, most plausibly to refer to the consummation of the will and plan of God.[93] "Fulfillment" in this sense, in a context in which ἀγάπη comes from the Spirit, means that the moral demands of the law no longer have any role for Christ-believers. For the law and the Spirit are stark alternatives: "If you are led by the Spirit, you are not under the Law" (Gal. 5:18). In the new era in Christ, the law is irrelevant to the moral dimensions of the life of those who have faith in him.

In Romans Paul explains how law and love are related in a manner that is consistent with, yet develops, his viewpoint in Galatians. To appreciate the point he is making in 13:8-10, we need to remember that earlier in Romans Paul had relied on the fourth commandment mentioned here, "Do not covet," to impart the fundamental problem with the Mosaic law. In chap. 7 he had explained how sin had manipulated the law to its own ends and produced all desire in Israel. In this process, the commandment "Do not covet" had had a programmatic significance: "I would not have known desire," says Israel (with whom Paul identifies), "unless the law had said 'You shall not covet.'" Apart from the law, sin was dead. Before the Mosaic law, Israel had been "alive," but with its arrival sin revived and Israel "died" (7:7-9). This explicitly negative picture of the law, with its emphatic assertion that the law had failed in its objective to provide life, even though Paul hastens to protest (too much?) that it is holy and just and good (7:12), had not come into sight in Galatians. In this letter, especially in Gal. 3:10-12, Paul suggests (admittedly in a compressed argument) that the problem with the law was that

Israelites had not kept it and that it was difficult (but perhaps not impossible in principle) to keep.[94] In Romans 7 Paul goes much further, setting out detailed reasons for the failure of the law and coming close to asserting that it was impossible to fulfill its demands.

While we have no reason to doubt that the law is summed up in the expression "You shall love your neighbor as yourself," Paul's explanation of the character of the law in Romans 7 inevitably entails that this noble ideal could not come into effect by operation of the law. When Paul says, therefore, that the person who loves has "fulfilled the law," he means that he or she has achieved the ideal of the Mosaic law, which was, however, never realized by that law. Someone who has faith in Christ is thus able to obtain the best that the law promised, although never delivered, but by an entirely different route.[95]

For these reasons, Paul's objective in concluding his discussion of ἀγάπη (13:8-10) with an explanation of its relation to the Mosaic law is readily understood within a social identity framework. Here he draws back from the attitudes and behavior that embody and manifest that defining virtue of the Christ-movement to remind his readers of its role in sharply differentiating them from the Israelite outgroup. By reminding them that the nature of existence in Christ is achieved by a route separate from that of the law, he carries on with his policy of portraying their identity, of telling them who they are, in relation to who they are not. In Christ they have been recategorized into a new group whose moral life rests on a new foundation and is distinct both from Israel and from the lifestyle of their non-Israelite neighbors, not only reflective Stoics but also the ordinary folk for whom idolatry, in the contexts of political and domestic religious practice, still had strong appeal.

Romans 13:11-14

To many commentators the temptation to apply the word "eschatological" to 13:11-14 has proved irresistible. Dunn is typical: "The opening phrase recalls the recipients to the eschatological perspective so basic to Christian self-understanding—not only a new but the final age of God's purpose," before he cites 3:26, 8:18, and 11:5, which have in common a reference to "the present time," presumably significant because they stand in contrast with "the age to come," although that phrase is never used by Paul and the only explicit contrast with the future appears in 8:18.[96] Later Dunn adds that "the eschatological tension is strongly marked" and that "the note of imminent expectation is equally strong."[97]

I have already had occasion in chapter eleven above to challenge recourse to "eschatology" in understanding Paul and have noted the different interpretation possible as to Paul's view of the future when one adopts an understanding of time in attunement with ancient Mediterranean views. To the extent that by "eschatological" is meant the pressures induced by a sense that the end is near, that God is about to intervene decisively in human experience with the second (and final) return of his Son, I submit that the case for 13:11-14 being eschatological has been greatly overstated and that some alternative and more appropriate framework is needed for this passage.

In 1932 C. H. Dodd noted that, whereas in 1 Thessalonians and even in 1 Corinthians Paul appeared to think that the arrival of the Lord would occur possibly within a few months and certainly within the lifetime of most present members of the movement, it was striking that in Romans there is no mention of the parousia of the Lord, except in these verses. He then made these telling observations: "The whole argument stands independent of any such expectation. The forecast of history in chapter 11 is hardly framed for a period of a few months or years. There is no suggestion of 'interim ethics' in 12.1—13.10. The positive value assigned to political institutions in 13.1-6 stands in contrast to the depreciation of family life in view of the shortness of time in 1 Corinthians 7."[98]

From this evidence he drew the following conclusions: "Clearly the urgent sense of the imminence of 'the End' was fading in Paul's mind as the years passed. He dwelt more and more on the thought that Christians were already living in the New Age, and the date at which it should be consummated became a matter of indifference. Only in the present passage the old idea of nearness of the Day of the Lord survives to give point to his moral exhortations." I submit that this is a reasonably accurate analysis (although Dodd too was working with modern notions of time that sharply differentiate the present from the future). Indeed, to this one might add the further consideration (to be explored below) that "eschatological teaching is minimal in the passage when the content is considered."[99] While the language and conceptuality of "eschatology" are inappropriate here, the social identity perspective being utilized throughout this volume offers a more promising resource for interpreting this passage.

In chapter two above I noted the place of the temporal dimension in the existence and maintenance of the identity of a group, and I applied these insights to 8:18-39 in chapter eleven. Members see the groups to which they belong as being generated over time. The very fact that we possess identities depends on our capacity to relate fragmentary experiences across temporal boundaries: "Even momentary self-images involve a simultaneous awareness of the present (self-in-context), the past and the anticipated future. . . . A sense of identity—of being oneself—hence necessitates both retroactive and proactive memory."[100]

As social actors the members understand the groups to which they belong as historical phenomena, stretching backward in time and forward into the future. One aspect of this is that the (future-oriented) actions of collectivities are often directed toward a future beyond the lifetimes of existing category members.[101] All this means that groups tell themselves who they are in part by imagining where they are going. Extrapolations of their group's future contribute to their sense of identity in the present. One aspect of this is that ingroup members are concerned to persuade other members to accept and endorse positively valued "visions" of what will happen to the ingroup in the future.[102] A social identity approach to time such as this (although reflecting an earlier development of this field of social psychology) has previously proved useful in relation to 1 and 2 Thessalonians.[103] How can it help with Rom. 13:11-14?

What Paul says in 13:11-14 is certainly predicated on a belief (which he presumably shares with his Roman audience) that a glorious destiny, which he calls "salvation" (σωτηρία), awaits them in a forthcoming time. Whereas elsewhere in Romans he mentions the future judgment of God (2:1-11), that judgment is not referred to here, probably because Paul is proceeding on the assumption that his addressees are and will be righteous when the final events occur and will not therefore be judged (as I have suggested in chapter seven). They will attain the eternal life, glory, honor, and peace promised to those who do good (2:7, 10). It is particularly noticeable that the horrors of the judgment are not cited here as a motivation for moral behavior in the meantime, even though that message comes through loud and clear in 2:1-10. The picture of the future in 13:11-14 is an unreservedly positive one. At the same time, just as we saw in relation to 8:18-39, the future here is organically connected with, and on the horizon of, the present. It is day to the present night; the latter inevitably gives way to the former.

Paul's point in the passage is that the Roman Christ-followers should be as they will one day become. The imagery of future salvation serves to tell them who they are or should be in the present, not to warn them that the future is near. Paul contrasts the day that is beckoning with the night that they are currently experiencing. They should be or become people of "the day," not of the night. This is primarily a means of reminding them who they are, of promoting the three dimensions of group belonging (cognitive, evaluative, emotional), people of the day, in contrast to who they are not, people who will not experience the glories of the day. Paul wants them to be people of the day ahead of time.

Consider the first part of the passage: "And this, knowing the time (καιρός), that already it is the hour for you to wake from sleep, for our salvation (σωτηρία) is now nearer than when we (first) came to have faith (ἐπιστεύσαμεν). The night is advanced; the day is near." There is no urgent sense of a pressing or imminent future here. That he says it is the hour to wake is just another way of saying the day (the key metaphor he needs) is near, a point he also makes explicitly. It is entirely self-evident, moreover, that salvation is now nearer than when they first believed. Paul's point is not that they need to get themselves in order because they have little time left, but rather that the anticipated future provides a model for their identity *right now!*

That is why he then proceeds: "Therefore let us throw off the works of darkness, and let us put on the weapons of light. Let us live our lives respectably as in the day, not in revelry and drunkenness, not in debauchery and sexual excess, not in dissension and jealousy. But put on the Lord Jesus Christ and make no provision for the flesh to satisfy its desires." The key expression for the existence that Paul endorses is εὐσχημόνως περι-πατήσωμεν, literally, "let us walk respectably." The verb περιπατέω is common in Paul to designate manner of life or lifestyle.[104] Within the theoretical framework adopted here it designates a particular identity, as also at 1 Thess. 2:12; 4:1, 12.[105] The instance at 1 Thess. 4:12 is also qualified by the adverb εὐσχημόνως ("in order that you might adopt a respectable identity in relation to outsiders").

Thus Paul's concern is that they should be Christ-followers of a particular type in the present, not that the Lord is about to return at any moment. The forthcoming has relevance in that it gives the present a particular character, not as the focus of ardent expectation and longing. Here we can see that the imagery of the Day of the Lord fuses with urban imagery (from Rome and other cities of the Greco-Roman world) of the distinction between the sobriety of day and the sinfulness that characterized the night, with its drunkenness, carousing, and fornication.

Conclusion

In chaps. 12–13 we see Paul providing for the benefit of the Christ-movement in Rome a detailed guide to the "norms," the identity descriptors that they should hold onto and manifest as followers of Christ. Perhaps the major area in which Paul saw room for improvement was in the relations between Judeans and non-Judeans within the congregations; to an area of the text that seems to relate to that issue, 14:1—15:13, we must now proceed.

14

The Weak and the Strong
(Romans 14:1—15:13)

Preliminary Issues concerning Romans 14:1—15:13

One of the most important milestones in the history of research into Romans came with the publication in 1971 of Paul Minear's short but potent monograph, *The Obedience of Faith*. As W. S. Campbell has correctly noted, it was only with this book that a full-blown situational reading of the letter finally appeared, based mainly on Romans 14–15.[1] The current chapter of this volume is devoted to 14:1—15:13. Its significance in relation to the Roman context into which Paul dispatched this letter will become manifest as the argument in this chapter develops.

Romans 14:1—15:13 gives all the appearance of conveying an integrated message to the recipients of Paul's letter that relates to the need for them to be unified and mutually accepting of one another. A prominent sign of this integration is the repetition of the key word "welcome" (προσλαμβάνεσθε) on four occasions in this section of the letter. Paul urges on his addressees the practice of welcoming at 14:1 and 15:7 and also observes as support for his argument that God (14:3) and Christ (15:7) have welcomed (προσελάβετο). Other indications of this communicative intent emerge in his exhorting them not to judge (14:13) one another and to think the same thing among one another according to Jesus Christ (15:5), and also in the scriptural quotation that proclaims a common rejoicing among non-Israelites and Israel (15:10). This message is especially directed to two subgroups of the Christ-movement in Rome who are identified as "the weak in faith" (ἀσθενοῦντα τῇ πίστει) and "the strong" (οἱ δύνατοι; 15:1), between whom there are differences of opinion over food, wine, and days.

It is also possible to point to strong connections between this part of the letter and chaps. 12–13. Both passages contain material that relates to the attitudes and behavior appropriate to members of the Christ-movement, what I am calling "norms" in a social identity sense or, more particularly, "identity descriptors." There are also some specific connections. For example, after the abundance of material relating to ἀγάπη within the movement in chaps. 12–13, it comes as no surprise when Paul comments at 14:15 that a person who behaves in the way he is censuring no longer walks in accordance with ἀγάπη. In other words, Paul is presenting the problems highlighted in 14:1—15:13 as a particular arena for the exercise or nonexercise of the ἀγάπη he has just dealt with at length in chaps. 12–13. There are also linkages between 14:1—15:13 and chaps. 1–11 and 15:14—16:27. Of particular importance, as we will see later, is the issue of bringing Judean and non-Judean Christ-followers together and the arrogant attitudes that the latter group were expressing toward the former.

Two initial questions arise in relation to 14:1—15:13. These concern whether Paul is appealing to actual problems he knew were besetting the Roman congregations and the identity of "the weak in faith" and "the strong." I will consider these issues in a provisional fashion, pending an interpretation of this part of the letter within the identity framework in a Roman cultural context used in the earlier chapters of this volume. This detailed interpretation occupies the second major section of this chapter.

An Actual Situation or a Literary Construct?

For some scholars, for example, Robert Karris, what Paul has to say about the weak and the strong in 14:1—15:13 is not based on strife within the Christ-movement in Rome but is better explained as general Pauline moral teaching that is adapted and generalized especially from Paul's earlier discussion in 1 Corinthians 8–10 and is addressed to a problem that might arise in any community.[2] Probably the most common view today, for good reason, however, is that Paul's remarks in Rom. 14:1—15:13 were directed toward problems he knew were affecting the Christ-movement in Rome. I will now set out basic support for this proposition, although it will be confirmed by the subsequent discussion in this chapter.

We have seen in chapter five above that Romans 16, which was always part of the letter sent to Rome, indicates that Paul knew a number of the Christ-followers of Rome, especially Prisca and Aquila, Epaenetus, and the mother of Rufus, and must have been in receipt of information from them. Some of this information was quite detailed; otherwise he would not have been able to say, for example, that a certain Mary had worked hard among them (16:6). Given this, it seems likely that Paul had received word of a problem in Rome that prompted him to include the material we now have in 14:1—15:13. Why would he risk sending such exhortations, which would have made him look ridiculous if there was no basis for them, unless he was not already sure of the difficulties he identifies?

John Barclay has suggested further considerations in favor of a particular context in Rome for this passage. These include the differences from 1 Corinthians 8–10, the space Paul devotes to the subject, his careful description of opposing positions, the prominence of the passage at the end of the section containing moral exhortation (which Barclay calls "paraenesis"), and the fact that he confidently numbers himself among the strong (15:1).

Barclay helpfully observes that the fact that Paul writes at a fairly general level does not weigh against this result, since for communities he had not founded "it would be presumptuous to write with instructions so specific as to give the appearance that he thought himself entitled to regulate their affairs in detail."[3] Reasoner has proposed an interesting argument along similar lines. He argues that the "strong" and the "weak" designations must have been current in Rome *before* Paul wrote the letter (and, I may add, he must have known about them from a Roman source), for the principal reason that it would have been counterproductive for him to drop these labels on the congregations.[4] Reasoner has also pointed out numerous respects in which the language of "strong" and "weak" would have been at home in the status-obsessed society that was first-century CE Rome.[5] It is most unlikely that whoever Paul was referring to as the "weak in faith" had applied that designation to themselves.[6] The terminology of "weak" and "strong" is probably an invention of the strong, and it is interesting that Paul adopts this language from the Roman congregation even though it reflects the stereotypical viewpoint of the strong.

The preferable view, therefore, is that Paul addresses an actual situation in Rome; he is not just generalizing on the basis of his experience in Corinth. As well as the positive reasons for this view just noted, the proposal of Karris has run into strong opposition, for example, from Karl Donfried, for his distinguishing 14:1—15:13 too easily from chaps. 12–13 and for the reason that his arguments that Paul has here modified 1 Corinthians 8–10 are not plausible on inspection.[7] Part of Karris's case involves denying the popular view that the weak are "Jews" and the strong are "gentiles." For him, the weak are simply weak and the strong simply strong.[8] This runs up against the problem that Rom. 15:7, which starts a section dealing with Judeans and non-Judeans, begins with the connecting word διό, meaning "therefore," which strongly links what has been said previously to what is to follow on this topic. Karris needs to have recourse to 1 Corinthians to address this problem! This brings us to the second initial question, concerning the identity of the strong and the weak.

The Identity of the Weak and the Strong

Who were the weak and the strong? One view is that they cannot be identified, with the position of the weak being regarded as the most problematic, since Paul identifies himself with the strong in 15:1.[9] Yet this seems a surprisingly meager position to adopt in face of the considerable amount of data given in the text and the extent to which it is possible to demonstrate connections between what he says here and what he sets out elsewhere in the letter in relation to identified subgroups of the Roman Christ-movement.

The vast majority of scholars, who do seek to identify the weak and the strong, have two broad options. The first considers that all concerned were members of the Christ-movement, but then this option subdivides into a variety of views on the representation of Judeans and non-Judeans among the groups. A second option, espoused by Mark Nanos and part of his overall thesis that the Christ-movement of Rome was still within the orbit of the Judean synagogues of the capital, argues that the weak were Judeans not connected with the Christ-movement.[10] I accept the former option. The main problem with Nanos's interesting and important suggestion in the context of the case I am making in this volume is twofold. First, chap. 16, in pointing unequivocally to Christ-followers meeting in houses when we know that the Judeans of Rome met in large, tailor-made *proseuchai,* suggests a separation between the Christ-movement and synagogues. Second, the only interest Paul shows in the rest of Romans is in bringing together under one common identity Judean and non-Judean members of the movement and, as we will see, this seems to be his aim in 14:1—15:13, with the houses where they gathered the proposed locus of this reconciliation.[11] This does not mean, however, that some Christ-followers were not still attending the Judean *proseuchai* in Rome; I return to that question below.

If, therefore, the strong and the weak were located within the Christ-movement, what was their precise character? The best indication probably does not come from the way they are described or the attitudes and actions attributed to them, which Paul Sampley wrongly suggests exhaust their identifiable characteristics.[12] For, as Joel Marcus has observed, the linkage between the "weak" and the "strong," on the one hand, and Judean and non-Judean subgroups among the Roman Christ-followers, on the other, is supported by the transition between 14:1—15:6 and 15:7-13. This transition is marked by use of the strong connective διό in 15:7, but also by the fact that in 15:8-9 Paul goes on to say that Christ has been the servant both of the circumcision on account of the promises God made to the fathers and of the non-Judeans on account of God's mercy.[13] Immediately after he quotes scripture to the effect that the non-Israelites should rejoice with Israel (literally "his people"). All this means that whatever Paul has been getting at in 14:1—15:6, it relates directly to his earlier interest in the separate subgroups of Judeans and non-Judeans and the fact that both of them have been incorporated within the new identity under God, as announced programmatically in 3:21-31 and elaborated on in the prototypical Abraham in chap. 4. Scholars such as Wayne Meeks and Sampley who resist the relevance of Paul's admonitions to these groups underestimate the interconnections between this passage and the rest of the letter, unlike others such as Robert Jewett who do not.[14] This line on the meaning of 14:1—15:13 also renders views that introduce issues that would be entirely new to this section of the letter (such as the idea of M. Rauer that the weak were non-Judean Christ-followers who abstained from meat and perhaps wine on certain days under the influence of pagan religions)[15] prima facie unlikely.

Yet this does not mean that we should rush to a crude identification of the weak with Judean Christ-followers and the strong with non-Judean Christ-followers. After all, Paul numbers himself among the strong, except in relation to their scorn for the weak (15:1). As mentioned above, the "strong/weak" terminology has probably been invented (or adopted) by the strong in Rome to reflect their stereotypical grasp of the situation in a way that would hardly have been welcomed by those they labeled as "the weak."[16] In spite of this, Paul allies himself with them. The critical factor in this perspective on the two groups is the Mosaic law. Paul says at 14:14, "I know and am persuaded in the Lord that nothing is unclean (κοινόν) in itself, but it is unclean for anyone who thinks it is unclean," and shares with the strong the conviction that the Christ-follower may eat anything (14:2, 20). So much for the Levitical food laws! As Barclay notes, "This constitutes nothing less than a fundamental rejection of the Jewish law in one of its most sensitive dimensions."[17] To adjudge how other Judeans contemporary with Paul (but not sharing his convictions on this matter) would react to such a sentiment, we need recall only the horror felt by Peter in being asked to eat something unclean (κοινόν), which he had never done before (Acts 10:14). This attitude is of a piece with Paul's assertion that he is no longer "under law" (ὑπὸ νόμον, Rom. 6:14-15) and his picture of the failure of the law to help Israel (with whom he identifies) in chap. 7.

We may deduce from this, therefore, that a central dimension to the identity of the strong is a belief that the Mosaic law does not bind the Christ-follower. While it was possible for an Israelite like Paul to hold this belief, we would expect it also to characterize many non-Judean Christ-followers, especially those who harbored arrogant attitudes toward Israel. The non-Israelites Paul addresses in 11:13-24, especially those he condemns in 11:18 for boasting over the Israelites who have been cut off from the olive tree, could not have had a positive regard for the law of Israel. No doubt they felt the same derision for the means by which Israel preserved its identity as a people as they evidently felt for the people themselves. We must envisage that they would have shared Paul's views that no food was impure and therefore include them among the strong.

As for the identity of the weak, the core of this group would most probably have been Judeans who had not come to Paul's view that the Mosaic law was not binding on Christ-followers. That there were people like this among the Christ-movement in Rome is demanded by the lengths to which Paul goes in chaps. 6–7 to argue that the law has no part to play in the attainment of righteousness. The Judean Christ-followers who needed convincing that Moses was no longer the route to righteousness would also hold the view that prescriptions in the law relating to food and holy days were still in force. Nevertheless, it is also possible that there were some non-Judeans, and in Rome these were "Greeks," who had taken on certain aspects of law observance, possibly relating to food and days. Thus, although the weak and the strong did not represent a tidy split between Judeans and non-Judeans, the differentiating factor was attitude to the Mosaic law, and it is likely that the core elements of each group were Judeans among the weak and Greeks among the strong.[18] That is why Paul can so smoothly proceed from calling for the mutual acceptance of weak and strong in 14:1—15:6 to a paradigmatic description of Christ's service to both Judeans and non-Judeans in 15:7-12.[19]

When one looks at the specific activities mentioned, this position is confirmed. Thus, although the Mosaic law does not prohibit the consumption of meat and wine (which has opened the door for a variety of other explanations as to the rationale of this abstinence), Judeans in non-Judean contexts did often restrict their diets to avoid eating meat and drinking wine, probably to avoid the possibility (or even the appearance) of contact with idolatrous practices connected with these substances.[20]

Social Identity and the Interpretation of Romans 14:1—15:13

Context of the Interpretation

Before I launch into an interpretation of 14:1—15:13, it will be useful briefly to recall aspects of the Roman context of the letter that were explored in chapters three, four, and five above. Paul was writing to a movement comprising members from different ethnic groups, Judeans and Greeks, who had clashed with one another, often violently, in various places around the Mediterranean for a century, with several examples having occurred not long previously, in 39–44 CE. The events in Alexandria in 38–41 had been particularly serious for the Judeans. Both groups no doubt contained members who nursed the ethnocentric and stereotypical antagonism toward other ethnic groups common in this culture. In addition, these people were living in a city with marked socioeconomic divisions, and they cherished attitudes to honor that easily accommodated feelings of envy and competitiveness toward those not members of one's ingroup, especially meaning one's kin and retainers living in the same house as oneself. Rivalry between families from the base of their households was a feature of Roman life at elite and nonelite levels. Yet the

Christ-movement met in just such households, unlike the Judeans in the city, who met each Sabbath in tailor-made prayer houses *(proseuchai)* at least as impressive as the mid-first-century example in the small town of Ostia. The forms of socialization associated with these different architectural settings for Judeans and Christ-followers also represented another point of difference in this environment.

The probability that such an unstable mix of factors would produce tension and even conflict within the Christ-movement was high, and there are indications in the letter prior to chaps. 14–15 that the probable had become the actual. The clearest example comes with Paul's rebuke of the non-Judeans in chap. 11: "Do not make honor claims over the branches" (11:18) and "Do not entertain haughty thoughts" (11:20). Paul had been trying to remind the two subgroups of their new common identity, but without seeking to erase their distinctive identities, throughout chaps. 1–11. In chaps. 12–13 he had begun to set out at a fairly general level attitudes and behaviors necessary for this new identity ("norms"/identity descriptors) that stressed the centrality of ἀγάπη. He had also exhorted them "not to think arrogantly" (μὴ ὑπερφρονεῖν), contrary to how they should think (παρ᾽ ὃ δεῖ φρονεῖν), but think (φρονεῖν) with self-restrained thinking (σωφρονεῖν; 12:3), to think in harmony toward one another (12:16).

The evidence just cited, however, does not support any idea that the Christ-followers of different ethnicity were completely estranged from one another. Non-Judeans boasting over Judeans (11:18) demands the presence of representatives from both subgroups. As Andrew Clarke has observed, the contact between Christ-followers "of different persuasions" was "sufficient to cause tensions." He also thinks that differing stances regarding food and holy days (which we will soon consider) presupposes situations where they were clearly in contact with one another.[21]

All this provides some key elements of the context within which we should seek to interpret 14:1—15:13.

Weak in Faith and the Contrast with Abraham

"Welcome the person who is weak in faith," Paul begins this section of his letter, "but not for disputes over opinions" (14:1). To those of his audience who have been listening closely to the letter as it was read out to them (perhaps by Phoebe), the expression "weak in faith" (ἀσθενοῦντα τῇ πίστει) would not have struck like a bolt from the blue. Earlier in the letter Paul had mentioned that Abraham had not "weakened in faith" (ἀσθενήσας τῇ πίστει) when God had promised that he would become the father of many nations. That Abraham was about one hundred years old and his wife Sarah was barren had not led him to distrust God. Instead he grew strong in faith (ἐνεδυναμώθη τῇ πίστει) and gave glory to God (4:16-20). As I have argued in chapter eight above, Paul presents Abraham as the prototypical believer in God and in this sense the ancestor of all who have faith in Christ, both non-Israelite and (in a noticeable divergence from the position in Galatians) Israelite (4:11-12).

Yet central to the way Paul portrays Abraham is the enormity of what Abraham was asked to believe—that a man one hundred years old with an old and barren wife would become the father of many nations. As Paul sees it, the condition of Abraham and his wife Sarah demands that he be strong, not weak, in faith, and this is precisely how he describes him, even if Genesis can allow Abraham a doubt or two.[22] Accordingly, Abraham is presented as the prototypical believer, not only to the extent that he embraces (in Paul's view) Israelite and non-Israelite but also in being strong, not weak, in faith. With this in mind, when Paul begins chap. 14 with the injunction to welcome the weak in faith, he is signaling that such a person has not reached a level of faith that Abraham had reached and is paving the way for the introduction of those who have. These are the people mentioned as the strong (οἱ δυνατοί) in 15:1, but whose presence may be divined earlier as those representing the converse viewpoint to the weak in the series of opposites that occupy chap. 14. To describe someone as "weak in faith" at the start of this section of the letter is to portray them in a negative way, as falling in the long shadow of failure to meet the standard set by Abraham.

Given that the weak are probably a group predominantly composed of law-observant Judean members of the movement, with possibly some Greeks, the comparison with Abraham would have hit particularly hard, perhaps as soon as they heard reference to Abraham *not* having been weak in faith in 4:19-20. The Judeans in view would have regarded Abraham as their ancestor by physical descent, and Paul was now referring to them using a designation—not their own—that highlighted their difference from the patriarch on a matter of the most fundamental importance.

Households and Welcoming

Paul's direction is: "Welcome the person who is weak in faith, but not for disputes about opinions" (14:1). The word for "welcome" here (προσλαμβάνεσθαι), aimed by Paul at his addressees again in 15:7 (and used of the action of God and Christ at 14:13 and 15:7, respectively), deserves our closest attention for the insight it offers into his communicative purpose. Fitzmyer explains the word as meaning "take to oneself, take into one's household," hence "welcome," "accept with an open heart."[23] It is the meaning of "take into one's household" that is particularly germane here. The only other time in his correspondence (apart from these four instances) Paul uses this word is at Phlm. 17, where it certainly relates to welcoming into a house. Similarly, Dunn says it has the force of "receive or accept into one's society, home, circle of acquaintances," and he also cites 2 Macc. 10:15 and Acts 28:2.[24]

This raises the intriguing possibility that Paul has in mind welcoming people into one another's houses. Certainly Rom 14:1: "Welcome . . . but not for disputes about opinions," seems to envisage some such welcome into a specific place, and the most likely place is the house of the one being urged to do the welcoming. Donfried notes that this verb is used to address someone who is not already in intimate communion with the one addressed (Phlm. 17; Acts 28:2).[25]

The phenomenon of households in Rome that are antagonistic to one another may well be in view here. In chapter four above I noted that where *inimicitiae* supplanted a former friendly relationship, the public declaration "would be accompanied by the announcement that the new *inimicus* was no longer welcomed in one's house."[26] It is probable that Paul, aware that *inimicitiae* (or some form of personal animosity like them) have been troubling the congregations in Rome, here prescribes the specific antidote for such a malady. Some owners of households in the movement and their friends and clients have presumably reached the view that the Mosaic law is not necessary. They have also expressed negative sentiments (which must have an ethnic dimension given the subject at issue) toward other members (from other households, Judean in the main) who still observe the law and, quite possibly, attend Sabbath meetings of Judeans in the *proseuchai* of the capital, and thus maintain a social base in the Judean community, while also taking part in the meetings of the Christ-movement.[27]

But does the use of the word προσλαμβάνεσθαι of God and then of Christ, not in a domestic context, militate against this particular sense? Probably not, for the reason that the very attribution of the same word to the activities of human beings and of God and Christ would suggest that its precise reference is likely to be different. Yet, in addition to the word προσλαμβάνεσθαι, there are also other signs in the text of a household context, in the use of words with the stem οἰκ-.

The most important of these is οἰκέτης at 14:4. The word means a domestic servant or slave. Yet this is the only time in his correspondence that Paul uses the word. He could just as easily have employed the usual term for slave (δοῦλος), as he does thrice elsewhere in this letter and in fourteen other places in his letters.[28] John H. Elliott offers an erudite note on the use of οἰκέτης in 1 Pet. 2:18 in his magisterial commentary on that letter.[29] Included in Elliott's treatment is the observation that the plural form οἰκέται at this point in 1 Peter "makes explicit the connection of these slaves to the 'household' *(oikos)* and thus signals the shift of focus from the civic (2:13-17) to the domestic realm."[30] In a Pauline context, where this is the only time that οἰκέτης appears, while δοῦλος finds seventeen examples, it is hard to resist the conclusion that Paul is also seeking to emphasize the household relevance of this material.

There is, indeed, a natural context within which this word had a literal significance in Rom. 14:1—15:13. I noted in chapter five above that the two groups of Christ-followers described as belonging to the households of Aristobulus and Narcissus in 16:10-11 were probably domestic slaves or perhaps freedmen. These people were, literally, οἰκέται. While this indicates something about the social level of some of the Roman Christ-followers, others, such as Prisca and Aquila, had a higher socioeconomic status.

Second, there is the use of the word οἰκοδομή at 14:19 and 15:2. The word originally meant the building of a house (οἶκος), a word that appears in 16:5. But, like the equivalent Latin word *aedificatio*, it acquired a figurative sense, "upbuilding" or "edification." It is a popular word with Paul. It usually has the figurative meaning, but on two occasions it is used literally.[31] In addition, the verbal form οἰκοδομέω appears soon after this passage, at 15:20, in the literal sense. It is possible, therefore, that in 14:19 and 15:2, while the meaning may be predominantly figurative, it is difficult not to exclude the additional sense of strengthening the various households (οἶκος) that made up the movement in Rome by improving their relations with one another.

Interpreting Romans 14:1-12

In the light of the above analysis, it is likely that in 14:1 Paul is urging the strong, who included some Greek and some law-free Judean Christ-followers, to make it a practice[32] of welcoming the weak, which included a core of law-observant Judean and perhaps some Greek Christ-followers, into their homes, but not for the purpose of arguing with them. Paul may either mean they should initiate this practice and go on with it, or continue with it but not on the basis that they should argue with the weak over what they should eat. The latter is the more likely alternative, both because, as noted above, Paul appears to be addressing a situation where the rival groups had not been completely estranged from one another and because of the manner in which he continues his argument in 14:2. This may suggest that the strong have more resources, and they host meetings, although since nothing suggests that the movement in Rome included members of the elite, we should not envisage an invitation to anything other than the ground floor of a reasonable *insula*.

The reference to "disputes" in 14:1 requires careful consideration. Although drawing on an area of social theory different from the one applied here (in his case that of Coser and Simmel relating to conflict) and speaking of another text (*First Clement*), William Lane has well described the sort of task Paul faced as follows:

> Conflict resolution does not normally occur of its own accord. It requires the intervention of a "specialist" in formulating solutions to intragroup conflicts. The "specialist" is a person with authority to determine and articulate the norms that are relevant to a discordant situation, who is capable of showing how these norms pertain to the basic values and experiences of any given group. The result is almost always increased group structure and institution building as a response to the challenge of existing social arrangements.[33]

This is accurate as far as it goes. Yet we are able to introduce more precision if we assess the problem in Rome in the light of the discussion in chapter two above concerning the role of debate in shaping group identity. A central insight of self-categorization theory (that allowed it to chart a different course from its social identity parent) is that intragroup consensus can never be assumed. Many groups contain divisions between members rather than consensus. This situation often generates an attempt by the members to achieve consensus, through argument, negotiation, and persuasion. On this view, expressed by Alexander Haslam and his colleagues, groups are more often caught up in the process of consensualization, the shared quest for agreement, rather than simply resting happily in a state of consensus.[34] Yet this seems altogether too benign a view for 14:1, and another recent social psychological proposal seems more pertinent to the problem Paul is addressing in Rome. Fabio Sani and Steve Reicher, while agreeing that debate is important in shaping group identity and prompting group action, question its restriction to the effort to achieve consensus. Sometimes, they propose, certain group members will see particular positions as incommensurable with their own to such an extent that to permit them would be to subvert the very nature of the group. Such an impasse may result in schism within the group.

The arguments (διαλογισμοί) mentioned by Paul in 14:1 seem to have as their likely consequence, in his estimation, schism rather than consensus. As someone hoping to exercise a leadership role over these Christ-believers—to push them in a direction concordant with the needs of the movement as a whole—he needs to take this discussion in hand and to persuade those indulging in these debates to desist from doing so. To see what is at stake here, it is helpful to recall the differentiation of ethnic identity into three separate though connected levels of abstraction (micro, median, and macro) formulated by

Fredrik Barth (mentioned in chapter three above). These levels correspond to the ordinary members of the group, the leaders of the group, and outsiders with power over the group. The micro level of ethnic identity focuses on persons and their interactions, the events of human lives, the management of selves in the context of relationships, demands, values, ideas, and symbols.[35] This is the level represented by those initiating or being subjected to the arguments referred to in 14:1, although the case that these are based on ethnic differences will be made below. Paul's intervention into the situation in Rome occurs at the median level, which is the arena of "entrepreneurship, leadership and rhetoric," where collectivities are set in motion. Processes at the median level intervene to modify people's attitudes and action on the micro level and fashion many aspects of the boundaries and dichotomies of ethnicity.[36] In 14:1 Paul signals the problem that will trigger his response, as an entrepreneur of the group's identity, in an argument that will unfold in this section of the letter until we reach 15:13.

As noted at the end of chapter two, in a context where there is disagreement (such as Paul introduces in 14:1 and develops thereafter) a leader is someone who has the skill, through argument, negotiation, and persuasion, to manage the debate, to neutralize views antagonistic to his or her own, and to stimulate a process of consensualization around a particular vision of group identity. This is what Paul is attempting in 14:1—15:13. The way Paul crafts his argument confirms the importance of his rhetoric in creating, installing, and maintaining a particular social identity among the Christ-followers of Rome.

In 14:2 we learn that the one who has faith eats everything and the one who is weak eats vegetables. The priority given to the former class in this formulation is striking. It is not immediately obvious whether Paul is here referring to joint meals of the Christ-movement or to meals by these two groups in their own settings. Yet probably the former is in view, since otherwise there would be no opportunity for the disputes mentioned in 14:1. As already noted, Paul seemed to be responding to dysfunctional gatherings of the Christ-movement in Rome rather than the total isolation of one group from another. Perhaps we should imagine gatherings in a strong person's house where there is a meal with meat and vegetables, but the weak will eat only the vegetables and are abused by the strong for doing so. This situation would help explain Paul's mention of "their table" as a snare and a trap in Rom. 11:9.

Paul admonishes the one who eats (= the strong), meaning eats other food in addition to vegetables, not to despise the one who does not eat this additional food (= the weak; 14:3). The word for "despise" (ἐξουθενέω) essentially refers to the scornful rejection of another from a position of perceived superiority, often in an intergroup context.[37] The attitude condemned is cognate with the boasting by the non-Israelites over the Israelites that Paul disapproves in 11:18. In both cases, the motivation is likely to be Greek ethnocentric dislike of Israelites triggered by their distinctive customs that depend on adherence to the Mosaic law. This behavior therefore provides a specific occasion for the interethnic tension that I have argued was an integral part of the exigence in relation to which Paul framed his message.

In their turn, the one who does not eat, the weak, must not judge the one who does, because God has welcomed him or her (αὐτόν). On this view the person God has welcomed (αὐτόν) is the eater of all, the strong one, because the judger is the one who will think God has not welcomed the other, as Dunn notes.[38] The aorist for God having welcomed him (προσελάβετο) may refer to the occasion on which he was received into the community, at baptism (see chapter nine above).

This point seems confirmed by 14:4. It is the judger (ὁ κρίνων), the weak, who is rebuked here as judging someone else's servant. It is only his master (κύριος) to whom a domestic servant is answerable. While this statement works well at a figurative level, it is also apt literally because of the presence of domestic slaves and servants in the congregations in Rome, as noted above.

The connection between a master and his domestic slave then prompts Paul to interpret the various attitudes to days and food as acceptable as long as everyone concerned acts in honor of *the* Lord (14:5-9). In Paul's picture of the connection between the two we have a reprise of the message of 8:31-39, albeit at a lower emotional intensity.

Romans 14:10-11 recapitulates the message of the previous verses. Judging (of strong by weak) and despising (of weak by strong) is ruled out, for everyone will stand before the dais of God. Everyone will have to give an account of her- or himself before God. My conclusion is reasonably consonant with the view ably championed by William Campbell that Paul is saying "Gentiles must not regard observance of the Jewish law as incompatible with Christian faith, and Jews must not regard it as essential to Christian faith."[39]

Interpreting Romans 14:13-23

Paul begins 14:13-23 with a warning against judging one another (which certainly includes the weak, even if here it also covers the attitudes of the strong), but his real target here is the strong, whose freedom with respect to what they eat is an obstacle and stumbling block to others, meaning the weak (14:13). Although nothing is unclean in itself, if by what you eat you cause your brother grief, you are not walking according to love (ἀγάπη) and will possibly cause the ruin of someone for whom Christ died (14:14-15). This would be inconsistent with the righteousness, peace, and joy in the Holy Spirit that are characteristic of the kingdom of God (14:17). They should pursue what makes for peace and mutual upbuilding. The faith that they have should be between themselves and God (14:22), that is, not thrust in the face of the weak. The problem is that if anyone has doubts about what to eat, here primarily referring to someone weak in faith who is persuaded (or shall we say, half persuaded) that it is all right to eat anything, that person is not acting in accordance with faith and is thereby condemned (14:23).

Paul's earnest entreaty to leave alone those who continue in their adherence to the Mosaic food laws may seem odd on the lips of someone who expressed the negative views toward the Mosaic code we find in chap. 7. Yet we have seen in several places in this volume that Paul is not seeking to erase subgroup identities in the cause of reminding them of the ingroup identity in Christ and under God that they share. He is content to explain why the law cannot produce righteousness, only faith can. In Romans 9–11 we saw the extent to which he was capable of activating the Israelite dimensions of his self-concept when the need arose. He probably considered that adherence to the food laws was not positively harmful to Christ-followers, that it was indifferent, and that to impose pressure on them might lead them into a position of bad conscience that would result in their ruin. Certainly he nowhere urged the weak to sever any connection they might have had with the Judean synagogues, which counts heavily against Watson's thesis that this loomed large in his intentions in the letter.[40]

Interpreting Romans 15:1-13

Paul begins the closing unit of this section by putting the onus firmly on the strong (a class among which he numbers himself) to help the weak and to please them (15:1). Each of them should please his neighbor for his good (15:2), for the purpose of "upbuilding" (οἰκοδομή), which, as noted above, most likely carries here a literal flavor of strengthening the households that were the bases for the Christ-movement in Rome, as well as the figurative sense of "edification." His use of "neighbor" (πλησίον) deserves comment. The word appeared a little earlier, in a quotation from Lev. 19:18 at Rom. 13:9: "You will love your neighbor (Ἀγαπήσεις τὸν πλησίον σου) as yourself," and in Rom. 13:10 following on from this: "Love (ἀγάπη) does no evil to a neighbor (πλησίον)." Apart from these three instances in chaps. 13 and 15, the only other time the word features in the Pauline corpus is at Gal. 5:14, in the same quotation from Lev. 19:18. In using the word πλησίον, therefore, Paul is reminding the strong of the need for them to act with ἀγάπη toward the weak. Paul had already made this point expressly at Rom. 14:15, when he told the same type of person (the strong) that if by what he ate he caused his brother grief, he was not walking according to love (ἀγάπη). Now he makes it by necessary implication. This is a further dimension to the links Paul creates between his teaching on love in 12:9—13:10 and the particular instruction on the strong and the weak in 14:1—15:13.

He summons the self-sacrifice of Christ as a model for what not pleasing oneself means. In 15:3 Paul quotes from Ps. 69:9, "The reproaches of those who reproached you fell on me." In the psalm the "you" referred to is God and the speaker has taken on himself reproaches meant for God. Paul interprets the speaker to be Christ, and his endurance of reproaches probably refers to his shameful death on the cross, not to his earthly life as well.[41] The references to shame in Ps. 69 just before this quotation (vv. 7-8) make this singularly appropriate as a scriptural allusion to crucifixion, the most shameful death of all. As noted elsewhere in this volume (see chapter nine), Paul does not present the life of the earthly Jesus as prototypical of those who believe in him, but here at least he is willing to present the self-sacrificial death of Jesus as a model of putting others before oneself.

Paul takes the opportunity afforded him by the citation of Ps. 69:9 to make a general commendation of Israelite scriptures (Rom. 15:4). They were written for "our instruction" (εἰς τὴν ἡμετέραν διδασκαλίαν), he asserts, in order that through their endurance and encouragement "we might have hope." Earlier in the letter Paul had argued that endurance led (via the character it produced) to hope. Now he repeats the theme in the context of scripture. Other Judeans, of course, would hardly acquiesce in the notion that their scriptures were given for the instruction of the Christ-movement. But in tendentious maneuvers like this Paul discloses how the collective memories of a people can be contested among different groups. What is at stake is not merely the interpretation of the past but, as clearly here, the role of those memories in understanding the present and in envisioning the future. Israelite scriptures were battlefields for rival groups bent on securing the victory that would preserve their respective identities.

The thought of the endurance and encouragement of scripture prompts Paul to utter a prayer to the God who embodies those qualities, but a prayer that well expresses the emphasis on the unity of the Christ-movement in Rome that has motivated his message throughout the letter: "May the God of endurance and encouragement grant to you to think the same thing among one another in accordance with Christ Jesus, in order that unanimously in one voice you may glorify the God and Father of our Lord Jesus Christ" (15:5-6). Here the expression for "think the same thing among one another" (τὸ αὐτὸ φρονεῖν ἐν ἀλλήλοις) is virtually identical to one found at 12:16 ("thinking the same thing among one another," τὸ αὐτὸ εἰς ἀλλήλους φρονοῦντες). This reflects the importance Paul attaches to the mental dimension of group behavior, possibly derived from his engagement with Greek philosophical ethics, especially of a Stoic kind, and also indicates another connection he is drawing between the general instruction in chaps. 12–13 and the particular problem of the strong and the weak. That he needs to pray that they should engage in a joint act of worshiping God makes best sense if the members of the Roman Christ-movement are not already doing so. For Paul the termination of dissension and conflict driven by ethnic and cultural animosity and focusing on pro and con attitudes to the Mosaic law, especially in relation to food, wine, and holy days, will climax in an act of joint worship where all members will, with one mind and one voice, glorify the one God. In line with my earlier argument, Paul probably envisaged this liturgy taking place in houses rented by some of the members in the city.

This emphasis on the glory of God becomes the stimulus for Paul's final injunction to them to welcome one another: "Therefore welcome one another, just as Christ welcomed you, for the glory of God" (15:7). Then follows the statement describing Christ as having become the servant of the Judeans to show that God has kept his promises to the patriarchs and the servant of the non-Judeans to show his mercy (15:8-9). Paul illustrates and reinforces this point with a string of scriptural quotations that speak of the place of the non-Judeans in the broad scheme of salvation, with v. 10 (a verbatim quotation from the LXX of Deut. 32:43) being particularly interesting in its image of non-Judeans and Judeans rejoicing in unison, an image that clearly reveals the underlying ethnic division that Paul has just said (Rom. 15:6) he wants to see ended: "Rejoice, foreign nations, with his people" (15:10).

Paul concludes this section of the letter with a prayer that the God of hope may fill them with joy and peace in their faith and that, by the power of the Holy Spirit, they may abound in hope.

Conclusion

The investigation conducted in this chapter has revealed the extent to which ethnic tensions, being worked out within domestic settings in the unique social milieu that was the Rome of the mid-first century CE, explained the problem of the weak and the strong to which Paul, from his knowledge of the situation in the city, felt obliged to respond. This was a vital area for him to exercise leadership over the Roman Christ-followers, to influence them in a manner that would enhance their contribution to the realization of group goals. He was faced with a situation where the argumentative discourse over food, wine, and holy days occurring within the movement threatened its stability. This prompted his intervention in a manner designed to push the members in a particular direction that would neutralize this particular issue.

The resources he brought to bear on this disorder were essentially the "norms" or identity descriptors he had formulated in general terms in Romans 12–13, especially ἀγάπη and its various characteristics. Paul sees the practice of this virtue as the key to the reconciliation of the rival groups. But he also recommends the need for them to think (φρονεῖν) in unison.

Yet Paul plainly views the strong as those who must give way most. The weak are not to judge them, but the initiative for resolving the disputes rests with the strong. This result bears on the important thesis that John Barclay has proposed in relation to this part of Romans. It is true, Barclay concedes, that Paul insists that he maintained the law (3:31), and in 14:1—15:6 he supports the right of the weak to observe Mosaic food and Sabbath laws. Nevertheless, since Paul regards some aspects of the law as wholly dispensable for Christ-believers, he is actually relativizing the significance of the Israelite cultural tradition by advocating that "Jewish Christians" associate freely with other "Christians" in the congregations, and this undermines the theological and intellectual foundation of this tradition:

> What Paul demands of these weak Christians is their commitment to a church in which the Jewish mode of life is tolerated but not required. . . . In demanding this toleration, Paul subverts the basis on which Jewish law-observance is founded and precipitates a crisis of cultural integrity among the very believers whose law-observance he is careful to protect. Such is the fundamental paradox of the passage we are studying.[42]

While this may have been the *effect* of what Paul was saying, the better view is that it was not what he *intended*. What seems to us an awkward compromise, or even a paradox, does so with the benefit of hindsight. Paul was not to know how long it would be until the final consummation. In other parts of the letter, in chaps. 9–11 especially, he had made much of his own Israelite identity and had made quite clear (in the visual imagery of the olive tree above all) that the Judean and non-Judean elements of the Christ-movement retained their distinctiveness, indeed the former had precedence. Their new common identity did not entail the dissolution of their valued subgroup identities.[43] Coupled to this was Paul's firm belief that Israel would continue in existence until the non-Judeans had come in, then Israel too would be saved (11:25-27). Paul may well have been relativizing the Judean tradition; his critique of the law in Romans represents a powerful sally in this direction. But he was not to know that the mixture of belief in Christ and acceptance of compliance with some aspects of the Mosaic law by some members that he agitates for among the Christ-movement in Rome was a solution that would ultimately not survive, and he did not in this letter deliberately seek to eliminate the difference between Judean and non-Judean. Miroslav Volf has reached a similar conclusion.[44] Perhaps Paul even thought that his encouraging non-Judean Christ-followers to eschew arrogant attitudes to Judean Christ-followers would carry over into their dropping animosity toward Judeans who had not turned to Christ. This type of result is a recognized feature of some recategorization exercises, as noted in chapter two.

Epilogue: Conflict and Identity

Sometime in the mid-50s of the first century CE, when Paul was in Corinth, he began dictating a letter to a scribe for delivery to the Christ-fearers of Rome, whose faith was well known around the Mediterranean. It was a long and serious letter and Paul meant it to be taken seriously, probably to be heard and reheard by the Roman Christ-followers.

But fifty years short of two millennia later we are still reading and rereading it, still struck by the compressed and difficult nature of its thought, still taken by its power to cut to the heart of what it means to be a Christian in this or any time. For while this was a communication addressed to the particular needs of nonelite, Greek-speaking people in the imperial capital, Judeans and Greeks, it has the capacity to touch the experience of the present, to burst through the barriers of historical contingency, and to speak across time and place.

Every Christian who senses the daunting contemporaneity of this first-century text, the circumstance of its being "so ancient and so new," to cite Augustine's description of God (*Confessions* 10.27), will wish to select some area of human experience where Romans manages to articulate a problem and to give voice to a solution. For me, Romans reveals its connection with the taproot of human experience in relation to violent ethnic conflict in the world. Across the globe groups differentiated on the basis of ethnicity mobilize to defend their patch against real or imagined threats to it, ache to avenge insults (again, real or imagined) that may be centuries old, or launch upon bouts of murderous aggression against other groups in their context, sometimes unprovoked by either ancient slights or modern oppression. With machetes, rifles, and bombs they invent new rituals to crystallize the identity of their group through the murder or maiming of large numbers of people ethnically different.

There is nothing new in this phenomenon. The ancient Mediterranean world was full of ethnic groups who ethnocentrically derided and, wherever possible, took action against the members of other ethnic groups. Romans did not like Greeks. Greeks did not like Romans. Both Romans and Greeks disliked Judeans. At times these simmering animosities flared up into bouts of violence, rioting, murder, and theft. In the period 38–41 CE there was a major blowup between the Greeks and Judeans of Alexandria, with the Greeks gaining the upper hand through the connivance or inertia of imperial officials and taking over Judean *proseuchai* and houses in the city.

The seriousness of ethnic conflict in both ancient and modern times imposes a considerable burden on those who would seek to understand its manifestations, let alone to mitigate them. The primary requirement is the need to bring appropriate theoretical resources to bear upon the data. For the reasons set out above, the constructivist and processual approach to ethnicity inaugurated by Fredrik Barth carries considerable explanatory power, including in relation to the various ethnic groups of the Mediterranean world of the first century. Such an approach, when linked to the manifestations of ethnicity characteristic of that time and place, demands that the group known by themselves and outsiders as *Ioudaioi* (even though they also called themselves Israelites) should be translated as "Judeans," not "Jews." Only "Judeans" does justice to its designation of a people who, whether they lived in Judea or in the numerous diaspora communities around the Mediterranean, were oriented toward Judea and its capital Jerusalem and, in particular, to its temple and to the God who was worshiped there in magnificent, aniconic austerity. At the same time, the phenomenon of "nested" and "dual identity" reminds us that people who regarded themselves as Judean in one context, for example, when they were attending Jerusalem to take part in the Passover ceremonies, might have activated other ethnicities they derived from other contexts, for example, by birth and upbringing in other places, such as Galilee or Idumea.

When Paul wrote to the Roman Christ-movement he was already familiar with some of its circumstances from contacts he had in the city, such as Prisca and Aquila, Epaenetus, and the mother of Rufus, whom he also regarded as his "mother." He knew that it was composed of Judean and Greek members from the nonelite section of Rome's foreign population. He knew there were several different congregations and that they met in the houses of the members with the most wealth. He may well have known that there were impressive *proseuchai* in Rome, so that the fact that the majority of Israel continued in much the same way as it had before the coming of Christ was all too obvious. He also knew that there was trouble in Rome, mainly caused by some of the Greeks adopting arrogant ethnocentric attitudes toward other members who still observed certain features of the Mosaic law, such as those relating to food, wine, and holy days, possibly exacerbated by the interfamilial competition common in Rome. This meant that on occasions when both the "strong" and the "weak" gathered in one place, the strong challenged the weak to justify their views, and the weak condemned the strong. The capacity for Greeks and Judeans to collide with one another, often in violent ways, had been conspicuous in many cities of the Greco-Roman East within Paul's lifetime. On the other hand, the movement in Rome was at least not being troubled by influential Judean members seeking to have the Greeks become circumcised and accept the law of Moses, a problem Paul had previously faced in Antioch and Galatia.

Paul was concerned about the tension and conflict in the Roman congregations not merely for the sake of the Christ-believers involved, but because they stood to get in the way of his preparations for his missionary journey to Spain. For that enterprise he was going to need considerable assistance from the Roman congregations, money and translators especially, and if he went to Spain and left the Roman church in chaos behind him, such support might not be forthcoming.

He also had another reason for writing the letter. He was about to travel to Jerusalem with money that had been collected by his congregations in Macedonia and Achaia, although not, revealingly, in Galatia. This was an extremely confrontational step on his part. For the collection told the entire Christ-movement that he had stuck to the bargain he had reached with the Jerusalem pillars some years before in Jerusalem (Gal. 2:1-10) even though they had not (Gal. 2:11-14). By presenting himself in Jerusalem with the money he would challenge them to abide by the agreement. He knew this challenge would not be well received. That is why he wanted the Roman believers to pray the collection would be acceptable to the movement in Jerusalem (Rom. 15:31). The embarrassment that was ultimately to be caused by his arrival there explains why Luke, describing the event much later in Acts 21, fails to mention that this was the purpose of Paul's visit.

At the same time, some of the animosity expressed toward Paul by Judean Christ-followers like those in Jerusalem who considered that adherence to the Mosaic law was an additional requirement to be imposed on non-Judean Christ-followers surfaces in the letter. The clearest instance is the nasty rumor that Paul advocates the commission of evil so that good may come of it (3:8); in other words, that he espouses the abandonment of the Mosaic law as part of the new dispensation. Such a charge was calculated to wound both Paul and the gospel he preached. In an oral culture like this, the use of slander was a standard technique for destroying a person's honor and thereby neutralizing him as a rival. Paul assumes that some of this malicious gossip has already reached Rome and that he must counter it. He must also hope that if he can get the Romans on his side, word will move from them to Jerusalem and this will assist him when he visits the city.

It is in this context, with a variety of issues and problems pressing on him, that Paul dictates his letter. To be successful he will need to exercise what we now call a leadership role over its recipients. That is, he will need to influence them in a way that pushes them as a movement in a certain direction that accords with his vision and sense of the requirements of the situation. He wants them to follow as he leads. He must cover both the problems internal to the Roman congregations and also those that relate to his reputation and to the allegations that he knows are current about him and his gospel, especially in relation to the Mosaic law. The vast majority of his addressees were illiterate, and he must rely on the oral presentation of the letter, possibly by someone like Phoebe whom he had previously schooled in its meaning, to achieve these effects.

His foundational insight is the need to remind his addressees, meaning all of the Judean and Greek members of the Christ-movement in the city, "all God's beloved in Rome, who are called to be holy" (1:7), not just some of them, who they are. He must invoke and explore for them the identity that they have acquired by entry into the movement, through faith expressed at baptism. Here, as with ethnicity, the invocation of a concept such as identity imposes a responsibility on interpreters carefully to model what is meant by it. The perspective on ethnicity I find useful in relation to Romans embraces the social identity theory pioneered by Henri Tajfel and the closely related self-categorization theory developed initially by John Turner.

While the identity Paul espouses for the Roman Christ-followers has cognitive, emotional, and evaluative dimensions, it focuses on one righteous God who righteouses those who have faith in his son, Jesus Christ, who has laid down his own life to break the power of sin in the world. To be righteous is how Paul encapsulates what this identity is like, in all its splendor. Yet this is an identity that transcends the fundamental ethnic division among them between Judeans and Greeks, a division made all too real by the division and conflicts that occur when they happen to gather together in domestic premises rented out by some of the members. Paul regards the unity that they must achieve as a direct expression of the oneness of God. It is a unity also capable of visual expression as the body of Christ or the olive tree. In the language of modern social identity theory, Paul's strategy amounts to an exercise in recategorization, the creation (or perhaps invocation) of a common ingroup identity.

Perhaps because of his previous experience in Galatia, where he had taken a tough line on Judeans but where he may not have won the day (since the Galatians had not contributed to the collection he is taking to Jerusalem even though he had directed them to), Paul seems to have hit upon an aspect of successful recategorization that is prominent in modern research into the resolution of intergroup conflict. The feature in question is that an attempt to bring two (sub)groups together under a superordinate identity is likely to fail if those conducting it take steps that threaten the preexisting (sub)group identities. The ideal conditions are where the two (sub)groups are equal in status but share different experiences or expertise. Paul's approach incorporates this insight, but with a slight switch. He aims to show that, prior to their recategorization as believers in Christ, the Judeans and Greeks are equal in respect to a negative status, their subjection to sin, although from entirely different routes—the Greeks apart from the law and the Judeans under the law. In this perspective, Rom. 1:18—3:20 is explicable as Paul's careful attempt to set out separately (and sequentially) the plight of Greeks and then Judeans. This is why the dominant metaphor in relation to non-Judeans (1:19-32) is Sodom and why Adam is not alluded to until later in the letter. One of the purposes served in this section of the letter is the elimination of any possibility that either of the two ethnic groups could accuse the other of being, prior to acquisition of the new identity, "holier than thou."

Yet Paul was interested not only in demonstrating the experience from which they had escaped, but also in elaborating upon the glorious new identity that they had attained. He begins this process in 3:21-31 by setting out its basis as righteousness for all who believe, Judeans and Greeks without distinction, who have faith in Jesus Christ who was put forward by God as an expiation in a process where the oneness of God guarantees that righteousness is offered impartially. Paul also brings God and Christ very close together. By attributing to Christ the language of "Lordship" that in the Old Testament is reserved for God, Paul brings Christ into the identity of God.

To solidify his message of the oneness of God and the unity of the Christ-movement Paul develops the image of Abraham as a prototype of the new identity in chap. 4. To do so, Paul must stage an audacious raid on the collective memory of Israel, by appropriating Abraham to the new group identity even though Judeans who had not turned to Christ would have contested this claim with great vigor. Yet here too it is clear that Paul's previous (probably unhappy) experience in Galatia, where, in similarly taking possession of Abraham for the new movement, he had come close to denying him any connection with Israel in the flesh, has led him to adopt a more moderate approach.

That Abraham was a figure from the past illustrates the extent to which shaping of identity must embrace a temporal continuity stretching across past, present, and future. The "we" with whose experience individual members of the group identify both predate and survive them. For Paul the key figures in the past were Abraham, on the positive side, and Adam and Moses, on the negative side. He creates a structure of "social time." This portrays Adam as the original point of failure (when sin entered the world), Abraham as an early success whose promise was to be fulfilled much later, Moses as representing a lost opportunity for Israel when the law he promulgated proved not to be strong enough for its noble purpose, and the death and resurrection of Christ as the vital triumphs in the temporal progression. Romans 5 marks the critical points concerning Adam, Moses, and Christ. Yet given the bleak period between Abraham and Christ the expression "salvation history" is hardly apposite for this structuring of time. Through the long years after Abraham, while sin rampaged through the human race, even winning a new lease of life with the Mosaic law, the promise lay dormant, only to come to life with Christ and those who had faith in him.

Paul's presentation of the Mosaic law is bleak. While he asserts that the law is holy and its commandments holy and just and good, the sad truth is that it has failed. Although it is a travesty of Paul's understanding to suggest that God sent the law in order that sin would increase (as if God would say "You shall not murder" *in order that* people would), that has nevertheless been its result. Sin used the law to its advantage. The law, in short, was not strong enough for the dirty job God gave it. While this might be thought to imply a question about the capability of God to produce so weak an engine of his will, this is not a question that Paul asks.

The status of the law must have been of more interest to the Judean component of Paul's audience than the Greek. It is beyond doubt that he wanted to offer a coherent explanation of his position so as to push them toward his view of the law. To do this he adopts a particular leadership tactic that makes good sense within a social identity framework. In chap. 7, in the "I" section in particular, he presents himself as prototypical of Israel's experience under the law. The "I" who speaks is Paul as representative of Israel, and there is no reason not to believe that this reflected his understanding of his past as he looked back on it after his coming to faith in Christ.

The converse to the lamentable predicament of Israel under the law is presented in chap. 8. Above all, Paul can point to the experience of the Spirit of God dwelling in those who are righteous. We must shed modern notions that have relegated the Spirit to the role of theological topos and imagine congregations where the presence of the Spirit was associated with an explosion of charismatic gifts, such as miracles, prophecy, glossolalia, interpretation, visions, and auditions. This represents the highest pitch of their common identity.

Yet their identity and the social time in which Paul structures it do have a future dimension. The believers may be enduring sufferings, but they are nothing compared with the glory that is being revealed to them (8:18). Sentiments such as this encourage advocates of Pauline "eschatology" to resort to the tension between the "now" and the "not yet." When we clear our gaze of the socially constructed notions of time that we think are natural, however, a different picture lights up. Paul depicts a "forthcoming" rather than a future, a forthcoming that is growing out of the present and exists on its horizon. His concern is with the inevitability of the transformation rather than with the time at which it will occur. He positively discourages speculation as to what it might be like (8:24). This results in a much more attenuated sense of the future than the one with which we are familiar, and one much closer to the understanding of Bultmann than of Käsemann if we wish to situate this issue in relation to traditional scholarly positions. Romans 8 ends with the powerful presence of God and Christ with the believer, now, rather than with visions of future glory.

The exaltation with which Paul ends chap. 8 stands in contrast to his feelings of desolation as he contemplates the fact that, by and large, Israel has failed to turn to Christ. The strong affiliation that Paul expresses for Israel in chaps. 9–11 well illustrates the central feature of self-categorization theory that a person's sense of self varies in particular group situations. Whereas the standard spectrum is from strongly group oriented at one end to strongly individualist at the other, the self can also vary between different groups. In chaps. 9–11 Paul's Israelite identity becomes salient on a number of occasions with remarkable strength. By so doing he created a link with all the Israelites in his audience, who were more likely to accept what he had to say about Israel if he could establish his credentials for speaking at all. The basic thrust of Paul's message in chaps. 9–11 is that God's promise to Israel has not failed but has been fulfilled in the form of the remnant who have come to faith in Christ. Yet as Paul nears the end of this section he begins to intimate both that the rest of Israel has a glorious future after all and that the Judean component of the Christ-movement is superior to the non-Judean component. The former aspect appears in his notion that God is provoking Israel to jealous concern to regain what is rightfully hers and that, in the end, she will do precisely that. The latter becomes clear in the image of the olive tree, where Paul's deliberate inversion of the usual pattern, of grafting cultivated branches into a wild stock (since wild branches do not produce ripe fruit), powerfully relegates the non-Judeans to second place in the economy of salvation and makes their boasting over the Judeans who have been cut off ridiculous indeed.

Within social identity theory, "norms" are values that define acceptable and unacceptable attitudes and behavior by members of the group. They tell members what they should think and feel and how they should behave if they are to belong to the group and share its identity. Once Paul has described the foundations and nature of the new identity, and dealt with certain issues (especially with respect to the character of the Mosaic law) that arise in consequence of his argument, it is quite natural for him to proceed to outline the norms, or descriptors, of that identity. This task occupies him in 12:1—15:13. He had previously followed the same course in Galatians, where his exposition of identity norms also appeared near the end of the letter (Gal. 5:13—6:10). A social identity perspective highlighting a group's norms provides an alternative to typical (yet problematic) treatments of such material in terms of "ethics" or "paraenesis."

Paul has a highly developed vision of these norms, centering on ἀγάπη, the distinctive love of the Christ-movement. This must have appeared as a countercultural force in this environment, especially in the climactic exhortation not to be conquered by evil but to conquer evil by good (12:21) that subverted the requirement on persons of honor to take vengeance on those who had harmed them. Nevertheless, Paul's vision has a strongly cognitive dimension, and he expands upon it in a way that may be helpfully compared and contrasted in detail with the Stoic approach to cognate issues. Encouraged, moreover, by the view expressed in the fourth century by the Pauline commentator Ambrosiaster that in this part of the letter Paul was interested in offering instruction on how to lead a good life, I find it reasonable to construe Paul's message on the norms of identity in Christ as a form of virtue ethics.

The need for ἀγάπη features in his discussion of the particular problem of attitude and behavior vexing the congregations of Rome, that involving the strong and the weak. These represented elements in the Roman Christ-movement who were, respectively, of the view that the Mosaic law on matters such as food, wine, and holy days was entirely irrelevant (an opinion entertained by some non-Judeans and certain Judeans, such as Paul himself) or that it should be observed (an opinion held mainly by Judeans but also possibly by some non-Judeans). One might expect that given his critique of the law earlier in the letter and his own view that he was free of it, Paul would have had little patience with the "weak." In fact, he urges the strong to express ἀγάπη toward them, by welcoming them into their homes and by not arguing with them about such matters. He wants Judean and non-Judean to unite in praise of God. If, as seems possible, the "weak" continued to have some form of association with the Judean communities in Rome meeting in their impressive *proseuchai*, there is no sign here that Paul is interested in discouraging them from doing so. His focus is totally on what is going on in the congregations of the Christ-movement.

The pro-Israelite dimension to Paul's thought evident in chap. 11 and 14:1—15:13 and the fact that he presents, in his metaphor of the olive tree especially, an image of a group that is a unity but differentiated as to its parts (with the Judean parts having precedence), falsify claims that Paul erases the difference between Judeans and non-Judeans. While it is probably going too far to say that Paul retains all existing social differences between the two groups and only advocates unity on a theological level, since the thrust of his thought undermines the cultural distinctiveness of Israel by its assertion that the Mosaic law is unnecessary for righteousness, Paul does not tell the Judean members of the Christ-movement to stop being Judeans. He does not ask them to sever any ties that they may have with the Roman synagogues, and he is tolerant of their continued practice of the Mosaic law, at least in regard to provisions relating to food, wine, and holy days. While one may admit that Paul's is a compromise position that was unlikely to last, it is nevertheless inaccurate to attribute to him the positive aim of destroying the differences between Judeans and non-Judeans. Throughout the letter he takes, indeed, the opposite course—as he must to bring these rival ethnic groups together—of acknowledging their different (sub)group identities at critical stages in the argument. Nor does he call the new identity he espouses "Israel."

We are left then with a letter that represents an elaborate and profound attempt to re-present the identity of the Christ-movement in a manner dominated by the recognition of ethnic difference. It is a communication in which the theological truth of the oneness of the God who righteouses all without distinction constitutes the foundation for the common identity advocated by Paul. In a world still torn by ethnic conflict, this is a message that will continue to resonate.

Notes

1. Romans and Christian Identity

1. See Kermode 1975: 44, in a work stimulated by T. S. Eliot's 1944 essay, "What Is a Classic?"

2. Achtemeier 1980: 125.

3. See Achtemeier 1980: 114–23; Esler 1998: 5–6.

4. See Achtemeier 1980: 120–23 (relating this evolving recognition to the issue of the inspiration of scripture); Esler 1998: 21–23.

5. Achtemeier 1980: 125.

6. The Manicheans explained the existence of evil on the basis of a struggle between light and darkness. They identified evil with the material world and believed that the only people who would be saved were those who, entirely by accident, had become receptacles for particles of light; see Steinmetz 1986: 14.

7. With particular reference to Romans 9, Augustine initially argued—in a text from 394 CE entitled *Propositions from the Epistle to the Romans* (*Expositio quarundam propositionum ex epistola ad Romanos*)—that whereas God calls the sinner and that this call cannot be merited by human activity, the response to this call, namely faith, lies wholly within the free will of the sinner. God's election of such a person is based on his foreknowledge that he or she will have faith. Following further consideration of Romans 9 and the difficulties that the plight of Jacob and Pharaoh mentioned in that text (9:11-13, 17) pose to such a high view of free will, Augustine soon abandoned the idea that election turns upon God's foreknowledge of man's faith as inconsistent with divine omnipotence. Instead he proposed, for the first time in *De diversis quaestionibus ad Simplicianum* (written c. 397) and repeated in other works, that human goodwill was itself elected by God. It was a divine gift, not a human achievement, even though this meant that the righteousness of God was incomprehensible, given that he inexplicably chose to remit from only some human beings the universally owed debt of damnation. See Fredriksen Landes 1982: x–xii; Steinmetz 1986: 14–17.

8. For the assistance Luther gained from Augustine's view that human goodness is a result of God's election, not its precondition, see Steinmetz 1986: 17–22.

9. Luther's detailed position on the letter appears in his *Lectures on Romans* (delivered from the spring of 1515 to the autumn of 1516: Oswald 1972: x), which are accessible in English translation in Oswald 1972. His *Preface to the Epistle of St. Paul to the Romans*, written c. 1522 (Woolf 1956: 274), represents a limpid summation of his views; it begins: "This epistle is in truth the most important document in the New Testament, the gospel in its purest expression" (see the text in Woolf 1956: 284–300).

10. Martin Luther, *Preface to the Epistle of St. Paul to the Romans*, in Woolf 1956: 284.

11. See McCormack 1995: 137.

12. Barth 1933: 6–7.

13. Achtemeier 1980: 125.

14. Achtemeier 1980: 149–50.

15. Achtemeier 1980: 151.

16. Stendahl 1962: 179.

17. See Esler 1998: 1–21.

18. Morgan 1995: 11.

19. The following statement by Morgan (1995: 61) comes close to this formulation: "Paul did not expect to be read centuries later, but he intended to say things that are generally true, not limited to some particular context."

20. See Morgan 1995: 93; Moxnes 1980: 15–31 and passim.

21. Morgan 1995: 11.

22. See Bassler 1991; Hay 1993; Hay and Johnson 1995; Johnson and Hay 1997.

23. Johnson and Hay 1997.

24. Dunn 1998: xvi. This book is 844 pages long.

25. Hay and Johnson 1997: xi–xii.

26. Roetzel 1999: 93–94.

27. Thus, meaning 1 in *Webster's Third New International Dictionary of the English Language Unabridged* (Chicago: Encyclopaedia Britannica, 1986), 2371, is "the rational interpretation of religious faith, practice, and experience"; and meaning 1.a in *The Oxford English Dictionary* (Oxford: Clarendon, 1989), 898, is the "study or science which treats of God, His nature and attributes, and His relations with man and the universe." The definition of *theology* as "the sum of beliefs held by an individual or group regarding matters of religious faith," etc., cited in the text, is meaning 2c in *Webster's*.

28. See Theissen 1999: 1.

29. See Dunn 1975.

30. Dunn 1998.

31. Dunn 1998: 2, 3.

32. Dunn 1998: 9.

33. Dunn 1998: 6.

34. Morgan 1995: 13.

35. Morgan 1995: 12–15.

36. See Betz 1991; Theissen 1999; Ashton 2000.

37. W. Smith 1991: 20–21.

38. W. Smith 1991: 25–31.

39. W. Smith 1991: 29.

40. W. Smith 1991: 32.

41. W. Smith 1991: 36–37.

42. W. Smith 1991: 44.

43. W. Smith 1991: 193–202.

44. See Esler 1995b: 4–8.

45. For this distinction see Malina 1994, 1996d; Esler 2001b: 25–26.

46. Donfried 1991b: xli.

47. Campbell 1991: 1.
48. See Donfried 1991b: xlii.
49. See Munck 1959.
50. See Campbell 1991: 2–3.
51. See Käsemann 1969a.
52. Campbell 1991: 5.
53. See Aguilar (1998: 38–50) for a description of the genocide.
54. On Saturday 9 June 2001 the London newspaper *The Times* reported (p. 13) that on the previous day two Rwandan nuns had been found guilty by a Belgian court of helping Hutu extremists to slaughter 6,000 Tutsis in the spring of 1994. On one occasion a nun was alleged to have actively assisted Hutu militia members to burn to death 700 people locked in her convent's health clinic.
55. F. Barth 1994: 27.
56. F. Barth 1994: 4.
57. For Yugoslavia see Volf 1996; for Rwanda see Aguilar 1998.
58. I am proceeding on the basis that the material in Rom. 1:19-31 reflects, if any actual behavior, that which Greek members of the Roman congregations had left behind on turning to Christ. Similarly, Romans 7 relates (see chapter ten below) to the previous experience of Israelites prior to conversion; in addition I do not accept the arguments of Augustine and Francis Watson (2000: 91–182) that the "desire" of Romans 7 is restricted to sexual desire.
59. Stanley 1996.
60. But see the introduction and some of the essays in Brett 1996 for the early application of social-scientific theory relating to ethnicity to various biblical texts.
61. See Assmann and Friese 1999b: 11: "In den letzen zehn Jahren hat sich das Wort 'Identität' in unserer Alltagssprache geradezu epidemisch ausgebreitet." The expression *Plastikwort* derives from Uwe Pörksen, whom they cite a little after this sentence.
62. For a good sample on this area generally, see the essays in Assmann and Friese 1999a; Gephart and Waldenfels 1999. In the field of NT studies this flourishing area is represented, for example, in the fine, theoretically informed exegesis by Börschel 2001; S. von Dobbeler 2001, 2002; Feldtkeller 1993; Vogt 1993; Wolter 1997, 2001.
63. See Walters 1993 for the former type and Campbell 1991: 98–121 for the latter, although both these books have real strengths in other ways and both appeared when the "ethnicity" revolution was barely beginning.
64. See Judge 1994: 363. He notes that the young knights whom Nero engaged to applaud his performances were called *Augustiani*.
65. J. Elliott 2000: 791. His entire coverage of *Christianos* (2000: 789–94) deserves the closest attention.
66. F. Watson 1986: 180–81.
67. See F. Watson 2000.
68. Moxnes 1980: 6.
69. Moxnes 1980: 40–41.
70. Bauckham 1998.

71. Bauckham 2002b: 4. He lists the extensive data on pp. 5–6 of this paper.

72. See Bauckham 2002b for the text. Bauckham is currently preparing an exhaustive two-volume monograph on his christological views.

73. See Esler 1998: 15.

74. See Roberts and Good 1993; Esler 1998: 16–17.

75. Interest in the rhetorical characteristics of Galatians was fostered by Betz 1975 (the ideas from which were utilized in Betz 1979) and has gathered apace since; see Esler 1998: 18.

76. Particularly worthy of attention is N. Elliott 1990.

77. Esler 1998: 18–19.

78. I am greatly indebted to Robert Keay, a doctoral student in the University of St. Andrews, for bringing this issue to my attention and to alerting me to much relevant literature.

79. An important source is Norden 1958, whom some, however, have thought overused the concept of Asianism. See Winterbottom 1996.

80. See the arguments by Duncan (1926) for Asianic rhetorical features in 1 Corinthians.

81. This explanation of "rhetorical situation" is dependent on Bitzer 1968; see Esler 1998: 17–18 for its relevance to Galatians. The concept is usefully discussed by Consigny 1974.

82. On this point I disagree with N. Elliott's view that a "rhetorical-critical analysis of Romans cannot have recourse to independent knowledge of the situation Paul confronted" (1990: 17).

83. This distinction is drawn by N. Elliott 1990: 18. His (erroneous) view that historical criticism looks "behind" a text is similar to the position of F. Watson 1994: 15.

84. See my explanation in Esler 1998: 21–22.

85. See Harris 1989; Hezser 2001.

86. I am indebted to Francis Watson of the University of Aberdeen for stressing this dimension to me during a conversation in December 2002.

87. Esler 1998.

2. Explaining Social Identity

1. Börschel 2001: 12.

2. See Börschel 2001: 12: "Am Anfang steht die Differenz, welche Identität konstituiert. Etwas 'ist' nur, indem es von anderem unterschieden ist" ("At the outset stands difference, which constitutes identity. Something 'is' only because it is differentiated from something else").

3. For a sample of recent research, with extensive bibliography, see Robinson 1996; Ellemers, Spears, and Doosje 1999.

4. For the historical development of the understanding of the individual and the group in social psychology, see Turner et al. 1987: 1–18.

5. Sherif and Sherif 1953; Sherif et al. 1955, 1961; the summer camp experiments are discussed in Brown 2000: 246–50.

6. See Tajfel et al. 1971.

7. See Turner 1999: 8.

8. Brown 1988: 42–48.

9. Brown 2000: 290.

10. Oakes, Haslam, and Turner 1994: 83, 211–13.

11. Condor 1996: 289–91.

12. Condor 1996: 302–3.

13. Condor 1996: 303.

14. Carr 1991: 113–14; cited at Condor 1996: 306.

15. Condor 1996: 306–7.

16. Cinnirella 1998.

17. Cinnirella 1998: 243.

18. I am using the concept as explained by Breakwell 1986: 22; a similar idea was enunciated by Halbwachs 1980.

19. Breakwell 1986: 22.

20. Halbwachs 1980. Halbwachs died in Buchenwald in 1945 (1980: 17). On Halbwachs see Namer 2000.

21. Billig 1990: 60.

22. Middleton and Edwards 1990b: 10: *"he who controls the past controls who we are."*

23. See Thelen 1989: 1127.

24. Middleton and Edwards 1990b: 10.

25. See Assmann 2000, 2002. Assmann prefers the description "cultural memory" (kulturelle Gedächtnis) for his version of this idea.

26. Hogg and McGarty 1990: 10–11.

27. See Esler 1998: 215–34.

28. Hogg and McGarty 1990: 11.

29. J. C. Turner et al. 1987: vii.

30. J. C. Turner et al. 1987: ix.

31. J. C. Turner 1999: 11.

32. J. C. Turner 1999: 11.

33. So Kawakami and Dion 1993: 526.

34. See Esler 1998.

35. Sani and Reicher 2000: 97.

36. Haslam et al. 1998.

37. Sani and Reicher 2000: 97.

38. Billig 1987.

39. Sani and Reicher 2000: 98.

40. Sani and Reicher 2000: 99.

41. Sherif et al. 1961.

42. See Gaertner et al. 1989; Gaertner et al. 1993; Dovidio et al. 1998; Gaertner et al. 2000.

43. Minard 1952.

44. See Brown 1996: 175–76; Brewer and Miller 1984: 288–99; Bettencourt et al. 1992. I have sought to interpret the parable of the good Samaritan as an example of decategorization; see Esler 2000b.

45. See Deschamps and Doise 1978.

46. Gaertner et al. 1993: 6.

47. See Gaertner et al. 1993: 21.

48. Gaertner et al. 2000: 133–34.

49. Dovidio et al. 1998: 117; Gaertner et al. 2000: 133.

50. Dovidio et al. 1998: 110.

51. Gaertner et al. 2000: 143.

52. Gaertner et al. 2000: 144–45. On the other hand, there are occasionally contexts in which it may be desirable, if possible, to eliminate the original group boundaries, for example, in corporate mergers or step-families perhaps, in which the continued existence of earlier group identities may be diagnostic of serious underlying problems; see Gaertner et al. 2000: 135–36.

53. Martyn 1997: 37–45.

54. Note that in 1 Cor. 16:1 Paul gives directions to the Corinthians in relation to the collection just as he said he had given to the congregations of Galatia. Yet in Rom. 15:26 he reports that Macedonia and Achaia have contributed, but there is no mention of Galatia. Presumably the Galatian congregations had failed to support Paul in this task.

55. The other three conditions are (a) there should be social and institutional support for the contact; (b) the contact should be sufficiently prolonged; and (c) the goals for the contact should have been mutually agreed; see Brown 1996: 181.

56. Dovidio et al. 1998: 117.

57. Hewstone and Brown 1986b; Hewstone 1996.

58. Gaertner et al. 2000: 145.

59. See Haslam 2001: 58.

60. See Schütz 1975: 240–42 especially; Holmberg 1978: 72–82.

61. Doohan 1984: 11–25.

62. Dodd 1999: 12, emphasis added.

63. Dodd 1999: 1–2.

64. Dodd 1999: 14.

65. Dodd 1999: 14.

66. Dodd 1999: 238.

67. I acknowledge my great debt to Haslam 2001 in this area.

68. Haslam 2001: 59.

69. See Burns 1978.

70. Fleishman 1953; Fleishman and Peters 1962.

71. Haslam 2001: 59.

72. Hemphill 1969; Cooper and McGaugh 1969; Haslam 2001: 60.

73. Haslam and Platow 2001: 214.

74. Fiedler and Garcia 1987; Haslam 2001: 60–62.

75. Haslam 2001: 62.

76. Haslam 2001: 63.

77. Hollander 1995.

78. Haslam 2001: 63–64.

79. Haslam 2001: 65.

80. Haslam and Platow 2001: 217.
81. Haslam and Platow 2001: 218.
82. Haslam 2001: 66.
83. Haslam 2001: 69.
84. Haslam 2001: 69; Hogg 1996.
85. Hogg 1996: 81.
86. Haslam 2001: 72.
87. Haslam and Platow 2001: 223.
88. Haslam and Platow 2001: 218.
89. Reicher and Hopkins 1996; Haslam 2001: 69.

3. Ethnicity, Ethnic Conflict, and the Ancient Mediterranean World

1. In this year "ethnicity" was introduced by sociologist W. Lloyd Warner as an alternative to "race" as a response to Fascism; on this see Sollors 1996: x–xliv. See Glazer and Moynihan 1975b: 1 for the oft-mentioned suggestion of 1953 as its year of appearance.
2. See Horowitz 1985.
3. B. Williams 1989: 401–2, 413–15.
4. Horowitz 1985: 98.
5. I rely on Jenkins (1997: 9–11) for this discussion of Weber and Hughes.
6. See Weber 1978: 389.
7. See Weber 1978: 390; Jenkins 1997: 10.
8. Hughes 1994: 91.
9. Jenkins 1997: 11.
10. I have discussed Barth's approach in relation to Galatians in Esler 1998: 78–82.
11. See Vermeulen and Govers 1994b: 2.
12. F. Barth 1969b: 15.
13. F. Barth 1969b: 14.
14. F. Barth 1969b: 14.
15. F. Barth 1969b: 11.
16. See Eriksen 1993: 92; Vermeulen and Govers 1994b: 3.
17. F. Barth 1969b: 13, emphasis added.
18. F. Barth 1969b: 15.
19. Hutchinson and Smith 1996b: 6–7.
20. See B. Williams 1989; Cornell 1996: 268–69; Roosens 1989; 1994: 83–84.
21. Parsons 1975: 60.
22. Roosens 1994.
23. Geertz 1963b; cited in Hutchinson and Smith 1996: 41–42.
24. See Gil-White 1999: 802.
25. Geertz 1963b; cited in Hutchinson and Smith 1996: 42.
26. See Eller and Coughlan 1993; cited in Hutchinson and Smith 1996: 45–51.
27. So Jenkins 1997: 45.
28. Gil-White 1999: 803.
29. Eller and Coughlan 1993; cited in Hutchinson and Smith 1996: 47–48.

30. See Esler 1995b: 4–8 (partly in debate with Susan Garrett espousing a Geertzian approach); Esler 1998: 1–21 (on reading Galatians interculturally).

31. J. M. Hall 1997: 19.

32. J. M. Hall 1997: 18.

33. S. Jones 1997: 74.

34. See Bell 1975; Ross 1980; Varshney 1995.

35. See Scott 1990; Jenkins 1997: 44–48.

36. F. Barth 1969b: 15.

37. Jenkins 1997: 45.

38. Jenkins 1997: 46.

39. J. M. Hall 1997: 19.

40. Gil-White 1999: 792.

41. F. Barth 1969b: 17.

42. F. Barth 1994: 12.

43. Gil-White 1999.

44. Barth 1994: 21.

45. See A. Cohen 1994a, 1994b. By way of autobiographical note, I should record that I first encountered the Barthian notion of ethnicity in 1993 when Anthony Cohen presented at the St. Andrews University Anthropology seminar a version of the paper he subsequently gave later that year at the Amsterdam conference (Cohen 1994a). Cohen's paper and my discussion with him afterward inspired my own initial application of ethnic theory to the NT (Esler 1996).

46. F. Barth 1994: 21.

47. This is a phenomenon well illustrated in the essays in Spickard and Burroughs 2000a.

48. For useful comments on the relationship between Jewish ethnicity and Jewish religion in the United States, see Gans 1994.

49. Waters 2000: 26–27.

50. This illustration would probably not work so well if we were to substitute Umbria for Sicily, since it is doubtful if any sense of identity shared by the people living in Umbria could be classed as ethnic. Such people could share some different identity, perhaps a "regional" one, where the only connection between them was one of geographic propinquity. This is an area (raised by Sean Freyne in a conversation we had in Dublin in December 2002) that would repay further research.

51. Stephan and Stephan 2000: 231.

52. J. N. Paden, writing in 1970 and cited in Okamura 1981: 452.

53. Stephan and Stephan 2000: 240.

54. Horowitz 1985: 144–47, 181–84.

55. Horowitz 1985: 143–44.

56. Sumner 1906: 12–13, cited from Reminick 1983: 7; I am indebted to Malina (2002) for this reference.

57. Horowitz 1985: 149.

58. Horowitz 1985: 151–60.

59. Horowitz 1985: 166.

60. Horowitz 1985: 171–81.

61. Horowitz 1985: 182.

62. Banton 1986: 49.

63. Robert Knox, *The Races of Men: A Philosophical Enquiry into the Influence of Race over the Destiny of Nations*. The second edition appeared in 1862. There is an excerpt in Augstein 1996a: 240ff.

64. Augstein 1996b: ix–x.

65. See Banton 1969, 1977.

66. Mason 1986: 7.

67. See Mason 1986: 6–7.

68. See Zimmerman 1988.

69. To cite only a few writers, see Sherwin-White 1967: 86–99; Stern 1988; Stendahl 1993 (even though in this essay he acknowledges that anti-Semitism was invented by Wilhelm Marr in the 1870s); Boyarin 1994, who attributes "anti-Semitism" to some first-century CE phenomena, for example, 1 Thess. 2:14 (p. 22), but denies that it affected Paul, when the whole concept is irrelevant to that period; and Roetzel 1999: 22.

70. Note the view of Sherwin-White (who nevertheless employs the word "anti-Semitism"): "Though Greeks and Latins refer to the Jews as an ἔθνος or a nation or a gens, i.e. a folk or a tribe, there is no genuinely racial or racist connotation. The distinction is political, social and religious, national rather than genetic" (1967: 99).

71. Balsdon 1979: 30–33.

72. See Balsdon 1979: 67 for a brief overview. For the primary sources see Stern 1974 and 1980; and for a full discussion see Gager 1983.

73. Sherwin-White 1967: 65.

74. Philo, *On Abraham* 107; ET in Yonge 1993: 420.

75. Almog 1988.

76. An interesting analogy here is the extent to which efforts to deal with so-called terrorists have been hindered by European and North American academics seeing their role to be not the dispassionate investigators of relevant phenomena through close involvement with primary data, but rather the defenders of liberal democracy content to demonize the subjects of their research and to limit their exposure to them; see Brannan, Esler, and Strindberg 2001.

77. Vermeulen and Govers 1994: 4–5.

78. Eriksen 1991.

79. Especially see Goudriaan 1992; Østergård 1992; Hall 1997; Pohl 1998b; and the essays in Malkin 2001a.

80. Malkin 2001b: 4.

81. This point is well made by Duling 2002/2003: 12.

82. Malina 2001: 58–80.

83. J. M. Hall 1997: 35.

84. Aristotle, *Politics* 1326.

85. J. M. Hall 1997: 35.

86. J. M. Hall 1997: 36.

87. Hesiod, *Catalogue of Women and Eoiae*, frg. 18; Evelyn-White 1936: 169.

88. E. Hall 1989: 7–8.

89. In 425 BCE Aristophanes parodied its opening chapters in one of his plays, *Acharnians* 515ff.

90. J. M. Hall 1997: 7.

91. J. M. Hall 1997: xiii.

92. J. M. Hall 1997: 17–33.

93. See Konstan 1997: 98, 100–106; Buell 2000: 244–45.

94. Petrochilus 1974: 17.

95. Walbank 1951: 46.

96. Petrochilus 1974: 20.

97. Hesiod, *Catalogue of Women and Eoiae*, frg. 4; see Evelyn-White 1936: 157.

98. Note Cicero in *Pro Flacco* 63: "who does not know . . . that there are three descent groups (*genera*) of Greeks? The Athenians are one of these, who were held to be Ionians, the second were called Aeolians and the third Dorians."

99. J. M. Hall 1997: 41.

100. J. M. Hall 1997: 36–38.

101. Malina 2001: 60–67.

102. See the discussion in Thomas and Stubbings 1962.

103. I omit "Judeans" from this list, to leave the discussion of this name until later. In citing these names I am not forgetting the continual need to be alert for Josephan tendentiousness; yet he provides these names during incidental illustrations in his argument and they do not fall under suspicion as central props in its logic.

104. The Macronians (Μάκρωνες) were a people of Pontus (Herodotus, *Histories* 2.104, etc.). Presumably their name derived from a territory called Μάκρων, but this word seems not to be attested in this sense.

105. These were a Pelasgian people who allegedly migrated to Italy and became the parent stock of the Etruscans. Tyrrhenia was another word for Etruria (Ovid, *Metamorphoses* 14.452).

106. Josephus, *Against Apion* 1.82.

107. W. H. S. Jones 1984: 113. On this type of material see Malina 1992.

108. W. H. S. Jones 1984: 115.

109. Malkin 2001b: 3.

110. E. Hall 1989.

111. E. Hall 1989: 110.

112. See, for example, Plato, *Republic* 4.427e 10–11.

113. See Plato, *Republic* 4.444b 7–8.

114. E. Hall 1989: 121–22.

115. E. Hall 1989: 103.

116. It is worth noting, however, that some claim that such a thing as Solomon's temple never existed and was an invention to fill in the myth of Israel's origins; see Thompson 1999. Certainly no archaeological remains of a temple prior to the one now called the Second Temple have been found in Jerusalem, but this could be the result of their having been entirely built over and subsumed into the later structure. It would have been rather odd if there were no Iron Age temple in Jerusalem.

117. Diodorus Siculus, *Bibliotheca Historica* 40.3; cited in Stern 1974: 26–9.

118. Josephus, *Against Apion* 1.179; see Stern 1974: 49–50. It is worth noting that

Stern insists on translating Ἰουδαῖοι as "Jews" here in spite of the express statement in the text linking the people and the land.

119. For Lysimachus see Josephus, *Against Apion* 1.305–10, in Stern 1974: 383–84. For Apion see Josephus, *Against Apion* 2.15–28, in Stern 1974: 395–97.

120. See Stern 1974: 337.

121. Weber 1978: 390; cited in Hutchinson and Smith, 1996: 36. For a fine treatment of diaspora peoples in contemporary society, including the Palestinians, see Klausner 1992.

122. See Freyne 2001: 185–86.

123. Cicero, *Pro Flacco* 28.67.

124. This work describes an embassy (of which Philo himself was a member) from the Judeans of Alexandria to the emperor Gaius (Caligula) in early 40 CE to complain of their persecution by the Greeks of the city. See the edition by Smallwood (1961). The passage in question is discussed in more detail in chapter four below.

125. For the whole passage see Philo, *Legatio ad Gaium* 156–57; ET in Smallwood 1961: 92.

126. Binder 1999: 488–89.

127. Philo, *In Flaccum* 46.

128. Esler 1987: 145–48. In contemporary cultures there is a tendency among the children and grandchildren of immigrants at times to feel less attached to the original homeland. But we should be chary of imputing such a phenomenon to ancient Judeans given that their dedication to maintaining distinctiveness in diaspora settings by sheltering within the "fence" of the Mosaic law has had few parallels, then or since.

129. Malina and Rohrbaugh 1992: 32–34, 168–69; 1998: 44–46; Pilch 1993; 1996; 1997; 1998; 1999: 98–104; Malina and Pilch 2000: 64–66; Malina 2000a; Horsley 1995; 1996; also see Hanhart 1995: 505.

130. Esler 1998: 4.

131. See Wahlde 2000: 49, who wants to retain "Jew" for "national use" and "Judean" for "regional use."

132. On these events see Brook 1999.

133. Josephus, *Judean War* 2:43.

134. Thackeray 1927: 339.

135. Contra Wahlde 2000: 49.

136. The problem is not so acute in German, since there the word for "Jews," *Juden*, at least conveys something of the inevitable connection to Judea. On the other hand, the problem of subsequent Jewish history obscuring the meaning of Ἰουδαῖοι is more pressing in Germany than anywhere (with the Gestapo order to Jews to leave their homes, "Juden 'raus!" ["Jews out!"], still echoing in the memory), so that the case for dropping *Juden* and using instead the word *Judäer* of the people is also strong.

137. See Esler 1994e: 125–30.

138. S. Cohen 1999: 69–106. Some of the ideas in this book appear in an earlier essay (Cohen 1990).

139. S. Cohen 1989: 17.

140. S. Cohen 1999: 5–6.

141. So F. Barth 1969b: 14, in a passage Cohen himself cites (1999: 5).

142. Cohen's reliance on Anthony Smith's 1981 four-element formulation, as opposed to Smith's later adoption of a six-element scheme in conjunction with John Hutchinson (as discussed above), emerges at 1999: 6–7.

143. A. Smith 1981: 66.

144. A. Smith 1986: 32: "*Ethnie* (ethnic communities) may now be defined as named human populations with shared ancestry myths, histories and cultures, having an association with a specific territory and a sense of solidarity." For religion as distinct from ethnicity, see Smith 1986: 34–37.

145. S. Cohen 1999: 6 n. 9, 7.

146. See Hutchinson and Smith 1996b: 6–7.

147. S. Cohen 1999: 8.

148. See W. Smith 1991 (religion as a post-Enlightenment concept); Malina 1986; 1994; 1996d; Esler 2001b (for the ancient Mediterranean position).

149. S. Cohen 1999: 71.

150. S. Cohen 1999: 72.

151. S. Cohen 1999: 6–7.

152. S. Cohen 1999: 73.

153. It is frequently translated "race," and I myself have previously entertained that possibility (Esler 2001b: 29 n. 10). The problems with the whole notion of "race," as set out above, suggest that "physical descent" is the best translation.

154. S. Cohen 1999: 73.

155. Josephus, *Judean War* 2:510 and 4:105.

156. Freyne 2000b: 130; he cites Josephus, *Judean War* 2:43, discussed above.

157. The same point about the reality of dual or nested ethnic identities can also be made against Richard Horsley's proposal (1995: 45 and passim) that there was a radical separation between Galileans and Judeans in Josephus's mind. There is no difficulty in their being, ethnically, both Galileans and Judeans. Yet at least Horsley has moved to the use of "Judeans" instead of "Jews." Horsley's proposal is subject to critique on other bases by Freyne 2000b: 26.

158. S. Cohen 1999: 78–81.

159. S. Cohen 1999: 8.

160. See Josephus, *Judean Antiquities* 20.142; S. Cohen 1999: 79.

161. See Kraemer 1989; M. Williams 1997. It must be noted that these contributions (especially Kraemer's) were produced before ethnicity theory was widely used in the field.

162. For the details, including primary references, for all of these occasions, see Stanley 1996: 101–3.

163. Stanley 1996: 105.

164. Malina 2002.

165. See Stanley 1996: 115–23.

166. Stanley 1996: 123.

4. The Context: Rome in the 50s CE

1. Lenski and Lenski 1987. For a general application of this model to Rome, see Esler 2000e: 11–12.

2. See Harris 1989 on the low literacy rates in the Roman world and Hezser's superlative analysis of the Judean situation (2001), with her advocacy of rates just as low (if not lower).

3. Malina 2000b: 43–45.

4. Malina 2001: 33–36.

5. Perhaps a metaphor will help. When we are flying in an airplane at 30,000 feet our view of the land below picks up only its larger features: lakes, mountains, plains, and so on. As we descend for landing we lose this big picture but begin to discern smaller aspects: individual buildings, trees, cars, even people. While a complete understanding of the landscape requires high and low altitude perspectives (indeed, a shuttling between both that may well reveal a higher view is challenged by lower-level data), the models discussed in the text are analogous to the former. Critics who oppose model use by advocating, for example, a Geertzian thick description of data (so Garrett 1992) or a "literary ethnography" (Lawrence 2002 and 2003), think the only way to fly, as it were, is a few hundred feet above the ground and thus deny themselves the broader perspective, for no convincing reason I can see. For a magisterial explanation of model use, see Elliott 1995: 36–50. Also see Esler 1995b: 4–8, in debate with the strongly argued and elegantly stated view of Garrett 1992, herself, of course, a creative interpreter of high ability (as in Garrett 1989). In spite of her unjustified (in my view) antipathy to generalizing about culture, Lawrence is a perceptive interpreter of texts.

6. Meggitt 1998: 18–29.

7. See Meggitt 1998: 29–39 for a valuable overview.

8. See the popular text by Lindsay (1960) and the important research by Jongman (1988) into the 153 wooden writing tablets once belonging to L. Caecilius Iucundus and by Franklin (1987, 1991, 1997a, 1997b) into the graffiti.

9. Cameron 1991: 30.

10. See Garnsey 1998b.

11. For seminal research into the Roman aristocracy, see Münzer 1999.

12. See Reasoner 1999: 45–63.

13. See Rohrbaugh 1991 and Malina 2000b: 26–45.

14. Malina 2001: 36.

15. Hopkins and Burton 1983a: 107–19 (for the late Republic); 1983b (for the early Empire).

16. Hopkins and Burton 1983b: 149–50.

17. Hopkins and Burton 1983b: 150.

18. Malina 2001: 34, 39.

19. See the various essays on patterns of friendship in the Greco–Roman world in Fitzgerald 1997, although the authors focus mainly on evidence in philosophical and literary texts and do not show much interest in the meaning of friendship within the characteristic patterns of Mediterranean culture.

20. Epstein 1987: 7.

21. Epstein 1987: 75.

22. Epstein 1987: 76.

23. Saller 1994: 72.

24. Saller 1994: 91.

25. Saller 1994: 92.

26. Epstein 1987: 4, where he also adds: "The exclusion of a former friend from one's house is attested in a couple of instances for the Republic but is likely to have been too commonplace to be reported regularly in the sources."

27. A fine example of this, for which I am grateful to Peter Oakes of the University of Manchester, is a collection of graffiti on a wall outside Region I Block X houses 3–4 in Pompei, in which a man of unknown occupation taunts a weaver for his alleged lack of amatory success (see *CIL* IV.3.I, nos. 8258, 8259).

28. See Versnel 1991 (covering Greek and Latin material); Winkler 1991.

29. Walker 1985: 45–46.

30. Meeks 1983: 31: "Evidently, besides conviviality the clubs offered the chance for people who had no chance to participate in the politics of the city itself to feel important in their own miniature republics."

31. Meggitt 1998: 34.

32. *ILS* 7457.

33. Saller 1994: 89.

34. Saller 1994: 93.

35. Frier 1980: 39–40.

36. See Yavetz 1952: 509–10, 514–17; Frier 1980: 26–33.

37. See Vitruvius, *De architectura* 2.8.7.

38. Strabo 5.3.7.

39. For details of dangerous methods of tenement construction and the risk of fire, see La Piana 1927: 207–13; Yavetz 1952: 508–12.

40. Yavetz 1952: 504.

41. The *Natural History* of Pliny the Elder (23/24–79 CE) is a valuable source for the crafts of the various ethnic groups in Rome and products sent to the provinces.

42. On *collegia* see Waltzing 1895–2000; La Piana 1927: 225–81; Kloppenborg and Wilson 1996.

43. La Piana (1927: 274–75), citing Waltzing 1895: 148, 215, and the list of *collegia domestica* in Waltzing 1899: 342ff. Waltzing's treatment is in 1899: 222–64.

44. La Piana 1927: 225.

45. Waltzing 1895: 255.

46. Meeks 1983: 31. See n. 23 above.

47. See Suetonius, *Divus Julius* 42: "Cuncta collegia, praeter antiquitus constituta, distraxit."

48. So Josephus, *Judean Antiquities* 14.215.

49. Suetonius, *Divus Augustus* 32; Waltzing 1895: 115–17.

50. La Piana 1927: 225.

51. See Coulston and Dodge 2001b: 10 n. 2, and the literature they cite.

52. Only citizens could receive the monthly wheat dole, and Philo tells us in *On the Embassy to Gaius* (156–57) that some Judeans did qualify.

53. For a succinct and well-documented discussion of resident aliens, see Elliott 2000: 476–83.

54. Note the view of La Piana (1927: 184–85): "Since there is no doubt that the Christians in Rome were for a long period mostly foreigners, and since it is also well known that the great majority of them belonged to the humbler social classes, the

study of the life and manners of the foreign multitudes in Rome during the early centuries of the empire might throw much light on the life of the Christian community itself."

55. See M. Williams 1994a: 182, who points out that the vast majority of the (poorer quality) scratched and painted epitaphs from the Judean catacombs in Rome were in Greek while most of the Latin ones were done on (more expensive) marble.

56. Juvenal, *Satire* 3.62–65.

57. La Piana 1927: 188–205.

58. This view, although doubted by La Piana (1927: 215), gains some archaeological support from the first-century levels extant beneath Santa Sabina, the exquisitely beautiful and well preserved fifth-century church on the Aventine (which has been in the hands of the Dominican order since the thirteenth century).

59. La Piana 1927: 215–21.

60. See map 1 in Noy 1995 for the location of these catacombs.

61. The figure is reproduced from Noy 1995: 574 by permission of Cambridge University Press.

62. As happened in 174 CE when the *statio* of the Tyrians in Puteoli, then declining in importance as Ostia grew, appealed to Tyre itself for financial help; see La Piana 1927: 255–65 for this incident and *stationes* generally.

63. La Piana 1927: 258.

64. Balsdon 1979: 31–32, 38.

65. So La Piana (1927: 228), who offers a useful summary of the position (1927: 226–34). Also see Sherwin-White 1967; Balsdon 1979, especially pp. 31–71 for data and discussion on the extremely negative Roman attitudes to Greek and other peoples.

66. La Piana 1927: 234.

67. Balsdon 1979: 161–92.

68. See Valerius Maximus, *Factorum ac dictorum memorabilium* 1.3.2. For a sample of the discussion of the Judeans in Rome, see Walters 1993: 28–29; Barclay 1996a: 282–319; Hedner-Zetterholm 2001. All of these writers use the words "Jew" and "Judaism." For reasons set out in the previous chapter, I submit that our expanding understanding of ethnicity in the ancient world means that such usage is difficult to defend for the first century CE and should be dropped.

69. Cicero, *Pro Flacco* 66.

70. The primary sources are Josephus, *Judean Antiquities* 18.65–84; Tacitus, *Annals* 2.85.4; Suetonius, *Tiberius* 36; Dio Cassius 57.18.5a. See the discussion in Brown 1983: 94; Barclay 1996a: 295, 298–301.

71. Barclay 1996a: 301.

72. See Williams 1994a: 178 and the evidence she cites.

73. See Williams 1994a: 165.

74. Frey 1936: 211–27.

75. Rutgers 1998: 49–54.

76. See Frey 1936: liii–cxliv (Introduction); Leon 1960; Williams 1994a, 1994b; Rutgers 1998: 45–71.

77. See Frey 1936: lxx.

78. Williams 1994a: 168.

79. See Frey 1936: lxx n. 3; Leon 1960: 139.

80. It remains possible that some later emperor was in mind, but that is far less likely than that the name refers to the first emperor who was particularly favorable to Judeans. Similarly, the Agrippa in question may have been Marcus Iulius Agrippa II, born in 27/28 and the son of Marcus Iulius Agrippa I, the Agrippa who as tetrarch of Galilee had John the Baptist beheaded. Agrippa II lived for a time in Rome and supported the Judean embassy to Claudius in 50 CE to complain of the Samaritans and the procurator Cumanus. Even so, it is more likely that his name would have been selected in the mid-first century CE to designate a Judean community than at any other time.

81. So Williams 1994b.

82. See Levinskaya 1996: 186.

83. Nanos 1996: 377.

84. Nanos 1999: 285–86.

85. Especially White 1996: 60–101; but also Meyers and Kraabel 1986: 177–89; Meyers and Strange 1981: 140–54.

86. See Binder 1999 for the position generally and Runesson 2001 for as authoritative a discussion of the synagogue at Ostia that we are likely to get in the regrettable absence of a final report on the excavation (conducted in the 1960s).

87. See Danker 1982.

88. Griffiths 1995.

89. So Horbury and Noy 1992: 215.

90. See Kraabel 1995: 99, 108, 112–15.

91. See Hengel 1966.

92. See Binder 1999: 307–17.

93. See the excellent discussion in Binder 1999: 233–54.

94. Meeks 1983: 80, citing Hengel 1966: 160–64; emphasis added.

95. See the edition by Smallwood 1961.

96. Philo, *Embassy* 156–57; ET by Smallwood 1961: 92, with modifications.

97. Philo, *Hypothetica*; for the Greek text see Gifford 1903a: 458; and for ET see Gifford 1903b: 389–90. For a study of synagogues and Sabbath observance see McKay 1994.

98. Philo, *Embassy* 158; ET by Smallwood 1961: 94.

99. Smallwood 1961: 24.

100. See Box 1939: xxxiii–xxxvii; Smallwood 1961: 36–43.

101. See *Against Flaccus* 21–101; *Embassy* 120–39.

102. See *Embassy* 121–33; *Against Flaccus* 44–62.

103. *Embassy* 132.

104. *Against Flaccus* 122–23.

105. See *Embassy* 134; *Against Flaccus* 42.

106. *Embassy* 134–35.

107. *Embassy* 132, 134.

108. See *Embassy* 133, 134; *Against Flaccus* 48–49.

109. *Against Flaccus* 53.

110. *Against Flaccus* 122–23.

111. See *t. Sukkah* 4:6; *y. Sukkah* 5, 1, 55a–b; *b. Sukkah* 51b; Levine (2000: 85) notes that although there is exaggeration here, the description is so detailed and unique that it should not be rejected out of hand as totally fanciful. Philo, after all, refers to a synagogue that was the "largest and most magnificent in the city" (*Embassy* 134). This was the one, mentioned in the text, in which the Greeks erected a bronze statue of someone riding a four-horse chariot. I am grateful to Stephen Catto of the University of Aberdeen for informing me of the rabbinic evidence.

112. On this interpretation see Courtney1980: 192; Duff 1904: 170.

113. See Duff 1904: ix–xviii.

114. I am grateful to my St. Mary's colleague, Professor Richard Bauckham, for alerting me to this significance of *proseucha* as a Greek loanword in Latin.

115. There are other references to beggars in Judean *proseuchai* in the Greek writers Artemidorus (mid- to late second century CE) in *Onirocritica* 3.53 (Stern 1980: 330), and Cleomedes in an astronomical text, written perhaps c. 360 CE (Stern 1980: 157–58); see Courtney 1980: 192.

116. The first- or second-century date was proposed by Collon 1940: 88, supported by Williams 1994a: 178 n. 88.

117. No. 531 in Frey 1936: 391.

118. An inscription from Panticape (now Kertsch) in the Crimea, on the northern shores of the Black Sea, and precisely datable to 80 CE, records a woman called Chreste manumitting her slave Heraclas in the *proseucha* so that he would be free to do as he liked, subject only to a duty of devotion and assiduity toward the *proseucha* with the agreement of her heirs and also under the joint guardianship of the *synagogue* of the Judeans (Frey 1936: no. 683). McKay (1994: 219) comments accurately in relation to this and two other similar inscriptions: "In all three inscriptions the synagogue of the Jews is referred to only in its civic function as a group with a memory, voice and power in the community. The buildings associated with these synagogues of the Jews are called *proseuchai.*"

119. See Binder 1999: 332; Runesson 2001.

120. See White 1997a and (more especially) 1997b.

121. Binder 1999: 331–32.

122. Binder 1999: 327. It is clear from the face of the inscription that the phrase "Mindis Faustus with his family" has been cut into the stone in place of the original donor a century later, possibly to record another donation.

123. Binder 1999: 335. For a discussion of this epigraphy see Runesson 2001: 85–92.

124. Binder 1999: 336.

125. So Nanos 1996: 377 n. 15.

126. From Runesson 2001: 79; floor plan of the first-century CE synagogue at Ostia (reprinted by permission of Anders Runesson), with names for parts of the building added (from Runesson 2001).

127. From Runesson 2001: 80; artistic reconstruction of the first-century CE synagogue building at Ostia by P. Lönegard, with the eastern wall adjusted by D. Mitternacht in accordance with Runesson 2002 (reprinted by permission of Birger Olsson and Anders Runesson).

128. It is represented in other periods in excerpts and epitomes by Zonaras and Xiphilinus.

129. Dio Cassius, *Historia Romana* 60.6.6; ET from Cary 1924: 383, but with the substitution of "Judeans" for "Jews" in translation of *Ioudaious*.

130. Suetonius, *Divus Claudius* 25.4; ET from Rolfe 1914: 53, but with the substitution of "Judeans" for "Jews" in translation of *Iudaeos*. The Latin is: "Iudaeos impulsore Chresto assidue tumultuantis expulit."

131. Orosius, *Historiarum adversus paganos libri VII*, 7.6.15–16. ET here by Slingerland 1997: 123 (replacing his "Jews" with "Judeans").

132. Slingerland 1992: 133–36.

133. Slingerland 1992: 134 n. 36.

134. Suetonius, *Nero* 10.

135. Slingerland 1992: 136–42; 1997: 123–29.

136. Slingerland 1991.

137. See Slingerland 1991, 1992.

138. Brown 1983: 100.

139. Tacitus, *Annals* 15.44.

140. See Slingerland 1997: 111–29, 203–41; Rutgers 1998: 193, admittedly without apparently having seen Brown 1983 (for which, see text).

141. Barclay 1996a: 305; Slingerland 1997: 97–110.

142. See Slingerland 1997: 81 (regarding Claudius securing the Judeans their rights); 1997: 16 (Claudius's "common plague" statement), both in reference to Claudius's settlement of the Alexandrian trouble as recorded in P. Lond. 1912.

143. See the helpful remarks by Brändtle and Stegemann 1998: 127.

144. See Brown 1983: 94, who notes that the smallest estimate of the Judean population in Rome he has seen is 10,000.

145. In addition, I have argued elsewhere (Esler 1987: 145–61) that certain difficulties in the early chapters of Acts are explicable on the basis that in the early Jerusalem days some diaspora Judean Christ-followers admitted non-Judean God-fearers to the movement, including joint table fellowship, possibly because of their manifesting the gifts of the Spirit (Esler 1994b), and that this caused problems with the Galilean core of the movement. If there were Romans among such God-fearers, they could have carried belief in Christ back to Rome.

146. This phenomenon can be seen time and again in Judean reaction to the preaching of the gospel as described in the Acts of the Apostles.

147. Watson (1986) argues that Paul is advocating maximal separation, while Nanos (1996) sees very little separation at all.

148. See Wiefel 1991 (originally published in German in 1970).

149. This area has been well developed by Young-Sung Jung (2000), and I have profited greatly from his discussion of the subject and from conversations with him.

150. Important literature in this area includes Hall 1966; Rapoport 1969, 1976a, 1977, 1982a, 1982b, 1990, 1994; Hillier and Hanson 1989; Kent 1990.

151. But for pioneering and provocative applications of spatial theory to Luke-Acts that do address most of these issues, see Jung 2000; O'Keefe 2002. For an honorable exception to the general disinterest in these questions that focuses on the

question of the housing conditions of the nonelite, although not directly related to Romans, see Jewett 1993.

152. Wallace-Hadrill 1997: 219.

153. See Wallace-Hadrill 1994, 1997.

154. Sack 1986.

155. Jung 2000.

156. Hall 1966.

157. Hillier and Hanson 1984.

158. Hillier and Hanson 1984: 180–82.

159. Hillier and Hanson 1984: 181.

160. The Greek writer Cleomedes referred to beggars who tended to gather in the courtyards *(aulai)* of the *proseucha;* see *De motu circulari* 2.1.91; for text and translation see Stern 1980: 157–58.

161. Binder 1999: 323.

162. Nanos (1999: 286–87), citing Josephus, *Judean Antiquities* 14.213–16.

163. La Piana 1927: 275.

164. See Claridge (1998: 284–88) for a discussion of San Clemente, with floor plans. This room, in a first-century *horrea* (warehouse), has a good claim to be the oldest extant interior space used for Christian worship.

165. See chapter fourteen below.

5. The Letter's Purpose in the Light of Romans 1:1-15 and 15:14—16:27

1. See chapter one above.

2. Minear 1971: 7.

3. I am grateful to Robert Jewett for bringing home to me the importance of this factor during conversations we had in Heidelberg in late October 2002.

4. Donfried 1991a. More recent discussion can be followed up in Miller 2000.

5. Stowers 1994: 30–33.

6. Stowers argues that the authors "encoded" in the text are "gentiles at Rome who know something about Jewish scripture and Jesus Christ" even though he cannot say who were its actual or "empirical" readers (1994: 22). N. Elliott believes the letter was "explicitly directed to a Gentile-Christian congregation" (1990: 7), yet also included "Jewish Christians" (1990: 32). Similarly Dunn 1988a: xlv.

7. The magnificence of Luther's translation of Romans is well brought out in his rendering of the opening four lines: "Paulus, ein Knecht Christi Jesu, berufen zum Apostel, ausgesondert, zu predigen das Evangelium Gottes, das er zuvor verheissen hat durch seine Propheten in der heiligen Schrift, von seinem Sohn Jesus Christus, unserm Herrn, der geboren ist aus dem Geschlecht Davids nach dem Fleisch, und nach dem Geist, der heiligt, eingesetzt ist als Sohn Gottes in Kraft durch die Auferstehung von den Toten" (translation in Nestle-Aland 2000: 409, *Das Neue Testament: Griechisch und Deutsch*).

8. For the notion of the Mediterranean as a recognizably distinctive part of the world in antiquity, see Esler 2000e: 3–9.

9. Jewett 1982b.

10. This is the view of Munck (1959: 200–209); N. Elliott 1990: 35, 71–72 (although he does not offer a detailed exegesis of these verses to support his position);

and Stowers 1994: 21. Although he favors the view that Paul was addressing a Roman audience "made up of a Gentile-Christian majority and a Jewish-Christian minority," Moo (1996: 13) nevertheless considers that Rom. 1:5-6 "appear to be decisive" for Paul's readers having been "Gentile Christians" (1996: 11).

11. Moo 1996: 53.

12. Dunn 1988a: 18.

13. Fitzmyer 1993: 238.

14. Dunn 1988a: 18–19.

15. Moo 1996: 61.

16. Dunn 1988a: 32.

17. On the other hand, note Robert Jewett's astute recognition of the "shameful" character of the word "gentiles" (1997: 261, 264).

18. His statement in Rom. 15:19 that he has fully preached the gospel of Christ "from Jerusalem as far round as Illyricum" probably relates to his activities during his two brief visits to the city that he describes in Gal. 1:18—2:10. Apart from these occasions, there is no sign in his own letters that he had evangelized in Judea by the time he wrote Romans.

19. Paul's statement at 1 Thess. 1:9 that his addressees "turned to God from idols to serve the living and true God" is best interpreted on the basis of an audience composed solely of non-Judeans, in spite of the different picture in Acts 17:1-9; see Esler 2001a: 1200.

20. See the valuable remarks by Meeks on this point (1983: 29). The picture in Acts, however, of Paul routinely commencing his mission in Judean synagogues is probably tendentious; see Esler 1987: 42. In a city like Thessalonika, with its wholly non-Judean congregation, Paul may have made initial contacts and preached the gospel as he plied his trade (probably among non-Judeans) in a leather worker's shop (see Hock 1980).

21. For a discussion of Paul as "apostle of the non-Judeans," see Strelan 1996: 303–6.

22. Here the function of the clause at the end of Gal. 2:9: "that we (should go) to the ἔθνη and they to the circumcision" is "primarily to emphasize the authority of Paul and Barnabas and the legitimacy of their gospel in one mission area, and that of the pillars in another, rather than simply to differentiate those areas. This point can be made with a colloquial translation of v. 9: 'so that we might do our thing among the Gentiles, while they did theirs among the Jews'" (Esler 1995d: 301).

23. Although my argument depends on much more than simply the prepositional phrase ἐν οἷς in v. 6, note Schlatter, correctly, on this verse: "He does not say that they are of Gentile extraction, for there are many Jews among them. For this reason he did not say ex hôn este kai hymeis" (1995: 11). Moo wrongly underestimates the force of the preposition (1996: 54).

24. Minear 1971: 2.

25. See Jewett 1988.

26. See Manson 1991 (originally expressed in 1938), especially at 13–15; and Marxsen 1968: 107–8. For a helpful overview of the discussion, see Jewett 1988: 147–48 and the literature he cites.

27. Gamble 1977.

28. See Ollrog 1980, whose arguments are summarized and adopted by Jewett 1988: 148.

29. Dunn is correct to insist on this translation of προστάτις as the only plausible one (1988b: 888).

30. See the arguments in Fitzmyer 1993: 85; Moo 1996: 2–3.

31. See Kearsley 1999 and Osiek 2004/5.

32. So Dodd 1932: 234–35; Dunn 1988b: 886; Jewett 1988: 151; Fitzmyer 1993: 729.

33. Minear 1971: 7.

34. Lampe 1991: 229–30.

35. So Jewett 1988: 151–52.

36. Note that Paul includes a greeting from Tertius, the scribe to whom he dictated the letter, in Rom. 16:22.

37. Aquila is described as a Judean from Pontus in Acts 18:2 and his wife is likely to have been Judean as well.

38. A point powerfully made by Bauckham 2002a: 165–69.

39. Bauckham 2002a: 170.

40. As made by Lampe 1991: 224–25.

41. A suggestion well made by Dunn 1988b: 11.

42. So Dunn 1988b: 893; contra, Lampe 1991: 225.

43. Moo 1996: 11.

44. "I must stress that I do not need to throw out chapter 16 in order to maintain a gentile audience in the text. . . . Ancient letters frequently send salutations to individuals who are not encoded readers" (Stowers 1994: 33).

45. The absolute centrality of honor as the primary value in ancient Mediterranean culture and the significance of this fact for NT interpretation was first set out by Malina in 1981 (3rd ed. 2001). Most current NT scholars probably accept this view, which is also now being expounded by classical scholars; see Lendon 1997; Barton 2001. For essays dealing with various aspects of honor in Romans, see Moxnes 1988a, 1988b, 1995; Jewett 1997.

46. See Nanos 1996.

47. Minear's five factions were: (a) the "weak in faith" who condemned the "strong in faith"; (b) the strong in faith who scorned and despised the weak in faith; (c) the doubters (cf. Rom. 14:23); (d) the weak in faith who did not condemn the strong; and (e) the strong in faith who did not despise the weak (1971: 8–15).

48. This was the case at Thessalonika (1 Thess. 1:1), Cenchreae (Rom. 16:1), and, in spite of its prominent divisions, at Corinth (1 Cor. 1:2; 2 Cor. 1:1). Moreover, the ἐκκλησίαι that Paul addresses in Gal. 1:2 may well have reflected a situation where there was a single ἐκκλησία in a number of Galatian towns.

49. Minear 1971: 7–8.

50. See Lampe 1987. Lampe has prepared an extensive revision of this text; see his *From Paul to Valentinus: Christians at Rome in the First Two Centuries* (Minneapolis: Fortress Press, 2003).

51. Lampe 1991.

52. Minear 1971: 24.

53. Lampe 1991: 230.

54. For example, see Brown 1983a: 108; Walters 1993: 130 n. 39.

55. Caragounis 1998: 252–60.

56. Brent 1995: 456.

57. Corinth had been refounded in 44 BCE by Julius Caesar as a Roman colony.

58. This is noted by Brent 1995: 400.

59. See Jewett 1993.

60 Fitzmyer 1993: 740–41.

61. As Brent, for example, points out (1995: 399), it is interesting to ask what connection the groups evident in Romans 16 have with the *tituli* churches of Rome documented in the fifth to sixth centuries CE in the *Liber Pontificalis* (1.3.10) where each church is described as a quasi-diocese with its own building, clergy, liturgy, and burial places. There are twenty-five such titular parishes in the proceedings of the Roman Synods from 499 to 595 (Lampe 1987: 302–4).

62. See Moxnes 1997b and 1997c for illuminating discussions of many of the factors involved in the varying relationships between cultural settings, families, and houses.

63. See Malina 2001 for the general position, and Lendon 1997 and Barton 2001 for Rome.

64. See 1 Cor. 1:10-17; 3:3; 11:18.

65. See Stanley 1996.

66. Lagrange 1931: 372: "One is astonished to find, after the greetings to the Romans and before those from Paul's companions, advice directed against the sowers of discord. . . . The context is definitely not natural."

67. Ziesler 1989: 349.

68. See Käsemann 1980: 416–17; Watson 1986: 102; Dunn 1988b: 901; Fitzmyer 1993: 745.

69. Dunn 1988b: 901.

70. Fitzmyer 1993: 745.

71. Moo 1996: 929.

72. Donfried 1991d: 51–52.

73. So Dunn 1988b: 901; Moo 1996: 929–30.

74. So Fitzmyer 1993: 744.

75. For summaries of the debate over the purpose of Romans, see Donfried 1991b; Jervis 1991: 11–28; Guerra 1995: 22–42.

76. Minear 1971: 2.

77. See his brilliant essay on gossip in the NT, Rohrbaugh 2001.

78. I am avoiding using the word "saints" because of the inappropriate connotations produced by the later history of this word.

79. See Esler 1998: 117–40, and an earlier version of the same argument in Esler 1995d.

80. Note the description of this at 2 Cor. 8:4: "the sharing in the ministry for the holy ones" (τὴν κοινωνίαν τῆς διακονίας εἰς τοὺς ἁγίους).

81. See Martyn 1997: 38–39. Georgi (1992: 49), on the other hand, and perhaps not so plausibly, suggests that "the Galatians—brought somewhat back to earth by

the admonitions made in Paul's epistle—had succeeded in disentangling themselves from the influences of the opponents."

82. For a lucid exposition of challenge-and-riposte, which was central to most social interactions in the ancient Mediterranean world, see Malina 2001: 33–36.

83. For a striking exception to this lack of interest, see the well-judged comments of Dunn 1988b: 879–80.

84. See Moo 1996: 910–11.

85. See Esler 1998.

86. Esler 1998.

87. For Luke-Acts see Esler 1987 (where I formulated the model of the movement from reform movement to sect); for John's Gospel see Esler 1994c.

88. This point has been made previously by W. S. Campbell (1991: 124): "the thesis proposed in this [sc. Watson's] book fits the Paul of Galatians better than of Romans."

89. Watson 1986: 178.

90. Nanos 1996.

91. Campbell 1991: 100.

92. Campbell 1991: 116.

93. Boyarin 1994: 22 unfortunately misses the fact that Paul could hardly have given vent to a racist attitude that came into existence only in the nineteenth century.

94. Boyarin 1994: 152.

95. It would be unhelpful to refer to the Judean ethnic group as "Judeanism" (still less as "Judaism") since "-ism" is not an ending we attach to ethnic groups in English, but rather to ideologies or religions. The word Ἰουδαϊσμός that appears in Gal. 1:14 refers to that part of Judean ethnic identity that relates to the observance of its laws and customs (as in 2 Macc. 2:21).

96. See Morgan 1995: 63, 72; Miller 2000: 178.

97. Haslam 2001: 58.

98. Jervis 1991: 158.

6. Common Ingroup Identity and Romans 1:1—3:20

1. For this summation of the nature of leadership see Haslam 2001: 58.

2. So Haslam (2001: 3–4), interpreting the views of E. P. Hollander.

3. See the valuable discussion of the opening of the letter in Jervis 1991: 69–85.

4. The contrast with the other undoubtedly authentic epistles is instructive. Paul often names someone else as coauthor of the letter (Sosthenes in 1 Cor. 1:1; Timothy in 2 Cor. 1:1, Phil. 1:1, and Phlm 1; Silvanus and Timothy in 1 Thess. 1:1); Galatians (1:1) is the only other letter naming him alone. The title "apostle" appears elsewhere at the start of 1 and 2 Corinthians and Galatians. The closest comparison to "slave of Christ Jesus" is the plural form, "slaves of Christ Jesus," of himself and Timothy in Phil. 1:1.

5. See Dodd 1932: 4–5; Dunn 1988a: 5; Moo 1996: 45 (who also properly warns of the dangers of seeking to define the traditions used too closely: 1996: 45–46).

6. Haslam 2001: 66.

7. This is an unusual word, only occurring elsewhere in the NT in 2 Cor. 9:5, where it means "promised" (of a gift) and is used of human agents.

8. That he does not use ἐκκλησία in addressing the Philippians suggests that this view can only be advanced cautiously.

9. See 1 Thess. 1:5 for Paul's statement of how his proclamation of the gospel in Thessalonika occurred with power and the Holy Spirit, by miracles and charismatic gifts (Esler 2001a: 1203). The same thing occurred in Galatia (Gal. 3:1–5). In 1 Cor. 14:18 he thanks God that he speaks in tongues more than any of the Corinthians. There is no doubt that charismatic phenomena created an exciting zone of Spirit-filled experience that was characteristic of his ministry and congregations.

10. Such as the one at Thessalonika; see 1 Thess. 3:2, where he employs the same word for "strengthen" used here—στηρίζω.

11. Käsemann 1980: 19.

12. As Moo thinks he is (1996: 62).

13. So Ziesler 1989: 66.

14. C. Barton 2001: 224.

15. So Ziesler 1989: 68. Other possibilities are that he held fast to the gospel, in spite of the sophistication of contemporary culture, or that the gospel was not destructive of ethical living (ibid., 67–68).

16. See Esler 1998: 141–77.

17. Bassler (1982) constitutes an exception to the majority view by arguing that the theme of 1:18—3:20 is divine impartiality, not universal human guilt.

18. Moo 1996: 92.

19. Wedderburn 1988: 36.

20. Moo 1996: 92.

21. See Tobin 1993.

22. Dovidio et al. 1998: 117; Gaertner et al. 2000: 133.

23. Campbell 1995: 272.

24. Gaertner et al. 2000: 143.

25. Dovidio et al. 1998: 117.

26. See Esler 2004b.

27. For a recent discussion of the "two ways" tradition (in relation to its appearance in the *Didache*), see Sandt and Flusser 2002. Their treatment of it as a "Jewish" tradition appears at 140–90.

28. See Horbury 2001: 652–53.

29. See Wis. 13:16 and the *Apocalypse of Abraham*, a work to be dated sometime shortly after 70 CE, which describes in chaps. 1–7 how certain idols, including some made by Abraham's father, succumb to various (rather comic) catastrophes, beginning with one that had fallen over.

30. Oakes, Haslam, and Turner 1994: 211.

31. Oakes, Haslam, and Turner 1994: 213.

32. See Fitzmyer 1993: 270; Käsemann 1980: 33 (in 1:18-32 "the spotlight undoubtedly falls on the Gentile world").

33. Hooker 1990: 78.

34. See Barrett 1962: 17–19; Wedderburn 1988: 119–20; Dunn 1988a: 72.

35. Hooker 1990: 78.

36. Wedderburn 1988: 119.

37. Käsemann 1980: 45.

38. Martin 1995: 334.
39. Stowers 1994: 86–87.
40. Martin 1995: 335.
41. See Esler 2004b.
42. For a recent discussion of the tradition see Fields 1997.
43. See Dover 1978: 172–73.
44. See Winkler 1990: 11.
45. Persuasive evidence for this comes from the coarse way in which Catullus boasts he is going to treat two men whom he labels as assuming a passive position in same-sex intercourse: "Pedicabo ego vos et irrumabo, Aureli pathice et cinaede Furi" (16.1-2).
46. See Esler 2004b.
47. I am ending this section with v. 6, since the μὲν . . . δέ construction in vv. 7–8 marks a new unit more clearly than the relative pronoun (ὅς) at the start of v. 6.
48. So Käsemann 1990: 52–57; Dunn 1988a: 78; Moo 1996: 125–27, to cite merely a few examples.
49. Stowers 1994: 102.
50. See Bassler 1982; note the full title of this book: *Divine Impartiality: Paul and a Theological Axiom.*
51. Contra Dunn 1988a: 146.

7. The Foundations of the New Identity (Romans 3:21-31)

1. Fitzmyer 1993: 343–44, 353.
2. Sanders 1983: 13–14 n. 18.
3. Von Dobbeler 1987.
4. See Dunn 1997. Also see Matlock 2000 on lexical issues in this debate.
5. For a British scholar who has also adopted the subjective meaning, see Hooker 1989.
6. See Hays 1993; Johnson 1982; Williams 1980, 1987.
7. These are Rom. 3:22, 26; Gal. 2:16 (twice), 20; 3:22; Phil. 3:9.
8. Tobin 1993: 300 n. 5.
9. For an unconvincing attempt to deny εἰς Χριστὸν Ἰησοῦν ἐπιστεύσαμεν at Gal. 2:16 their plain meaning, see Williams 1987: 442–44.
10. Hays 1997: 55.
11. Williams 1987: 446.
12. Hays 1997: 51–52.
13. For a balanced assessment of Arianism see Rankin 2000.
14. This debate is well illustrated in Hick 1977.
15. Note the typically balanced view of Wiles 1977: 8: "The absence of incarnational belief would not simply destroy this mediatorial function altogether. It would still be possible to see Jesus not only as one who embodies a full response of man to God but also as one who expresses and embodies the way of God towards men."
16. Charles Monroe Sheldon's *In His Steps: "What Would Jesus Do?"* was first published in 1896, and has gone through numerous reprints. I am indebted to Robert Jewett for alerting me to the importance of this work in this discussion.

17. Ziesler 1989: 114, emphasis added.

18. See Reumann 1982.

19. See Esler 1998: 141–77.

20. Käsemann 1980: 112.

21. Käsemann 1980: 112.

22. I am using quotation marks because in my own experience, outside the context of this particular discussion, the word "forensic" is generally limited in its usage (as opposed to its dictionary definitions) to phrases such as "forensic psychiatry," "forensic science," and "forensic investigation," with "judicial" being the usual epithet for the decisions of judges. "Forensic" in relation to a decision by a judge in court sounds odd to my ears. Perhaps there is some difference here between British/Australian usage on the one hand and U.S. usage on the other? Or perhaps biblical scholars everywhere in the anglophonic world have adopted an epithet they think appropriate to the decisions of judges in ignorance of the usage of lawyers themselves?

23. Käsemann 1980: 113.

24. Ziesler 1972.

25. Similarly Morgan 1995: 25.

26. Ps. 143:2 cannot be summoned against this conclusion. Pace Betz (1979: 118), the eschatological judgment is *not* in view in that psalm, "since the psalmist, beset by enemies, is there simply beseeching God not to condemn him but to come to his aid—and soon (cf. v. 7)" (Esler 1998: 251 n. 1). It is possible that Paul alludes to Ps. 143:2 in Gal. 2:16 and Rom. 3:20. Yet in both cases he does not inform his audience that he is doing so, perhaps a wise course given that the particular point he wants to make, that righteousness does not come from works of law, is nowhere to be found in Ps. 143:2. Paul also alters LXX πᾶς ζῶν to the expression πᾶσα σάρξ, which is much closer to his own thought, but which rather disguises the possible source of the expression. Indeed, in Gal. 2:16 he even omits ἐνώπιόν σου from the psalm. Nor does Paul mention the element of judgment present in it. Its attraction for him was not in any connection between righteousness and judgment, final or otherwise. It was because this was the only place in scripture that expressed the idea that no one will be righteoused (using the verb δικαιόω), even though the addition of "by works of the law" is a Pauline addition. Indeed, Paul may have intended no allusion to the psalm but it merely subconsciously provided him with the raw material for expressing a particular idea.

27. Matera 1992: 93.

28. Lagrange 1931: 122–33; Esler 1998: 160–64 (relating to data in the LXX) and 160–77 (specifically on Galatians).

29. Exod. 23:7; Deut. 25:1; 2 Sam. 15:4; Ps. 81:3 (LXX; "gods" who judge); Isa. 1:17; 5:23; Ezek. 44:24; Sir. 42:2.

30. See Exod. 23:7 and Isa. 5:23. For a discussion see Esler 1998: 150–51, 161.

31. See Gen. 38:26; 44:16; Job 33:32; Ps. 72:13 (LXX); Jer. 3:11; Ezek. 16:51–52.

32. Sir. 1:21; 7:5; 10:29; 13:22; 18:22; 23:11; 26:29; 34:5; see Esler 1998: 162.

33. Lagrange 1931: 123–31.

34. Ps. 18:9 (LXX); 50:4 (LXX); Isa. 42:21; Sir. 18:2.

35. Ps. 142:2 (LXX); Mic. 7:9; Isa. 43:9, 26; 50:8, 11.

36. There is judicial imagery in Ps. 142:3; Mic. 7:9; and Isa. 43:9, but not in Isa. 43:26; 50:8; 53:11.

37. See Esler 1998: 149–50.

38. See Esler 1998: 153–59.

39. Morgan 1995: 71.

40. Morgan 1995: 71.

41. Esler 1998: 141–77.

42. Esler 1998: 160–90.

43. For the feebleness of "judicial" interpretations of δικαιοῦν, see Esler 1998: 160–64.

44. See Prov. 10:2; 11:4, 5, 21, 30; 12:28; 13:2, 6; 14:34; 15:5, 9, 29; Ps. 36:6 (LXX).

45. Job has the next largest number of occurrences of ἀσεβής, about 40 examples in total.

46. Fitzmyer 1993: 278.

47. Malina 2001: 32–33.

48. See Esler 1998: 82–86, 164–69.

49. Esler 1998: 165–69.

50. Esler 1998: 176.

51. Käsemann 1980: 102.

52. As noted earlier in this chapter, there is little difference between use of the present passive form of the verb δικαιόω and the epithet δίκαιος; that is why I have translated δικαιοῦσθαι in this verse as "righteous" and not "righteoused."

53. Moxnes 1980: 6.

54. Moxnes 1980: 34.

55. Moxnes 1980: 40–41.

8. Abraham as a Prototype of Group Identity (Romans 4)

1. A version of the material in this chapter was presented as a paper in the Social World seminar at the British New Testament Conference meeting in Cambridge on 6 September 2002. I am grateful for responses made on that occasion by the participants, especially William Campbell, Gerald Downing, David Horrell, and Halvor Moxnes, none of whom, however, is responsible for the views expressed here.

2. It has been suggested (by Borgen 1965: 47–50; and van der Minde 1976: 78–83) that the chapter represents a midrash on Gen. 15:6, which is prominent throughout the argument; but it is doubtful if applying this label helps us to understand Paul's communicative purpose any better.

3. See the discussion (and references) in Moxnes 1980: 103–5.

4. Dodd 1932: 64.

5. Watson 1986: 139.

6. Moxnes 1980: 103.

7. Examples include Käsemann ("Abraham . . . is the prototype of the justification of the ungodly and, as the Gentile Christians prove, is thus also the father of justified ungodly" [1971: 89]), Hanson ("he is the prototype of believing Christians" [1974: 62]), Dunn ("For within the Judaism of Paul's day Abraham had long been lauded as,

in effect, the prototype of the devout Jew" [1988a: 226]), and Adams ("It is recognized by scholars that Abraham serves for Paul in Romans 4 as, in some respects, a prototype of Christian faith" [1997: 65–66]).

8. A. von Dobbeler 1987: 133–45. Dobbeler shows how Paul presents Abraham as an example *(Beispiel)* of four different types of people: those who rely not on works but on God's mercy (4:1-8), the uncircumcised righteous (4:9-12), the recipients of the promise apart from law (4:13-17), and the person of righteous, unshakeable faith (4:18-22).

9. See Smith and Zarate 1990: 245.

10. Smith and Zarate 1990: 246.

11. This is the subject of Smith and Zarate 1990.

12. Outgroup homogeneity is a common but not inevitable feature of intergroup relationships; see Brown 2000: 285–90.

13. Cinnirella 1998.

14. For the difficulties with asserting an historical basis for Abraham in the second millennium BCE, see Van Seters 1975.

15. This is the title of the novel by T. H. White.

16. Cinnirella 1998: 232.

17. In Rome this is expressed in the notion of *mos maiorum* and the extraordinary rituals for honoring ancestors practiced by elite families especially, so that even in the imperial period such families preserved crafted images of their ancestors in their homes.

18. Bruce Malina mounted a strong argument for our need to read biblical texts within the perspective of "Mediterranean time" rather than "Swiss time" as long ago as 1989 (reprinted as Malina 1996b), but the fundamental challenge he thus posed to much biblical interpretation has been insufficiently addressed by most scholars.

19. Condor 1996: 289–91.

20. Carr 1991: 113–14; cited at Condor 1996: 306.

21. See Halbwachs 1980. Halbwachs died in Buchenwald in 1945.

22. Billig 1990: 60.

23. Middleton and Edwards 1990b: 10: *"he who controls the past controls who we are."*

24. Billig 1990: 62.

25. See Assmann 2000 and 2002 for the basic theory and numerous applications.

26. For the potential in Assmann's position see his absorbing monograph on Moses (1997).

27. In a speech delivered to 3,000 U.S. marines at Camp Pendleton, California, on 28 August 2002, Donald Rumsfeld said: "It wasn't until each country got attacked that they said: 'Maybe Winston Churchill was right, Maybe that lone voice expressing concern . . . was right'" (*The Times,* 29 August 2002, p. 18). The criticism by a number of British commentators (see *The Guardian,* 29 August 2002, p. 3) mainly argued that Rumsfeld greatly oversimplified Churchill.

28. The notion of "the processing of the past" derives from David Cohen (1994: 4, 245) and I have applied it recently in a study of the book of Judith (Esler 2002).

29. See Thelen 1989: 1127.

30. Middleton and Edwards 1990b: 10.

31. For this characteristic of stereotypes see Oakes, Haslam, and Turner 1994: 83, 211–13.

32. See Malina 2001: 58–67, who does not suggest that individuals were unimportant (an impression one gets from Burnett 2001), but that they derived meaning from group belonging in ways that he rightly argues are not (at the appropriate level of abstraction) characteristic of North Atlantic cultures.

33. Shils 1981.

34. Shils 1981: 12.

35. Keesmaat 1999: 17.

36. Fishbane 1985: 6.

37. Fishbane 1977: 286.

38. Keesmaat 1999.

39. Fishbane 1985: 15.

40. Fishbane 1985: 16.

41. Hays 1989.

42. Hays 1989: 1–21.

43. Hays 1989: 20–21. He is quoting Michael Fishbane.

44. Hezser 2001.

45. See Dunn 1988a: 276–77.

46. See Goppelt 1972: 251–52. I put quotation marks around "eschatological" because I consider this word has passed its expiration date in biblical studies; see chapter eleven below.

47. Goppelt 1972: 250.

48. Dovidio et al. 1998: 117; Gaertner et al. 2000: 133.

49. Gaertner et al. 2000: 144–45.

50. Watson 1986: 178.

51. Boyarin 1994: 22.

52. For a survey of Abraham in "Jewish" literature see Hansen 1989: 175–99; Moxnes 1980: 117–69 (especially covering Philo).

53. *Pss. Sol.* 9:8–9; ET by Wright 1985: 661.

54. See Moo 1996: 256.

55. See Halbwachs 1980: 80 for this dimension of collective memory.

56. Halbwachs 1980: 85–86.

57. So Schwartz 1990: 81–82, drawing particularly on Lowenthal 1985: 209–10.

58. So Schwartz 1990: 82, drawing especially on Shils 1981: 31–32.

59. So Dunn 1991: 304.

60. Philo, *On Abraham* 276; ET in Yonge 1993: 434.

61. As a few examples see Barrett 1982b; Barclay 1987: 87–88; Hansen 1989: 98, 112, 170–74; Siker 1991: 31–35.

62. Moxnes notes (1980: 125) that the "collection of Scriptures consisting of the Law, the Prophets and the Writings has been more or less established at the very latest by *c.* 200 B.C."

63. Käsemann 1971: 96.

64. Philo, *On Abraham* 5; ET in Yonge 1993: 411.

65. Hansen comes close to this when he writes in relation to the use of Israelite scripture concerning Abraham in Galatia: "The argument from authority is not only an argument from the authority of Scripture; it is also an argument from the model of Abraham's faith" (1989: 112).

66. Barclay 1987: 87–89; for a more ample use of Galatians as a source of knowledge of its context, see Esler 1998: 61–68 (largely in critique of the extremely minimalist positions of Lyons 1985 and Hall 1991) and passim.

67. Siker 1991: 34.

68. See Hansen 1989: 171.

69. See Esler 1998: passim for the general position, and pp. 92–116 for the problem with mixed table fellowship.

70. Barrett 1982b.

71. Esler 1998: 173.

72. See Gen. 12:3, 7; 13:15; 17:7, 16; 22:18; 24:7.

73. I have elsewhere commented on the significance of these arguments in Paul's assertion of a positive social identity for his Galatian congregations; see Esler 1998: 173–75, 209–15.

74. Siker 1991: 49 and 213 n. 63.

75. Tobin 1995: 441–42.

76. Breakwell 1986: 47–48.

77. Breakwell 1986: 128–47.

78. Rohrbaugh 2001.

79. See A. von Dobbeler 1987: 133–35 on these verses.

80. Richard Hays has suggested (1985) that we should repunctuate this question to read, "What then shall we say? Have we found Abraham (to be) our forefather according to the flesh?" This interesting view is unconvincing (although Hays has found a supporter in Cranford [1995: 75–76]), since none of the other instances in Romans of the initial expression τί (οὖν) ἐροῦμεν that he cites for introducing a break before εὑρηκέναι is followed by an infinitive and, more importantly, because we would then have Paul asking a question not taken up in Romans 4. I assume that Paul has used the perfect infinitive (εὑρηκέναι) to indicate that the discovery that Abraham made has a continuing validity in the present. This use of the perfect infinitive is thus part of Paul's argument that Abraham is a prototype of faith (as argued here).

81. For this latter meaning I rely on Gal. 3:3, where Paul, in reference to his converts' interest in being circumcised, says: "Having begun with the Spirit, are you now ending with the flesh (ἐν σαρκί)?"

82. As E. P. Sanders has pointed out (1983: 21), the only two places in the LXX connecting πίστις and a δικ- root word are Gen. 15:6 and Hab. 2:4.

83. This perspective was reasonably labeled as "the new perspective" by Dunn (see his essay "The New Perspective on Paul"; Dunn 1990: 183–241). But given that over twenty-five years have now elapsed since Sanders brought it to the attention of the scholarly world, the label "new" is hardly appropriate except for those who prefer endless iteration of the known to the discovery of the unknown. The recognition that Paul is speaking of the works of the Mosaic law and not human action generally has

become what research scientists call "background technology," as opposed to "foreground technology," which refers to ideas currently at the forefront of research and pushing knowledge in new directions. For an analysis of Romans 4 using Sanders's perspective mediated through Dunn, see Cranford 1995.

84. Dunn 1988a: 200. He does not offer any explanation of the meaning of "type" or "model" in this context, however.

85. *Damascus Document* 3.2–3; ET in Martínez 1994: 34.

86. Moxnes 1980: 130–64. Yet, as noted above, Philo still insists on Abraham as the "first author and founder of our nation; a man according to the law as some persons think, but, as my argument has shown, one who is himself the unwritten law and justice of God" (*On Abraham* 276; ET in Yonge 1993: 434). On the different meanings of πίστις for Philo and Paul see Käsemann 1980: 107, 112.

87. See Esler 1998: 165–69; and chapter seven above.

88. Moo 1996: 266.

89. See the comments of A. von Dobbeler 1987: 135–36 on these verses.

90. Here περιτομῆς is an epexegetic genitive (Moo 1996: 268). There is a clear allusion to the phrase εἰς σημεῖον διαθήκης in Gen. 17:11.

91. See Wright 1991 for an important expression of this view. For an anti-covenantal reading of Paul much closer to the view taken in this volume, see Martyn 1991.

92. A. von Dobbeler 1987: 136: "Die abschliessende Bezeichnung Abrahams als πατὴρ ἡμῶν fasst die beiden Gruppen (Juden- und Heidenchristen) unter der einen Vaterschaft Abrahams zusammen" ("The final designation of Abraham as 'our father' unites both groups [Judeans and non-Judean Christians] under the fatherhood of Abraham").

93. Ambrosiaster, *Commentarius in epistulam ad Romanos*, on 4:12 (Vogels 1966: 137): "hoc dicit, quia credens Abraham primus factus pater est circumcisionis, sed cordis, non tantum eorum, qui sunt ex eius origine, sed et eorum, qui similiter credunt ex gentibus. Secundum carnem enim Iudaeorum pater est, secundum fidem vero omnium credentium."

94. A. von Dobbeler's valuable comments on Rom. 4:13–22 are worth close attention (1987: 136–40).

95. Rom. 4:13, 14, 16, 20; 9:4, 8, 9; 15:8. The cognate verb ἐπαγγέλλομαι appears once, at 4:21.

96. See Moo 1996: 274.

97. Although his expression is not particularly clear, Paul probably does not mean here Judeans outside the Christ-movement but the Judean members; see the arguments to this effect by Moo 1996: 278–79.

98. So Dunn 1988a: 215.

99. So Moo 1996: 277.

100. Luz 1967: 322.

101. Martyn 1991: 172.

102. Adams 1997.

103. See A. von Dobbeler 1987: 140–42 for "Die Anwendung des Abraham-Beispiels auf die christliche Gemeinde" ("The application of the example of Abraham to the Christian community").

104. Käsemann 1980: 106–11.

9. The New Identity in Christ: Origin and Entry (Romans 5–6)

1. Theissen 1987: 179.

2. It is important to note that ἵνα clauses can express result as well as purpose; see n. 21 below.

3. MacDonald 1990: 86.

4. See Moxnes 1980: 41–45.

5. See chapter eleven.

6. See McDonald 1990: 89: "It is in 5.1-11, that, for the first time in the letter, Paul describes the life of faith."

7. So Ziesler 1989: 139, for the reason that this form of love is spelled out in vv. 6-8.

8. See chapter eleven.

9. See Dunn 1988a: 252.

10. Fitzmyer 1993: 412.

11. Black 1984.

12. This view depends on the admittedly disputed step of giving ἐφ' ᾧ in Rom. 5:12 a causal sense; see the discussion by Fitzmyer 1993: 413–17; Moo 1996: 321–22.

13. Bultmann 1955a: 252.

14. Esler 1998: 195, 197.

15. See Dunn 1988a: 276–77.

16. See Goppelt 1972: 251–52. See the discussion on types and prototypes in chapter eight above.

17. See my discussion of πίστις Χριστοῦ in chapter seven above.

18. Dunn 1988a: 277.

19. "Adam then is the type of the one to come to this extent, that already God then decreed in mystery that one Christ should rectify the sin committed by one Adam" (Ambrosiaster, *In epistulam ad Romanos* [Vogels 1966: 179]).

20. John Chrysostom, Migne's *Patrologia Graeca* 60:478.

21. For my detailed argument that this is a result and not a purpose clause, that the more likely meaning is that the law slipped in with the result that sin increased, not with that purpose, see Esler 1998: 240–43 (an appendix devoted to Rom. 5:20-21). I continue to be amazed by the number of commentators who are comfortable with the idea that Paul imagined God gave the law *in order that* transgression would multiply (so Hübner 1984: 26; Moo 1996: 347). This view has the consequence that God forbade his people from serving other gods *in order that* they would do so, or from committing adultery or murder *in order that* they would. For further discussion on this point (including the suggestion that this idea attributes to God so unique a perversity as a lawgiver as to raise a doubt as to whether "God" is an appropriate name for such an entity), see Esler 1998: 196–97.

22. The same point should be made of the third question of this type (discussed in chapter ten below) at Rom. 7:7 ("What shall we say then? That the law is sin?"). It is easy to imagine that opponents of Paul who advocated the circumcision of Christ-followers (not that there is any sign that they were yet active in Rome) would allege that

he subscribed to the sentiments in 6:1, 15, and 7:7, so that here he "is answering objections to his theology that he himself has anticipated" (Theissen 1987: 181). In overreacting against the more mechanical types of "mirror-reading" Paul, scholars (such as Lyons 1985) have themselves forgotten that ancient rhetoricians, not surprisingly, advised those making a case to practice "anticipation" (προκατάληψις; *praesumptio*), which is "the method by which we shall counteract the ill-feeling which is against us by anticipating the adverse criticisms of our audience and the arguments of those who speak against us" (Aristotle, *Rhetorica ad Alexandrum* 1432b). Romans 3:8 constitutes direct evidence that this was a live issue for Paul as far as his Roman audience was concerned.

23. See Sani and Reicher 2000.

24. *Pace* Moo's remarkable argument that Paul essentially leaves baptism behind at v. 4 (1996: 355, 359–67).

25. So Meeks 1983: 150.

26. See Hartman 1992: 584–85. On the other hand, the representation of Jesus receiving the Spirit on this occasion (in addition to the bare fact of his baptism) is, in my view, almost certain to be the product of a tradition intent on homologating the experience of Jesus in the Jordan with the facts of early baptism, which included immersion and receipt of the gifts of the Spirit. I hope to develop this argument elsewhere.

27. Hartman 1992: 585.

28. This is clearest in Mark 1:10: "and immediately coming up out of the water (ἐκ τοῦ ὕδατος) he saw the heavens being rent asunder."

29. Meeks 1983: 151.

30. *Did.* 7:1.

31. Note that at the beginning of Vision 1 of the *Shepherd of Hermas*, a text from Rome datable to the late first or early second century CE, the narrator starts by mentioning that he saw a woman named Rhoda bathing in the river Tiber and helped her to get out.

32. Tertullian, *De baptismo* 4; ET in Souter 1919: 50. For a valuable recent discussion of Tertullian, see Wright 2000.

33. For the historicity of Peter's martyrdom in Rome under Nero, see the persuasive discussion of the sources (including some not usually cited in this regard) by Bauckham 1992.

34. On this point see Easton 1934: 25.

35. Hippolytus, *Apostolic Tradition* 21.1–2; ET by Easton 1934: 45 (whose sentence enumeration is adopted here). For further discussion of the *Apostolic Tradition*, see Botte 1963; Cumming 1976; and now Bradshaw, Johnson, and Phillips 2002.

36. Hippolytus, *Apostolic Tradition* 21.20.

37. Meeks 1983: 151, 237 n. 49.

38. See Fagan 1999: 24–29. The woman named Rhoda in Vision 1 of the *Shepherd of Hermas* (see note 31 above) was naked or near naked when the narrator helped her from the Tiber.

39. Hippolytus, *Apostolic Tradition* 21.11–20.

40. Tertullian, *De baptismo* 4; ET in Souter 1919: 50.

41. *Did.* 7:2–3. ET (slightly modified) in Holmes 1989: 153.

42. Holmes 1989: 153 n. 26.

43. Dunn 1970: 226–27 and passim.

44. As Craig Koester notes (2001: 311), however, reception of the Holy Spirit could also occur before baptism, as in Acts 10:44-48 (although this is clearly anomalous and Peter has those affected baptized immediately) or in connection with the laying on of hands that happened after baptism (Acts 8:17; 19:6).

45. Dunn 1970: 225–26.

46. John Pilch has written extensively on altered states of consciousness; see Pilch 2002 and the literature he cites.

47. See Esler 1994b: 37–51, drawing especially on Goodman 1972.

48. Esler 1994b: 41.

49. Goodman 1972: 15.

50. Goodman 1972: 72, 74.

51. See Koester 2001: 313–14.

52. Meeks 1983: 151–52.

53. See Goodman 1972 passim.

54. Cullmann 1950: 29.

55. Hippolytus, *Apostolic Tradition* 18.3; ET by Easton 1934: 43.

56. Hippolytus, *Apostolic Tradition* 22.5–6; ET by Easton 1934: 48. Note that the practice of a "holy kiss" had begun in Paul's time (cf. 1 Cor 16:20).

57. A. von Dobbeler 1987.

58. Elliott 2000: 673.

59. Levine and Moreland 1994.

60. Rupert Brown 2000: 24–34.

61. See chapter eleven.

62. See chapter thirteen.

63. See McVann 1991: 334–35.

64. See van Gennep 1960; Turner 1969.

65. Turner 1969: 95.

66. Brown 2000: 31.

67. McDonald 1990: 88.

68. Dunn 1988a: 314.

69. See Cullmann 1950: 47–55 ("Baptism and Faith").

70. So Wedderburn 1987: 40–41.

71. See Hartman 1992: 586.

72. See Acts 2:38; 3:16; 10:48; 19:5; cf. 1 Cor. 1:13, 15. The subject is helpfully discussed by Hartman 1992: 586–87. In time, as trinitarian notions developed, baptism was in/into the name of the Father, Son, and Holy Spirit, as in Matt. 28:19 and later in Hippolytus's *Apostolic Tradition*.

73. Wedderburn 1987: 54, 59.

74. Lagrange well expresses the effect of the imagery of this rite of passage (1931: 144): "Le baptême était une image de la mort, parce qu'on était complètement plongé dans l'eau; quand on sortait de l'eau, on venait à une nouvelle existence" ("Baptism was an image of death, because one was completely plunged into water; when one left the water, one came into a new existence").

75. So Ziesler (1989: 159): "doubtless the act of baptism is what is meant."

76. Moo 1996: 373, 376–77.

77. To speak of δεδικαίωται as "transfer language," a usage pioneered by E. P. Sanders (1983: 10) and utilized in relation to this verse by John Ziesler (1989: 161), is problematic for the reason that the word refers not merely to the passage from one identity to another but to the continuation in that new identity thereafter.

78. "Il s'agit de la vie nouvelle du chrétien, non de la résurrection future" ("It concerns the new life of the Christian, not the future resurrection") (Lagrange 1931: 148).

79. Moo 1996: 364. Moo eliminates baptism from Rom. 6:5-10 and seeks to downgrade its importance in chap. 6.

80. Wedderburn 1987: 49, citing Rom. 7:4, 6; 2 Cor. 5:14; Gal. 2:19, 5:4; 6:14. Moo is of much the same opinion (1996: 363–65).

81. Moo 1996: 364.

82. Blass and Debrunner (Funk 1961: 119) note that with the genitive it means "'Through' of space, time, agent."

83. Wedderburn 1987: 392.

84. Wedderburn 1987: 396.

85. Moo 1996: 363–64.

86. Lévi-Strauss 1972: 237.

87. Eliade 1959.

88. Gell 1992: 28–29.

89. Baum 1968: 143.

90. Byrne 1981: 563.

91. Hartman 1992: 588.

92. Schweitzer 1998: 125.

93. See Malina 2001: 58–67; the first edition of this work (1981) was the *fons et origo* of this insight.

94. Boyarin 1994: 22–23, 180–200.

95. Brendan Byrne describes the slave imagery, perhaps a trifle euphemistically, as "rather unattractive" (1981: 564).

96. Gal. 1:10; Phil. 1:1.

97. Moo, indeed, wrongly suggests (1996: 400, 403) that ἐλευθερωθέντες relates to "conversion," in line with his downgrading of the significance of baptism.

98. Israelite sinfulness (meaning contravention of the law) on its own would be appropriately described as παρανομία. Admittedly, the noun παρανομία occurs in the New Testament only at 2 Pet. 2:16, but its verbal paronym παρανομέω appears on the lips of the Lukan Paul at Acts 28:3.

99. In 1 Thessalonians, a letter written to a non-Israelite audience who had previously practiced idolatry (see 1 Thess. 1:9 and Esler 2001a: 1200), Paul had employed ἀκαθαρσία to designate the sinful world that his converts had left behind (1 Thess. 4:7) but that also represented a continuing temptation from their proper state of holiness (cf. ἁγιασμός at 1 Thess. 4:3, 7; and ἁγιωσύνη at 3:3). See Esler 1998: 157–58.

100. See Esler 2001a: 1207; 1998: 157–58.

101. So Hauck 1965: 428. Fitzmyer's comment (1993: 451) that although what Paul is describing in Rom. 6:19b "may seem to be typically pagan vices," nevertheless

"the Qumran Essenes repudiated the same in their Jewish confrères (1QS 3:5; 4:10, 23-24)," does not weigh against the view that Paul here intends a non-Judean referent, since this is based on his own and wider Judean usage, not that of a sectarian document from an entirely different context that frequently stigmatized Judeans who were not Essenes in language similar to that applied by mainstream Judeans to non–Judeans.

10. Pauline Leadership and Group Exemplification in Romans 7

1. To recapitulate, Rom. 1:18—2:5 are relevant primarily to non-Israelite Christ-followers and Rom. 2:17—3:20 to Israelite ones. But, as argued in chapter five above, both groups were likely represented in the original audience(s) of the letter when Phoebe (presumably) brought it to Rome (Rom. 16:1-2) and, possibly, went around the various groups in Rome reading it aloud to them (perhaps offering helpful tips from Paul on its meaning as she did so?).

2. Such people could either be visitors, as certainly in Antioch (Gal. 2:11-14) and Corinth (2 Cor. 11:4), and possibly in Galatia, or locals, as Nanos (2001) has now argued was the case in Galatia. Also cf. Phil. 3:2-3.

3. Haslam 2001: 58.

4. Smith and Zarate 1990: 246.

5. See Stowers 1981.

6. Haslam and Platow 2001: 228.

7. Haslam and Platow 2001: 66.

8. B. Dodd 1999: 18–29.

9. B. Dodd 1999: 23.

10. For the distinction between exemplar and prototype, see Smith and Zarate 1990; and chapter three above.

11. So Dunn 1988a: 359. Paul assumes a case where the husband has not exercised the right of divorce given to him (but not her) by Deut. 24:1. The fact that νόμος is anarthrous is no obstacle to this interpretation in light of the many other references to the Mosaic law in Romans without the definite article (2:12, 13, 14, 23, 25; 3:20, 21, 28, 31; etc).

12. In Roman law a widow had to mourn her husband and remain unmarried for twelve months after her husband's death (Dunn 1988a: 360, citing Corbett 1969: 249). On the other hand, Roman women could divorce freely.

13. As suggested by Käsemann 1980: 187.

14. See Nanos 1996 for a case that the Roman Christ-movement was closely connected with the Judean community. Stowers 1994, on the other hand, has an improbably small role for Judeans in Romans.

15. That Paul is able to refer to his fellow Israelites as "my brothers" emerges at Rom. 9:3-4 (there actually those outside the Christ-movement), even though he uses the same expression in relation to all of his addressees in Rome in 15:14.

16. The antecedent of ἐν ᾧ at the start of 7:6b is νόμος in 7:6a.

17. This conclusion, it is worth noting, suggests that "those who know the law" is an inapposite description of the totality of Christ-followers in Rome and thus weighs against all of the non-Judean Christ-followers having previously been synagogue-attending God-fearers who would thus have acquired knowledge of the law.

18. For the possibility of ἵνα starting a result, rather than a purpose, clause, see chapter nine above.

19. As well as in 1 Cor. 9:7; Gal. 5:22; Phil. 1:11, 22; 4:17.

20. I am interpreting τὰ παθήματα τῶν ἁμαρτιῶν as an objective genitive akin to ζῆλος θεοῦ, "zeal for God" (Rom. 10:2), and ζῆλος τοῦ οἴκου σου, "zeal for your house" (John 2:17); see Funk 1961: §162. This avoids Paul making an admission as to personal sinfulness (as he does not concede he succumbed to the desires) at this point. Support for this approach is found in Rom. 6:12, where Paul urges against letting sin reign in one's mortal body through obedience to its desires (ἐπιθυμίαι); presumably, therefore, if one does not succumb to desires, one avoids sinfulness.

21. See Dunn 1988a: 359; Fitzmyer 1993: 456.

22. Dunn 1988a: 363.

23. Haslam et al. 1998: 216.

24. Thus J. L. Martyn has plausibly argued (1997: 37–45) that in Romans Paul is seeking to rectify problems that had arisen because of the way he sought to persuade the Galatians to adopt his understanding of the meaning of the gospel, so that Romans can be seen as the first interpretation of Galatians. Support for Martyn's view exists in the description by T. H. Tobin (1995) of the remarkable differences between Paul's presentation of Abraham in Galatians (as the ancestor of non-Israelite Christ-followers) and in Romans (as the ancestor of all Christ-followers, Israelite and non-Israelite).

25. Haslam and Platow 2001: 228.

26. Cinnirella 1998: 243 and passim.

27. See chapter eight above.

28. Accusative: vv. 11, 23, and 24; dative: vv. 8, 10, 13 (twice), 17, 18 (twice), 20, 21 (twice); and genitive: vv. 18 and 23 (thrice).

29. These three classes of "I" statement represent an adaptation of Theissen's scheme (1987: 191). The use of ἐγώ elsewhere in Paul and in other ancient Greco-Roman literature was taken up by Kümmel in his 1929 argument for a fictive or rhetorical "I" and has recently been reconsidered by Theissen (1987: 191–201).

30. There is a useful summary of Kümmel's argument in Westerholm 1988: 53–65. Also see the discussion in B. Dodd 1999: 222–23.

31. See chapter nine above.

32. At Rom. 8:2 the reference to liberation "from the law (νόμος τῆς ἁμαρτίας) of sin and death" is not a reference to the Mosaic law (contra Dunn 1988a: 418–19). Here νόμος means something more like "authority" or "demand," as immediately prior to this at 7:23, 25, where the phrase νόμος τῆς ἁμαρτίας also occurs, but is clearly differentiated from the Mosaic law (which is equivalent to the law operative in the speaker's mind) by the word "different" (ἕτερος), in 7:23 (so, correctly, Moo 1996: 462–64).

33. Also in Philo, De decalogo 173, desire is described as the fountain of all iniquities.

34. This is the case even though Paul had previously used the word ἐπιθυμία in a general sense of desires, which if obeyed, caused sin (Rom. 6:12).

35. For the role of the Mosaic law to stimulate life, see Deut. 30:15-20.

36. See my discussion of the proper interpretation of Rom. 5:20-21 in Esler 1998: 240–43; and in chapter nine above.

37. Esler 1998: 198–200.

38. C. Dodd 1932: 107. Fitzmyer (1993: 464) also cites Bruce, Deissmann, Gundry, Jeremias, Kühl, Packer, Weinel, and Zahn as holding this view.

39. Paul tells us in Phil. 3:5 that he was circumcised on the eighth day, but one would assume such an early circumcision even without this statement because of the law of Lev. 12:3.

40. Israelite parents sought to give their children a thorough knowledge of the law from their earliest years; see Philo, *On the Embassy to Gaius* 210; Josephus, *Against Apion* 2.178.

41. Segal 1990: 241–45.

42. Kümmel 1929: 74–84.

43. B. Dodd 1999: 223.

44. See Esler 2001a: passim.

45. See Sanders 1990: 42–43; 1993: 105–10.

46. See Lyonnet 1962; Wedderburn 1978; Watson 1986: 151–53; Dunn 1988a: 399–403; Hill 2001: 1097.

47. Käsemann 1980: 196.

48. See Theissen 1987: 202–11; and N. T. Wright 1991: 197: "The primary emphasis of the argument is on Israel, not Adam: what is being asserted is that when the Torah arrived it had the same effect on her as God's commandment in the Garden had on Adam."

49. Theissen 1987: 203.

50. Moo 1986: 124. Romans 5:13-14 is the crucial evidence for Moo's opinion.

51. See chapter nine above.

52. This is similar to the conclusion reached by Moo 1986: 128.

53. Dunn 1988a: 383.

54. Martin 1995. Also see Esler 2004b.

55. Kümmel 1929.

56. Fitzmyer 1993: 465.

57. Modern advocates include Stauffer 1964b; Lambrecht 1974; N. T. Wright 1980: 145–60; Moo 1986.

58. See Condor 1996; Cinnirella 1998.

59. See Condor 1996: 306; Carr 1991: 113–14.

60. So Cranfield 1975: 334–47, 355ff.; Dunn 1988a: 403–12.

61. Theissen 1987: 183.

62. See Seifrid 1992: 321.

63. Dunn 1988a: 376.

64. See the discussion in Dunn (1988a: 398–99), who does not consider Rom. 7:25b to be misplaced.

11. The Exalted Character of the New Identity (Romans 8)

1. See Coetzer 1981 for structuration arguments.

2. There is a difficult textual problem at this point with σε ("you," singular) appearing in a number of important textual witnesses (especially the Alexandrian א and B), with "me" (με) represented in A and D. The *lectio difficilior* is σε and would normally be preferred for that reason. But here it seems just too difficult. Paul has not

previously addressed the totality of his Roman audience in this way, having used the second person singular σύ of a representative non-Judean at 2:3 and of a representative Judean at 2:13. He used the second person plural ὑμεῖς at 7:4 and will do so again at 8:9. On the other hand, με represents a natural continuation of his language in chap. 7. A likely explanation for the σε is that it is the product of dittography after ἠλευθέρωσεν, which precedes it.

3. Rom. 1:4; 5:5; 7:6.

4. Rom. 1:3; 2:28; 4:1; 6:19; 7:5, 18, 25; at 3:20 σάρξ means "person."

5. See Ziesler 1989: 200.

6. Consider this view of Dunn (1988a: 441): "It is much more likely, then, that Paul sharpened up the antitheses for paraenetical reasons because he wanted to make clear to his readers that the choice already made in conversion needs to be reaffirmed and renewed in the religious and ethical decisions of daily life." Explanations of this type are rejected by Moo 1996: 486.

7. Moo 1996: 486.

8. See Esler 1998: 208–9.

9. See Esler 1994b for an explanation of effects of the Holy Spirit in the light of comparable modern phenomena and an argument that although the Cornelius episode in Acts 10 may not be historically accurate in its details, it does reflect the historical likelihood that it was the manifestation of charismatic gifts by non-Judeans that persuaded Judean Christ-followers to allow them to join the movement. See Forbes 1997 for the unique character of the charismatic phenomena of the Christ-movement in the ancient Mediterranean world.

10. The shift from indicative to imperative (admittedly in meaning and not in mood) is noted by Schmithals 1988: 274. Some scholars, such as Moo (1996: 493), attach 8:12-13 to the preceding section.

11. See Greenspahn 1994.

12. For a superlative exposition of this parable in its ancient cultural context, see Rohrbaugh 1997.

13. Malina 2001: 82.

14. For an introduction to this area see the essays in Moxnes 1997a, his own contributions (Moxnes 1997b, 1997c), and Osiek and Balch 1997.

15. See Dunn 1988a: 447; Schmithals 1988: 277; Moo 1996: 497–98.

16. See the fine explanation of the word by Dunn 1988a: 453–54.

17. Malina 2001: 32.

18. Moo 1996: 504, 509.

19. Meeks 1983: 188.

20. Bultmann 1957: 38.

21. Bultmann 1957: 42 (citing Rom. 14:17; 2 Cor. 5:17; 6:2; Gal. 4:4, 6).

22. Bultmann 1957: 43–47.

23. Bultmann 1957: 151–52.

24. Käsemann 1969b: 131. The words "the position of humanity in the new dispensation" represent Käsemann's word "anthropology," which is an unfortunate usage given that it now has a very different meaning in connection with one of the social sciences.

25. Käsemann 1969b: 131–37.

26. See Carmignac 1970–1971: 364–70; 1979: 133–34.

27. Kvanvig 1988: 40, 56.

28. See Weiss 1985 (1892); Schweitzer 1968 (1906).

29. Carmignac 1970–1971: 390 ("Since this term is a source of confusion, why not abandon it? Since this notion perverts the biblical notion of the kingdom of God, why retain it any longer?").

30. Sanders 1993: 183.

31. Malina 1997: 84.

32. Condor 1996: 289–91.

33. This conundrum has been well observed by Beker 1980: 170; Lindars 1984/85: 766–67.

34. See Munn 1992; Adam 1990, although Adam has also surveyed the anthropological and sociological dimensions (1994).

35. Gosden 1994: 2.

36. Gosden 1994: 3.

37. Adam 1990: 16.

38. Malina 1996b.

39. See Durkheim 1915; Mead 1959; Gurvitch 1963; Sorokin 1964; Schutz 1971.

40. Evans-Pritchard 1969 (1940); Lévi-Strauss 1963, 1966, 1969; Leach 1961; Gell 1992.

41. Durkheim 1915: 11.

42. Gell 1992: 4.

43. Gell 1992: 5–14. Durkheim accepted a rationalist approach to understanding reality and rejected the empiricist alternative. He considered that the "categories," the very general concepts held by many philosophers to underpin all discursive thought (such as number, cause, space, and time), are basic thought forms and do not derive from experience. Moreover, he considered that the source of these categories was not (as with Descartes) the certainty of the lone *cogito,* but the collective activity of each particular group. His view is close to that of Kant, except "that whereas, for Kant, reason is an aspect of nature, for Durkheim reason is an aspect of society" (Gell 1992: 8).

44. Gosden 1994: 122.

45. Evans-Pritchard 1969 (1940). Gell regards these as corresponding to microcosm (the domestic grazing routines) and macrocosm (1992: 16–18).

46. Evans-Pritchard 1969 (1940): 108.

47. Lévi-Strauss 1963, 1966, 1969; see Gell 1992: 23.

48. Gell 1992: 25.

49. Gell 1992: 24.

50. Gell 1992: 26–27.

51. Lévi–Strauss 1972: 236–37.

52. Eliade 1959.

53. Gell 1992: 28–29.

54. Leach 1961: 31.

55. See Gell 1992: 33–36.

56. See Nowotny 1975; Bourdieu 1979; Adam 1990: 134.

57. Hägerstrand 1985.

58. Malina 1996b.

59. Adam 1990: 138–39.

60. Hohn 1984: 49–104.

61. Dundes 1984.

62. See Wilson 1975: 292–306; Brown 1991: 431–36.

63. See Burridge 1969; Worsley, 1970; Williams 1976.

64. Esler 1994b.

65. Esler 1993: 186–87.

66. Malinowski 1948: 100.

67. Malinowski 1948: 101.

68. Wallman 1992: 16.

69. Doty 1986: 44–94.

70. Moo 1996: 508; also cf. p. 509, where he states Paul is engaged in "the exposition of the future glory to be enjoyed by the believer."

71. Bartsch 1968: 42.

72. Byrne 1986: 165.

73. See Dunn 1988a: 471 on why this is the best solution. Contra Byrne 1986: 166–67, who suggests Adam.

74. The word ματαιότης appears some thirty times in Ecclesiastes (LXX).

75. Byrne 1986: 166.

76. See Malina 1996b: 194.

77. Malina 1996b: 195.

78. Ibid.

79. Käsemann 1980: 237–38.

80. The dative τῇ . . . ἐλπίδι is modal or associative, not instrumental (= "by means of hope"); see Dunn 1988a: 475.

81. Malina 1996b: 190.

82. The extraordinary view of Käsemann (1980: 238) that by τῇ . . . ἐλπίδι Paul meant to "provide a pointed attack on enthusiasm" shows just how far his tendentiousness in this area has taken him. There is no sign whatever of an adversative at the start of v. 24 that would be necessary for such a view to have any validity.

83. Baumgarten 1975: 176; Dunn 1988b: 476.

84. Dunn 1988b: 477.

85. A respectable variant has instead God as the subject of this clause (so RSV).

86. Moo 1996: 536.

87. Byrne 1986: 176.

88. Lagrange 1931: 217 ("a sort of song of anticipated triumph").

89. See the references in Dunn 1988b: 502–3.

90. Moo 1996: 504; Meeks 1983: 188.

12. Israel and the Christ-Movement (Romans 9–11)

1. For a helpful discussion of the history of research into Romans 9–11, see Gorday 1983: 1–13 (and his ample footnotes thereto on pp. 243–56). Also see Johnson 1989: 110–23.

2. C. H. Dodd 1932: 148–50.

3. See Bultmann 1995a, 1995b.

4. Baur 1873: 327.

5. See Johnson 1989: 113 for references to the views along these lines of Christiaan Beker, Nils Dahl, Johannes Munck, Krister Stendahl, and others.

6. Guerra 1995: 145.

7. Hays 1989: 34.

8. See Johnson 1989: 110–75; 1997.

9. See Turner et al. 1987.

10. Sani and Reicher 2000: 99.

11. Haslam 2001: 58.

12. Haslam 2001: 66.

13. Haslam and Platow 2001: 218.

14. Note Dunn 1988a: 519: "Also striking is Paul's involvement, both in the problem he poses and its solution (9:1-3; 10:1; 11:13-14)."

15. The imperfect tense of ηὐχόμην represents the use of the imperfect to express possibility (here corresponding to "I could have . . ."), even though such a prayer is not carried out (see Funk 1961: §§358–59).

16. Here "foreigners" is a correct translation of ἔθνεσιν, because Paul is speaking to non-Israelites but using a designation current only in Israelite circles. He could have referred to them as "Greeks" but does not do so.

17. See Turner et al. 1987: 44.

18. Turner et al. 1987: 44.

19. See Bell 1994: 178.

20. See Bell 1994: 174, and the literature he cites.

21. Piper 1983: 7.

22. See Michaelis 1968: 168.

23. Dunn (1988b: 338) and Moo (1996: 572) suggest "fail." The latter meaning is suggested by Michaelis 1968: 169, who points to the use of the cognate word διαπίπτω at Josh. 21:45: "Nothing failed (διέπεσεν) from all of the good words which the Lord spoke to the children of Israel; everything came to pass."

24. Noted by Michaelis 1968: 169.

25. So Käsemann 1980: 261; Dunn 1988: 539; Cranfield 1979: 473. For others, it has a more limited role. See Aageson 1986: 268.

26. Käsemann 1980: 260–61.

27. Holmberg 1978: 205–7.

28. Johnson 1989: 110–75; 1997.

29. Johnson 1997: 239.

30. This is the point at issue; when Moo (1996: 572) expresses the issue with the question "Has God revoked these blessings and gone back on his word to Israel?" he is importing into the text something that is not necessarily there—that God has broken his promises. The issue is whether God's word has been successful, and this involves Israel's reception of it as well as God's intentions.

31. The suggestion in Acts 28:21 that the Judean leaders in Rome had heard nothing adverse to Paul up to the time of his arrival in the city is unlikely to be historical.

32. Dunn 1988b: 539.

33. Berger and Luckmann 1967.

34. Bell 1994: 185.

35. Johnson 1989: 139.

36. Exod. 9:16 runs as follows: καὶ ἕνεκεν τούτου διετηρήθης, ἵνα ἐνδείξωμαι ἐν σοὶ τὴν ἰσχύν μου, καὶ ὅπως διαγγελῇ τὸ ὄνομα μου ἐν πάσῃ τῇ γῇ.

37. I am translating ἔθνη in 9:24 to bring out that Paul is describing this group using an Israelite term, not a self-designation of these people.

38. Though note that there are also Israelites as numerous as sand on the shore in Hos. 1:10.

39. Isa. 28:16 reads: Ἰδοὺ ἐγὼ ἐμβάλλω εἰς τὰ θεμέλια Σιὼν λίθον πολυτελῆ, ἐκλεκτὸν, ἀκρογωνιαῖον, ἔντιμον, εἰς τὰ θεμέλια αὐτῆς, καὶ ὁ πιστεύων οὐ μὴ καταισχυνθῇ. Isa. 8:14 reads: Κἂν ἐπ᾽ αὐτῷ πεποιθὼς ᾖς, ἔσται σοι εἰς ἁγίασμα, καὶ οὐχ ὡς λίθου προσκόμματι συναντήσεσθε, οὐδὲ ὡς πέτρας πτώματι.

40. The same expression appears also at 1 Pet. 2:8, a reading closest to that of the translations of Aquila, Symmachus, and Theodotion; see Elliott 2000: 430.

41. Barrett (1982b: 144–45) takes the view that the stumbling stone is the law, while Wright considers that it consists of the law and Christ (1991: 244).

42. See Sanders 1977 and 1983.

43. Sanders 1983: 36.

44. See Cranfield 1979: 506–10; Gundry 1985: 17; Bell 1994: 189–91.

45. Strengthening my point is that a number of textual witnesses read νόμου after ἔργων.

46. See the helpful discussion by Ziesler 1989: 252–54.

47. As Bell inevitably suggests (1994: 188).

48. Moo 1994: 636.

49. Especially see Badenas 1985.

50. Badenas 1985: 79.

51. Moo 1996: 639, with the analysis in n. 41.

52. The word is used in an adverbial phrase meaning "fully" in 2 Cor. 1:13 and with the entirely different sense of "tax" on two occasions in Rom. 13:7.

53. Badenas 1985: 144–51.

54. Moo 1994: 641.

55. See Moo 1994: 641.

56. See Esler 1998: 203–4.

57. Badenas 1985: 36.

58. See chapter eight.

59. This means I must demur from the important thesis of N. T. Wright 1991.

60. See chapter eight.

61. This should not be taken to suggest that Paul did not subscribe to an exaltation of Christ that took the form of an ascension into heaven, as advocated by Luke and John, since he mentions the position of Christ at the right hand of God in Rom. 8:34. Rather, Paul is saying that one need not go to heaven to find Jesus in order to be saved.

62. Hays 1989: 163.

63. See Hays 1989; Keesmaat 1999.

64. So also Bell 1996: 90–92.

65. Bell 1994: 5–7.

66. Malina 2001: 109.

67. See Elliott 1988, 1990, 1991, 1992, 1994.

68. Pilch and Malina 1993: 56.

69. Malina 2001: 126.

70. The instances of φθόνος are at Wis. 2:24; 6:23; 1 Macc. 8:16; 3 Macc. 6:7.

71. Examples include Deut. 29:20; 4 Kgs. 19:31; Isa. 9:7; 37:32; Ezek. 23:25; 36:6.

72. But note Wis. 2:24: "...ecause of the envy of the devil death came into the world."

73. See Malina 2001: 126.

74. Bell 1994: 95–104.

75. Bell 1994: 200–285.

76. Moo 1996: 668.

77. So Schlatter 1995 (1935): 219; Käsemann 1980: 299 ("At the commencement of the new dialogue Paul declares his solidarity with his people as in chs. 9 and 10. Also here he does not do it out of patriotism [Jülicher]. He does it to prove his thesis. He himself as an Israelite of the seed of Abraham is a living example of God's will to save"); Moo 1996: 673.

78. Dunn hits the mark when he writes that the notion "that Paul puts himself forward in a representative capacity (God has not rejected his people because he has not rejected me!) both misses and cheapens the point." Dunn suggests that Paul is claiming, rather, to express "an authentically Jewish viewpoint" (1988b: 635), and this is close to the view taken here.

79. Dunn (1988b: 641) has an excellent discussion of the scriptural sources.

80. See Dunn 1988b: 641, citing Cranfield.

81. For example, Moo 1996: 682–83.

82. Minear 1971: 78–79.

83. See chapter fourteen.

84. Here, as elsewhere, we must not automatically assume that ἵνα has a final sense.

85. Schmidt 1968: 884.

86. Contra Moo 1996: 688, who suggests Paul "seems already to have in mind Gentile readers." At this point he has Israelite Christ-followers primarily in mind. Moreover, he has in mind listeners rather than readers.

87. See the discussion on this point in chapter five.

88. That is, by God; so Moo 1996: 693.

89. Gale 1964.

90. See Esler 1998: 201–2.

91. Räisänen 1986: 145, fn. 84. For my view on Paul's understanding of the law in Romans, see chapters nine and ten.

92. The first of these alludes to Num. 15:17-21, which mentions an ἀπαρχὴ φυράματος, although that passage does not refer to the transmission of holiness from initial part to final whole.

93. Moo 1996: 698.
94. Boyarin 1994: 22–25.
95. For the full argument see Esler 2003b.
96. C. H. Dodd 1932: 180.
97. Baxter and Ziesler 1985: 26.
98. Baxter and Ziesler 1985: 27.
99. Baxter and Ziesler 1985: 26.
100. Note Stuhlmacher 1994: 168; and Bryan 2000: 181, although they cite Columella for the view, and it is unclear if they have read Baxter and Ziesler 1985.
101. Pansiot and Rebour 1960: 21.
102. Pansiot and Rebour 1960: 14.
103. Forbes 1982: 254–55.
104. Foxhall 1990: 98.
105. Frankel 1999: 36.
106. Kent 1948.
107. Foxhall 1990: 97.
108. For the text of the inscription see Durrbach 1926: 166 (no. 366 B, lines 8-25), and for a discussion see Kent 1948: 288.
109. Davies 1984b: 160.
110. Davies 1984b: 161.
111. See Dunn 1988b: 683.
112. See Mussner 1984: 34.
113. Dunn 1988b: 697–98.
114. Dunn 1988b: 701–2.
115. So Dunn 1988b: 518, 539.
116. Note the interesting idea of Martyn (1991: 178–79) that maybe Romans 9–11 is meant to clarify or perhaps even slightly modify the cryptic expression "Israel of God" in Gal. 6.16, where it refers to the former "Jews" and former "gentiles" who live in the new creation.

13. Descriptors of the New Identity (Romans 12–13)

1. For these three formulations see, in turn, Moo 1996: 744; Dodd 1932: 188; Black 1973: 150.
2. Käsemann 1980: 323; Fitzmyer 1993: 638.
3. See Esler 2003a. In this article I also argue that taking this route does not entail denying the fundamental insight of Martin Luther that we are who and what we are because of the God who righteouses us.
4. "Post tractatum enim legis et fidei et populi Iudaici et gentilis ad vitam bonam agendam hortatur." For the Latin text see Vogels 1966: 393.
5. See Esler 2004a.
6. William S. Campbell, in the course of an illuminating essay on Rom. 12:1—15:13, also uses the word *norms* of the material in Romans 12, although he approaches them from a different perspective (Campbell 1995).
7. The other instances of παρακαλῶ (12:8) in Romans have rather the meaning "to encourage," "to comfort," "to console," while the cognate noun παράκλησις

(15:4, 5) means "encouragement," "comfort," or "consolation," a meaning also reflected in the related word συνπαρακαλέομαι in 1:12, there denoting mutual encouragement. These different meanings are represented in relation to παρακαλῶ and παράκλησις throughout their ancient Greek usage (Schmitz 1967).

8. The verb οἰκτείρω appears uniquely in the NT at 9:15 ("I will have mercy"). The plural οἰκτιρμοί probably reflects Hebrew *rahamim* (used often in Hebrew Scripture in relation to God: Dunn 1988b: 709).

9. Moo 1996: 748.

10. The translation is taken from the RSV, slightly altered to have "rational" instead of "spiritual" in 12:1, to restore the "and" at the beginning of 12:2, and to alter "world" to "age."

11. The only other examples of λατρεία in the NT are at John 16:2 and Heb. 9:1.

12. Thompson (1991: 82) connects λατρεία in Rom. 12:1 with the cognate verbal form in 1:25, but misses λατρεία itself at 9:4.

13. Relevant passages include Isa. 1:11-20; Hos. 6:6; Amos 5:21-24; Ps. 51:17; 69:30-31; Sir. 35:1-2. There could also be a Stoic background, in the notion of the Logos, the all-pervasive reason that links humanity to the divine, but this does not exclude a significance for Judeans, since this idea was familiar to Philo (cf. *Spec. Laws* 1.227) and other reaches of Hellenistic Judean tradition; see Ziesler 1989: 293.

14. Moo 1996: 752.

15. Dunn 1988b: 710.

16. So Dunn 1988: 712.

17. "Si corpora nostra incontaminata servemus, dissimiles a saecularibus, qui voluptatibus student" (Vogels 1966: 393).

18. Ziesler 1989: 294.

19. Dunn 1988: 66.

20. Grundmann 1964: 260.

21. Annas 1993: 445.

22. Esler 2004a.

23. Note Bertram 1974: 232: "In R. 12:3 the paronomasia with the fourfold φρονέω directs us to salutary σωφρονέω . . . in place of dangerous ὑπερφρονέω."

24. For the first proposal see JB; for the second see RSV; Dunn 1988b: 719; Fitzmyer 1993: 644.

25. Moo 1996: 759.

26. 4 Macc. 13:1; 14:11; 16:2.

27. See the essay on envy in Malina 2001: 108–33, a new feature of the third edition of this now classic work on the NT in its ancient Mediterranean context. Also see the discussion of envy and jealousy in chapter twelve above.

28. See Esler 2004a.

29. This is the view, for example, of Dunn 1988b: 721–22; and Fitzmyer 1993: 645–46. The position of Moo (1996: 760–61) that Paul is speaking of "basic Christian faith as given equally by God to all" does not adequately address the signs of differentiation in the text, for example, the statement at 12:6: "Having gifts that differ according to the grace given to us, if prophecy in proportion to faith."

30. Another possible translation (there is no need to decide this difficult point here) is "the one who cares."

31. See Esler 2004a.

32. This is the central meaning of "prophecy" for the Christ-movement. This type of prophecy was spontaneous and had an unstructured immediacy of inspiration and thus differed from the more formalized prophetic ritual of Greco-Roman shrines (Dunn 1988b: 727). This is the only mention of prophecy in Romans, but its priority here accords with statements he makes elsewhere (1 Cor. 14:1, 39; 1 Thess. 5:19-20).

33. Moo 1996: 764.

34. Moo 1996: 759.

35. So RSV.

36. Lagrange (1931: 301) also saw a division in the text between vv. 16 and 17.

37. So Black 1989 (and before him Talbert 1969/70), unwisely followed by Dunn 1988b: 738; Fitzmyer 1993: 652; Moo 1996: 773–74 (though with some caveats).

38. Ong 1982: 37. Also see Osiek 1998: 162–63 for an important discussion of this feature in relation to the *Shepherd of Hermas*.

39. The participial expression "being beloved (ἠγαπημένοι) by God" does occur, however, at 1 Thess. 1:4.

40. Stauffer 1964a: 50.

41. Some textual witnesses have "love of God" or "love of God in Christ" here, but these variations are probably due to harmonization with similar phrases in 5:5 and 8:39.

42. Dunn 1988a: 253.

43. Dunn 1988a: 265.

44. So Dunn 1988b: 878; Fitzmyer 1993: 725; Moo 1996: 909. This meaning is suggested by the comparison with 5:5 and by the context of 15:30, where Paul is appealing to fellow Christ-followers.

45. Dunn 1975a: 294.

46. For the argument on this point see Esler 2003a, 2004a.

47. Although σπουδή and its paronyms can refer to "haste" (Harder 1971), for Paul it has the sense of eagerness; see Esler 1998: 251 n. 22.

48. Best 1972: 67.

49. Esler 2001a: 1206.

50. For 1 Thessalonians see my discussion in Esler 2001a: 1208; for Galatians see Esler 1997; 1998: 218–34; 2000a.

51. See M. B. Thompson 1991: 94.

52. M. B. Thompson 1991: 94–95.

53. I assume that underlying the dative τοῖς ταπεινοῖς in 12:16 is a masculine, not a neuter, plural.

54. See Esler 2004a.

55. See Dunn 1988b: 747.

56. See Esler 1987: 175.

57. Rathbone 1996: 604.

58. M. B. Thompson 1991: 96.

59. See Esler 2004a.

60. Vogels 1966: 407 (on Rom. 12:15).

61. These two parenthetical exhortations have been mentioned above but are included here for completeness.

62. See Esler 2004a.

63. These include Qumran texts, such as *Damascus Document* 9:2-5; *Rule of the Community* (1QS10:17-18); as well as *2 En.* 50:3-4 and *T. Gad* 6:7; see Yinger 1998.

64. The Latin runs "Mandatum enim in lege erat: diliges proximum tibi et odio habebis inimicum tibi" (Vogels 1966: 411).

65. Esler 2000c: 335–36.

66. See M. B. Thompson 1991: 107; Yinger 1998: 84–85.

67. *Joseph and Aseneth* 28:9-10.

68. *Joseph and Aseneth* 29:10-14.

69. *Joseph and Aseneth* 23:9; ET in Burchard 1985: 240.

70. *Joseph and Aseneth* 29:3.

71. *Sentences of Pseudo-Phocylides* 76-78; ET by van der Horst 1985: 577.

72. Thompson 1991: 96–105.

73. Thompson 1991: 107.

74. See the references in Yinger 1998: 95, n. 93.

75. Yinger 1998: 74.

76. His brief remark in relation to such language (1998: 86) that "all" can be limited to the members of an ingroup is unpersuasive.

77. Yinger 1998: 74.

78. For a good account of scholarship on this section of the letter, see N. Elliott 1995: 218–21.

79. Dunn 1988b: 759.

80. See Tacitus, *Annals* 13.50-51; Suetonius, *Nero* 10.1; for discussion see Stuhlmacher 1976; Reasoner 1999: 38–39.

81. Nanos 1996: 289–336.

82. See Sherwin-White 1963: 8–11.

83. Strabo, *Geography* 2.5.8; Winter 2002: 83–84.

84. Reasoner 1999: 161.

85. See N. Elliott 1995: 220–26.

86. The word reappears, however, at 14:10 and 15:30.

87. The commandments occur at Exod. 20:13-15, 17, and Deut. 5:17-19, 21, although Paul's order differs slightly.

88. See Esler 2003a.

89. Dunn 1988b: 775.

90. Dunn 1988b: 781.

91. Esler 1998: 203–4.

92. Dunn regards "the works of the law" as comprising only part of the law, namely, those components that served as its "boundary markers," as opposed to the law as a whole, including its ethical teaching; see my discussion in Esler 1998: 182–84.

93. Moule 1967–68.

94. Esler 1998: 187.

95. Moo reaches a similar conclusion to this (though for different reasons), namely, that the love command replaces these commandments, rather than simply focusing them by setting forth a demand that is integral to each of them (1996: 815–17).

96. Dunn 1988b: 784.

97. Dunn 1988b: 792.

98. Dodd 1932: 209.

99. Fitzmyer 1993: 682.

100. Condor 1996: 303.

101. Condor 1996: 306–7.

102. Cinnirella 1998: 235.

103. Esler 2001a: 1209; 2001b: 1217–18.

104. Moo 1996: 366.

105. Esler 2001a: 1205.

14. The Weak and the Strong (Romans 14:1—15:13)

1. Minear 1971; Campbell 1991: 5. Minear's own proposal, that five groups could be discerned in Romans 14–15, has not found many supporters; nevertheless the book is full of insights that have now become part of the framework for Romans research.

2. See Karris 1991; for other supporters of positions similar to this, see the useful *status quaestionis* discussion in Reasoner 1999: 1–23. Meeks (1987) also takes a view of the passage that sees it extending beyond the situation in Rome.

3. Barclay 1996b: 289.

4. Reasoner 1999: 57. He also notes a verse of Horace where it is suggested that to observe the Sabbath is weak (1999: 54).

5. Reasoner 1999, p. 61 and passim.

6. So Marcus 1989: 73.

7. Donfried 1991e: 108–9.

8. Karris 1991: 77–81.

9. See the discussion in Reasoner 1999: 1–23, citing Lietzmann, Dodd, and Sampley (see Sampley's 1995 essay) as having doubts about identification.

10. See Nanos 1996: 85–165. Neil Elliott (1999) also argues for the weak being "non-Christian Jews."

11. Gagnon (2000) has criticized Nanos's proposal as to the identity of the weak on other grounds.

12. Sampley 1995: 41–42.

13. Marcus 1989.

14. See Meeks 1987: 297; Sampley 1995; Jewett 1985.

15. Rauer 1923: 76–184.

16. See Marcus 1989: 74 for this view.

17. Barclay 1996b: 300.

18. So Minear 1971: 9; see Marcus 1989: 69 for a similar view. Campbell has a somewhat similar view, but sees more scope for the argument to exist among non-Judean Christ-followers (1995: 270–78).

19. For a conclusion on the issue similar to this one, see Horrell 2002: 67.

20. Note Dan. 1:8-16; Jdt. 12:1-4 (though there she uses her own wine); Esth. 4:17x LXX; Josephus, *Life* 40; see Barclay 1996b: 294–95; Horrell 2002: 67.

21. Clarke 2002: 110.

22. Genesis 17:17: "Then Abraham fell on his face and laughed, and said to himself, 'Shall a child be born to a man who is a hundred years old? Shall Sarah, who is ninety years old, bear a child?'"

23. Fitzmyer 1993: 689.

24. Dunn 1988b: 798. He also suggests that what is in view is "the everyday recognition and practice of brotherhood, not an official act of reception," which is correct as far as it goes, but it misses the domestic architectural context implied.

25. Donfried 1991e: 110.

26. Epstein 1987: 4.

27. This suggestion is made by Barclay 1996b: 306. Campbell is undecided "whether we should envisage the Christians who feel obligated to a Jewish lifestyle as being *part* of a synagogue or, alternatively, as comprising a separate assembly of Jews who had faith in Jesus" (1995: 275).

28. See Rom. 1:1; 6:16, 17, 20.

29. Elliott 2000: 513–16. He also covers the entire phenomenon of slavery in the ancient Mediterranean world.

30. Elliott 2000: 513.

31. Figurative: 1 Cor. 14:3, 5, 12, 26; 2 Cor. 10:8; 12:19; 13:10; literal: 1 Cor. 3:9; 2 Cor. 5:1.

32. The present, rather than the aorist, imperative looks to an action that goes on over a period of time.

33. Lane 1998: 239.

34. Haslam et al. 1998.

35. Barth 1994: 21.

36. Barth 1994: 21.

37. See Mark 9:12; Luke 18:19; 23:11; Acts 4:11; 1 Cor. 1:28; 6:4; 16:11; 2 Cor. 10:10; Gal. 4:14; 1 Thess. 5:20.

38. Dunn 1988b: 803.

39. Campbell 1995: 283 (original emphasis removed).

40. See Watson 1986.

41. So, correctly, Moo 1996: 868.

42. Barclay 1996b: 308.

43. See Campbell 1995.

44. Volf 1996.

Bibliography

Abrams, Dominic, and Michael Hogg, eds. (1990). *Social Identity Theory: Constructive and Critical Advances*. New York: Harvester Wheatsheaf.

Achtemeier, Paul J. (1980). *The Inspiration of Scripture: Problems and Proposals*. Biblical Perspectives on Current Issues. Philadelphia: Westminster.

Adam, Barbara (1990). *Time and Social Theory*. Cambridge: Polity.

——— (1994). "Perceptions of Time." In Ingold 1994: 503–26.

Adams, Edward (1997). "Abraham's Faith and Gentile Disobedience: Textual Links between Romans 1 and 4." *JSNT* 65: 47–66.

Aguilar, Mario (1998). *The Rwanda Genocide and the Call to Deepen Christianity in Africa*. Eldoret, Kenya: AMECEA Gaba.

Almog, Schmuel, ed. (1988). *Anti-Semitism through the Ages*. Trans. Nathan H. Reisner. Oxford: Pergamon.

Ashton, John (2000). *The Religion of Paul the Apostle*. New Haven: Yale Univ. Press.

Assmann, Jan (1997). *Moses the Egyptian: The Memory of Egypt in Western Monotheism*. Cambridge: Harvard Univ. Press.

——— (2000). *Religion und kulturelles Gedächtnis: Zehn Studien*. Munich: Beck.

——— (2002). *Das kulturelle Gedächtnis: Schrift, Erinnerung und politische Identität in frühen Hochkulturen*. 4th ed. Munich: Beck.

Assmann, Aleida, and Heidrun Friesse, eds. (1999a). *Identitäten: Erinnerung, Geschichte, Identität 3*. Frankfurt: Suhrkamp.

——— (1999b). "Einleitung." In Assmann and Friesse 1999a: 11–23.

Augstein, Hannah Franziska (1996a). "Introduction." In Augstein 1996b: ix–xxxiii.

——— (1996b). *Race: The Origins of an Idea, 1760–1850*. Bristol: Thoemmes.

Badenas, Robert (1985). *Christ the End of the Law: Romans 10.4 in Pauline Perspective*. JSNTSup 10. Sheffield: Sheffield Academic Press.

Baldry, H. C. (1965). *The Unity of Mankind in Greek Thought*. Cambridge: Cambridge Univ. Press.

Balsdon, J. P. V. D. (1979). *Romans and Aliens*. London: Duckworth.

Banton, Michael (1969). *Race Relations*. London: Tavistock.

——— (1977). *The Idea of Race*. London: Tavistock.

——— (1986). "Epistemological Assumptions in the Study of Racial Differentiation." In Rex and Mason 1986: 42–63.

Barclay, John M. G. (1987). "Mirror-Reading a Polemical Letter: Galatians as a Test Case." *JSNT* 31: 73–93.

——— (1996a). *Jews in the Mediterranean Diaspora: From Alexander to Trajan (323 BCE–117 CE)*. Edinburgh: T & T Clark.

——— (1996b). "'Do we undermine the Law?' A Study of Romans 14.1—15.6." In Dunn 1996: 287–308.

Barrett, C. K. (1962). *From First Adam to Last: A Study in Pauline Theology.* London: Black.

———— (1982a). *Essays on Paul.* London: SPCK.

———— (1982b). "The Allegory of Abraham, Sarah, and Hagar in the Argument of Galatians." In Barrett 1982a: 154–70.

———— (1982c). "Romans 9.30—10.21: Fall and Responsibility of Israel." In Barrett 1982a: 132–53.

Barth, Fredrik, ed. (1969a). *Ethnic Groups and Boundaries: The Social Organization of Culture Difference.* London: George Allen and Unwin.

———— (1969b). "Introduction." In Barth 1969a: 9–38.

———— (1994). "Enduring and Emerging Issues in the Analysis of Ethnicity." In Vermeulen and Govers 1994: ¹1–32.

Barth, Karl (1933). *Epistle to the Romans.* Trans. of the 6th German edition by Edwyn C. Hoskyns. London: Oxford Univ. Press.

Barton, Carlin A. (2001). *Roman Honor: The Fire in the Bones.* Berkeley: Univ. of California Press.

Barton, John (1998). *Ethics and the Old Testament.* London: SCM.

Barton, John, and John Muddiman, eds. (2001). *The Oxford Bible Commentary.* Oxford: Oxford Univ. Press.

Barton, Stephen C. (2001). "The Epistles and Christian Ethics." In Gill 2001: 63–73.

Bartsch, Hans-Werner (1968). "The Concept of Faith in Paul's Letter to the Romans." *BR* 13: 41–53.

Bartsch, Hans Werner, and Reginald H. Fuller, eds. (1964). *Kerygma and Myth: A Theological Debate.* Vol. 1. London: SPCK.

Bassler, Jouette M. (1982). *Divine Impartiality: Paul and a Theological Axiom.* SBLDS 59. Chico, Calif.: Scholars Press.

————, ed. (1991). *Pauline Theology.* Vol. 1: *Thessalonians, Philippians, Galatians, Philemon.* Minneapolis: Fortress Press.

Bauckham, Richard J. (1992). "The Martyrdom of Peter in Early Christian Literature." In *ANRW.* Part II: *Principate.* Vol. 26.1: 539–95.

———— (1998). *God Crucified: Monotheism and Christology in the New Testament.* Didsbury Lectures for 1996. Grand Rapids: Eerdmans.

———— (2002a). *Gospel Women: Studies of the Named Women in the Gospels.* Grand Rapids: Eerdmans.

———— (2002b). "Paul's Christology of Divine Identity." Paper delivered to the Pauline Epistles Section of the SBL annual meeting, Toronto, 25 November 2002.

Baum, Gregory (1968). "Baptism." In Adolf Darlap, ed., *Sacramentum Mundi: An Encyclopedia of Theology.* Vol. 1. London: Burns & Oates. 136–46.

Baumann, Gerd (1999). *The Multicultural Riddle: Rethinking National, Ethnic, and Religious Identities.* London: Routledge.

Baumgarten, J. (1975). *Paulus und die Apokalyptik.* WMANT 44. Neukirchen-Vluyn: Neukirchener Verlag.

Baur, Ferdinand Christian (1873). *Paul the Apostle of Jesus Christ: His Life and Works, His Epistles and Teachings.* Trans. A. Menzies. Edinburgh: Williams and Norgate.

Baxter, A. G., and Ziesler, J. A. (1985). "Paul and Arboriculture: Romans 11.17-24." *JSNT* 24: 25–32.

Beker, J. Christiaan (1980). *Paul the Apostle: The Triumph of God in Life and Thought.* Philadelphia: Fortress Press.

——— (1985). "Suffering and Triumph in Paul's Letter to the Romans." *HBT* 1/7: 105–19.

Bell, D. (1975). "Ethnicity and Social Change." In Glazer and Moynihan 1975: 141–74.

Bell, Richard H. (1994). *Provoked to Jealousy: The Origin and Purpose of the Jealousy Motif in Romans 9–11.* Tübingen: Mohr/Siebeck.

Berger, Peter L., and Thomas Luckmann (1967). *The Social Construction of Reality: A Treatise in the Sociology of Knowledge.* Garden City, N.Y.: Doubleday.

Bertram, Georg (1974). "φρήν, etc." In *TDNT* 9: 220–35.

Best, Ernst (1972). *A Commentary on the First and Second Epistles to the Thessalonians.* Black's New Testament Commentaries. London: Adam & Charles Black.

Bettencourt, B. A., M. B. Brewer, M. R. Croak, and N. Miller (1992). "Cooperation and the Reduction of Intergroup Bias: The Role of Reward Structure and Social Orientation." *Journal of Experimental Social Psychology* 28: 301–9.

Betz, Hans Dieter (1975). "The Literary Composition and Function of Paul's Letter to the Galatians." *NTS* 21: 353–79.

——— (1979). *Galatians.* Hermeneia. Philadelphia: Fortress Press.

——— (1991). "Christianity as Religion: Paul's Attempt at Definition in Romans." *Journal of Religion* 71: 315–44.

Bilde, Per, Troels Engberg-Pedersen, Lise Hannestad, and Jan Zahle, eds. (1990). *Religion and Religious Practice in the Seleucid Kingdom.* Aarhus: Aarhus Univ. Press.

———. (1992). *Ethnicity in Hellenistic Egypt.* Aarhus: Aarhus Univ. Press.

Billig, Michael (1987). *Arguing and Thinking: A Rhetorical Approach to Social Psychology.* Cambridge: Cambridge Univ. Press.

——— (1990). "Collective Memory, Ideology and the British Royal Family." In Middleton and Edwards 1990a: 60–80.

Binder, Donald D. (1999). *Into the Temple Courts: The Place of Synagogues in the Second Temple Period.* SBLDS 169. Atlanta: Society of Biblical Literature.

Bitzer, Lloyd F. (1968). "The Rhetorical Situation." *Philosophy and Rhetoric* 1: 1–14.

Black, C. Clifton (1984). "Pauline Perspectives on Death in Romans 5–8." *JBL* 103: 413–33.

Black, Matthew (1973). *Romans.* New Century Bible. London: Oliphants.

Borgen, Peder (1965). *Bread from Heaven.* NovTSup 10. Leiden: Brill.

Börschel, Regina (2001). *Die Konstruktion einer christlichen Identität: Paulus und die Gemeinde von Thessalonich in ihrer hellenistisch-römischen Umwelt.* Berlin and Vienna: Philo.

Botte, Bernard (1963). *La Tradition Apostolique de Saint Hippolyte.* Münster: Aschendorffsche.

Bourdieu, P. (1979). *Algeria 1960.* Cambridge: Cambridge Univ. Press.

Boyarin, Daniel (1994). *Paul: A Radical Jew.* Berkeley: Univ. of California Press.

Bradshaw, Paul F., Maxwell E. Johnson, and L. Edward Phillips (2002). *The Apostolic Tradition: A Commentary.* Hermeneia. Minneapolis: Fortress Press.

Brändtle, Rudolf, and Ekkehard W. Stegemann (1998). "The Formation of the First 'Christian Congregations' in Rome in the Context of the Jewish Congregations." In Donfried and Richardson 1998: 117–27.

Brannan, David W., Philip F. Esler, and N. T. Anders Strindberg (2001). "Talking to 'Terrorists': Towards an Independent Analytical Framework for the Study of Violent Substate Activism." *Studies in Conflict and Terrorism* 24: 3–24.

Breakwell, Glynis M. (1986). *Coping with Threatened Identities.* London: Methuen.

Brent, Allen (1995). *Hippolytus and the Roman Church in the Third Century: Communities in Tension before the Emergence of the Monarch-Bishop.* Supplements to Vigiliae Christianae 31. Leiden: Brill.

Brett, Mark G., ed. (1996). *Ethnicity and the Bible.* Biblical Interpretation Series 19. Leiden: Brill.

Brewer, M. B., and N. Miller (1984). "Beyond the Contact Hypothesis: Theoretical Perspectives on Desegregation." In Miller and Brewer 1984: 281–302.

Brook, Kevin Alan (1999). *The Jews of Khazaria.* Northvale, N.J.: Aronson.

Brown, Dee (1991 [1971]). *Bury My Heart at Wounded Knee: An Indian History of the American West.* London: Vintage.

Brown, Raymond E. (1983a). "Part Two: Rome." In Brown and Meier 1983: 87–210.

——— (1983b). "Not Jewish Christianity and Gentile Christianity but Types of Jewish/Gentile Christianity." *CBQ* 45: 74–79.

——— and John P. Meier (1983). *Antioch and Rome: New Testament Cradles of Catholic Christianity.* New York: Paulist.

Brown, Rupert (1988). *Group Processes: Dynamics within and between Groups.* Oxford: Basil Blackwell.

——— (1996). "Tajfel's Contribution to the Reduction of Intergroup Conflict." In P. Robinson 1996: 169–89.

——— (2000). *Group Processes: Dynamics within and between Groups.* 2nd ed. Oxford: Blackwell.

Bryan, C. (2000). *A Preface to Romans: Notes on the Epistle in Its Literary and Cultural Setting.* Cambridge: Cambridge Univ. Press.

Buell, Denise Kimber (2000). "Ethnicity and Religion in Mediterranean Antiquity and Beyond." (Review of Baumann 1999; Cohen 1999; and Hall 1997), *Religious Studies Review* 3: 243–49.

Bultmann, Rudolf (1955a). *Theology of the New Testament.* Vol. 1. Trans. Kendrick Grobel. London: Chapman.

——— (1955b). *Theology of the New Testament.* Vol. 2. Trans. Kendrick Grobel. London: Chapman.

——— (1957). *History and Eschatology.* Gifford Lectures for 1955. Edinburgh: Edinburgh Univ. Press.

——— (1964b). "New Testament and Mythology: The Mythological Element in the Message of the New Testament and the Problem of Its Re-Interpretation." In Bartsch and Fuller 1964: 1–44.

Burchard, C. (1985). "Joseph and Aseneth (First Century B.C.–Second Century A.D.): A New Translation and Introduction." In Charlesworth 1985: 177–247.

Burnett, Gary W. (2001). *Paul and the Salvation of the Individual.* Leiden: Brill.

Burns, J. M. (1978). *Leadership.* New York: Harper & Row.

Burridge, Kenelm (1969). *New Heaven, New Earth: A Study of Millenarian Activities.* Oxford: Blackwell.

Byrne, Brendan J. (1981). "Living Out the Righteousness of God: The Contribution of Rom 6:1—8:13 to an Understanding of Paul's Ethical Presuppositions." *CBQ* 43: 557–81.

———— (1986). *Reckoning with Romans: A Contemporary Reading of Paul's Gospel.* GNS 18. Wilmington, Del.: Michael Glazier.

Calhoun, J. B., ed. (1982). *Environment and Population: Problems of Adaptation.* New York: Praeger.

Cameron, Averil (1991). *Christianity and the Rhetoric of Empire: The Development of Christian Discourse.* Sather Lectures 51. Berkeley: Univ. of California Press.

Campbell, William S. (1981). "The Freedom and Faithfulness of God in Relation to Israel." *JSNT* 13: 27–45.

———— (1991). *Paul's Gospel in an Intercultural Context: Jew and Gentile in the Letter to the Romans.* Frankfurt: Lang.

———— (1995). "The Rule of Faith in Romans 12:1—15:13: The Obligation of Humble Obedience to Christ as the Only Adequate Response to the Mercies of God." In Hay and Johnson 1995: 259–86.

Capes, David B. (1992). *The Old Testament Yahweh Texts in Pauline Christology.* WUNT 2/47. Tübingen: Mohr/Siebeck.

Capozza, Dora, and Rupert Brown, eds. (2000). *Social Identity Processes: Trends in Theory and Research.* Thousand Oaks, Calif.: Sage.

Caragounis, Chrys C. (1998). "From Obscurity to Prominence: The Development of the Roman Church between Romans and *1 Clement.*" In Donfried and Richardson 1998: 245–79.

Carmignac, Jean (1970–1971). "Les Dangers de l'Eschatologie." *NTS* 17: 365–90.

———— (1979). *Le Mirage de l'Eschatologie: Royauté, Règne et Royaume de Dieu sans Eschatologie.* Paris: Letouzey et Ané.

Carr, David. (1991). *Time, Narrative, and History.* Studies in Phenomenology and Existential Philosophy. Bloomington: Indiana Univ. Press.

Cary, Ernest (1924). *Dio's Roman History.* Vol. 7. LCL. New York: Putnam.

Chapple, A. L. (1984). "Local Leadership in the Pauline Churches." Ph.D. thesis, Univ. of Durham.

Charlesworth, James H., ed. (1983). *The Old Testament Pseudepigrapha.* Vol. 1: *Apocalyptic Literature and Testaments.* Garden City, N.Y.: Doubleday.

————, ed. (1985). *The Old Testament Pseudepigrapha.* Vol. 2: *Expansions of the "Old Testament" and Legends, Wisdom and Philosophical Literature, Prayers, Psalms and Odes, Fragments of Lost Judeo-Hellenistic Works.* Garden City, N.Y.: Doubleday.

Cinnirella, Marco (1998). "Exploring Temporal Aspects of Social Identity: The Concept of Possible Social Identities." *EJSP* 28: 227–48.

Claridge, Amanda (1998). *Rome: An Oxford Archaeological Guide.* Oxford: Oxford Univ. Press.

Clarke, Andrew D. (2002). "Jew and Greek, Slave and Free, Male and Female: Paul's Theology of Ethnic, Social and Gender Inclusiveness in Romans 16." In Oakes 2002: 103–25.

Coetzer, W. C. (1981). "The Holy Spirit and the Eschatological View in Romans 8." *Neotestamentica* 15: 180–98.

Cohen, Anthony P. (1994a). "Boundaries of Consciousness, Consciousness of Boundaries." In Vermeulen and Govers 1994: 59–79.

——— (1994b). *Self Consciousness: An Alternative Anthropology of Identity*. London: Routledge.

Cohen, David William (1994). *The Combing of History*. Chicago: Chicago Univ. Press.

Cohen, Shaye J. D. (1989). "Crossing the Boundary and Becoming a Jew." *HTR* 1989: 13–33.

——— (1990). "Religion, Ethnicity, and 'Hellenism' in the Emergence of Jewish Identity in Maccabean Palestine." In Bilde et al., 1990: 204–23.

——— (1999). *The Beginnings of Jewishness: Boundaries, Varieties, Uncertainties.* Berkeley: Univ. of California Press.

Cohn-Sherbok, Dan, and John Court, eds. (2001). *Religious Diversity in the Greco-Roman World: A Survey of Recent Scholarship*. Biblical Seminar 79. Sheffield: Sheffield Academic Press.

Collins, John J., and Gregory E. Sterling, eds. (2001). *Hellenism in the Land of Israel.* Christianity and Judaism in Antiquity Series 13. Notre Dame, Ind.: Univ. of Notre Dame Press.

Collon, S. (1940). "Remarques sur les quartiers juifs de la Rome antique." *Mélanges de l'École Française de Rome* 57: 72–94.

Condor, Susan (1996). "Social Identity and Time." In P. Robinson 1996: 285–315.

Consigny, Scott (1974). "Rhetoric and Its Situations." *Philosophy and Rhetoric* 7: 175–86.

Cooper, J. B., and J. L. McGaugh (1963). "Leadership: Integrating Principles of Social Psychology." In Gibb 1969: 242–50.

Corbett, P. E. (1969 [1930]). *The Roman Law of Marriage*. Oxford: Clarendon.

Cottrel, A. B., and J. A. Ross, eds. (1980). *The Mobilization of Collective Identity.* Lanham, Md.: Univ. Press of America.

Coulston, Jon, and Hazel Dodge, eds. (2000a). *Ancient Rome: The Archaeology of the Eternal City*. Oxford University School of Archaeology Monograph 54. Oxford: Oxford University School of Archaeology.

——— (2000b). "1. Introduction: The Archaeology and Topography of Rome." In Coulston and Dodge 2001a: 1–15.

Courtney, E. (1980). *A Commentary on the Satires of Juvenal.* London: Athlone.

Cranfield, C. E. B. (1975). *A Critical and Exegetical Commentary on the Epistle to the Romans*. Vol 1: *Introduction and Commentary on Romans I–VIII*. ICC. Edinburgh: T & T Clark.

——— (1979). *A Critical and Exegetical Commentary on Romans*. Vol. 2: *Commentary on Romans IX–XVI and Essays*. ICC. Edinburgh: T & T Clark.

Cranford, M. (1995). "Abraham in Romans 4: The Father of All Who Believe." *NTS* 41: 71–88.

Cullmann, Oscar (1950). *Baptism in the New Testament*. Trans. J. K. S. Reid. SBT 1/1. London: SCM.

Cumming, Geoffrey (1976). *Hippolytus: A Text for Students*. Grove Liturgical Study 8. Bramcotte: Grove.

Danker, Frederick W. (1982). *Benefactor: Epigraphic Study of a Graeco-Roman and New Testament Semantic Field*. St. Louis: Clayton.

Davies, Glenn N. (1990). *Faith and Obedience in Romans: A Study in Romans 1–4*. JSNTSup 39. Sheffield: Sheffield Academic Press.

Davies, W. D. (1984a). *Jewish and Pauline Studies*. Philadelphia: Fortress Press.

——— (1984b). "Paul and the Gentiles: A Suggestion Concerning Romans 11:13-24." In Davies 1984a: 153–63, 356–60. Reprinted from *Paganisme, Judaïsme, Christianisme: Influences et Affrontements dans le Monde Antique: Mélanges offerts à Marcel Simon*. Paris: de Boccard, 1978. 131–44.

Deschamps, J.-C., and W. Doise (1978). "Crossed Category Memberships in Intergroup Relations." In Tajfel 1978: 141–58.

Dobbeler, Axel von (1987). *Glaube als Teilhabe: Historische und semantische Grundlagen der paulinischen Theologie und Ekklesiologie des Glaubens*. WUNT 2/22. Tübingen: Mohr/Siebeck.

Dobbeler, Stephanie von (2001). "Auf der Grenze: Ethos und Identität der Matthäischen Gemeinde nach Mt 15, 1-20." *Biblische Zeitschrift* 45: 55–78.

——— (2002). "Die Versammlung 'Auf Meinen Namen Hin' (Mat 18:20). Als Identitäts- und Differenzkriterium." *NovT* 44: 209–30.

Dodd, Brian (1999). *Paul's Paradigmatic 'I': Personal Example as Literary Strategy*. JSNTSup 177. Sheffield: Sheffield Academic Press.

Dodd, C. H. (1932). *The Epistle of Paul to the Romans*. Moffatt New Testament Commentary. London: Hodder and Stoughton.

Doise, W. (1976). *L'articulation psychosociologique et les relations entre groupes*. Brussels: de Boeck. ET = (1978) *Groups and Individuals: Explanations in Social Psychology*. Cambridge: Cambridge Univ. Press.

Donfried, Karl P., ed. (1991a). *The Romans Debate*. Rev. ed. Edinburgh: T & T Clark.

——— (1991b). "Introduction 1977: The Nature and Scope of the Romans Debate." In Donfried 1991a: xli–xlvii.

——— (1991c). "Introduction 1991: The Romans Debate since 1977." In Donfried 1991a: xix–xxii.

——— (1991d). "A Short Note on Romans 16." In Donfried 1991a: 44–52.

——— (1991e). "False Presuppositions in the Study of Romans." In Donfried 1991a: 102–25.

Donfried, Karl P. and Peter Richardson, eds. (1998). *Judaism and Christianity in First-Century Rome*. Grand Rapids: Eerdmans.

Doohan, H. (1984). *Leadership in Paul*. GNS 11. Wilmington, Del.: Glazier.

Doty, William G. (1986). *Mythography: The Study of Myths and Rituals*. Tuscaloosa: Univ. of Alabama Press.

Dover, K. J. (1978). *Greek Homosexuality*. London: Duckworth.

——— (1993). Review of Cohen 1991 in *Gnomon* 42: 657–60.

Dovidio, John F., Ana Validzic, and Samuel L. Gaertner (1998). "Intergroup Bias: Status, Differentiation, and a Common In-Group Identity." *JPSP* 75: 109–20.

Duling, Dennis (2003). "'Whatever Gain I Had . . .': Ethnicity and Paul's Self-Identification in Phil. 3: 5-6." In David B. Gowler, L. Gregory Bloomquist, and Duane F. Watson, eds., *Fabrics of Discourse: Essays in Honor of Vernon K. Robbins*. Harrisburg, Pa.: Trinity Press International.

Duff, J. D., ed. (1904). *D. Iunii Iuvenalis Saturae XIV: Fourteen Satires of Juvenal.* Cambridge: Cambridge Univ. Press.

Duncan, Thomas Shearer (1926). "The Style and Language of Saint Paul in His First Letter to the Corinthians." *BSac* 83: 129–43.

Dundes, Allen (1984). *Sacred Narrative: Readings in the Theory of Myth.* Berkeley: Univ. of California Press.

Dunn, James D. G. (1970). *Baptism in the Spirit.* London: SCM.

———— (1975). *Jesus and the Spirit: A Study of the Religious and Charismatic Experience of Jesus and the First Christians as Reflected in the New Testament.* London: SCM.

———— (1988a). *Romans 1-8.* WBC 38A. Dallas: Word.

———— (1988b). *Romans 9-16.* WBC 38B. Dallas: Word.

———— (1990). *Jesus, Paul, and the Law.* Louisville, Ky.: Westminster John Knox.

———— (1991). "What Was the Issue between Paul and 'Those of the Circumcision'?" In Hengel and Heckel 1991: 295–313.

———— (1997). "Once More, PISTIS CHRISTOU." In Johnson and Hay 1997: 61–81.

———— (1998). *The Theology of Paul the Apostle.* Edinburgh: T & T Clark.

Durkheim, Emile (1915). *The Elementary Forms of the Religious Life.* London: Allen & Unwin.

Durrbach, Félix, ed. (1926). *Inscriptions de Délos: Comptes des Hiéropes (Nos. 290-371).* Paris: Librairie Ancienne Honoré Champion.

Easton, Burton Scott (1934). *The Apostolic Tradition of Hippolytus. Translated into English with Introductory Notes.* Cambridge: Cambridge Univ. Press.

Eliade, Mircea (1959). *Cosmos and History: The Myth of the Eternal Return.* Trans. W. R. Trask. New York: Harper & Row.

Eliot, T. S. (1945). *What Is a Classic: An Address Delivered before the Virgil Society on the 16th October 1944.* London: Faber & Faber.

Ellemers, Naomi, Russell Spears, and Bertjan Doosje, eds. (1999). *Social Identity: Context, Commitment, Content.* Oxford: Blackwell.

Eller, J. D., and R. M. Coughlan (1993). "The Poverty of Primordialism: The Demystification of Ethnic Attachments." *ERS* 16: 181–202.

Elliott, John H. (1988). "The Fear of the Leer: The Evil Eye from the Bible to Li'l Abner." *Forum* 4/4: 42–71.

———— (1990). "Paul, Galatians and the Evil Eye." *Currents in Theology and Mission* 7: 262–73.

———— (1991). "The Evil Eye in the First Testament: The Ecology and Culture of a Pervasive Belief." In David Jobling, Peggy L. Day, and Gerald T. Sheppard, eds., *The Bible and the Politics of Exegesis: Essays in Honor of Norman K. Gottwald on His Sixty-Fifth Birthday.* Cleveland: Pilgrim. 147–59.

———— (1992). "Matthew 20:1-15: A Parable of Invidious Comparison and Evil Eye Accusation." *BTB* 22: 52–65.

———— (1994). "The Evil Eye and the Sermon on the Mount: Contours of a Pervasive Belief in Social Scientific Perspective." *BibInt* 2: 51–84.

———— (1995). *Social-Scientific Criticism of the New Testament.* GBS. Minneapolis: Fortress Press.

——— (2000). *1 Peter: A New Translation with Introduction and Commentary.* AB 37B. New York: Doubleday.

Elliott, Neil (1990). *The Rhetoric of Romans: Argumentative Constraint and Strategy and Paul's Dialogue with Judaism.* JSNTSup 45. Sheffield: Sheffield Academic Press.

——— (1995). *Liberating Paul: The Justice of God and the Politics of the Apostle.* Sheffield: Sheffield Academic Press.

——— (1999). "Asceticism among the 'Weak' and the 'Strong' in Romans 14–15." In Vaage and Wimbush 1999: 231–51.

Engberg-Pedersen, Troels (2000). *Paul and the Stoics.* Edinburgh: T & T Clark.

Epstein, David F. (1987). *Personal Enmity in Roman Politics 218–43 BC.* London: Crook Helm.

Eriksen, Thomas Hylland (1993). *Ethnicity and Nationalism: Anthropological Perspectives.* London: Pluto.

Esler, Philip F. (1987). *Community and Gospel in Luke-Acts: The Social and Political Motivations of Lucan Theology.* SNTSMS 57. Cambridge: Cambridge Univ. Press.

——— (1993). "Political Oppression in Jewish Apocalyptic Literature: A Social-Scientific Approach." *Listening: Journal of Religion and Culture* 28: 181–99.

——— (1994a). *The First Christians in Their Social Worlds: Social-Scientific Approaches to New Testament Interpretation.* London: Routledge.

——— (1994b). "Glossolalia and the Admission of Gentiles into the Early Christian Community." In Esler 1994a: 37–51.

——— (1994c). "Introverted Sectarianism at Qumran and in the Johannine Community." In Esler 1994a: 70–91.

——— (1994d). "Millennialism and Daniel 7." In Esler 1994a: 92–109.

——— (1994e). "The Social Function of 4 Ezra." In Esler 1994a: 110–130.

——— (1994f). "Sorcery Accusations and the Apocalypse." In Esler 1994a: 131–46.

———, ed. (1995a). *Modelling Early Christianity: Social-Scientific Studies of the New Testament in Its Context.* London: Routledge.

——— (1995b) "Introduction: Models, Context and Kerygma in New Testament Interpretation." In Esler 1995a: 1–20.

——— (1995c). "God's Honour and Rome's Triumph: Responses to the Fall of Jerusalem in 70 CE in Three Jewish Apocalypses." In Esler 1995a: 239–58.

——— (1995d). "Making and Breaking an Agreement Mediterranean Style: A New Reading of Galatians 2:1-14." *BibInt* 3: 285–314.

——— (1996). "Group Boundaries and Intergroup Conflict in Galatians: A New Reading of Gal. 5:13—6:10." In Brett 1996: 215–40.

——— (1997). "Family Imagery and Christian Identity in Gal. 5.13—6.10." In Halvor Moxnes, ed., *Constructing Early Christian Families: Family as Social Reality and Metaphor.* London: Routledge. 121–49.

——— (1998). *Galatians.* London: Routledge.

——— (2000a). "'Keeping it in the Family': Culture, Kinship and Identity in 1 Thessalonians and Galatians." In Henten and Brenner 2000: 145–84.

——— (2000b). "Jesus and the Reduction of Intergroup Conflict: The Parable of the Good Samaritan in the Light of Social Identity Theory." *BibInt* 8: 325–57.

———, ed. (2000c). *The Early Christian World.* Vol. 1. London: Routledge.

———, ed. (2000d). *The Early Christian World.* Vol. 2. London: Routledge.

——— (2000e). "The Mediterranean Context of Early Christianity." In Esler 2000c: 3–25.

——— (2001a). "1 Thessalonians." In Barton and Muddiman 2001: 1199–212.

——— (2001b). "Palestinian Judaism in the First Century." In Cohn-Sherbok and Court 2001: 21–46.

——— (2002). "Ludic History in the Book of Judith: The Reinvention of Israelite Identity." *BibInt* 10: 107–43.

——— (2003a). "Social Identity, Virtue Ethics and the Good Life: A New Approach to Romans 12:1—15:13." *BTB* 33: 51–63.

——— (2003b). "Ancient Oleiculture and Ethnic Differentiation: The Meaning of the Olive-Tree Image in Romans 11." *JSNT* (forthcoming).

——— (2004a). "Paul and Stoicism: Romans 12 as a Test Case." *NTS* 50 (forthcoming).

——— (2004b). "The Sodom Tradition in Romans 1:18-32." *BTB* 34 (forthcoming).

Evans-Pritchard, E. E. (1969 [1940]). *The Nuer.* Oxford: Oxford Univ. Press.

Evelyn-White, Hugh G. (1936). *Hesiod, the Homeric Hymns and Homerica.* LCL. Cambridge: Harvard Univ. Press.

Fagan, Garrett G. (1999). *Bathing in Public in the Roman World.* Ann Arbor: Univ. of Michigan Press.

Faraone, Christopher A., and Dirk Obbink, eds. (1991). *Magika Hiera: Ancient Greek Magic and Religion.* Oxford: Oxford Univ. Press.

Feldtkeller, Andreas (1993). *Identitätssuche des syrischen Urchristentums: Mission, Inkulturation und Pluralität im ältesten Heidenchristentum.* Göttingen: Vandenhoeck & Ruprecht.

Fiedler, F. E., and J. E. Garcia (1987). *New Approaches to Effective Leadership.* New York: Wiley.

Fields, Weston W. (1997). *Sodom and Gomorrah: History and Motif in Biblical Narrative.* Sheffield: Sheffield Academic Press.

Fiore, Benjamin. (1986). *The Function of Personal Example in the Socratic and Pastoral Epistles.* Analecta biblica 105. Rome: Pontifical Institute Press.

Fishbane, Michael (1977). "Torah and Tradition." In Douglas A. Knight, ed., *Tradition and Theology in the Old Testament.* Philadelphia: Fortress Press. 275–300.

——— (1985). *Biblical Intepretation in Ancient Israel.* Oxford: Clarendon.

Fitzgerald, John T., ed. (1997). *Greco-Roman Perspectives on Friendship.* SBL Resources for Biblical Study 34. Atlanta: Scholars Press.

Fitzmyer, Joseph A. (1993). *Romans: A New Translation with Introduction and Commentary.* AB 33. New York: Doubleday.

Fleishman, E. A. (1953). "The Description of Supervisory Behaviour." *Journal of Applied Psychology* 67: 523–32.

Fleishman, E. A., and D. A. Peters (1962). "Interpersonal Attitudes, Leadership Attitudes, and Managerial Success." *Personnel Psychology* 15: 43–56.

Forbes, Christopher (1997). *Prophecy and Inspired Speech in Early Christianity and Its Hellenistic Environment.* Peabody, Mass.: Hendrickson.

Forbes, H. A. (1982). *Strategies and Soils: Technology, Production and Environment in the Peninsula of Methana, Greece.* Ann Arbor: Univ. Microfilms.

Fortna, Robert T., and Beverly R. Gaventa, eds. (1990). *The Conversation Continues: Studies in Paul and John in Honor of J. Louis Martyn.* Nashville: Abingdon.

Foxhall, Lin (1990). "Olive Cultivation within Greek and Roman Agriculture: The Ancient Economy Revisited." Ph.D. dissertation, Univ. of Liverpool.

Frankel, Rafael (1999). *Wine and Oil Production in Antiquity in Israel and Other Mediterranean Countries.* JSOT/ASOR Monograph 10. Sheffield: Sheffield Academic Press.

Franklin, James L., Jr. (1987). "Pantomimists at Pompeii: Actius Anicetus and His Troupe." *American Journal of Philology* 108: 95–107.

——— (1991). "Literacy and the Parietal Inscriptions of Pompeii." In J. H. Humphrey, ed., *Literacy in the Roman World.* Ann Arbor: Journal of Roman Archaeology. 77–98.

——— (1997a). "Vergil at Pompeii: A Teacher's Aid." *Classical Journal* 92: 175–84.

——— (1997b). "Cn. Alleius Nigidius Maius and the Amphitheatre: Munera and a Distinguished Career at Ancient Pompeii." *Historia* 96: 434–47.

Fredriksen Landes, Paula (1982). *Augustine on Romans: Propositions from the Epistle to the Romans; Unfinished Commentary on the Epistle to the Romans.* Texts and Translations 23. Chico, Calif.: Scholars Press.

Frey, J.-B., ed. (1936). *Corpus inscriptionum iudaicarum.* Vol. 1. *Europe.* Rome: Pontificio Istituto di Archeologia Cristiana.

Freyne, Sean (2000a). *Galilee and Gospel: Collected Essays.* WUNT 125. Tübingen: Mohr/Siebeck.

——— (2000b). "Behind the Names, Samaritans, *Ioudaioi.*" In Freyne 2000a: 114–31.

——— (2001). "Galileans, Phoenicians, and Itureans: A Study of Regional Contrasts in the Hellenistic Age." In Collins and Sterling 2001.

Frier, Bruce W. (1980). *Landlords and Tenants in Imperial Rome.* Princeton: Princeton Univ. Press.

Funk, W. Robert (1961). *A Greek Grammar of the New Testament and Other Early Christian Literature.* A translation and revision of the ninth-tenth German edition of F. Blass and A. Debrunner incorporating notes by A. Debrunner. Chicago: Univ. of Chicago Press.

Furnish, Victor Paul (1968). *Theology and Ethics in Paul.* Nashville: Abingdon.

——— (1979). *The Moral Teaching of Paul.* Nashville: Abingdon.

Gaertner, Samuel L., Jeffrey Mann, Audrey Murrell, and John F. Dovidio (1989). "Reducing Intergroup Bias: The Benefits of Recategorization." *JPSP* 57: 239–49.

Gaertner, Samuel L., John F. Dovidio, Phyllis A. Anastasio, Betty A. Bachman, and Mary C. Rust (1993). "The Common Ingroup Identity Model: Recategorization and the Reduction of Intergroup Bias." *ERSP* 4: 1–26.

Gaertner, S. L., M. C. Rust, J. F. Dovidio, B. A. Bachman, and P. A. Anastasio (1996). "The Contact Hypothesis: The Role of a Common Ingroup Identity on

Reducing Intergroup Bias among Majority and Minority Group Members." In J. L. Nye and A. M. Bower, eds., *What's Social about Social Cognition: Research on Socially Shared Cognition in Small Groups*. Thousand Oaks, Calif.: Sage. 230–60.

Gaertner, Samuel L., John F. Dovidio, Jason A. Nier, Brenda S. Banker, Christine M. Ward, Melissa Houlette, and Stephanie Loux (2000). "The Common Ingroup Identity Model for Reducing Intergroup Bias: Progress and Challenges." In Capozza and Brown 2000: 133–48.

Gager, John G. (1983). *The Origins of Anti-Semitism*. New York: Oxford Univ. Press.

Gagnon, Robert A. J. (2000). "Why the 'Weak' at Rome Cannot Be Non-Christian Jews." *CBQ* 62: 64–82.

Gale, Herbert M. (1964). *The Use of Analogy in the Letters of Paul*. Philadelphia: Westminster.

Gamble, Harry (1977). *The Textual History of the Letter to the Romans: A Study in Textual and Literary Criticism*. Grand Rapids: Eerdmans.

Gans, Herbert J. (1994). "Symbolic Ethnicity and Symbolic Religiosity: Towards a Comparison of Ethnic and Religious Acculturation." *ERS* 17: 577–92.

Garnsey, Peter (1998a). *Cities, Peasants and Food in Classical Antiquity: Essays in Social and Economic History*. Edited with addenda by Walter Schiedel. Cambridge: Cambridge Univ. Press.

———— (1998b). "Aspects of the Decline of the Urban Aristocracy in the Empire." In Garnsey 1998a: 91–106.

Garrett, Susan (1989). *The Demise of the Devil: Magic and the Demonic in Luke's Writings*. Minneapolis: Fortress Press.

———— (1992). "Sociology of Early Christianity." In *ABD* 6: 89–99.

Geertz, Clifford, ed. (1963a). *Old Societies and New States*. New York: Free Press.

———— (1963b). "The Integrative Revolution: Primordial Sentiments and Civil Politics in the New States." In Geertz 1963a: 105–57. (Partially reproduced in Hutchinson and Smith 1996: 40–45).

———— (1973a). *The Interpretation of Cultures*. New York: Basic.

———— (1973b). "Ethos, Worldview and the Analysis of Sacred Symbols." In Geertz 1973a: 126–41.

Gell, Alfred (1992). *The Anthropology of Time: Cultural Constructions of Temporal Maps and Images*. Oxford: Berg.

Gennep, Arnold van (1960). *The Rites of Passage*. Trans. Monika B. Vizedom and Gabrielle L. Caffee. (French original 1908.) Chicago: Univ. of Chicago Press.

Georgi, Dieter (1992). *Remembering the Poor: The History of Paul's Collection for Jerusalem*. A revised English version of the 1965 German original. Nashville: Abingdon.

Gephart, Werner, and Hans Waldenfels, eds. (1999). *Religion und Identität: Im Horizont des Pluralismus*. Frankfurt: Suhrkamp.

Gibb, C. A., ed. (1969). *Leadership: Selected Readings*. Harmondsworth: Penguin.

Gifford, Edwin Hamilton (1903a). *Eusebii Pamphili: Evangelicae Preparationis Libri XV*. Part 1. Oxford: Clarendon.

———— (1903b). *Eusebius: Preparation for the Gospel*. Part 1. Translated from a Revised Text. Oxford: Clarendon.

Gill, Robin, ed. (2001). *The Cambridge Companion to Christian Ethics.* Cambridge: Cambridge Univ. Press.

Gil-White, Francisco J. (1999). "How Thick Is Blood? The Plot Thickens . . . : If Ethnic Actors Are Primordialists, What Remains of the Circumstantialist/Primordialist Controversy?" *ERS* 22: 789–820.

Glazer, Nathan, and Daniel P. Moynihan, eds. (1975a). *Ethnicity: Theory and Experience.* Cambridge: Harvard Univ. Press.

——— (1975b). "Introduction." In Glazer and Moynihan 1975a: 1–26.

Goodman, Felicitas D. (1972). *Speaking in Tongues: A Cross-Cultural Study of Glossolalia.* Chicago: Univ. of Chicago.

Goppelt, Leonhard (1972). "τύπος, etc." *TDNT* 8: 246–59.

Gorday, Peter (1983). *Principles of Patristic Exegesis: Romans 9–11 in Origen, John Chrysostom, and Augustine.* Studies in the Bible and Early Christianity 4. New York: Mellen.

Gosden, Christopher (1994). *Social Being and Time.* Oxford: Blackwell.

Goudriaan, Koen (1992). "Ethnical Strategies in Graeco-Roman Egypt." In Bilde et al. 1992: 74–99.

Greenspahn, Frederick E. (1994). *When Brothers Dwell Together: The Preeminence of Younger Siblings in the Hebrew Bible.* New York: Oxford Univ. Press.

Griffiths, J. Gwyn (1995). "Egypt and the Rise of the Synagogue." In Urman and Flesher 1995: 3–16. (Reprinted from *JTS* 38 [1987] 1–15.)

Grundmann, Walter (1964). "δόκιμοι, etc." *TDNT* 2: 255–60.

Guerra, Anthony J. (1995). *Romans and the Apologetic Tradition: The Purpose, Genre, and Audience of Paul's Letter.* Cambridge: Cambridge Univ. Press.

Gundry, Robert H. (1985). "Grace, Works and Staying Saved in Paul." *Bib* 66: 1–38.

Gurvitch, G. (1963). "Social Structure and the Multiplicity of Times." In E. A. Tiryakian, ed. *Sociological Theory, Values, and Sociocultural Change.* London: Free Press of Glencoe. 171–85.

Gustavson, James M. (1970). "The Place of Scripture in Christian Ethics: A Methodological Study." *Interpretation* 24: 430–55.

Hägerstrand, T. (1985). "Time and Culture." In Kirsch, Nijkamp, and Zimmerman 1985.

Halbwachs, Maurice (1980). *The Collective Memory.* Trans. Francis J. Ditter Jr. and Vida Yazdi Ditter, with an introduction by Mary Douglas. (ET of 1950 French original.) New York: Harper.

Hall, Edith (1989). *Inventing the Barbarian: Greek Self-Definition through Tragedy.* Oxford: Clarendon.

Hall, Edward T. (1966). *The Hidden Dimension.* Garden City, N.Y.: Doubleday.

Hall, Jonathan M. (1997). *Ethnic Identity in Greek Antiquity.* Berkeley: Univ. of California Press.

Hall, Robert (1991). "Historical Inference and Rhetorical Effect: Another Look at Galatians 1 and 2." In Watson 1991: 308–20.

Halperin, David (1989). *One Hundred Years of Sexuality and Other Essays on Abraham in Galatians.* JSNTSup 29. Sheffield: Sheffield Academic Press.

Hanson, Anthony T. (1974). "Abraham the Justified Sinner." In *Studies in Paul's Technique and Theology.* Grand Rapids: Eerdmans, 52–66.

Harder, Günther (1971). "σπουδάζω, σπουδή, σπουδαῖος." In *TDNT* 7: 559–68.

Harris, William V. (1989). *Ancient Literacy*. Cambridge: Harvard Univ. Press.

Hartman, Lars (1992). "Baptism." In *ABD* 1: 583–94.

Haslam, S. Alexander (2001). *Psychology in Organizations: The Social Identity Approach*. Thousand Oaks, Calif.: Sage.

Haslam, S. Alexander, John C. Turner, Penelope J. Oakes, Craig McGarty, and Katherine J. Reynolds (1998). "The Group as the Basis for Emergent Stereotype Consensus." *ERSP* 8: 203–39.

Haslam, S. Alexander, and Michael J. Platow (2001). "Your Wish Is Our Command: The Role of Shared Social Identity in Translating a Leader's Vision into Followers' Action." In Hogg and Terry 2001: 213–28.

Hauck, Friedrich (1965). "Ἀκάθαρτος, etc." In *TDNT* 3: 427–31.

Hawthorne, Gerald F., with Otto Betz, eds. (1987). *Tradition and Interpretation in the New Testament: Essays in Honor of E. Earle Ellis for His Sixtieth Birthday*. Grand Rapids: Eerdmans.

Hay, David M., ed. (1993). *Pauline Theology*. Vol. II: *1 and 2 Corinthians*. Minneapolis: Fortress Press.

Hay, David M., and E. Elizabeth Johnson, eds. (1995). *Pauline Theology*. Vol. III: *Romans*. Minneapolis: Fortress Press.

Hays, Richard B. (1983). *The Faith of Jesus Christ*. SBLDS 56. Chico, Calif.: Scholars Press.

———— (1985). "'Have We Found Abraham to Be Our Forefather according to the Flesh?' A Reconsideration of Rom 4:11." *NovT* 27: 76–98.

———— (1986) "Relations Natural and Unnatural: A Response to John Boswell's Exegesis of Romans 1." *Journal of Christian Ethics* 14: 184–215.

———— (1989). *Echoes of Scripture in the Letters of Paul*. New Haven: Yale Univ. Press.

———— (1996). *The Moral Vision of the New Testament: Community, Cross, New Creation: A Contemporary Introduction to New Testament Ethics*. Edinburgh: T & T Clark.

———— (1997). "ΠΙΣΤΙΣ and Pauline Theology: What Is at Stake?" In Johnson and Hay 1997: 35–60.

Hedner-Zetterholm, Karin (2001). "The Jewish Communities of Ancient Rome." In Olsson, Mitternacht, and Brandt 2001: 131–40.

Hemphill, J. K. (1969). "The Leader and His Group." In Gibb 1949: 223–50.

Hengel, Martin (1966). "Die Synagogeninschrift von Stobi." *ZNW* 57: 145–83.

Hengel, Martin, and Ulrich Heckel, eds. (1991). *Paulus und das antike Judentum: Tübingen-Durham-Symposium im Gedenken an der 50. Todestag Adolf Schlatter*. Tübingen: Mohr/Siebeck.

Henten, Jan Willem van, and Athalya Brenner, eds. (2000). *Families and Family Relations as Represented in Early Judaisms and Early Christianities: Texts and Fictions*. Studies in Theology and Religion 2. Leiden: Deo.

Hewstone, Miles (1996). "Contact and Categorization: Social Psychological Interventions to Change Intergroup Relations." In Macrae et al. 1996: 323–68.

Hewstone, Miles, and Rupert Brown, eds. (1986a). *Contact and Conflict in Intergroup Encounters*. Oxford: Blackwell.

———— (1986b). "Contact Is Not Enough: An Intergroup Perspective on the 'Contact Hypothesis.'" In Hewstone and Brown 1986a: 1–44.

Hezser, Catherine (2001). *Jewish Literacy in Roman Palestine.* Texts and Studies in Ancient Judaism 81. Tübingen: Mohr/Siebeck.

Hick, John, ed. (1977). *The Myth of God Incarnate.* London: SCM.

Hill, Craig C. (2001). "Romans." In Barton and Muddiman 2001: 1083–108.

Hillier, Bill, and Julienne Hanson (1984). *The Social Logic of Space.* Cambridge: Cambridge Univ. Press.

Hock, Ronald F. (1980). *The Social Context of Paul's Ministry: Tentmaking and Apostleship.* Philadelphia: Fortress Press.

Hogg, Michael A. (1996). "Intragroup Processes, Group Structure and Social Identity." In P. Robinson 1996: 65–93.

——— and Craig McGarty (1990). "Self-Categorization Theory and Social Identity." In Abrams and Hogg 1990: 10–27.

Hogg, Michael A., and D. J. Terry, eds. (2001). *Social Identity Processes in Organizations.* New York: Psychology Press.

Hohn, H.-W. (1984). *Die Zerstörung der Zeit. Wie aus einem göttlichen Gut eine Handelsware wurde.* Frankfurt: Fischer Alternativ.

Hollander, E. P. (1995). "Organizational Leadership and Followership." In P. Collett and A. Furnham, eds., *Social Psychology at Work.* London: Routledge. 69–87.

Holmberg, Bengt (1978). *Paul and Power: The Structure of Authority in the Primitive Church as Reflected in the Pauline Epistles.* Lund: Gleerup.

Holmes, Michael W., ed. (1989). *The Apostolic Fathers.* Trans. J. B. Lightfoot and J. R. Harmer. 2nd ed. Leicester: Apollos.

Hooker, Morna D. (1989). "ΠΙΣΤΙΣ ΧΡΙΣΤΟΥ." *NTS* 35: 321–42.

——— (1990). *From Adam to Christ: Essays on Paul.* Cambridge: Cambridge Univ. Press.

Hopkins, Keith, ed. (1983). *Death and Renewal.* Sociological Studies in Roman History 2. Cambridge: Cambridge Univ. Press.

Hopkins, Keith, and Graham Burton (1983a). "Political Succession in the Late Republic (249–50 BC)." In Hopkins 1983: 31–119.

——— (1983b). "Ambition and Withdrawal: The Senatorial Aristocracy under the Emperors." In Hopkins 1983: 120–200.

Horbury, William J. (2001). "The Wisdom of Solomon." In Barton and Muddiman 2001: 650–67.

Horbury, William J., and D. Noy (1992). *Jewish Inscriptions of Graeco-Roman Egypt.* Cambridge: Cambridge Univ. Press.

Hornblower, Simon, and Antony Spawforth, eds. (1996). *The Oxford Classical Dictionary.* 3rd ed. Oxford and New York: Oxford Univ. Press.

Horowitz, Donald L. (1985). *Ethnic Groups in Conflict.* Berkeley: Univ. of California Press.

Horrell, David G. (2002). "Solidarity and Difference: Pauline Morality in Romans 14:1—15:13." *Studies in Christian Ethics* 15: 60–78.

Horrell, David G., and Christopher M. Tuckett (2000). *Christology, Controversy and Community: New Testament Essays in Honour of David R. Catchpole.* NovTSup 99. Leiden: Brill.

Horsley, Richard A. (1995). *Galilee: History, Politics, People.* Valley Forge, Pa.: Trinity Press International.

———— (1996). *Archaeology, History, and Society in Galilee.* Valley Forge, Pa.: Trinity Press International.

Horst, P. W. van der (1985). "Pseudo-Phocylides (First Century B.C. – First Century A.D.): A New Translation and Introduction." In Charlesworth 1985: 564–73.

Hübner, Hans (1984). *Law in Paul's Thought.* (ET of 1978 German original.) Edinburgh: T & T Clark.

Hughes, E. C. (1994). *On Work, Race, and the Sociological Imagination.* Ed. L. A. Coser. Chicago: Univ. of Chicago Press.

Hursthouse, Rosalind (1999). *On Virtue Ethics.* Oxford and New York: Oxford Univ. Press.

Hutchinson, John, and Anthony D. Smith, eds. (1996a). *Ethnicity.* Oxford: Oxford Univ. Press.

———— (1996b). "Introduction." In Hutchinson and Smith 1996a: 3–14.

Ingold, Tim, ed. (1994). *Companion Encyclopedia of Anthropology.* London: Routledge.

Jenkins, Richard (1997). *Rethinking Ethnicity: Arguments and Explorations.* London: Sage.

Jervis, L. A. (1991). *The Purpose of Romans: A Comparative Letter Structure Investigation.* Sheffield: Sheffield Academic Press.

Jervis, L. A., and P. Richardson, eds., (1995). *Gospel in Paul: Studies on Corinthians, Galatians, and Romans for Richard N. Longenecker.* JSNTSup 108. Sheffield: JSOT Press.

Jewett, Robert (1982b). "Romans as an Ambassadorial Letter." *Int* 36: 5–20.

———— (1985). "The Law and the Co-Existence of Jews and Gentiles in Romans." *Int* 39: 341–56.

———— (1988). "Paul, Phoebe, and the Spanish Mission." In J. Neusner et al., eds., *The Social World of Formative Judaism and Christianity: Essays in Tribute to Howard Clark Kee.* Philadelphia: Fortress Press. 142–61.

———— (1993). "Tenement Churches and Communal Meals in the Early Church: The Implications of a Form-Critical Analysis of 2 Thessalonians 3:10." *BR* 38: 23–42.

———— (1997). "Honor and Shame in the Argument of Romans." In Virginia Wiles, Alexandra Brown, and Graydon F. Snyder, eds., *Putting Body and Soul Together: Essays in Honor of Robin Scroggs.* Valley Forge, Pa.: Trinity Press International. 25–73.

Johnson, E. Elizabeth (1989). *The Function of Apocalyptic and Wisdom Traditions in Romans 9–11.* SBLDS 109. Atlanta: Scholars Press.

———— (1997). "Romans 9–11: The Faithfulness and Impartiality of God." In Johnson and Hay 1997: 211–39.

Johnson, E. Elizabeth, and David M. Hay, eds. (1997). *Pauline Theology.* Vol. IV: *Looking Back, Pressing On.* SBLSymS 4. Atlanta: Scholars Press.

Johnson, Luke Timothy (1982). "Rom. 3:21-26 and the Faith of Jesus." *CBQ* 44: 77–90.

Jones, Siân (1997). *The Archaeology of Ethnicity.* London: Routledge.

Jones, W. H. S., trans. (1984). *Hippocrates.* Vol. 1. LCL. Cambridge: Harvard Univ. Press.

Jongman, Willem (1988). *The Economy and Society of Pompeii*. Amsterdam: Gieben.

Judge, E. A. (1994). "Judaism and the Rise of Christianity: A Roman Perspective." *TynBul* 45: 355–68.

Jung, Young-Sung (2000). "From Temple to House-Church in Luke-Acts: A Lukan Challenge to Korean Christianity." Ph.D. dissertation, Univ. of St. Andrews.

Karris, Robert (1991). "Romans 14:1—15:13 and the Occasion of Romans." In Donfried 1991a: 65–84.

Käsemann, Ernst (1968). "A Critical Analysis of Phil. 2.5-11." *Journal for Theology and the Church* 5: 45–88.

——— (1969a). *New Testament Questions of Today*. Trans. W. J. Montague and Wilfred F. Bunge. London: SCM.

——— (1969b). "Primitive Christian Apocalyptic." In Käsemann 1969a: 108–37.

——— (1969c). "Worship in Everyday Life: A Note on Romans 12." In Käsemann 1969a: 188–95.

——— (1969d). "Principles of the Interpretation of Romans 13." In Käsemann 1969a: 196–216.

——— (1980). *Commentary on Romans*. Trans. and ed. Geoffrey W. Bromiley. Grand Rapids: Eerdmans.

Kawakami, Kerry, and Kenneth L. Dion (1993). "The Impact of Salient Self-Identities on Relative Deprivation and Action Intentions." *EJSP* 23: 525–40.

Kearsley, R. A. (1999). "Women in Public Life in the Roman East: Iunia Theodora, Claudia Metrodora and Phoebe, Benefactress of Paul." *TynBul* 50: 203–5.

Keesmaat, Sylvia C. (1999). *Paul and His Story: (Re)Interpreting the Exodus Tradition*. JSNTSup 181. Sheffield: Sheffield Academic Press.

Kent, John Harvey (1948). "The Temple Estates of Delos, Rheneia, and Mykonos." *Hesperia* 17: 243–338.

Kent, Susan, ed. (1990). *Domestic Architecture and the Use of Space: An Interdisciplinary Cross-Cultural Study*. Cambridge: Cambridge Univ. Press.

Kermode, Frank (1975). *The Classic*. London: Faber & Faber.

Kirsch, G., P. Nijkamp, and K. Zimmerman, eds. (1985). *Time Preferences: An Interdisciplinary Theoretical and Empirical Approach*. Berlin: Wissenschaftcentrum.

Klausner, Samuel Z. (1992). "Diaspora in a Comparative Perspective: Toward a Definition of Religion." In M. Mor, ed., *Eretz Israel, Israel and the Jewish Diaspora: Mutual Relations*. Studies in Jewish Civilization 1. New York: University Press of America. 194–221.

Kloppenborg, John S., and Stephen G. Wilson, eds. (1996). *Voluntary Associations in the Graeco-Roman World*. London: Routledge.

Koester, Craig R. (2001). *Hebrews: A New Translation with Introduction and Commentary*. AB 36. New York: Doubleday.

Konstan, David (1997). "Redefining Ancient Greek Ethnicity." *Diaspora* 6: 97–110.

Kraabel, Alf Thomas (1995). "The Diaspora Synagogue: Archaeological and Epigraphic Evidence since Sukenik." In Urman and Flesher 1995: 95–126. (Reprinted from H. Temporini and W. Haase, eds. [1979] *ANRW. Principat, Religion. Judentum: Allgemeines; Palästinisches Judentum*. II. Vol. 19.1. Berlin and New York: de Gruyter, 477–510.)

Kraemer, Ross S. (1989). "On the Meaning of the Term 'Jew' in Greco-Roman Inscriptions." *HTR* 82: 35–53.

Kraft, Robert A., and George W. E. Nickelsburg, eds. (1986). *Early Judaism and Its Modern Interpreters.* Philadelphia: Fortress Press.

Kümmel, Werner Georg (1929). *Römer 7 und die Bekehrung des Paulus.* Leipsig: Hinrichs. (Reprinted as *Römer 7 und das Bild des Menschen im Neuen Testament.* Theologische Bücherei 53. Munich: Chr. Kaiser, 1974.)

Kvanvig, Helge S. (1988). *Roots of Apocalyptic: The Mesopotamian Background of the Enoch Figure and of the Son of Man.* WMANT 61. Neukirchen-Vluyn: Neukirchener Verlag.

La Piana, G. (1927). "Foreign Groups in Rome During the First Centuries of the Empire." *HTR* 20: 183–403.

Lagrange, M.–J. (1931). *Saint Paul: Épitre aux Romains.* 4th ed. Paris: Gabalda.

Lambrecht, Jan (1974). "Man Before and Without Christ: Romans 7 and Pauline Autobiography." *Louvain Studies* 5: 18–33.

Lampe, Peter (1987). *Die stadtrömischen Christen in den ersten beiden Jahrhunderten: Studien zur Sozialgeschichte.* Tübingen: Mohr/Siebeck. ET = (2003). *From Paul to Valentinus: Christians at Rome in the First Two Centuries.* Trans. Michael Steinhauser. Ed. Marshall D. Johnson. Minneapolis: Fortress Press.

——— (1991). "The Roman Christians of Romans 16." In Donfried 1991a: 216–30.

Lane, William L. (1998). "Social Perspectives on Roman Christianity during the Formative Years from Nero to Nerva: Romans, Hebrews, *1 Clement.*" In Donfried and Richardson 1998: 196–244.

Laurence, Ray (1997). "Space and Text." In Laurence and Wallace-Hadrill 1997: 7–14.

Laurence, Ray, and Andrew Wallace-Hadrill, eds. (1997). *Domestic Space in the Roman World: Pompeii and Beyond. Journal of Roman Archaeology,* Supplementary Series 22. Portsmouth, R.I.: Journal of Roman Archaeology.

Lawrence, Joy Louise (2002). "Matthew—A Literary Ethnography: An Anthropological Reading of Matthew's Constructed World." Ph.D. thesis, Univ. of Exeter, England.

——— (2003). *An Ethnography of the Gospel of Matthew: A Critical Assessment of the Use of Honour and Shame in New Testament Studies.* WUNT 165. Tübingen: Mohr/Siebeck.

Leach, Edmund (1961). *Rethinking Anthropology.* London: Athlone.

Lendon, Jon E. (1997). *Empire of Honour: The Art of Government in the Roman World.* New York: Oxford Univ. Press.

Lenski, Gerhard, and Jean Lenski (1987). *Human Societies: An Introduction to Macrosociology.* 5th ed. New York: McGraw-Hill.

Leon, Harry J. (1960). *The Jews of Ancient Rome.* Morris Loeb Series. Philadelphia: Jewish Publication Society of America.

Levine, Lee I. (2000). *The Ancient Synagogue: The First Thousand Years.* New Haven: Yale Univ. Press.

Levinskaya, Irina. (1996). *The Book of Acts in Its Diaspora Setting.* The Book of Acts in Its First Century Setting 5. Grand Rapids: Eerdmans.

Lévi-Strauss, Claude. (1963). *Structural Anthropology.* New York: Basic.

——— (1969). *The Elementary Structures of Kinship.* Boston: Beacon.

——— (1972). *The Savage Mind.* London: Weidenfeld & Nicolson.

Lindars, Barnabas (1984/85). "The Sound of the Trumpet: Paul and Eschatology." *Bulletin of the John Rylands Library* 67: 766–82.

Lindsay, Jack (1960). *The Writing on the Wall: An Account of Pompeii in Its Last Days.* London: F. Muller.

Luz, Ulrich (1967). "Der alte und der neue Bund bei Paulus und im Hebräerbrief." *EvT* 27: 318–36.

Lyonnet, S. (1962). "L'histoire du salut selon le ch 7 de l'épître aux Romains." *Bib* 43: 117–51.

Lyons, George (1985). *Pauline Autobiography: Toward a New Understanding.* SBLDS 73. Atlanta: Scholars Press.

Macrae, C. N. , C. Stangor, and Miles Hewstone, eds. (1996). *Stereotypes and Stereotyping.* New York: Guilford.

Malherbe, Abraham J. (1986). *Moral Exhortation: A Greco-Roman Sourcebook.* LEC. Philadelphia: Westminster.

Malina, Bruce J. (1986). "Religion in the World of Paul: A Preliminary Sketch." *BTB* 16: 92–101.

——— (1992). "Is There a Circum-Mediterranean Person: Looking for Stereotypes." *BTB* 22: 66–87.

——— (1994). "Religion in the Imagined New Testament World: More Social Science Lenses." *Scriptura* 51: 1–26.

——— (1996a). *The Social World of Jesus and the Gospels.* London: Routledge.

——— (1996b). "Christ and Time: Swiss or Mediterranean." In Malina 1996a: 179–214. (This essay originally appeared in *CBQ* 51 [1989] 1–31.)

——— (1996d). "Mediterranean Sacrifice: Dimensions of Domestic and Political Religion." *BTB* 26: 26–44.

——— (1997). "Jesus as Astral Prophet." *BTB* 27: 83–98.

——— (2000a). "Three Theses for a More Adequate Reading of the New Testament." In Lawler, Michael G., and Gail S. Risch, eds., *Practical Theology: Perspectives from the Plains.* Omaha: Creighton Univ. Press. 33–60.

——— (2000b). *The New Jerusalem in the Revelation of John: The City as Symbol of Life with God.* Collegeville, Minn.: Liturgical.

——— (2001). *The New Testament World: Insights from Cultural Anthropology.* 3rd ed. Louisville: Westminster John Knox.

——— (2002). "We and They in Romans." *HvTSt* 58: 608–31.

Malina, Bruce J., and John J. Pilch (2000). *Social-Science Commentary on the Book of Revelation.* Minneapolis: Fortress Press.

Malina, Bruce J., and Richard L. Rohrbaugh (1998). *Social-Science Commentary on the Gospel of John.* Minneapolis: Fortress Press.

——— (2003). *Social-Science Commentary on the Synoptic Gospels.* 2nd ed. Minneapolis: Fortress Press.

Malinowski, Bruno (1948). "Myth in Primitive Psychology." In *Magic, Science and Religion and Other Essays.* Garden City, N.Y.: Anchor. 93–148.

Malkin, Irad, ed. (2001a). *Ancient Perceptions of Greek Ethnicity*. Washington, D.C.: Center for Hellenic Studies and Trustees for Harvard University.

———— (2001b). "Introduction." In Malkin 2001a: 1–28.

Manson, T. W. (1991). "St. Paul's Letter to the Romans—and Others." In Donfried 1991a: 3–15.

Marcus, Joel (1989). "The Circumcision and Uncircumcision in Rome." *NTS* 35: 67–81.

Martin, Dale B. (1995). "Heterosexism and the Interpretation of Romans 1:18-32." *BibInt* 3: 332–55.

Martínez, Florentino García (1994). *The Dead Sea Scrolls Translated: The Qumran Texts in English*. Trans. Wilfred G. E. Watson. (ET of 1992 Spanish original.) Leiden: Brill.

Martyn, J. Louis (1991). "Events in Galatia: Modified Covenantal Nomism Versus God's Invasion of the Cosmos in the Singular Gospel: A Response to J. D. G. Dunn and B. R. Gaventa." In Bassler 1991: 160–79.

———— (1997). *Theological Issues in the Letters of Paul*. Edinburgh: T & T Clark.

Marxsen, Willi (1968). *Introduction to the New Testament*. Trans. G. Buswell. Philadelphia: Fortress Press.

Mason, D. (1986). "Introduction: Controversies and Continuities in Race and Ethnic Relations Theory." In Rex and Mason 1986: 1–19.

Matera, Frank J. (1992). *Galatians*. Sacra Pagina 9. Collegeville, Minn.: Liturgical.

McCormack, Bruce L. (1995). *Karl Barth's Critically Realistic Dialectical Theology: Its Genesis and Development 1909–1936*. Oxford: Oxford Univ. Press.

McDonald, Patricia M. (1990). "Romans 5.1-11 as a Rhetorical Bridge." *JSNT* 40: 81–96.

McKay, Heather A. (1994). *Sabbath and Synagogue: The Question of Sabbath Worship in Ancient Judaism*. Religions in the Graeco-Roman World 122. Leiden: Brill.

McVann, Mark (1991). "Rituals of Status Transformation in Luke-Acts: The Case of Jesus the Prophet." In Neyrey 1991: 333–60.

Mead, G. H. (1954 [1925]). *The Philosophy of the Present*. La Salle: Open Court.

Meeks, Wayne E. (1983). *The First Urban Christians: The Social World of the Apostle Paul*. New Haven: Yale Univ. Press.

———— (1986). *The Moral World of the First Christians*. LEC. Philadelphia: Westminster.

———— (1987). "Judgment and the Brother: Romans 14:1—15:13." In Hawthorne with Betz 1987: 290–300.

———— (1993). *The Origins of Christian Morality: The First Two Centuries*. New Haven: Yale Univ. Press.

Meggitt, Justin J. (1998). *Paul, Poverty and Survival*. Edinburgh: T & T Clark.

Meyers, Eric M., and A. Thomas Kraabel (1986). "Archaeology, Iconography, and Nonliterary Written Remains." In Kraft and Nickelsburg 1986: 175–210.

Meyers, Eric M., and James F. Strange (1981). *Archaeology, the Rabbis, and Early Christianity*. Nashville: Abingdon.

Michaelis, Wilhelm (1968). "πίπτω, etc." In *TDNT* 6: 161–73.

Middendorf, Michael Paul (1997). *The "I" in the Storm: A Study of Romans 7*. St. Louis: Concordia.

Middleton, David, and Derek Edwards, eds. (1990a). *Collective Remembering*. London: Sage.

———— (1990b). "Introduction." In Middleton and Edwards 1990a: 1–22.

Migne, J. P. (1862). *Patrologia Graeca*. Vol. 60. Paris.

Miller, James C. (2000). *The Obedience of Faith, the Eschatological People of God, and the Purpose of Romans*. SBLDS 177. Atlanta: Society of Biblical Literature.

Miller, N., and M. B. Brewer, eds. (1984). *Groups in Contact: The Psychology of Desegregation*. New York: Academic Press.

Minard, R. D. (1952). "Race Relationships in the Pocahontas Coal Field." *Journal of Social Issues* 8:29–44.

Minde, H.–J. van der (1976). *Schrift und Tradition bei Paulus*. Munich: Schöningh.

Minear, Paul S. (1971). *The Obedience of Faith: The Purposes of Paul in the Epistle to the Romans*. SBT 2/19. London: SCM.

Moo, Douglas J. (1986). "Israel and Paul in Romans 7.7-12." *NTS* 32: 122–35.

———— (1996). *The Epistle to the Romans*. NICNT. Grand Rapids: Eerdmans.

Morgan, Robert (1995). *Romans*. New Testament Guides. Sheffield: Sheffield Academic Press.

Moule, C. F. D. (1967–1968). "Fulfilment Words in the New Testament: Use and Abuse." *NTS* 14: 293–320.

Moxnes, Halvor (1980). *Theology in Conflict: Studies in Paul's Understanding of God*. NovTSup 53. Leiden: Brill.

———— (1988a). "Honour and Righteousness in Romans." *JSNT* 32: 61–77.

———— (1988b). "Honor, Shame and the Outside World in Paul's Letter to the Romans." In Neusner 1988: 207–18.

———— (1995). "The Quest for Honor and the Unity of the Community in Romans 12 and in the Orations of Dio Chrysostom." In Engberg-Pedersen 1994: 203–30.

————, ed. (1997a). *Constructing Early Christian Families: Family as Social Reality and Metaphor*. London and New York: Routledge.

———— (1997b). "Introduction." In Moxnes 1997a: 1–9.

———— (1997c). "What is Family? Problems in Constructing Early Christian Families." In Moxnes 1997a: 42–65.

Munck, Johannes (1959). *Paul and the Salvation of Mankind*. (ET of German original, 1954.) London: SCM.

Munn, Nancy D. (1992). "The Cultural Anthropology of Time: A Critical Essay." *Annual Review of Anthropology* 21: 93–123.

Münzer, Friedrich (1999). *Roman Aristocratic Parties and Families*. Trans. Thérèse Ridley. Baltimore: Johns Hopkins Univ. Press.

Mussner, Franz (1984). *Tractate on the Jews: The Significance of Judaism for the Christian Faith*. Translated, with an introduction, by Leonard Swidler. Philadelphia: Fortress Press.

Namer, Gérard (2000). *Halbwachs et la mémoire sociale*. Paris: L'Hartman.

Nanos, Mark D. (1996). *The Mystery of Romans: The Jewish Context of Paul's Letter*. Minneapolis: Fortress Press.

———— (1999). "The Jewish Context of the Gentile Audience Addressed in Paul's Letter to the Romans." *CBQ* 61: 283–304.

Nestle-Aland (2000). *Das Neue Testament: Griechisch und Deutsch.* Stuttgart: Deutscher Bibelgesellschaft and Katholische Bibelanstalt.

Neusner, Jacob, et al., eds. (1988). *The Social World of Formative Christianity and Judaism: Essays in Tribute to Howard Clark Kee.* Philadelphia: Fortress Press.

Neyrey, Jerome H., ed. (1991). *The Social World of Luke-Acts: Models for Interpretation.* Peabody, Mass.: Hendrickson.

Norden, E. (1958 [1898]). *Die Antike Kunstprosa.* Two volumes. 5th ed. Stuttgart: B. G. Teubner.

Nowotny, H. (1985). "From the Future to the Extended Present: Time in Social Systems." In Kirsch, Nijkamp, and Zimmerman 1985.

Noy, David (1995). *Jewish Inscriptions of Western Europe.* Vol. 2: *The City of Rome.* Cambridge: Cambridge Univ. Press.

Oakes, Penelope J., S. Alexander Haslam, and John C. Turner (1994). *Stereotyping and Social Reality.* Oxford: Blackwell.

Oakes, Peter, ed. (2002). *Rome in the Bible and the Early Church.* Carlisle: Paternoster.

Okamura, Jonathan Y. (1981). "Situational Ethnicity." *ERS* 4: 452–65.

O'Keefe, Anne (2002). "The House as Key to Understanding Acts (the Micro-Text) within Its Roman Imperial Context (the Macro-Text)." Ph.D. dissertation, Trinity College Dublin.

Ollrogg, Wolf-Hennig (1980). "Die Abfassungsverhältnisse von Röm 16." In D. Lührmann and G. Strecker, eds., *Kirche: Festschrift Günther Bornkamm zum 75. Geburtstag.* Tübingen: Mohr/Siebeck. 221–44.

Olsson, Birger, Dieter Mitternacht, and Olof Brandt, eds. (2001). *The Synagogue of Ancient Ostia and the Jews of Rome: Interdisciplinary Studies.* Stockholm: Svenska Institutet i Rom.

Ong, Walter (1982). *Orality and Literacy: The Technologizing of the Word.* London: Methuen.

Osiek, Carolyn (1998). "The Oral World of Early Christianity in Rome: The Case of Hermas." In Donfried and Richardson 1998: 151–72.

——— (2004/5). "*Diakonos* and *Prostatis:* Women's Patronage in Early Christianity." Chapter in forthcoming book by Osiek and Margaret MacDonald.

Osiek, Carolyn, and David L. Balch, eds. (1997). *Families in the New Testament: Households in the New Testament World.* Louisville: Westminster John Knox.

Østergård, Uffe (1992). "What Is National and Ethnic Identity?" in Bilde et al. 1992: 16–38.

Oswald, Hilton C., ed. (1972). *Luther's Works.* Vol. 25: *Lectures on Romans; Glosses and Scholia.* St. Louis: Concordia.

Pansiot, Fernand Paul, and Henri Rebour (1961). *Improvement in Olive Cultivation.* Rome: Food and Agriculture Organization of the United Nations.

Petrochilus, N. (1974). *Roman Attitudes to the Greeks.* Athens: N. Petrochilus.

Pilch, John J. (1993). "Jews or Judeans: A Translation Challenge." *Modern Liturgy* 20: 19.

——— (1996). "Jews and Christians: Anachronisms in Bible Translations." *Professional Approaches for Christian Educators (PACE)* 25: 18–25.

———— (1997). "Are There Jews and Christians in the Bible?" *HvTSt* 53: 1–7.

———— (1998). "No Jews or Christians in the Bible." *Explorations: American Interfaith Institute/World Alliance of Interfaith Organizations* 12: 3.

———— (1999). *The Cultural Dictionary of the Bible.* Collegeville, Minn.: Liturgical.

———— (2002). "Altered States of Consciousness in the Synoptics." In Stegemann, Malina, and Theissen 2002: 103–17.

Pilch, John J., ed. (2001). *Social Science Models for Interpreting the Bible: Essays by the Context Group in Honor of Bruce J. Malina.* Biblical Interpretation Series 53. Leiden: Brill.

Pilch, John J., and Bruce J. Malina, eds. (1993). *Biblical Social Values and Their Meaning.* Peabody, Mass.: Hendrickson.

Piper, John (1983). *The Justification of God: An Exegetical and Theological Study of Romans 1:1-23.* Grand Rapids: Baker.

Pohl, Walter (1998a). "Introduction: Strategies of Distinction." In Pohl and Reimitz 1998: 1–15.

———— (1998b). "Telling the Difference: Signs of Ethnic Identity." In Pohl and Reimitz 1998: 17–69.

Pohl, Walter, with Helmut Reimitz (1998). *Strategies of Distinction: The Construction of Ethnic Communities, 300–800.* Leiden: Brill.

Raepple, Eva Maria (2001). "The Metaphor of the City in the Book of Revelation: A 'Textual Image' and Incentive for Imagination." Ph.D. dissertation, Univ. of St. Andrews.

Räisänen, Heikki (1986). *Paul and the Law.* Philadelphia: Fortress Press.

Rankin, David (2000). "Arianism." In Esler 2000c: 975–1001.

Rapoport, Amos (1969). *House Form and Culture.* Englewood Cliffs, N.J.: Prentice-Hall.

———— ed. (1976a). *The Mutual Interaction of People and Their Built Environment: A Cross-Cultural Perspective.* The Hague: Mouton.

———— (1976b). "Socio-Cultural Aspects of Man-Environment Studies." In Rapoport 1976a: 7–35.

———— (1977). *Human Aspects of Urban Form: Toward a Man-Environment Approach to Urban Form and Design.* Oxford: Pergamon.

———— (1982a). *The Meaning of Built Environment: A Nonverbal Communication Approach.* Beverley Hills: Sage.

———— (1982b). "The Effect of Environment on Behaviour." In Calhoun 1982: 200–211.

———— (1990). "Systems of Activities and Systems of Settings." In Kent 1990: 9–20.

———— (1994). "Spatial Organisation and the Built Environment." In Ingold 1994: 460–502.

Rathbone, Dominic W. (1996). "Food Supply." In Hornblower and Spawforth 1996: 604.

Rauer, M. (1923). *Die 'Schwachen' in Korinth und Rom nach den Paulusbriefen.* Biblische Studien 21. Freiburg: Herder.

Reasoner, Mark (1999). *The Strong and the Weak: Romans 14.1—15.13 in Context.* SNTSMS 103. Cambridge: Cambridge Univ. Press.

Reicher, Stephen, and Nicolas Hopkins (1996). "Self-Category Constructions in Political Rhetoric: An Analysis of Thatcher's and Kinnock's Speeches Concerning the British Miners' Strike (1984–5)." *EJSP* 26: 353–71.

Reminick, Ronald A. (1983). *Theory of Ethnicity: An Anthropologist's Perspective.* Lanham, Md.: Univ. Press of America.

Reumann, John (1982). *"Righteousness" in the New Testament: "Justification" in the United States Lutheran-Roman Catholic Dialogue.* Philadelphia: Fortress Press.

Rex, John, and David Mason, eds. (1986). *Theories of Race and Ethnic Relations.* Cambridge: Cambridge Univ. Press.

Roberts, R. H., and J. M. M. Good, eds. (1993). *The Recovery of Rhetoric: Persuasive Discourse and Disciplinarity in the Human Sciences.* Charlottesville: Univ. Press of Virginia.

Robinson, D. W. B. (1970). "'Faith of Jesus Christ': A New Testament Debate." *Reformed Theological Review* 29: 71–81.

Robinson, Peter, ed. (1996). *Social Groups and Identities: Developing the Legacy of Henri Tajfel.* Oxford: Butterworth Heinemann.

Roetzel, Calvin J. (1999). *Paul: The Man and the Myth.* Personalities of the New Testament. Minneapolis: Fortress Press.

Rohrbaugh, Richard L. (1991). "The Preindustrial City in Luke–Acts: Urban Social Relations." In Neyrey 1991: 125–49.

——— (1997). "A Dysfunctional Family and Its Neighbors: Luke 15:11-32." In V. G. Shillington, ed., *Perspectives on the Parables: Images of Jesus in his Contemporary Setting.* Edinburgh: T & T Clark. 141–64.

——— (2001). "Gossip in the New Testament." In Pilch 2001: 239–59.

Rolfe, J. C. (1914). *Suetonius.* Vol. 2. LCL. New York: Macmillan.

Ross, J. A. (1980). "The Mobilization of Collective Identity: An Analytical Overview." In Cottrel and Ross 1980: 1–30.

Runesson, Anders (2001). "The Synagogue at Ancient Ostia: The Building and Its History from the First to the Fifth Century." In Olsson, Mitternacht, and Brandt 2001: 29–99.

——— (2002). "A Monumental Synagogue from the First Century: The Case of Ostia." *Journal for the Study of Judaism in the Persian, Hellenistic, and Roman Periods* 33: 171–200.

Rutgers, Leonard Victor (1998). *The Hidden Heritage of Diaspora Judaism.* Contributions to Biblical Exegesis and Theology 20. Leuven: Peeters.

Sack, Robert David. (1986). *Human Territoriality: Its Theory and History.* Cambridge Studies in Historical Geography 7. Cambridge: Cambridge Univ. Press.

Saller, Richard P. (1994). *Patriarchy, Property and Death in the Roman Family.* Cambridge Studies in Population, Economy, and Society in Past Time 25. Cambridge: Cambridge Univ. Press.

Sampley, J. Paul. (1991). *Walking between the Times: Paul's Moral Reasoning.* Minneapolis: Fortress Press.

——— (1995). "The Weak and the Strong: Paul's Careful and Crafty Rhetorical Strategy in Romans 14:1—15:13." In White and Yarbrough 1995: 40–52.

Sanders, E. P. (1977). *Paul and Palestinian Judaism.* Philadelphia: Fortress Press.

——— (1983). *Paul, the Law, and the Jewish People.* Philadelphia: Fortress Press.

——— (1990). *Jewish Law from Jesus to the Mishnah: Five Studies.* Philadelphia: Trinity Press International.

——— (1993). *The Historical Figure of Jesus.* London: Penguin.

Sandt, Huub van de, and David Flusser (2002). *The Didache: Its Jewish Sources and Its Place in Early Judaism and Christianity.* Compendia Rerum Iudaicarum ad Novum Testamentum. Minneapolis: Fortress Press.

Sani, Fabio, and Steve Reicher (2000). "Contested Identities and Schisms in Groups Opposing the Ordination of Women as Priests in the Church of England." *British Journal of Social Psychology* 39: 95–112.

Schlatter, Adolf (1995 [1935]). *Romans: The Righteousness of God.* Trans. Siegfried S. Schatzmann. (ET of the 4th edition of *Gottes Gerechtigkeit: Ein Kommentar zum Römerbrief.*) Peabody, Mass.: Hendrickson.

Schmidt, Karl Ludwig (1968). "πταίω." In *TDNT* 6: 883–84.

Schmithals, Walter (1988). *Der Römerbrief: Ein Commentar.* Gütersloh: Gütersloher Verlagshaus Gerd Mohn.

Schmitz, Otto (1967). "παρακαλέω, παράκλησις." In *TDNT* 5: 773–99.

Schofield, M., and Gisela Striker, eds. (1986). *The Norms of Nature: Studies in Hellenistic Ethics.* Cambridge: Cambridge Univ. Press.

Schutz, A. (1971). *Collected Papers.* Vol. 1: *The Problem of Social Reality.* Ed. M. Natanson. The Hague: Nijhof.

Schütz, John (1975). *Paul and the Anatomy of Apostolic Authority.* SNTSMS 26. Cambridge: Cambridge Univ. Press.

Schwartz, Barry (1990). "The Reconstruction of Abraham Lincoln." In Middleton and Edwards 1990a: 81–107.

Schweitzer, Albert (1968 [1906]). *The Quest of the Historical Jesus: A Critical Study of Its Progress from Reimarus to Wrede.* Trans. W. Montgomery. New York: Macmillan.

——— (1998 [1931]). *The Mysticism of Paul the Apostle.* Trans. William Montgomery. Baltimore: Johns Hopkins Univ. Press.

Schwimmer, Erik, ed. (1976). *"The Vailala Madness" and Other Essays.* St. Lucia, Queensland: Univ. of Queensland Press.

Scott, G. M., Jr. (1990). "A Resynthesis of the Primordial and Circumstantialist Approaches to Ethnic Group Solidarity: Towards an Explanatory Model." *ERS* 13: 147–71.

Sheldon, Charles Monroe (1935 [1896]). *In His Steps: "What Would Jesus Do?"* New York: Grosset & Dunlap.

Segal, Alan (1990). *Paul the Convert: The Apostolate and Apostasy of Saul the Pharisee.* New Haven: Yale Univ. Press.

Seifrid, Mark A. (1992b). "The Subject of Rom 7:14-25." *NovT* 34: 313–33.

Sherif, M., and C. W. Sherif (1953). *Groups in Harmony and Tension: An Integration of Studies on Intergroup Relations.* New York: Octagon.

——— (1969). *Social Psychology.* New York: Harper & Row.

Sherif, M., B. J. White, and O. J. Harvey (1955). "Status in Experimentally Produced Groups." *American Journal of Sociology* 60: 370–79.

Sherif, M., O. J. Harvey, B. J. White, W. R. Hood, and C. W. Sherif (1961). *Intergroup Conflict and Cooperation: The Robber's Cave Experiment.* Norman: Univ. of Oklahoma Book Exchange.

Sherwin-White, A. N. (1963). *Roman Society and Roman Law in the New Testament.* Oxford: Clarendon.

——— (1967). *Racial Prejudice in Imperial Rome.* Cambridge: Cambridge Univ. Press.

Shils, Edward (1957). "Primordial, Personal, Sacred and Civil Ties." *British Journal of Sociology* 8: 130–45.

——— (1981). *Tradition.* London: Faber and Faber.

Siker, Jeffrey S. (1991). *Disinheriting the Jews: Abraham in Early Christian Controversy.* Louisville: Westminster John Knox.

Slingerland, H. Dixon (1997). *Claudian Policymaking and the Early Imperial Repression of Judaism at Rome.* South Florida Studies in the History of Judaism 160. Atlanta: Scholars Press.

Smallwood, E. Mary (1961). *Philonis Alexandrini: Legatio ad Gaium. Edited, with an Introduction, Translation, and Commentary.* Leiden: Brill.

Smiga, G. (1991). "Romans 12:1-2 and 15:30-32 and the Occasion of the Letter to the Romans." *CBQ* 53: 257–73.

Smith, Anthony D. (1981). *The Ethnic Revival.* Cambridge: Cambridge Univ. Press.

——— (1986). *The Ethnic Origins of Nations.* Oxford: Blackwell.

Smith, Eliot R., and Michael A. Zarate (1990). "Exemplar and Prototype Use in Social Categorization." *Social Cognition* 8: 243–62.

Smith, Wilfred Cantwell (1991 [1962]). *The Meaning and End of Religion.* Minneapolis: Fortress Press.

Soderlund, S., and N. T. Wright, eds. (1999). *Romans and the People of God: Essays in Honor of Gordon D. Fee on the Occasion of His 65th Birthday.* Grand Rapids: Eerdmans.

Sollors, Werner (1996). *Theories of Ethnicity: A Classical Reader.* Basingstoke: Macmillan.

Sorokin, P. A. (1964). *Sociocultural Causality, Space and Time: A Study of Referential Principles of Sociology and Social Science.* New York: Russell & Russell.

Souter, Alexander (1919). *Tertullian's Treatises: Concerning Prayer, Concerning Baptism.* New York: Macmillan.

Spickard, Paul, and W. Jeffrey Burroughs, eds. (2000a). *We Are a People: Narrative and Multiplicity in Constructing Ethnic Identity.* Philadelphia: Temple Univ. Press.

——— (2000b). "We Are a People." In Spickard and Burroughs 2000a: 1–19.

Stack, J. J., ed. (1986). *The Primordial Challenge: Ethnicity in the Contemporary World.* New York: Greenwood.

Stanley, Christopher D. (1992). *Paul and the Language of Scripture: Citation Technique in the Pauline Epistles and Contemporary Literature.* SNTSMS 74. Cambridge: Cambridge Univ. Press.

——— (1996). "'Neither Jew Nor Greek': Ethnic Conflict in Graeco-Roman Society." *JSNT* 64: 101–24.

Stauffer, Ethelbert (1964a). "ἀγαπάω, etc." In *TDNT* 1: 35–55.

———— (1964b). "ἐγώ." In *TDNT* 2: 550–51.

Stegemann, Wolfgang, Bruce J. Malina, and Gerd Theissen, eds. (2002). *The Social Setting of Jesus and the Gospels*. Minneapolis: Fortress Press.

Steinmetz, David C. (1986). *Luther in Context*. Bloomington: Indiana Univ. Press.

Stephan, Cookie White, and Stephan, Paul (2000). "What Are the Functions of Ethnic Identity?" In Spickard and Burroughs 2000a: 229–43.

Stendahl, Krister (1962). "Contemporary Biblical Theology." In G. A. Buttrick, ed., *The Interpreter's Dictionary of the Bible*. 4 vols. New York: Abingdon. 1: 418–32.

———— (1993). "Anti-Semitism." In Bruce M. Metzger and Michael D. Coogan, eds., *The Oxford Companion to the Bible*. New York: Oxford Univ. Press. 33–34.

Stern, Menahem (1974). *Greek and Latin Authors on Jews and Judaism*. Vol. 1: *From Herodotus to Plutarch*. Jerusalem: Israel Academy of Sciences and Humanities.

———— (1980). *Greek and Latin Authors on Jews and Judaism*. Vol. 2: *From Tacitus to Simplicius*. Jerusalem: Israel Academy of Sciences and Humanities.

———— (1988). "Antisemitism in Rome." In Almog 1988: 13–25.

Stowers, Stanley K. (1981). *The Diatribe and Paul's Letter to the Romans*. SBLDS 57. Chico, Calif.: Scholars Press.

———— (1994). *A Rereading of Romans: Justice, Jews, and Gentiles*. New Haven: Yale Univ. Press.

Strehlow, T. (1947). *Aranda Traditions*. Melbourne: Melbourne Univ. Press.

Strelan, Rick (1996). *Paul, Artemis, and the Jews in Ephesus*. BZNW 80. Berlin: de Gruyter.

Stuhlmacher, Peter (1976). "Zur historischen Situation und Intention von Röm 13, 1-7." *ZTK* 73: 131–66.

———— (1994 [1989]). *Paul's Letter to the Romans: A Commentary*. Trans. Scott J. Hafemann. Louisville: Westminster John Knox.

Sumner, William G. (1906). *Folkways: A Study of the Sociological Importance of Usages, Manners, Customs, Mores, and Morals*. Boston: Ginn.

Tajfel, Henri, ed. (1978). *Differentiation between Social Groups: Studies in the Social Psychology of Intergroup Relations*. London: Academic Press.

Tajfel, Henri, Michael G. Billig, R. F. Bundy, and C. Flament (1971). "Social Categorization and Intergroup Behaviour." *EJSP* 1: 149–77.

Talbert, C. H. (1969/70). "Tradition and Redaction in Romans 12:9-21." *NTS* 16: 83–94.

Thackeray, H. St. J. (1926). *Josephus: The Life, Against Apion*. LCL. Cambridge: Harvard Univ. Press.

———— (1927). *Josephus: The Jewish War, Books I–III*. LCL. Cambridge: Harvard Univ. Press.

Theissen, Gerd (1987). *Psychological Aspects of Pauline Theology*. Trans. John P. Galvin. Philadelphia: Fortress Press.

———— (1999). *The Religion of the Earliest Churches: Creating a Symbolic World*. Trans. John Bowden. Minneapolis: Fortress Press.

Thelen, David (1989). "Memory and American History." *Journal of American History* 75: 1117–29.

Thomas, Helen, and Frank H. Stubbings (1962). "Lands and Peoples in Homer." In Wace and Stubbings 1962: 283–310.

Thompson, Michael B. (1991) *Clothed with Christ: The Example and Teaching of Jesus in Romans 12.1—15.13.* JSNTSup 59. Sheffield: JSOT Press.

Thompson, Thomas L. (1999). *The Mythic Past.* New York: Basic.

Tobin, Thomas H. (1993). "Controversy and Continuity in Romans 1:18—3:20." *CBQ* 55: 298–318.

——— (1995). "What Shall We Say That Abraham Found? The Controversy behind Romans 4." *HTR* 88: 437–52.

Tonkin, Elizabeth, Maryon MacDonald, and Malcolm Chapman, eds. (1989). *History and Ethnicity.* ASA Monographs 27. New York: Routledge.

Turner, John C. (1999). "Some Current Issues in Research on Social Identity and Self-Categorization Theories." In Ellemers, Spears, and Doosje 1999: 6–34.

Turner, John C., with Michael A. Hogg, Penelope J. Oakes, Stephen D. Reicher, and Margaret S. Wetherell (1987). *Rediscovering the Social Group: A Self-Categorization Theory.* Oxford: Blackwell.

Turner, Victor (1969). *The Ritual Process: Structure and Anti-Structure.* Ithaca, N.Y.: Cornell Univ. Press.

Urman, Dan, and Paul V. M. Flesher, eds. (1995). *Ancient Synagogues: Historical Analysis and Archaeological Discovery.* Vol. 1. Studia Post-Biblica 47. Leiden: Brill.

Vaage, Leif E., and Vincent L. Wimbush, eds. (1999). *Asceticism and the New Testament.* London: Routledge.

Van Seters, John (1975). *Abraham in History and Tradition.* New Haven: Yale Univ. Press.

Varshney, Ashutosh (1995). *Ethnic Conflict and Rational Choice: A Theoretical Engagement.* Cambridge: Center for International Affairs, Harvard University.

Vermeulen, H., and C. Govers, eds. (1994a). *The Anthropology of Ethnicity: Beyond "Ethnic Groups and Boundaries."* Amsterdam: Het Spinhuis.

——— (1994b). "Introduction." In Vermeulen and Govers 1994a: 1–9.

Versnel, H. S. (1991). "Beyond Cursing: The Appeal to Justice in Judicial Prayers." In Fararone and Obbink 1991: 60–106.

Vogels, Henricus Iosephus, ed. (1966). *Ambrosiastri Qui Dicitur Commentarius in Epistulas Paulinas. Pars Prima. In Epistulam ad Romanos.* CSEL 86. Vienna: Hoelder-Pichler-Temsky.

Vogt, Thea (1993). *Angst und Identität in Markusevangelium: Ein textpsychologischer und sozialgeschichtlicher Beitrag.* Göttingen: Vandenhoeck & Ruprecht.

Volf, Miroslav (1996). *Exclusion and Embrace: A Theological Exploration of Identity, Otherness, and Reconciliation.* Nashville: Abingdon.

Wace, Alan J. B., and Frank H. Stubbings, eds. (1962). *A Companion to Homer.* New York: St. Martin's.

Wahlde, Urban C. von (2000). "'The Jews' in the Gospel of John: Fifteen Years of Research (1983–1998)." *Ephemerides theologicae lovanienses* 76: 30–55.

Walbank, F. W. (1951). "The Problem of Greek Nationality." *The Phoenix* 5: 41–60.

Walker, Susan (1985). *Memorials to the Roman Dead.* London: Trustees of the British Museum.

Wallace-Hadrill, Andrew (1994). *Houses and Society in Pompeii and Herculaneum.* Princeton, N.J.: Princeton Univ. Press.

———— (1997). "Rethinking the Roman Atrium House." In Laurence and Wallace-Hadrill 1997: 219–40.

Wallman, Sandra, ed. (1992). *Contemporary Futures: Perspectives from Social Anthropology.* ASA Monographs 30. London: Routledge.

Walters, J. C. (1993). *Ethnic Issues in Paul's Letter to the Romans: Changing Self-Definitions in Earliest Roman Christianity.* Valley Forge, Pa.: Trinity Press International.

Waltzing, Jean P. (1895–1900). *Étude historique sur les corporations professionelles chez les Romains.* 4 Vols. Louvain: Peeters.

Waters, Mary C. (2000). "Multiple Identities and Identity in the United States." In Spickard and Burroughs 2000a: 23–40.

Watson, Duane F., ed. (1991). *Persuasive Artistry: Studies in Rhetoric in Honor of George A. Kennedy.* JSNTSup 50. Sheffield: JSOT Press.

Watson, Francis (1986). *Paul, Judaism and the Gentiles: A Sociological Approach.* SNTSMS 56. Cambridge: Cambridge Univ. Press.

———— (2000). *Agape, Eros, Gender: Towards a Pauline Sexual Ethic.* Cambridge: Cambridge Univ. Press.

Weber, Max (1978 [1922]). "Ethnic Groups." *Economy and Society.* Vol. 1. Guenther Roth and Claus Wittich, eds. Berkeley: Univ. of California Press. 385–98. (Partially reproduced in Hutchinson and Smith 1996: 35–40.)

Wedderburn, A. J. M. (1978). "Adam in Paul's Letter to the Romans." *Studia Biblica* 3: 413–30.

———— (1987). *Baptism and Resurrection: Studies in Pauline Theology against Its Graeco-Roman Background.* WUNT 44. Tübingen: Mohr/Siebeck.

———— (1988). *The Reasons for Romans.* Studies of the New Testament and Its World. Edinburgh: T & T Clark.

Weiss, Johannes (1985 [1892]). *Jesus' Proclamation of the Kingdom of God.* Edited and introduced by R. H. Hiers and D. L. Holland. (ET of 1892 German original.) Chico, Calif.: Scholars Press.

Westerholm, Stephen (1988). *Israel's Law and the Church's Faith: Paul and His Recent Interpreters.* Grand Rapids: Eerdmans.

Wetherell, Margaret (1996). "Constructing Social Identities: The I Individual/Social Binary in Henri Tajfel's Social Psychology." In P. Robinson 1996: 269–84.

White, L. Michael (1996 [1990]). *The Social Origins of Christian Architecture.* Vol. 1: *Building God's House in the Roman World: Architectural Adaptation among Pagans, Jews and Christians.* HTS 42. Valley Forge, Pa.: Trinity Press International.

———— (1997a). *The Social Origins of Christian Architecture.* Vol. 2: *Texts and Monuments for the Christian Domus Ecclesiae in Its Environment.* HTS 42. Valley Forge, Pa.: Trinity Press International.

——— (1997b). "Synagogue and Society in Imperial Ostia: Archaeological and Epigraphic Evidence." *HTR* 90: 23–58.

White, L. Michael, and O. Larry Yarborough, eds. (1995). *The Social World of the First Christians: Essays in Honor of Wayne A. Meeks.* Minneapolis: Fortress Press.

Wiefel, Wolfgang (1991 [1970]). "The Jewish Community in Ancient Rome and the Origins of Roman Christianity." In Donfried 1991a: 85–101.

Wiles, Maurice (1977). "Christianity without Incarnation?" in Hick 1977: 1–10.

Williams, B. F. (1989). "A Class Act: Anthropology and the Race to Nation across Ethnic Terrain." *Annual Review of Anthropology* 18: 401–44.

Williams, F. E. (1976). "The Vailala Madness." In Schwimmer 1976.

Williams, Margaret H. (1994a). "The Organisation of Jewish Burials in Ancient Rome in the Light of Evidence from Palestine and the Diaspora." *ZPE* 101: 165–82.

——— (1994b). "The Structure of Roman Jewry Re-considered: Were the Synagogues of Ancient Rome Entirely Homogeneous?" *ZPE* 102: 129–41.

——— (1997). "The Meaning and Function of *Ioudaios* in Graeco-Roman Inscriptions." *ZPE* 116: 249–62.

Williams, Sam K. (1980). "The *Pistis Christou* Formulation in Paul." *NovT* 22: 248–63.

——— (1987). "Again *Pistis Christou.*" *CBQ* 49: 431–47.

Wilson, Bryan R. (1975). *Magic and the Millennium.* London: Paladin.

Wilson, Walter T. (1991). *Love without Pretense: Romans 12.9-21 and Hellenistic-Jewish Wisdom Literature.* WUNT 2/2. Tübingen: Mohr/Siebeck.

Winkler, John J. (1990). *The Constraints of Desire: The Anthropology of Sex and Gender in Ancient Greece.* New York: Routledge.

——— (1991). "The Constraints of Eros." In Faraone and Obbink 1991: 214–43.

Winter, Bruce (2002). "Roman Law and Society in Romans 12–15." In Oakes 2002: 66–102.

Winterbottom, Michael (1996). "Asianism and Atticism." In Hornblower and Spawforth 1996: 191.

Wolter, Michael (1997). "Ethos und Identität in paulinischen Gemeinden." *NTS* 43: 430–44.

——— (2001). "Die ethische Identität christlicher Gemeinden in neutestamentlicher Zeit." *Marburger Jahrbuch Theologie* 13: 61–90.

Woolf, Bertram Lee (1956). *Reformation Writings of Martin Luther.* Vol. 2: *The Spirit of the Protestant Reformation.* London: Lutterworth.

Worsley, Peter (1970 [1957]). *The Trumpet Shall Sound: A Study of "Cargo" Cults in Melanesia.* London: Paladin.

Wright, David (2000). "Tertullian." In Esler 2000d: 1027–47.

Wright, N. T. (1980). "The Messiah and the People of God: A Study in Pauline Theology with Particular Reference to the Argument of the Epistle to the Romans." Ph.D. dissertation, Oxford University.

——— (1991). *The Climax of the Covenant: Christ and the Law in Pauline Theology.* Minneapolis: Fortress Press.

Wright, R. B. (1985). "Psalms of Solomon (First Century B.C.): A New Translation with an Introduction." In Charlesworth 1985: 639–70.

Yavetz, Z. (1952). "The Living Conditions of the Urban Plebs in Republican Rome." *Latomus* 17: 500–517. (Reprinted in Seager 1969: 162–79.)

Yinger, Kent L. (1998). "Romans 12:14-21 and Nonretaliation in Second Temple Judaism: Addressing Persecution within the Community." *CBQ* 60: 74–96.

Yonge, C. D. (1993). *The Works of Philo: Complete and Unabridged.* New updated edition. Peabody, Mass.: Hendrickson.

Ziesler, John (1989). *Paul's Letter to the Romans.* TPI New Testament Commentaries. Philadelphia: Trinity Press International.

Zimmerman, Moshe (1988). "From Radicalism to Antisemitism." In Almog 1988: 241–54.

Zizioulas, John D. (1993). *Being as Communion: Studies in Personhood and the Church.* Crestwood, N.Y.: St. Vladimir's Seminary Press.

Index

Aaron, 232–33

Abba, 247, 248

Abraham, 24, 31; as a prototype of group identity, 175, 177–78, 269, 346; as prototypical for Judeans, 178–80; in Galatia, 180–84; as a possible self, 180; role of his memory in social contest, 181; Abrahamic descent in Galatia, 182–83; Paul's view threat to Judean identity, 183; his righteousness, 184–88; Abrahamic descent including Judeans in Romans 184–85; as prototypical for Judeans 189; his circumcision 189; and common ingroup identity 190, 346; and monotheism 190; promise made to him, 191–92; as a former idolater, 193; his faith, 193; his contemporary relevance, 194, 286; like root of olive tree, 305; not weak, but strong in faith, 345–46

Adam, non-presence in Rom. 1:18-32, 148–49; cause of sin and death, 199, 228, 234, 261; as type of one to come, 200–201; not negative prototype, 201; typological features, 201–2; contrast with Jesus Christ, 202; not alluded to in "I" voice of Romans 7, 233–36

agapé, in Rom. 12:9-21, 316–30; described in thirty statements, 317; aural repetition in Rom. 12:9-21, 318–19; product of Paul's oral proclamation, 319; meaning elsewhere in Romans, 319–21; God's love, 320; Christ's love, 320; as fulfillment of law, 321, 333–35; and the Spirit, 321–22; distinguished from spiritual gifts, 322; and social identity, 322–30; expressive of ingroup identity, 322–23; hospitality, 325–26; in relation to civic and political authorities, 330–33; final instruction in Rom. 13:8-10, 333–35; in relation to weak and strong, 351–52

Alexandria, 90–93

Ambrosiaster, on Abraham, 191; how to lead a good life, 308

ancestry: *See* ethnicity

Antioch, incident at, 129, 133

anti-Semitism, anachronistic for ancient world, 12; nineteenth-century origin, 52; non-existence in Greco-Roman world, 52–53; relation to mistranslating *Ioudaios*, 62–63. *See also* race

apocalyptic, Käsemann and, 250; an outmoded term, 251–52; history of use, 251; inappropriate for Paul, 263

apostle: *See* Paul

Aquinas, 7

Aquila, 107, 118, 121–22, 340

Architecture, relation to origins and character of Christ-movement, 102–7; differences between Judeans and Christ-followers, 103–7; space as structuring relationships, 104; territoriality, 104; sociofugal and sociopetal space, 104; distributive and non-distributive space, 104–5;

the Temple in Jerusalem, 105; house churches and Romans 16, 120–25; contrast between house churches and Judean *proseuchai*, 122–23

Aristeas, Letter of, 146, 164

Aristotle, 16, 21; Aristotelian ethics, 308, 322

Asa, 233

Augustine, use of Romans 1, 7; God's love, 320; free will, 366 n. 7

Augustus, 91

Australian Aboriginal people, 256

authority: *See* leadership

baptism, and sin, 202; origin and practice, 203–9; of John, 204; remission of sins, 204; total immersion, 204; living water, 204; Peter's baptizing in Tiber, 204–5; nakedness during, 205; occasion for receipt of Holy Spirit, 206, 245–46, 321; ecstatic states, 206–7; glossolalia, 207; presence of community, 208–9; and social identity, 209–21; Paul's teaching on, 212–17; breaking power of sin, 212; into Christ, 213; link to Christ's death and resurrection, 213–17; ritual effect, 215–16; Christ present, 216; union with Christ, 217; in Christ, 217. *See also* rituals

barbarians, 61. *See also* Greeks

Barth, Fredrik: *See* ethnicity

Barth, Karl, 1, 5

biblical texts, 2

"blameless" (Phil. 3:6), 232–33

blessing, result of righteousness, 164, 167, 187, 188; of Abraham, 188–91

boasting: in Mediterranean culture, 168

body, analogy of, 313–14; to illustrate warning against despising, 316

boundaries: *See* ethnicity

brotherly love, 324–25. *See also agapê*

brothers, 138

Caligula, Gaius, 87

Calvin, John, 7

cardinal virtues, 61

catacombs: *See* Judeans

Chalcedon, 159

Challenge-and-riposte: *See* cultural context, collection

charismatic authority: *See* leadership

Chrestus, 98, 100. *See also* Claudius, Judeans

Christ: *See* Jesus Christ

Christ-movement, origins in Rome, 100–102; Wiefel's thesis about origins in Rome, 102; influence on character of architecture, 102–7; dissension in Rome, 107–8; tension between house churches in Rome, 123–25; fundamental beliefs, 136

Christian: *See Christianos*

Christian identity: *See* identity

Christianos: meaning and translation "Christ-lackey," 12; "Christian" as anachronistic in first century CE, 12–13; not first-century ingroup designation, 12–13; translation as "Christ-follower," 13

circumcision, not a requirement of Pauline congregations, 114; Judean status, 153; heightened importance in Maccabean period, 180; role in Galatia, 181–82; and Abraham, 184, 189

classic texts, meaning, 1; Romans as a classic, 1, 3; continuing impact, 3

Claudius, 87, 98–100

canonical texts, 1

cargo cults, 258

civic and political authorities, proper attitude to, 320–33; taxation, 332

cognitive alternatives: *See* social identity

cognitive dimension to Romans, 12, 310, 311, 312, 313, 314, 345, 353–54

collection, 129–30; as an illustration of challenge-and-riposte, 130–31; in Rom. 12:13, 326

collective memory: *See* memory

collegia: See Rome

common ingroup identity, and the purpose of Romans, 133, 142; recategorization/common ingroup identity and conflict reduction, 30–33, 133, 142–43, 269, 309; need to retain subgroup identities, 30–31, 178; equal status on different dimensions, 31–32, 144, 145, 152, 153–54, 300; recategorization in Romans, 32–33, 140, 142, 154; Paul not eradicating difference between Judeans and non-Judeans, 132–33, 143,145, 178, 218, 269, 307, 355–56; righteousness and common ingroup identity, 168; and monotheism, 169; presentation of Abraham, 171–94; Abraham as prototype of, 184–94; Abraham and monotheism, 190; its origin, 196–99; its character, 197–98; its exalted character, 243–67, 279, 264, 312; emotional dimension, 198; and the body of Christ, 218; and the Holy Spirit, 243–49, 279; expressed in olive tree image, 300; expressed in body analogy, 313–15; common worship as climax, 354. *See also* social identity

conflict: *See* ethnic conflict, social identity

contesting identity: *See* identity

covenant, climax of, problem with, 189, 193, 285–86; no development of law, 285. *See also* salvation history

creation, waiting for revelation of sons of God, 260–61; and birth pangs, 261; link to group identity, 262

crucifixion, Paul's understanding, 160; enabling existence of group, 160; shame of cross, 201; breaking power of sin, 212

cultural context, of Romans, 17; ancient Mediterranean, 54; dominant features, 78. *See also* collection

cultural distance, 2

curses *(defixiones): See* envy

dais of God, 266

day of wrath: *See* judgment

death, meaning and effect of, 200, 230

decline of civilization narrative, 149

diaspora, 64

distributive and non-distributive space: *See* architecture

dual ethnic identities: *See* ethnicity

Durkheim, Emile, views on time, 254–55; rationalist understanding, 405 n. 43

end of law, Christ as: *See telos*

ecstatic phenomena: *See* Holy Spirit

elite: *See* Rome

emic, distinguished from etic, 8

entrepreneurs of identity: *See* leadership

envy, provoking Israel to jealousy, 288; usage in LXX, 288; meaning, 288; jealousy contrasted with envy, 288–90; jealousy and envy in relation to honor and "limited good," 288–90; evil eye, 289, 291; curses, 289; meaning of envy, 289; meaning of jealousy, 289–90; jealousy defensive or aggressive *(aemulatio)*, 290; Deut. 32:21, 290–91; Israel concerned with what is rightly hers, 292, 296, 297; olive tree and provocation of Israel to jealousy, 305

Esau, 279, 280

eschatology, unhelpfully elastic term, 156; approaches of Bultmann and Käsemann, 250; an outmoded term, 251–52, 267, 335–36; history of use, 251; use by scholars, 254. *See also* future

ethics: unhelpful in relation to Romans? 312, 315, 323; *also see* identity descriptors, social identity

etic: *See* emic

ethnic conflict, 10; breakup of Yugoslavia, 10, 53; atrocities in Kosovo, 10, 41, 46; slaughter of Tutsis by Hutus in Rwanda, 10, 41, 46, 53; in Northern Ireland, 10, 41, 44; over Kashmir, 10; in Israel/Palestine, 10, 41, 54; as major world evil, 10–11; reconciling Judeans and Greeks in Romans, 12; prevalence in modern world, 40; in Sri Lanka, 41; in a social identity framework, 50–51; reasons for two groups usually being involved, 51; in ancient Mediterranean world, 54; between Greeks and Judeans, 74–76, 344; relevance of Greek/Judean conflict to Romans, 74–76; Roman dislike of foreigners, 86; in Rom. 16:17-20, 125–28; Israel's failure to turn to Christ, 277; an aspect of "this age," 310

ethnicity, resurgence of, 10; contextual factors in salience of, 10; link to identity, 11; usually undefined, 11; full explanation, 40–76; provisional definition, 40–41; nomenclature, 40; interactive and self-ascriptive approach to, 41–43; Max Weber's approach, 41; Everett Hughes's approach, 41–42; Fredrik Barth's approach, 42–43; role of boundaries, 42–43; cultural features as signaling not constituting boundaries, 42–43; ethnic cultural features, 43–44; myth of common ancestry, 44; connection with homeland, 44; religion as an ele-

ment, 44; primordialism, 44–49; Clifford Geertz and primordial attachments, 45–46; reconciling Barthian and primordial understandings, 46–48; micro, median, and macro ethnic levels, 48–49, 349–50; dual and multiple ethnicity, 49–50, 123; distinguished from race, 51–53; in the ancient Mediterranean world, 53–76; Greek ethnic identity, 54–61; meaning of *ethnos*, 54–55; Barthian approach to Greek ethnicity, 55–58; Greek ethnic identity in first century CE, 56–57; *Graeci*, 57–58; the territorial dimension to Greek names for ethnic groups, 58–60; ethnic nomenclature in Homer's *Catalogue of Ships* and Josephus's *Contra Apionem*, 59; Hippocrates on the effect of environment, 59–60; dual Greek ethnic identities, 60; Judean ethnic identity, 62–74. *See also* ethnocentrism, Judean ethnic identity, Rome

ethnocentrism, meaning of, 50; in ancient world, 76; Judean, 145

ethnos: *See* ethnicity

eucharistic meal, 208

Evans-Pritchard, E. E., 255

Eve, 199, 235

evil eye: *See* envy

expiation, 159

faith, of Roman congregations, 138; and righteousness, 140–41, 153, 155–57; social character, 156–57; in Jesus Christ, 157–59, 282; proto-Arian implications of subjective view, 158–59; and Abraham, 185; positive role for, 192; and baptism, 208; affirmed in baptism, 212; comes from hearing, 288; measure of, 313–14

fama: See Rome

flesh, life in, 244–45
food, theme in Romans 14, 126; in
    Rom. 16:17-20, 127–28. *See also*
    table-fellowship
free will, 1
future, Paul's attitude to in current dis-
    cussion, 249–50; problems with
    current discussion, 250–52; myths
    of, 253, 258–59; culturally condi-
    tioned attitudes to, 257; Northern
    European and North Atlantic atti-
    tudes to, 257; Mediterranean atti-
    tudes to, 257–58; as culmination of
    presently occurring forces, 258,
    263–64; problem with "now and
    not yet" formula, 261–62, 265;
    hope, 263; present in Rom. 13:11-
    14, 336–68. *See also* future hope,
    time
future hope, 249–67

garden, of Eden, 199
Geertz, Clifford: *See* ethnicity
Gentiles, 12, 75. *See also* non-Judeans
Ghost Dance, 258
glossolalia: *See* baptism
God: *See* faith, Jesus Christ, monothe-
    ism, righteousness, theology
gospel, 111, 136, 138, 139; and social
    identity, 139–41; and shame,
    139–40; different gospel not yet in
    Rome, 222
gossip, 184
Graeci: See ethnicity
graffiti, 81
Greeks, attitudes to non-Greeks, 61;
    Paul's attitude toward, 138. *See also*
    ethnicity
grief, 326

Halbwachs, Maurice, 24, 174, 370 n.
    20
heirs, 247, 248
Hellen, 56, 58. *See also* ethnicity
historical-critical analysis, necessity of,

2; not concerned with what "lies
    behind" a text, 16; meaning to
    original audience, 16–17
historical setting of Romans, 8–9
Holy Spirit, 14; gifts of, 138; content
    of righteousness, 167; gift of, 197;
    received at baptism, 206–8,
    245–46; ecstatic states, 206–7,
    246, 262; and group identity,
    243–49; life in, 244–45; group dif-
    ferentiation, 245; link to divine
    sonship, 248; experienced in pre-
    sent, 262–63, 264; problem with
    gifts at Corinth absent, 316; and
    agapê, 321–22, 334
Homer, 59
hope, and the future, 263; in relation
    to *agapê*, 324
honor, Paul not shamed by gospel,
    139; blushing as sign of dishonor,
    139; challenge-and-riposte in rela-
    tion to Abraham, 184; gossip, 184;
    honorable families, 248–49; com-
    petitiveness and envy, 313; avoid-
    ance of agonistic, honor-related
    conduct, 316, 324–25, 327; coun-
    tercultural inversion, 325. *See also*
    cultural context
house churches, in Rome, 120–22;
    contrast with Judean *proseuchai*,
    122–23; tension between, 123–25;
    ethnicity as exacerbating tensions,
    124–25; relation to hospitality,
    346–48; household imagery in
    Romans 14–15, 347–48
Hughes, Everett: *See* ethnicity
Hutus: *See* ethnic conflict

"I" voice (Rom. 7:7-25), meanings of
    "I" statements, 227; *status quaestio-
    nis*, 227–28; of pre- or post-conver-
    sion Paul, 231; Phil. 3:6 not
    excluding Pauline connection,
    231–33; not reference to Adam,
    233–36; not reference to humanity

in general, 236–37; as showing
Paul's identification with Israel,
237–38

identity, Christian identity and ethnic
conflict, 10; link to ethnicity, 11; a
"plastic" word, 11, 19; usually
undefined, 11; broad approach to,
11; recent research in Germany, 19;
contesting identity within groups,
27–29; threats to, 183; coping
strategies against threats, 183–84;
righteousness as referring to privileged identity, 164, 166; regional,
373 n. 50

identity descriptors, and norms,
20–21; social identity norms as a
useful alternative to ethics, 21;
body analogy, 315; alternative to
indicative/imperative distinction,
315; *agapê* as, 323–30; in Romans
14–15, 339–40, 355. *See also* social
identity

idolatry, 147, 310

impartiality of God, 151–52, not only
theological but social, 152

impurity, 220–21. *See also* lawlessness

In His Steps: "What Would Jesus Do?",
159

inimicitiae: See Rome

insulae: See Rome

intertextuality, nature of, 176–77;
problems with, 177, 181

intragroup phenomena, *See* social
identity

intercultural communication, its reality, 2–3

Isaac, 279

Ishmael, 280

Israel, group attitudes on failure to
turn to Christ, 276–78; privileges
of, 273; not equated with Christ-
movement, 279; continued existence, 286; rejection of the gospel,
287–293; need to be concerned
with what is rightly hers, 292–93; a

remnant survives, 293–96; spiritual
stupor continuing, 294–95; second
chance for, 296–98; future salvation of, 296; coming redemption
of, 305–6

Israel/Palestine: *See* ethnic conflict

Jacob, 279

jealousy: *See* envy

Jerusalem, origins of Christ-movement, 101; Paul anticipating trouble, 116. *See also* Paul

Jesus Christ, identification with God
in Romans, 14–15, 159; source of
Paul's apostleship, 137; as object of
faith, 157–59, 282; role in establishing new common identity,
196–97; death and its effects,
198–9, 240; not a prototype in
relation to faith, 201; contrast with
Adam, 202; present in baptism,
216; in Christ, 217–18; body of
Christ, 218; teaching on nonretaliation, 329; his self-sacrifice, 353.
See also crucifixion

Jew, as mistranslation of *Ioudaios*, 62;
Kingdom of God, 260; his love,
320. *See also* Judeans

Job, 232

Joseph and Aseneth, 328–29

joy, 197

Judeans, "Jew" as anachronistic in first
century CE, 12; Judean ethnic identity, 62–74; Barthian approach, 62;
correct translation of *Ioudaios*,
63–68; answering objections to
"Judean" for *Ioudaios*, 68–74; link
to Judea, 63–67; diaspora experience, 64–66; anachronism in use of
Jew, Jewish, 67; critique of Shaye
Cohen's use of "Jew" and "Jewish,"
68–74; in Rome, 86–97; history
and organization in Rome, 86–88;
settlement in Trastevere, 87; Judean
catacombs in Rome, 85 (diagram),

87–88; dating of Judean catacombs, 87; Judean organization from catacomb epigraphy, 88; synagogues, 88; hierarchy and honor in synagogues, 88; Judean synagogues in Rome, 88–97, 331–32; Judean synagogues in Alexandria, 90–93; *proseucha* near Tullian wall, 94; first century CE synagogue at Ostia, 94–97; under Claudius, 98–100; sources for impact of Claudius, 98–99; expulsion by Claudius, 91–100; date of expulsion, 99–100; how they divided the world, 113; addressed by Paul in Romans, 112–13, 119; equal to non-Judeans in sin, 143–54; plight of, 152–53; sinfulness of, 152–53; disinherited from Abrahamic descent in Galatians, 183; in Romans 7, 145. *See also* ethnic conflict, ethnicity, Rome

judgment, coming, 150–52, 161; day of wrath, 151; events of, 151; last, 160, 187, 249; not for the righteous, 162, 266; in Romans 8, 266

Junia: *See* Romans

Juvenal, 93–94

Kant, Immanuel, 21

Kashmir: *See* ethnic conflict

Kingdom of God, 260

kinship, 247

Kneale, Matthew, 52. *See also* race

Knox, Robert, 51. *See also* race

Kosovo: *See* ethnic conflict

law, Mosaic, absence of law, 152; under the law, 152; problem in relation to non-Judean righteousness, 169–70; and Abraham, 186; Paul's coherent view of, 200, 228–29; not the cause of wrongdoing, 202; and Judeans, 223–24; effect of, 229–30; negative view in

Galatians, 229, 285; more positive view in Romans, 229; its holiness and goodness, 230, 239; Sinai event, 230; effect of sin, 239; irrelevance for Christ-followers, 239–40; its uselessness in relation to sin, 240–41; not productive of righteousness, 282–83; legalism absent from Romans, 282–84; no development of, 285; Christ in radical discontinuity with, 285; replaced by Christ, 286–87; fulfilled by *agapê*, 333–35; not binding on Christ-followers, 343; not banned for Judean Christ-followers, 351–52

lawlessness, and non-Judeans, 220–21. *See also* impurity

leadership, in social identity perspective, 33–39, 223–24; current approaches to authority and leadership in Paul, 33–35; Weber on charismatic authority and institutionalization, 33; overview of social-scientific approaches, 35–36; followership, 36; social identity and self-categorization approach, 36–39; in relation to shared social identity, 37, 223; use of ingroup prototypes, 37, 223; Paul as exemplar of group, 224, 226; leaders as entrepreneurs of identity, 38, 223, 242, 350; in Romans, 133, 222–42; Paul's task, 135, 136, 137–39; in Romans, 222–42. *See also* "I" voice (Rom. 7:7-25)

Leach, Edmund, 256

Lévi-Strauss, Claude, 254–56

literacy: *See* oral culture

love: *See* agapê

Luther, Martin, use of Romans, 1; understanding of righteousness, 160; and "I" voice, 228; and Augustine, 366 n. 8; on Romans, 366 n. 9; God's righteousness and Christian identity, 410 n. 3

Mactar inscription: *See* Rome

Manicheans, determinism, 1; beliefs, 366 n. 6

Marr, Wilhelm, 52. *See also* race

Mediterranean context: *See* cultural context, ethnic conflict

Melanchthon, Philip, 9

memory, role of classic and canonical texts, 1; collective memory, 22, 24, 174–75, 176, 177; remembering, 24; Israelite scriptures as repository of collective memories, 136–37, 180, 266; contestation, 137, 174, 176, 186, 286–87, 353; and proto-types, 174; Assmann's "cultural memory," 174; processing the past, 174–75. *See also* social identity, time

mirror-reading, 181; usefulness of, 397–98 n. 22

myths, and the future, 253, 258–59; millennial/millenarian, 258; func-tionalist approaches, 259; conflict-oriented, 259; prescriptive versus proscriptive types, 259; future myth in 1 Thessalonians, 253, 260; future myth lacking in Romans, 253, 260, 263

monotheism, in Romans, 14; Jesus Christ and, 14–15; and recatego-rization into one identity, 169, 190, 269. *See also* Jesus Christ

Nero, 87; and the Christ-movement in Rome, 101; and Peter, 205

nonelite: *See* Rome

non-Judeans, in Roman congregations with Judeans, 112–15; Judean antipathy to, 113; Paul's interest in, 138–39; equal to Judeans in sin, 143–54; the target of Rom. 1:19-32, 145–50; idolatry of, 147; addressed at Rom. 11:13, 297; arrogance toward Israel, 300

norms: *See* identity descriptors

Northern Ireland: *See* ethnic conflict

olive tree metaphor, discussion of, 298–305; an image of the Christ-movement, 300; rejuvenation of failing trees, 301; character of olive trees, 301; grafting, 301–2; Theophrastus on grafting, 302; olive groves on Delos, 303; image of recategorization, 305

oracles of God, 153

oral culture, and understanding Romans, 17–18; low ancient liter-acy rates, 17; listening to Romans in its order, 17–8; low literacy rates, 177; mnemonic/aural pat-terning in Rom. 12:9-21, 316

Orwell, George, 24

Ostia synagogue, 90, 94–97, 123; first-century date, 95; plan, 96; artistic reconstruction, 97

P46, 116

parousia, 260

patron and client: *See* cultural context

Paul, effort in writing Romans, 17; his knowledge of the Roman situation, 17, 110; learning from experience, 31; aware of Judean/Greek ethnic conflict, 76; as entrepreneur of identity, 109; interest in non-Judeans, 113; evangelism to Judeans, 114; producing mixed congregations, 114; his future plans, 115–16; proposed journey to Spain, 115–16; need for help in Spain, 115–16, 223, 326; likely trouble in Jerusalem, 116; people mentioned in Chapter 16, 118–19; worried about possible arrivals in Rome, 125; his right to speak to the Romans, 133; his circum-stances dictating Romans, 135; establishing his leadership creden-tials, 135–39; his initial greetings,

135–37; apostle, 135–36; representative of shared identity, 136; Christ as source of his apostleship, 137; building an emotional bond with audience, 137–39; as a figure of controversy, 142; understanding of Jesus' crucifixion, 160; understanding of righteousness, 163–68; defining himself in relation to ingroup, 196, 212; slander about him, 203; leadership role, 222–42; as group exemplar, 224; and ecstatic phenomena, 246; personal statements in Romans 9–11, 270–71, 293; connecting with Judean identity, 272–73, 284; his heart with Israelites, 297–98; and Stoic ethics, 208; allies himself with strong in Rome, 343. See also "I" voice (Rom. 7:7-25)

Peter, 204–5

Phoebe: See Romans

Pompeii, 81, 82; graffiti, 379 n. 27

Pompey, 86

possible selves: See social identity

potter, 280–81

primordialism: See ethnicity

primogeniture, 247

Prisca, 107, 118, 121–22, 340

promises, fulfillment theme in Romans, 136; to Abraham, 191–92; and social identity, 192; children of, including non-Israelites, 279

proseucha see Judeans, Ostia, Rome

prototype, of ingroup, 37, 172; definition, 172; and possible social identities, 172; Abraham as, 175. See also leadership, social identity

race, as anachronistic of ancient world, 12; distinguished from ethnicity, 51–53; nineteenth–century origin of the concept, 51–52; non-existence of the concept in the ancient

Greco-Roman world, 52–55. See also anti-Semitism

reading, the approach to Romans in this volume, 18, 109

Rebecca, 279

recategorization: See common ingroup identity, social identity

reform movement, 132. See also sect

religio: See religion

religion, role of experience, 5; as a framework for Romans research, 6–7; history of the word, 7; meaning of religio, 7; as a modern, not ancient, notion, 7–8; embedded religious phenomena in ancient world, 8; political and domestic forms in ancient world, 8; problems with use in relation to Paul, 8; as an element in ethnicity, 44; not the basis for Northern Ireland tension, 44

resurrection, 298

rhetoric, character of in Paul's work, 15–17; recent rise in New Testament research, 15; problem of excessively technical approaches, 16; neglect of Asiatic variety, 16; meaning of rhetorical situation, 16; rhetorical situation in Rome, 110; Paul's use for group identity, 224

rhetorical situation: See rhetoric

righteousness, initial mention, 140; of God, 140–41, 156, 163, 164; relation to group identity, 140, 282–83; and unrighteousness, 145; basic outline, 155–57; semantic field, 156; meaning in current discussion, 159–63; and God's act, 160; change of behavior, 161; non-judicial use of verb "to righteous" in LXX, 162–63; Paul's understanding of, 163–68; danger of overstressing, 163–64; redacted out of 1 Thessalonians, 163, 167; in Galatians, 164; to denote blessed and privileged

identity, 164, 167, 187, 188; data
in the LXX, 165–66; a form of
ascribed honor, 167; necessary
when writing to Judeans and non-
Judeans, 167; as contributing to
common ingroup identity, 168;
and Abraham, 185–86; a present
condition, 161, 187; fragility of,
218; of the works variety, 282–83
rituals, distinguished from ceremonies,
210–11; of initiation, 211–12; liminal stage, 211; bringing the past
into the present, 216
Romans (the letter), history of scholarship, 9; theological dimension,
13–15; significance of the letter
frame, 109–111; reading the last
chapters first, 110; debate over the
letter, 110; the rhetorical situation,
110; problem with "encoded" readers, 110–11; connecting with
Judeans and non-Judeans, 111–15;
Chapter 16 as integral, 116–17;
ethnic subgroups in Chapter 16,
117–20; Phoebe as bearer and
reader, 117–18, 135, 345; Junia,
118; no mention of synagogues,
119–20; house churches and Chapter 16, 120–25; Minear's view on
five groups in Rome, 120; purpose,
128–34; Paul's advocacy of sectarianism, 132; positions of Watson,
Nanos and Campbell, 132–33
Rwanda: See ethnic conflict
Rome, elite and nonelite inhabitants,
77; collegia, 77; macrosociological
model of elite and nonelite, 78; no
middle class, 78; dominant cultural
features, 78; sources for nonelite,
79; the elite, 79–81; upper and
lower nobility, 79; agonistic social
relationships, 79–80; concern for
fama, 79; competition in elections,
79–80; inimicitiae, 80, 108; houses
to advertise honor, 80–81; houses

and inimicitiae, 81, 347; nonelite,
81–84; sharing values of elite, 81;
nonelite housing, 82–83; the Mactar inscription, 82; atrium houses,
82; types of insulae, 82, 107; poor
living conditions of nonelite,
82–83; craftsmen's shops, 83; voluntary associations (collegia),
83–84; collegia tenuiorum, 83, 106;
collegia domestica, 83, 106–7; Julius
Caesar, Augustus, and collegia,
83–84; ethnic groups, 84–86; population, 84; resident aliens, 84;
Judeans, 84; areas inhabited by foreigners, 84–85; pomerium, 84;
Aventine, 84; Trastevere, 84; stationes, 86; Roman dislike of foreigners, 86; history and
organization of Judeans in Rome,
86–88; Judean proseuchai, 88–97,
345; custom built synagogues,
89–90, 278; proseucha near Tullian
wall, 94; origins of Christ-movement in Rome, 100–102; effect of
Christ-followers reaching Rome,
101; Wiefel's thesis about origins in
Rome, 102; dissension within the
Christ-movement, 107–8; plurality
of congregations, 120–21; house
churches, 120–21; lateness of
monarchical bishop in Rome, 121;
struggle between house churches,
123–25; ethnicity as exacerbating
tensions, 124–35, 344–45

Sabbath, 91
Sacrifice, 310
salvation, 199
salvation history, 192–93, 194,
285–86
San Clemente, 106, 122
Santa Sabina (on the Aventine), 380 n.
58
Sarah, 31, 279–80
schism: See social identity

scripture, Israelite, oracles of God, 153; special status of, 180; container of sacred memories, 181; and Abraham, 185; as battleground, 177, 181, 185–56; preference for lowly, 325

sect, 132

self-categorization theory: *See* social identity

Sentences of Pseudo-Phocylides, 329

Sinai, 230, 234, 236, 238

sinfulness, as common plight, 141; explanation of the gift of righteousness, 142; Adam as a cause, 199; universal blame, 200; not the result of Paul's views, 203; different for Judeans and non-Judeans, 218–19; not a consequence of grace, 219–21

slavery, imagery, 219–20

social identity, basic meaning of, 11; and Romans generally, 12, 315; link to theological dimension to Romans, 13–14; and monotheism in Romans, 14; full explanation, 19–39; and intergroup phenomena, 19–22, 311–12; general outline, 19–20; influence of Henri Tajfel, 19–20; effect of categorization into groups, 20; summer camp experiments, 20, 29; minimal group experiments, 20; definition, 20; meaning of stereotyping, 21–22; Judean stereotyping of outgroups, 146–47; Paul's stereotyping of Judeans, 283; and time, 22–24, 28; groups and time, 22–23; possible selves and cognitive alternatives, 23, 252–53; self-categorization theory, 24–27, 184–85, 271–72; intragroup phenomena, 24–27; distinction between personal and social identity, 25; definition of self-categorization, 25; mobile selves in self-categorization theory,

26, 184–85; relevance of self-categorization to Romans, 26; process of consensualization, 27–28, 349; contestation and schism, 28, 349; reducing tension and conflict within groups, 29–30; leadership in social identity perspective, 35–39; ethnic conflict in a social identity framework, 50–51; Paul's leadership, 136; prototypes from the past, 173; Abraham as a possible self, 180; promises to Abraham, 192. *See also* identity, identity descriptors, common ingroup identity, leadership, memory, righteousness, time

socialization into group, phases 209; reconnaissance, 209–10; change of self-concept, 210; initiation, 210–11; and *agapê,* 322–30

sociofugal and sociopetal space: *See* architecture

Sodom, tradition underlying Rom. 1:18-32, 145, 149–50, 166; samesex relations between women, 150, 281

Solomon's temple, 375 n. 116

sons of God, 246–49; Mosaic law context in Galatians, 248; Holy Spirit context in Romans, 248

Spain: *See* Paul

Sri Lanka: *See* ethnic conflict

stationes: *See* Rome

stereotyping: *See* social identity

Stoicism/Stoic ethics, 308, 312, 313, 315, 322, 325, 326, 327, 335, 354

strong: *See* weak

summer camp experiments: *See* social identity

synagogues: *See* Judeans, Rome

table-fellowship, problem with, 131; table as a snare, 295; table as a snare in the Roman context 295–96

Tajfel, Henri: *See* social identity
telos, meaning in relation to Christ, 284–86
Temple in Jerusalem, attraction to Judeans, 66–68; nature of space, 105
territoriality: *See* architecture
theologian: *See* theology
theology, Pauline, 3; questionable appropriateness to Paul, 4; problem with, 4; different meanings of, 4; role of theologians, 4; unhelpful focus ideational dimension of religion, 4, 5, 6; Paul's theology as problematic, 4–5; "theologian" as inappropriate for Paul, 5–6; Anselm's definition of, 6; link to social issues in Romans, 13–4; importance of Abraham account, 171; dictionary definitions, 367 n. 27. *See also* Jesus Christ, Holy Spirit
Tiberias (emperor), 87
time, and social identity, 22–24, 28, 252–53; recent interest by social identity theorists, 22; groups as ongoing processes over time, 22–23, 336–37; social time, 23–24; and prototypes, 172; prototypes and examples from the past, 173; and social reality, 173; future hope, 249–267, 336–37; anthropology of, 253; sociology of, 253; as socially conditioned, 253; social-scientific analysis of, 254–56; different views on the future, 257. *See also* future, memory
titulus church, 122, 387 n. 61. *See also* San Clemente, Santa Sabina
tradition, current understandings of, 175–76; contested tradition, 176
Trastevere: *See* Judeans, Rome
tree of life, 199
Tutsis: *See* ethnic conflict
two-ways tradition, 146

Utilitarians, 21

vengeance, to be left to God, 327; context in Israelite tradition, 327–29; extension of nonretaliation to everyone, 327–28; nonretaliation and teaching of Jesus, 329
virtue ethics, 21

weak, and strong as actual groups in Rome, 340–41; present in Rome before Paul wrote, 341; identity of weak and strong, 341–44; Paul allies himself with strong, 343; attitude to Mosaic law as central distinction, 344; weak as not measuring up to Abraham, 346
Weber, Max: *See* ethnicity, leadership
word of God, 273–74; connection with social aspects, 274–75
worship, 310

Yugoslavia: *See* ethnic conflict

CPSIA information can be obtained
at www.ICGtesting.com
Printed in the USA
LVOW03s0035150318

569899LV00012B/119/P